1 8 6 5
ALABAMA

1865
ALABAMA

From CIVIL WAR to UNCIVIL PEACE

CHRISTOPHER LYLE MCILWAIN SR.

The University of Alabama Press
Tuscaloosa

The University of Alabama Press
Tuscaloosa, Alabama 35487-0380
uapress.ua.edu

Copyright © 2017 by the University of Alabama Press
All rights reserved.

Hardcover edition published 2017.
Paperback edition published 2024.
eBook edition published 2017.

Inquiries about reproducing material from this work should be addressed to the
University of Alabama Press.

Typeface: Bembo

Cover image: Ruins of CSA Naval Foundry, Selma, Alabama, burnt April 5, 1865;
Alabama Department of Archives and History
Cover design: Michele Myatt Quinn

Paperback ISBN: 978-0-8173-6193-8

A previous edition of this book has been cataloged by the Library of Congress.
ISBN: 978-0-8173-1953-3 (cloth)
E-ISBN: 978-0-8173-9136-2

Our modern wars make many
unhappy while they last and
none happy when they are over.
—Johann Wolfgang von Goethe,
September 6, 1787

Contents

List of Figures   ix

Acknowledgments   xi

Introduction   1

PART I. THE FINAL DOOM OF SLAVERY   5

1 "The Fever of Your Imagination"   7

2 "Treason—Treason—Treason!!!"   18

3 The "Peace Bubble"   26

Part II. THE FINAL DOOM OF ALABAMA'S INDUSTRIAL ECONOMY   39

4 The Will Is Wanting   41

5 The Society of Loyal Confederates   53

6 The Wedding Party   66

7 "Satan's Kingdom Is Tumbling Down"   75

PART III. THE FINAL DOOM OF STATE SOVEREIGNTY   87

8 "When This Cruel War Is Over"   89

9 "Glorious News"   110

10 "A Lull in the Tempest"   120

11 "Most Prominent and Influential Loyal Men"   132

12 "Diabolical"   143

13 The Liberator   160

14 "A Radically, Sickly, Deathly Change" 168

15 "The Rump of the Confederacy" 178

16 "The South As It Is" 187

17 The Legacy of 1865 203

Abbreviations 213

Notes 215

Bibliography 303

Index 355

Figures

1. Robert Jemison   11

2. William Russell Smith   19

3. John Forsyth   23

4. Jefferson Davis   27

5. John Archibald Campbell   28

6. Abraham Lincoln, 1860   31

7. Abraham Lincoln, 1865   31

8. Thomas Hill Watts   45

9. James Harrison Wilson   51

10. Nathan Bedford Forrest   55

11. John Tyler Croxton   71

12. Ruins of Naval Foundry at Selma   79

13. Maximilian I of Mexico   94

14. *The Peacemakers* by George Peter Alexander Healy   95

15. Andrew Johnson   99

16. Benjamin F. Butler   101

17. Frederick Douglass   108

18. William Gannaway Brownlow   112

19. Ulysses S. Grant   130

20. William Hugh Smith   138

21. Lewis Parsons   163

Acknowledgments

I am grateful to my wonderful wife, Anna, and my children, Elizabeth and Christopher, to whom this book is dedicated. As with my first book, *Civil War Alabama*, Dr. Guy Hubbs, Dr. Michael Fitzgerald, Dr. George Rable, Dr. Ben Severance, and others gave sound advice and assistance that greatly improved the manuscript. I owe them much.

I am also obliged to the many librarians and archivists who provided assistance. Special thanks go to the staffs at the Alabama Department of Archives and History, the Tuscaloosa Public Library, the Birmingham Public Library, the Tutwiler Collection of Southern History, the Huntsville–Madison County Public Library, the Mobile Public Library, the Alabama Supreme Court Library, the Hoole Special Collections Library, Bounds Law Library and Gorgas Library at the University of Alabama, Auburn University Library of Special Collections and Archives, the Lawrence County Archives, the Dallas County Public Library, the Mervyn H. Sterne Library at the University of Alabama in Birmingham, Duke University, the Southern Historical Collection at the University of North Carolina, and the National Archives.

Last and certainly not least, I am grateful for the skills of my legal assistant, Bonnie Sutton, who painstakingly typed and retyped the manuscript through its myriad permutations and revisions. Her loyalty and dedication will never be forgotten.

Introduction

> Instead of hating their own leaders they hate ours. They do not realize
> that such men as Mason, Yancey, Davis, and Toombs led them, for selfish
> purposes, into this sea of blood; they followed these leaders willingly,
> believe in them still, and insist that the North brought on the war by
> illegal encroachments, which they were bound in honor to resist.
>
> —Whitelaw Reid, *After the War*

In 1912, one of Alabama's many twentieth-century historiopropagandists, John Witherspoon DuBose, posited the period 1865 to 1874 as crucial in understanding the plight of Alabamians. The year 1912 was when his series of rambling and often inaccurate newspaper articles, later republished in a 1940 book, *Alabama's Tragic Decade: Ten Years of Alabama, 1865–1874*, were first published in the Birmingham *Age-Herald* newspaper.[1] DuBose, a South Carolina native who had been a Marengo County, Alabama, planter before the Civil War, indicted the federal government and the Republican Party of that era for all of Alabama's ills. He maintained that the Republican-dominated federal government had, among other things, wantonly destroyed the state's economy during the Civil War, prevented a prompt postwar recovery, and inexcusably and maliciously sought to elevate the "already healthy and happy" freed slaves to equality with the white population.[2] It was a yarn most white Southerners were taught and readily accepted.[3]

If DuBose had simply focused on 1865, however, he would have realized—and likely did realize—that his conclusions were flawed. That was Alabama's critical year. At its conclusion a young Mobile, Alabama, woman, who had served as a Confederate nurse, wrote that 1865 had "developed the fate of the South. Time has revealed the utter loss of all our hopes" and begun a "new era, midst poverty, tears, and sad memories of the past."[4] Like the cornerstone of a great building laid in a Masonic ritual, 1865 is the foundation to an accurate understanding of Alabama's present.

It may be presumptuous to maintain that one particular year was the most critical in Alabama's history. An argument can be made that 1819, the year Alabama was admitted to the Union, was extremely important;[5] that 1837, the year of an economic panic that led to years of depression, was particularly crucial;[6] that 1861, the year Alabama seceded from the Union, was momentous;[7] that 1901, the year Alabama's current constitution was adopted, was most decisive;[8] or that 1970, the first year that African Americans were elected to the Alabama legislature since the Reconstruction Era, was most pivotal.[9]

For several reasons, however, 1865 was unique and seminal.[10] The actions and inactions of Alabamians during those twelve months were the cause of many self-inflicted wounds that haunted them for the next century. The focus here will be on four consequences of imprudent decision making and conduct: (1) the immediate and unconditional—as opposed to gradual or compensated—emancipation of the slaves; (2) the destruction of Alabama's remaining industrial economy; (3) a significant broadening of Northern support for suffrage rights for the freedmen; and (4) an acute and lengthy postwar shortage of investment capital.

The labor of dependent, apolitical slaves had been a decisive component of Alabama's antebellum agricultural economy. The institution of slavery was also an essential mechanism for controlling the black population, and in the view of many white Southerners, a way of protecting the white populace from violent retribution.[11] Before the war began, Alabama was slowly moving toward an industrial economy, with railroads being built to access the mineral wealth of central and northeast Alabama and various towns vying to become the so-called Pittsburgh of the South.[12] The demand for weapons during the Civil War had accelerated this process, increasing mining and iron-making facilities in the mineral districts and manufacturing in several areas.[13] The end of the war would require these economic assets to retool for peace-time pursuits, but that would necessitate far less capital than if the state were forced to start the industrialization process all over again. Taking another economic leap forward at the conclusion of the war, however, would require significant investment capital and, as in the antebellum period, that could only come from capital markets in the North or Europe.[14] That was possible only if Alabama evidenced a high degree of political stability and social harmony. Capital, it was generally held, "avoids revolution" and "shuns all uncertainties," instead seeking "security, protection and the guarantees of stable institutions."[15]

The grinding effects of war had already substantially degraded the agricultural and industrial economy of north Alabama before 1865 dawned. Slaves had been freed, and farming animals and implements and manufacturing facilities destroyed along with the homes of many Confederates and Unionists.[16] Scores of the freedmen in that region either joined the Union army or, through their labor, aided the Union war effort.[17] They would understandably expect at least the equal rights accorded citizens as their just reward, and some looked for reparations of sorts.[18]

Due to a combination of geography and Union military strategy, however, the much more significant economic assets of central and south Alabama were still unscathed in January 1865. They were, however, the most important remaining military targets in the Deep South. Their destruction was deemed necessary to end the Confederacy's ability to make war—and to convince die-hard Southerners that further resistance through guerrilla warfare was futile. When efforts to reach a peace accord failed, the loss of those assets was assured. At least Pres. Abraham Lincoln had urged charity for all in his second inaugural address in 1865, and maybe he would actively promote a regeneration of Alabama's economy after destruction came, while shielding the South from radical political reconstruction. But then he, too, was gone. His shocking loss in 1865 also strengthened currents in the North for revenge and an increased desire to impose black suffrage on the South as a form of punishment and national security. Andrew Johnson, Lincoln's successor, did not support that policy either, and this encouraged white Southerners to resist social and political change for the freedmen. The resulting power struggle contributed to the type of political and social disharmony that discouraged essential capital flows to Alabama. This all haunted the state for over a century.

One of the purposes of this book is to provide a sifting analysis of what really happened in Alabama in 1865 and why it happened. Relevant events outside Alabama are woven into the narrative. Another purpose is to demonstrate that, contrary to the myths manufactured by some early historians like John DuBose, the decisive events that made 1865 so important for Alabama were not necessarily brought on by the North. They were, in fact, quite avoidable if Alabama's political leadership had been savvier. But as if Providence were controlling and guiding Alabama's destiny, these events occurred despite a host of forces pulling in the opposite direction. And they are critically important in understanding how Alabama came to be as it is today.

I

THE FINAL DOOM OF SLAVERY

Timeline: January 3, 1865–March 11, 1865

January 3, 1865	Confederate general John Bell Hood's remaining army arrives at Corinth, Mississippi, following the Battle of Nashville.
January 5, 1865	Union troops reach Walker County, Alabama.
January 8, 1865	University of Alabama president Landon Garland gives prowar speech in Tuscaloosa.
January 10, 1865	Unionist guerrillas attack Jasper, Alabama, and burn the county courthouse.
January 13, 1865	Preston and Montgomery Blair meet with Confederate president Jefferson Davis to encourage peace talks.
January 14, 1865	*Richmond Sentinel* accuses members of the Confederate House of Representatives of treason.
January 16, 1865	William Russell Smith withdraws from the Confederate house.
January 21, 1865	Union general William T. Sherman orders Union general George Thomas to prepare for an invasion of central and south Alabama.
January 31, 1865	US House approves the Thirteenth Amendment, submitting it to the states for ratification.
February 3, 1865	Hampton Roads Peace Conference fails.
February 11, 1865	Unionist guerrillas burn the St. Clair county courthouse.
February 13, 1865	Prowar meetings take place in Selma, Talladega, and Mobile.
February 14, 1865	Unionist guerrillas raid Barbour County.
February 20, 1865	Confederate house adopts slave soldier bill.
February 23, 1865	Prowar meeting held in Montgomery.
March 1, 1865	Society of Loyal Confederates meets in Mobile.
March 4, 1865	Pres. Abraham Lincoln gives second inaugural address.
March 11, 1865	Prowar meeting held in Tuscaloosa.

1

"The Fever of Your Imagination"

One of the many flaws of historian John Witherspoon DuBose's *Alabama's Tragic Decade* is that, in making his argument for Alabama's righteousness and for Northern sins, he conveniently skips over any detailed discussion of the Civil War. His first chapter, in fact, begins in May 1865.[1] Much happened in the first four months of that year that undermines DuBose's conclusions.

As 1865 dawned and the end of the Civil War neared, Confederate Alabama was a sitting duck. Her sister states Mississippi, Tennessee, and Georgia had already been substantially overrun by Union forces and were virtually impotent. North Alabama was occupied. Mobile Bay had fallen to the Union navy a few months earlier.[2] The Confederate Army of Tennessee under Gen. John Bell Hood might have provided Alabama some defense, but it had left Alabama in November and been defeated and nearly annihilated by Union forces under Union general George Henry Thomas at the Battle of Nashville on December 16, 1864.[3] The implications of this debacle were quickly realized in Richmond, Virginia, the Confederacy's capital. Gen. Josiah Gorgas, a future president of the University of Alabama, wrote that if Hood's army were "defeated & demoralized" as the Northern press was trumpeting, "there is no force to cover Alabama & Georgia, & the enemy may penetrate these states at his leisure."[4]

What was the true mental state of Hood's beaten and retreating army? Alabamian Edward Norphlet Brown, a quartermaster, had written to his wife, Fannie, on Christmas Eve from Bainbridge, Alabama, on the north side of the Tennessee River, where frantic efforts were being made to cross the river and escape capture by pursuing Union forces. Brown revealed to her that the Yankees had "routed our army & drove it pell mell from the battle ground." There was, he continued, "never such a rout in modern times." In the process, "Hood lost eighty-two pieces of artillery, about ten thousand men & not less than fifteen thousand small arms." Brown described the survivors as "entirely demoralized" and "worn down" and the army "ruined." As a result, he concluded, "the cause of the South is sadly on the wane & I fear we shall be subjugated."[5]

Word of Hood's defeat had reached some others in Alabama by the time Alabamians ushered in the New Year. "We arrive at the painful conclusion that General Hood's expedition to Tennessee has been most disastrous," wrote the worried editor of the Greensboro *Alabama Beacon*.[6] The people were no less out of sorts. Hear their voices:

> We hear bad news now, namely, that Hood has fallen back to Corinth. I am much depressed and dread the coming of the enemy. If it was only the Lord's will that we could have peace, how thankful I certainly would be.[7]

> Give my love to all the connexion [*sic*]. Pray fervently for me. And oh kiss my sweet children for me, for in all probability I will never get to do it myself. I cannot help but grieve.[8]

> I frankly acknowledge that I trimble [*sic*] for the denouement of the great tragedy, and fear that we are approaching that point when according to holy writ destruction will inevitably follow—a house divided against itself.[9]

> What a contrast between this and a New Year's morning five years since, before the advent of this miserable war! Then the house echoed with many voices crying to each other. "I wish you a Happy New Year!" But, this morning, each child seems to know and feel by common consent there is no happy year in store for us, and all such expressions are hushed.[10]

> The year has come around with excitement and trouble for the poor downtrodden people of Alabama.[11]

> Another year has come and gone and yet this cruel war is raging. I can see no prospect for peace but all things are possible with God and He can make war cease when He thinks best. Christmas and New Years Days, times for joy and festivity, have passed but they brought no joy to me.[12]

> Although woe and desolation stare at us every way we turn, the heart of the patriot is as firm as ever, and determined that, come what may, he

"THE FEVER OF YOUR IMAGINATION" / 9

will never yield. There is no doubt but we have some among us whose love of self forbids their minds to rise above the dank sod upon which they tread; men who have never known what it is to experience a thrill of pleasure, when listening to the "patriot's moving story, shedding for freemen's rights his generous blood." Such we have among us; but, thank the Giver of all good, they are in the minority.[13]

The year is closed without the least prospect of closing the war, suffering, sadness and gloom cover the land, no one knows the end, humanity seems to have fled, immorality prevails to an alarming extent, food is scarce and if the war continues we may look for scenes among our people to equal the spanish and french troubles.[14]

Instead of a New Year's dinner, that was promised to us in the paper, we got nothing but flour to day, not any meat at all. But so long as we get enough to live on, no matter what, we will not complain.[15]

Everybody is depressed and somber. Military events have as in '62 & 63 closed against us. Still gaiety continues among the young people, & there is much marriage & giving in marriage.[16]

The poor rebels went up into Tennessee and were defeated. I am so disappointed for I was sure they would be victorious, which they would have been had they only held their ground about twenty-four hours longer. They had invested Nashville and would have soon been in it; but Hood's army had been taught to retreat and fight and would not fight without running. It was the worst defeat our army ever experienced and I hope the last.[17]

And to the chagrin of the editor of the transplanted and now Selma-based *Chattanooga Rebel*, "just now the croakers are in the hey-day of their carnival. Everything has gone wrong. They knew it and told you so."[18]

But the Selma-based Jackson *Mississippian* joined other members of the Alabama press in misrepresenting the capability of Hood's degraded army to defend Alabama. It was "in a good fighting condition," wrote its editor.[19] The *Chattanooga Rebel* agreed, declaring that "all the Yankee reports about the demoralization of the [Army of Tennessee] are mere fabrications."[20] Edward Brown had earlier warned his wife not to put credence in positive war news in the press. "This is all inflation gotten up to encourage."[21]

In what may also have been misinformation, one of Hood's many deserters claimed that Hood and his retreating troops had been ordered to Tuscaloosa in west central Alabama to reorganize his "shattered army." The story was telegraphed from Union-occupied Courtland, Alabama, and quickly became national news, thereby placing an even larger target on the City of Oaks and its military academy at the University of Alabama.[22] Whether Hood had actually received such an order is unknown, but it is interesting that a large wagon train of Hood's carrying his army's supplies and pontoons was intercepted and captured by a detachment of General Thomas's cavalry just south of Russellville, Alabama, reportedly while on its way to Tuscaloosa.[23]

As many Confederate civilians from across the South who had already fled to Tuscaloosa had concluded,[24] Tuscaloosa was a very logical destination for a force seeking refuge from an enemy approaching from the north or west side of the rain-swollen Black Warrior River, which in essence served as a broad moat to protect the town. Unless the attacking force brought pontoons, all the defenders had to do was dismantle the privately owned river bridge between Tuscaloosa and Northport, thereby in essence raising the drawbridge over the moat. Bringing pontoons in from the north or west would be very difficult for an aggressor. As a Nashville correspondent to the *Chicago Journal* put it, Tuscaloosa "was the old capital of the State, but is now a country village, and there is not a pike leading to the place. The bad state of the roads, Davis and Hood thin[k]s will prevent pursuit; and perhaps it will."[25] In addition to its isolation and relative inaccessibility, Tuscaloosa was a good base of supply given the war-related factories in the area and the availability of river transportation to and from Mobile in the winter and spring. Tuscaloosa was also a satisfactory staging area to protect the mines and foundries in nearby Jefferson and Shelby Counties and the important war-related industries to the southeast in Selma.

If Hood and his exhausted army were headed toward Tuscaloosa, they never made it any farther than Tupelo, Mississippi.[26] According to a report wired to Confederate president Jefferson Davis by Confederate general Richard Taylor, Hood's "army needs rest, consolidation, and reorganization. Not a day should be lost in effecting these latter. If moved in its present condition," Taylor concluded, "it will prove utterly worthless; this applies to both infantry and cavalry."[27] In a subsequent telegram to Davis, Taylor was even plainer. "My telegram of the 9th expressed the conviction that an attempt to move Hood's army at this time would complete its destruction."[28] Taylor was not exaggerating. According to the diary of one of Hood's men who had returned after being away on medical leave for some weeks, "it is enough to discourage the stoutest and most hopeful spirits to listen to the conversation of the men who participated in the recent campaign in Tennessee. They are utterly despon-

"The Fever of Your Imagination" / 11

Figure 1. Robert Jemison. Alabama Department of Archives and History.

dent and would hail with joy the prospect of peace on any terms." They were "fully convinced the Confederacy is *gone*."[29] Hood's announcement that he had been relieved of command did not improve their morale.[30]

If the remnant of the Army of Tennessee had reached Tuscaloosa, one wonders what type of reception they would have received. Even before Union general William Tecumseh Sherman's devastating march through Georgia and Hood's crushing defeat in Tennessee, there were strong signs that many Tuscaloosans were anxious for peace and would settle for the best terms available. Most probative in this regard was the fact that planter-industrialist Robert Jemison (fig. 1), a highly influential community leader who had been elected to the Confederate Senate in 1863 and taken his seat in December of that year,[31] had chosen not to return to Richmond when the Confederate Congress last convened on November 7, 1864.[32] Possibly more telling, Jemison's decision does not appear to have generated any public controversy for almost three months, and even then it was only from *Mobile Advertiser and*

Register editor John Forsyth in Mobile, not the local press.[33] Forsyth, Alabama's foremost Confederate propagandist, wondered whether Jemison's absence might be "owing to private business," but in any case Forsyth called on Jemison to resign his senate seat and "leave it to some man who has time to devote to the public service. If from any other reason, the public has a right to know."[34] And know the whole public and the nation soon would. In three months, the Richmond *Dispatch* would publish a list of public men in the South that the *New York Tribune* alleged were "in favor of reconstruction on the basis of the Union and the Constitution"—code words for reunion with slavery intact—and one of the nine Alabamians on the list was Jemison.[35]

Not long after Jemison's no-show in Richmond, former Whig Tennessee governor Neil Smith Brown appeared in Tuscaloosa to attempt to revive the spirit for war and independence there. According to the *Tuscaloosa Observer*, Brown addressed a group at a church in Tuscaloosa, warning of the horrors that would flow from emancipation and confiscation under Lincoln's regime if the South ever stopped fighting and submitted to his control:

> What a state of society would we then have? Ourselves impoverished, our negroes among us and on an equality with us, our lands in the hands of Yankee owners, who would farm them with our negroes at nominal wages. Such was now the sad picture in Tennessee and those border States that the Yankees hold. What has been will be again. Were we willing to submit to such degradation? Were the sons of those noble pioneers, who converted the wilderness into these smiling gardens and fruitful fields—who erected these temples to God—these courts of justice—these educational institutes, and these happy homes, amidst the attack of a savage foe, willing to yield our noble heritage to the vandal foe—the hated Yankee? Are we too craven to defend it? No! Never! We will conquer our independence, or we will die.[36]

Up to that point, however, the Confederate army alone had already suffered an estimated 146,845 casualties, and more recently Hood's army had suffered thousands more.[37] It was later estimated that 35,000 Alabamians in the Confederate army had been killed or wounded since the war began.[38] Some of the grim consequences of those stunning losses were staring Tuscaloosans in the face. Episcopal bishop Richard Hooker Wilmer, a strong supporter of the Confederacy, had visited Tuscaloosa to preside over the dedication of a new orphanage sponsored by the Episcopal Church. War had caused the innocent children terrible, life-altering losses for which there was no adequate compensation. Guilt may in part explain the fact that $50,000 had been raised in west Alabama (more than $8,000 in Tuscaloosa) to underwrite the construction and operation of the home.[39] Other religious organizations engaged in fund-raising efforts for orphanages around Alabama were experiencing the same outpouring of support.[40] But even more children would eventually become orphans unless the fighting stopped.

Morale on the home front in other parts of Alabama was also poor. Some members of the Alabama press were openly blaming Davis for their predicament.[41] Samuel Pickens, a soldier from west Alabama who was serving in Gen. Robert E. Lee's Army of Northern Virginia, noted that men returning from home "give a deplorable account of the sentiments of the people in Ala. & also in Ga. & So. Ca. Everybody whipped & despairing of our cause: wanting peace on any terms, reunion, submission—anything. How shameful!" He hoped it was "only a temporary fit of despondency caused by the disastrous campaign of Hood, the bold & well nigh unopposed march of Sherman, and the utter demoralization of our (Hood's) army down there."[42] Similarly, a worried soldier who had just rejoined Hood's army noted that "it is well known that Georgia is taking the initiatory steps looking to *submission*—at least the matter is being discussed in primary meetings held for that purpose, and I know that her course is approved and even applauded in the army." In fact, he continued, "shameful though it be . . . three-fourths of the Army of Tennessee, and perhaps as great a proportion of the citizens of Georgia, Alabama and Mississippi, are in favor of peace on any terms, no matter how ignominious they may be."[43]

Support for the Confederacy in Tuscaloosa was probably not renewed or enhanced by a speech given there in early January 1865 by University of Alabama president Landon Garland, who also served as superintendent of the Corps of Cadets there. Garland declared that "God intends that we shall be free, but He will have no subterfuges. By no foreign intervention, by no Great Western chimera, are we to be disenthralled, but by a Daniel-like endurance in a fiery furnace, by a baptism in blood, by heroic martyrdom and sacrifice are we to be brought forth into the light of liberty." Perhaps not receiving the reaction from the crowd that he had expected to his oratory, Garland observed that "some are gloomy and downcast" and asked was it "because of Hood's reverse" or "because Sherman's army has swept" over Georgia? "Were this the cause," he continued, "your despondency might soon be remedied." Then Garland unwisely resorted to ridicule, accusing his audience of being unenthusiastic for "a graver reason. You are demoralized, in fact subjugated; your patriotism sinks within you at the idea of four more years of war; you shrink appalled at this carnage, its wastings and confiscations, and think the price of liberty too high, even if paid in Confederate money; you hoped that

Hood would winter his forces on the banks of the Ohio, and that Sherman would be annihilated before he reached Atlanta. Very well; your expectations were unreasonably high, and disappointment has been the inevitable result—you have to blame the fever of your imagination."[44]

But it was not their imagination that Confederates—from President Davis on down—had earlier made these very unrealistic predictions and thereby created now unmet expectations.[45] Now, promises of future success would fall on deaf ears. Under the circumstances, one course for Tuscaloosans interested in their town's economic future was to avoid the Union army's attention while the war played itself out elsewhere. That appears to have been Robert Jemison's course of action. But the news about Hood retreating to Tuscaloosa had foiled this strategy by putting the name of the town back into the Northern press for the first time in months. Try as they might to take a position of neutrality, Tuscaloosans knew that the war was coming ever closer to them. On January 5, while chasing some of Hood's other wagon trains, Union general James Harrison Wilson's troopers had come as far south as Nauvoo, Alabama, in nearby Walker County.[46] Shortly thereafter, a company of "Tories"—Unionist guerrillas—raided Jasper, the county seat of Walker County, burning the courthouse, jail, and several other buildings, along with the records of the tax collector and assessor and the court clerk.[47] Unless peace came quickly, the next thrust would more than likely reach and destroy Tuscaloosa. Tuscaloosans, as well as all other Alabamians, knew that was not far off.

Not long after Garland's ill-advised lecture, General Sherman ordered Union general George Henry Thomas, the victor over Hood at Nashville, to prepare for the invasion. Sherman envisioned it including "an army of 25,000 infantry and all the cavalry you can get, under Wilson." This force was to move to "some point of concentration about Columbus, Miss., and thence march to Tuscaloosa and Selma, destroying [the] former, gathering horses, mules (wagons to be burned), and doing all the damage possible; burning up Selma, that is the navy-yard, the [Selma and Meridian] railroad back toward the Tombigbee, and all iron foundries, mills and factories."[48]

There was no effort by the Union military to keep this plan a closely guarded secret. On the contrary, perhaps to intimidate Alabama into capitulating, while at the same time tying down Confederate forces in the Deep South so they could not be sent east to reinforce Lee and fight against Sherman and Union general Ulysses S. Grant, the Northern press teemed with reports about the coming offensive and, generally speaking, those reports were quite accurate. It was said that Thomas had established his headquarters east of Florence, Alabama, on the south side of the Tennessee River at Eastport,

Mississippi, and was making plans for a full-scale invasion of Alabama as far south as Selma, Cahaba, and Montgomery. Part of this invasion force would include Wilson's huge cavalry corps, which had already begun establishing its base at Gravelly Springs, Alabama, a tiny village just north of the Tennessee River and a few miles east of Florence. The only detail not given was the date for the invasion,[49] but it was known in Alabama as early as January 1865 that the attack was imminent and, according to the *Montgomery Mail*, then only "prevented by the impassable nature of the roads" caused by spring rains.[50]

It is, therefore, clear that what would happen to Tuscaloosa as well as a few other central and south Alabama towns in less than ninety days was no surprise by any means to Tuscaloosans or any other Alabamians.[51] "Indeed," as the Montgomery-based *Memphis Appeal* declared, "there is no excuse for [surprise] now, for the Yankees have themselves boasted so much of their purposes, that such as are unenlightened now as to the dangers which threaten Alabama, will remain ignorant until the gridiron is planted on their faces in the very heart of the State."[52]

And the Northern press certainly did boast, uniformly assuring that taking Alabama would be relatively easy. According to an Ohio editor, "there is no adequate militia force in the State to make resistance, as the Legislature failed to make any provisions for calling out what little remains." "Nor will the people of Alabama probably make any more determined resistance than did the people of Georgia, who actually made no resistance at all."[53] A Chicago editor agreed, reporting that "the 50,000 cavalry under Thomas and [Kentucky-born Union major general Edward Richard Sprigg] Canby will sweep over the states of Mississippi and Alabama as soon as the weather will permit, and many places now nominally held by the rebels will fall into our hands, and numerous railroads, at present useful to the enemy, will be destroyed, and two or three rivers of great importance will be opened to our gunboat fleet; but all this will require no serious fighting; it will not be war, as that term has been understood the last three years; only a mere raid will be required."[54]

That this would be the case was even more likely after Davis's adamant insistence that most of Hood's remaining force be moved east to try to stop Sherman's juggernaut through the Carolinas toward Richmond. In Davis's telegram to Confederate general Richard Taylor at Meridian, Mississippi, Davis explained that "Sherman's campaign has produced bad effect on our people. Success against his future operations is needful to reanimate public confidence."[55] But according to all accounts, Hood's defeats in Tennessee had also "produced bad effect" on Alabamians and Mississippians.[56] From north Alabama, former Alabama Confederate congressman J. L. M. Curry wrote to Alabama governor Thomas Hill Watts that the "public mind is depressed beyond what I have known at any antecedent period of this war. The demoralization in the Army, fearful beyond description, is exceeded by demoralization at home."[57] The withdrawal of the Army of Tennessee from the region was certain to further undermine morale and thereby force those on the fence to opt for peace on any terms available, particularly if the institution of slavery could somehow be preserved.

Even before this, an anonymous author calling himself "Planter" had given further evidence of how critical slavery was to what many expected for a just and honorable peace. In "How to Stop the War and Save the Institution of Slavery," a letter published in the *Selma Reporter*, Planter proposed two methods to negotiate a conclusion to the war that maintained slavery. First, he advocated a national convention to be attended by delegates, selected by the governors of each state, to decide the issues. "These delegates are to be old men that have not worn a star, bar, stripe or tape during this war," he wrote. If this method did not work, he continued, "let the Governors of the States convene the different State Legislatures so that people may be authorized to elect delegates to the State convention that something may be done for the good of our country in this dark hour of her history."[58] The desire to negotiate toward this purpose was widespread. A Montgomery correspondent to the *Mobile Advertiser and Register* denounced a "class of negotiators and reconstructionists who are now clamoring so loudly for peace through the agency of 'diplomatists and newspapers.'"[59] He was likely referring to, among others, the course of the now openly propeace *Montgomery Mail*, whose editor had recently opined that without "providential interference"—which was unlikely—the Confederacy simply could not prevail.[60]

Was making the perpetuation of slavery an essential negotiating point realistic? After all, had not Lincoln issued his Emancipation Proclamation freeing the slaves in the insurrectionary states on January 1, 1863, and then publicly refused to withdraw it on several occasions since then?[61] And had not Lincoln announced in his December 1864 annual message that he would push for the adoption by Congress of the Thirteenth Amendment, which abolished slavery throughout the nation?[62] Yes, and that was the reason why Planter proposed to circumvent Lincoln (and Davis) by urging a convention of governor-selected delegates, whose constituents might be willing to trade the Union and peace for slavery. But the idea of such a convention seemed just as far-fetched. As a Mobile newspaper pointed out, most of the Northern governors were members of Lincoln's political party, and an open break by them with his policy was unlikely.[63]

Some Southerners had, therefore, given up on slavery and simply wanted peace. A Georgia woman, writing to her sister in Alabama, said that "I believe that this war will last until we are thoroughly scourged and purified from the evil that predominates in our land. It will not last always however, and we can alone trust in God. If my precious husband and brothers can be spared this is all I ask, and I do pray that God will see fit to bring them safely through this war."[64] Little did she know that the South's peculiar institution also still had life, thanks in part to the efforts of another Tuscaloosan.

2

"Treason—Treason—Treason!!!"

Under the circumstances, those Alabamians who still sincerely clung to the cause of independence were arguably not in touch with reality. Certainly not among that class was Confederate congressman William Russell Smith (fig. 2), another Tuscaloosan on the *New York Tribune*'s list of reconstructionists in the South.[1] Like Robert Jemison, Smith had attempted to prevent the state from seceding in 1861, but unlike Jemison, Smith had returned to his seat in the Confederate house during its current session, although possibly under duress. Several months earlier, Smith had unsuccessfully attempted to get his wife and family out of the crumbling Confederacy and to her mother's home in Maryland, but his plan had been foiled by Confederate provost officials in Alabama.[2] After Smith returned to Richmond in November 1864, however, they were permitted to leave and, according to John Forsyth, passed by way of Mobile through enemy lines in early January 1865.[3]

With his family in the clear, Smith then gained national attention, as well as the hatred of Confederates, when he stood in the Confederate house and advocated for peace talks with the North. He later wrote, "When my judgment became convinced that the Southern cause was hopeless, I considered it my duty to feel for terms of accommodation."[4] In early January 1865, an opportunity to achieve Smith's goal presented itself when a private but very prominent Northerner, Francis Preston Blair Sr., traveled to Richmond to meet with Davis and other Confederate officials in an effort to kindle peace talks.[5] Interestingly, Blair's trek to Richmond had been preceded by exiled Huntsville Unionist Jeremiah Clemens's visit to Washington, DC, reportedly on a mission to advise Lincoln on the means of accomplishing peace in Alabama and to apply once again for appointment as the state's military governor.[6] As both Blair and Clemens were Democrats before the war, it is possible they met and discussed what it would take to convince Southerners, sick of the bloodshed but fearful of the sudden abolition of slavery, to abandon

Figure 2. William Russell Smith. Alabama Department of Archives and History.

the Confederate government. That, feared die-hard Confederates like John Forsyth, was an offer of a plan for gradual emancipation.[7]

A gradual process had been used by several Northern states to end slavery there during the antebellum period. New York, for example, had enacted legislation at the turn of the century providing that children born to slave mothers were free but were required to serve an apprenticeship, and all slaves would be totally free on July 4, 1827.[8] If slavery in the South were to end, many Southern slave owners preferred this approach as opposed to sudden emancipation. Would the North allow gradual emancipation in exchange for an end to the bloodletting?

Abolitionists were opposed to it, as were many in the Republican Party. In a speech in Nashville on January 12, vice president elect Andrew Johnson of Tennessee, a former slave owner, declared his absolute opposition to any delay in the emancipation process, although he was not opposed to a period of apprenticeship.[9] But some believed Lincoln was willing to consider it. According to newspaper accounts, before going to Richmond, Francis Blair had met with Lincoln and obtained an assurance not only that peace commissioners could be appointed to meet with commissioners selected by the Confederacy to negotiate a peace accord but that Lincoln was, surprisingly, willing to deal on the issue of gradual emancipation. The New York *World* reported that Lincoln "does not insist upon immediate abolition, but he does insist that measures be taken to secure its extinction within a reasonable length of time."[10]

Following Blair's arrival in Richmond on January 11, but before meeting with Jefferson Davis, he consulted with members of the Confederate House Committee on Foreign Affairs, of which William Russell Smith was a member. According to the diary of Jehu A. Orr of Mississippi, another member of that committee, Blair revealed that in exchange for peace and re-union, Lincoln would not only be favorable to the concept of gradual emancipation but receptive to the idea that it could be drawn out over a period as long as thirty years.[11] That would have allowed slavery in the South to continue until 1895. Southern optimists could remind any skeptics that in late 1862 Lincoln had proposed a plan for gradual *and* compensated emancipation that would have allowed slavery until 1900.[12] They could also cite his statements several months *after* the issuance of his Emancipation Proclamation that he was willing to accept gradual emancipation and in fact believed it to be "better for both white and black."[13] No evidence has been found that Alabama slave owners were the least bit skeptical.

The next day, Smith's committee issued a secret report to an executive session of the house. It was rumored to contain a call for the appointment by the Confederate Congress, *not* Davis, of commissioners to go to Washington, DC, to negotiate a peace accord.[14] According to a revealing public letter Smith subsequently wrote to his constituents, Smith was "under the deepest conviction that there are not one hundred men in the [Tuscaloosa congressional] District who would object to it."[15] Smith's estimate of the level of support for peace negotiations back in Tuscaloosa was similar to that contained in an anonymous letter from Tuscaloosa that later appeared in the *Montgomery Mail*. According to its author, "four-fifths of the people think we must have peace soon or we are ruined. If the war continues six months, we will have to accept any terms that the North proposes."[16]

The contents of the committee's report were apparently leaked to Davis and, as the entire nation would soon learn, pandemonium broke loose in Richmond. As Alabamians read in their newspapers, the *Richmond Sentinel*, which was considered to be Davis's primary organ in the Confederate capital, published with approval a letter it provocatively titled "Treason—Treason—Treason!!!" in which an anonymous author lambasted all of the members of the Committee on Foreign Affairs. He charged them with disloyalty and "treachery of the most infamous character" for having proposed a "disorderly, ruinous and fatal proposition" having "neither dignity, honor or safety" to "open irregular negotiations, through commissioners, with Mr. Lincoln for peace." He was certain that the "people of the Confederacy generally, would not allow themselves to be sold by traitorous Congressmen after this fashion."[17]

The publication of this letter incensed several members of the committee and, on January 17, Congressman Orr had the House clerk read it to the entire body, following which he warned that "denunciation will be met by defiance. This movement," he revealed, "is not in the hands of timid or time serving men. Sustained, as they are, by a volume of sentiment in the country and in the army, and by their own sense of duty, they are determined that, in some form, the statesmanship of the country shall be invoked in an honest effort to end this carnival of death by negotiation." With obvious reference to Davis, Orr concluded that the "statesman who would refuse to do this is a hideous moral deformity." Then a Georgia congressman moved to suspend the rules so he could introduce a resolution denying disloyalty and resolving that the allegations to the contrary "merit the emphatic rebuke and unqualified denunciations of this House." When a vote was taken on the motion to suspend, however, it failed to even gain a majority (ayes, 32; noes, 36), much less the two-thirds vote required to suspend the rules. Therefore, the resolution could not be considered at that point.[18]

In a letter, William Russell Smith explained that "when this was announced, I felt extremely indignant," having "expected protection" from the House, "and not abandonment." Therefore, he continued, "I immediately determined to withdraw from the House, not willing to sit there under the shadow of an impeachment."[19] Smith rose and, addressing the Speaker of the House, declared that he considered the vote on the motion to suspend "as, to some extent endorsing the *Sentinel*, and as long as that vote stands as the sense of this body, I can take no part in its deliberations." Smith then formally withdrew from the House, and in the letter to his constituents stated that "I expect to return home as soon as I can close up my business here."[20]

The last propeace member of the Confederate House who had withdrawn from that body out of frustration was a former Alabamian, Henry Stuart Foote of Tennessee.[21] In an effort to negotiate a peace settlement, Foote had attempted to leave the Confederacy with his wife before Christmas of 1864. But as was reported nationally, Foote was arrested by Confederate authorities in Virginia before crossing the Potomac River and was returned to Richmond.[22] With Smith's wife and family already in Maryland, Smith may have considered that destination, and John Forsyth suspected that was Smith's actual motive for withdrawing from the House. Smith, declared Forsyth, "must rest under the grave suspicion of a purpose to fly from what he considered a sinking ship," especially given his family's recent departure.[23] Forsyth was probably not alone in his suspicions, and Smith was likely closely watched in the ensuing weeks as a result.[24]

It is also possible that Smith did initially intend to return to Alabama to bolster the peace movement. Henry Foote later revealed that there was a "solemn compact entered into between the almost entire Congressional delegation from Tennessee—nearly a majority of that from N[orth] Carolina, Georgia and Alabama, and a portion from Mississippi and Virginia that if peace was not restored there that they would in defiance of Davis and the War faction stump their respective States for an immediate reunion with the federal States."[25] But whether Smith was a member of that compact is unknown.

Word of Lincoln's reported stance on gradual emancipation meanwhile spread like wildfire.[26] It caused great consternation in the North among those who favored immediate emancipation and who feared that Lincoln would concede on this issue in order to achieve peace. The *Mobile Advertiser and Register* had earlier reported that two-thirds of Alabamians would agree to that.[27] As a consequence, proabolition Republicans in Congress redoubled their efforts in the US House of Representatives to have the joint resolution proposing the Thirteenth Amendment adopted. According to the New York *World*, the "radicals distrust Mr. Lincoln; they wish to head off all probability of his making a peace that does not include the extinction of slavery."[28]

News of Lincoln's rumored position on gradual emancipation also reached Alabama. In traumatized north Alabama, Franklin County lawyer Joshua Burns Moore, a reconstructionist, noted the receipt of information from a friend that "Lincoln has sent Com's to Richmond to try and negotiate terms of peace upon the following terms, 'The Southern States go back into the Union, no confiscation, full amnesty, emancipation at the end of 30 years.'" According to Moore, "such propositions would be accepted I believe by 3/4th of the Southern people and by 3/4th of the secessionists themselves." With obvious contempt, Moore concluded: "So much for secession. After desolating the country, [the secessionists] are willing to crouch like dogs to save their necks from the halter, and their property from confiscation."[29]

Although John Forsyth (fig. 3) was certainly no croucher, that was exactly how he saw public sentiment in south Alabama. To him that was a major problem. In an editorial titled "Our Danger," he candidly admitted that "the Confederate cause is at this moment passing through its most dangerous crisis. Large numbers of the people—perhaps, upon a fair poll, the majority—are heart-sick of the war, and willing to end it upon terms which would have been scouted at as treasonable two years, or even one year ago." He was particularly surprised that "even the class of slaveholders, having the deepest pe-

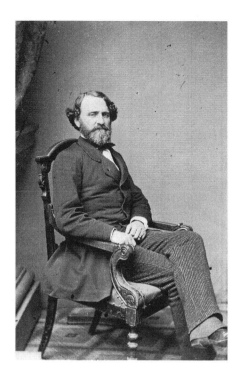

Figure 3. John Forsyth. Courtesy of the Library of Congress, Prints and Photographs Division.

cuniary stake in the success of the struggle for independence, are ready to make sacrifices the mention of which a short time ago would not have been tolerated. We have not a doubt that the country, including the slave-proprietors, large and small, would compromise to-day for peace and independence on the basis of a gradual and universal emancipation of the blacks. We may go further, and say that large numbers would be willing to give up all their cherished thoughts of independence, and exchange the institution for naked peace, upon terms of reconstruction."[30]

Many Alabamians were in the process of doing just that. According to an Associated Press dispatch, it was "whispered" that President Lincoln met with "two Alabama peace envoys" on January 19 and that "the President was giving his mind to the endeavors from both sides of the line of war to bring about a settlement."[31] The *Chicago Tribune* reported that these two unidentified envoys were "authorized to visit Washington by a secret association, embracing at least two-thirds of the people of the State, and who are resolved to overthrow the rebellion at the earliest moment possible."[32] The following day, what General Thomas described as a "deputation of citizens of North Alabama" met with him at his base at Eastport, Mississippi, to "consult with me as to the best mode of bringing their section back in the Union." According to his report of the meeting to Assistant Secretary of War Charles Anderson Dana, Thomas advised the group to "call a convention of the people living north of the Tennessee River, and adopt the necessary measures in convention for re-establishing civil law in their district, and then to make a petition to the President to be admitted into the Union as a section of Alabama, prepared in all respects to perform their duties as loyal citizens of the Government of the United States, acknowledging the *practical* abolition of slavery [sometimes a euphemism for gradual emancipation through apprenticeship], and expressing a desire that the institution may never be restored; then to send a delegation to Washington with a copy of the proceedings of their convention and their petition to lay before the President." As Thomas advised Dana, "I think these people are sincere, and hope they may be encouraged to reorganize civil authority in their district, believing it will greatly facilitate any future efforts that may be made to re-establish civil authority in the State of Alabama, and its restoration to the Union."[33]

At about the same time, Jean Joseph (J. J.) Giers of Morgan County, who for some time had been serving as a spy for the Union army, had a clandestine meeting somewhere on the road between Decatur and Moulton with a group that included Confederate general Philip Roddey's chief of staff. Roddey's brigade, which was primarily composed of men from northwest Alabama, was the only regular Confederate military organization left in north Alabama. Neutralizing it was important to the peace process, especially given Watts's message to the Alabama legislature in November 1864 threatening violent retribution for any internal effort to engineer reunion.[34] As Giers explained in his January 26 report to General Grant, "but a squad [of Confederate soldiers] in a county is sufficient to check any popular movement [toward reconstruction] outside the federal lines." During the meeting Giers was informed that the linchpin of the deal for Roddey's acquiescence in reconstruction was an agreement on a plan of gradual rather than immediate emancipation. Giers was also told that not just north Alabama but "three-fourths of the State" could be convinced to, in essence, secede from Alabama.[35]

According to Giers's report, the process would begin with an effort to "communicate with Governor Watts first, and should no result come from it, to make a movement, civil and military, to immediately organize a State government," presumably similar to the means by which West Virginia had been created earlier in the war. In exchange, slavery would be abolished over a period of years, thereby avoiding the destruction of "the life of the community by convulsions and a total derangement of the entire order of things political, social, moral and economical" that would be wrought by the "abrupt" and "instantaneous emancipation of 500,000 slaves."[36] Perhaps to seal the deal with Roddey himself, the Union military agreed to attempt to procure for him a full pardon and to orchestrate a large prisoner exchange regarding former members of Roddey's brigade, all of which appears to have been arranged in record time.[37]

Word of these collaborative activities by Roddey's men may have gotten back to Confederate general Richard Taylor, who was the commander of the military department that included north Alabama. Taylor reportedly had secret agents deployed in Alabama and "no branch of Government Officials have been more assiduous in their duties than those gentlemen attached to the secret service. They are, or seem to be, ubiquitous."[38] Without expressly citing concerns about disloyalty, Taylor requested his superior, Confederate general P. G. T. Beauregard, to obtain authorization from the War Department in Richmond to "delocalize" and move Roddey's brigade out of north Alabama "for the good of the service."[39] Davis became personally involved in this decision and, ironically, initially nixed the proposed redeployment, explaining that "on each occasion when this officer has been sent with his command to distant service, serious calamity to Alabama has followed."[40] Roddey may have attempted to prove his value in his present location by reporting on what he claimed were impending military movements by the enemy. For example, he informed the Confederate commander in Columbus, Mississippi, of ongoing preparations by Union troops in Huntsville for an offensive from Huntsville toward Tuscaloosa and then Selma.[41] As will be seen, this information was not accurate; the attack would ultimately originate from northwest Alabama.

While the final decision on Roddey was pending before Confederate authorities, however, electrifying news of events many assumed would finally lead to peace reached Alabama and the rest of the nation (or nations). Expectations of the end of the conflict for which so many had prayed would be at their highest in years, but those expectations would be cruelly dashed.[42]

3
The "Peace Bubble"

Our vice-president and others have gone to Washington to make peace arrangements. God speed them.

—Sarah Espy

For my own part I have very little confidence in the ability of our Commissioners to make peace—so if it comes I will only be the more rejoiced because it will be totally unexpected.

—Hubert Dent

How much I desire to see my dear wife and sweet little daughters, hope that peace will soon be made & all of us sent home to stay with our much loved ones the balance of our days.

—James Lanning

Old Frank Blair left last week, and on Sunday morning (yesterday) three so-called peace commissioners started off for Washington. They are Judge Campbell, Mr. Hunter and Mr. Stephens. Will anything come of it? I doubt it. They have no credentials nor authority but go simply to see whether anything can be agreed on, or hit on, as a basis for negotiations.

—Gen. Josiah Gorgas

I have not heard any news lately; but hope we will soon hear that best of all news, Peace.

—Sally Independence Foster

A rumor had swept Alabama and the rest of the South in late 1864 that Jefferson Davis (fig. 4) had died, prompting one war weary Alabama soldier, Grant Taylor, to declare that "I believe his death would be a great blessing to the Confederacy."[1] His death would certainly have been a great blessing to peace advocates in Alabama. For that very reason, William Nugent, a Mississippi soldier who heard the same rumor while serving in South Carolina, wrote to his wife that he hoped it was "without foundation." Mindful of his plantation in the Mississippi Delta, Nugent explained that Davis was "the only man I know of who has the ability and nerve to carry us safely through this revolution and if his place is supplied with [Confederate vice president Alexander] Stephens I fear the consequences. Our Vice President has still a

Figure 4. Jefferson Davis. Courtesy of the Library of Congress, Prints and Photographs Division.

little of the old Leaven left and might in a pinch be disposed to reconstruct on old Abe's plan," and "without slavery little of our territory is worth a cent." This lawyer-planter was adamant that "there can be no peace as long as the alternative of abolition is presented to us."[2]

The rumors of Davis's demise were baseless. And with reluctance, he had finally bowed to intense public and political pressure by appointing commissioners to meet with commissioners from the North to discuss peace terms.[3] So optimistic that Davis's Confederate commissioners—John Archibald Campbell (fig. 5) of Alabama, Alexander Stephens, and Confederate senator Robert Mercer Taliaferro Hunter of Virginia—would be successful in this endeavor, William Russell Smith decided to return to his seat in the Confederate Congress.[4] What Smith and other Alabama peace advocates did not immediately realize was that what would become known as the Hampton Roads Peace Conference was merely intended by Davis as a pretense to silence the peace movement.[5] Rather than engaging in good faith negotiations, which implied compromise on both sides, Campbell and the other Confederate commissioners were only authorized to make a single take-it-or-leave-it offer of

Figure 5. John Archibald Campbell. Courtesy of the Library of Congress, Prints and Photographs Division.

peace with independence.[6] Davis knew this offer would not be accepted, but when it was rejected, he could claim that he had tried and failed to reach a negotiated peace, that Lincoln had negotiated in bad faith, and that continued resistance was the South's only option.[7]

This explains why Alabama Confederates like John Forsyth were likewise optimistic about the results of the upcoming conference. "If they fail," he wrote in an editorial, "the mouths of peace men should be forever closed, for it will then be conclusive that the only hopes of the country will rest in its courage and its arms."[8] The *Selma Reporter* saw another positive benefit in failed peace negotiations; it would lead to foreign recognition and possibly intervention pursuant to international law. According to the *Reporter*, Lincoln's agreement to treat with appointed Confederate commissioners implied "practical and substantial recognition of us as a defiant *de facto* republic, if not as an independent people; and whatever may be the result of the negotiations, we must henceforward stand before the world admitted by our enemy to be a political organization having substantial rights that must be made the subject of treaty and mutual agreement."[9]

But the homesick and war-weary soldiers on both sides actually believed that there would be fruitful negotiations for peace. According to the Richmond *Dispatch*, as the Confederate commissioners made their way from Richmond toward Hampton Roads, "our troops set up such a cheering as never was heard before, and continued it until the Commissioners were out of sight, and were within the federal lines, when the clamor was immediately caught up by the federal troops, who cheered and hurrahed until they were hoarse, and amid the deafening shouts of the two armies, the Commissioners went on their way."[10] Samuel Pickens, an Alabama soldier in the Confederate Army of Northern Virginia, noted that the news of peace talks "is very agreeable" and "we can't help entertaining some hope" for peace. "God grant they may meet with success, & this lamentable strife cease." He was realistic, however, admitting that "there is really little grounds for hope of any acceptable terms from the Yankees after the successes they have recently met."[11]

To understand what happened at Hampton Roads on Friday, February 3, 1865, it is helpful to recall that all of the participants, including Lincoln and William Seward, were lawyers and therefore familiar with the age-old process of how hotly contested lawsuits are settled. Neither side opens the bidding with their best offer. Instead, initial offers are intentionally outside the expected settlement range. Their primary purpose is to feel out the other side and determine where the median or middle ground is. Given this, it was no surprise that when Campbell et al. offered to settle based on Confederate independence, Lincoln's initial reply did not include an offer to resolve the most important issue—slavery—through a process of gradual emancipation. Lincoln instead counteroffered that the insurrection would simply cease and federal authority be allowed to resume in the South.[12]

But according to several sources, Lincoln did suggest to the Confederates propositions they could make that would receive positive consideration. Despite having publicly expressed delight less than forty-eight hours earlier regarding the January 31 adoption by the US House of Representatives of a resolution favoring submission of the Thirteenth Amendment to the states,[13] Lincoln (and Seward) indicated means by which the ratification of that amendment could be defeated or delayed. One suggestion was for the Southern states to cease fighting, convene their legislatures, and vote against ratification. Another was for those legislatures to vote to ratify the amendment on a prospective basis only, such that it would not take effect for several years. Lincoln also indicated a willingness to sweeten the deal by recommending to Congress that slave owners be compensated for the loss of their "property."[14]

Why would Lincoln compromise on this basis when the end of the war seemed so near? Just a few days earlier, Secretary of the Navy Gideon Welles had written in his diary that "the President, with much shrewdness and much good sense has often strange and incomprehensible whims. Takes sometimes singular and unaccountable freaks."[15] But there were also several very rational possible reasons. Horace Greeley had written to Lincoln in 1864 imploring him to initiate peace negotiations, describing the country as "bleeding, bankrupt [and] almost dying"[16] It was no better in 1865 from a financial standpoint. After expending over $3.35 billion on the war, the national debt had ballooned from a manageable $648 million in 1860 to a whopping $2.6 *billion* and was still rising.[17] Lincoln also knew what much of the Northern public did not about the nation's financial health: that the cost of the war was far exceeding revenues and that if the government continued to spend at its current rate of $838 million per year, the national debt would rise to the staggering, unprecedented level of $2.7 billion by the middle of 1865. The truth had been withheld from the public to avoid a decrease in morale,[18] but in January 1865 the venerable *Merchants' Magazine and Commercial Review* described the nation's finances as "inflated like an immense balloon, and showing signs of collapse." It predicted that unless radical changes were made in terms of significant tax increases, the current of debt would "hurry" the nation to bankruptcy.[19] Despite Union victories in Georgia and Tennessee, the war continued and expenses rose with the deaths on the battlefield. Moreover, comparing Lincoln's photographs at the beginning of the conflict (see fig. 6) with those of more recent vintage (see fig. 7) clearly reflects that the war had taken a tremendous emotional toll on him. Quite simply, the war-weary Lincoln wanted to end the bloodshed and avoid a national financial collapse.[20]

As the lawyers on the Confederate side probably noted, Lincoln's suggestions had superficial appeal. If secession were not legal and the states composing the Confederacy were actually still in the Union as Alabamians knew some in Congress believed, the legislatures of at least some of those states would have to ratify the Thirteenth Amendment for it to be legally adopted.[21] As the *Cincinnati Gazette* pointed out, with thirty-six states to be counted, twenty-seven would be necessary to achieve ratification, and only twenty-five had not attempted to secede. Three of those, Kentucky, New Jersey, and Delaware, all slave states, were considered unlikely to ratify the amendment. So even if the legislatures of the already substantially reconstructed states—Tennessee, Louisiana, and Arkansas—voted to ratify, and their votes were counted, the amendment would still fail unless at least two of the Kentucky–New Jersey–Delaware trio voted for ratification.[22] Chances were, at least two of those states could be convinced to vote against ratification by a pledge from the South to stop fighting. In fact, both Delaware and Kentucky subsequently rejected the amendment even without that assurance.[23]

The remarkable suggestions made by Lincoln and Seward to block or delay the effect of the Thirteenth Amendment were theoretically viable, but not foolproof. The unknown variable was how the US Supreme Court would ul-

Figure 6. Abraham Lincoln, August 13, 1860. Photograph by Preston Butler. Courtesy of the Library of Congress, Prints and Photographs Division.

Figure 7. Abraham Lincoln, February 5, 1865. Photograph by Alexander Gardner. Courtesy of the Library of Congress, Prints and Photographs Division.

timately rule on the now-blazing issue of the legality of secession.[24] Forsyth correctly characterized this conundrum as the "Yankee Dilemma,"[25] and its political implications would beguile efforts to reconstruct the nation when the war finally ended. If the US Supreme Court ruled that secession was legal and that the Southern states were therefore out of the Union and not to be counted in determining the number of states needed to ratify, then the Thirteenth Amendment would easily be adopted despite opposition from the South. However, if secession were deemed legal, then the North's war against the South was arguably illegal, as was the huge war debt that had been accumulated *and* the taking of slaves without compensation. Given this, as well as Northern public opinion generally, it was more probable that the Court would decide that secession was illegal, that the war was legal, and therefore that three-fourths of *all* the states would have to ratify the Thirteenth Amendment before it was binding. Meanwhile, slavery would be perpetuated for the foreseeable future unless the Supreme Court upheld the legality of Lincoln's Emancipation Proclamation, a legal question about which Lincoln himself expressed uncertainty[26] and regarding which even Alabama Unionists would later differ.[27] Having been a member of the US Supreme Court, John Archibald Campbell understood the constitutional issues and the likely possible outcome. It is not surprising, therefore, that Campbell was favorable to Lincoln's suggestions,[28] and it is possible that after the conclusion of the conference he communicated this either directly or indirectly to peace advocates back in Alabama.

Lincoln's actual settlement offer at Hampton Roads—reunion—was not a bad faith proposal of the sort that oftentimes terminates negotiations. In order to receive a better offer than this, however, the Confederates had to make a counteroffer. No lawyer bids against himself, and Lincoln could not have been expected to do so. But attorney Jefferson Davis, himself well schooled in the art of negotiation, had anticipated this and made clear to the commissioners beforehand that they were not authorized to make that next offer. In addition, unlike Lincoln, Davis had not accompanied his commissioners to Hampton Roads and, therefore, could not be lobbied by Campbell and the others for additional settlement authority. In retrospect, President Lincoln should not have agreed to meet unless the ultimate decision-maker on the Confederate side, Jefferson Davis, was also present.[29] In any event, after almost four bloody years of war, the Hampton Roads peace talks terminated after only four hours.[30]

As William Russell Smith later wrote, the "party in power [in the South] held the doctrine 'Independence or Extermination.' It would listen to nothing else with patience."[31] A disappointed pro-Confederacy teenage girl who was a member of a prominent Florence, Alabama, family wrote that "our commissioners returned without effecting anything. The yanks would not agree to our terms, and we would not agree to their peace terms. It seems that we will have war four years longer, but oh! Lord may it not be so."[32] A saddened Greensboro lawyer, Augustus Benners, wrote that the "hopes for peace which some cherished have been disappointed—& it seems that the dreadful war will last still longer." Letters home from two members of an Alabama regiment confirm the existence of this sentiment. One wrote of the "intense feeling of insubordination" that pervaded the army, and another declared that he was "for peace" and never wanted to hear any "war speakers" ever again.[33] "May God help us—& give us strength to endure its terrible inflictions."[34] A worried Alabama officer in the Army of Northern Virginia wrote home of hundreds of desertions and of a possible impending bloody mutiny. "The men," he wrote, "speak openly of the 'muskets having the power' and of their determination not to submit to military authority much longer."[35] Whether a majority of Alabama troops shared these sentiments is unknown. Capt. Edward Crenshaw, an Alabamian from a prominent Black Belt family who was serving in Virginia, had a different viewpoint. But this may have been based on misinformation supplied by Confederate officials to the troops. He wrote that "President Lincoln refused to treat with the Confederate States while in arms. He requires us to lay down our arms and submit before he will make any terms with us. And before we do this I hope that we will fight until the last man, woman, and child in the South is slain. Better death than dishonor."[36]

The discouraging outcome at Hampton Roads had been anticipated by some Alabama Unionists. Before the newspapers ever reported the result, Joshua Burns Moore wrote that he "put not one particle of confidence" in the "various rumors of armistice, proposals of peace, etc." On the contrary, he continued, "I believe if Lincoln were to propose to Davis to make peace and let the states all come back with every right they originally had under the Constitution, Davis would refuse to even listen to it. Davis, and those who like him command this war, set out for a Southern Confederacy, and nothing but the total cutting to pieces and scattering of the Southern armies will divest their minds of this one idea. No matter what suffering it brings. No matter upon whom the hardships may fall."[37]

The sentiment among many south Alabama Unionists was the same. A correspondent in Montgomery noted with disgust the presence of a "peace party in our midst."[38] Before Hampton Roads, he had probably correctly surmised that they were plotting to surrender the town if the Yankees approached, as had the mayor of Savannah, Georgia, Dr. Richard Arnold, who thereby saved that city before Sherman attacked. "It has been whispered that the handful of croakers and submissionists that infest this city had an informal meeting to see how many could be found to follow the cowardly and traitorous example of the Arnolds of Savannah. The meeting was too slim to be chronicled by the peace organ of the city"—a reference to the *Montgomery Mail*—and there was "no chance for diplomatists and newspapers to undertake the task of effecting a peace from such scanty and uncertain materials." "It was," he concluded, "a dirty flash in the pan and so died out in its own smoke."[39] But that yearning for peace had not died out. Shortly after Hampton Roads, the same correspondent complained that this group was "ever clamoring 'peace,' 'peace,' like old John Hook shouting 'beef,' 'beef,' through our camp in the war of the Revolution." Even worse, "one of this class was heard to say a few days since, 'If the President did not accept the terms offered, they (the speculators, we suppose) would make him.' This is the patriotism of the peace-on-any-terms party."[40]

A much more sympathetic Tuscaloosa correspondent to the *Montgomery Mail* agreed that the chance for peace on "fair terms" was now, not later, and advocated that Governor Watts call a convention so that the people could express their views. However, he concluded, "Governor Watts will not move unless compelled."[41] Consistent with the plan earlier proposed by Roddey's chief of staff to J. J. Giers, an effort was made by Alabama Unionists to convince Watts to issue a call for a convention or for a special session of the legislature. A group that included another of Roddey's men, Col. James M. Warren, a prewar merchant in Lawrence County,[42] had gone to Montgomery to meet and reason with Watts on this topic.[43] They were unsuccessful.[44]

Watts was likely aware of strong rumors on the street and in the press that if he convened the legislature, Unionists such as Joseph C. Bradley of Huntsville would introduce peace resolutions. According to reports, these resolutions would declare the Ordinance of Secession adopted in 1861 to be a nullity; call on Alabama officials to take the necessary oath to support the constitution of the United States; provide for congressional elections; and recall all Alabamians in the Confederate army.[45]

Roddey appears to have attempted to use a subterfuge to convince Watts to call the legislature together. In a letter to Watts, Roddey reminded him of the upcoming state elections in August 1865 and warned him that, unless Confederate soldiers were authorized by the legislature to vote outside the counties of their residence, the growing peace party in Alabama would control the elections. Watts, however, did not take the bait. He replied to Roddey that "I have been aware, for some time of the organization of which you speak." In fact, Watts continued, "I know many of the leaders of it & have my eyes on them." Then Watts correctly noted that a constitutional amendment would be required to change the law regarding voting procedures but falsely claimed that the adoption of such a change could not be accomplished before August. As Watts acknowledged in his letter, if he called the legislature into special session, it could adopt measures scheduling a constitutional convention. There, as Watts well knew, the delegates could make the change Roddey claimed he desired. But it would also give peace advocates a path to accomplish their entire program. Watts was not about to allow that. He declared to Roddey that "the matter you suggest cannot be accomplished."[46]

The next step in the Unionists' plan in Alabama was to begin an armed revolt and then organize a loyal state government. A correspondent to the *Chicago Tribune* predicted that if Watts's defiance continued, "then look for a revolution. The people have fully weighed the responsibility of the situation, and they are determined to end the rebellion so far as their State is concerned, and they will be backed by 40,000 Union cavalry, and a fair force of infantry, though not half that number will be needed."[47] Signs of armed insurgency were already appearing. On the night of February 11, what a south Alabama newspaper described as a "band of tories and negroes, 60 to 100 strong" invaded Ashville in St. Clair County and "liberated 15 political prisoners" from the jail before burning the county courthouse. They also killed the captain of a reserve cavalry unit, wounded another, and killed the local agent for collection of the tax-in-kind.[48]

Reports regarding Roddey's involvement in a revolutionary movement were also beginning to appear in the Northern press.[49] In a widely cited article, a pro-Union St. Louis, Missouri, newspaper unwisely reported that it had learned from a military official fresh from Tennessee that "Brigadier-General Roddey, who has earned a high reputation during the war as a partisan cavalry commander, and who has co-operated with Forrest in several important operations, grew tired of the contest a few weeks ago. He found means to communicate with the federal authorities, and through them procured a full pardon from the President as a condition precedent to laying down his arms. His pardon was forwarded to Gen. Thomas's headquarters by Mr. Lincoln last week, and by this time, doubtless, is in the hands of the repentant rebel for whom it was prepared."[50] A Nashville correspondent to the *Chicago Journal* noted that "so intense are the sufferings of the people" in Alabama that "they demand immediate relief; and unless Gov. Watts grants it, or shows a disposition to make peace, he will be ousted by a counter revolution; and that counter revolution will be led by no less a person than Gen. Roddey. He is at the head of a considerable force, and he is only awaiting the conclusion that the Governor will arrive at; and he will not tarry much longer."[51]

If Confederates in Alabama had any doubts about the accuracy of these reports, all they had to do was read the clumsy denials in the *Nashville Union*. "The last sensation rumor comes from one of the St. Louis papers, and is to the effect that Gens. Clanton and Roddy [*sic*] are about to come over with bag and baggage, &c. A friend who ought to know, tells us that these reports are utterly false, and that these Generals are now as determined rebels as ever. These reports may have originated from the fact that they both are very humane and honest men, and exceedingly honorable and courteous in their occasional intercourse with the federal authorities. Gen. Roddy [*sic*] has always treated our prisoners with the utmost kindness and consideration; and all speak highly of him. Union men and their families have never been treated by him with cruelty, but their opinions, if not openly expressed, have been respected."[52]

Roddey and his men were eventually ordered to change their base to Tuscaloosa, thereby ending their ability to easily communicate with the Union army and its agents in north Alabama. At least they would not be sent east to fight against Sherman.[53] Tellingly, however, according to a report to General Thomas, some of Roddey's men *refused* to go and remained in Lawrence County.[54] But even if those objectors remained, they would have been insufficient in number to provide the military might necessary to protect a separatist movement from retaliation by Confederate guerrillas or the detachments from Maj. Gen. Nathan Bedford Forrest's cavalry corps that were being sent in to replace Roddey's men in north Alabama.[55]

Forsyth was obviously ecstatic about the failure of the peace talks at Hampton Roads. "Exit another peace bubble, exploded! The Commissioners went, talked and came back with Abe's ultimatum—peace on the sole condition of submission to the Constitution and laws of the Union—that is to say, submission to the unbridled will of enemies who hate us to the point of extermination. This brings us back to the point we started from four years ago. This is the ultimatum which the advocates of the war have declared all along we had to confront. Well, the issue is plain enough now. He who runs may read, and the partisan of negotiation and diplomacy is henceforth the open champion of his country's everlasting disgrace and the enslavement of its people. The croakers are fairly cornered, and we look at least for the spirit of the rat which under the same circumstances turns upon its enemies and fights with desperate determination."[56]

The *Selma Dispatch* was likewise glad that the "agony of suspense, to a great many of our people, is over." Now, "if the reconstruction and 'peace at any price' elements" were not silent, "they must be silenced by popular sentiment and the power of the Government. A man that now talks of peace on any terms offered by the enemy talk [*sic*] cowardice and treason." Henceforth, it concluded, "we look for a grand uprising of the whole people, and the exhibition of determined patriotism and manhood of which this people are capable. Who can doubt the successful establishment of the Government of the Confederate States if there is a universal resolve among our people to that end."[57] The Selma-based *Chattanooga Rebel* declared that, "henceforth every man is either for absolute submission, or for the best and bravest and most forcible resistance we can make to [Lincoln's] insolent and inhuman demands. If we are not cowards, we ought now to be united on the platform of resistance to the bitter end." But, it concluded, "with God as our shield, we may safely rely on a united people to achieve their independence."[58] A correspondent in Montgomery agreed. "Well! The protracted agony is over. The clamorers for peace by negotiation have had their experiment." Now "the sentiment of our people throughout the country should be, 'war to the knife, and the knife to the hilt,' until our would be oppressors are forever driven from our soil."[59]

And with that, slavery was doomed to end sooner rather than later. Just two months hence a Northern editor would conclude that "Providence has permitted this war to be protracted until the great cause of it—slavery—has been destroyed by the actions of both parties—the South as well as the North."[60] Slavery, however, would not be Alabama's only loss.

II
THE FINAL DOOM
OF ALABAMA'S
INDUSTRIAL ECONOMY

Timeline: March 21, 1865–April 12, 1865

March 21, 1865	General Wilson's force begins the invasion of Alabama from Lauderdale County.
March 24, 1865	Wilson's force reaches Russellville, Alabama.
March 25, 1865	James Holt Clanton is wounded while trying to stop an invasion force from Pensacola, Florida.
March 28, 1865	Wilson's force reaches Jasper, Alabama.
March 30, 1865	Wilson's force reaches Elyton, Jefferson County, Alabama.
April 1, 1865	Richmond, Virginia, falls to General Grant.
April 2, 1865	Selma falls to Wilson's force.
April 3, 1865	Tuscaloosa falls to Gen. John Tyler Croxton's force.
April 4, 1865	Lincoln visits Richmond.
April 9, 1865	Lee surrenders his army to Grant at Appomattox, Virginia.
April 12, 1865	Montgomery and Mobile are surrendered to Union forces.

4

The Will Is Wanting

Die-hard Confederates were still full of very brave talk, but their words did nothing to provide the manpower and resources necessary to replenish the Confederate war effort and fight off the huge Union army strike force everyone knew was massing to invade central and south Alabama. Now even the man affectionately called the War Eagle, Nathan Bedford Forrest—still the darling of the Deep South press—was having difficulties retaining and recruiting men to fight for the cause.[1] His cavalry corps had been crippled by desertions during the course of Hood's demoralizing retreat from Tennessee,[2] and there were rumors in the press that Forrest had since been "stabbed by one of his men while [Forrest was] chastising a brother of the assassin."[3] Forrest's brother denied this,[4] but given the contents of a lengthy and rambling telegram Forrest sent to Gen. Richard Taylor from Corinth, Mississippi, there may have been some truth to the rumor.

Forrest had learned that the remnant of Hood's army was being sent to Georgia and that Forrest and his men would be charged with the responsibility of defending Mississippi and Alabama from the expected invasion. Rather than boldly undertaking this challenge, Forrest replied by revealing to Taylor that his forces were inadequate because of casualties, as well as the fact that many of his men had "taken advantage of all the confusion and disorder attending the hasty retreat of a beaten army, and are now scattered through the country or have gone to their homes." He also curiously added that he wanted to be temporarily replaced so he could travel to Richmond, in part to discuss matters with the War Department and also as "a recreation to myself." Forrest wrote that "the latter is much needed, as I have had no rest or relief from duty since I came into this department."[5]

Whether Forrest's request for recreation was granted is unknown. But news of his unorthodox method of rebuilding his corps would soon appear in the press. According to one admiring Alabama editor, Forrest resorted to making threats to burn the houses of skulkers and deserters unless they went into his ranks.[6] Not reported in Alabama were the executions of those who subsequently deserted.[7] But such were the times, and as Forrest is said to have put it, he had been left alone to "hold the bag in this section," and it was a "pretty big bag."[8]

The Montgomery-based *Memphis Appeal* assured that there were enough eligible men outside the army in Alabama to "encircle as with a Chinese Wall" the entire state. "The will, the WILL, is alone wanting."[9] The *Montgomery Advertiser* and other Alabama newspapers had recently reported that over 18,000 Alabama men were not subject to conscription because they either qualified for exemptions (1,315 of whom were "overseers and agriculturalists" and 162 as "editors and newspaper employees") or had been detailed because of their expertise in certain essential trades or businesses.[10] Many of these men had, before the war, made what the disgusted editor of the *Mobile Tribune* called "little addresses" with "great ardor" and "a wonderful degree of eloquence" indicating "they were ready at any moment to sacrifice themselves for the general good. Cannon and camp life, and Minie muskets had then no terror for them. They were minute men, ready at any moment's notice, to take up their guns and die in the 'last ditch' to save the country." Now, however, "it is pretty well known that even in [Montgomery], there are hundreds of men who, whilst having a profound love for the country, and hatred of the federals, would not stop their daily profits for a few days, in order to do something, somehow, for the cause."[11]

Others believed that the necessary troops were already in the army but not being properly utilized. One Montgomery correspondent wrote: "Why there are a *thousand* able-bodied men idling about this little City of Montgomery, many of whom have never been in the army, others, after a brief campaign, have found some softer place where they now ingloriously recline."[12] Among those to whom he may have been referring was brigadier general and prewar Montgomery lawyer James Holt Clanton. In mid-December a Union army raiding party of about two thousand men from Pensacola struck the critically important but curiously undefended rail junction at Pollard in south Alabama. Clanton was supposedly on sick leave in Montgomery at the time, while the remaining members of his brigade were deployed in Mississippi. Clanton's friends at the *Montgomery Advertiser* covered for him by publishing an article portraying him as a hero in the incident. The editor wrote that Clanton "received the summons to organize a force at Pollard to resist the advance of the enemy" and "immediately repaired to Pollard," where, "mustering such recruits as he could find thereabouts among the citizens and soldiers, made up a company of about forty men, with whom he held the Yankee force in check." Clanton "displayed his usual gallantry having his horse killed under him, his bridle reins shot in two just below his hand, and a hole through his handkerchief."[13] As other reports would reveal, however, the Union force had already destroyed the telegraph, railroad infrastructure, and supplies at Pollard and were returning to Florida before they ever met any significant resistance, which was made by troops sent from Mobile.[14]

Clanton was certainly not alone in seeking a "softer place" to "ingloriously recline," and that desire appears to have intensified after Hood's defeat in Tennessee. The *Selma Dispatch* admitted that a "remarkable depression" was "apparent among our people," who were now "laboring under demoralization never before exhibited in this war."[15] John Forsyth agreed that the "demoralization in which our danger lies does exist to a lamentable, if not an alarming extent." Although he believed that its cause lay in the fact that men had gotten soft since the American Revolution,[16] there was another reason. The bankrupt Confederacy was not paying its soldiers, causing hardships to their families and as a consequence sparking a surge in additional desertions.[17] Grant Taylor confided in a letter to his wife that "if I live God being my helper I intend to come home next April if I do not get a furlough before then and they do not pay me off or I will be caught and brought back in the attempt."[18] It did not go unnoticed by the common man that those with more money or better connections were being allowed to hold cushy positions or to avoid service altogether. Lest they forgot, peace advocates were quick to remind them that this was a rich man's war and a poor man's fight.[19] Further proving this point, as rumors of an attack on Mobile grew stronger,[20] wealthy parents of boys on the verge of being conscripted were sending their sons to Europe through Mexico until the war was over.[21]

Well-to-do people in the army were making themselves useless as leaders by escaping in other ways. What was called the "fatal vice of drunkenness among army officers" had become such a problem in Mobile that the local Committee of Safety had been "memorialized by a large number of the citizens" urging "some vigorous measures of reform upon the authorities." Wrote Forsyth, "It is high time, for liquor has been the author of a prolific crop of disasters to our arms."[22] Governor Watts, according to a young officer from Eufaula, "closed up the liquor shops" in Mobile, "but plenty of whiskey is still afloat in the city."[23] Forsyth suggested that the prevalence of the vice of drunkenness would be reduced if Mobile could be "relieved of the enormous evil of a host of supernumerary officers without duties to restrain them from the temptations of dissipation." There were simply too many officers who were "adrift without commands in the field or duties in the bureaux," and their numbers "will be immensely increased, when the regiments come to be consolidated." The solution to this problem, he shockingly concluded, was the adoption of the policy of "enlisting negro troops" and putting them "under the charge of experienced and veteran officers, who could soon initiate them in the principles and practice of the school of the soldiers."[24]

But as future Alabama Republican John Pennington was advising North Carolinians, prudence dictated that Alabama Confederates reassess whether Confederate independence was even possible at this point.[25] They knew that the invasion of the state was imminent;[26] that the available military force was inadequate to stop it, even if the loyalty and dedication of the remaining troops were not suspect; that armed resistance would likely result in the retaliatory destruction of cities, towns, and valuable infrastructure, just as was then occurring in South Carolina on Sherman's relentless march from Georgia toward Virginia; and that Davis's hard-line stance on a peace accord guaranteed the worst outcome because it precluded a negotiated resolution of the conflict on any realistic basis. Sadly for Alabama, very little prudence was being exercised by public leaders in Alabama at this point. This fact, and their irrational public pronouncements, would virtually invite the coming invasion and its terrible consequences. For this, Alabama Unionists would never forgive or forget.[27]

After Hampton Roads, Alabama governor Thomas Hill Watts (fig. 8) told a large audience in Montgomery that "when the report of our commissioners announcing the ignominious terms of peace presented to us by Lincoln, was made in the capital of the Confederate States, on the soil of old Virginia, the indignant response [of those in Richmond] brought a thrill of joy to my heart."[28] Ominously, many Northerners felt the same way. A revengeful Vermont editor probably spoke for many when he declared that "now that the peace movement has ended in talk, and the well-meant endeavors of a few tender-hearted men have come to nought, as we supposed they would, we hope that all this nonsense about making peace with traitors and rebels, thieves and robbers, while they still have deadly weapons in their hands, is at an end; and that Grant and his Generals with their mighty forces will go forward conquering and to conquer until Lee and his armies are vanquished, and the power of the Confederacy completely broken."[29]

Sherman was already busy executing that public will with a vengeance. Newspaper reports of the massive scale of destruction by his men during their march through South Carolina instilled an intense degree of anxiety and depression among Confederates in Alabama.[30] In January, the First Alabama Cavalry, USA, a unit composed primarily of Alabama Unionists that was now under the command of a future Alabama Republican, Maj. Francis L. Cramer, had been made a part of the Third Brigade of Cavalry, commanded by Col. George E. Spencer, which in turn was part of Sherman's newly formed

THE WILL IS WANTING / 45

Figure 8. Thomas Hill Watts. Alabama Department of Archives and History.

Third Cavalry Division under the command of the flamboyant Union brigadier general Judson "Kill Cavalry" Kilpatrick. His division had crossed the Georgia–South Carolina line,[31] and as South Carolinians were soon to discover, the rules governing plundering and the destruction of private property had changed for the worse, most spectacularly represented by the fate of the state capital, Columbia, on the anniversary of Davis's inauguration as president of the Confederacy in Montgomery in 1861.[32] Spencer and his men appear to have had nothing to do with that particular town's fiery demise that night; Kilpatrick and his cavalry were apparently somewhere between Lexington and Alston.[33] Reports regarding their activities do not indicate they ever entered Columbia.[34]

Spencer's Alabamians would have relished the opportunity to exact vengeance on South Carolina secessionists in their own state capital. Not only had South Carolinians been instrumental in agitating the sectional conflict during the antebellum period that ultimately led to the war but their seemingly senseless failure to capitulate had prolonged the war and necessitated more fighting, dying, and maiming. One of the many resulting casualties was Union colonel Wager T. Swayne, a Yale-educated Ohio lawyer who was the son of US Supreme Court associate justice Noah Swayne. Wager Swayne, who had served in north Alabama prior to Sherman's Atlanta campaign, had commanded an Ohio infantry regiment in that campaign and there succeeded in making it through Sherman's march across Georgia without injury. But he was severely wounded not long after Sherman's advance from Savannah toward South Carolina and as a result lost a leg. Perhaps mindful of the important role of the Supreme Court in the postwar period, Lincoln nominated him to the rank of full brigadier general to fill the vacancy occasioned by the resignation of that rank by Vice President Andrew Johnson.[35] After the war ended, Swayne would return to Alabama to serve as assistant commissioner of the "Bureau of Refugees Freedmen, and Abandoned Lands for Alabama,"[36] an agency established by Congress that many South Carolina and Alabama planters would blame for their inability to treat the freed slaves as unfreed slaves.[37]

There is little doubt that the Alabama troopers hoped to send a message to the leaders back home that, absent capitulation, South Carolina's fate would be Alabama's. By reporting on the destruction in South Carolina, the Alabama press unwittingly served to communicate that message on a regular basis.[38] After reading those reports, one still committed young lady in Mobile, Kate Cumming, wrote that "the very name of Sherman brings up woe and desolation before us. The beautiful city of Columbia, South Carolina, had been laid in ruins by him and his hirelings. Bands of marauders, black and white, are sent through the country to do their worse on the helpless inhabitants." South Carolina had "indeed been scourged," she related, "because they say she was a sinner above all the rest." But, she concluded hopefully, "there is a day of reckoning for the evil-doer," although she asked "Lord how long shall the wicked triumph."[39] Augustus Benners, the less committed Black Belt lawyer-planter, was less interested in vengeance and more in ending the conflict. "Oh that this horrid war would close." "God of Heaven," he wrote a few days later, "send us reconciliation and peace."[40] It would not be long before Cumming joined him in this refrain, writing "O, how terrible is this cruel, cruel war! When will it cease?"[41] So with a widow in northeast Alabama, Sarah Espy, whose sons were in the Confederate army. "O' that this cruel war was indeed over, and all could be at peace at home."[42] And with James Mallory, a planter in central Alabama who had little sympathy for South Carolinians, who asserted that those "people mostly brought on this unne[ce]ssary war and are now reaping the sorrows of it." He also recognized that "we soon will have our sorrows," noting that "Sherman has not been opposed yet to even harass him, the remnant of Hoods poor shattered army is going that way but to no purpose, for Sherman will not have a check until he meets Lee's forces in Virginia." Like the others, Mallory prayed that "God in his mercy do something to save our poor and suffering army and people and bring this war to a close in his own way and for his own glory."[43]

The situation in Alabama and throughout the Confederacy cried out for leadership, statesmanship, and diplomacy. As the pro-Democrat and vehemently anti-Lincoln New York *World* pled in vain, "the politic thing for the South to do is disband its armies, peacefully insisting on its rights under the constitution [code words for opposing emancipation and the Thirteenth Amendment], but not prejudicing those rights by setting up untenable claims."[44] With South Carolina having already reaped the whirlwind of the destructive war its sons had helped ignite, it was obvious that Alabama was soon to fall unless the *World*'s advice was heeded. Assistant adjutant-general of Alabama, Jones Mitchell Withers, wrote from Montgomery to recently appointed Confederate secretary of war John C. Breckinridge that as a consequence, the "tone of public feeling" in Alabama "is most lamentably despondent. The old Unionists and reconstructionists (mostly of the Douglas faction) have seized on late reverses and been most active in charging them all on the President as their author, in having removed General Johnston" in 1864 from command of the Army of Tennessee and replacing him with Hood. "The straggling, scattered, undisciplined, disorganized condition and consequent lawless conduct of the Army of Tennessee in passing through the state has unfortunately added much to the success of disloyal efforts to increase despondency, spread discontent, and organize opposition to the Government and to the continuance of the war. Deserters and stragglers by the hundreds are now scattered broadcast throughout the State, and such is the state of public sentiment that in half the counties in the State they can remain with impunity."[45]

As evidenced by Watts's cavalier comments, Alabama's officials and public figures, most of whom had never fired a shot in anger, but who had the most to lose financially if the cause was lost, seemingly tried not to allow the conflict to end. Former Alabama Confederate senator C. C. Clay Jr. of Huntsville, who after involvement in various clandestine activities in Canada on behalf of the Confederacy, had unwisely returned to the South (but not Alabama) on February 3, 1865.[46] He wrote a public letter to a friend in Montgomery that "we must trust in God and our own virtues for deliverance, or lose all that is worth living for or dying for. If our people knew all that avails them, if conquered, they would gladly offer up all their blood and treasure to avert that greatest of all calamities. I am sure that no bondage, from that of the Israelites to this day, of which history makes mention, was so humiliating and galling as ours will be, if we yield to any terms of peace that do not embrace our independence of the North. But I fear that many of our people do not believe this, and indulge in the fatal and base delusion that they may enjoy their [slave] property and their most essential liberties under Yankee domination."[47]

Efforts were underway to attempt to change that mindset. The Montgomery-based *Memphis Appeal* reported that the Selma-based *Chattanooga Rebel* "brings us the gratifying information that some of the leading and most influential citizens of that portion of Alabama have already taken the initiatory steps towards the inauguration of a system of public meetings, with a view of arousing the people to a realizing sense of the magnitude of the present crisis, and the importance of at once, and without further delay, making the most effective preparations to resist and beat back the tide of invasion which will certainly be poured upon us at an early day. The best popular speakers are to be appointed to address the people at the various places to be hereafter indicated by public announcement."[48]

In Mobile, Confederates such as John Forsyth as well as a refugee secessionist from north Alabama, David Hubbard of Lawrence County, issued a call for a public meeting to "bring to the aid of our cause and country all the available means at our disposal."[49] That gathering, which took place at the local theater, was described as the "largest meeting that ever assembled in Mobile" and featured a number of speakers, including Forsyth and Confederate district judge William Giles Jones. Forsyth chaired the meeting and reportedly addressed those in attendance "in a stirring appeal to their reason, urging them to a united action for a vigorous prosecution of war, and the abandonment of all ideas of reconstruction." Jones declared that it was "foolish to cry out peace when we should cry out war! war!" He also expressed hostility to all Unionists, alleging they were traitors "and as such should be treated." The "croakers," Jones "compared to frogs in a mud puddle."[50] Several resolutions were adopted at this gathering, including one asserting that "manly resistance and honorable death" were preferable to the "abject submission required for us" by Lincoln and declaring "our unalterable resolve to fight it out to the bitter end, with 'victory or death' inscribed on our banners." Last, but presumably not least, the group resolved that "we believe in God—in His perfect wisdom, goodness, justice and power; and that although He hath chastened us, He hath not given us over to the will of our enemies; but that as He hath bruised, so He will heal; and if we do the deeds of brave, earnest, God-fearing men, the light of glorious peace, and the blessings of renewed prosperity will soon be vouchsafed to our now bleeding and oppressed country."[51]

On the same night as the meeting in Mobile, Confederates were conducting a similar gathering at the Selma City Hall. According to the Selma-based *Mississippian*, the building was "literally filled to overflowing with the *chivalry* of our city, and interspersed with a goodly number of the fair sex." Among others, future Alabama Republican Alexander White delivered what the local press called a "soul-stirring and eloquent address"[52] and announced his intention to "stump the State for the purpose of rousing up the slumbering energies of the people."[53] White's next harangue occurred at Jacksonville, where he was joined by former Confederate congressman J. L. M. Curry.[54] The content of White's speech in the Methodist Episcopal Church there likely gives some insight into his remarks at Selma. According to the Talladega *Democratic Watchtower*, "Mr. White showed by argument too conclusive to admit to controversy, that reconstruction was impossible; that separate State action [for peace] was a fa[l]lacy; that submission was, on many accounts, more destructive to the peace, quiet and interest of the country, than active warfare; and that the road to the wealth and happiness of the Southern people, was in a vigorous prosecution of the war." He declared that "there was no cause for despondency; the records of the past [were] full of instances of much more intense suffering on the part of those struggling to be free, than the people of the Confederacy have yet been called upon to endure, and that united action on the part of the southern people, would ensure success to our arms and secure peace and independence."[55]

In order to motivate the populace, Alabama Confederates frequently suggested that the Yankees harbored immoral intentions, thereby pressuring Alabama women to push men to fight. "In this fearful issue, no class of human beings have so much at stake as the women of the South," wrote one Alabama editor. "There are truths—there are threatened evils which we are not permitted to describe, but which all good and well informed ladies can imagine for themselves." But, he continued, if it was made known that "you will not recognize, nor receive into your social circles, any man who is improperly absent from his command, or evades the proper service of his country, 40,000 soldiers will be added to our ranks," and with this "we are redeemed" and the "war will end."[56]

With all of this irrational defiance among the press and civilian leaders in control of Alabama, achieving peace would have to be done the hard, much more destructive way. Another raid of Unionist guerrillas was made, this time through Dale County where they had been active for several months despite brutal efforts to suppress them.[57] Significantly, however, there is no evidence that any economic assets useful to the state's postwar economy were destroyed during this expedition. But for reasons that are unclear, the anticipated general uprising by north Alabama Unionists did not materialize. Most of Roddey's men had finally reluctantly left north Alabama and, in accordance with new orders from the Confederate military, were then moving toward Selma by way of Tuscaloosa.[58] Unionists south of the Tennessee River were thereby left exposed to Confederate retaliation. According to a report of the Union commander at Decatur, Gen. Robert S. Granger, Confederate guerrillas in north Alabama took advantage of Roddey's absence and were "conscripting, murdering, burning cotton and houses of Union men," prompting "Union men and deserters" hiding in the mountains south of the Tennessee River to seek enlistment in the Union army "for one year to serve in Alabama."[59] However, it would take too long to train them into an effective fighting force. Thus, the task of conquering a peace in Alabama would necessarily devolve on the Union military, meaning that the state's remaining economic assets would be in great jeopardy.

The Selma *Mississippian* was already reporting that vice president elect Johnson, among other civilian leaders, had been urging General Thomas "to commence a movement upon Alabama at an early moment," and that a "correspondent of the Memphis *Argus* from Eastport, says the army has received marching orders."[60] Indeed, the day after the war meetings in Mobile and Selma, Grant issued the fateful order whose execution threatened to set back Alabama from an economic standpoint for generations. Grant directed Thomas to form as large a cavalry force as possible in north Alabama to make an expedition to Tuscaloosa and Selma in order to, among other things, "destroy the enemy's line of communications and military resources."[61] Events would, meanwhile, increase the chance of the members of this large cavalry force interpreting the term "military resources" very broadly.

While the commander of that cavalry force, Gen. James Harrison Wilson (fig. 9), had established his headquarters at "Wildwood," the Lauderdale County plantation home in which prewar Unionist George Smith Houston of Limestone County had been raised,[62] his men were certainly not living through this bitterly cold winter, or the monsoon rains that followed, in the lap of luxury. According to Jerome Quinn, a member of an Illinois unit under Wilson's command, they built themselves shanties because their pup tents were "comfortless habitations, even at Gravelly Springs in the alleged Sunny South." And like most soldiers enduring bad weather and a long, bloody war, they were not happy campers. Quinn wrote that Wilson was "unpleasantly despotic" and forced his unenthusiastic and unappreciative mounted infantrymen to drill incessantly on the fine points of cavalry tactics. In addition, the Union army's supply system to Gravelly Springs initially functioned very poorly. Quinn wrote that the men were forced to subsist on half rations of "hard tack and sow-belly," while the horses were "provided with abundant forage." As a consequence, he continued, "some of the boys purloin corn from their steeds and make hominy." Even after a month at Gravelly Springs, Quinn noted that it "is still a-rainin', and the boys are still a-grumblin'." Wilson's men knew the end of the war was near and they just wanted to get it over with. Quinn wrote that "this camp life is monotonous, and we are longing for more

The Will Is Wanting / 51

Figure 9. James Harrison Wilson. Engraving by J. A. Lowell and Co. Courtesy of the Library of Congress, Prints and Photographs Division.

active service." A few days later he noted that "the boys are clamorous for the campaign to open."[63] But prolonged, unprecedented poor weather conditions had made the roads impassable, and thereby prevented and delayed their march for several weeks.[64]

Not surprisingly, Confederate civilians in the area became the victims of the soldiers' frustration during their frequent scouting expeditions. Joshua Burns Moore noted that one of his Confederate neighbors "complains awfully of the treatment f[ederals] gave him; took his corn and fodder and he says left him without bread; that they cursed and abused him. Told him he was a leading *secesh*." Moore had no sympathy for the man, declaring that he "ought not to complain of anything they do [to] him as he was an awful secessionist, ready for the war, and ringing the church bell in high glee, when Ala[bama] went out of the Union. I suppose on short [food] allowance as he is, he must regret that ever the State seceded."[65]

In Montgomery, the editor of the *Memphis Appeal* thought he had a solution to this menace from north Alabama. "There is a strong nucleus of gallant and tried veterans at the front [a reference to Forrest and Gen. Hylan Lyon's men] in North Alabama and North Mississippi, and around these the reserves should rally as speedily as possible before they are driven back, and one-half the State is in possession of the enemy. Selma and Montgomery can be better defended at the threshold of the State than in the woods immediately around those cities. Thomas should be met at the start, and the territory of the State contested inch by inch. He should be harassed and opposed at all times, and every foot of soil wet with the blood of his vandals."[66] As far as can be determined, however, this editor did not practice what he preached. Neither he nor any county reserves from central or south Alabama went off to north Alabama. In fact, no effort whatsoever was made by the Confederate military or the state militia to force Wilson's cavalry corps out of Lauderdale County before his invasion began.

One reason for this is that there were simply insufficient active troops to protect Alabama from all of the threats it faced. In addition to the impending raid from north Alabama, Grant had ordered Maj. Gen. Edward Canby to proceed from New Orleans with an amphibious force to take Mobile and then move toward Selma and Montgomery. Canby's plan was to land a portion of this force on the eastern shore area of Mobile Bay and proceed north to the Confederate garrisons at Spanish Fort and then Fort Blakely. Most of the rest of the force, which was composed of, among others, five thousand black troops as well as Louisiana Unionists under the command of a New Yorker, Gen. Frederick Steele, were to land at Pensacola, make a feint toward Montgomery as far as Pollard, Alabama, and then march west down the Mobile and Great Northern Railroad to link up with Canby and invest Mobile.[67] In order to divert attention from Mobile and give the illusion that Selma and Montgomery were actually the primary targets, raiding parties from Pensacola had already begun making raids up the Alabama and Florida Railroad before Steele ever arrived, forcing the Confederates to commit men from the port city away from the area of the main invasion. As the *Montgomery Advertiser* reported, one such expedition occurred on February 23 and resulted in the capture of a Confederate cavalry picket command near Milton, Florida, several miles southeast of Pollard.[68]

The signs were very ominous, but Governor Watts still had the opportunity to avert disaster by calling the legislature into special session and seeking a separate peace. Instead, he, future Republican Samuel Farrow Rice, and other die-hard Confederates called for a public meeting in Montgomery to pump up morale by giving false hope of victory and a glimpse of the public's supposedly nightmarish fate if reconstruction occurred. During that meeting, which fittingly took place in a theater, Watts did his very best Patrick Henry impression, encouraging those in the audience to choose death rather than submitting to "such terms as Lincoln demanded."[69] Some foolishly would, but others had no choice.

5
The Society of Loyal Confederates

At about the same time that Watts addressed residents of Montgomery, John Forsyth was forming an organization in Mobile designed to provide means for prolonging the war indefinitely: the Society of Loyal Confederates. According to the published prospectus of the new group, its objects included not only benevolence toward the soldiers and their families but also the encouragement of an "energetic prosecution of the great struggle in which we are engaged for liberty and independence."[1] Exactly how this would translate into action was not initially clear, but themes from Forsyth's newspaper provide telling clues.

After the nightmare in Tennessee and the corresponding surge in demands for peace negotiations, Forsyth had published a letter from his newspaper's Montgomery correspondent praising members of Hood's defeated army who had supposedly recently "sworn *eternal war* against the ruthless invaders and destroyers of our country. When no longer able (if that day should ever come) to meet the foe with large armies like his own, our gallant soldiers will retire to the mountain fastness, and to the wide-spreading jungles of our lowlands, and from these retreats they will continue the war while an enemy's foot pollutes our soil."[2] Forsyth certainly liked the idea, and the following day he had published an editorial glorifying the future roles of these guerrilla patriots:

> Standing camps of the enemy will be established at important points, to protect the Yankee land pirates who will be engaged in cultivating our stolen lands with the assistance of our stolen negroes. Around these forts and these plantations the Mosby's of a future generation will hover, writing in characters of blood and fire on every unprotected point, the record of their undying hate of the Yankee. The wives and children of the partisans, meanwhile, withdrawn to mountain fastnesses or inland districts and towns, will rest secure under the protection of the veterans of the first years of the war, no longer qualified for the daring raid, the

impetuous charge or the rapid flank march.... Yet we shall survive, and our children after us, and these, as they become able to rein a steed or aim a rifle, will accept it as their lot in life to revenge a father's death or to emulate the achievements of a heroic sire and grandsire, to win in stricken fields the applause of their comrades and the smiles of the fair.[3]

Forsyth's views regarding guerrilla warfare were adopted or at least shared by others. For example, in February, Jefferson Davis's organ in the Confederate capital, the *Richmond Sentinel*, declared that "if our affairs should come to the worse, and we should not be able to man large regular armies in the field, we would, by guerrilla warfare, make the South too hot to hold [by] the Yankee intruding landlords. They would be watched, ambushed, and shot down by night and by day like beasts of prey. Few who would find themselves, their wives, and little ones driven from their homes, would hesitate if necessary, to way-lay the wandering Yankee robbers. No armies from the North could put down such warfare as this, if we fight but half as well as most other nations similarly situated have fought."[4]

In the minds of most Confederates, the perfect person to lead the guerrillas in the Deep South was Nathan Bedford Forrest (fig. 10), who would soon be promoted to the rank of lieutenant general.[5] His home state of Tennessee had already experienced more than its share of destructive guerrilla raids, and those attacks were on the increase. The same was occurring in north Alabama.[6] A South Carolina editor reported that Confederate "guerrillas are doing a very active and lucrative business, and as soon as the woods are green, and blankets can be thrown aside," Alabama, Mississippi, and Tennessee "will furnish 10,000 men to bushwhack Thomas's army on every mountain, and retard his movements through every pass and defile."[7] This prediction was likely mere propaganda, but there were fears within the Union high command that Forrest would simply revert to guerrilla warfare even if the regular Confederate armies were forced to surrender during the coming campaign and that he would have some degree of success. These fears were behind Sherman's instructions to Thomas that with the impending invasion of Alabama, "I would like to have Forrest hunted down and killed."[8] Objectively, the threat of guerrilla warfare was also a primary reason why the South's war-making capacity had to be totally destroyed even if its regular armies surrendered.

The War Eagle finally recovered a portion of the men who had deserted him during the retreat from Nashville,[9] thanks in part to the use of very unorthodox and brutal tactics but more importantly his never-to-yield swagger. In a stirring address to his men and members of the public, he bragged about

Figure 10. Nathan Bedford Forrest. Alabama Department of Archives and History.

the accomplishments of his forces during the war and then informed them that he was "ready to lead you again to the defence of the common cause." He appealed to them "by a remembrance of the glories of your past career; your desolate homes; your insulted women and suffering children; and above all, by the memory of your dead comrades—to yield a ready obedience to discipline, and to buckle on your armor anew for the fight. Bring with you the soldier's safest armor—a determination to fight while the enemy pollutes your soil—to fight until independence shall have been achieved—to fight for home, children, liberty and all you hold dear."[10] He would soon issue a public letter—published in its entirety in Forsyth's newspaper—declaring his intention to fight "as long as there is a man left to fight with, or anything left to fight for."[11] In reply to those who argued that reconstruction was the only way to avoid destruction, Forrest warned that: "'Reconstruction' would require the soldier to destroy the proud ensigns of his glory, to stack his arms, lower his head in dishonor, and pass under the yoke of abolition tyranny. It would require confiscation, imprisonment and death! It would turn into our families bands of detectives to ferret out the household secrets! It would suppress the freedom of speech—deprive us of arms and the elective franchise. Every office would be filled by Yankees, the churches by Yankees, tory (or negro) preachers, and we would be made the slaves of our slaves, who would be lurking spies over all our conduct. Our homes, land, property ALL taken from us! I cannot see how continued resistance will bring upon us greater destruction."[12]

Even if he led the guerrillas in the field, those forces would require two things that were in increasingly short supply: war materiel and a will to fight on. The pro-Confederacy press had hinted for over a year that an alliance with the embattled, French-supported imperial government of Austrian prince Ferdinand Maximilian in Mexico was in the works.[13] Barring that, private funds would be required if the Confederate government failed. Forsyth described the demoralization that was inexorably bringing the Confederate war effort to a halt as "a noxious weed" that had "over spread the fair fields of the South" and if not gotten rid of would "well nigh choke out every manly and noble sentiment."[14] But to kill that aggressive weed, someone would have to provide the young knights who would continue the joust with the hated Yankees with sustenance, the means to support their families, and war materiel. The bankrupt Confederate government was ostensibly no longer in position to fill those basic needs, and as a result many soldiers were being forced to serve without pay, leading to a very high desertion rate during this final phase of the war. In order to avert a mass mutiny, some private citizens were already independently stepping forward to donate funds to be paid to those soldiers.[15] Creating a formal private organization to unite and more efficiently direct and encourage these support efforts appears to have been one reason for the conception in Mobile of the Society of Loyal Confederates.[16]

Resorting to guerrilla warfare was at best a fallback position. It was much more preferable to continue to field large regular armies if at all possible.[17] That was becoming increasingly difficult, however, particularly as reconstruction sentiment continued to grow after Hampton Roads. During a speech at the organizational meeting of the Gulf City Club of Loyal Confederates at Mobile on March 1, Forsyth, who chaired the meeting, indicated that the purposes of the organization also included dealing with the peace element. What was needed, he urged, was to reform public opinion on the chances for success against the Yankees, have unity of action to strengthen the cause, and "drive laggards to duty."[18] As he explained in an editorial two days later, if "eight men stay at home, dodge all public service, and devote themselves to their own private affairs, while two go to the front, the contest is necessarily protracted, if not fully desperate."[19]

In a sense, the Confederacy was in precisely the same position as it had been exactly four years earlier. Alabama had seceded in January 1861, but it was well known that an underground reconstruction movement was then afoot. Therefore, allegedly at the insistence of a Black Belt Alabama lawyer-secessionist, James Graham Gilchrist of Lowndes County, this movement

THE SOCIETY OF LOYAL CONFEDERATES / 57

was stopped in its tracks by an avoidable act that outraged the North—firing on Fort Sumter in April 1861—thereby precluding any amicable settlement of the sectional conflict and forcing the "laggards" to fight through several years of bloody war.[20] More recently, another Black Belt Alabama lawyer-secessionist, George Washington Gayle of Dallas County, had promoted another such act—the assassinations of Lincoln, Johnson, and Seward—that he disingenuously represented would lead to peace by March 1, 1865. As Gayle's widely published advertisement made clear, all he needed was $50,000 up front, with $950,000 to be paid after the dirty deeds were done.[21] Execution of such a plan would again force those "laggards" to fight for their lives in order to avoid retributive slaughter.

The evidence allows only speculation regarding whether another of the purposes of the Society of Loyal Confederates was to raise this bounty money. It is clear that the society was formed during the month leading up to Gayle's promised "peace" deadline and that one of its functions was to raise money to promote the war effort. In fact, the stated goal of Forsyth's mother organization in Mobile was to raise $1 million, exactly what Gayle had requested be pledged.[22] It is also clear that Forsyth hated Lincoln and seemed to be obsessed with ultimately reporting on Lincoln's demise. As if stalking Lincoln from a distance, Forsyth had, for over a year, regularly reported on Lincoln's public appearances and movements in Washington, DC, including those at theaters.[23] He had also published information regarding a failed attempt to kidnap or kill Lincoln while he was staying at the Soldiers' Home in Washington, DC. Obviously frustrated when security around the president was then tightened, Forsyth sneeringly ridiculed Lincoln for having been "frightened out of the Soldiers' Home back to the White House."[24] Gayle had published his advertisement in the *Selma Dispatch* eleven days later, and six days after that Forsyth gave voice to Gayle's proposal on the front page of the *Mobile Advertiser and Register:* "A citizen of Cahaba advertises in the Selma Dispatch for $1,000,000, and says if the citizens of the Southern Confederacy will furnish him that amount he will cause to be taken the lives of Abe Lincoln, W. H. Seward and Andy Johnson, and restore peace to the country by the 1st of March next."[25]

Since then, Forsyth had repeatedly charged Lincoln with having encouraged a spirit of genocide.[26] "He means, if he can, by brute force to trample this people out of existence, appropriate their lands and goods, and repopulate this land with colonies of people and soldiers from the North."[27] After the failure at Hampton Roads, Forsyth blamed Lincoln and told his readers that "Abe pricks us with the point of the sword; he strikes us with the flat of the blade, and exclaims, 'fight, rebel, coward and scoundrel, or give me your property, your freedom and your life.'"[28] In announcing the purpose of the Society of Loyal Confederates, Forsyth echoed these themes, declaring that he was "fully satisfied that if we failed in establishing our independence, history would record that we were suicides. We have the power, and have only to exercise that power to secure success."[29] If he truly believed all of this, engaging in an assassination conspiracy was certainly not out of the question. After all, targeting the enemy's government officials was a logical guerrilla tactic.

No one was assassinated by March 1 or even by the inauguration of Lincoln on March 4. But Lincoln had unwittingly increased the chances that that would occur through his much-anticipated second inaugural address.[30] The *Nashville Press* had expressed hope that the president would be "so guided and influenced by wisdom and moderation as to bring the country safely through the dangers and complications with which it is still environed. The new Administration will most especially need the support of all who desire to see peace and order restored throughout the land, as there is a strong element in the immediate party of the President which appears determined to embarrass him unless he yields to their malignant and destructive policy."[31] For months, north Alabama Unionist Jeremiah Clemens had emphatically recommended this moderate approach in letters from Philadelphia to the Lincoln administration. "Offer pardon to *all*, not even excepting the arch traitor, Davis, himself," wrote Clemens shortly after the presidential election. Davis "*will not accept*," he predicted, "but the effect would be *to alienate from him the affections of the people—to deprive him of their confidence—to destroy his power to deceive them*—to let them clearly understand that he, & his satellites, *are alone responsible* for the slaughter of their sons, & the desolation of their homes."[32]

Alabama Confederates sincerely hoped and predicted that Lincoln would instead announce a much more vindictive policy. A few days before the inauguration, a correspondent in Montgomery noted that "the second inauguration of the great rail splitter" would soon take place and that some "suppose that he will signalize that event by some special act of clemency, in imitation of the crowned heads of Europe." However, he continued, "we believe Abe Lincoln incapable of a just and righteous act, and as destitute of humanity and generosity as the Gorilla of Africa, which he so nearly resembles. But as good old Father Ritchie used to say, nous verrons'" (We shall see).[33]

Well, they would soon see, or at least read, the tack Lincoln would take. And there was good reason to believe that, because of the immense political capital he had amassed up to this point, whatever it was would be embraced by many in the North. On the morning of the inauguration, the editor of the *New York Herald* incisively described Lincoln as "a most remarkable man. He may seem to be the most credulous, docile and pliable of backwoodsmen, and

THE SOCIETY OF LOYAL CONFEDERATES / 59

yet when he 'puts his foot he puts it down firmly,' and cannot be budged." Lincoln, he continued, "has proved himself in his quiet way, the keenest of politicians, and more than a match for his wiliest antagonist in the arts of diplomacy. He upsets, without an effort, the most formidable obstacles of caucuses and congresses, and seems to enjoy as a huge joke the astonishment of his friends and enemies. Plain common sense, a kindly disposition, a straight forward purpose and a shrewd perception of the ins and outs of poor, weak human nature, have enabled him to master difficulties which would have swamped almost any other man." The editor concluded that "with the most cheering prospects before him, this extraordinary rail-splitter enters upon his second term the unquestioned master of the situation in reference to American affairs at home and abroad."[34]

Lincoln's Bible-based rhetoric directed toward the South and published in most Southern newspapers was quite conciliatory, encouraging his listeners, and the millions of Southerners who would read his address in their newspapers in the following days, to "judge not, that we not be judged," to act "with malice toward none, with charity for all," to "bind up the nation's wounds," and "to do all which may achieve and cherish a just and lasting peace among ourselves."[35] What people do not say is often as important as what they do say. Significantly, despite the fact that black suffrage was becoming an issue,[36] Lincoln did not advocate political rights for the black population or any other policy that would challenge the prevailing political or economic supremacy of the white people in the South.[37]

Even worse for Confederate diehards attempting to increase war spirit in the South, the prowar faction of the Northern press favored Lincoln's conciliatory direction. The author of a letter to the editor of one midwestern newspaper observed that Lincoln lived "in the hearts of his countrymen, beloved and respected, all anxious to do him honor. His mild, firm gentle nature winning respect everywhere, he goes forth peacefully and calmly at the call of his countrymen to discharge for another term the duties of the Chief Magistracy."[38] One editor was so moved that he was led to recall the Old Testament verse in Genesis: "And the Angel of the Lord called unto Abraham out of Heaven a second time."[39] Probably guessing correctly at Lincoln's strategy, the *New York Tribune* praised Lincoln's address, agreeing "now is the fittest time for putting forth manifestations of generosity, clemency, magnanimity, which, however they be spurned by the Rebel chiefs, are certain to exert a great and salutary influence among their duped, disgusted, despairing followers."[40] The *Tribune* also assured those flagging followers that "the nation asks for justice, and for every measure which its future security may require; but it does not ask and it has never asked, for indiscriminate, blind, and bloody revenge. There is no feeling more alien than this to the Northern mind."[41] An editor in Montana agreed: "On the one side, all is hope and assurance of success; on the other, misery, ruin and despair. When the last blow shall be struck, and the earthquake voice of victory rises uncontrolled, may the mercy and kindness of the victors hallow forever the memory of their valiant deeds."[42] Two different Ohio editors advocated that the New Testament passage in Lincoln's inaugural address advising "malice toward none" and "charity for all" should be "engraven on every heart."[43] The editor of the venerable Washington, DC, *National Intelligencer* described these words as "distinguished for patriotism, statesmanship, and benevolence, and deserve to be printed in gold."[44]

There is evidence Lincoln's approach was having a direct effect on rank and file Confederate troops in the field, particularly among the nonslaveholders, who had feared execution as traitors in the aftermath of a Confederate capitulation but could now assume from Lincoln's address and prior public comments that they would receive amnesty. A Philadelphia correspondent claimed that meetings had been held in various regiments within General Robert E. Lee's vaunted Army of Northern Virginia "in which there was a free interchange of opinions, and fair and satisfactory vote as to whether the soldiers would return to the Union and enjoy peace upon the basis of the propositions submitted by President Lincoln at [Hampton Roads]." A "considerable desire to return to the old Government was shown." According to the same source, votes taken on this issue revealed a majority in favor of reunion on these terms, but the officers of these regiments suppressed the results and instead sent resolutions to the Richmond newspapers wherein their men purportedly pledged themselves to "an unwavering and protracted prosecution of the war until rebel independence should be received."[45] Defeatism was spreading, even among the sons of slaveholders, who held Lee in great esteem. William McClellan, a member of a prominent Limestone County family, wrote to his brother Robert from a camp near Petersburg, Virginia, that "I am low down. I can see but little hope for these confederate states in these times."[46]

The ultimate political statement—desertions to the enemy—could not be fully suppressed, even in Lee's army. According to one Confederate deserter, Lee "has promised thirty days furlough to every man who shoots another attempting to desert. This does not stop them; 'how soon we can get out of the lines' is the common talk in every tent in every company." Those that remained "agree to fire high when we run." According to the same man, after finding out the truth about Lincoln's peace proposal presented at Hampton Roads, "our boys said the terms were good enough for them, and they were not going to fight anymore just to save their leaders, and this I found when I went to the front was the feeling throughout the army."[47] Another deserter reportedly declared that, under the circumstances, they "would be fools to remain any longer to be killed," and still another confirmed that "one half of Lee's army would desert, or surrender, if an opportunity offered to do so without their getting killed."[48] Meanwhile, the remnants of Hood's shattered army had that opportunity and were still taking it. According to the *Nashville Union*, "the boys who were duped into going into Jeff. Davis' war for the benefit of the rich at the expense of the poor, are rapidly finding out their blunder, and returning [to Uncle Sam]. On Thursday twenty-seven rebel deserters came in at this place, and yesterday eighteen more."[49] And who could blame them? Edward Norphlet Brown, who was then marching with that army through Georgia in pursuit of Sherman, wrote to his wife from Georgia's capital that the "people are as badly whipped as any I have met in all my travels. I have not met a man since I left Macon [Georgia] who was not willing to accept Lincoln's ultimatum."[50] If the civilian population were prepared to quit, why fight on?

The Confederate army was not the only element of the Confederacy showing signs of disintegration. John Archibald Campbell wrote to Alabama reconstructionist Benjamin Fitzpatrick telling him that the Confederate cause would soon collapse and advising the former governor and US senator to "take measures for the restoration of Alabama to the Union."[51] Fitzpatrick ultimately would. Rumors were emanating from Richmond of a possible coup.[52] Three days after Lincoln's inaugural address, the *Richmond Enquirer* was almost hysterical about the "rumors of Senatorial committees approaching the President [Davis] to submit terms of submission? Is that report true? Are any Senators or Representatives whipped? Have they approached the President to press upon him any such base proposition? Is there any plan on foot to force the President to compromise with subjugation or resign? Is there any one else ready to volunteer resignations in case he is forced to vacate his place, and if he does who is proposed to fill that place?" Perhaps in an effort to kill the conspiracy by exposing some of the participants, the editor revealed that there was, in fact, a "plan on foot to force Mr. Davis to resign, and that Mr. [Alexander] Stephens had consented to resign, so that Mr. [R. M. T.] Hunter, as President of the Senate, would become President." The editor hoped this plan had "miscarried," but if not "the conspirators may understand that if they should succeed they will have placed a barren sceptre in their grip, thence to be wrenched by an unlineal hand, no son of theirs succeeding."[53] Hunter publicly denied involvement in the scheme but, without expressing loyalty to Davis, suggested instead that it was "to the Chief Ruler of the Universe that [the people] should look for aid in the mighty struggle in which they are engaged."[54] Confederate general Josiah Gorgas, a future University of Alabama president, was also incensed at the members of the Confederate Senate and had an antidote for their rampant rationality. "Pity a few could not be taken out and hung or shot."[55]

In sum, wrote the editor of the *Cleveland Leader*, the "Confederacy is a hollow shell, and the shell is crushed."[56] This was in part due to the fact that the number of peace advocates was increasing thanks to Lincoln's conciliatory approach. A Wisconsin editor hoped that "a few months more will, in all probability, suffice to trample out the last vestige of organized martial resistance to the authority of the Union, and ABRAHAM LINCOLN will, we trust and believe, retire at the end of four years more from his great office amid the plaudits of a united, happy and prosperous people. So mote it be."[57] The end of the rebellion would come in a matter of weeks rather than months. Thanks to Lincoln, those working behind the scenes in the South, trying to convince skeptics that continued resistance was unnecessary for self-preservation, had some ammunition to work with. They could affirm that, as a bulwark to extremism from the victors, Lincoln was indeed the "very best friend" the white South had, just as a Tennessee legislator would later describe him.[58] A member of Lincoln's cabinet would say the same thing, revealing that "Mr. Lincoln at every cabinet meeting counseled forbearance, kindness and mercy" toward the South.[59] As a Pennsylvania editor would recall, with Lincoln "the Rebels" had "hope of an easy step from treachery satiated to the performance of duty under the old Government; without him they have little to hope save through the gallows and the felons-cell."[60]

Southern Unionists were energized and redoubled their efforts to lay the groundwork for peace. According to the *Nashville Union*, Jeremiah Clemens was in the process of returning from Philadelphia to Alabama where "loyal men are earnestly at work" planning for reconstruction. "About twenty counties of North Alabama, comprising all that region running from North Mississippi to the Northern part of Georgia, are now and have always been at heart loyal to the United States. The people anxiously look for the time when they shall be delivered from rebel rule, and enabled to show their faith by their deeds."[61]

From the safety of Union-controlled Jackson, Mississippi, Selma Unionist and future Alabama Republican John Hardy was voicing editorial criticism in the *Jackson News* of the Confederate Congress's recent decision to adopt legislation authorizing the use of slaves as soldiers, instead of calling for peace "upon the best terms that can be extended to us." After all, he wrote, arming the slaves was "a total abandonment of the chief object of this war, and if the institution is already irretrievably undermined, the rights of the States are buried with it." Therefore, he concluded, "why fight one moment longer, if the object and occasion of the fight is dying, dead or damned."[62] Other future Republicans at the propeace *Montgomery Mail* also used their positions to undermine public confidence in the Confederate war effort.[63] They published a letter by an anonymous author warning that "some persons, to revive our drooping spirits, are continually reminding us of the old Revolutionary war—of the great difficulties our forefathers had to contend with, greater than ours—of their fortitude, and their final triumphant success. But they forget that it was France which saved the United States in the old Revolutionary War." Therefore, the author concluded, "without assistance these Confederate States will not be able to gain their independence."[64] As one Alabama Confederate correctly surmised, the purpose of these types of editorials was to "poison the minds of the people by unceasing abuse of the Government, and by a constant depreciation of our means of defense."[65]

Given the circumstances, such overt anti-Confederate activities in the Heart of Dixie were still very dangerous and risked violent retribution or arrest and confiscation. As a consequence, the efforts of many Unionists were still much more subtle. This was the case in Tuscaloosa, whose loyalty to the cause was seen by outsiders as being, at best, "speckled."[66] Tuscaloosa's secretly Unionist mayor and future Republican Obediah Berry cleverly used Jefferson Davis's designation of March 10 as a day of "Public Fasting, Humiliation and Prayer, with Thanksgiving," to focus the community on achieving peace rather than fighting. In a proclamation he urged all to "visit the several places of Divine Worship, refrain from all secular pursuits, and with one accord, be in humble submission before the Footstool of the Most High." While there, said Berry, they should "implore His pardon for our manifold sins; that His sustaining grace may be given to our people, and His Divine Wisdom may direct our rulers, and graciously take our cause into His own hand, and mercifully establish for us, a lasting, just, and honorable peace."[67]

But not everyone in Tuscaloosa saw it that way. On the same day Berry's proclamation was published in the *Tuscaloosa Observer*, its editor called attention to a "war meeting" to be held in a few days at the Tuscaloosa County courthouse. "Let there be a general awakening of the people—a re-kindling of the same spirit that animated the hearts of the people in '61, and revolutionary sires of '76," he asked. "Throw off your apathy, and swear, upon the altar of your country, that you will never be willing to truckle to the indolent foe that is aiming at your subjugation and utter ruin. Never let it be said that you bowed the suppliant knee to the fell destroyer, who is riding rough-shod, over our beautiful but bleeding country, visiting it with fire and sword, and sparing neither age, sex, nor condition."[68]

Avoiding this collateral damage may have been one of Tuscaloosa lawyer-Unionist E. W. Peck's goals at this point.[69] Peck, who had been born in the North, certainly did not want everything he and other local Unionists had built in Tuscaloosa over the last several decades to be lost as a result of a failure of leadership in Alabama. In order to avoid that, it was essential that Union forces preserve the war-related facilities in the area so they could later be converted to peacetime pursuits. For that to happen, the Union force would need to have good intelligence about the location of not only those assets but also the defensive measures being taken to protect them. With that information, the defenses could be quickly neutralized and those assets saved. Peck may have been one of several sources of this information. In the weeks leading up to the invasion, General Wilson made use of spies in Alabama to gather strategic intelligence,[70] and according to one account, Peck had been in contact with Union spies at some point during the war. A member of the First Alabama Cavalry, USA, is said by family lore to have carried messages between Peck and several Union generals and was almost caught near Peck's home but made his escape across the Black Warrior River.[71]

Union spies were also busy in Alabama's capital, and they may have been mystified by what they saw. What a Montgomery correspondent called "another glorious gathering of the true and loyal citizens" took place in Montgomery on March 9.[72] Two days later Montgomery residents, including Governor Watts, met to organize a Society of Loyal Confederates there.[73] Former Alabama Supreme Court chief justice William Parish Chilton was named the group's president, and future Alabama Republican Samuel Farrow Rice and others were appointed to a committee to "solicit subscriptions in aid of the patriotic and benevolent objects of this society."[74] Reportedly, between fifteen thousand and twenty thousand dollars was subscribed during this initial meeting.[75]

That very day, the aforementioned War Meeting in Tuscaloosa convened, during which the now familiar litany of proindependence resolutions were proposed and, of course, unanimously adopted. The primary focus of the meeting may have been to simply ward off an attack on the town and the associated destruction of the property of some of the elites in attendance such as Robert Jemison, rather than to prolong the Confederacy and achieve independence. One of the resolutions represented that the threatened raid on Tuscaloosa "may, in all probability, be repelled, or averted, by concert of action." An address by the group issued to the people called for "every man and boy who can carry a gun" to come forward for local defense and pledged "to all who enroll themselves, that *they will not be taken out of their county*."[76] However, those in attendance also heard an address by David Hubbard, who had traveled from Mobile to Tuscaloosa with a copy of the prospectus of the Society of Loyal Confederates, advocating the formation of a society there. Resolutions organizing a branch were adopted and, seemingly ironically, Jemison was elected president of the society. The new organization was called the Rodes League of Loyal Confederates in honor of the late Robert Rodes, a Tuscaloosa resident, civil engineer, and Confederate general who had been killed in action in Virginia earlier in the war.[77]

Now there would be yet another income stream to fund whatever the "patriotic objects" of the society might be, and more local branches of this organization would soon form elsewhere in the South.[78] But whether enough money would be raised in time to make a difference was unknown, although the fund-raising activity up to this point may have been enough to demonstrate the society's bona fides to those interested in earning blood money. Coincidentally or not, in the weeks after praise for the society began appearing generally in the Southern press, assassins, including John Wilkes Booth and Alabama native Lewis Thornton Powell, a former member of Confederate general John Singleton Mosby's guerrillas, were taking the step of casing Ford's Theatre in Washington, DC—some of them even watching a play from the presidential box—and then meeting to discuss strategy in a private room at a local saloon. They would soon hide a cache of weapons in Mary Surratt's local boardinghouse, where some of them stayed while planning their scheme.[79]

Meanwhile, Union forces were moving to take Alabama out of the war by destroying its remaining industrial base.[80] It would soon all be over. But it should always be remembered that, with rational leaders in Alabama, all of this might have been avoided.

6
The Wedding Party

North Alabamians had gotten the bloody war they did not want and had gone profoundly backward economically. Adding injury to insult, up to this point south Alabama had generally avoided the hard hand of war. As Joshua Burns Moore wrote, "North Ala. voted overwhelmingly against [secession,] and for three years she has suffered the most terrible the mind can conceive of. While in South Ala. they have been speculating upon our misfortunes and calling us terms [of derision]."[1] Moreover, efforts by north Alabamians to convince Governor Watts, another member of the south Alabama planter elite, to seek a separate peace had been rudely dismissed and ignored.

By this point in the war, even Confederate civilians in north Alabama seemed to have had a gut full.[2] A Nashville correspondent, who had recently returned from Florence and Tuscumbia in northwest Alabama, wrote that he had observed "no rebels in that region, save an occasional person, at home on 'fence furlough,' trying to gin his cotton, or shirk further service. This rebellion is utterly 'played' [out] in this region, as regards hopes. Deserters flock in daily and report large numbers in the interior, skulking from Hood, Roddey and Forrest."[3] The depressed and despondent mental state of current and former Confederates in the region was matched by the visible reduction in the standard of living and prosperity of these once vibrant towns. The people had worked hard in the antebellum period to raise the capital necessary to build the Memphis and Charleston Railroad, had celebrated the completion of its construction, and were riding its economic engine until the secessionists had brought on what Joshua Burns Moore called the "most disgraceful war ever inaugurated and the most causeless." "In fact," he charged, it was "commenced for no real injury whatever."[4] Wrote a Nashville correspondent, "Desolation reigns supreme" at Tuscumbia and Florence. "Not a store, hotel, or grocery open in all their borders. A perpetual Sabbath invests those towns, and grass grows in their unfrequented streets."[5] He did not mention that virtually all of the manufacturing facilities that had been put in operation in north Alabama prior to the war were long ago burned to the ground.[6]

Soon it would be central and south Alabama's turn to suffer. As Generals Wilson and Canby put in motion their gigantic pincer movement from opposite ends of the state in March 1865, it was evident that there was nothing stopping them from sending the rest of Alabama back to the pioneer days. Yet John Forsyth assured his readers that, despite what they were hearing about the advancing enemy, "our authorities are prepared for them, and a Sherman march into the interior of Alabama without opposition, is a thing not to take place. Whenever it is tried somebody 'will be hurt.'"[7] But as the *Montgomery Advertiser* reported just three days later,[8] General Wilson was at that very moment moving south between Russellville and Jasper in north Alabama on his own Sherman-style raid and facing *less* than token resistance, much less a prepared defensive force.[9]

Some of the populace had initially assumed that Nathan Bedford Forrest's cavalry corps would intercept and easily defeat Wilson as he came south.[10] But the War Eagle had relied on misinformation that Wilson would first attack Columbus, Mississippi, before moving toward Tuscaloosa and Selma and was therefore waiting at his base near West Point, Mississippi, when Wilson began his march.[11] As a result, Forrest was unable to meet Wilson in the mountains of north Alabama where his hit-and-run tactics would have likely been more effective against Wilson's much larger force than in the relatively flat terrain further south. Although by as early as March 25, newspapers as far away as Philadelphia, Pennsylvania, were reporting Wilson's advance,[12] Forrest apparently did not learn that Wilson was underway until March 27,[13] meaning he would be very lucky to reach Wilson before he demolished Selma. Meanwhile, as Forsyth had arrogantly predicted, somebody would be hurt—Tuscaloosa, Elyton, and much of the rest of central Alabama.

At least Tuscaloosa had the Black Warrior River to protect it, as long as the truly simple and basic precaution of demolishing enough of the wooden toll bridge between Tuscaloosa and Northport was taken. At least as early as Monday, March 27, Tuscaloosans were well aware that Wilson was coming. On March 30, the *Tuscaloosa Observer* reported that "on Monday evening last, our town was in a considerable stir created by official intelligence that the Yankees, in heavy force, were at Jasper, Walker County, the preceding day, and it was thought their destination was Tuscaloosa."[14] According to a correspondent from Mobile on the scene, the local post commander, twenty-eight-year-old Maryland-born Col. Aaron Bascum Hardcastle had "no troops and none were within calling distance." Therefore, Hardcastle "dispatched couriers to the country" to call for volunteers. In response "by Tuesday noon some six hundred men, including the [university] Cadets, were under arms, stationed for fight, with three pieces of artillery, and defied the raiders to attempt to cross the Warrior!"[15] Although Hardcastle was an 1861 graduate of the US Military Academy at West Point and a veteran of several battles including Shiloh, he did not live up to his name by dismantling the bridge or even a portion of it sufficient to prevent the Yankees from using it to cross the raging Black Warrior River.[16]

Tuscaloosa, however, temporarily dodged a bullet when Wilson opted to veer east after reaching Jasper in order to prevent Forrest from flanking him and to instead move on Elyton in adjacent Jefferson County.[17] The *Tuscaloosa Observer* assured that the reason for this change in direction was that the Yankees were afraid to tangle with the Tuscaloosa County militia and University of Alabama Cadets, declaring that they "gave Tuscaloosa the go by" because they "deem[ed] it advisable."[18] A Mobile correspondent agreed, writing that the "enemy deflected east, as they were not willing to try it on!"[19] With false bravado, the *Observer* concluded by assuring its nervous readers that "we can safely say, from the unanimous spirit that was in evidence on this occasion, that whenever a raid by the enemy is attempted on Tuscaloosa it will be met with a bold and determined resistance" and further that "we should not be surprised to hear if these audacious raiders were soon brought to grief by our cavalry, who, by this time, are in hot pursuit of them."[20]

Forrest was indeed in hot pursuit. Tuscaloosa, however, was not his priority. He was leading a portion of his men toward Finch's Ferry on the Black Warrior River near Eutaw, Alabama, approximately thirty-five miles west of Tuscaloosa, with the intention of going directly to the infinitely more important (to the Confederacy) industrial town of Selma. The plan was for one of Forrest's brigades under Gen. William Hicks "Red" Jackson to cross the river at Tuscaloosa and then proceed east to attempt to flank Wilson well north of Selma.[21] In fact, the need for Jackson to cross the river at Tuscaloosa may have been the reason Hardcastle had not yet ordered the bridge to be at least partially demolished. Forrest and his men were ultimately forced to use the bridge at Tuscaloosa as well, possibly because high water from spring rains had made the river unfordable at Finch's Ferry. Forrest reached Tuscaloosa on the afternoon of March 29,[22] but after his crossing there was no apparent military reason to leave the bridge totally intact. At this point, no one in Tuscaloosa knew whether Wilson's change of direction toward Elyton was a mere feint to be followed by another change back toward Tuscaloosa. In fact, Wilson did not reach Elyton until the next day, March 30,[23] so anything was still possible. Moreover, as Hardcastle would telegraph Gen. D. W. Adams at

Selma on April 2, he received what he considered to be credible intelligence that a large force of "7,000 infantry and some cavalry were encamped at Eldridge Post-office (fifty-five miles north of Tuscaloosa) night before last," meaning Friday, March 31. Hardcastle reported that he had "scouts upon the road" looking for this new threat from the north,[24] but once again he inexplicably failed to order the demolition of the bridge, and Yankees north of the river would, in fact, arrive on April 3.

One can only speculate on the reasons for this fundamental omission in defense strategy that would have such grave consequences for Tuscaloosans. It is possible that Hardcastle had been ordered to keep the bridge intact to facilitate future Confederate troop movements between Mississippi and Alabama, but that does not explain why he did not at least issue another call for the militia when he learned on April 2 of the force that recently arrived at Eldridge. The same is true regarding the theory advanced by some that the omission was justified by his receipt on April 1 of a telegram from General Jackson reporting that he had defeated a Union force east of Tuscaloosa at Trion (now Vance) that had been moving from Elyton toward Tuscaloosa on the *south* side of the Black Warrior River. Jackson suggested that Hardcastle "assure the fair ladies of Tuscaloosa that the tread of the vandal hordes shall not pollute the streets of their beautiful city."[25] As previously mentioned, Hardcastle received information about the new threat *north* of the river the next day on April 2, giving him an opportunity to once again put Tuscaloosa on high alert, marshal the available militia and cadets, and "raise the drawbridge" over the virtual moat protecting Tuscaloosa, thereby making the town impregnable from any force approaching from the north.

Curiously, Hardcastle would later report to his superior that the Yankee's subsequent arrival was "sudden and unexpected" and that "I hope you may believe what I avow, that I did the best I could with the means I had."[26] Based on the available evidence, these representations were false and he knew they were false. In making them, was he merely covering for himself or perhaps something else? Suspiciously, as far as can be determined he was never criticized by Tuscaloosans for his actions or inactions.

Although of course sheer speculation, this evidence raises the question whether he may have been part of a secret understanding to voluntarily surrender the town as long as neither civilians nor private property were molested. Given the number of Unionists in and around the town, it is reasonable to believe that idea was at least considered by some of the residents. If so, it is also logical that the idea gained traction among some key area elites after Forrest and his men galloped through town on their way to save Selma, leaving Tuscaloosans to essentially fend for themselves against the Yankees. Men like Robert Jemison, who owned a majestic mansion known as Cherokee in the town *as well as* the toll bridge in question, had a lot to lose if the outcome in Tuscaloosa was more like that in Columbia, South Carolina, than Savannah, Georgia,[27] where the mayor had surrendered to Sherman's forces and thereby succeeded in preventing its destruction. Several prominent Tuscaloosans of northern birth were in the same economic situation as Jemison. For example, New York–born Dr. Sewell Jones Leach, who was a member of E. W. Peck's church, was part owner of the Leach and Avery Foundry. Connecticut native Elisha Sage Olmstead operated a hat factory across the river in Northport. Both facilities had produced goods for the Confederate war effort. Similarly, New Jersey–born Charles Foster, another member of Peck's church, owned a large tanyard and shoe shop in Tuscaloosa that had been in business for almost thirty years and made shoes for the Confederates. Several other northern-born merchants depended for their livelihood on the ability of customers from Northport and the rest of the northern part of the county to cross Jemison's bridge to reach their stores.

All Tuscaloosa businessmen, including Jemison, also had a stake in preserving the University of Alabama, which, contrary to the postwar slant by some historians, was a very legitimate military target. As previously discussed, the Union military was attempting to end the war and avoid a period of protracted guerrilla fighting, and the only means of accomplishing this result was to completely destroy the Confederacy's war-making capacity. The university had not only produced officers and soldiers for the Confederacy throughout the war but its Board of Trustees had provided financial support by squandering approximately $100,000 of its endowment on purchases of Confederate bonds and treasury notes.[28] Everyone anticipated that the university would be destroyed if the war continued. All were aware of the destruction in 1863 of the military school at LaGrange College in north Alabama by Union forces, and Landon Garland had written that same year to then-governor John Gill Shorter predicting that if "the enemy should ever reach this place, they would not leave at this University one brick standing upon another."[29] More recently, in Lebanon, Tennessee, Confederate cavalry under Gen. Joseph Wheeler had destroyed the Presbyterian-supported Cumberland University, including its respected school of law, as well as some educational academies in that middle Tennessee town. According to the *Mobile Advertiser and Register*, the deed was done because the buildings "were occupied by negroes" (black soldiers) and by "Yankee school marms," who were teaching the young "how to shoot."[30] Despite the fact that the state universities in both Mississippi and Georgia had already chosen to suspend their op-

Figure 11. John Tyler Croxton. Courtesy of the Library of Congress, Prints and Photographs Division.

erations,[31] the University of Alabama was still open for business and giving lessons in this same art.

One of the university's future trustees, Unionist circuit judge William S. Mudd of Elyton, certainly recognized that the institution was in grave danger. One of E. W. Peck's former protégés and a future Alabama Republican, Mudd had left Tuscaloosa on March 28 and returned to Elyton where he ate lunch with General Wilson at his plantation mansion, Arlington, on March 30. There they discussed Tuscaloosa's defenses, among other things. Perhaps trying to convince Wilson not to bypass Tuscaloosa and to instead accept its surrender, Mudd told Wilson that the town was only lightly defended by militia and University of Alabama Cadets.[32] Wilson was convinced and had dispatched a 1,500-man brigade back to Tuscaloosa under the command of a Kentucky lawyer, Brig. Gen. John Tyler Croxton (fig. 11).[33] Although the written order by Wilson to Croxton stated that Croxton was to destroy the University of Alabama and several other war-related facilities in the Tuscaloosa area, there is reason to believe that this order may have been verbally conditional on the town refusing to surrender without bloodshed. As will be seen, Wilson would largely spare Montgomery from destruction when it surrendered, and so he must have possessed that level of discretion from his superiors. Moreover, it is very unlikely Mudd would have provided strategic information to Wilson without an assurance that the campus would be unharmed. However, for Tuscaloosa to surrender, Hardcastle had to either have been part of a surrender plot or somehow very distracted from his duties. Either scenario is consistent with what happened and what would happen in the coming, anxiety-filled days.

Croxton and his men arrived at the Northport side of the bridge at approximately eleven o'clock on the night of April 3.[34] He later reported that a few workers were then in the process of removing some of the bridge's floor boards but only an estimated twenty feet had been taken out. Conveniently, there was apparently only a small force guarding the bridge, and they had no artillery in sight.[35] Many of the local men who might have been defending the bridge were attending the wedding reception of a Confederate officer, James A. Carpenter, and the daughter of Dr. Sewell Jones Leach, for whom one of E. W. Peck's daughters, Lydia, had served as a bridesmaid earlier in the evening.[36] Contrary to local lore, that reception was not held at Dr. Leach's home, which was close to the river, but instead occurred some distance away from the bridge at Robert Jemison's mansion.[37] Whether this was also part of a surrender plot is unknown, but in retrospect, it was a serviceable distraction for Hardcastle, who was likely invited and in attendance with his subordinate officers. During this final phase of the war, events like weddings, which reminded people of their peacetime pursuits and the continuity of life, were irresistible.[38]

As has perhaps been the case in all generations, others were elsewhere actively engaging in assuring the continuity of life, not necessarily within the blissful bounds of marriage. One of Croxton's men would later recall that they had seen a light burning in a house in Northport, and when they investigated, they found one of Jackson's couriers "sparking his best girl." Pretending to be Confederate soldiers, they yelled to him to "come out of that." When he came outside, the courier, not recognizing their uniforms because it was dark, informed them of the true nature of the meager defenses of the bridge. Specifically, he confirmed that there was "a guard of two sentinels at the entrance of the bridge, and at the farther end a reserve guard of 20 men, and beyond, two pieces of artillery in the street opposite the livery stable of Mr. Evans. After he had given us all the information we desired he was told to hold up his hands."[39]

The information provided by this startled soldier was likely consistent with what Croxton already knew from spies who had been in Tuscaloosa.[40] If he had expected stiff resistance, he and most of his brigade would have stormed the bridge immediately. With his knowledge that defense of the

THE WEDDING PARTY / 73

bridge would be light or nonexistent and a desire to prevent plundering of private property, he elected to hold 90 percent of his force in reserve on the Northport side of the river until after Tuscaloosa's mayor, Obediah Berry, formally surrendered the town the next day.[41] In fact, Croxton had intended to delay his entry into Tuscaloosa until dawn on April 4, which would have resulted in even less risk of harm to his men as well as civilians. By then, even the soldiers who had attended the Carpenter-Leach wedding party would be sound asleep.[42] But the beginning of demolition efforts on the bridge forced Croxton to advance his timetable, and he ordered a Michigan company to take the bridge and enter the town. This force charged the bridge, and after a very brief exchange of volleys the guardsmen beat a hasty retreat.[43] One of Croxton's men recalled the scene at the wedding reception at the Jemison mansion when the party's uninvited guests literally crashed it in the presence of a vast crowd of people. "One of [Gen. Richard] Taylor's Majors, from Mobile, was taking unto himself a wife in the person of one of Tuscaloosa's fair daughters, and when the boys in blue appeared on the carpet there was wild commotion and running to and fro in hot haste. Carriages in waiting were quickly entered and whirled away at a gallop, while the 'vandal horde' was mean enough to shoot down the horses as they ran." Along with all of the other captured Confederate soldiers, "the bridgegroom was sent to the guardhouse."[44]

Unfortunately for Tuscaloosa, shortly after midnight a small number of university cadets were unwisely marched up from the campus by either university president Landon Garland or the university's military instructor, Col. James T. Murfee. They briefly exchanged volleys with the invaders, before retreating to the university and then to Hurricane Creek nine miles east. They should not have been brought downtown in the first place. As one of Croxton's men recalled over twenty-five years later, "while many of us in [our] brigade were mere youths, we had often heard the zip of the bullet and felt the nip of the grayback, and knew what battle meant." But "those boys [in the Cadet Corps] and their bright uniforms were for the drawing room or holiday parade." He expressed sincere regret that any were casualties and "hoped that the shot that did it was accidental."[45] Be that as it may, the result was that by the time all resistance had ceased, Croxton's force had suffered a few dozen casualties, sealing the fate of the university and other enterprises, even though Mayor Berry then formally surrendered the town.[46]

During the night, Croxton's main force on the Northport side of the river initiated the process of destroying war-related facilities by burning the Olmstead hat factory.[47] At dawn, these men crossed the bridge and entered Tuscaloosa. As far as can be determined, there was then no resistance and the town was peaceful.[48] Nonetheless, his men proceeded east toward the university, arriving at nine o'clock in the morning, and then began the fiery destruction of several buildings, including the barracks where the cadets lived, the classrooms where they were taught, and the rotunda that housed the library where they studied. These soldiers did not destroy university facilities that had no apparent connection with military instruction, such as the observatory constructed under the oversight of Prof. F. A. P. Barnard in the 1840s or the homes of the president or faculty members. The amount of destruction was actually *less* than Garland had earlier predicted.[49] In the afternoon, Croxton's demolition teams turned their attention to the manufacturing facilities in the downtown area. Among others, the Leach and Avery Foundry, Charles Foster's tanyard, the cotton mill, cotton warehouses, and a niter factory were torched.[50] By contrast, the Hospital for the Insane, which had been used to treat prisoners and soldiers, was spared.[51] In addition, no effort was made to destroy the old state capitol, the county courthouse, the county jail, retail businesses, private schools, or private homes and only a minimal amount of looting occurred.[52] Nonetheless, coupled with Croxton's destruction of the river bridge upon his departure on April 5, Tuscaloosans had already suffered enough from an economic standpoint for the omissions and commissions of others. Indeed, thanks to a war that many Tuscaloosans had opposed, thirty years of industrial development in the City of Oaks had just gone up in smoke.[53]

According to local lore, when Croxton left Tuscaloosa, some gathered at a flagpole in the town with a few soldiers and "danced around the pole, singing 'Dixie' and the 'Bonnie Blue Flag.'"[54] But the only Tuscaloosans who had any reason to dance were the slaves, many of whom had celebrated Croxton's arrival. One of his men recalled that "while we were there the negroes flocked into the city in countless numbers," crying that "the day of jubilee am come!"[55]

7
"Satan's Kingdom Is Tumbling Down"

Bent came home yesterday, left his command at Montevallo. . . . Bent is the bluest man I've seen. I think he has lost almost all hope of the success of the Confederacy. Says as things are now he don't see how we can continue the struggle much longer. The enemy occupy so much territory, have destroyed railroads, institutions & manufactories to such an extent that he don't see how our armies can be sustained. I fear his doubts are but too well founded; since Hood's retreat I have had very little hope of our ultimate success, tho' I try hard to look at the bright side & keep up a hopeful spirit. The bare thought of defeat & its consequences is so dreadful that I try to avoid it as much as possible.

—Mary Fielding

By April 1865, there was no reason for Confederates to dance anywhere in Alabama. While Croxton was having his way in Tuscaloosa County, most of Wilson's men were busy systematically destroying the state's economic assets in central Alabama.[1]

Because of the presence there of iron ore, coal, and limestone in great abundance, there was an industrial corridor of mining and manufacturing facilities from Jefferson County south through Shelby County and Bibb County that produced malleable iron from iron ore mined in the area for use in weapons, munitions, and naval manufacturing facilities in Selma.[2] If the mines, blast furnaces, and rolling mills could have survived the war, they would have been invaluable for the production of iron rails and other products necessary for the completion of Alabama's railroad network. The absence of modern, versatile transportation facilities had heretofore stunted the growth of the iron industry.[3] Now the failure to stop the war led to the destruction of this industrial corridor and prevented Alabama from taking a quantum leap forward from an economic standpoint when the fighting stopped.

Wilson's forces began the destruction in Jefferson County on March 30, destroying the blast furnaces and related buildings, machinery, and equipment of the Red Mountain Iron and Coal Company at Oxmoor. Next was the Cahawba Iron Works at Irondale.[4] On the way to Tuscaloosa, a detachment of Croxton's force had already destroyed the Roupes Valley Iron Works at Tannehill, which included three blast furnaces, a foundry, a steam plant, and a tannery.[5] In Shelby County stood the blast furnaces and rolling mill of the Shelby County Iron Manufacturing Company, said to be the largest supplier of iron to the arsenal at Selma. Along with the Helena Rolling Mill, it was soon a thing of the past, as was the Central Rolling Mill at Helena and the approximately three thousand tons of coal stockpiled there.[6] Then it was on to Bibb County on March 31 where Wilson's forces made quick work of the blast furnaces and rolling mill at the Bibb Naval Furnace at Brierfield near the Ashby station of the Alabama and Tennessee Rivers Railroad to Selma, as well as the Little Cahaba Furnace.[7]

Selma, the Queen City, had been the Holy Grail of Deep South military targets for Union commanders ever since it had become a center of weapons manufacturing earlier in the war.[8] Among the products of its large arsenal, blast furnaces, rolling mills, and powder factory was everything needed to fight on land and water.[9] Selma's significance to the Confederate war effort was evidenced by the fact that it had been placed under Forrest's defense umbrella for over a year. In an effort to stop Wilson's southbound surge toward Selma, Forrest had rallied a relatively smaller force near Ebenezer Church at what is now Stanton, Alabama (in a part of Bibb County that is now in Chilton County), approximately twenty-six miles north of Selma. Battle was joined on Saturday, April 1, 1865, and Wilson's superior forces ultimately prevailed. The War Eagle, who came very near being killed,[10] retreated through Plantersville and toward what he may have hoped were impregnable fortifications at Selma.[11]

Those fortifications, which Forrest first saw on the Sabbath morning of April 2,[12] were very impressive. But unlike Tuscaloosa, Selmans did not have the benefit of a river between them and the oncoming troops. The Alabama River was *south* of their town, and thus also hampered any organized retreat. With the aid of slave labor, a giant semicircle of fortifications reaching from bank to bank had been built. Overcoming them would require an attacking force from the north (Wilson's direction) to approach over a cleared and flat area, then scale fortifications that included ditches, stockades, and parapet walls, theoretically all under constant fire from artillery and soldiers in rifle pits utilizing an inexhaustible supply of munitions produced in Selma.[13] The problem for the Confederates was that there were a grossly inadequate number of soldiers to man these defenses, even with the men under Forrest, Roddey, and others combined.[14]

Gen. Richard Taylor had traveled by train to Selma from his base in Meridian, Mississippi, in order to personally inspect and plan the defenses. Upon his arrival the mayor, Dr. John H. Henry, a future Republican, had urged that the town be surrendered. Taylor refused to permit this but set an odd example when he later hopped aboard the last train that left town before the Yankees arrived.[15] As was the case at Tuscaloosa, the Confederacy was forced to rely primarily on civilians to make a defense. In an effort to spur volunteers from among the traditionally reserved and unenthusiastic Selma business community, the transplanted *Chattanooga Rebel* warned Selmans in its April 1 edition that the "enemy in force is in our vicinity, and is now engaged in the work of devastating the country above, and destroying some of the most important interests upon which the prosperity of Selma begins. Already we have information of the destruction of valuable iron works and coal mines, the loss of which will be severely felt, and it is certain that they will continue their depredations until every iron work in that section is destroyed if they are not driven off, and that they will finally attack either this city or Montgomery, and perhaps both." Given this, its editor implored, "will the men of this section sit tamely down and unresistingly permit this iniquitous work to go on, or will they vindicate their manhood by unsheathing their swords in defense of their rights and their liberties, and the protection of their families and their homes?"[16]

For most Selmans, the answer to that question was apparently in the affirmative. The *Chattanooga Rebel* reported that "the roads in all directions were lined with fleeing citizens, soldiers and officers, traveling in a hurry to escape the 'wrath to come.' Large quantities of whiskey were guzzled to maintain their normal condition."[17] As a consequence, Forrest issued a decree ordering all civilian men to either take their places in "the works" or go "into the river." To enforce his order, soldiers were detailed to search the town, and those unfortunates who were rounded up were deployed at the front and center of the defense structure.[18]

This was not wise strategy. Not surprisingly, the reluctant civilian warriors of Selma ultimately proved to be the weak links in Selma's defenses. After Wilson began his frontal attack on Sunday, April 2, at approximately five o'clock in the afternoon, the civilians, according to one of Wilson's troopers, "began to falter and gradually quit their places behind the breastworks, leaving broad gaps." When Wilson's force hit those gaps, the civilians ran for their lives. The militia threw "away their arms, and were swiftly seeking their horses, and divesting themselves, as they fled, of all that would betray their late connection to the defense of Selma."[19] Several contemporary Southern sources confirm there was what they called a "disgraceful stampede."[20] One older man did not run, but he did not fight either. "I was in the trenches when Wilson came. Everybody was. I just watched both ways, and when I saw how the cat was jumping, I threw my musket as far as I could, dropped down as if I was killed and walked into town after the Yankees."[21] The precise length of the "battle" of Selma is unknown, but most contemporary accounts put it somewhere between fifteen minutes and one hour.[22] The engagement ended quickly, but for those who survived, the running away had just begun. The Northern press initially reported that Forrest and Roddey had been captured,[23] but thanks to darkness and confusion, they along with several other Confederate officers and soldiers were able to make their escape, moving east toward Burnsville, then north toward Plantersville, and finally west to Marion in Perry County.[24]

Meanwhile, the Selmans who remained witnessed chaos and pandemonium, contributed to in large part by the fact that the retreating Confederate forces set fire to an estimated twenty-five thousand bales of cotton in downtown Selma before they left.[25] Predictably, the fire spread, wiping out not only a large portion of the business district but also the offices of most of the local newspapers, several homes, and the Episcopal Church. As had occurred in Tuscaloosa to a more limited extent, the poor, including members of the slave population, took advantage and went on a looting spree.[26] The outcome of the nightmare that Sunday night might have changed if Wilson's troops had been inclined to stop any of this, but their discovery of large amounts of whiskey presumably made them even more willing to take out their frustrations on Selma. As a hotbed of secession sentiment for over a decade, and the manufacturing center of weaponry that had brought death to their comrades, relatives, and neighbors, Selma, in their minds, deserved the same treatment accorded to South Carolina.[27]

Over the next eight days, 2,700 captured Confederate soldiers and civilian militiamen imprisoned in a cotton warehouse in Selma that had previously housed federal prisoners were treated to repeated renditions of "Dixie" by Wilson's band. Wilson's engineers, meanwhile, executed their plan to totally destroy the industrial facilities in the area, including the vitally important railroad tracks, shops, and depots, as well as the foundries.[28] A report published in a military newspaper, the *Federal Union,* and printed on the *Chattanooga Rebel*'s press, declared that the "capture of the arsenals and Government works, and their destructions, together with the burning of the iron and coal works on our route, has put a sharper thrust to the heart of the rebel leaders, than would even the capture of Richmond"[29] (fig. 12).

Not all Alabamians were sympathetic to Selma's plight, particularly north Alabamians. In fact, to some it was simple, retributive justice that had been a long time coming. "Now I wonder how they feel" and "how they think," wrote Joshua Burns Moore of the large nest of Dallas County secessionists that had dominated the Black Belt and the state for years. "They ought to give these fellows hell. They are the ones that carried this State out of the Union."[30]

Figure 12. Ruins of CSA Naval Foundry, Selma, Alabama. Burnt April 5, 1865. Alabama Department of Archives and History.

Selma's fall stunned many Alabamians, however, including those fighting elsewhere. Within two days of Selma's occupation, A. H. Whetstone, a soldier from Autauga County serving in the eastern theater, wrote that he had received "awful news from Alabama this morning. *Selma* gone up. Great God. What's next. I feel awful upon the reception of this verry unwelcome news. I wish I had something to steady my nerves."[31] He was not alone in this respect.

As the shock wore off, blame had to be assessed by Confederate propagandists. Overwhelming force was not cited. Instead, it was simply a failure of some of Forrest's subordinates.[32] For example, referring to Generals James R. Chalmers and Red Jackson, the Meridian *Clarion* alleged that "some of Forrest's officers did not come to time," meaning arrive in Selma on time, "and some of his men disgraced themselves. This is the secret of our failure." But, its editor assured, "by this time Forrest may have found all his men," and "if so, the enemy is doomed."[33] In Mobile, the *Army Argus and Crisis* expressed the same level of optimism. "Forrest, we learn, is making rapid preparations to rout the enemy 'horse, foot and dragoon.' He will do it."[34]

But Forrest had fought his last, possibly for reasons that have never been suspected. Ironically, it appears that this may have been an unintended consequence of the doomed president of the United States doggedly practicing what he had preached in his recent inaugural address, despite opposition from within his own political party and cabinet. Not long before Selma was taken, the *Washington* (DC) *Chronicle*, which was widely perceived to be Lincoln's semiofficial organ, had editorialized in favor of leniency toward Confederate leaders, particularly "if a series of bloody battles can be prevented which would result in the death or wounding of thousands of loyal men and as many conscripts in the rebel army who have no sympathy with the rebellion." In a telegraphic report (which he apparently received, despite the ongoing war, within five days or less of its publication) on the editorial, Forsyth's newspaper stated that "the Washington Chronicle of the 24th has a peace article which advocates a liberal policy towards the rebel leaders, to prevent further bloodshed."[35] This was a very controversial policy announcement, as it had been preceded by significant debate between several other major Republican Party organs. Some objected to announcing anything regarding this burning issue before peace was conquered for fear it would show weakness. Some others, including many Southern Unionists, were adamantly opposed to amnesty and pardons for political and military leaders of the Confederacy.[36] But Lincoln was determined to bring about a forgiving peace.

Then, as reported apparently for the first time in Alabama by the *Montgomery Mail*, Richmond was captured on April 3, sending Davis on the run, setting off wild celebrations in the North, and inspiring new hopes among many that the end was near.[37] In addition, as Lincoln likely hoped, public opinion in the North appeared to be trending in the direction of leniency toward the South. What the *New York Tribune* described as "urgent appeals to the President for an exhibition of magnanimity and clemency" were made by key members of the Northern press so that guerrilla warfare could be avoided, and "every one still clinging to the tattered, trailing flag of Disunion shall be supplied with reasons for quitting that unholy service and casting himself unreservedly on the mercy of his aggrieved and lately imperiled but victorious and placable country."[38]

Given the chaos and disorganization that now gripped the dispersed Confederate high command, the question of peace was finally in the hands of individual Confederate field commanders, who were freed from the restraining influence of the now fleeing, but still defiant, Davis. On April 8, the day after Grant requested Lee's surrender, General Wilson met privately with Forrest under a flag of truce at the Cahaba, Alabama, plantation home of Unionist Thomas M. Mathews.[39] As had been the case with Roddey in north Alabama in January, the "reported" topic of the meeting, negotiation of prisoner exchanges, was sometimes actually a cover for the exchange of ideas between field commanders regarding how to end the conflict without further senseless loss of life. Given the image Forrest had cultivated for himself, it is reasonable to assume that he required all present to permanently maintain the secrecy of the actual discussions, so it is not surprising that there is no direct evidence the two reached an accord. However, there is strong circumstantial evidence that

"Satan's Kingdom Is Tumbling Down" / 81

Wilson likely made Forrest an offer he could not refuse. Wilson later recalled that after they concluded their private meeting, they began "treating each other like old acquaintances, if not old friends."[40] It is interesting that when Wilson's force subsequently left Selma, crossed the Alabama River on a pontoon bridge, and on April 10 began moving *east* through Lowndes County toward Montgomery, the man who had become famous for chasing down Union colonel Abel Streight's brigade two years earlier and who the newspapers were now confidently reporting would revenge Selma and repulse the invaders, *did not follow* Wilson.[41] On the contrary, the War Eagle moved his force in the *opposite* direction *west* toward Gainesville, Alabama, where he would quietly remain until the end of the war.[42] In what may have been the quid pro quo, Forrest was very surprisingly never punished for the atrocities at Fort Pillow as many in the North still fervently wished, much less killed as General Sherman had directly ordered in January.[43]

Wilson's march from Selma toward Montgomery was very destructive. Six months later a shocked Northern correspondent reported that "a man, though a fool," could still have followed Wilson's track. A "tropical tornado never left more distinct traces of its course through the jungle than this same raid has through the heart of Alabama."[44] The only real resistance Wilson encountered on his way to Montgomery was an ambush by the remnants of the Seventh Alabama cavalry, but those in the ambuscade were quickly routed.[45]

On April 9, the propeace *Montgomery Mail* had published an editorial encouraging the citizens of Montgomery to cease resistance and simply acquiesce in the takeover of the town when Wilson's force arrived.[46] But that very day, Governor Watts issued a public proclamation warning that "base and cowardly fears but invite the enemy to destroy you all." He defiantly declared that the "military authorities here are determined to defend the city of Montgomery" and that "the seat of government shall not be surrendered as long as there is a reasonable hope of defending it."[47] Wilson and his men therefore initially assumed that they would have a much tougher fight on their hands when they reached the Cradle of the Confederacy.[48] Meanwhile, Watts likely delighted area temperance advocates when he prohibited the sale of liquor within ten miles of Montgomery. He was one-upped by the Montgomery city council, which adopted an ordinance to send all liquor to a designated location out of town. As one approving correspondent put it, "if the Yankees come here and can get liquor, good bye to Montgomery."[49]

But on April 11, when it became apparent that Watts's final call for volunteers from the region to come to the capital's defense had largely fallen on deaf ears and that Forrest was not riding to the rescue, the Confederate military shocked and angered even reluctantly sober local pro-Confederates by opting to burn approximately eighty-five thousand bales of cotton valued at $12 million that was stored there and then skedaddling to Columbus, Georgia. Despite Watts's macho liberty-or-death declarations less than a month earlier, he was not inclined to stay behind and fight. He was instead among the refugees, including what a pro-Confederacy Georgia newspaper called "original secesh," who left Montgomery with the departing Confederate soldiers. Watts did not stop running in Columbus but instead fled all the way to Eufaula, Alabama.[50]

A correspondent with the *New York Herald* later reported that a "committee of citizens waited upon [Confederate] General Adams previous to the evacuation" and that during their ensuing meeting Adams "refused to allow the committee to go out and meet the Union Generals."[51] The identity of the members of this committee, which was obviously attempting to obtain permission to surrender Montgomery in order to save it, is unknown. However, given the active and apparently very extensive Union spy network in Alabama, it is very likely Wilson was being kept apprised of these developments in Montgomery. The town's mayor, W. L. Coleman, and a delegation of citizens that included Milton Saffold and other Unionists would surrender the town without a shot being fired. According to one account, after Confederate forces evacuated the town, the "Mayor . . . with a deputation of citizens had made preparations to meet the enemy under a flag of truce, and obtain protection for the undefended city."[52] According to this same account, the delegation left Montgomery on the night of April 11,[53] and other sources indicate that the meeting with the commander of Wilson's forward unit occurred near the Catoma Creek west of the city on the road to Hayneville at approximately three in the morning on April 12.[54] A correspondent of the *New York Herald* reported that the group was "received with great courtesy" and an agreement was reached to surrender Montgomery.[55]

A few hours later, a squad of mounted Union soldiers reportedly "dashed into Main Street, and rode up to the Capitol, where they formed a line. In about half an hour General [Edward] McCook, at the head of his columns, accompanied by the Mayor and committee of the [city] Council, rode into Court House Square, and from thence to the Capitol. Very soon thereafter the US flag was floating from the Capitol dome, the Court House, the telegraph office, and from the Exchange Hotel, where General McCook established his headquarters. The flag of truce and the battle flag of the advance were placed one on each side of the Capitol stairs."[56] A Montgomery resident, Sarah Follansbee, wrote at the time that the town was spared, "some said because no defence was made." Later that morning, she continued, "it was made known by a printed placard that the city of Montgomery having been surrendered into a protection of the United States, all private property would be respected, except such as required by military necessity."[57]

This was fortunate for Montgomery residents, certainly when compared to the bad hands that had recently been dealt to Selma and Tuscaloosa in response to resistance. Although some war-related industries and the railroad depots were ultimately destroyed,[58] the Union soldiers who began passing through Montgomery on their way to Columbus, Georgia, on the morning of April 12 were not given the pleasure of destroying the capitol building where Alabama's secession was orchestrated and the Confederacy was born.[59] If they had been, it is certainly possible that the town's designation as the state's capital might have been jeopardized, possibly to Tuscaloosa's advantage given that the old capitol building there had not been harmed and no one had the money to build another anywhere else.

But as would be repeatedly demonstrated in the coming months, magnanimity by the victors was not necessarily met by a spirit of reconciliation and renewed loyalty. The still mindlessly defiant editors of the *Montgomery Advertiser* told their readers after the Yankees had left town for Georgia that "we have no cause to despair. During four long years of the most terrible warfare, we had been spared, and whilst our brethren in other sections of the country saw their homes invaded, their fields laid waste, we have lived in peace and plenty, knowing of but its general effects upon the country at large, but not feeling its terrors at home." Surprisingly, they also maturely conceded that it "was just and proper, perhaps, in the eyes of Providence, that we, too, should feel the heel of the invader on our cherished soil, and as terrible as may be this visitation we have still cause to be thankful." They further recognized that it could have been much worse. "Whilst other cities have been reduced to ashes and their inhabitants left homeless wanderers, we have been spared in our homes, our families have been respected, and now chastened by misfortune we can look back to the past and enquire whether we have done all our duty, whether the chastisement was not deserved?"[60] But the *Advertiser's* editors, as well as some other Alabama editors, refused to acknowledge that the Confederate cause was lost, at least until the Yankees returned to occupy the town ten days later.[61]

While the dramas in Tuscaloosa, Selma, and Montgomery were playing out, the fate of Alabama's largest city, Mobile, was also being decided. As planned, the coordinated nature of the movements from the north and the south, coupled with the aforementioned destruction of portions of the Alabama and Florida Railroad between Pollard and Greenville,[62] prevented Confederates in either region from reinforcing each other. As a result, Union general Canby was basically unmolested during his pounding, thirteen-day siege of Spanish Fort, ultimately forcing the Confederates to evacuate the facility on April 8.[63]

Three days before Spanish Fort fell, John Forsyth had assured his readers that it would take the Yankees "five years and three months to take Mobile."[64] On April 9, however, Canby and Steele teamed their forces in a successful assault on the unfortunate Confederate defenders of Fort Blakely. Thanks to the 1864 massacre at Fort Pillow, some of those defenders were shown no quarter by Steele's black infantrymen.[65] The fall of Fort Blakely placed Confederate forces in Mobile in jeopardy of being cut off, and so on the same day Montgomery was evacuated, the Confederates evacuated Mobile. On the fourth anniversary of the Confederate attack on Fort Sumter, Mobile's mayor, Robert H. Slough, wisely agreed to surrender it to Union forces. They occupied the city on April 13.[66]

Perhaps with Forsyth in mind, the editor of the Washington, DC, *National Republican* responded to a telegraph report of this news by remarking that "Satan's Kingdom is tumbling down, glory hallelujah."[67] The *Register* as well as the other Mobile newspapers temporarily ceased publication, and so Union general Gordon Granger, the departmental commander, authorized a correspondent of the pro-Union *New Orleans Times* to begin publication of the *Mobile News*, apparently on Forsyth's presses.[68] As one might expect, the editorial slant of this new entrant in the Mobile press was definitely not Forsythesque. Its editor urged the citizens to "submit cheerfully" to occupation forces.[69]

After concluding further resistance was futile, Lee also formally surrendered unconditionally to Grant on April 9.[70] Several riders, including a future Alabama governor, twenty-year-old Maj. Thomas Goode Jones of Montgomery, were sent from Confederate lines with white flags of truce to initiate the process of the surrender of Lee's Army of Northern Virginia. In accordance with Lincoln's prior instructions, Lee and his soldiers were allowed to return to their homes "not to be disturbed by the United States authority so long as they observe their parole and the laws in force where they may reside." At the time, it was hoped in the North this would trigger a series of mass surrenders by Confederate forces elsewhere over the next several weeks.[71]

While most Northerners, of course, rejoiced, the reaction of Alabamians to the Confederate collapse depended on their level of support—financial or emotional—for the Confederacy. Josiah Gorgas, who had married into a prominent Alabama family, wrote that the loss was "of a character so overwhelming that I am as yet unable to comprehend it. I am as one walking in a dream, & expecting to awake."[72] Confederate civilians also expressed shock and disbelief. Elizabeth Meriwether, a refugee from Memphis who was living

"Satan's Kingdom Is Tumbling Down" / 85

in Tuscaloosa at the time, later recalled that "when news of Lee's surrender reached Tuscaloosa the citizens stood about on the streets almost stunned," and some suspected that the report "was merely another vile Yankee invention!"[73] An aptly named teenage girl in Florence, Sally Independence Foster, wrote that "I feel very sad, for I heard yesterday that we had been defeated at Richmond, though hope with all my heart it is not so."[74] In Huntsville, Mary Chadick, who had noted that "our hearts sink within" and that "several ladies had to go to bed in consequence" of the fall of Richmond, wrote, "Oh, my God, can this be true?" when word of Lee's capitulation arrived.[75] Similarly, Kate Cumming wrote that "none of our people believe the rumors, thinking them as mythical as the surrender of General Lee's army. They look upon it as a plot to deceive the people."[76]

Ostensibly in order to discourage defeatism, at least one Alabama newspaper, the *Demopolis Herald*, was still publishing denials of Lee's surrender three weeks after it had occurred. Its editor claimed that "a general armistice has been agreed upon between the United States and the Confederate States" and that "our heart is full to overflowing at the glorious prospect now dawning for the independence of the South." He also ridiculed Unionists and reconstructionism, asking "where will be the long faces now? Were the caterwauls continually assailing those who have held fast to the faith that independence and liberty would be the final inestimable boon of their country?"[77]

By contrast, like many other north Alabama Unionists, Joshua Burns Moore naively concluded that "one thing is certain. The secessionists have had their run. The race is over."[78] But was it really over? Instead, would the remaining Confederate forces under Generals Johnston and Taylor refuse to surrender? Would the fanatics now go to Mexico and attempt to stage a comeback? Jefferson Davis was then attempting to make his way to the trans-Mississippi region, probably to Texas.[79] Would Confederates who had not initially supported secession, but who had fully invested in the cause from a financial, physical, and emotional standpoint to keep the Confederacy and, therefore, slavery alive, now continue the fight by joining the mass guerrilla movement Forsyth and others had been advocating?[80] After Mobile was taken, a gang of guerrillas reportedly stormed the Battle House Hotel in an effort to assassinate General Gordon Granger, who had established his headquarters there.[81] Had there been sufficient damage to the South's capacity to make war to prevent either of these nightmare scenarios?

For Unionists, those were not the only pressing questions.[82] Even if warfare stopped, would there really be peace? What would happen to the secessionists and the Confederate military and political leaders? Would treason really be made odious, as Andrew Johnson had pledged, or would they get off scot-free? William Yancey was gone, but was the political and economic power of surviving Alabama Confederates like Watts, C. C. Clay, J. L. M. Curry Jr., Forsyth, and other loyal Confederates to be broken? If so, who would fill the power vacuum and control policies in the postwar period?

Alabamians faced other significant social, economic, and legal challenges. Most basically, given the interruption of the planting season, how would sufficient food be produced to prevent starvation in the coming months? What would happen to the freed slaves? How would they be controlled? Who would care for them? What rights would they have? Could the greatly inflated Confederate currency still be used as legal tender, at least until Yankee greenbacks became commonly available? Would the state redeem the millions of dollars of bonds issued by the state or the Confederacy to finance the war? Would Alabama ever recover its antebellum standard of living, or would it forever remain a dead cock in the pit from an economic standpoint? All anyone could say with certainty was "*nous verrons*," and that much would depend on Lincoln.

III
THE FINAL DOOM
OF STATE SOVEREIGNTY

Timeline: April 14–December 20, 1865

April 14, 1865	Lincoln is shot.
April 15, 1865	Lincoln dies at 7:20 a.m.
April 15, 1965	Andrew Johnson is sworn in as president.
April 18, 1865	Sherman reaches a peace accord with Johnston.
April 24, 1865	Johnson disapproves the Sherman-Johnston accord.
April 26, 1865	John Wilkes Booth is killed.
April 26, 1865	Johnston surrenders his army to Sherman on the same terms as Lee.
April 27, 1865	USS *Sultana* disaster kills over 1,500 passengers.
April 29, 1865	Johnson removes trade restrictions over most of the South.
May 4, 1865	Taylor surrenders his army to Canby.
May 10, 1865	Trial of the surviving Lincoln assassins begins.
May 10, 1865	Davis is captured in Georgia.
May 12, 1865	C. C. Clay Jr. surrenders in Georgia.
May 25, 1865	Explosion occurs at ammunition depot in Mobile, Alabama.
May 29, 1865	Johnson announces his reconstruction policy, issuing his Proclamation of Amnesty and his proclamation appointing a provisional governor for North Carolina.
June 21, 1865	Johnson appoints Talladega lawyer Lewis Parsons as provisional governor of Alabama.
July 5, 1865	Assassination conspirators found guilty.
July 7, 1865	Sentences of conspirators are carried out.
July 20, 1865	Parsons issues a proclamation setting an election of delegates to a constitutional convention.
August 31, 1865	Delegates are elected in Alabama.
September 12, 1865	Alabama constitutional convention assembles in Montgomery.
September 30, 1865	Alabama constitutional convention adjourns.
October 1, 1865	Connecticut voters reject an amendment to the state constitution that would have provided for black suffrage.
October 8, 1865	Black residents hold an insurrection in Jamaica.
November 6, 1865	North Alabama businessman Robert Miller Patton is elected governor.
November 10, 1865	Henry Wirz is executed.

November 20, 1865	Alabama legislature convenes.
December 4, 1854	US Congress convenes.
December 5, 1865	Johnson gives his annual message.
December 13, 1865	Alabama governor Patton is inaugurated.
December 18, 1865	Thirteenth Amendment abolishing slavery is declared ratified.
December 20, 1865	Patton is authorized by the Johnson administration to take reins of power, thereby ending the provisional government in Alabama.

8
"When This Cruel War Is Over"

All business is suspended, the future is dark we rely too little on God, our only help.

—James Mallory

The village is in Clarke County [Alabama]. There is some wealth about here and the people seem very kind. As I close this entry the tones of a piano are filling the house with music, and a sweet young woman's voice is singing "When This Cruel War Is Over."

—William Pitt Chambers

For Alabama's own loved dead,
Though humbler be their names,
Why should the selfish tear be shed?
They are now God's and fame's.
Rest, Irby, Webb, Jones, Hobbs and Hale,
Rest, Jewett, Summers, Moore,
Inge, Garrott, Lomax, Pelham, Baine,
On death's triumphant shore.

—Alexander Beaufort Meek

In 1864 the editors of the *Montgomery Advertiser* had extolled the virtues of the war in terms of its diversification of Alabama's economy. "We see the results everywhere in the improved condition of our mechanical and manufacturing industry, notwithstanding the heavy drain of the war upon *the labor of the country.*" Despite the fact that most of the capital for those advances had come from the Confederate and state governments for war-related purposes, the editors assured that "after the war we expect to see the most rapid development of our resources ever witnessed in any country."[1]

Perhaps if the Unionists' steadfast predictions of ultimate ruin had been heeded by the secessionists at the beginning of the conflict or by Confederates like Davis and Watts near the end, these expectations might have been fulfilled. Even without the potent economic engine of war and despite limited outside capital, there was irrefutable evidence that Alabama had been moving slowly but surely toward an industrial economy during the antebellum period.[2] But as would occur eighty years later as the result of Allied efforts to destroy Germany's war-making capacity,[3] the Union military's efforts to accomplish precisely the same goal in a more primitive fashion had already succeeded in wiping out most of those gains in north Alabama, and Wilson's raiders in particular had eliminated much of what remained in central and south Alabama.[4]

As a correspondent for the *Cincinnati Commercial* proudly described it:

> The last strongholds of the rebellion were captured by Wilson's raid. Next to the Tredegar Works, at Richmond, the principal source of supply to the rebels of the munitions of war, were the vast iron works, and rifle and pistol factories, besides the extensive cotton factories, employed in the manufacture of rebel clothing, found and destroyed, in Alabama. A rebel ram, nearly ready for sea, was also destroyed, with arsenals, armories, accouterments, shops, paper-mills, &c. In addition, the railroad from Selma to Blue Mountain, connecting with the iron works; also, the Montgomery and Georgia Railroad and an immense quantity of rolling-stock were torn up and burned. On the Montgomery road thirty-six culverts and a large amount of track suffered for treason. The effect of these terrible fires in the rear of the Confederacy cannot be over-estimated. They effectually consumed the propagative quality of the last dragon's tooth, and sundered every nerve of the last ganglion of rebellion.[5]

Nonetheless, literally and figuratively, Alabama's ace in the hole had always consisted of the rich, largely untapped, mineral deposits buried in central and north Alabama outside the plantation counties, and those, as well as other natural assets, were still in place.[6] At this point the prudent goal for Alabama's leaders should have been to focus on rebuilding its economy and avoid anything that might antagonize the North any further than it already was.

As a Georgia editor would later advise,

> This war has not been without its good results. For forty years the North and South have been quarreling through their politicians; we will not call them statesman, for they do not deserve the name. Words have at last lead to blows; and now since the fight is over, we view each other in a true light—we know each others strength, resources and weak points. We have advanced fifty years in thought, and exploded several grey headed old errors, that were thought to be great truths, because they were generally believed to be true. The South especially, knows now her weak points, [and] if she is wise, she will profit by her sad experi-

ence in war. She has found out that her strength consists not alone in negroes and cotton bags; in fact, that her cotton was no strength at all in war, but a powerful producer of wealth to a certain class in times of peace. Commerce and the mechanical arts must be encouraged by us—no longer must we talk of what we ought to do, but do it. This war will give an impetus to Southern minds and Southern character. Internal improvements and direct trade will now receive our attention in a substantial manner. Our great mineral resources should not be overlooked. In fact we feel that a new field of thought will take possession of us, and that we will forget the negro and cotton in some degree in the pursuit of other callings that invite us to assure a road to wealth.[7]

This was excellent advice. But given the millions of dollars of destruction caused by Union forces to Alabama's economic assets over the past four years, fulfilling these aspirations would cost money that neither Alabama nor the South as a whole possessed, at least not in tender legal in the eyes of the US government.[8] But as before the war, Northern capitalists did have it, although it would take some doing to convince them to trust Alabamians or any other Southrons once again.[9]

This lack of trust was arguably justified. Some Alabamians had been outspoken agitators and leaders of the secession movement during the decade prior to the war, and after secession Alabama had served as the venue for the creation of the Confederate government. Alabamians had served in the Confederate cabinet and as the home of the Confederacy's first national capital. The order to fire on Fort Sumter had been sent by an Alabamian (Leroy Pope Walker) from Alabama, triggering a war that had resulted in the deaths of hundreds of thousands of Northerners. Many Alabamians had fought for the Confederacy and then used the conflict as a reason to withhold payments for prewar debts to Northern creditors. In addition, commerce raiders such as the CSS *Alabama* and the CSS *Tuscaloosa* had caused millions of dollars of damage to Northern shipping. Alabamian C. C. Clay had been involved in planning terrorist strikes in Northern cities from sanctuaries in Canada. Most recently, despite the fact that the war was clearly unwinnable in the western theater after the devastation of Hood's army in Tennessee, Alabama had refused to capitulate, requiring even more Northerners to die in order to subdue her and further bloating a nearly crippling US war debt. Hence, it was only natural that as a means of destroying the economic power of what Northerners perceived were planter aristocrats calling these shots, they were determined to punish by destroying the institution of slavery and other economic assets. Given all of this, convincing Northern capitalists to now build up Alabama and the other Southern states from an economic standpoint would not be easy.[10]

A strong profit motive could eventually overcome hate, as would the need for tax revenues to pay the immense federal war debt, but much would depend on whether the war ended on a positive note and the South returned like the proverbial prodigal son instead of a haughty, entitled teenager. Assuming it did the former, and with Lincoln's public assurances just over a month earlier of malice toward none and charity for all, there was reason in Alabama and the rest of the South for guarded optimism.[11] In the coming days, Lincoln further demonstrated by his words and conduct that this optimism was justified. And in retrospect, it appears clear that if his sentiments had been allowed to be translated into prolonged action throughout his second term in office, the vanquished South might have been substantially resurrected from an economic standpoint within a reasonable period of time. With a resumption of capital flows from a charitable North to rebuild and further develop Alabama's transportation and industrial base, a new and improved version of the antebellum model—the New Alabama—could be created. For this reason, Lincoln was not necessarily the best friend of those freed slaves now desiring equality, but he certainly was the most important Northern friend the white South had.[12]

Tragically, however, Lincoln's days were numbered. As the conspiracy indictment to which Cahaba, Alabama, lawyer George Washington Gayle later pled guilty would allege,[13] in December 1864 Gayle had advertised in a Selma newspaper for contributions amounting to $1 million to procure the assassinations of Lincoln, Vice President Andrew Johnson, and Secretary of State William Seward. The audacity of his proposal and the amount of the bounty for the job had contributed to it being reprinted in newspapers all over the country and even abroad in the last four months.[14] Secretary of War Edwin Stanton would later reveal to the nation that a group of assassins, who had conspired to commit the crimes of the millennium, had been planning since "before the fourth of March" and that "it would seem that they had for several days" before the plan was put into execution "been seeking their chance, but for some unknown reason it was not carried into effect" until the night of April 14.[15]

One reason was that Lincoln had been in Virginia meeting with Alabamian John Archibald Campbell, the Confederate assistant secretary of war but also a reconstructionist, who had tellingly not fled Richmond when the Confederates evacuated on April 3.[16] As the national press would soon be reporting, when Campbell asked Lincoln how the Union could quickly be reunited, Lincoln had shockingly suggested as a first step that the existing, but recently adjourned, wartime Virginia legislature (instead of the rival Union-loyal government led by provisional governor Francis Pierpont) be reconvened so it could then recall all Virginia soldiers from the Confederate army, thus pulling the rug out from under Lee and his then still-retreating army.[17]

For most Northern "Radical" Republicans and Southern Unionists, allowing any "rebel legislature" to ever meet again was a very bad idea. Instead, they understandably insisted that governmental power in the South should henceforth be exercised only by men loyal to the Union.[18] Lincoln certainly recognized that what he was suggesting to Campbell would be met with a torrent of criticism. So why did he do it? It was not from purely charitable motives. There is substantial evidence that Lincoln, like his generals, was very concerned that unless leniency was shown, a guerrilla war would follow the end of conventional warfare, and that this fear shaped his vision of reconstruction policies.[19] And for good reason. The press in Alabama and elsewhere had long conditioned Confederates to prepare for a guerrilla war if conventional warfare ended. It was, they were reminded, the means by which their forefathers had finally bested the British in the South.[20] And it had proven successful at an early point in the war when Union forces invaded north Alabama. There it had cost Lincoln one of his most popular generals, Robert L. McCook of Ohio.[21] According to a correspondent in Tennessee, then military governor Andrew Johnson had viewed McCook's remains in Nashville and was "visibly affected by the sight of his late friend."[22] Despite being subject to a black flag (under which condition they would take no prisoners and show no clemency) if caught, guerrillas continued their sporadic attacks in 1865 and they were usually quite effective.[23] Guerrillas who attacked a train near Cumberland, Tennessee, in April would have bagged Johnson if he had not changed his mind about returning home and remained in Washington, DC.[24]

Guerrilla warfare was the next phase expected by many Confederates and Union commanders.[25] According to the memoir of Brig. Gen. Cullen Andrews Battle, a prewar Tuskegee, Alabama, lawyer, even Robert E. Lee had long "expressed the belief that in the mountains of Virginia he could carry on the war for twenty years." After Grant cut off his retreat, however, Lee had rejected that bloody option and surrendered his army.[26] But would his men abide by and respect his change of heart, especially given that Jefferson Davis had not expressly and publicly ruled out this brand of warfare? And what about the soldiers serving under other commanders?

The threat of a long and bloody period of guerrilla warfare was magnified by the possible availability of Mexico as a staging area for Confederate forces.[27] France had saddled Mexico with an imperial government, headed

Figure 13. Maximilian I of Mexico, ca. 1864. Courtesy of the Library of Congress, Prints and Photographs Division.

by Emperor Ferdinand Maximilian (fig. 13), who had been installed in that position by French emperor Napoleon III and a large contingent of French soldiers. It was a violation of the Monroe Doctrine that the US government had protested from the outset but not yet challenged militarily for fear of provoking French recognition of the Confederacy.[28] The press in Alabama and elsewhere had spread the rumor that such recognition was just around the corner. Despite numerous Confederate overtures,[29] however, Napoleon had not yet given official recognition to Davis's government. But Napoleon and Maximilian had given it covert support.[30] The US government was well aware of these activities and had given covert military and financial support to a rival Mexican government under Benito Pablo Juarez with the intention of ousting Maximilian and the French from Mexico after the Confederacy's capitulation.[31] But Maximilian was still hanging on, and so were the hopes of die-hard Confederates.

Just as troubling was the nation's financial situation. The country had survived, but it was still in great economic distress and the effusion of treasure and blood had to stop. Financially and emotionally it could not afford to further prosecute any significant war, much less one with, or supported by, a foreign power.

"When This Cruel War Is Over" / 95

Figure 14. *The Peacemakers* by George Peter Alexander Healy, 1868. This painting shows the March 1865 meeting among Pres. Abraham Lincoln, Lt. Gen. Ulysses S. Grant, Maj. Gen. William T. Sherman, and Rear Adm. David D. Porter aboard the *River Queen* off City Point, Virginia. They were discussing prospects of peace during Grant's siege of Richmond, just a few weeks before the Civil War ended. Courtesy of the Library of Congress, Prints and Photographs Division.

To some degree the South's return to prosperity would benefit the nation as a whole, but its continued prostration only encouraged Southerners to look at extreme options. Among others, the pro-Lincoln *New York Times* was therefore calling for Lincoln to return the South to "great prosperity." "At all events, we trust our government will do its best to clear the way."[32] That prosperity was exactly what Alabama needed to overcome its long ordeal in the Confederacy, and every piece of available evidence suggests that Lincoln was not only willing but anxious to "clear the way." For example, the US Military Railroads Construction Corps was already in the process of rebuilding Southern railroads.[33]

Lincoln had previously communicated his views of postwar policies to his military commanders, free from influence from advisers and outsiders, during a meeting on March 27 and 28 at Grant's headquarters at City Point, Virginia, with Grant and Sherman, as well as Adm. David Dixon Porter (fig. 14).[34] During that meeting, the matter of the political wrangling in Washington,

DC, over peace terms came up, and Lincoln emphasized that his goals were to end the war as soon as possible without the effusion of more blood and to quickly get the Confederate soldiers *and* their officers back home so they could resume their prewar private lives and would not be tempted to engage in guerrilla warfare. To encourage this, none of the Confederate leaders— not even Davis—were to be punished. In order for Lincoln to avoid political pressure from Northern hardliners, he suggested that those leaders be permitted to escape from the country into exile without his prior knowledge.[35] Those that chose to remain would, nonetheless, receive leniency.

On April 6, when Lincoln met with Alabamian John Archibald Campbell in Richmond, he reiterated the terms he had proposed at Hampton Roads. There is also evidence that Lincoln repeated his suggestion that the Southern legislatures could vote against, and thereby defeat, ratification of the Thirteenth Amendment. This was the same earlier-mentioned meeting where Lincoln authorized the wartime Virginia legislature to convene.[36]

When news became public of Lincoln's authorization, it ignited a firestorm of controversy.[37] The editor of the *Cleveland Leader* was indignant. He declared that allowing this "will awake grave thoughts in the minds of all loyal men[.] Is *this* to be the punishment of treason—*this* to be the reward for four years of bloody rebellion—*this* the example to be made of leading traitors; that the rebel legislature of Virginia, who have been foremost and loudest in traitorous action, who hurried the State out of the Union against her will, who have oppressed and persecuted the true-hearted loyalists, black and white, through the State, who have been elected because of their conspicuous and notorious subservience to the rebel cause—that *these* scoundrels, forsooth, shall still rule the reconstructed and purified State of Virginia?"[38] Montgomery Unionist William Crawford Bibb went so far as to travel to Washington, DC, to meet with Lincoln and deliver a letter requesting that he retract his permission for the Virginia legislature to meet. "The careful avoidance of offence," wrote Bibb, "will add to your own popularity at the same time that it will tend to the pacification of the country. We who have borne the heat & burthen of the day are deeply interested in the quiet settlement of this matter. If it is not carefully dealt with, we the conservatives of the South will be the sufferers."[39]

Other Alabama Unionists were also adamant that traitors should no longer hold positions of authority. For example, although Jeremiah Clemens had never been a member of the Alabama legislature during the war, his vote for the Ordinance of Secession in the 1861 secession convention, and brief service shortly thereafter as the head of Alabama's militia, had been raised by Alabama Unionists as disqualifiers in his bid to receive Lincoln's appointment as Alabama's military governor.[40] In an effort to overcome this opposition, Clemens had recently written a public letter denying that he ever "gave in my adhesion to the doctrine of secession." Instead, he wrote, there "never was an hour when I did not pronounce it treason." He also explained that although he was appointed "Major General and Commander of all the [militia] forces of Alabama in 1861," he had taken "no oath of office of any kind" and "did not organize the Alabama troops." In sum, he claimed he had maintained an "unfaltering attachment to the Union" and "labored to preserve it while it existed and to restore it when it had been violently disrupted."[41] However, the stigma of disloyalty surrounding him had apparently stayed Lincoln's hand in appointing Clemens Alabama's military governor. If Clemens were disqualified in the eyes of Unionists, the majority of the members of the Alabama legislature certainly were, especially given their failure to ever actually adopt any measure expressly calling for an end to the war.

Lincoln ultimately did withdraw his permission for the Virginia legislature to convene.[42] But the *New York Tribune* revealed that "the President still expressed his determination of evincing a great nation's magnanimity and forgiveness where the executive clemency is sincerely and penitently asked."[43] While rumors swirled in the North that peace negotiations with the Confederates were also underway, Lincoln had remained at City Point safe from criticism until April 9. He even rebuffed efforts by Seward, Johnson, Sen. Charles Sumner, and other worried Republicans to interfere with him there.[44]

According to the diary of Gideon Welles, Lincoln remained obsessed over the threat of guerrilla warfare after he returned to Washington, DC. Two days before Lincoln died, he emphasized to Welles his continuing concern about the guerrilla threat. "Civil government must be reestablished, [Lincoln] said, as soon as possible; there must be courts, and law, and order, or society would be broken up, the disbanded armies would turn to robber bands and guerrillas," and this, Lincoln concluded, "we must strive to prevent." This could be done by establishing provisional governments and it was clear to Lincoln that they must be of the sort white Southerners would support. Wrote Welles, Lincoln's idea was that "prominent and influential men" in the South "had better come together and undo their own work."[45] Was it intended by Lincoln that such men would also make decisions regarding issues like black suffrage?

While the nation pondered that question, Forsyth announced in his Mobile newspaper that the members of the Society of Loyal Confederates in Alabama had raised $1 million. Forsyth, who would never be indicted as a conspirator with George Washington Gayle, represented that this money was to be "directed to the payment of Government arrearages to the Confederate troops serving in this State."[46] But by this point that was not necessary; $1 million had already reached Alabama and was on deposit with Confederate officials in Tuscaloosa.[47] Whether John Wilkes Booth and his gang were aware that the bounty had been amassed is unknown, but it is clear that they were motivated by a large financial reward. There is evidence Booth had received money from someone in the Northeast and that he had a bank account in Canada that reflected a deposit from someone in England.[48] There is also evidence that some of the conspirators had bragged that they would become rich and would soon do something that would be reported in the newspapers.[49] After Gayle's assassination advertisement was published, Booth also alluded to a great "speculation" in which he was involved,[50] and the day before the assassination reportedly told an acquaintance he had something big "on his hands" and "there was a great deal of money in it."[51]

One of their targets, Andrew Johnson (fig. 15), had also recently traveled to Richmond[52] and following his return to Washington, DC, had appeared in public at a giant, spontaneous celebration of the fall of Richmond on the southern portico of the Patent Office where he had given a brief speech.[53] According to the report of that speech in the *Washington* (DC) *Chronicle*, he discussed his thoughts on postwar policy, telling the large crowd in attendance that he was "in favor of leniency"—a change from his days in Tennessee—except with regard to the "evil doers," who he declared should be punished. But when some in the crowd shouted their agreement, he seemed to return to his earlier Old Testament stance. "Treason," he declared, "is the highest crime known in the catalogue of crimes, and for him that is willing to lift his impious hand against the authority of the nation—I would say death is too easy a punishment." In conclusion, he announced that he favored "the halter to intelligent, influential traitors," but "to the honest boy, to the deluded man, who has been deceived into the rebel ranks, I would extend lenience."[54] In the eyes of the assassins, such retributive comments must have made him an even more righteous target, and there was a certain segment of the Republican Party who, despite his tough rhetoric, would likely not shed any tears over his loss.

Johnson had only begrudgingly come to Washington, DC, for his inauguration because he was furious that Congress (whose members were then present in the audience) had bowed to the will of the Radical Republicans by resolving that Tennessee's electoral votes from the 1864 election would not be counted, thereby suggesting that Tennessee's senators and congressmen would not be admitted to Congress following their upcoming election.[55] As Alabamians had read in their newspapers, many in the North alleged with

Figure 15. Andrew Johnson. Courtesy of the Library of Congress, Prints and Photographs Division.

some justification that Johnson was drunk during his inauguration address in which he had basically informed key Radical Republicans that they had gotten too big for their britches.[56] Since then, there had been multiple calls for the resignation or impeachment of the man Forsyth subsequently ridiculed as the "Caesar of the dunghill,"[57] and this, in turn, presaged very combative relations between the executive branch and the Republican-controlled Congress over state sovereignty should Johnson be forced to lead the nation.[58] It had also heartened Northern Democrats, as well as Confederate Alabamians, who were looking a few chess moves ahead and searching for any and every means of dividing their opposition.[59]

Barring Johnson's resignation or impeachment, most Radical Republicans probably concurred with an editorial from the *Cincinnati Commercial* that was reprinted in the Alabama press praying that "He who controls the lives of men and destinies of nations preserve the life of Abraham Lincoln, and spare the country the humiliation it would be made to feel in the contingency of Andrew Johnson's assumption of the reins of Government."[60]

Confirming that prayer works, Lincoln had survived his trip to Virginia,[61] but, following his return, he quickly resumed his risky pattern of appearing in public without adequate security. On April 10 he made two brief appearances from the White House before adoring crowds ecstatic over Lee's surrender to Grant the prior day. His remarks were happy, lighthearted, and calculated to avoid any hint of ridicule or malice toward the South and instead to allow passions to continue to cool.[62] That did not matter to Booth, who was present in the crowd with Alabama native Lewis Powell. He urged Powell to shoot Lincoln then and there but Powell thought it was too risky.[63] The following morning Booth readied himself for the challenge by taking target practice at a local shooting gallery.[64]

Meanwhile, some Radical Republicans were busy agitating the public about punishment for the rebels and granting equal rights to the freed slaves, rhetoric sure to irritate Confederates and potentially make Lincoln's task of reconciliation much more difficult.[65] A case in point was Union major general Benjamin Franklin Butler (fig. 16), perhaps the least photogenic public figure of the nineteenth century. Butler was a lawyer-politician from Massachusetts who the president had, for strictly political reasons, commissioned a major general. But in January 1865 Lincoln unceremoniously relieved him from command at the behest of Grant and ordered him to go home.[66] Shortly after Lincoln's return from Virginia, Butler made a fire-and-brimstone speech from the balcony of Willard's Hotel in Washington, DC, in which he pandered to the vindictive side of his audience, while at the same time encouraging a political and social outcome in the South that he certainly knew would antagonize not only most white Southerners but also his commander in chief. Butler, who the South had nicknamed "Beast" for his actions as commander of occupation forces in New Orleans"[67] and who Lincoln had (according to some accounts) once similarly described as being "as full of poison gas as a dead dog,"[68] declared that there were "four classes of men in the rebellious States" and explained "what shall be done with them." First, said Butler, were those educated at West Point, who should "suffer the same penalty for deserting which the government and the law have enforced upon so many of our soldiers for the same crime." Second, there were the members of Congress who had resigned when their states seceded, who Butler suggested should be permanently disenfranchised and disqualified from holding office. Third were the soldiers "in the ranks of the rebellion," who Butler said ought to be forgiven. Fourth and finally (in Butler's mind) were the freed slaves—"the true Union men of the South"—who deserved "liberty and equality under the laws forever."[69] In light of his comments on this and other occasions, the fact that he and fellow outspoken Radical Republi-

Figure 16. Benjamin F. Butler. Courtesy of the Library of Congress, Prints and Photographs Division.

cans, such as Charles Sumner or Thaddeus Stevens, were not also on Booth's hit list is some additional evidence that Booth and the other conspirators were strictly conforming to Gayle's prescription.

It is highly unlikely that Lincoln would have regretted their loss, since he probably recognized that the execution of his own plans would be much easier in their absence. But even without their timely demise, Lincoln likely believed he could overcome what a correspondent of the *Cincinnati Gazette* described as the "active and influential minority of the radical Republicans who are disposed to resist the settlement of existing difficulties upon the terms and in the manner indicated by the President and Gen. Grant." As that correspondent concluded, the "desire of the people for a settlement—speedy and final—upon the easiest possible terms, will, it is believed, sustain the President."[70]

Perhaps in an attempt to neutralize Butler, Lincoln had agreed to meet with him at the White House on the morning of April 11. The press later confirmed that "Butler had a lengthy audience with the President to-day."[71] Historians have debated the content of their private discussions during that "lengthy audience," but there is evidence they reached a mutual understanding. Butler solicited Lincoln's assistance regarding an investigation by the US

Treasury Department of Butler for corruption in connection with missing money and involvement in cotton smuggling during his previous command.[72] According to Butler, Lincoln, under pressure by Butler's Radical Republican allies to appoint him military governor of Virginia,[73] enlisted Butler's participation in a leadership capacity in connection with a secret black colonization project intended to reduce the possibility of a race war in the South after the war ended. Butler would later recall that Lincoln stated that he "can hardly believe that the South and North can live in peace, unless we can get rid of the negroes." The plan, according to Butler, was to seed a foreign colony by involuntarily deploying 150,000 black troops to the Panama isthmus to work on an American canal and then having the federal government later fund the voluntary relocation there of their families.[74]

Perhaps not coincidentally, while Lincoln's administration had been lobbying Congress to adopt the Thirteenth Amendment earlier in the year, it had also tasked Union general Dan Sickles to travel to Panama, where he had arrived on January 22. The purpose of his trip was not made clear to the public, but a few weeks later a Panamanian newspaper, the Panama City *Mercantile Chronicle*, reported that Sickles was attempting to acquire land on which the US government intended to colonize thousands of the freed slaves. "The object of the Americans," it continued, was to "remove these poor people from a country which has been thrown into a state bordering on destruction, through their presence there in the condition of slaves. To have these people as freed men in the Southern States after the war, it may have been concluded, would be a constant cause of irritation to the former masters, inducing disaffection and turmoil as successors to a restoration of the Union." It was the Lincoln government's "wish, therefore, to settle them in one of the neighboring and friendly states where the laws of the country will guarantee them safety, and where it will be easy for the United States Government to extend a protecting hand to them in any hour of extremity."[75]

This report did not appear in the American press until March 6, two days after Lincoln's second inauguration and Congress's adjournment. At that point it was reprinted in several major newspapers, including the *New York Times*, the *New York Herald*, the *Hartford Courant*, and the *Boston Herald*.[76] Interestingly, however, neither Lincoln nor anyone within his administration ever publicly denied the accuracy of the report. Even more incredibly, the report did not incite any public debate or cause Sickles to be withdrawn.[77] It was as if colonization of the freed slaves had been assumed all along.

If the exchange between Lincoln and Butler truly occurred, the apparent result would have been seen by white Southerners as shrewd lawyer-

"When This Cruel War Is Over" / 103

ing on Lincoln's part. Given the Treasury Department investigation, Lincoln clearly had Butler over a barrel. As Butler likely realized, if Lincoln refused to intervene, not only would Butler's future political career as a darling of the Radical Republicans be in jeopardy but he risked disgrace and imprisonment. On the other hand, if he played ball with Lincoln on the colonization project, he might still lose face among some Radical Republicans for whom colonization was anathema, but he would avoid jail and receive a new military assignment through which he could redeem himself by leading black troops and perhaps creating a utopia for them in Central America. At the same time, Lincoln would get Butler out of the country and therefore out of Lincoln's hair as far as the process of reconstruction was concerned. Lincoln's desire to quickly achieve this goal may explain why, immediately following his meeting with Butler on April 11, he did intervene in the investigation of Butler. For his part, Butler wisely refrained from public criticism of Lincoln's important prepared speech later that night and quietly left Washington, DC, three days later.[78]

To say the least, that speech was not in the genre of Butler's tough talk the prior day.[79] Lincoln did not even hint at the concepts of disenfranchisement, disqualification, or punishment of any other sort. He did not mention colonization either. Instead, he began by reminding the thousands in attendance that for the "gladness of heart" and the "hopes of a righteous and speedy peace," "He from whom all blessings flow must not be forgotten." Then Lincoln wisely praised General Grant and "his skillful officers and brave men," whose efforts gave "us the cause of rejoicing."[80] Grant, as Lincoln well knew, had just taken the potential heat from Radical Republicans by negotiating a surrender with Lee under which not even those high-ranking Confederates like Lee, who had attended West Point and led the Confederate enemies to victories that had killed tens of thousands, would be prevented from returning to their homes unpunished. Grant could take the heat; he was a bona fide war hero at the top of his game and was already being compared to Napoleon.[81] The *New York Tribune* heartily endorsed those terms, declaring that "Gen. Grant was as wise as he was generous in granting such liberal terms," which it correctly assessed he had done "with and by the advice of President Lincoln, who, we are confident, will proceed in the line of magnanimous policy thus indicated if he is not overruled by bad advisors and deterred by what he mistakes for public opinion." And as its editor noted, an important precedent had been set. If Lee and men like him were allowed to "go in safety to their homes, with a pledge that they shall remain 'undisturbed' so long as they shall continue to deport themselves loyally and quietly, how can you fail to treat with equal lenity those who may hereafter surrender? If these ought not to be tried and punished, who should be? Nay: with what show of fairness can you put others on trial for their lives, yet allow these to go free?"[82]

Recognizing his own broad popularity, Lincoln also took the opportunity in his address to defend the process by which some Southern state governments had already been reconstructed under his "ten percent" plan announced in December 1863. This appears to have actually been a pretext for signaling his future policy on the status of the freed slaves. Focusing on Louisiana, Lincoln somewhat disingenuously noted that its new constitution did not "adopt apprenticeship for freed people," but he did not mention that this method of control he had earlier suggested was not prohibited either and therefore could later be implemented by the newly elected legislature.[83] That the new Louisiana constitution did not guarantee black suffrage probably assured that it would occur. But Lincoln expressed no concern about that feature of the constitution either. "It is also unsatisfactory to some that the [elective] franchise is not given to the colored man," he observed. "I would myself prefer that it were now conferred on the very intelligent and those who serve our cause as soldiers." But as he noted, that was not material. Lincoln announced that the "*sole* object to the [federal] government, civil and military, in regard to those States, is to again get them into" what he called the "proper practical relation with the Union." Thus, he said, "let us all join in doing the acts necessary to restore the proper practical relations between these States and the Union." Lincoln cleverly tied this call for prompt restoration to the ratification of the still-pending Thirteenth Amendment, which he noted arguably required approval by three-fourths of all the states and not merely those that had not seceded. As he pointed out, Louisiana's new government had already given its approval to that amendment, and to retrench now would mean one less vote for ratification.[84] Hence, for abolitionists and those who simply wanted the slave power in the South broken, there was a big carrot encouraging rapid restoration without black suffrage.

Lincoln did not take this opportunity to address the issue of executive clemency. There were still troops fighting in the field, and some commentators had cautioned that he not go further at this point in terms of making a general proclamation of amnesty. Wrote the editor of the *Army and Navy Journal*, "It is well to be merciful, but let us not be hasty. Our soldiers should have an opportunity to thoroughly finish their work before the civil power is brought in to interfere with them in any form. A firm, even-handed judicious military rule is the one at present best adapted to the sections from which the flag of Rebellion has been so recently driven. It is the rule, too, which is the most likely to educate into a new allegiance to whose loyalty is worth the most to us. Too hasty tenders of restored citizenship are most likely to secure the venal allegiance of those with whom patriotism and speculation are terms nearly synonymous."[85]

Although Lincoln's April 11 address is frequently cited as evidence of his strong, unqualified support for extending political rights to the freed slaves, supporters of black suffrage were actually crestfallen.[86] According to one newspaper correspondent in attendance, the speech "has caused a great disappointment and left a painful impression. It was mentioned in the crowd in explanation of a passage in his remarks, that Mr. Lincoln was opposed to the extension of the suffrage to colored men."[87] US Supreme Court chief justice Salmon Chase, a strong advocate of black suffrage, also expressed disappointment.[88] As he certainly knew, if majority-black Louisiana resumed its original relationship to the Union as Lincoln sought, an amendment of the federal constitution would be required to impose black suffrage there. Given the difficulty with which the Thirteenth Amendment was finally adopted by representatives of the free states in Congress, passing such an amendment any time soon—much less having it ratified by the states—was very unlikely. Thus, for black suffrage advocates, Lincoln's stance was tantamount to the death knell of equal suffrage—barring some unforeseen event.

On the other hand, Lincoln's speech received high marks from the mainstream Republican press. "We breathe freely since reading this great and good speech," wrote the editor of the Washington, DC, *National Intelligencer*. It "seems also to reflect the present spirit of the more influential among the Republican newspapers." Lincoln, he concluded, "has opened wide the gate to restoration; and thus far, he has grandly performed his part."[89] According to a Connecticut editor, the "one sole object for which the war on our side was accepted and prosecuted, has been and now is Restoration—not 'Reconstruction'—of the Union," and the president, "in his straight-forward, practical way, is for reaching that end with the least possible delay—the least possible waste of time and temper in discussion of non-essential abstractions—the least possible complication with side issues which nervous theorists and pragmatical spouters might seek to thrust into undue prominence in connection with it."[90]

The "non-essential abstraction"—to most—of black suffrage did not seem to be of importance to the editor of the *New York Times* either. In modern times targeted by conservatives for alleged ultraliberalism, the *Times* was actually in the forefront of opposition to black suffrage in the spring of 1865. In February, its editor had argued that not only was the question of deciding who should vote an "essential state right" with which Congress could not interfere but the former slaves were "hardly more competent to vote upon public questions than the beasts of the field."[91] The *Times*'s editor conceded that "whether the Southern states, if restored at once to their full State rights, would not abuse them by an oppression of the black race" was an important factor in deciding the degree of "discretionary power that should be accorded" to them. But he also maintained that the "great end is to get every Southern State back, so that it shall perform the same obligations, and exercise the same rights, identically that are performed and exercised by every Northern State." However, he did at least allow the fact that since the "black race" had rendered assistance to the government in the time of danger, this "entitled them to its benign care,"[92] but not necessarily social equality or political rights.

The *New York Tribune* remarked that Lincoln's April 11 address "will be regarded as reserved and indecisive by some" but concluded that he "is evidently determined to do whatever he deems fairly within his power to restore our country speedily to peace and heal the wounds inevitably infected by years of gigantic and desolating Civil War. We cannot doubt that further and more conclusive proofs of this will speedily be given, and that the progress of pacification and restoration will henceforth be rapid and unbroken."[93] In this regard, on the day after the speech, the *Cleveland Leader* again declared that "the time has come, as we believe, for the President to address the *people* of the rebellious States, inviting them to return to their allegiance, and promising them mercy and protection if they do so." The rebellion was "dead" and "all that remains is to pursue a liberal and generous policy, *not* toward the Confederate government or the traitors who constituted it, but toward the oppressed and abused people of the rebellious States."[94] The *New York Tribune*'s editor agreed. "We entreat the President promptly to do and dare in the cause of Magnanimity. The Southern mind is now open to kindness, and may be magnetically affected by generosity. Let assurance be once given there is to be a general Amnesty and *no* general Confiscation. This is none the less the dictate of mercy. What we ask is that the President say in effect, 'Slavery having, through Rebellion, committed Suicide, let the North and the South unite to bury its carcase [*sic*], and then clasp hands across the grave' "[95] Meanwhile, he continued, the nation rejoiced in the fact that, finally, the "path of Peace opens pleasantly before us. . . . The road before us smiles only with Summer sunshine." Furthermore, "a new world is born, and the Sun of Peace rises in splendor to send abroad over the land its rays of warmth and light! Never before had [a] nation so much cause for devout Thanksgiving; never before had a people so much reason for unrestrained congratulation and the very extravagance of joy."[96]

Of course, no one could know whether these editorials reflected the views of the common man in the North, but it is obvious that the white South was receiving good vibrations. Indeed, this likely explains why, two days after Lincoln's April 11 speech, the still-fleeing Davis finally authorized Johnston to initiate purposeful and compromising peace negotiations with Sherman, a process Johnston formally began by having a note delivered to Union general Kilpatrick under a flag of truce in North Carolina on the fateful night of April 14.[97] As if giving reassurance to Davis that he had made the correct decision, the Washington, DC, *National Intelligencer*'s April 14 edition included an editorial that ridiculed the Radical Republican positions on reconstruction that conflicted with Lincoln's view that "submission is restoration, amnesty, and peace." There were "some who would prefer to talk *now* about who should be hung" and "push to the foreground, with violent zeal, questions about negro suffrage, *based on the hypothesis that the South will continue to be traitors*, no matter to what oaths of allegiance they may swear, and that there *is a sufficient amount of treason in the North to blend therewith*, and destroy the *country* (party?) unless this shall be countervailed by black suffrage, as a sort of equipoise against certain other votes." However, assured the editor, "the only thought of the *people*, whose representative Mr. Lincoln has, thus far proven himself to be, is, to restore peace, to bring back Union, and to provide, by wise, affectionate, liberal, practical statesmanship, for the perpetual unity and fraternity of these States. Standing on this platform, the President may safely defy the storm. If he shall now develop such firmness as the winds of contention shall be unable to shake, then his mission will be vindicated, as that of a man raised up to save his country."[98]

Undisputed evidence confirms that Lincoln intended to do just that. During his last cabinet meeting, which occurred on the morning of his assassination, he expressed relief that Congress had adjourned until later in the year and that its radical elements would not be able to interfere with his plan. Also according to Gideon Welles, Lincoln reiterated his commitment to state sovereignty on the question of black suffrage. "He wished [Louisianans] had permitted Negroes who had property, or could read, to vote; but this was a question which they must decide for themselves. Yet some, a very few of our friends, were not willing to let the people of the states determine these questions, but, in violation of first and fundamental principles, would exercise arbitrary power over them." These "humanitarians," Lincoln complained, sought to "break down all state rights and constitutional rights." Therefore, he concluded, "we must make haste to do our duty" before Congress convened in December.[99] From this it is possible that if Congress later attempted to pass legislation undermining what Lincoln had wrought, he might veto it— just as he had the Wade-Davis bill a year earlier.[100]

Figure 17. Frederick Douglass, April 26, 1870. Photograph by George Francis Schreiber. Courtesy of the Library of Congress, Prints and Photographs Division.

Needless to say, many of those who had battled for decades for emancipation and most recently for suffrage rights for the freed slaves were deeply dismayed and disillusioned.[101] Former slave and now civil rights leader Frederick Douglass (fig. 17) would later recall that the nation was "in danger of losing a just appreciation of the awful crimes of this rebellion."[102]

Massachusetts's US senator Charles Sumner similarly complained to US Supreme Court chief justice Salmon Chase that Lincoln met his argument that Davis and others ought not be pardoned by repeatedly quoting the biblical passage "'Judge not that ye be not judged.'" The president, Sumner wrote, was "full of tenderness."[103] The concern was that in Lincoln's haste for an amicable reconciliation with the South, he would ignore the apparently widely recognized problem inherent in a democracy of denying voting rights to substantial minorities.[104]

But thanks to the series of decisive Union victories in Alabama, Virginia, South Carolina, North Carolina, and elsewhere over the last ninety days, the conciliatory themes enunciated by Lincoln, and the terrible destruction to some Southern cities and towns, the attitudes of even some Northern abolitionists toward the South were increasingly charitable during the first two weeks of April 1865.[105] Shortly after the fall of Richmond, the famous pro-abolition minister, Henry Ward Beecher, preached a very remarkable sermon of love and reconciliation at his Plymouth Church in Brooklyn, New York. That sermon was based on passages from the Book of Judges regarding the virtual destruction of the "tribe of Benjamin" by the other tribes of Israelites following a battle that started over the murder of the wife of a Levite by some members of the tribe of Benjamin. As Beecher noted, the members of the tribe of Benjamin "were so despoiled and impoverished and so pitiable in their distress as to excite the compassion of their destroyers." Grief "overtook them," and the Lord directed them to take steps to restore the tribe of Benjamin. "We have come together in circumstances like it in our time," Beecher said. "I suppose there are whole regions in the South where the entire male population is cut off. Along the seaboard we can give essential relief, but all along the route of Sherman's army, the description given by the prophet is eminently applicable: 'Before him was the garden of Eden, and behind him was the desert.' We can send our sons and daughters—our wealth, our prayers, and sympathies must go forth in the missionary work of teaching and resuscitating." In the same sermon, Beecher expressed opposition to all acts of punishment and retribution. "Let us take care that we do not fall into the easy sin of vengeance under the plea of justice. Few men can afford to be just until they first learn how to love. I hear many men say this war ought not to be ended until the principal traitors are hung, and that a sour apple tree should take the place of Haman's gallows upon which should swing the archtraitor Jeff Davis." But, Beecher averred, the South had already suffered enough, and the penalty had already been paid. Thus, much like Lincoln, he urged that Davis should simply be allowed to "go away where he'll be by himself, powerless to [do] injury," while others should neither be expatriated nor disenfranchised.[106]

If Lincoln had lived, he would have probably continued to preach this same gospel of reconciliation from the bully pulpit of the presidency and likely done so successfully. But this was apparently not God's will and as a consequence Alabama would suffer even more. As one devout Alabama planter, James Mallory, would later conclude, "God no doubt has a purpose in the affair and will punish us in a way to make us humble and subservient to him."[107]

9

"Glorious News"

Reports of the April 14, 1865, assassination of Lincoln and attempted assassination of William Seward (Andrew Johnson's assassin lost his courage) reached Alabama fairly quickly.[1] Some Alabamians publicly expressed their approval.[2] The *Chattanooga Rebel*, which had resumed publication in Selma shortly after Wilson's force had left for Montgomery, published an editorial that would be reprinted in several Northern newspapers in the coming weeks asserting that both Lincoln and Seward had gotten what they deserved. In particular, Lincoln, whom the editor ridiculed as a "political mountebank and professional joker, whom nature intended for the ring of a circus, but whom a strange streak of popular delusion elevated to the Presidency," had "gone to answer before the bar of God for the innocent blood he has permitted to be shed, in his efforts to enslave a free and heroic people."[3] In Huntsville, after the commander of the occupying Union force ordered the residents to place black crape on their front doorknobs as a sign of mourning, many refused and one put a "great big Negro doll" on his knob.[4] The *Demopolis Herald* reported the president's death under the headline "Glorious News"[5] and a few days later falsely claimed that the news of Lincoln's assassination had caused one hundred thousand of Grant's men to desert, thereby forcing Grant to seek an armistice with Lee that would end in Southern independence. "The downfall of Lincoln ends the war," it declared.[6] But for the South in general, and Alabama in particular, it was anything but glorious news.[7] On the contrary, it would turn out to be the worst possible news for most white Alabamians.

Like the attack on Fort Sumter four years earlier,[8] the bombing of Pearl Harbor on December 7, 1941, and the terrorist attacks on September 11, 2001, the Lincoln assassination was a shocking hinge event that fundamentally changed the course of American history. Although not noted by historian John Witherspoon DuBose, it quite naturally let loose feelings of outrage and revenge that had been decreasing in intensity with each passing day.[9] An Ohio editor wrote that the "foul and cowardly assassination" had "aroused more universal execration than any deed in history" with the exception of "the crucifixion of Christ."[10] While some ministers around the country would soon be attempting to explain Lincoln's Good Friday assassination in New Testament terms on Palm Sunday,[11] they were forced to attempt to overcome thirty-six hours of Old Testament rage that did not stop even then.[12]

A Philadelphia editor correctly predicted that, as a consequence, there would be a "widespread and determined desire to put a stop at once to any disposition to deal leniently with rebels and traitors." Henceforth, there would be a "prevalent belief that with such a spirit abroad in the south magnanimity is a crime and a blunder. The result, therefore, will be not less a terrible calamity to the south than to the nation."[13] As the *New York Evening Post* put it, the "whole nation mourns the death of its president, but no part of it ought to mourn that death more keenly than our brothers of the South."[14] Now, wrote an Ohio editor, the policy "shall be 'an eye for an eye, and a tooth for a tooth.'"[15] After four years of bloody war, that was a lot of eyes and teeth.[16]

As the Alabama press would soon be reporting, within hours after Lincoln was pronounced dead, Chief Justice Salmon P. Chase administered the oath of office to Andrew Johnson, swearing him in as president at the Kirkwood Hotel in Washington, DC.[17] The "renegade demagogue," as Forsyth had denounced Johnson a year earlier,[18] had a well-earned reputation for opposition to disloyalty and for the promotion of the interests of unconditional Unionists. The latter group were, in his mind, entitled to rule over the disloyal and extract financial restitution from them. For those who had truckled to treason, Johnson's ascension to the presidency was a nightmare.[19]

In the eyes of Confederates, Johnson's punitive rule as military governor of Tennessee had spawned the even more militant Unionist governor William G. Brownlow (fig. 18) as his successor.[20] Elected governor of Tennessee in March 1865, Brownlow openly acknowledged his continuing hatred for Confederates. "I am one of those at the south who believe this war has closed out two years too soon," he wrote. "The rebels have been whipped," he continued, "but not whipped enough."[21] Brownlow was busily dealing out the whippings. He had been pushing a radical agenda that included not only immediate emancipation of their slaves but also disenfranchisement of former Confederates and a dystrophic future for them of ruinous civil lawsuits, criminal prosecutions, and murder. Just as worrisome, Brownlow did not rule out extending voting rights to the freedmen at some point in the not too distant future.[22] Was "Brownlowism," as it was known, to be the fate

Figure 18. William Gannaway Brownlow, ca. 1862. Photograph by Frederick Gutekunst. Courtesy of the Library of Congress, Prints and Photographs Division.

of Alabama's Confederates? That would now largely depend on Johnson and whom he appointed to serve as provisional governor, which, in turn, would be influenced in part by his own degree of outrage over the assassination.

In a brief address following the inauguration, Johnson ominously declared that "my past history, in connection with the rebellion by which the whole land had been afflicted, will foreshadow what my future course will be."[23] Based on that "past history" it was generally assumed the "South had more hope from Lincoln's clemency than they can look for from his successor."[24] Even the minister who would eulogize Lincoln at his burial in Springfield, Illinois, was sure that the "traitors will probably suffer by the change of rulers, for one of sterner mold, who himself has deeply suffered from the Rebellion now wields the sword of justice."[25] Like their brethren in other Southern states, Alabama Unionists certainly hoped so. Joshua Burns Moore predicted that the "leaders of secession" would learn that Johnson "would arrest, try, convict and hang them and confiscate their property to repay Union men what they had lost at [their] hands." Johnson, he continued, had "lived in East Tenn." and "knows what Union men suffered there. He feels the indignities he recd. at the hands of the rabid secessionists, and my judge is he will be a most dangerous customer for them to deal with. Well," he concluded, "an inaugurater [sic] of civil strife—necessarily stakes his life and property upon success. If the leaders have brought upon themselves destruction, it is no more than they have been instrumental in bringing upon thousands who did not ever have a voice in the terrible war they originated."[26]

Radical Republicans in the North could not have agreed more. Some even appeared to be glad that the weak-kneed (to them) late president was finally out of their way.[27] In a widely reported speech at a meeting in New York City less than a week after the assassination, Benjamin Butler praised the deceased president and blamed the rebellion for, "with a blind hate," striking down "in cold silence the most forgiving, the most lenient, the most gracious friend that the misguided men of this rebellion ever had in this country." But then Butler characterized Lincoln's death as a "dispensation of God's good providence" and coldly declared that there was "no occasion of despondency." Lincoln, he said, had "driven out the life and spirit of the rebellion" but "it is for us to take care of the soul (Cheers)." Lincoln had been the "first victim of clemency." Now, "punishment should be visited upon them who have caused this great wrong. The nation," he declared, "demands it," the "widowed wives of those fallen soldiers sleeping in southern soil cry out for it," the "insulted majesty of the nation has determined upon it, and woe be to him that gets in the path of justice and of the execution of the law."[28] Ironically, given what would happen two years later (when Butler was one of the leaders of efforts to impeach Johnson), Butler also expressed confidence in Johnson. He "feels as you and I do—I know it—on the subject." Johnson, he pointed out, "has had a nearer view of it than we have had. It has been at his hearth-stone, and he had almost his roof-tree blazing over him. And every one ought to know that he is not only able, but willing and desirous that it should be dealt with as we would have it dealt with. And, therefore, let every man be of cheer. (Cheers)."[29]

How would Butler and men like him have the South dealt with? In the immediate aftermath of the assassination, the heretofore moderate *New York Times* was now calling for a "class revolution" in the South that would "grind" the Southern aristocracy to "powder."[30] The guiltiest parties should, according to its editor, be executed, and the remaining "bad men" disqualified from state and federal office.[31] Also in the heat of the moment, the *New York Herald*, a heretofore racially conservative newspaper that was the most widely read in the nation, went a step further and advocated "the concession of negro suffrage in the reconstruction of the insurgent states" because it would "effectually spike the last gun of Northern abolitionists, and will expel or neutralize the fire-eating political elements of the south for all time to come. Indeed," it continued, "nothing half so effective could be employed as negro suffrage to weed out the intractable secessionists from the Southern states."[32] In sum, the Lincoln administration had armed the freed slaves with guns to help defeat the Confederacy, but thanks to Booth an increased number of citizens in the outraged North now intended to arm them with the right to vote and thereby, through mass vote dilution, have them protect themselves, the Union, as well as newly formed Union-loyal state and local governments in the South. The former slaves would be able to purge those governments of men who had attempted to organize a separate nation to keep them enslaved.[33]

Frederick Douglass rejoiced in a speech less than a month after Lincoln's death: "To-day, to-day as never before this North is a unit! (Great applause) To-day, to-day as never before, the American people, although they cannot have indemnity for the past—for the countless treasure and the precious blood— yet they resolve to-day that they will exact ample security for the future! (Cheers.)"[34] Similarly, a speaker in South Carolina observed a few days later that "the nation's loss is the colored man's gain, and Abraham Lincoln is the martyr."[35] Thus, from the prospect of racial *inequality* during Lincoln's second term of office, the former slaves were seemingly on the cusp of achieving political equality and in some cases—majority-black states like Louisiana, Mississippi, and South Carolina, and majority-black counties in Alabama and elsewhere—political dominance.[36]

As recently as January 10, 1865, Andrew Johnson had declared that he favored immediate, not gradual, emancipation but not black suffrage in Tennessee. He said at the same time that he favored either the apprenticeship or colonization of the black population to Mexico or some other country free of race discrimination.[37] Lincoln had had the gravitas and political capital to allow the Southern states to make their own choice on suffrage. But even if Johnson personally agreed with Lincoln's approach—which he did—he was a comparative political lightweight and was not seen as a bulwark who could withstand the rejuvenated forces of political radicalism.[38] And after the assassination, would he even try to do so?

The bitter fruits of Lincoln's passing were manifesting themselves, confirming Butler's admonition to those who got in the way of his self-prescribed "path of justice" for the South. Ironically, one of the first unwitting targets of this backlash was the man who had made Georgians and other Southerners howl, William Tecumseh Sherman. Apparently based on Lincoln's guidance at City Point less than a month earlier, Sherman had used Johnston's April 14 peace overture as an opportunity to obtain a comprehensive settlement that included more than just the unconditional surrender of all remaining Confederate armies in the field. Even after learning of Lincoln's death, which he clinically termed in one of his communications to Johnston "this new and unforseen complication,"[39] Sherman had proceeded to negotiate a tentative agreement on multiple issues. Among other things it included terms requiring Johnson to recognize the existing state governments in the Confederacy, to guarantee the political and property rights of all Southerners, and to forego criminal prosecutions.[40]

If this agreement had been ratified by Johnson, radically inclined provisional governors similar to Tennessee's Brownlow could not have been appointed and Alabama's governor Watts and the wartime Alabama legislature would have been left in control of affairs in the state. Almost certainly, one of the consequences of this would have been Watts's call of a special session of the legislature to vote against ratification of the Thirteenth Amendment, a result now unacceptable to most Northerners. Confederates would also have been in position to adopt legislation favorable to, or protective of, their interests. Needless to say, black suffrage would not have been an option. Other measures might have included immunity under state law for wartime torts and criminal acts committed in the name of the Confederacy[41] and the imposition of taxes to redeem all of the otherwise worthless money and bonds issued by the Confederacy and the states that had been used to fund the war effort, millions of which were in the hands of Confederates. Unionists were also concerned that Confederates would regulate who would vote and who would be qualified for public office and would discriminate against them for failure to serve in the Confederate military.[42] Furthermore, Unionists feared that Confederates with an axe to grind against them would be able to retaliate without concern for punishment from a criminal justice system manned by judges, district attorneys, and sheriffs who had been elected or appointed during Watts's regime. Jury venires as well would be composed of men selected by those officials for their wartime loyalty to the Confederacy.

Sherman's primary motive, as explained in a report issued on the same day as Butler's speech, was one that had earlier led Lincoln toward his conciliatory course. "There is great danger," Sherman wrote, "that the Confederate armies will dissolve and fill the whole land with robbers and assassins, and I think this is one of the difficulties that Johnston labors under. The assassination of Mr. Lincoln shows one of the elements in the rebel army which will be almost as difficult to deal with as the main armies."[43] Three days earlier,

Virginia's governor had made what an Alabama soldier described as a "strong Southern speech . . . counseling Guerilla warfare" to a group of soldiers in Greensboro, North Carolina.[44]

Davis, who was still on the run, had wisely agreed to the proposed terms,[45] but Sherman would have to send to Washington, DC, for ratification. Sherman entrusted the delivery of the settlement paperwork to Alabama native Henry Hitchcock Jr., a member of his staff who was the son of a late Alabama Supreme Court associate justice.[46] Under the circumstances one wonders whether young Hitchcock was reminded of the old axiom about killing the messenger as he departed Durham Station, North Carolina, on April 18. Sherman, however, was blissfully optimistic, writing one of his subordinates that "I have no doubt that I have this day made terms with Johnston that will close the war and leave us only to march home."[47] The timing of Hitchcock's arrival in Washington, DC, on the evening of April 21 could not have been worse.[48] Lincoln's initial funeral ceremonies had taken place there on April 19, but the city was still in mourning. And on April 21 Lincoln's funeral train departed up the East Coast to New York on its long and depressing trip back to Illinois.[49] That very day, Johnson, who had recently learned that he, too, had been a target of the assassins,[50] had given a widely reported address to a delegation from Indiana reaffirming his desire to punish and "impoverish" traitors and also destroy their "social power." Eliciting applause, Johnson also vowed that "every Union man and the Government should be remunerated out of the pockets of those who have inflicted this great suffering upon the country. (Applause)."[51] Given recent publicity for George Gayle's advertisement, Johnson had a million more reasons to feel that way.

That night, Johnson as well as Lincoln's holdover cabinet considered the documents Hitchcock had delivered. They predictably disapproved and repudiated the proposed agreement. Not only that, but Grant was ordered to personally communicate the decision to Sherman and also to supersede Sherman and to "direct operations against the enemy" from Sherman's headquarters.[52] Grant returned to North Carolina with Hitchcock but refused to execute this humiliating slap in the face. Instead, according to Hitchcock, when he and Grant reached a point approximately thirty miles from Sherman's headquarters, Grant sent him ahead with a written communication notifying Sherman of the government's decision and directing Sherman to resume offensive operations unless Johnston agreed to the same terms of surrender as Lee had earlier accepted.[53]

Despite Grant's discreteness and delicacy, when word of the disapproved agreement was leaked to the *New York Times* and other newspapers, Sherman, the national hero, temporarily became Sherman, the national disgrace.

Some implied that he might have taken a bribe from Davis's partisans to allow Davis and them to escape to Mexico with Confederate gold. Others asserted that Sherman was just plain crazy.[54] But Sherman's motives were arguably entirely pure and rational. As he explained his concerns to Grant, "I now apprehend that the Rebel Armies will disperse; and instead of dealing with six or seven states, we will have to deal with numberless bands of desperadoes headed by such men as Mosby, Forrest, Red Jackson, & others who know not, and care not for danger or its consequences."[55] Sherman was incensed, as the public would soon learn, and would never forgive Secretary of War Edwin Stanton and the Radical Republicans for inspiring these insults, a factor that would play a role in the dynamics of the reconstruction process in the coming years.[56]

Sherman was not the only victim of the postassassination riptide. Alabama Unionists, who had been yearning to implement various versions of the Tennessee reconstruction model and who were awaiting the surrender of Confederate forces in Alabama before risking a public movement, were initially unaware that they too were being pulled away from that shore and out into a very uncertain and bewildering sea. According to the diary of Joshua Burns Moore, Moulton lawyer and Unionist Thomas Peters met with Moore and Franklin County lawyer, William Skinner, at Skinner's home near Russellville on Sunday, April 23. "We all agreed the war was about at an end," wrote Moore. But the main topics of conversation appear to have been the fate of "the rabid secessionists of South Ala." and "what is to be done" with the slaves. Moore, like many north Alabamians, was extremely bitter toward the secessionists, as well as Watts, and counted on Johnson's pledge to "give those fellows hell."[57]

The more difficult problem Unionists faced related to the freed slaves. Slavery was "at an end," Moore wrote, and he was glad of it. "Let it go—we have in exchange a government. Rather than have the trouble I have had for the last 4 years, [I] had 50 negroes, I'd give them all [up]. I have been the slave myself, to keep them fed and clothed—but I have done it and now I am ready to let them go. They have never been of any advantage to me—I have made nothing with them and never would." Although freeing the slaves relieved men like Moore of the expense of their support and upkeep, it also created difficult challenges for all Southern society, both white and black members. Moore indicated that he, Peters, and Skinner also discussed these issues on April 23. The following day Moore mused: "What is to be done with them—turn them loose and a white man can't live amongst them. To some extent they must be controlled and taken care of. P. thinks a gradual emancipation would be infinitely better."[58]

Moore would later record his thoughts regarding initiatives to be pushed once a Union-loyal legislature could be convened. He looked upon slavery "as gone, gone, gone, beyond the possibility of help" but maintained that "stringent police laws" needed to be passed to "govern the negroes" because "they must be controlled in some way or white people cannot live amongst them." In addition, the legislature must "refuse to let them vote or hold office or to testify against a white person," explaining that "those who know the negro, his dullness—his stupidity—his mendacity, will know that these measures are absolutely necessary for the security in person and property of the whites."[59] A Virginia Unionist, John Minor Botts, agreed, but at least publicly enunciated a more politically palatable excuse that would be repeatedly plagiarized in the coming years. Black suffrage, he contended, would simply perpetuate the authority of the "old slaveholders" because "the negroes would be dependent on them for employment" and would, therefore, "be guided by them in regard to voting." This would continue to be the case, he maintained, "until the negroes become educated and independent enough to think for themselves."[60]

Most of the slaves were not only illiterate but products of a system of total dependency that had theoretically provided for their basic needs from cradle to grave. Lincoln had also recognized that releasing them had a number of serious implications for them and for white people.[61] In a letter issued by Lincoln in early 1863 only a week after his final Emancipation Proclamation, he explained that Southern whites "need not to be hurt by it" and suggested that they "adopt systems of apprenticeship for the colored people, conforming substantially to the most approved plans of gradual emancipation."[62] Presumably these "most approved plans" would at a minimum require the employer to provide compensation and basic medical care to the apprentices and their families in exchange for control of the apprentice's labor during the apprenticeship period.

One of the principal problems with an absolutely free labor system was that in the nineteenth century no employer was required to pay a minimum wage, much less provide health benefits to their employees.[63] Another was the absence of a federal government-run welfare system to support the young or the elderly who were unable to work.[64] One South Carolina diarist wrote that the "Negroes are a good riddance. A hired man is far cheaper than a man whose father and mother, his wife and his twelve children have to be fed, clothed, housed, nursed, taxes paid and doctors' bills."[65] Lincoln had supported Congress's creation of the Bureau of Refugees, Freedmen and Abandoned Lands, a stopgap measure to temporarily fill this void. At the time of its creation on March 3, 1865, however, this Freedmen's Bureau, as it was better known, was designed to expire one year after the end of the war.[66] After that one year, Lincoln expected black people (and Southern white people) to either work for a living or die off. Several contemporary sources indicate that at the Hampton Roads Peace Conference in February, Lincoln had told the Confederate commissioners a homespun parable about an Illinois hog farmer to illustrate his vision of the necessary work ethic of the freed slaves. To feed the hogs, the farmer planted a large field in potatoes. When the potatoes matured, he turned his entire herd into that field with the expectation that they would dig up the potatoes when they became hungry. When asked what would happen in the winter when the ground froze, the farmer replied, "Well, it may come pretty hard on their snouts, but I don't see but that it will be root hog or die!" Some adherents of Darwinism in the North and the South predicted that without the structure and support provided by some sort of system besides the free market, the black race would in fact gradually disappear or die out, just as had many Native Americans east of the Mississippi River.[67] Consistent with this theory, the *New York Herald* would soon observe that the mortality rate among the former slaves was "from all accounts increasing."[68] Some in the South and the North may have hoped that would be the case, but others, for either selfish or charitable reasons, did not.[69]

In any event, the ability of Alabamians, through their state government, to design and be legally free to implement what they considered the appropriate system to address the issue of race was seemingly undermined by Lincoln's death. In fact, rather than the black population being "controlled and taken care of," white people in the twenty majority-black counties in Alabama would soon have reason to fear that the freed slaves would ultimately be in control of them. And in the heat of the moment that was now perfectly acceptable with an increasing number of opinion makers in the North.[70]

From their perspective, white Southern Unionists and Confederates alike were now in an impossible situation. On one hand, they seemingly had no bargaining position whatsoever and no peaceful means by which to resist the imposition of black suffrage. Violent resistance would be interpreted as evidence of a continuing rebellious spirit in the South, thereby justifying even more harsh reconstruction measures and killing any desire of Northern capitalists to invest in Alabama or the other Southern states. On the other hand, acquiescing in the impending political and social revolution threatened to give the balance of political power in Alabama to the putative black electorate, who consisted of poor, illiterate former slaves who might choose to grind their own axes and thereby possibly trigger a nightmarish race war. Thus, Lincoln's death was most *in*glorious news indeed, and its repercussions would haunt Alabama's politics and economic recovery for the next century.

10
"A Lull in the Tempest"

Of a more sensational character, however, are the reports of the assassination of President Lincoln and Secy. Seward. Should these reports prove true, and they seem well authenticated, I am fearful the war will be prosecuted more barbarously than ever, for I have a poor opinion of the moderation of such a man as Andrew Johnson who, it is reported, was installed as President on the 15th inst.

—William Pitt Chambers

America was never a hospitable place for the losers of a revolution or a rebellion.[1] Even after the Second Treaty of Paris in 1783, many colonists who had opposed the American Declaration of Independence in uniform or as civilians and remained loyal to the British king George III—the original "Tories"— were often brutally assaulted, murdered, had their properties confiscated, or were outright robbed. In order to avoid continued persecution, over one hundred thousand of them went into exile elsewhere.[2] Native Americans were later treated in much the same way but on a much broader scale and were ultimately forced to leave their ancestral lands.[3] Incidentally, when World War II officially ended in 1945, millions of German soldiers were incarcerated, as were a number of Nazi government officials and other leaders, a number of whom would be tried before military tribunals and executed. Even after the release of the survivors, many of the Nazis were excluded from positions of influence in postwar government at the national and local levels, as well as in many businesses.[4]

As the *Chicago Tribune* noted, Lincoln had had "the will and power to shield" the South from such harsh outcomes, but with that shield gone, the manner of his passing encouraged many in the North to call for the exercise of all of these options.[5] Speaking of "Rebel Leaders," a Kansas editor warned that "spare the leaders of the rebellion, and for every one of their forfeited lives thus spared, thousands of good citizens may hereafter suffer death by a second rebellion. Which shall be done, make an example of the leading traitors now? or, by sparing them, expose thousands of our children to the bloody graves of a second set of traitors? We think but one answer will come up from the American people: Let the leaders perish for the good of the country."[6]

Johnson repeatedly affirmed his now famous declaration to make treason "odious," and this had become an article of faith as far as many Alabama Unionists were concerned.[7] But he had not yet revealed exactly how he would go about it as the tumultuous month of April 1865 came to an end. On May 1, however, Johnson ordered that a military commission be organized, ostensibly to try only those immediately involved in the conspiracy to assassinate Lincoln, Seward, and himself.[8] The following day, however, he issued a proclamation calling for the arrest of Davis, as well as C. C. Clay and other Confederate agents who had been based in Canada during the war, alleging that they had been the masterminds behind that conspiracy.[9] In order to encourage a diligent search for them, rewards were offered, and General Wilson posted handbills in Georgia announcing that those who apprehended and delivered Davis to federal military authorities could also keep the cache of Confederate gold and silver reputed to be carried in Davis's wagon train.[10] During the massive manhunt, Davis, while trying to escape to Texas, would be captured in Georgia a little over a week later by Wilson's forces.[11] Clay, who had also been planning to leave the country, decided on the advice of his attorney, former Mobile, Alabama, lawyer Phillip Phillips, to instead voluntarily turn himself in to Wilson's forces in Georgia.[12] Shortly after Clay's arrest, the Washington, DC, correspondent of the *Boston Journal* reported that "positive information has been received here that Clement C. Clay of Alabama, who was in Canada last fall and winter, reached Richmond on the day before its evacuation by the rebels, and there are reasons for believing that he carried tidings of the atrocious plot for the murder of the President, the agents of which, excepting perhaps Booth, were the mere hirelings of the slave power."[13]

As if Davis's and Clay's problems were not serious enough already, news of a failed but nonetheless shocking germ warfare scheme in which they were alleged to have been involved surfaced at this time and further enraged the nation. According to newspaper accounts, bedding and clothing used by yellow fever victims were shipped from Bermuda to New York, Philadelphia, and other major Northern population centers in order to start a deadly epidemic.[14] In the coming weeks, news reports of testimony being taken in connection with the Lincoln assassination linked Clay with other acts of terrorism during the war.[15] Graphic reports were, meanwhile, circulating in the North regarding the appalling physical condition of prisoners of war released from Confederate prisons like that at Cahaba, Alabama, and Andersonville, Georgia, for which Confederate officials would be blamed.[16] Many of the surviving Cahaba prisoners tragically died in a terrible steamboat accident on the Mississippi River while being transported back to their homes and were therefore not seen by the Northern public. Some former Confederates in Alabama may have seen this incident as a grim blessing in disguise.[17]

Southerners assumed punishment of Confederates would extend beyond those suspected of being involved in the assassination conspiracy. As had long been the case with Southern Unionists,[18] Northerners were voicing a strong desire to punish Southern governors who had led their states through secession and war. An Ohio editor declared that "every one of these rebel Governors is just as guilty as Jefferson Davis himself. Every one of them has seconded, with every means within his power, the measures of that chief of traitors. Every one of them deserves to die the death of a traitor."[19] Perhaps anticipating this, Florida governor John Milton, an original secessionist, had already committed suicide at his plantation near Marianna two weeks before Lincoln's assassination.[20]

Given that news of Milton's means of escape appeared in the Alabama press, one wonders whether any of Alabama's three wartime governors considered this dark option.[21] After all, each of them had committed treason and were subject to capital punishment. The first, Andrew Barry Moore, had certainly facilitated the act of secession that brought on the war. First, he acceded to the demands of the secessionists in 1860 that a convention be called, and then he scheduled the election of convention delegates in December of that year. Before the convention had even met, much less voted on whether the state ought to secede, Moore had also ordered the seizures of Forts Morgan and Gaines in Mobile Bay and the federal arsenal at Mount Vernon.[22] His was a clear-cut case of treason, and Moore was arrested in May 1865 and taken aboard the USS *Constitution* to Savannah, Georgia, where he was confined in a military prison at Fort Pulaski.[23] Moore's successor, John Gill Shorter, had carried the torch for the Confederacy and the increasingly unpopular Davis with such conviction that it cost him his bid for reelection in 1863. But perhaps the federal government felt that was punishment enough, for no evidence has been found that Shorter was arrested after the war ended.[24] Shorter's successor, Thomas Hill Watts, did not get off quite that easily. Rather than seeking a peace accord after his landslide election in 1863—as many of those who voted for him instead of Shorter had expected—Watts had essentially picked up where Shorter left off. Even when Watts and everyone else in the nation knew that Wilson and Canby would soon be attacking Alabama in overwhelming force in the spring of 1865, he failed to at least attempt to end Alabama's involvement in the war before the destruction of its remaining industrial base. Not surprisingly, therefore, soon after his plantation home near Greenville was destroyed by federal troops on their way from

Mobile to Montgomery, it was reported nationally that he was arrested. For some unknown reason, however, he was released on parole within a week or two thereafter.[25] Nonetheless, economically he was a broken man and would later file a petition to be declared bankrupt.[26]

Under the terms of surrender extended to and accepted by General Lee on behalf of the Army of Northern Virginia, he and his men were allowed to return to their homes, where they were to be unmolested by the federal government as long as they abided by their paroles and the laws where they resided.[27] Although these terms had been negotiated before Lincoln's murder, they were somewhat surprisingly used as the template for the later surrender by Johnston on behalf of the Army of Tennessee. At this point former members of the Confederate armed forces were fearful that the Johnson administration would not abide by that now seemingly hyperlenient term or would instead seek the eye-for-an-eye and tooth-for-a-tooth brand of justice for which some were now clamoring. But the government also allowed Gen. Richard Taylor to surrender his army at Citronelle, Alabama, on May 4—the very day Lincoln was buried in Illinois—on the same basis as had Lee and Johnston.[28] Yet, any illusion that Confederate military figures were safe was dispelled three days later when Wilson had Confederate captain Henry Wirz, the former commander of the Confederate prison facility at Tuscaloosa and most recently the horrific prison camp at Andersonville, Georgia, arrested and taken to Washington, DC.[29] And with the military tribunal called for by Johnson methodically proceeding toward guilty verdicts,[30] it appeared that constitutional guarantees such as due process and the right to trial by jury would likely be ignored along with the surrender terms.[31]

The Northern press reported a speech by abolitionist Wendell Phillips in New York City in which he called for the summary banishment of a thousand secessionists because it was "not safe that those thousand men should dwell in North America." Congress, he continued, should enact legislation selecting another thousand "leading men of the South" to banish from the United States. The property of the banished, he continued, as well as that of "a thousand or two thousand more"—the "subordinate actors"—should be confiscated and given to "the loyal white man and black man."[32]

To an editor in Cleveland, Ohio, it was a foregone conclusion that "Jefferson Davis must die." That, he was certain, was the "unanimous verdict of the North" because Davis was "universally regarded as the Great Traitor." But Lee should suffer the same fate, the editor wrote, because he was "the wickeder and baser of the two." It was "selfish ambition that led [Lee], Judas like to betray his country."[33] If Lee, whom Grant had released on parole, would face capital punishment, who else would be exposed?

It was, therefore, for good reason that uncertainty as to the depth and breadth of the roundup, and the ultimate fate of the arrestees, had all current and former Confederates in Alabama on edge. Probably because of the Confederacy's own propaganda earlier in the year that Lincoln intended to exterminate the white South, this had been the case even before Lincoln's assassination. Humorously, the propeace *Montgomery Mail* cracked that when Wilson's force had entered the capital in early April, the city was "filled with the simon-pure and the unadulterated war-shriekers, who had howled the children of their neighbors into the gay carnival of death," but suddenly those shriekers had begun to sing a very different tune. "We noticed men of every shade of political opinion, from the veriest 'blood-drinker' and simon-pure, to the most unadulterated victim of suspicion, bowing and cringing for military protection."[34]

After Lincoln's assassination, these feelings of dread and panic greatly intensified. William McLin Brooks, who had served as president of Alabama's secession convention in 1861, feared he would be arrested and told Josiah Gorgas that he was considering fleeing.[35] When the Northern press focused on a passage in J. L. M. Curry's so-called Rebel Manifesto of 1864 from the Confederate Congress that advocated "measures of retaliation" for alleged illegitimate acts of war,[36] Curry quickly found God once again. After he registered his righteously indignant public protest against the implication that he had ever actually favored retaliatory tactics,[37] it was announced in the *Selma Times* that the now twice born-again former north Alabama politico was resuming his work as a minister, this time permanently.[38]

A correspondent to the *New York Times* reported strong disappointment among even some Southerners that the late archsecessionist William Lowndes Yancey was not around to face the music. "I discover among all classes a feeling of antipathy against Wm. L. Yancey, which appears very strange to me. In referring to the probability of hanging Davis, it is a common thing to hear people say they wish Yancey had not died—he was the man to hang. He was the most prominent secession leader in the South," and "his promises to pay the expenses of the war with a ten cent piece, and wipe up the blood with his handkerchief, are often repeated now, and his memory is held in anything but a sacred reverence."[39]

At this early point, the South appeared to some to be in such a frightened and pliable state of mind that public opinion could be molded to accede to not only disenfranchisement of Confederates but enfranchisement of the freed slaves—*if* the North was a "unit" on those issues as Frederick Douglass believed or hoped. Although no proponent of black suffrage, Joshua Burns Moore was certain that the "rabid secessionists of South Ala." could "see the handwriting on the wall" regarding forthcoming punishment of a lethal sort. He predicted they too "will crouch down like whipped spaniels and beg for mercy—like they have done every where."[40] One north Alabamian who certainly fit that whipped-puppy description was Huntsville lawyer and former Confederate secretary of war Leroy Pope Walker, who was actively lobbying Alabama Unionists to support his application for a presidential pardon.[41]

Tuscaloosa Unionist E. W. Peck would later testify that Confederates "would have believed themselves very leniently treated if they could have been assured that they would not have their property confiscated and their lives taken." Peck was also certain "they would have been willing to have relinquished their future political privileges."[42] An Alabama correspondent to the *New York Herald* made the same observation. "At first, when they saw and felt that they were conquered—that they had no hope save in the magnanimity and liberality of their conquerors—when they saw the South one vast desolation of destruction, their fair fields a wilderness and their mansions ruined castles, from which the owl hooted and the bittern [a migratory marsh bird in the heron family] mourned—they had reached the acme of despair. In this woeful condition they clung to the government like drowning men to straws and cried 'enough! enough!' most lustily. They considered that they had forfeited all their rights under the constitution by engaging in rebellion, and consequently prayed for mercy."[43] Historian Walter Fleming, whose style of slanted history undoubtedly influenced John Witherspoon DuBose, wrote in his *Civil War and Reconstruction in Alabama* that the "paroled Confederate soldier returned to his ruined farm and went to work to keep his family from extreme want." No one, claimed Fleming, "thought of further opposition to the United States."[44]

Some Confederates might have felt this way, but not all. Although on May 17, Roddey and his men had officially surrendered, some reportedly improperly retained much of their supply of weaponry.[45] Other Confederates in Alabama were actually still battling on. Union transports on their way from Mobile up the Alabama River to Selma were repeatedly fired into near Cahaba, resulting in a retaliatory raid by General Steele's cavalry that destroyed a portion of the Selma and Meridian Railroad near Demopolis.[46] According to other military reports, "organized parties of marauders" were "operating in Winston, Walker and other counties of North Alabama, burning houses [and] murdering Union men."[47] There was also a telegraphic report that "100 rebels, under Capt. Bill Forrest," bushwhacked a Union cavalry unit near Memphis, Tennessee, causing the death of several.[48] Ominously, there were widespread rumors that Nathan Bedford Forrest was planning a return to the field of battle.[49]

When pressed into a corner by threats of execution or a social and political revolution, would Confederates come out fighting? The thoughts of the guerrilla bands had haunted the dead president in the last several months of his life. Grant and his former adversary, Lee, certainly thought the Confederates might form guerrilla bands.[50] As Sarah Espy in north Alabama put it, "the cause is hopeless. I fear the South through the influence of her leaders has committed a great wrong. Now innocent people must suffer for it." Nonetheless, she also felt "crushed to earth by this great sorrow, and look[ed] to the future with dread for I think we have every thing to fear if we are subjugated as I suppose we are. O' how dark looks all to me, and what is to be the end of it." What appeared to be the end of the war might be merely a cruel illusion. She concluded her diary entry by writing that "I have fears that it is only 'a lull in the tempest' and will be resumed with added fury."[51] Consistent with this, a Confederate surgeon from Missouri who was serving in the trans-Mississippi region west of the Mississippi River wrote that he hoped the North would "agree on honorable terms of capitulation; otherwise, there is no alternative but to fight on to the bitter end."[52]

That fight would be very difficult. The *Mobile News* reported that the pen used by General Taylor to sign the surrender documents was a "steel point lashed to an althea twig with a white cotton thread—emblematic of the straits to which the people of the rebellion have been reduced."[53] But although pen had been put to paper, there was no guarantee that all of the men would resign themselves to the fact that the war was over. Some certainly would. A south Alabama woman later recalled that "as I sit in the twilight and drift back in the past, it is not easy to restrain tears, as memory views those soldiers in their worn gray, marching home, sad and depressed, with the cause they had so warmly espoused, lost."[54] Studies have shown that even members of the victorious Union army were suffering from depression and other symptoms associated with posttraumatic stress disorder.[55] One can only imagine the extent of this malady in the defeated and demoralized Confederate army. This may in part explain the large number of patients at the insane asylum in Tuscaloosa and elsewhere in the postwar years. As a Tuscaloosa newspaper would later observe, the "amount of insanity at the South since the war is alarming. Many of the Asylums are so full as to be compelled to refuse admittance to new cases."[56] Those with mental disabilities who returned to Alabama were not necessarily assured of treatment at the Tuscaloosa asylum. Like all other state agencies, it was insolvent and very close to closing its doors.[57]

Many of the mentally or physically wounded appear to have been anxious to simply obtain their paroles and go home. One of General Taylor's men stationed near Cuba, Alabama, had previously resigned himself to the fact that "*we have failed. It is painful, it is humiliating to write the record; after all, we must give it up and own that we are whipped!*" After being notified of Taylor's surrender, he seemed to rationalize it as God's will. "Thus ends the Confederacy! I have loved it well and given my best service to establish it among the nations of the earth. But it has all been in vain so far as national independence is concerned. There are doubtless lessons in it for our good, as well as for the good of all the people of America, and I seem to realize more and more that God's hand is in it and that He has ordered it well." After moving to Meridian, Mississippi, where many of the Confederates in this region were turning in their weapons and receiving their paroles, he concluded with some relief that "this act ends the 'Rebellion' *east* of the Mississippi River."[58]

Especially after what had occurred since Lincoln's death, however, there was some sentiment among Confederates from Alabama and elsewhere to go much further west, cross the Mississippi River, and continue the struggle in the Trans-Mississippi Department from staging areas in southern Texas and northern Mexico, possibly with the support of the French government.[59] One told Mary Boykin Chesnut that "they were bound for the Rio Grande, and intended to shake hands with Maximilian, Emperor of Mexico."[60] A letter to William Seward reported that after the fall of Richmond "many declared themselves subjects of Maximillian, openly, [and] used the most bitter declarations against their own country."[61] A Houston, Texas, editor called for Confederates to rally in the Lone Star State. Lee's surrender was no reason for yielding or "manly despair," he wrote, because Texas could "redeem the cause of the Confederacy from its present perils."[62] Telegraphic reports in the Northern press reported that civilians in Texas were meeting and voting to continue the war.[63]

And as the *Mobile News* was reporting, Confederate general Kirby Smith, commander of the Trans-Mississippi Department, had issued an appeal to his men to "sustain the old cause" and "stand by your colors," assuring them "you have hopes of succor from abroad" and "will surely receive the aid of nations who already deeply sympathize with you."[64] Word of Smith's continued defiance reached Confederate soldiers far and wide, including some from Alabama still held as prisoners of war in Maryland. One wrote of rumors that Smith was "determined to fight it out" and that he had even denounced General Lee and "all east of Miss. as traitors, & called upon soldiers to stand to their colors but a little longer & they would [re]ceive foreign aid."[65]

Confederate general John Bankhead Magruder issued a similar appeal, assuring Texans that continued resistance there would lead to "your brethren beyond the Mississippi" rising and waging battle, thereby forcing any invading force to withdraw in order "to recover the territory which he occupied, but has not conquered." Texas, he claimed, "will be thus redeemed, and the war will be renewed with greater vigor than ever, upon the soil of Virginia, South Carolina and their sister states, made sacred by the blood of a hundred thousand brave men, shed in the noblest and holiest cause—that of freedom and right against oppression and wrong!"[66]

Continuing this theme, Henry W. Allen, the wartime governor of Louisiana, issued a public appeal to the "Soldiers of Louisiana, of Texas, of Arkansas, and Missouri" to "continue in an attitude of armed defiance, and to fight with the utmost of our strength, fortitude and energy." In addition to suggesting that foreign aid was likely, he represented that, in turn, "our resistance here in the west will assist and hasten a reactionary movement in the states east of the Mississippi, so that while we engage here a federal army our brothers there may rally, reorganize and renew the fight, as they will assuredly do." To him, there was no other choice. Referring to President Johnson, Allen warned that "he who now, not by the grace of God, is called to preside over the destinies of the people of the United States, will show no leniency, no mercy whatever to the supposed traitors." He reminded all of Johnson's earlier declarations regarding the fate of those who had committed treason.[67] A Confederate senator from Texas, Williamson S. Oldham, concurred. He had previously issued a widely published public letter recommending the use of guerrilla tactics to fill the Northern people with "terror and consternation" and obtain revenge for Yankee outrages."[68]

These appeals resonated with some Alabama Confederates.[69] Planter James Mallory in Talladega County observed that the "war seems to be closed by the U.S. throwing troops enough through the country to stop it." But with obvious disdain he also wrote that "all the prominent men are making across the Mississippi no doubt to continue a useless struggle that has already caused the death of thousands, suffering and sorrow, the loss of millions of property, [and] brought disorder and lawlessness through the land with the fear that order will never be again restored."[70] A Chambers County man revealed that a number of locals "can't be reconciled to living under the old government" and were "preparing to emigrate" to Mexico.[71] Confederate nurse Kate Cumming, on her way back home from Georgia to Mobile, crossed paths with several soldiers from Missouri who, she wrote, "were outlawed by their own state, and were on their way to join Kirby Smith."[72] One obviously proud commander of Confederate troops based at Blue Mountain (now Anniston), Alabama, later recalled that his men "were ready for desperate deeds, to leave forlorn homes, to fight to the last gasp, if fighting was possible." In his opinion, "for Mexico and the guerrilla warfare carried on there, the world could not furnish their equals. They were ready to become Soldiers of Fortune, and were entitled to rank with the best the world had ever seen."[73]

General Grant certainly recognized the continuing threat from the trans-Mississippi region. He wrote to President Johnson that "I regard the act of attempting to establish a monarchical government on this continent in Mexico by foreign bayonets as an act of hostility against the Government of the United States. If allowed to go on until such a government is established, I see nothing before us but a long, expensive and bloody war, one in which the enemies of this country will be joined by tens of thousands of disciplined [Confederate] soldiers, embittered against their Government by the experience of the last four years."[74] Grant was convinced that a permanent peace could not be had as long as the French were in Mexico, and he was the foremost proponent of an aggressive policy in the region. In order to lay the groundwork for an invasion of Mexico and attempt to stop the flow of Confederates to it, he issued an order to Maj. Gen. Philip H. Sheridan on May 17, 1865, to take command of a large force that would be deployed to Texas and to establish a strong presence on the Rio Grande as a "first preliminary."[75] Orders were also given to prevent Confederates east of the Mississippi River—especially the leaders—from crossing the river and going to Texas or Mexico.[76]

Despite Grant's persistent lobbying of Johnson, however, Secretary of State Seward prevented the immediate issuance of an invasion order, giving him more time to use bluffs of military action and other means of diplomatic pressure to force a voluntary departure of the French.[77] This did not mean, however, that Johnson ignored the threat of a new Confederate uprising. On the contrary, his concern in this regard may provide a key to explaining some of his subsequent actions for which historians have been searching ever since.[78] He may have sided with Seward at this particular point, but on most strategic matters Johnson was very closely aligned with Grant (fig. 19).[79] And as historian William Blair concluded, Grant "wanted the war to end without provoking guerrilla action, renewed fighting, or alliances [by Confederates] with the French in Mexico. The situation south of the border was an especially sore spot with the United States; many officials were concerned that harsh treatment of former Confederates might chase them into the arms of the French and Mexican monarchists who conducted the war against the liberals under Benito Juarez."[80]

While Johnson pondered how to prevent this and avoid another costly war, a steady stream of Confederate officers, soldiers, and civilians continued to emigrate to Mexico in the coming months, thereby increasing concerns in the United States even further.[81] All they needed were respected leaders. Ala-

Figure 19. Ulysses S. Grant at his headquarters in Cold Harbor, Virginia, June 11 or 12, 1864. Courtesy of the Library of Congress, Prints and Photographs Division.

bama's most notorious guerrilla leader, John Pemberton Gatewood, was already en route.[82] He had been a terror to Union forces and Unionists alike from his base in Cherokee County during the war. Confederates who preferred black flag tactics in this next phase of the war were sure to find a kindred spirit if they joined his band.[83]

Nathan Bedford Forrest had actually been indicted for treason in Tennessee in March 1865. Despite his periodic efforts in the press to explain the incident at Fort Pillow away,[84] he was still seen as a war criminal by many. An Ohio newspaper called him the "King of the Cannibal Islands" and declared that "poetic justice requires that he meet with a violent death."[85] Black troops stationed in Memphis were reportedly planning to do the honors.[86] Thus, one would have assumed that he was a prime candidate for at least a self-imposed exile in Mexico, if not active involvement in the widely anticipated Franco-American conflict.[87] A Southern newspaper later reported that, according to an officer in Jefferson Davis's escort, Davis's plan was to "go to Mississippi, and there rally on Forrest, if he is in a state of organization, and it is to be hoped that he is; [but] if not, we will cross the Mississippi river and join Kirby Smith, and there carry on the war forever."[88]

Consistent with this plan, there is evidence that at least two Southern governors went to Gainesville, Alabama, to plead with Forrest to rededicate himself to the cause. But he is said to have abruptly retorted that "you may do as you damn please, but I'm a-going home" and added that "any man who is in favor of a further prosecution of this war is a fit subject for a lunatic asylum."[89] The efforts to enlist Forrest to go west did not cease, however, although the tactics of the proponents took a feminine twist. The *Nashville Union* reported receiving a letter from Mobile stating that "two rebellious ladies of Gainesville, Ala., recently went to Forrest, and reproach[ed] him after the manner of their sex, for giving up."[90] Forrest was still unmoved. Suggesting even further that Forrest had cut some sort of favorable deal with the federal government during the final weeks of the war, he publicly counseled his men against emigration and instead to take their paroles and go home. As the future head of the Ku Klux Klan told his men at Gainesville in his widely reported final order, "it is your duty and mine to lay down our arms [and] submit to the 'powers that be'—and to aid in restoring peace and establishing law and order throughout the land."[91] Forrest received his own parole, went to his Mississippi plantation (instead of back to the still hostile environment of Memphis), and was never arrested pursuant to the indictment or otherwise prosecuted.[92] Following his example, most of Forrest's men also took their paroles and went homeward.[93]

But if President Johnson intended to entirely eliminate the threat south of the border through negotiation with Napoleon instead of war, it would take a considerable amount of time—in fact until 1866. Logically, one means of buying that time was to somehow lessen the pressures that were compelling Confederates to go west in the first place. This, in turn, would require Johnson to tone down his retaliatory rhetoric and for federal policy on reconstruction to again soften and become less threatening. If he went too far, however, he might risk his presidency in the riptide of postassassination rage[94] and also alienate the affections of Southern Unionists. The alternative was an end to the lull in the bloody tempest. Having experienced the threat of guerrilla warfare in Tennessee, Johnson certainly knew that was not an option the nation could afford. The groundwork for avoiding it was already being laid, but it would merely prolong the lull.

11

"Most Prominent and Influential Loyal Men"

North Alabama remained the most overtly prounification region in the state. While the federal government worried over the continuing threat west of the Mississippi River, efforts to take advantage of that sentiment were being made through regional and local military commanders and members of the wartime peace movement.[1] General Robert Granger, the Union commander of the District of North Alabama, had issued a proclamation advising the citizens in his district to "meet together to devise means to re-establish their courts, and to take into their own hands, through the laws of the State, the suppression of all lawlessness, the re-establishment of law and order, and the giving of security to life and property."[2] Unstated was who would serve in official capacities—judges, district attorneys, sheriffs, court clerks, jurors—in this reanimated justice system, a question vital to Alabama Unionists. At about this same time Maj. Gen. George Thomas answered another important question in a companion proclamation to north Alabamians in which he declared that the law to be henceforth applied was "the Alabama Code before the rebellion," meaning that wartime legislation was to be ignored.[3] More foreshadowing of President Johnson's ultimate policy can be seen in the fact that no proclamations to Alabama citizens during this early period have been located that mention, much less encourage, black participation in these meetings. By contrast, none that have been found discouraged participation by Confederates, making it easy for them to infiltrate the process under the guise of renewed loyalty.

In south Alabama, where all Confederates were not yet under the control of occupation forces, some resistance was still being expressed and recriminations against Unionists were the order of the day. Referring to the two editors of the *Montgomery Advertiser*, the Unionists of the *Montgomery Mail* charged that the "proscriptionist sneaks back after the storm has passed and begins anew the pernicious work of agitation." Although these "agitators do not represent the public sentiment of this community" and instead con-

"Most Prominent and Influential Loyal Men" / 133

stituted the "fag end of a corrupt and almost extinct political clique whose spleen and malignity increases as their mischievous career is shortened," they still had the power to "do mischief" by using "their wagging tongues which would swallow the federal oath with the same eagerness that they spit forth the venom and slander" in order to "build up a party of opposition."[4]

But the trial of those who had executed the plot to assassinate Lincoln and Seward, which was then in progress in Washington, DC,[5] coupled with the arrests of Davis, Clay, and other high-ranking Confederates, provided a helpful spur to loyal sentiment in the South.[6] Beginning in early May a concerted effort was made in other parts of Alabama to, in the words of the *Mobile News*, encourage the people to "return at once to their fealty to the old government, assemble, and declare that they are ready and willing to help and sustain that government" so that the government would, "in return, help sustain and protect them."[7]

Protection against guerrilla reprisals was extremely important to this process. Joshua Burns Moore noted that "there will be a time soon I hope when men can speak out what they have thought and felt for years. The time is however not now. His life would be taken if he speaks his sentiment."[8] Not long thereafter, a guerrilla leader in north Alabama made news when he audaciously sent word to General Granger in reply to General Thomas's proclamation that he and his men refused to surrender. A cavalry unit was sent to capture them, yet as Unionists and deserters had demonstrated during the war, north Alabama was chock full of good hiding places.[9] After some of this particular band were caught, however, the balance decided to surrender. Most were paroled at Huntsville, although three of the group, who were said to be "noted bushwhackers," were "tied to trees and shot."[10] Other guerrilla bands were still out there, so Granger proclaimed that meetings of citizens for the purpose of reestablishing civil law in his district would "receive such military protection as they deem necessary." At the same time, he imposed the duty on "every good citizen to use his influence, and exert all his authority to put down every opposition, openly or secretly, against the Federal Government." He also warned that as "war no longer exists in this district," then "such persons as are secretly seeking the lives of their fellow-citizens can no longer be regarded as belligerents, but as murderers and assassins, and will be fit associates for Booth and his band of conspirators."[11] This soon became official federal policy throughout the South.[12]

One of the first reported public assemblies to take place in Alabama in 1865 occurred in the north Alabama town of Courtland on Tuesday, May 2, 1865, and it was apparently undisturbed. According to a cryptic telegram by J. J. Giers to Granger, it was "a splendid meeting,"[13] A correspondent of the *Nashville Union* reported that "a flag of truce" had "left Decatur, under [Union] Colonel [William Henry] Fairbanks, for the purpose of making known to the rebels the decision of General Thomas in reference to those who still continue in arms against lawful authority of the Federal Government." After reaching a point a few miles from Courtland, this group, which included Giers, "were met by a party of rebels under command of Major [James M.] Warren," an officer in Roddey's command. After what was described as a "parley" between the two commanders, it was "decided to proceed to Courtland where an informal mass meeting was held."[14]

Despite the manner in which the correspondent portrayed the incident, it is very unlikely this was a chance encounter. Warren was one of several north Alabamians who had gone to Montgomery in the waning months of the war to plead with Governor Watts to end Alabama's involvement in the conflict before it was too late. Given what had happened since then, it is very unlikely Warren's viewpoint had changed. He was still a dedicated peace activist in regular contact with Giers and other Unionists in the area. He and they likely put out the word that a Union meeting would take place, explaining why, according to the correspondent, "some three hundred citizens, soldiers, and ladies were present, all mingling with apparent satisfaction at Courtland that day."[15]

Convincing most of Roddey's remaining men still in this region to stop fighting was probably seen as a simple matter. But just in case, Warren addressed the crowd first. According to the newspaper correspondent, Warren told them that "further resistance on the part of the south was useless, and he would accept the same terms '*Granted*' to Lee, and would surrender his forces on Saturday the 13th inst." Warren also declared that "the people must begin to restore civil law, and recommended 'coercion' if they refused to do so." The correspondent noted that "these declarations were received without a dissenting voice, while the rebels frankly acknowledged that they were 'whipped.'" Giers was the next speaker and "after a few preliminary remarks read the order of Gen. Thomas, which was favorably received." Finally, likely preselected "citizens and residents" played their important roles in the presentation. According to the correspondent, Lawrence County lawyer and Unionist "Judge [Thomas] Peters, Rev. E.M. Swoope, and Col. [Richard Orrick] Pickett [another officer who had served under Roddey] recommended an abandonment of the contest and submission to the supremacy of the laws." Somewhat smugly, the correspondent concluded his letter by reporting that "everything passed off pleasantly, and the *Jonneys* [*sic*] seemed glad of the prospect of returning home. Upon every hand we see signs of returning loy-

"Most Prominent and Influential Loyal Men" / 135

alty, and ere long the voice of the loyal people of Alabama will again be heard mingling with the repentant wailings of a fast expiring Confederacy."[16]

A similar meeting took place in Somerville, then the Morgan County seat, on May 13, and another in Moulton on May 15. According to the *Louisville Journal*, the "rebellion was conceded to be dead, and the people expressed themselves in favor of yielding quiet submission to the laws of the federal Government."[17] No record has been found indicating that Thomas Peters attended these meetings or addressed the crowds,[18] but he did address a large gathering on May 23 at the Franklin County courthouse at Frankfort, where local Unionists, selected to form a resolutions committee, met to frame resolutions favoring restoration and calling for a state constitutional convention.[19] The content of Peters's speech is unknown but he may have begun by informing the crowds that Taylor had surrendered all Confederate forces in Alabama to Canby on May 4,[20] that Jefferson Davis was arrested on May 10, and that as far as Alabamians were concerned, the war was over. Peters may also have outlined what he understood would be the process of political reconstruction and the need to support that process so that civil government could be initiated as quickly as possible.

It is possible that Peters and at least some of those present were aware of reports in the press that President Johnson might be planning to appoint a sixty-three-year old Athens resident, future Republican Daniel Havens Bingham, as Alabama's military governor.[21] Bingham was a Vermont native who had graduated from Norwich University in 1824, after which he had taught school and served as a civil engineer in connection with the first railroad in North Carolina, before being hired to engineer various railroad projects in south Alabama in the 1830s. During the mid- to late 1840s, Bingham had engineered projects in Arkansas, but he had returned to Alabama and edited a newspaper in Athens, the *Athens Herald*, in which he promoted the construction of the Tennessee and Alabama Central Railroad in the 1850s. Like Thomas Peters, Bingham had been a vocal opponent of secession and in 1862 he had left the state, but his precise wartime activities are unclear. It is probable, however, that at some point Bingham became connected with Andrew Johnson's growing Unionist organization in Tennessee, which may explain Bingham's service at the end of the war in appointive positions like the US Treasury Department and as a member of the Board of Visitors of the US Military Academy at West Point, New York.[22]

Significantly, Bingham seemed to be a proponent of Tennessee Brownlowism. He revealed some of his intentions in a widely published letter to the editor of the *New York Herald*. In order to prevent political power from being retained by what he called the "slave dynasty," Bingham opposed the establishment of provisional governments manned by slave owners who, "willingly, knowingly and anxiously, went into rebellion and have employed all their energies, influence and wealth" to destroy the government or even those who initially opposed secession but subsequently acquiesced or supported the Confederacy. In addition, Bingham declared, "the slaveholding rebels must be disfranchised," at least temporarily. They must undergo "a probationary state that will insure their fidelity to the constitution and laws of our country; or to use a Southern provincialism, that when again they join the Church of the nation, 'they must give unmistakable evidence that they have got religion.' "[23] The Unionist state government in Tennessee would soon adopt legislation to this effect.[24] According to Governor Brownlow, "without a law to disfranchise Rebels, and a force to carry out the provisions of that law," Tennessee would "pass into the hands of the Rebels, and a terrible state of affairs" was "bound to follow."[25] Bingham obviously concurred.

Earlier in the spring of 1865, when rumors surfaced that President Lincoln might appoint former Huntsville lawyer Jeremiah Clemens as Alabama's military governor, Bingham had written a fiery letter to the editor of the pro-Republican *Nashville Times and True Union* blasting Clemens for his disloyalty to the Union. "Next to William L. Yancey the State of Alabama is much indebted to [Clemens] for the blight, ruin, desolation, poverty and misery, growing out of this dreadful civil war, brought about by his perfidy and treachery in selling himself, and his constituents in the [Alabama] Convention of 1861 to the behest of secession, in consideration for which he received and held, during the first year of the rebellion, the office of Rebel Major-General, and Commander-in-Chief of the military forces of the State of Alabama."[26]

Ironically, Clemens's own letters to Andrew Johnson unwittingly supported Bingham's contention that Clemens was not fit to execute reconstruction policy. In late 1864, Clemens, who then still owned over one hundred slaves, had emphasized to then-vice president elect Johnson that "you must have *men* in the Governorship not seekers of popularity among slave holders."[27] A week after Lincoln's assassination, Clemens urged Johnson to "give us a Governor who will not traffic with treason in any of its ramifications—who is not leagued with cotton speculators, or *with a worse gang*, who while claiming to be Union men, yet cling to the rotten system of slavery, & stickle at any pacification except upon the terms of the Constitution *as it is*, & the Union *as it was*."[28] By those very standards, Clemens did not possess the right stuff. His antebellum political career, which saw him reach the US Senate as a Democrat with the help of south Alabama Whig planters in the legisla-

"Most Prominent and Influential Loyal Men" / 137

ture, was replete with examples of his efforts to protect and advance the interests of slaveholders.

In an effort to justify his seemingly prosecession conduct in 1861, Clemens had authored a novel published in early 1865 titled *Tobias Wilson: A Tale of the Great Rebellion*, in which the narrator explained to a yeoman farmer in north Alabama that he had acquiesced in secession in order to make "an united and determined front." The "old Union will never be restored, but a better Union will spring from its ashes."[29] But many believed a true Unionist would have remained loyal to the existing Union and sought change through the constitutional process. Moreover, if Clemens had actually been motivated by a desire to fashion a more perfect Union, that Union, in his mind, was one where the institution of slavery would be protected by even more constitutional safeguards. The act of secession, for Clemens and men like him, was a strategic move to force the North to agree to these safeguards, and in their minds reconstruction would soon follow on that basis.[30] As Clemens had discovered, however, trafficking with treason even to this extent had placed the South on a slippery slope. The attack on Fort Sumter had sent Alabama over the cliff, and, as Bingham contended, led to the calamity from which Alabama was now suffering.

As far as can be determined, Clemens did not receive the appointment as Alabama's military governor. And as would be reported nationally, he died on May 20 of congestion of the lungs shortly after his return to Huntsville from Philadelphia.[31] According to an admiring acquaintance, Clemens "regretted [his] error" and "was ready to make any sacrifice to atone for it, and to repair whatever injury may have resulted from it." Clemens "died as full of love for the Union, and confidence in its future greatness and prosperity, as any of those who have presumed to pass judgment upon his honesty, and to deny him the full measure of trust to which he was entitled."[32]

Clemens's death did not necessarily mean that Bingham would be appointed Alabama's provisional governor. Another possibility was thirty-nine-year-old Randolph County lawyer and Unionist William Hugh Smith (fig. 20), who like Bingham had been forced to seek exile outside Alabama during the war. He became associated with a brigade in Grant's army under the command of Gen. Grenville Dodge and helped one of Dodge's subordinates, Col. George Eliphaz Spencer, recruit Alabama Unionists to the First Alabama Cavalry, USA.[33] Smith had, so far, refrained from revealing what his policies might be if he were appointed provisional governor of Alabama, but it was assumed that they would differ little from Bingham's. A Northern editor noted that conservatives considered Smith "as having been too good a Union man in the past to hold so prominent a position now," but his appointment "would,

Figure 20. William Hugh Smith. Alabama Department of Archives and History.

it is represented, gratify nearly the entire loyal element of that State, and insure the inhabitants safety and quiet in their homes, and an early and complete pacification and return to prosperity."[34] Smith's supporters appealed to President Johnson's known identification with the common man. One of the pro-Smith memorials Johnson received portrayed Smith as not only an undeniably loyal man but also "the poor man's friend and champion."[35]

For many Alabama elites, that sounded much too much like Brownlowism, a nightmare they could not countenance.[36] A movement had, therefore, been initiated to avoid that scenario by convincing Johnson that the appointment of a provisional governor for Alabama was not necessary to accomplish his legitimate goals and that Governor Watts should be allowed to call the Alabama legislature into special session to address those issues. This movement included not only Confederates, but also several prominent wartime reconstructionists—Unionists who had promoted peace during the war conditional on the continuation of slavery. It was a classic example of politics making strange bedfellows, but it came with benefits to reconstructionists willing to cross the line.

This particular conservative movement had first manifested itself in late April 1865. On May 1, the post commander at Montgomery, Gen. Frederick Steele, reported that he had been approached by the "first men of Alabama,

"Most Prominent and Influential Loyal Men" / 139

members of the state government included," who were "anxious to assemble the legislature for the purpose of calling a convention to annul the ordinance of secession. They say that all parties are now united on this subject, and that two thirds of the people of the State will take up arms to put down the rebels if allowed to do so."[37] Among those who signed a petition to this effect that was presented to Steele were men who were no doubt carefully selected for their apparent Unionism but who were primarily from the planter class. They included reconstructionists Lewis E. Parsons, Joseph C. Bradley, Alexander B. Clitherall, and Milton Saffold. One notable exception was wartime Unionist martyr Charles Christopher Sheats, whose surprising support for this proposition may explain why his initial role in the reconstruction process was not as prominent as one would have expected—he crossed the line with his support for convening the rebel legislature.[38]

A few days later, General Canby reported from Mobile to Secretary of War Stanton that he had received similar overtures. Canby was by this "satisfied that, if permitted, the Legislature of the State of Alabama" would "at once call a convention, which, in twenty-four hours after its organization, will undo all that has been done in the past four years, and settle favorably and definitively all questions that conflict with the supreme authority of the Government of the United States." Canby advised that in his judgment "it will be wise to use the policies and the agencies which now control."[39]

With the ice having been broken, efforts were initiated to create the illusion of widespread public support for this extraordinary idea that the late president had ultimately rejected. On May 10, Selma lawyer William McKendree Byrd addressed Dallas County residents at Selma in the first of several rallies of elites that took place in Alabama over the next several weeks.[40] According to news accounts "Judge Byrd, an influential citizen, made a short address, in which he said the war had decided two questions—secession and slavery—and both adversely to the South. He councelled [sic] conciliation and moderation, and said it greatly depended on the generosity and magnanimity of the visitors whether Constitution and harmony would be permanent and substantial." Those in attendance reportedly adopted a resolution requesting Watts to "call the Legislature together with a view of the State resuming her former position in the Union."[41] Not surprisingly, the post commander at Selma reported that "these are the sentiments of the people generally hereabouts."[42] They also, he added, wanted gradual emancipation, seemingly a pipedream at this point.[43]

The day after the meeting in Selma, another occurred in Montgomery at the county courthouse. There the resolutions committee included representatives of three diverse groups. The south Alabama reconstructionists included Montgomery residents Milton Saffold, J. J. Seibles, Marion A. Baldwin, George Goldthwaite and W. J. Bibb, each of whom had historic connections to Benjamin Fitzpatrick. North Alabama was also represented by reconstructionists Lewis Parsons of Talladega and Joseph C. Bradley of Huntsville. Original secessionists had a representative too: wartime governor John Gill Shorter.[44] After what was described as a short absence, the committee returned with a preamble and two resolutions. One expressed an "earnest desire of the people to resume their former relations to the Union." The other pledged "our earnest and zealous co-operation in the work of restoring the State of Alabama to her proper relations with the Union at the earliest practicable moment" and denounced the murder of Lincoln and the assault on Seward.[45] These resolutions were unanimously adopted, but neither the resolutions committee nor those at the meeting could reach unanimity on the mechanics of reconstruction to be recommended to Johnson.

It was agreed that a delegation would be appointed from among "*our most intelligent and influential citizens* to proceed to Washington City, and confer with the authorities there upon matters touching the immediate resumption of our position in the Union." They also would send a letter to Johnson proposing the method to be used. But the committee was divided over that issue. The majority drafted a letter to Johnson requesting him to permit Watts to "convene the legislature for the purpose of calling a convention of the people, in order to restore the State of Alabama to her political relations with the United States." But if Johnson were unwilling to approve this course, he was requested to appoint a military governor "from among the *most prominent and influential* loyal men of our State, and invest him with such authority as may enable him to call such convention for the purpose proposed." In other words, no Brownlows should be appointed. Joseph Bradley presented the committee's "minority report" that simply recommended that Johnson authorize Watts to convene the legislature in the same manner as the majority had suggested. Among other considerations, this minority, which included Lewis Parsons, apparently did not want to chance the appointment of a military governor, presumably no matter how "prominent and influential" he might be.[46] Rather than forcing a vote on which letter to send, it was agreed that persons at the meeting would sign whichever they preferred and that both letters would be placed at a local drugstore where members of the public could likewise sign either. Then an appointed delegation would deliver them to Washington, DC.[47] Eight prominent men were appointed delegates at the meeting, including Milton Saffold, Joseph Bradley, and Lewis Parsons. Most departed Montgomery by riverboat, reached Mobile by May 17, and

"Most Prominent and Influential Loyal Men" / 141

then after a trip to New Orleans, boarded an ocean steamer on May 22 for New York with the intention of taking a train down to Washington, DC.[48]

Unconditional Unionists opposed to the Montgomery plan were not willing to sit idly by while their future was stolen. They sounded the alarm and attempted to warn Johnson using every means possible. The editor of the *Mobile News* ridiculed the idea of the Alabama legislature being convened, noting that "all of the late violent secessionists and exterminators, including Gov. Watts, Ex-Gov. Shorter, [Supreme Court associate justice John Dennis] Phelan and Sam Rice, concur in and heartily approve the movement."[49] George Spencer, now a Union general engaged in occupation duties in north Alabama, wrote to Johnson warning that "several delegations of former politicians working in the interest of the rich and rebels and at heart hating both the Gov't and yourself, with the deadliest hatred" were "going to visit you."[50] Similar concerns were voiced by J. J. Giers in a letter to Johnson. The delegation was composed, he wrote, of "representatives of the old Slave Aristocracy, who would again rule us if they could." Even worse, their plan actually consisted of "*overtures*' from Gov. Watts and other rebels."[51]

At a gathering in Huntsville, prewar Unionists and future Republicans David Campbell Humphries and Nicholas Davis condemned the idea of Watts and the current legislature having any role in the reconstruction process. Future Republican governor David Peter Lewis, then a Huntsville lawyer, offered a resolution calling that scheme a "derogation of the rights of the Union men of this State and an endorsement of a principle dangerous in itself, as such legislature [which included Joseph Bradley and Lewis Parsons] is composed of a majority of secessionists elected in the midst of this rebellion." According to a newspaper account, this resolution was adopted. Nicholas Davis then proceeded to Washington, DC, to meet with Johnson and rebut the other delegation.[52]

Prewar Unionist and future Democratic governor George Smith Houston of Limestone County was also opposed to the wartime legislature being convened. He advocated new elections to fill all political offices. At a public meeting in Athens, Houston proposed resolutions that were expressly premised "upon the hypothesis that Confederate legislation and acts are null and void and never were of force" and insisted that the prewar Alabama Constitution and laws and the "same form of government as existed previous to the passage of the ordinance of secession are in as full force and power as they have ever been." Hence, according to Houston, all that was necessary was to fill the various offices by proper election "with men of capacity, integrity and patriotism."[53] Houston then began his own trek to Washington, DC.[54]

The trajectory of Alabama's future was at stake. Would the south Alabama plan prevail, thereby dashing the hopes of most Unionists that a new day would dawn for them? Or would unconditional Unionists finally gain control of their own destiny, including the manner with which the disloyal would be dealt? Would wartime loyalty be a decisive factor in Johnson's decision making, or would other considerations predominate? Much would depend on whether Johnson concluded that Lincoln's assassination and subsequent events had changed the political calculus of reconstruction.

12

"Diabolical"

Let Every man swear on his blade,
That he will not sheath nor stay it,
Till from point to hilt it glow
With the flush of Almighty vengeance,
In the blood of the felon foe.

—Jason Phillips, *Diehard Rebels*

Andrew Johnson's historical legacy pales when compared to that of Abraham Lincoln, primarily as a result of his reconstruction policies.[1] This is quite ironic because it can be argued that in 1865 Johnson attempted to execute virtually all of Lincoln's initiatives.[2] For example, just as Lincoln had expressed his desire that Louisianians consider adopting limited, qualified black suffrage, Johnson would make the same suggestion to Mississippians.[3] Johnson's blueprint for postwar provisional governments was also basically identical to Lincoln's.[4] The only real difference in policy, at least as far as 1865 is concerned, is that Johnson was adamant that restoration of a state required its immediate—not gradual—emancipation of the slaves and ratification of the Thirteenth Amendment. Voting against it was not an option. But like Lincoln, Johnson believed that peace, reunion, and the abolition of slavery, not the political or social reconstruction of the South, were the primary objectives of the federal government. And like Lincoln, Johnson seems to have recognized that the key in that regard remained convincing Confederate soldiers to go home and return to peacetime pursuits, rather than go to Texas and Mexico.

The *New York Times* spoke for mainstream Republicans when it agreed that the "nation, as a whole, is weary of carnage, and utterly opposed to plunging into an unnecessary and frivolous war" with Maximilian and the French.[5] Pushing a radical agenda would be counterproductive to that goal.[6] After all, Confederates pondering whether to stay or go west arguably had enough problems at home.[7] To a south Alabama woman it certainly seemed there was nothing for the paroled soldiers at home, and therefore nothing to lose by going west.[8] In many cases these men would be returning to communities physically and emotionally devastated by the effects of war and governed by martial law imposed by occupation troops who might one day come and arrest them.[9]

Seeking release by way of a writ of habeas corpus would not be an option because civilian courts could not conduct proceedings; perhaps for the first time ever the Alabama Supreme Court did not conduct its June term of court.[10] But to some the fact that the courts were not functioning may have seemed like a godsend. The *New York News* estimated that the merchants of New York alone were owed $150 million by Southern debtors for prewar debts.[11] As one Alabama newspaper noted, "there are claims and cases enough in the Southern States to occupy the courts for the next twenty-five years, but all questions at issue between the people must remain until the sitting of the courts."[12] This was not a problem merely in the state court system. Alabama's lone federal judge, Lincoln appointee Richard Busteed of New York, had not yet chosen to come to Alabama to open his court and in fact would not until late fall.[13] Even if he had convened his court on the day Taylor formally surrendered all Confederate forces in Alabama, however, operation of the court would have been hampered by the fact that most of the members of the legal profession in Alabama were effectively barred from practicing in federal courts by virtue of a law adopted by Congress in January 1865. That law, which applied throughout the country, required an oath of wartime loyalty called a "test oath" as a prerequisite to being admitted to practice in any federal court.[14]

All of this, of course, meant that the surviving lawyers who counted on courtroom work to put bread on the table would have to continue to go without. According to a wartime editorial by a sympathetic Columbus, Georgia, editor whose readership included Alabamians, the "lawyers are the only profession, as a class, that we know of, who have not and are not making money during our political struggle. They may, and doubtless do, when they get a case, charge more than they ever did before, but they get so few cases that, after all, they make comparatively nothing." Demonstrating that this editor was probably neither a lawyer nor a happy client, he expressed hope that "when this accursed war shall cease, our people will have learned to live together without litigation" and "like a band of brothers we shall go forth a living example of freedom, peace and fraternity in the world."[15] Needless to say, that would never happen, but at least with the courts still closed, some potential defendants were safe for the time being.[16]

This surprisingly frank editor was probably not a physician, a mechanic, or a merchant either or apparently seeking their purchase of advertising space in his newspaper. "People will get sick, and must necessarily take medicine, and a doctor is indispensable to administer it, and the doctors are charging three or four times the old prices for visits." The "mechanics are getting a large advance on former prices, and pay their laborers much higher wages. The merchants have all turned speculators, and nearly all of them have made their fortunes. Whiskey sellers are asking, and find ready sale for their foul decoctions at ten times the old prices. But the poor lawyers get nothing to do, however industrious and constant they are at their post."[17]

Most of those wartime profits had been accumulated as a result of the hyperinflation caused by the vast overissue of Confederate treasury notes. But as a Louisiana editor lamented, those notes were not even worth the paper they were printed on except as novelties.[18] One Alabamian mourned that "everything I had [and] all my effects had been converted into Confederate money and hence of course when the Confederacy went up a spout all I had went up with it and I am left perfectly destitute."[19] He was not alone. The editor of the *Mobile News*—which was established by occupation forces— reported that "one man bought one thousand and eighty dollars of it yesterday for 'four bits.' " The editor had no sympathy for those Southerners left holding worthless bags of wartime currency. He somewhat flippantly pointed out that the fact that "people are burdened with it—cursed with it" was simply a consequence of the pursuit of "a wrong course." The "United States Government," he declared, "cannot be expected to recognize it as currency, or as possessing any value whatever; and people engaged in business of whatever nature cannot be expected to touch or handle it, in payment of any kind of indebtedness."[20]

This, coupled with the other circumstances surrounding the crushing outcome of the war, had the members of all of these professions and vocations very despondent. A correspondent to a Wisconsin newspaper observed that Mobile, Alabama's largest city, "is a sad picture to contemplate. The stores look a thousand years old. They were something of the appearance of old castles to be seen in some of the countries of Europe. They are empty and forsaken, except here and there an old man seated like some faithful sentinel at his post. Shelves are forsaken of their silks, and occupied only with the flies and the dust." "The people," he continued, "look sad and sorry. The best people of the city are poor, and poorly clad. There is no money save the scrip of the Confederacy. The people are distressed. No money except coin and greenbacks will pass. They have little of the former—none of the latter. We have witnessed such sorrow over this order of things as we do not again desire to see. Soldiers of the Union army, who were expected to burn and destroy, have been seen to empty their haversacks, distributing their coffee and bread to starving women and children."[21]

Kate Cumming wrote that she "looked at my roll of Confederate money, and put it away with a sigh. Memories," she sadly concluded, "of what it once was came crowding in on me."[22] In Dallas County Mary Ann Hall wrote to her sister complaining that her region was "in a terrible condition—the planters have no money—no crops and many of them nothing to sell. I consider the South ruined for this generation."[23] Similarly, James M. Williams of Mobile, a Confederate officer who had emigrated to the South in 1858 and settled with his Southern wife in Mobile, wrote that "business here is utterly ruined for a long time to come; those who were rich are poor now as myself."[24] At about the same time, Augustus Benners noted that "our condition is a very sad one—the money of [the] Confederacy has ceased to have any purchasing value and want of provisions is getting to be a very serious matter. What distresses are still in store for us God only knows. May he give us strength to endure whatever may befall."[25] As Tuscaloosan James Robert Maxwell later recalled, the merchants in Tuscaloosa opened their stores, "but there was little traffic going on. All stocks of goods and hardware that people could find use for had long since been trafficked off. It was only a sort of bartering trade, and had so been for the last two years of the war."[26] The only subject of commerce at this early point was "country produce from Tuskaloosa and contiguous counties."[27] Out-of-state businessmen who visited the Florence area in northwest Alabama reported that the "people are very poor, and yet swearing they would rather starve than sell their cotton at 12 and 10 cents, the price now offered them. They report the little towns up the Tennessee River quiet enough for country church-yards."[28] The area south of the Tennessee River between the Mississippi line and Decatur was described as being "along the main roads, almost a desert. The hot breath of war swept over it time and again; many of its residences were burned; the fences were destroyed, and many of its fair fields, once covered year after year by luxuriant crops of cotton, are now overgrown with weeds and broom-sedge."[29]

Given the collapse of the Confederate currency, the Union army occupation forces were actually an important early source of aid and economic stimuli.[30] For example, not long after the arrival in Montgomery of an army paymaster and numerous iron chests reportedly containing $7 million,[31] a Montgomery correspondent remarked that "greenbacks are becoming quite plentiful by reason of the recent payments to the Fifteenth Army Corps, and the monetary pressure which had for a month or so existed, had almost subsided."[32] Even so, the multiplier effect of this economic activity was slow, and many white and black people were on the verge of starving.[33] The *New York Herald*'s Montgomery correspondent reported that the people were so desperate that the military had to step in to provide rations to the civilian population in the area. "The number of rations issued daily, to white people, is 2,000, and to colored, 5,000. Many of the white people receiving rations are of the most respectable families."[34] Statewide there were 135,000 white paupers who were "barely kept alive" by salt and meal from the federal commissary, wrote one reporter. The war, he concluded, "has played sad havoc with the poor of Alabama."[35] White Alabamians actually received more rations than the black population.[36]

In some cases, medical care was also provided by military personnel and, according to a Vermont editor, this demonstrated to Alabamians that "not only 'the devil is not so black as he is painted,' but that in fact he is not a devil at all."[37] As a result, once fears about mass, indiscriminate exterminations in retribution for Lincoln's death had subsided, some white citizens actively cultivated good relations with their white captors.[38] To the chagrin of some, announcements of wedding engagements between some women and Union officers would later be forthcoming.[39] Others, however, remained bitter and virulently angry. "Even on their way to the Government commissary to procure rations," wrote a very disturbed reporter for the *New York Times* who had just completed a journey from Mobile to Montgomery and back, "they abuse the Government and the people of the United States. Terms as unmerciful as any we have heard were used by this mad people."[40]

Confederates could not ignore that the Yankees also provided them a critically important security force. The chaos left in the wake of the disintegration of the Confederacy had encouraged armed bands to rob and otherwise terrorize citizens in several parts of the state.[41] Kate Cumming was horrified that "the country is filled with lawless men, whom defeat has made reckless," and "they steal from friend and foe."[42] In addition, there were fears that once freed, the slaves would finally rise and seek revenge from white people for lifetimes of exploitation[43] and that black troops would seek vengeance against former Confederate soldiers.[44]

At least temporarily, domestic cotton prices in the North were still spiked upward to approximately fifty cents per pound in May 1865 because of the lingering pent-up demand caused by the Union naval blockade.[45] There was still quite a bit of cotton from prior crop years hidden and otherwise stored in Alabama despite efforts by the Confederate military to destroy it.[46] In fact, estimates were as high as half a million bales.[47] But title to much of the cotton had been transferred to the Confederate government in exchange for bonds at an early part of the war, and it was therefore subject to confiscation by the federal government and sale for its benefit.[48] According to a report from the post commander at Demopolis, the captured records of the Confederate cotton agent there indicated that there were "something more than 10,000 bales of Government cotton on plantations within from five to twenty miles of Demopolis."[49] But as the secretary of the US Treasury would later learn to his dismay, it was unlikely that much of the proceeds of its sale would make its way into federal coffers. One reason for this was that, by hook or by crook, a lot of it was now hidden, "came up missing," stolen, or could no longer be identified as property of the Confederacy.[50] In cases where the federal government was successful in locating, identifying, and seizing what it believed was Confederate cotton, the prior owners would oftentimes assert claims contesting the Confederacy's title and therefore the right of confiscation by the government.[51] Hilary Abner Herbert, who returned to his south Alabama law practice, would later fondly recall that a legal "scramble" began for this cotton and the money it would beget, and this "gave much business to lawyers."[52]

There was also cotton in private hands to which title was uncontested,[53] but local offers for it were initially low, and transporting it to distant markets in the early summer of 1865 was very problematic.[54] Given the time of year, the Black Warrior River was virtually unnavigable.[55] While some areas did have reliable river transportation, the extensive damage and wear and tear to the railroad system, which had been built in part to serve the planters in the antebellum period, and the absence of competition, had caused river freight charges to skyrocket.[56] Virtually every railroad in the state had suffered damages to some key portion, and functioning engines and cars were in very short supply.[57] The cost of repairing those railroads was immense and in the absence of outside capital, sufficient cash flow necessitated that the charges for railroad transportation over the existing tracks be extremely high.[58] Although the presence of occupation troops was offensive to some, pragmatic business leaders in occupied towns that had previously been served by a railroad were much more receptive, especially when post commanders, who needed dependable transportation at a reasonable price with which to supply their troops, began detailing their men and laborers to make repairs to those roads.[59] As one Ohio soldier stationed near Huntsville wryly put it, "the rebels are anxious to have the assistance of the United States to repair their roads, while at the same time a large majority of them most cordially wish you at a warmer place than Alabama."[60] In any event, this occupation policy gave the affected communities like Huntsville, Decatur, Tuscumbia, Selma, Montgomery, and Mobile a head start out of the gate in the economic competition that would eventually resume. Because military necessity apparently did not require the construction of *new* roads, towns like Tuscaloosa would remain in their relatively inferior positions from a transportation standpoint for the foreseeable future, stunting their potential for postwar growth.[61]

Alabama planters still owned productive land, especially in the Tennessee

Valley and the Black Belt, but producing a new cotton crop in 1865 would prove very difficult. It was not only late in the planting season but in addition to the normal cost of production, north Alabama had been "almost entirely stripped of horses, mules, wagons, &c" by the Union army before the war ended.[62] The recently rejuvenated *Selma Times* reported similar problems in south Alabama. "The teams of most planters have been so reduced by the Confederate and federal forces, as to have crippled them in all their farming operations. Nearly all the planters along the route of Gen. Wilson, through Alabama, which extended over a wide circuit of the richest portions of the State, were stripped of their teams, at a time when they were pitching their crops, and they have had to rely, to cultivate such as they planted at that time, upon broken-down stock they were enabled to collect up."[63] Replacing these animals and the worn out and dilapidated farming gear, tools, and implements would be very difficult and in some cases impossible in the short run. Prior to the war, the antebellum credit practice of factors and other creditors lending money to planters secured by future crops had saddled the planter class with huge debt loads to Southern and Northern creditors, who were now anxious to collect the existing debt as soon as the court system began functioning and who were meanwhile very reluctant to make new loans.[64] Until credit markets began functioning again, the significant amount of funds necessary to replace these items and to plant crops would have to be paid for with cash on the barrelhead, but as previously mentioned, the planters' Confederate money was now worthless.[65] Even if they were among the few who had prudently hoarded a nest egg of specie during the war, weather and pests were still beguiling challenges, and the summer of 1865 was to be very hot and very dry.[66]

The planters' traditional labor force was now theoretically free to leave and, therefore, in the planters' minds less reliable.[67] Josiah Gorgas wrote that the freedmen "are in a state of excitement & jubilee not yet knowing what responsibilities their new condition brings with it."[68] As the editor of the *Selma Times* explained, "cotton cannot be made except by close diligent attention. A few days lost, at certain crises in the crop, destroys the prospect, and when once raised, it cannot be saved except by hard, persevering labor." But, he concluded, "in our opinion the negro will not raise cotton unless he is forced to labor. He is too indolent and idle by nature voluntarily to bestow the requisite amount of toil."[69] Augustus Benners wrote that there was "great gloom hanging over the people by reason of the destruction of the labor system of the country—no one knows what to depend upon or what to do." "And with reduced stock and negroes demoralized a crop looks impossible."[70] Similarly, James Mallory noted that "in full harvest, the crop is good," but "it will not likely all be saved as the negroes are leaving rapidly [and] those remaining do but little work." As a result, "should the wheat be neglected and the full corn crop not be made much suffering will be the result."[71] Robert Jemison complained to a Union officer predicting that some former slaves could not be convinced to do anything other than "skulk & hang around our plantations, killing our stock, depredating & stealing generally.[72] A Georgia editor reported a case where a planter had contracted with freed slaves to provide agricultural labor in exchange for wages, and they "went to work, but soon quit to go fishing." From this, the editor concluded that "unless there is some controlling power, Sambo cannot be depended upon."[73]

Some military officers in the regular army, as well as those assigned to the Freedmen's Bureau, attempted to fill this role by either allowing former masters to utilize traditional methods to enforce labor discipline or by actively encouraging the freed slaves to contract with their former masters to work their lands.[74] Rev. Basil Manly wrote to his sister that the post commander of Tuscaloosa "was a Kentuckian" and, as a result, "domestic arrangements" with "our servants" had not been interfered with or disrupted and "things go on as before."[75] The federal official in charge of the Freedmen's Bureau office at Demopolis reportedly told a group of between 1,500 and 2,000 former slaves that they "were free, but that freedom did not imply an exemption from labor, and the liberty to do as they pleased." On the contrary, he made clear, "their new situation increased their obligations to labor assiduously and faithfully, and to deport themselves correctly. Labor was their lot, and those who expected to live idleness would be made to work."[76] Similar remarks were made by the post commander at Selma. Even the military-subsidized *Federal Union* declared that "a negro is a negro and will not work unless compelled by some whip or spur other than his necessities or delicate sense of honor. He should be free to make his own contracts, but after that authority should be given his employer to make him work."[77] If they refused to make a contract, occupation commanders utilized other means. In Mobile and Montgomery, for example, federal vagrancy regulations were promulgated and strictly enforced in order to force the freedmen to find employment.[78]

These lessons in capitalism did not always take. Perhaps this was because the slaves had the indelible memories of their former masters exhibiting their own freedom by what appeared to be world-class idleness.[79] And as a number of Lawrence County residents reported, many former slaves had the impression that "the lands of the country ought to be divided between them" and had been encouraged to believe this by "designing or ignorant men."[80]

Following a mass meeting in Guntersville in mid-May called by the Yankees, Catherine Fennell wrote that she was "not so sorry" about the announcement that slavery would be immediately abolished. The slaves "were so much trouble and now we will not feel the responsibility for their comfort." In fact, she mused that it would have been better to have "given up slavery at the beginning" and "stayed in the Union but it is too late now." She noted with some satisfaction that, although they would be paid wages, "the poor negro will have to work harder than ever." She also wrote that one of the slaves who had attended the meeting was "very much disappointed when the Yanks told him 'They were free but better to work for their masters and receive wages.'" The man, according to her, "thought they would tell him 'You are free— go home and get a good horse or anything you want from your Mistress and [live] in ease and like a gentleman.'"[81]

Some would not live at all.[82] According to the equally smug editor of the *Selma Mirror*, the "negroes who congregated in such hot haste in Selma immediately after Wilson's raid, and who a short time were so jubilant over their freedom, are now dying like sheep with the rot, insomuch that scarcely a day passes that we do not hear of several that have shuffled off this mortal coil." The editor obviously believed that their freedom was to blame. "They are without guardians, and their inability to take care of themselves involves their probable extinction, ere the lapse of a century."[83] Northern Democrats encouraged this abolition-equals-death mentality. Slavery, to the abolitionists, "was a bad thing," wrote an Indiana editor, "but freedom is a thousand times worse."[84]

In some areas, the presence of cooperative post commanders and bureau officials could not cure the labor problem. The area of northwest Alabama south of the Tennessee River between the Mississippi line and Decatur was said to be "nearly depopulated" of former slaves. "It is estimated that nearly ten thousand were carried off and ran away during the second and third years of the war," wrote one correspondent.[85] This same phenomenon had taken place in south Alabama in the last several weeks as Union forces moved through the Black Belt. According to a *New York Tribune* correspondent writing from Montgomery after accompanying a march from Mobile, the "negroes hailed us as deliverers" and "thronged the highways, almost impeding our march." They refused requests that they remain with their masters, declaring that "da was going to be free." This was particularly the case for one elderly man the correspondent encountered, who had been "born in the North, and a free man, [but] had been kidnapped at the age of 15 and had been held in slavery *sixty-three* years."[86] An estimated five thousand had followed the soldiers to Montgomery, over two thousand of whom enlisted in the Union army."[87]

Even if all of these hurdles to making a cotton crop could somehow be overcome, the dynamics of the international cotton market had materially and permanently changed in response to the wartime blockade. Due to foreign competition from cotton produced in India and Egypt, prices in England were already nearing depressed, prewar levels.[88] When Southern cotton came into the international market, foreign and domestic prices were sure to erode even further,[89] making cotton planting an even less profitable venture than before the war. As far as slavery was concerned, an elderly Columbus, Georgia, man would lament that "the people of the South have killed the goose that laid the golden egg."[90] But Alabamians would discover that the same could be said for the South's antebellum cotton monopoly.[91] As a Washington, DC, editor put it, the "cotton monopoly and the reign of King Cotton have been destroyed by the very means which were taken to perpetuate it and to bring all nations to its feet."[92] Cotton "*may* recover the throne," said the *Montgomery Mail*, "but the old monarch is very shaky."[93] Many planters were even more pessimistic and maintained that "the day of cotton planting is passed."[94]

As a consequence, the values of Southern lands had plummeted. A Selma correspondent of the *New York Herald* reported that "fine plantations, including buildings, can be bought at from three to five dollars an acre, which was worth fifty dollars an acre before the war."[95] Outside the Black Belt, land values were even lower. Alabama was not alone in this regard. The *Herald's* correspondent in Virginia reported that "land in Virginia and North Carolina, which before the rebellion could not have been purchased for less than one hundred and fifty dollars per acre, can now be had for two dollars and two dollars and a half per acre."[96] The *New York Times* predicted that Yankees would soon "over-spread the South like locusts,"[97] but for land-poor planters desperate for cash, this postbellum epidemic of Alabama Fever was a mixed blessing. Newcomers who brought money also might bring unwanted ideas about how Southern society ought to work.[98]

Economic alternatives to cotton planting were few. Alabama's transition from an agricultural to an industrial economy had been rudely and spectacularly halted and reversed with the destruction of manufacturing plants, mines, furnaces, rolling mills, and foundry facilities by Union raiders beginning in 1862 and concluding with Wilson's raid.[99] The minerals were still there, but taking advantage would require a massive rebuilding project for which Alabama desperately needed capital, and now accumulating that capital would be even more difficult.[100] Not only had the South's wartime paper money become worthless, and its "hard money" or specie been substantially depleted, but the ability to accumulate and generate capital through local banking institutions had been severely limited by Congress's enactment during the war of rational and legitimate banking legislation designed to curb inflation and insure the stability of banks and the currency.[101] Gone were the days when planters and local businessmen were free to pool their individual capital and to, with authorization from their state legislatures, create banks that issued negotiable notes in amounts far exceeding their specie reserves. Now, in accordance with this federal legislation, the emphasis was on "national" banks having mandatory minimums of capital reserves, and a "national currency" at least for now capped at $300 million.[102] By the time the war ended, the number of national banks chartered in the North had already spoken for most of this currency cap amount, meaning that few national banks (only in Huntsville, Montgomery, Selma, and Mobile in 1865) would be created in Alabama, and those would have relatively small lending capacities.[103]

The Alabama victims of secession and war expressed their frustration as well as their intense animosity toward those who had led the state to destruction.[104] "Four years since," wrote the saddened editor of the *Montgomery Mail*, "the South was in the enjoyment of a prosperity and social quiet and happiness unequaled in the history of any people whose society rested on a slave basis." Indeed, "with a climate not only favorable to the maintenance of life without much exertion, but courting an indulgence in tropical ease and eastern luxury, a soil in admirable adaption to those ends, and a peculiar labor system that sympathized and affiliated with the people, the climate and the soil, it sustained the Southern sybarite in his lounging, lordly *abandon*." That era was now gone. "But what to-day is the picture? It bears no drawing in detail. We can only give a few prominent points in the scene and forbear. The baronial hall in ashes, the bones of its lord lie whitening on the hills, and its sons and daughters, outcasts and wanderers in the valleys. These we say, are the prominent points in the picture, the relief is drawn in colors of humiliation and degradation, unequalled in the history of any christian people of modern days."[105]

Similarly, Mary Fielding in north Alabama wrote that "to think that after all we have endured, lives lost, the untold suffering of thousands of widows and orphans, that it should be for nothing, worse than nothing, 'tis almost unendurable."[106] These same thoughts also haunted Kate Cumming, who had consistently supported the Confederacy while serving as a nurse. "O I felt so sad! Visions of the terrible past would rise in review before me—the days, weeks and months of suffering I had witnessed—and all for naught. Many a boyish and manly face, in the full hey-day of life and hope, now lying in the silent tomb."[107] These feelings were, of course, not exclusive to Alabamians. A Georgian wrote in his diary what many were thinking: that the war had been "begun in too much haste and fought with such dreadful loss for four long years. It grieves me to think of what the South has suffered and lost, *for what?* For a lot of worthless niggers, which now are worse than worthless."[108]

Augustus Benners, who had prayed for peace for years, knew that the consequences of the failed revolution had not yet all revealed themselves. "What distresses are still in store for us God only knows."[109] Georgiana Walker, a woman from Montgomery whose husband and family had chosen to get out of the country, wrote that the "allotted time of man is not enough for us to hope to see our Country what it once was. Our children's children may behold that day; but many a year must roll around before the ravages of this frightful War have passed away; before the broken hearts are healed;—that can never be—these must also pass away and new ones take their places."[110]

Some blamed Jefferson Davis and others for leading them to chaos and ruin.[111] Sarah Follansbee, a young schoolteacher in Montgomery, wrote that she heard the "instigators of secession" denounced soon after the war ended.[112] Joshua Burns Moore concluded that it was the "most disgraceful war ever inaugurated and the most causeless," having been "commenced for no real injury whatever."[113] Josiah Gorgas wrote that while dining with a previously wealthy Greene County planter, "it struck me very uncomfortably that his convictions should be so largely interladed with retrospection of his opposition to the doctrine of secession, & the necessary deduction that we fought so valiantly & bled so freely in a cause radically wrong."[114]

James Mallory wrote that "we are in an awful condition as a people, two or three hundred thousand of our best men killed or disabled, millions of property destroyed, millions more to go, our slaves rendered useless and a future pest, with a grinding debt on this generation, the people demoralized and wicked beyond any thing, all to gratify a few wild politicians."[115] Sarah Espy wrote that "I fear the South through the influence of her leaders has committed a great wrong. Now innocent people must suffer for it."[116] The editor of the *Montgomery Mail* was more pointed when he expressed relief that the "secession movement has been entirely crushed, and its advocates sentenced to silence and to shame." It was, he wrote, "a proper retribution, and the law of retribution is inexorable in its decrees."[117]

Some ordinary folk took their revenge against those who had brought on the war. As Parthenia Hague, a south Alabama woman, recalled, the war had "caused riches to take to themselves wings and fly away."[118] The majority of white Alabamians who were consistently or "truly" loyal to the Union comprised hard-working yeoman farmers, craftsmen, and laborers; and these "Yahoos," as Confederates had openly dubbed them during the war, had harbored prewar resentments about a variety of economic, social, and political issues. And as historian Michael Fitzgerald notes, the later hardships, brought on by secession, war, conscription, the tax-in-kind and other wartime measures, and now by poverty and starvation, had radicalized them to the point that former elites in various parts of the state had very good reason to be worried for their safety.[119] Even after the surrender of Confederate military forces in Alabama in early May, southeast Alabama was reportedly "full of returning rebel soldiers, much incensed against rich and leading rebels who had urged and forced them into the rebel army, leaving their families to suffer in their absence."[120] Kate Cumming wrote that those soldiers declared to one of their victims that "they had been fighting for four years to save his property, and now had a right" to take it.[121] South Alabama Unionists in Covington County, led by Alfred Holly, began organizing what the federal commander at Pensacola, Florida, called "armed companies against the rebels." The "greatest excitement prevails all over that county," he reported.[122] Similarly, Sarah Espy in northeast Alabama wrote that "the Tories are in the vicinity" and had taken a man hostage until "they could find his son," who they charged had "taken their property." Two days later she noted that this "band had captured [the son] yesterday and compelled him to make restitution." She did not indicate whether the son paid the "Tories" for their loss or whether they took it out of his hide.[123] A Confederate senator from Texas attempting to make his way through Alabama to Mexico later wrote of similar unrest in Randolph County. Unionist guerrillas made a retaliatory raid, burning the courthouse, jail, and several private houses in Wedowee on the night he stayed nearby.[124]

Radical sentiments also found expression even in the plantation counties. A Union army surgeon at the post in Selma wrote that paroled Confederate soldiers returning to the Talladega region were "breathing vengeance against the 'bombproof'" and were "openly defiant to what they themselves called the 'd____d old secesh,' robbing them of mules, cattle and provisions, and with quivering lips telling me all the long catalogue of wrong and outrage of the last four years. Several murders had already occurred, and many more have since happened. They that took the sword have fallen by the sword. Last Saturday two wealthy and prominent citizens were hung, and the gang have announced a 'proscribed list' of six others. Understand," he concluded, "this is not guerrilla warfare—it is Corsican vendetta. I can and do go freely through all the country without danger. But the rich cannot."[125] Similarly, a correspondent to the *Montgomery Mail* reported that "scarcely a decent house in middle Alabama" had avoided the work of looters, "from the finger ring to the household provisions."[126] In Montgomery, Ellen Blue wrote that her father had received word that his brother "was coming down here with his family, and I know it must be for protection. There are reports of a terrible state of affairs in Macon Co.—bush whacking, promiscuous killing, retaliation, etc."[127]

In addition to all of these disincentives to Confederate soldiers returning to their homes, Lincoln's murder assured that notions of mass disenfranchisement and black suffrage had their powerful supporters in the North.[128] In early May, Benjamin Butler had given a widely reported speech at the Loyal League Club in New York City in which he pointed to the "success of the bold original action of President Johnson in bringing Tennessee, as a loyal State, into the Union, by the votes of those only who had ever remained loyal, in heart, and rejecting all those who had participated in the rebellion." To Butler, limiting the right to vote in this fashion was "the key to the whole difficulty." He also advocated that any person who had held "military, civil or diplomatic office, under the so-called Confederate States, or either of them, or been any agent thereof during the rebellion, should have no political rights in the State, but should be and remain alien thereto forever."[129] He was all for including the freedmen in the class of those sharing political rights, later declaring in a speech in Boston that although he admitted their "want of intelligence and cultivation," they knew enough to be right during the war and "to be loyal; and that is a great deal more than his master did."[130]

But Mary Jane Chadick of Huntsville noted a fearful consequence of the "vindictive spirit at Washington now operating against the unfortunate people of the South." She warned that Northerners "had better take the advice of such men as Gen. Lee, who tells them 'unless they pursue a mild, generous policy toward the South, the war is not at an end!' "[131] Kate Cumming in Mobile made similar comments in her diary. Referring to reports of President Johnson's pledge to an Indiana delegation to punish traitors, she wrote that "it seems to have struck dismay to many a heart, and if he carries out what he says in it, I am confident the war is not over yet." She had "watched the countenances of some men, who I have been told never favored the war or secession, and I think they expressed a determination that, if there should be another war, they would assist in it, heart and soul."[132]

Andrew Johnson realized the existence of this sentiment. On May 12 and 13, Confederate forces had fought a Union army force at the Battle of Palmetto Ranch in Texas near the Rio Grande, the border with Maximilian's Mexico.[133] A few days before that battle, one of the die-hard Confederate soldiers stationed there had written his sister that "Andy Johnson calls for blood" and predicted that under Johnson "we are to be animals, slaves of our own slaves." Confederate soldiers would not be allowed to vote, he continued, and "blacks would elect other blacks to hold office." There was, he concluded, "nothing left to us but to fight."[134] And fight they had, *defeating* the Union force—with the aid of French volunteers.[135]

The nation was graphically reminded that continuing hostilities also remained a real possibility east of the Mississippi River by a shocking incident that occurred in Mobile, Alabama, on May 25.[136] According to Southern news accounts, five white employees of the Union Ordnance Department, along with thirty black Union soldiers and others, had been at work at a large ammunition depot in a downtown Mobile warehouse on the corner of Lipscomb and Commerce Streets. The ordnance—which consisted of, among other things, two hundred tons of ammunition, including thirty tons of gun powder—was a portion of that recently surrendered by General Taylor at Gainesville, Alabama.[137] A huge explosion occurred, creating what the horrified local newspaper editor then at work at his desk colorfully described as a shock that "made the city tremble like an aspen, shaking every building to its foundation." The crash of broken glass, he wrote, "was heard in every direction, and falling walls made the earth resound like the rumbling of an earth quake."[138] Another survivor, a Union soldier apparently somewhat further away, reported hearing "a deadened sound, like the distant report of a heavy gun, and was remarking upon it to a comrade, at the same time looking to the northeast, when the crash came like the concentration of a hundred thunderbolts, and up before my astonished vision rose that vast and rapidly spreading 'pillar of cloud and fire' combined, while prominent in the fearful gloom sprang yelping shell, bursting bombs and flame-streaming cartridges, with the rushing of a mighty wind and sound as of many waters, razing massive structures to the earth, while showers of flying missiles made one feel that *Lucifer* had again declared war with Michael and the hosts of Heaven, and was opening a 'masked battery,' or that a volcanic eruption like to that of Vesuvius of old, which entombed Pompeii and Herculaneum, had burst forth in our midst."[139]

The sound of the blast was heard one hundred miles away and the blast radius was huge. It totally destroyed eight nearby blocks of buildings, as well as several ships at the nearby wharf, and killed hundreds of civilians, Union soldiers, and recently paroled Confederates, burying many of them in the ruins. In the efforts to recover the living and the dead, thousands of responders were forced to contend with not only burning buildings but exploding shells, shrapnel, and bullets that "whistled through the air." Many of the bodies recovered were said to be "so burned and mutilated that recognition is impossible" and some were "so blackened that it was with difficulty their friends and relatives could identify them even when not disfigured by mutilation."[140]

Initial public speculation (as well as that of some historians) was that this tragic incident was caused by one of the workmen accidentally dropping a "percussion" shell.[141] But General Canby was suspicious and appointed a court of inquiry to attempt to determine the true cause. The *New Orleans Times* then electrified the nation when it reported that a man named John Jackson Wall had confessed to being part of a demolition team led by a "rebel major" who on the night before the explosion had "placed torpedoes between the buildings containing powder." According to Wall, "the major afterward lighted a [long] fuse of a shell connected with the infernal arrangement." It was also discovered that the US Customs House, another symbol of federal authority, had been booby trapped. "Torpedoes have also been discovered in the rooms of the Custom House," reported the *New York Times*, "so arranged as to explode on opening the doors. Others have been found concealed in desks in the same building."[142]

From this it appeared evident to some in the North that the fighting spirit of Loyal Confederates was still alive in Alabama and elsewhere. As a shocked Ohio editor put it in an editorial he titled "Diabolical," the "fiendish spirit which actuated the rebel leaders in inaugurating the rebellion, led them to starve and practice inhuman barbarities upon helpless prisoners in their hands, and to assassinate our beloved President, still continues to show itself as the war draws to a close."[143] To Union military officials, it must have been particularly disturbing that the Mobile terrorists did not consider federal troops to be out-of-bounds in their efforts to resist possible radical changes in Alabama's political and social framework, despite the devastating effect it would have on the state's ability to attract badly needed capital. More basically, the incident in Mobile indicated to some that the war might not actually be over after all, or even if that war was, another might suddenly explode on the war-weary North and the nearly bankrupt federal government in the not too distant future. Indeed, some in the North would soon be fearfully referring to the "next war."[144]

But the nation could not afford war with anyone. In response to continuing, repeated entreaties from General Grant for authorization to forcibly oust the French from Mexico, Johnson's cabinet members responded with an emphatic "No!" Secretary of the Navy Gideon Welles wrote that Secretary of the Treasury Hugh McCullough "at once declared that the Treasury and the country could not stand this nor meet the exigency which another war would produce."[145] Even Confederate leaders recognized the absence of a war option for Johnson's administration.[146]

Given these factors, what was the appropriate reconstruction policy to be pursued by the federal government? Should the radical program be followed? Should members of the Confederate military above a certain rank be banished and their property confiscated for their treason? Would that make the lingering threat from Mexico worse? Should each of the leading civilian officials of the Confederacy be tried and executed? If not, and all were allowed to remain, should their civil and political rights be terminated? Would this increase the risk of guerrilla warfare? Was it safe to press the issue of black suffrage or white disenfranchisement, or was it too dangerous not to?

As events of the coming years would reveal, despite Lincoln's murder and subsequent incidents like this in Mobile, Northerners were actually not a monolithic unit on these particular issues.[147] And like Lincoln, Johnson could see logical reasons to avoid a punitive policy despite his preassassination stance. Once the mantle of leadership was passed to him and he had to walk in Lincoln's shoes, he quite naturally followed Lincoln's path. For this he would soon be praised by Alabama Confederates but reviled by Radical Republicans and many future historians.

13
The Liberator

On May 29, 1865, four days after the blast in Mobile, President Johnson caused a figurative explosion when he issued two proclamations initiating what would later be called Presidential Reconstruction.[1] One provided amnesty from federal prosecution to most—but not all—former Confederates. Fourteen classes of individuals were excepted, including several categories of Confederate and state officials, as well as "all persons who have voluntarily participated in [the] rebellion, and whose estimated value is over $20,000." Some saw the property restriction as unnecessarily punitive, but even those subject to the exceptions could apply to Johnson for a special pardon.[2]

The other proclamation issued that day provided the framework for the restoration of North Carolina. Among other things, it contained an appointment of a wartime peace advocate as provisional governor and authorized him to appoint interim state and local officials and call for the election of delegates to a convention to rewrite the state's constitution.[3] Rather than leaving it to the provisional governor to decide whether the freedmen could vote, however, Johnson's proclamation provided that the electorate was restricted to those "who *are loyal* to the United States, and no other," who had taken the oath prescribed in Johnson's amnesty proclamation, and who met the legal qualifications to vote in force in the state "*prior to* secession." This, of course, necessarily excluded blacks from the election of delegates.[4]

It is submitted here that, for reasons of national security arising from the presence of the French and Confederates in Mexico, Johnson never revealed his true motivation for not granting limited suffrage rights to blacks.[5] Expressing fear of Napoleon would have been unwise. Thus, when a Frenchman questioned William Seward regarding the failure to grant suffrage rights, Seward made no mention of challenges south of the Rio Grande. He instead explained it in constitutional terms.[6] Johnson, likewise, publicly maintained that secession was illegal and a nullity and that Tennessee, Alabama, and the other Southern states had, therefore, never legally left the Union or lost their existence or rights. Under the constitution, the right to determine who could vote and who could not was held by the state and not by the federal government.[7] Several Northern editors, including that of the *New York Times*, agreed with Johnson on this point.[8] So did Northern Democrats and most white Alabamians. Joshua Burns Moore expressed great pleasure that "Johnson wisely takes ground in favor of states rights." Moore declared that it was "all nonsense to talk about equalizing a negro with a white man, and I am glad Johnson has the boldness to stem this torrent of fanaticism, and lay down the broad doctrine, that the states are to settle it for themselves."[9]

Unbeknownst to the general public, Johnson had done more than that. Rather than drawing only from white troops then stationed in the Deep South to man an occupation force in Texas, his administration had sent tens of thousands of black soldiers there from as far away as Virginia, as well as many from Alabama. In fact, black troops there outnumbered white troops by three to one. As one historian has noted, the failure to muster out the black troops permitted the government to maintain control over them while reducing tensions with white Southerners.[10] This deployment put the black troops that much closer to the Isthmus of Panama, where Gen. Daniel Sickles was still attempting to negotiate a deal for land.[11] And even if those negotiations did not bear fruit, the black soldiers could be permanently deployed in Mexico—as Johnson had earlier envisioned—if Juarez failed to oust Maximilian and the French and an invasion were necessary.[12] This was also consistent with, and perhaps a product of, the recommendations of racial conservatives in the North, such as Montgomery Blair, who saw Central America as a reservation for America's black population.[13] With word of Sickles's mission by now in the press, it is not surprising that many black soldiers expressed bitter opposition to being transferred to Texas.[14]

Anticipating Johnson's announcement, a Pennsylvania editor gave fair warning that Southrons had best "profit by this forbearance and clemency" and use the opportunity to work to return to prosperity. "An abuse of the kindness," he declared, "would ensure the severest visitations of justice."[15] But by his apparent kindness Johnson did himself no favors. Indeed, in retrospect, Johnson's failure to disenfranchise a sufficient number of former Confederates and enfranchise at least those freedmen whom Lincoln had personally preferred to have the right to vote—"the very intelligent and those who served our cause as soldiers"—would be his undoing as well as that of the antebellum notion of broad state sovereignty. All it would now take to incite Congress to trespass on that sovereignty was for former Confederates to give evidence of continuing disloyalty, such as dealing unfairly with the freed-men or white Unionists or committing other such acts. Johnson's failure to take action about that might also lead to his impeachment.[16]

On May 30, J. J. Giers wrote to Johnson warning that "the rebels have sud-denly faced about, and making up inactivity and shrewdness what they want in loyalty, no doubt hope to regain by the ballot box, what they have lost by the cartridge box."[17] The only chance to avoid that scenario in Alabama was for Johnson to appoint a provisional governor who would perform the tasks Johnson chose to avoid. That governor could be the fire wall to this outcome through his power to issue regulations further restricting the electorate. If, as in Tennessee, that power were exercised to exclude the disloyal from the elec-torate voting on the delegates to a constitutional convention, that convention could, in turn, adopt constitutional provisions imposing temporary or per-manent restrictions on the right to vote. Providing for limited black suffrage was also a theoretical possibility.

On the other hand, if the white electorate were not restricted by the provi-sional governor, those white people in states like Alabama who had remained loyal throughout the war could be outvoted in the election for delegates to the constitutional convention and could not hope to have constitutional re-strictions on the electorate imposed. As a consequence, they would be forced to either live under the rule of their wartime enemies, a fate to which they were adamantly opposed,[18] or as some were already predicting, push for black suffrage of a broader sort in order to bolster their voting strength.[19] Thus, for Alabamians of all stripes, the key was who Johnson would appoint if, as ex-pected, he chose to apply the North Carolina blueprint to Alabama.

In early June, Johnson began a series of meetings about that topic with the recently arrived interest groups of Alabamians in Washington, DC. All of the details of these discussions are not known, but according to several ac-counts, Johnson immediately rejected the idea of the wartime Alabama legis-lature convening to begin the reconstruction process. He, in fact, was report-edly "emphatic in the declaration that a delegation from any organization in the state of Alabama, in any way connected with the old order of things, during the period of the rebellion, could not be recognized by the execu-tive, nor any propositions for restoration, from such party or organization, be for a moment entertained."[20]

The response of the group to these comments is unknown, but over the next hour and a half they must have been very convincing regarding their wartime loyalty. They may have also emphasized the importance of eco-nomic prosperity to the success of reconstruction and the necessity of involv-ing influential businessmen, planters, and especially railroad promoters in the

Figure 21. Lewis Parsons. Alabama Department of Archives and History.

process of rebuilding and regenerating Alabama's economy. It is also possible they raised the threat posed by the Radical Republicans to Johnson's chances of election to a full term in 1868 and may have stressed that his continued opposition to black suffrage would allow them to marshal support for him in Alabama and elsewhere in the South, thereby foiling the radicals.

Johnson must have been impressed because at the conclusion of the meeting he reportedly suggested that the group "consult together and propose or recommend such persons from among the friends of the National Government in Alabama, any one of whom might be acceptable for the appointment of provisional governor, to guide him in the appointment of such officer."[21] Over the next several days this process boiled down to two candidates, Lewis Parsons (fig. 21) and William Hugh Smith. Given Johnson's choice as Alabama's US district attorney, former Selma lawyer James Quinton Smith, some might have assumed that William Hugh Smith was a prohibitive favorite.[22] James Quinton Smith had been imprisoned by Confederates during the war and, like William Hugh Smith, been forced to seek exile outside Alabama.[23] Both Smiths (they were not related) had good reason to deal sternly with Confederates and to protect Unionists. In this same class of Johnson's early Alabama appointees was former Selma newspaper editor John Hardy, who Johnson appointed to be Alabama's US marshal. Hardy, who had been the target of William Yancey's retaliatory prosecutions for criminal libel in the months leading up to Alabama's secession, also ultimately left the state.[24]

Johnson's appointment of Andrew Jackson Hamilton as Texas's provisional governor on June 17 was consistent with these appointments. Hamilton, a native of Huntsville, Alabama, who had emigrated to Texas during the antebellum period, had been an outspoken Unionist who was forced during the war to seek exile. President Lincoln appointed him to the rank of brigadier general and he organized a Union cavalry regiment that saw action in Texas.[25] Hamilton, as his course in Texas would demonstrate, harbored great animosity toward secessionists and would vigorously oppose their resumption of political control.[26]

William Hugh Smith was cut from this same cloth. And as Alabama Unionists like Daniel Havens Bingham correctly pointed out, Lewis Parsons had not experienced the same degree of oppression as Smith and others during the war. Rather than seeking exile or fighting for the Union, Parsons had chosen to remain in Alabama and serve in the legislature, which meant he had sworn an oath to support the Confederate government.[27] Thus, from the standpoint of public perception and President Andrew Johnson's political future, William Hugh Smith was arguably the clear choice for the post of provisional governor of Alabama. Many Alabama Unionists were among those taken by surprise when rumors began to surface in the press that Parsons would receive the appointment. Even after that appointment was made on June 21, several interposed protests and attempted to convince Johnson to withdraw his decision.[28]

Parsons's commitment to the Confederate cause had never been strong; he had even been a leader of the proslavery faction of the wartime peace movement. But Alabama Confederates saw him as at worst the lesser of two evils. As the editor of the *Mobile News* observed, "the late rebels [were] satisfied that he would not malignantly pursue or sacrifice them."[29] In other words, Parsons was no Brownlow and this may have been the decisive factor in Johnson's mind.[30] When it appeared that Johnson might have been reconsidering Parsons's appointment, and Parsons did not immediately return to Alabama, the proelite members of the Alabama press began to express a degree of anxiety.[31] But Johnson finally decided to leave Parsons in the saddle and in his proclamation appointing Parsons gave him the same broad powers and authority the provisional governor of North Carolina had received.[32]

The Black Belt press in Alabama praised Parsons's appointment.[33] The *New York Times*, the *New York Tribune*, and many other Northern newspapers also endorsed Johnson's choice.[34] But Johnson's tack was not so well-received by others in the North. On the contrary, support for Congress taking control of the reconstruction process was growing. At a rally at Faneuil Hall in Boston, resolutions were adopted expressing the importance of performing the task of reconstruction "well" rather than "quickly," that "no one in the South be allowed to vote who are not loyal and that none should be excluded from voting because of their race or color."[35]

Although the protests of Alabama Unionists and Northern supporters of black suffrage at this point were probably not a product of concerted action, it must have begun to become evident to both groups that, with the appointment of Parsons, their interests were becoming aligned. Moreover, as former Confederates began to assert themselves rather than leave the country, a coalition of these two groups and increasingly disillusioned Northerners was seemingly inevitable.[36]

Johnson might have been able to undermine the formation of such a coalition and avoid the backlash that General Sherman had already experienced by delaying the process of pardoning Confederates. A person who was excepted from amnesty was not only subject to federal prosecution for treason but could not vote or hold political office without first receiving a pardon. Thus, Johnson's amnesty proclamation had the initial effect of temporarily disenfranchising an indeterminable amount of the white electorate in Alabama. Another effect of being excluded from amnesty was that, unless pardoned, a Confederate's property was potentially subject to seizure under federal confiscation laws adopted during the war.[37]

As a consequence, some Confederates sought exile overseas, and this process of expatriation under duress was strongly encouraged by some Southern Unionists.[38] It was during this period that entrepreneurs began advertising in the Alabama press for settlers to migrate to Brazil.[39] Some others chose a different means of escape from life's new set of tribulations. For example, less than a month after Johnson issued his proclamation, Virginia archsecessionist Edmund G. Ruffin Sr., who was said to have fired the first shot at Fort Sumter in 1861, garnered national attention when he committed suicide at the home of his son near Danville, Virginia. According to a Richmond newspaper, Ruffin left a suicide note stating "that he could not live under the Government of the United States—that he preferred death to doing so."[40] Ruffin was not the only one.[41] Joshua Burns Moore wrote that a man who had been "in low spirits since the war" cut his own throat with a pocket knife "near the carroted [sic] artery, completely separating the windpipe."[42]

But the problem with delaying the pardon process was that the Confederate leadership might continue to opt for going to Mexico. Most recently, Gen. Kirby Smith had formally surrendered his scattered army on June 2, but after Johnson's proclamation he and others had crossed the Rio Grande and joined Confederates already there. More were on the way.[43] The *Selma Times* published a letter to an Alabamian from Cadmus Wilcox, one of Lee's generals, explaining his response to Johnson's amnesty proclamation. "On the 15th of June I saw Johnson's proclamation, and left the next day for [Mexico City], reaching here July 16th. I left with many regrets, but my sister was entirely willing, rather than have me stay and beg Andy's pardon, for having done only what I felt to be my duty, and what I have never felt any compunctions of conscience for doing."[44]

Would these military leaders play the pied piper and draw the amnestied rank and file Confederate soldiers to them? The French certainly hoped so.[45] Johnson was apparently unwilling to take that chance. He began issuing pardons even before his provisional governors had had the opportunity to call for the election of delegates to constitutional conventions.[46] His apparently liberal policy was destined to get him even deeper in hot political water. "The executive has in too many instances used the pardoning power for the enlargement of men who should either have been kept in duress, or hanged higher than Hicks the pirate," complained one irate, classically educated Northerner. His response to pardon applications from Southerners would be very different. "I would say, in the language of the great dramatist, 'A halter pardon them, and hell gnaw their bones.'"[47]

The fact that some prominent Alabamians had neither been amnestied nor pardoned did not preclude them from quietly using their influence behind the scenes and working through others in order to achieve political goals. For example, as would be the case throughout the Reconstruction era, Governor Watts's fingerprints were all over the strategy of elites, beginning with the aforementioned launch of the delegation sent to Washington, DC, to meet with Johnson regarding the implementation of a restoration plan for Alabama. Former military leaders, such as the still-recuperating James Holt Clanton, also retained considerable influence over men who had served within their commands during the war. Unless Parsons did the unexpected, virtually all Confederate soldiers below the rank of colonel would be allowed to vote.[48]

Johnson had taken a huge political risk when he attempted to execute Lincoln's reconstruction policies even after the toxic uproar in the North over Lincoln's assassination. By ignoring demands by a vocal, growing minority of Northerners for black suffrage in the South and appointing planter-lawyer-politician Parsons as Alabama's provisional governor, Johnson became the target of intense criticism.[49] As John Forsyth accurately observed, Johnson was in "danger of being left without support to his administration in the legislative branch of the Government. We have seen what it is for a President to be Tylerized. It is a position full of difficulty and official embarrassment."[50]

By incurring this risk, Johnson had ironically earned the right to be considered the best friend the Alabama planter class had in the federal government.[51] In a letter to Johnson, one Alabamian who was a supporter of Parsons paid Johnson the ultimate compliment by comparing Johnson to an iconic Tennessee figure. He praised Johnson for having "as much of the nerve of Andrew Jackson in your composition, as any man I ever knew, and your course, as far as it has unfolded itself is making you scores of friends."[52] John Forsyth agreed and predicted that Johnson would "deserve the title of 'Liberator'"[53]

By contrast, the type of common man who had supported Jackson was becoming increasingly disillusioned as Johnson's surprisingly conciliatory plan unfolded. Even in Tennessee, where most of the white population appreciated Johnson's stance on black suffrage, his approval rating among Unionists had plummeted. A resolution in the Tennessee House of Representatives supportive of Johnson's reconstruction policies was tabled on a vote of 39 ayes to 23 nays.[54] In order to avoid being "Tylerized" on a national basis, Johnson needed Alabama and the rest of the South to respond in a respectful manner and one that would not be seen as offensive to the still-grieving North. There would be no tolerance for acts of disloyalty or oppression toward Unionists or black people. Would or could the South oblige?

14
"A Radically, Sickly, Deathly Change"

I know that the men who are guilty of these proceedings felt, as they
fought against the government, that if they were defeated they lost
everything, and that even their lives were forfeited to the national
authority. They would have been grateful last May to be permitted to
exist. Now a little kindness has revived the tiger-appetite, and they will
fight for everything they went to war to win.

—A very eminent rebel

A review of the Northern press during this period indicates that the South
was on probation and under intense scrutiny. Was a truly loyal New South
emerging, or were the South's occasional professions of loyal sentiment merely
a subterfuge, cloaking a reemergence of the slaveocracy planter class that
would again become a dangerous political force once the South resumed its
original position in Congress and the national electorate? And once restored
to political equality with the North, would Southerners again disrupt the
Union and bring on a second civil war if they did not get their way?[1]

If a majority of Northerners were convinced of the South's sincerity, it
is at least possible that Johnson's plan of restoration might have succeeded
even without a grant of political rights to the freed slaves.[2] But the fact that
no Southern state had voluntarily surrendered, and that the North had been
forced to conquer a peace only a few months earlier, was persuasive evidence
to some of lingering Confederate nationalism, as was Lincoln's assassination
after Lee's surrender, which was still influencing Northern public opinion
even after the execution of several of the assassination conspirators.[3] Loyalty, not merely human rights, was the key, and Alabamians would be judged
by their actions.[4] Fortunately for those consistent Unionists in Alabama who
were already concerned about the direction of Johnson's policies, as well as
for Northern proponents of equal rights who saw black suffrage as the only
long-term, permanent solution to the loyalty problem, those policies had given
Alabamians broad latitude on a wide variety of issues that confronted them
and with regard to which they could give evidence of what was actually in
their hearts. And Northern correspondents were present in Alabama as well
as other Southern states to report as well as interpret events for their curious
and increasingly dubious readers.[5]

"A Radically, Sickly, Deathly Change" / 169

As would be demonstrated over and over again in the coming decades, however, magnanimity and mercy from the federal government was seen by a certain segment of Confederates as a sign of weakness that encouraged contemptuousness and arrogance to replace fears for their personal safety and property. As E. W. Peck later observed, "it seemed to me that they then discovered that there was a door open by which they could again acquire power; and they immediately changed their feelings, their conversation, and their course of conduct."[6] Other Alabamians noted this same reaction.[7]

Violence and terrorism were a part of that conduct. Part of the motivation was revenge. A South Carolina diarist noted widespread recrimination over the South's defeat and predicament. There was, she wrote, "such a hue and cry, everybody blamed somebody else." But she disagreed with only part of that sentiment. "I cry: Blame every man who stayed at home and did not fight."[8] Consistent with this, a subordinate reported to General Granger in Huntsville, Alabama, that "organized parties of marauders" were "operating in Winston, Walker and other counties of North Alabama, burning houses, murdering Union men, &c."[9] The Tuscumbia *North Alabamian* confirmed this, reporting that "bushwacking and robbing are prevalent in the mountains between Tuscumbia and Tuscaloosa."[10] A Black Belt Unionist, Anthony Dillard, complained to President Johnson that the "secessionists are very strong here, & are still disposed to run over the Union men." They were, he continued, even boasting that "so soon as the federal soldiers leave, they will kill the Union men."[11]

The freedmen in the South were also the victims of violence.[12] Reports of murders, maiming, assaults, and the burning of homes and churches were regular staples in the Northern press.[13] One black victim in south Alabama who had had his ears cut off said that the two former Confederate soldiers who did it claimed that "five thousand of them had formed a clan" to kill black people "without detection."[14] A shocked correspondent in south Alabama reported to a Washington, DC, newspaper that "to kill a 'nigger' is nothing more than to kill a pig. It is an everyday occurrence here, even by boys."[15] A Washington County resident wrote to Governor Parsons that many of the perpetrators were young, former Confederate soldiers who were "taking out their anger on the 'damned' nigger." This type of violence against the black population would continue for decades.[16]

Some Northerners seeking to settle in Alabama were subjected to discrimination in business and social relations, thereby frustrating efforts to attract critically important capital and skilled labor to Alabama. Among other things, some planters who were fearful that these newcomers might also bring with them threatening social, political, and economic ideas—especially in terms of the freed slaves—refused to sell them land.[17] A New Yorker wrote to Parsons that "the impression" existed in the minds of many "European & Northern men of the U.S. that the Southern people do not desire the settlement among them of persons from the non-slave holding states."[18]

Influential Confederates were, meanwhile, resuming their positions in Alabama society. Episcopal bishop Richard Wilmer issued a pastoral letter to the clergy and laity of the Diocese of Alabama that shockingly prohibited the use of a passage in the standard, prewar liturgical prayer for the "President of the United States and all in civil authority." Wilmer claimed that this passage somehow implied a desire for "a long continuance of military rule."[19] At least on the surface, Wilmer's very controversial stance in this regard was senseless. The president for whom Wilmer forbade prayer was the very person who was attempting to institute conservative civil governments in the South as soon as possible and certainly before Congress convened and tried to stop him. Johnson, therefore, arguably deserved Southern prayers more than anyone else. The military commander in Alabama ultimately became so fed up with Wilmer's refusal to revoke his pastoral letter that he created a national sensation by suspending Wilmer and all of the Episcopal rectors in Alabama from conducting religious services. According to the order, which was later withdrawn, Wilmer's stance demonstrated "a factious and disloyal spirit, and is a marked insult to every loyal citizen within the Department."[20]

The voices of Confederate wartime Alabama editors were also beginning to again be heard as they resumed their positions at their presses and attempted to shape public opinion. Among those was the fanatical founder just a few short months earlier of the Society of Loyal Confederates, John Forsyth.[21] The pro-Union editor of the *Mobile News* warned that the "old wireworkers have already arranged who are to go to the [constitutional] convention to be called, who are to fill every office to be recreated or restored, [and] how Governor Parsons' administration is to be swayed and controlled in their interest."[22] For good reason, conservative Republicans in the North would place much blame on the Southern press for the North's perception of the mental state of Southerners.[23]

Confederates had little to fear from Governor Parsons. Thomas Peters would later write to Thaddeus Stevens that Parsons "professes loyalty & practices anything else" and thought it "his highest honor to act as the tool of the Secessionists."[24] In Parsons's very first proclamation he figuratively bent over backwards to conciliate them. The "appeal to arms," Parsons declared, "has been made and decided against *us*, but not until our sons and brothers had exhibited a degree of courage and endurance which commands the respect and admiration of the world." Nothing was said by Parsons about the bravery of their foes or Alabama Unionists. Parsons also did not condemn the secession leaders or the act of secession, much less assert that it was unconstitutional or even a bad idea. Instead, he merely allowed that the "right of secession for the purpose of establishing a separate Confederacy, based on the idea of African slavery, has been fully and effectually tried, and is a failure."[25]

For many Alabama Unionists these comments went too far. The editor of the *Mobile News* was struck by Parsons's reference to the bravery of Confederate soldiers and the war having been decided against "us." Such expressions, he wrote, "are quite out of place in the commencement of a 'Proclamation' of a Governor pretending to be loyal to that Government against which those persons were fighting, whom, he says, have challenged 'the respect and admiration of the world.'"[26] Parsons's remarks in this regard also raised the eyebrows of Northerners. One editor noted that Parsons "becomes slightly confused in the use of pronouns." He added that it "should not be a matter of surprise . . . that a man so recently heartily aiding rebellion was not so far metamorphosed instantly by a federal appointment as not to occasionally speak of the rebellion, as *his* side of the contest."[27]

Further evidence in support of this conclusion came very quickly when Parsons addressed the issue of who would man state and local offices in Alabama during the tenure of his provisional government.[28] Like most Northerners, consistent Unionists in Alabama believed that secession had been illegal and that, as a result, the wartime government was illegal and wartime public officials ought to be removed. But Parsons created an uproar when he took the position of Confederates and announced that he would leave most local officials in office.[29] "Causidicus," an anonymous correspondent to the *Huntsville Advocate*, may have spoken for many Unionists when he wrote that the "wholesale appointment of the *de facto* State officials of Alabama is surely not the first step to take in building up and consolidating a party in the state honestly desirous of restoring the State to her federal duties, and binding her heart to the Union—the Arc of her salvation." "Secession and treason," he declared, "cannot be rendered odious by continuing their favorites in the offices which were earned by their zeal for the rebellion, and their avowed hatred of the federal Union." Such men, he concluded, "are not the proper agents to be employed in rekindling the fires of patriotism in the hearts of the people."[30]

To an Alabama correspondent of the *New York Herald*, the vocal support of Confederates for Parsons's decision was quite revealing. The "lion's skin was stripped completely off the ass," he wrote. He warned that "it is evident that a change—a radically, sickly, deathly change—has come o'er the spirit of the dreams of the people in the South." At one time, he recalled, they were pleading for mercy, but now they "demand their rights." The cause of this change in attitude, he averred, was that they had returned "like the sow to her wallow, and the politicians who led them into the rebellion are leading them today into anarchy and misrule, as sure as the earth revolves around the sun."[31]

Parsons also sometimes appointed Confederates to political office in lieu of qualified Unionists. When, for example, the mayor of Mobile, Robert L. Slough, resigned his office in protest over a federal military requirement that allowed black people to testify in municipal court proceedings over which he presided, Parsons passed over local Unionists to select John Forsyth—of all people—to replace him.[32] President Johnson was concerned about the direction of events in Alabama, and he sent Parsons a telegram trying to find out what was going on. Parsons's reply did not defend the wholesale reappointment of local officials that had the most direct contact with the citizenry except to say that he had reserved the right to "remove [officials] for disloyalty or other good cause." But Parsons also admitted that only a few such holdovers had been removed. He further claimed that in cases of special appointments— probate judges, sheriffs, circuit court judges, and other "higher officers of the County & State"—"union men have received preference in every instance, where one reasonably qualified would accept the office."[33] This was not totally true,[34] yet Johnson made no effort to redirect Parsons, much less remove him.[35]

Parsons then issued a proclamation that facilitated the pardon of Confederates who were not entitled to amnesty, thereby making some of them eligible to vote and serve as delegates to the constitutional convention. By this point, Johnson had established a system whereby the governor and attorney general of each Southern state would first receive applications for pardon and then make a recommendation to him, which he generally followed. Parsons declared that applicants were to answer a series of questions that would identify them as original secessionists, early warmongers, or wartime persecutors of Unionists.[36] The implication was that those who did not fit in these categories would receive his blessing, but even original secessionists began receiving pardons.[37] Forsyth, among others, praised Parsons for establishing a system whereby those seeking a pardon could receive it "with as little delay as possible."[38] Very quickly, according to Josiah Gorgas, the capitol in Montgomery "was filled with people seeking to see the Governor, chiefly on matters of 'pardon.'" Some elites wanted to speed up the process even further. Parsons's secretary of state, William Garrett, to whom Parsons had delegated the task of processing pardon applications, was willing to do so—allegedly for a price. Johnson's already-criticized policy for liberality in pardons was dealt another major black eye when Garrett was accused of accepting bribes and forced to resign.[39]

Perhaps the only thing Johnson did that had the potential for limiting the ability of elites to control the constitutional convention actually further revealed their continuing sentiment toward the perpetuity of slavery. Those who were amnestied or pardoned were required to appear before Union army officers to not only demonstrate their loyalty but also to take an oath, which required them to pledge their loyalty to the nation and to swear that they would abide by the Emancipation Proclamation. Submitting in this fashion to former enemies was difficult enough for some Confederates.[40] But giving the oath was particularly distasteful for members of the planter class who still clung to notions of gradual emancipation or at least compensated emancipation. Some refused to register to vote.[41] Others who were opposed to emancipation registered but did not vote in the election of delegates. A correspondent from a Southern newspaper observed that people in Selma "seemed to care but little whether they get back into the Union or not, and a great many seem to prefer the present state of affairs to a re-establishment of a State Government, and a return to the Union."[42]

But others feared that delegates infected with Brownlowism—what the *Montgomery Weekly Advertiser* would later call "agrarian Radicalism"[43]—might otherwise dominate the convention, and so they urged all to register and vote. Forsyth instructed that it was the duty of every man "to qualify himself as a voter under the proclamation of the President, and when election day comes, to cast his vote intelligently and conscientiously for members of the Convention." There were enough "good citizens" qualified to vote, Forsyth assured, "to control the election and thus secure the right sort of Constitution for the State." Above all, Alabamians could not "permit the State to pass into the hands of weak and unprincipled men, who may make shipwreck of all that is dear to us as a people." And whether the new state government the people instituted "shall be liberal, wise and conservative, or whether it shall be narrow, radical and burdensome," Forsyth concluded, "will depend upon the sort of men we send to represent us in that body."[44]

Some of the issues important to Forsyth and others like him were also of critical importance to Northerners who questioned the sincerity of the South's expressions of resumed loyalty. How the South responded would, in essence, serve as a litmus test on the validity and effectiveness of Johnson's plan of restoration. One critically important issue was the fate of Alabama's $16 million war debt.[45] If the delegates decided to pay that debt, wrote the editor of the *Washington* (DC) *Chronicle*, it would be seen in the North as a "fresh act of hostility to the United States Government."[46] Joseph C. Bradley reported to Johnson there was a faction in Alabama who wanted to do just that.[47] An Alexandria, Alabama, man wrote to Parsons that some in his region "seem to be willing to *fight* again if the state refuses to pay their "[John] Gill Shorter Treasury notes."[48] But to men like Forsyth, payment of the war debt was a solemn matter of "honor and plighted faith," and repudiation would not only financially ruin the creditors (many of whom were located in Mobile) but also harm the state's credit in foreign and domestic capital markets.[49] *Huntsville Advocate* editor William Bibb Figures, a wartime Unionist, aware of this sentiment, urged all Unionists to step forward and deny control of the state to south Alabama economic elites, who held most of this debt. He reminded his readers how the "money power" had "seized the reins of government, usurped power and wielded it to the loss of the liberties of the people" in 1861 and warned them that "in the very act of restoration" the money power was "again trying to steal from the many for the benefit of the few."[50] The war debt, wrote Figures, was not a legitimate obligation of the people and instead was a product of the "bastard secession State Government created to aid in overthrowing the United States." Besides, he added with a populist flair, the debt was "held mainly by money corporations, speculators, blockade runners, capitalists, those in and out of the State who have made money out of the war, etc., who now want to tax the people to make their investments good!"[51]

The economic and social addiction to slavery was also very difficult for some to overcome. There were worrisome signs that the slaveocracy, which was blamed by many Northerners and Alabama Unionists for having orchestrated secession and which created that debt and killed the President, was attempting to resurrect itself. A Calhoun County man wrote to Parsons that extremists there were "still confident that the U.S. will have a fight with England & France in Mexico and long for an opportunity to be revenged." Barring that, he continued, "they are confident . . . the former owners of slaves will be compensated or that they will have forty years to emancipate the slaves."[52]

This confidence was based on constitutional arguments and an expected alliance with Northern Democrats. One mutual goal was to have the Emancipation Proclamation rendered unconstitutional,[53] making slavery still a lawful institution.[54] If the US Supreme Court upheld the constitutionality of the Emancipation Proclamation, some former slave owners nonetheless believed that by joining forces with Northern Democrats, they might be successful in asserting claims for millions of dollars of compensation. These claims would be based on the "takings" clause of the US Constitution, which requires the federal government to pay just compensation for the taking by it of private "property" without the consent of the owner.[55] Significantly, however, if the state of Alabama, rather than the federal government, committed the "taking" by outlawing slavery, then any claim for compensation would be against the state. That was not a promising alternative because the state was flat broke, with a grand total of $532.39 of specie on deposit.[56] Therefore, these slave owners were very opposed to any act by the constitutional convention or subsequent legislatures that might jeopardize such a claim for compensation, such as the adoption of an ordinance abolishing slavery, or even the ratification of the federal Thirteenth Amendment.[57] According to Joseph C. Bradley's report to President Johnson, the former secessionists would even go so far as to oppose the action of the convention "being submitted to the people for their ratification—or rejection—because they do not want the amendment to the Constitution of the U[nited] States agitated, which will surely be done & the Legislature instructed to vote for it, if the *laboring classes* have a chance to act."[58]

Class-based animosity toward the planter element was certainly made more acute by some of the impassioned rhetoric it used. Elites unabashedly confirmed the true reason why the "laboring classes" had been forced to sacrifice so heavily over the last four years. "If that convention should abolish [slavery]," pled the editor of the *Mobile Tribune*, "it will be ignoring the war, which was, in some measure, made for its defense. It will do more—insult the memory of the dead who fought so bravely, but vainly, in its defense." The editor reminded his readers that "we owe something to the dead." Therefore, he concluded, the "citizen of the South who would tread without reverence on the grave of a Confederate soldier has no manhood."[59]

The freedmen knew what was in store for them if and when slavery was abolished, but without the right to vote, they could do little about it. Regardless of whether Unionists or Confederates prevailed, the black population and their Northern sympathizers knew that discriminatory black codes were going to be adopted. This was seemingly the fervent hope of most of the Black Belt planter class.[60] And some north Alabama Unionist planters were of the same mind. Shortly before the election, a correspondent for the *New York Times* reported that he had overheard a prominent Huntsville Unionist remark that "'these niggahs won't work. We have to pass State laws to force them to work.'" "Coming from such a source," the correspondent concluded, "I recognize it as a very important assertion, as evidencing the animus of the reconstruction (or office-taking) loyalty and Unionism of the South."[61]

All Alabama freedmen could do was hope that this new form of slavery would be averted by federal intervention. Those who could read or were learning to read were likely aware of newspaper reports in the Alabama press of promising comments made at Fourth of July celebrations in the North. Speeches were made by some members of Congress pledging to reverse the trend of events by denying admission of Southern representatives and senators to Congress until their state governments enfranchised the former slaves.[62] This stance appears to have had increasingly strong support among a segment of the Northern populace.[63] The author of a letter to the editor of the *New York Times* claimed that the "great body of the people are quite willing the rebel States should be reconstructed in ten years, and they are not willing that they should return with the whole political force of ten States thrown not only against the Administration, but against freedom, humanity, and civilization; in one word, to undo, if they can, all that four years of bloody and successful war has accomplished."[64]

Secretary of State Seward, by now having recovered sufficiently from his wounds to resume his duties, wrote to the American consul in France that two "parties are organizing here for ulterior political action. It is unmistakeable," he continued, "that immediate enforcement of negro suffrage upon the states which rebelled by the conquering loyal states is to be the platform of one. Decided and minatory action towards France in regard to Mexico another."[65]

Northern Democrats, sensing an opportunity to divide their opponents using race as a wedge issue and at the same time reclaim their traditional support among Southern voters, rallied to support Johnson on his restoration policy and his refusal to impose black suffrage.[66] Their burning desire to finally regain the White House and political hegemony would not only encourage Johnson to stay the course but would also inspire and encourage the ugly, violent, race politics in the South for which the region would ultimately become infamous. Forsyth had already begun channeling Democratic Party propaganda to his readers, beginning with a reminder of what he called "the favorite thought and political postulate of the late [Illinois senator and Democrat] Stephen A. Douglas, that 'THIS IS A WHITE MAN'S GOVERNMENT.'" He went on to warn that the nation's "days as a Republic are finished whenever the stream of influence and power, flowing from the masses through the ballot box, is poisoned by the confluence with the ignorance, idiosyncrasies and alienism of the African blood."[67]

As part of his standard propaganda portfolio during the war, Forsyth had repeatedly predicted that Northern Democrats in the Midwest would rise in revolt against the East over efforts to fight the war to end slavery instead of merely to save the Union.[68] He now assured his readers that Northern Democrats would come to the South's rescue if Northern Republicans attempted to impose black suffrage. If those "Radicals" did not cease their agitation for goals separate from reunion, he warned, "it takes no prophet to foretell that future civil war is in store for this land, and that when it begins again, it will not be a sectional conflict, but one that will be waged in the name of eternal justice, and will spread from the Penobscot to the Rio Grande."[69]

In sum, evidence available to the North seemed to strongly indicate that sentiment in Alabama and elsewhere in the South had changed for the worse since the surrender of the Confederate armies. But there were no scientific polling results available to confirm this. The only thing close would be the election of delegates to the Southern constitutional conventions and the votes of the delegates on the critical issues. Would the results confirm or assuage Northern concerns?

15
"The Rump of the Confederacy"

The North was watching very closely. An influential Pennsylvania congressman, William Darrah Kelley, expressed the concerns of many Northerners regarding the social and political trends in the South and their potential effects on the nation as a whole. "It is of primary importance to the country," he wrote, "that the people of the North and their representatives, in whom, as belligerent conquerors, the Government of the whole country is for the time being vested, shall understand the purposes and temper of the vanquished before our military power be withdrawn from the conquered territory and its people admitted to a potential voice in the common Government."[1]

This caution was arguably justified. It had been only a few months earlier that war was raging and fanatics had murdered the nation's president. Events had demonstrated that hate and disloyalty followed the surrender of the Confederate armies and that a significant threat of a renewal of hostilities still existed by virtue of the presence of many Confederate leaders south of the Rio Grande. The Northern press reported that a Confederate general, Sterling Price of Missouri, had been appointed a "Major-General in Maximilian's service, and empowered to raise a cavalry force of 30,000 from among the men of the disbanded Southern armies."[2] If a disloyal element were admitted into Congress, according to Kelley, they could "filibuster away a whole session" and thereby block legislation "necessary for the nation's health."[3]

This possibility was adding even more fuel to the fires of black suffrage. "Public opinion is rapidly ripening," wrote a group of Bostonians to President Johnson. Justice demanded that suffrage rights be accorded to the freedmen and so did the nation's security. "In the conflicts which threaten us we shall need their ballots quite as much as we needed their bullets in the conflicts of war."[4] There was another benefit to delaying reconstruction: it might give Northern public opinion more time to ripen. But were the ballots of the freedmen necessary to maintain national security? That was the question.

What was the temperature of Alabama Confederates on Election Day? Josiah Gorgas was among those full of bitterness. "This is the bitter end of four years of toil & sacrifices," he wrote. "What an end to our great hopes! Is it possible that we were wrong? Is it right after all that one set of men can force their opinion on another set? It seems so, & that self government is a mockery before the almighty. *He* permits it or refuses it as seems good to him." But Gorgas, who was trying to begin an iron-making business in Alabama for which he would need Northern capital, was also pragmatic. "Let us bow in submission," he concluded, "& learn to curb our bitter thoughts."[5]

Historian John Witherspoon DuBose wrote that "the election of August 3 transpired in quiet."[6] This, too, is inaccurate. Some Alabamians simply could not contain their animosity. In Greensboro, two former Confederate soldiers shot two Union soldiers, killing one from Illinois and wounding another.[7] As historian G. Ward Hubbs observes, the shooting "was as much a political statement protesting the new government as retribution against rude bullies."[8] Front pages of Northern newspapers were also marred by reports of an attack made by the sheriff of Cherokee County and his posse on a squad of Union soldiers that resulted in the death of one of the soldiers and the wounding of another.[9] Then came news of the murder of a US Treasury agent in Selma.[10]

Other events were also worrisome. White Alabamians did not march to the polls en masse and vote for Unionist candidates. Only slightly fewer than fifty-seven thousand Alabamians had registered to vote, and of that number fewer than thirty thousand cast their ballots.[11] Although apathy was not necessarily the main reason for this low turnout, the turnout was not interpreted as a promising sign in the North, which did not want the product of the convention to be repudiated later as having been the work of a minority.[12]

The results of the election were also disconcerting.[13] Joseph C. Bradley's report to Governor Parsons from north Alabama in the aftermath of the election was not reassuring. "You can not comprehend our condition up here," Bradley wrote. "The fire" of secessionism "is not all out." Secessionists were threatening Union men with harm once federal occupation troops were removed, and Confederate veterans "are just as hostile in feeling as ever." One of C. C. Clay's brothers, J. Withers Clay, who had been the fanatical editor of the wartime *Huntsville Confederate*, was suspected of being the "editor in disguise" of the *Huntsville Independent* newspaper, which Bradley called a "Copperhead Sheet." Most recently, John Drake, whom Bradley described as having been "Crazy for Disunion" and "no friend of President Johnson," had been elected from Madison County over the Unionist candidate, David

Campbell Humphreys. "We are in a bad fix," Bradley concluded, and "the election of Drake shows it."[14]

One of the bitter fruits of these trends would soon manifest itself in the critically important capital markets of the Northeast. John Whiting, a Montgomery businessman who was there seeking to borrow money on behalf of the state of Alabama, wrote to Parsons from New York City of his relative lack of success. He had obtained loans for the state "on many previous occasions," without significant problems, but was now encountering unprecedented "difficulties in negotiation." From this it was evident that lenders had little confidence in the viability of the government President Johnson had orchestrated in Alabama.[15]

The day before the Alabama convention was scheduled to meet, Levi Lawler, an Alabamian who was in Washington, DC, seeking a pardon, wrote to Parsons describing the "delicate" political situation there. Although Lawler believed Johnson's policies were still favorable to the South and that conservative Northerners supported him, "the radical Republicans are for blood & confiscation. The issue [between them] is gradually being made up & will soon assume a tangible form." Lawler warned that "if the policy of President Johnson is defeated, I see no hope for us. With confiscation & negro equality death would be a blessing." For this reason, Lawler sincerely hoped that "our convention will act with the utmost prudence and wisdom." Otherwise, a "false step might produce disastrous consequences." Lawler was particularly concerned about how the delegates would approach the issue of slavery. "It is idle to hope that slavery can, under any circumstances, be restored. It & the Confederacy have gone down together, never to be resurrected. Now," he concluded, "it behooves us to endeavor to save what is left" and "do nothing which will weaken [Johnson] in his efforts to benefit us."[16]

A south Alabama editor expressed these same concerns in an editorial titled "Look before You Leap." It was, he wrote, "vastly important" that "as far as allowed to act," Alabamians "act with wisdom, discretion and judgment." He observed that some Northerners "manifest a willingness to stop our punishment where it now rests, and not grind down as does the other class, seeking to crush the whites and give up the country to the negroes." Therefore, he urged, "let the accusation that there is still a purpose on the part of the South to be refractory, and not to perform her duty be hushed." Above all else, he advised, avoid anything that might support the impression that Johnson and Northern Democrats were "endeavoring to introduce States into the Union whose citizens are not to be trusted."[17]

The concerns of Alabama moderates were justified. Planters made up the largest class of delegates (eighty-three of ninety-nine),[18] meaning that there would be strong allegiance to the ways and means of the antebellum paradigm that had served planters so well. Proof of this came quickly when Madison County's John Drake reiterated his opposition to the ratification of the Thirteenth Amendment. The shocked editor of the *Nashville Union* declared "woe unto ye, Alabamians, if it follows the advise of such men as this General Drake!"[19]

Not all delegates were so impractical. Former US senator Benjamin Fitzpatrick, a prewar Democratic Party moderate who had never publicly supported the Confederate war effort, was unanimously elected president of the convention when it convened on September 12 in Montgomery.[20] But as Northerners noted, Fitzpatrick was no unconditional Unionist. He had publicly advised Alabamians to secede in 1861 and then walked out of Congress. And despite this, Johnson had pardoned Fitzpatrick, with whom he had served in the US Senate, and thereby put him in position to be elected as a delegate to the convention from Autauga County.[21] Fitzpatrick was, nonetheless, a good choice to preside over this group of men.

Joshua Burns Moore, who had been elected over an original secessionist from Franklin County, wrote that the "convention is a body of very moderate men, in point of ability—but a few of real ability—a good many chuckle heads so far as I can judge them."[22] Moore may have been referring to some who were not in touch with reality. A Mobile correspondent reported at the outset of the proceedings that "I have already discovered great diversity of views and opinions on the vital questions to be acted on by the Convention" and that there was a possibility this would "lead to extended and, I fear, excited debates in the Convention."[23] His fears were well-founded. Several members of the Northern press were there as witnesses and to report to their skeptical readers back home.[24] They would not have to wait long for disturbing news.

On September 15, the delegates took a test vote on an issue of great importance to the North and to many of Alabama's wartime Unionists: the repudiation of the state's war debt.[25] Repudiation lost at this point by a vote of 58–34.[26] "To us," wrote the shocked editor of the *New York Tribune*, "this debt is an abomination."[27] The editor of the equally influential Washington, DC, *National Republican* agreed, adding that "that Convention is badly in need of a Cromwell. It is manifestly the Rump of the Confederacy."[28] A Nashville editor was similarly incensed and not a little stunned. "This is incomprehensible. Is it possible that the Alabama Convention does not know that the repudiation of the 'Confederate States debt' is not an open question? They have no control over it. If they do not repudiate it, as the Tennessee Convention did, Congress will repudiate for them, in very decided terms."[29]

The day after the repudiation test vote open conflict began over the burning issues of slavery and secession.[30] Lawyer and Confederate diehard Alexander White of Talladega became a lightning rod for criticism and ridicule when he led efforts to have the convention forego the passage of an ordinance declaring the abolition of slavery in Alabama.[31] The debate over the secession ordinance ostensibly revolved around whether it should simply be declared null and void or whether—as Unionists asserted—it should also be condemned as illegal.[32]

While those issues were being debated over the next several days, a new issue was imprudently raised. As reported in the Northern press, a delegate had the audacity to offer a resolution calling for the appointment of a committee to procure the delegates' signatures for a petition for the pardon of Jefferson Davis, which was to be forwarded to President Johnson.[33] Not only was this topic far outside the expectations of Johnson but when seventy-nine delegates signed the petition it seemed to demonstrate widespread Confederate tendencies and further embarrass Johnson.[34]

Johnson did not follow Oliver Cromwell's example and issue an order proroguing the convention. That might have undermined his entire restoration policy and given fresh impetus to the exodus of Confederates to Mexico. The *New York Journal* had recently reported on the "arrival in Mexico City of large numbers of Confederate officers."[35] But Johnson did opt to play a more subtle form of hardball to nudge the delegates in the right direction. Alarmed Alabamians in Washington, DC, including Leroy Pope Walker, wrote to Parsons and Benjamin Fitzpatrick that Johnson was adamant that the convention properly address the key issues. Otherwise, "he neither has the power nor the wish to restore us."[36] In addition, Daniel Pratt, an Autauga County industrialist who was in Washington, DC, attempting to obtain a pardon, telegraphed Fitzpatrick on September 21 warning that "the reports from the Alabama Convention have not made a favorable impression here" and that the "pardon of Alabamians has been stopped."[37] US district attorney James Quinton Smith and US marshal John Hardy were, meanwhile, unleashed to initiate confiscation proceedings against those elites who had not yet been pardoned.[38] Elites caught in the middle of this vise could also expect indictments for treason.[39]

Johnson's heavy-handed strategy worked. Over the next several days, the key issues of slavery, secession, and the war debt were resolved.[40] Pratt then received his pardon, and Johnson ordered the cessation of all confiscation actions.[41] Seward blissfully wrote that "our system of reduction of men and expense, and of restoration of order and harmony seems to be succeeding very well."[42] But the public relations damage had already been done; in the eyes of many Northerners, Alabama had done only most of what it was forced to do and no more.[43] As one editor noted, the "spirit in which the act has been performed" was "quite as important as the act itself, for the real question to be settled when the States present themselves to Congress as petitioners for admission to the House and Senate, is whether they come with loyalty in their hearts as well as loyalty on their lips."[44]

And once again, the issue of loyalty implicated and gave more force to the argument for black suffrage.[45] So did the manner in which the convention addressed the issue of black rights—or failed to address it.[46] Historian John Witherspoon DuBose inaccurately claims that the "freedmen under the new state constitution possessed every civil right enjoyed by white minors and white women."[47] The convention had, not surprisingly, tabled a petition submitted by black residents in Mobile praying for the right of suffrage and all other rights and immunities of citizenship.[48] But despite urging from Johnson and Parsons,[49] the convention did not enact any ordinance whatsoever guaranteeing any civil rights to the black population, instead punting that task to the next Alabama legislature.[50] And in the same ordinance in which the destruction of slavery was acknowledged, it was made the duty of the legislature to adopt not only laws that would protect the freedmen with regard to their "rights of persons and property" but to "guard them and the State against any evils that may arise from their sudden emancipation."[51] A concerned Wisconsin editor wrote that Northerners were "curious to know what evils this convention apprehends from sudden emancipation, and how they propose to guard against them." It was understood that most white Alabamians would never see black suffrage rights as a remedy for the consequences of freedom. Instead, it was suspected that restrictions, rather than rights, would more likely be the order of the day.[52]

Historian W. E. B. Du Bois posed a critically important counterfactual in his classic work *Black Reconstruction in America*. Suppose, he wrote, a Southern state had granted black people conditional suffrage, that is, "with a high property qualification, or the ability to read and write, or service in the army, or all these." Du Bois was sure—that "there cannot be the slightest doubt"— that "such a program" would have changed history. It would, he continues, have "gathered enough support in the North to have made the history of Reconstruction not easy and without difficulty [for the black population], but far less difficult than it proved to be." But, Du Bois astutely concluded, the white South at this time was lacking in "far-seeing leadership" and "even some common sense."[53] In the long term, this would prove to be another boon to the freedmen.

Even the positive actions the Alabama convention reluctantly took were placed in jeopardy by the fact that the delegates did not adjourn sine die. Instead they adopted a resolution of adjournment providing that the president of the convention could call the delegates together again at any point on or before September 24, 1866.[54] Was this a means to allow for the adoption of additional measures deemed necessary to gain admission into Congress, or was it to allow for the repeal of what had been wrought if admission were denied?

Parsons compounded Alabama's image problem by, at the request of the convention, reinstituting the prewar state militia system that had produced many of the companies that formed the early regiments of the Confederate army.[55] And on September 30, the day the convention adjourned, a resolution was adopted requesting Johnson to withdraw all federal occupation troops from the state.[56]

Despite all of this, Johnson sent a telegram to Parsons approving the delegates' work. "The proceedings of the convention," Johnson declared, "has [sic] met the highest expectations of *all* who desire the restoration of the Union." It will "result as I believe in a decided success."[57] This was wishful thinking of the highest order.

The pro–black suffrage *New York Independent* was delighted with the animus on display during the Alabama constitutional convention. "The Alabama State Convention has adjourned. Better for President Johnson's plans had it never met!," wrote its editor. The whites, he continued, "are still at heart the same enemies of liberty as during the rebellion; the blacks are still the only trustworthy basis of loyalty in seven states." And he hoped that would continue to be the case because it would ultimately undermine the president's plan. "So let [the South] for a while be arrogant, defiant, disloyal, impertinent—the worse, the better! 'Give more madness, Lord!' "[58]

The *New York Times*, which was still generally supportive of Johnson's plan of restoration, had hoped that any issues of loyalty might be put to rest by Alabama voters ratifying the constitutional ordinances reluctantly adopted by the convention. "The moral effect of an overwhelming popular majority," wrote its editor, "would be exceedingly valuable." Among other things, it would "add much to the faith of the North in the reality of the wonderful change of Southern conviction and feeling which many can scarcely credit. It would have its weight, too, we believe, with Congress, and facilitate the readmission of Southern representation. Such an attestation of loyalty, rolling upon Congress like an oceanic surge, would leave little disposition to stand out on minor details."[59] But there would be no such surge to sweep away Northern concerns; a majority of the Alabama delegates had voted against

"The Rump of the Confederacy" / 185

conducting this plebiscite.[60] To House Speaker Schuyler Colfax of Indiana, it raised the specter of the ordinances being later revoked.[61] And others, including an editor in Maine, were sure that the "reptile of secession was only scotched, not killed." The "only security," therefore, was for Congress to "give every loyal man the full influence of his ballot against the still disloyal and discontented aristocrats of the South."[62]

The *New York Times* still disagreed. The freedmen were simply too ignorant to be accorded the right to vote. And besides, it maintained, Alabama's legislature would, by its actions, demonstrate that the state was both loyal and willing to execute federal policy by doing justice to "that race whom circumstances have made the wards of the government." Its editor confidently predicted that the legislature to be elected would make "a clean sweep of the old black codes, . . . giving to the blacks substantially the same equality with the white men before the law that prevails in the Northern States."[63] Would that happen or would there be more madness?

Black Alabamians likely assumed the latter, but they also may have recognized that this might be a blessing in disguise. And some had been organizing for the future. They had begun with peaceful, nonthreatening Fourth of July celebrations and a conciliatory barbecue in honor of Governor Parsons later that month.[64] In the fall, eyebrows in white communities were raised when some black church members began leaving white churches and associating themselves with the African Methodist Episcopal Conference.[65] Then political activists that the white press was darkly calling "black agitators" were brought to public attention as potential provocateurs of black unrest and racial violence.[66] This all incited fears in the white community that the failure of the Alabama constitutional convention to guarantee any rights whatsoever to the black population would bring on a revolt.[67] News of a bloody race riot in Jamaica made those fears even more acute.[68] But fear did not translate into conciliation. Instead, it engendered only threats of retaliation. "If to avoid both work and want," wrote John Forsyth, black people chose to "follow the Jamaica example, he only hastens his exit, for then the sword comes in to expedite the work of disease and famine."[69] With militia units forming around the state, that was no idle threat.

These sentiments only made Radical Republicans more determined. Horace Greeley, in an editorial in his *New York Tribune*, warned that "the rebels will not concede one jot or tittle toward reconstructing a Union that does not eternize slavery and strengthen the power of the slaveholders." These "gentlemen of the South mean to win," he asserted. "They meant it in 1861 when they opened fire on Sumter. They meant it in 1865 when they sent a bullet through the brain of Abraham Lincoln. They mean it now. The moment we remove the iron hand from the Rebels' throats they will rise and attempt mastery. . . . Therefore, we not only break faith with the negro, but with the true Union men—with those who went into the caves with Andrew Johnson, and with him suffered for their principles. The first fruits of reconstruction promise a more deplorable harvest, and the sooner we gather the tares, plow the ground again and sow new seed, the better."[70]

16
"The South As It Is"

You may talk of peace with the Yankee
But never of friendship or love;
Were it so, the souls of our brothers
Would upbraid you from Heaven above
You may talk of peace with the Yankee,
For Heaven hath mercy and rods;
But not where slumbers our young chivalry,
The untomb'd demi-gods!
You may talk of peace with the Yankee,
But never of friendship or love;
Will you beg the roused lion for pity?
The kite for protection, O dove?
O dove! Oh don't!

—Anonymous

Despite all of the troubling evidence of seemingly reluctant, merely pragmatic loyalty emanating from Alabama and the rest of the former Confederate states, some political pundits in the North still predicted that Congress
would admit loyal Southern representatives when it convened in December
1865 even though no Southern state had provided for black suffrage in their
constitutional conventions. All that would be necessary, it was said, was that
the Southern states elect congressmen and senators who could take the requisite federal test oath of wartime loyalty and that their newly elected legislatures ratify the Thirteenth Amendment and enact laws protecting the freedmen in their civil—not political—rights.[1]

One of the main reasons for optimism by racial conservatives throughout the nation was the result of a referendum in Connecticut on October 2.
The Connecticut legislature had earlier unanimously ratified the Thirteenth
Amendment, but a majority of the electorate voted against a state constitutional amendment giving black citizens in that state the right to vote.[2] It was
assumed, based on this, that because black suffrage was supposedly unpopular in most of the North, the North would not impose it on the South.[3]
Given this, a Washington, DC, correspondent wrote that the South had "the

game . . . in its own hands."[4] Abolitionist Wendell Phillips sadly conceded as much in a series of speeches in the Northeast titled "The South Victorious."[5]

If the South, in fact, had "the game" in its own hands, it could also fumble it away. Alabamians knew this. They recognized they would soon be given an opportunity to demonstrate to Congress what an anonymous correspondent to the *Huntsville Advocate*, who called himself "Madison," called "our *positive* (and not white washed) loyalty" in the upcoming state and congressional elections.[6] Madison warned Alabamians that if they elected former Confederates, it would constitute a "positive avowal on our part of decided hostility to the Government of the United States." In that case, Alabama's representatives would be denied admission to Congress and black suffrage might, in time, be imposed as punishment.[7] A correspondent to the *Montgomery Mail* agreed. "Civis" wrote that "it is simply a question of representation or not, and that means a question between remaining under military rule, with its Freedmen's Bureau and other accompaniments, or returning to our old status."[8]

It is debatable whether, by its actions over the past year, the South had any chance of avoiding that negative fate regardless of the wartime loyalty of its elected representatives. But if the year 1865 in Alabama is indicative of anything, it is that too many of Alabama's political leaders were either blind or deliberately indifferent to the consequences of their actions. One possible outcome was staring Alabama elites in the face. The militant populism that was part and parcel of William Brownlow's Tennessee had become increasingly violent and bloody. A conservative Nashville editor charged that Brownlow, whom he called a ruffian, a blackguard, a bully, and a poltroon, had created a "social hell" for Confederates grounded in his "hatred of rebels."[9] It was being reported in Alabama that Tennessee Confederates there were "frequently robbed, tied up to trees and cruelly whipped, burned out of their houses, and often murdered, without the slightest attempt on the part of the authorities to punish or put a stop to these inhuman outrages."[10] In an editorial titled "The Civil War in Tennessee," a Mobile editor accused Brownlow of encouraging violence and declared that "so long as this wild man is allowed to add to his own pernicious personal influence the prestige of almost unlimited official power, Tennessee will acquire for demoniac and sanguinary political rancor, a celebrity yet unattained by any country."[11] Reports would soon reach Alabama that Brownlow was vowing to support black suffrage if necessary to prevent Confederates from retaking political control of the state.[12]

If Presidential Reconstruction failed and Congress imposed its own plan, did Tennessee's condition presage Alabama's? Any rational person had to consider that a real possibility. The same is true with regard to another threat, this one made by Pennsylvania congressman Thaddeus Stevens. As reported in the Alabama press, Stevens advocated the confiscation of the property of "every rebel belligerent whose estate was worth $10,000, or whose land exceeded two hundred acres in quantity." Then the government would divide the land into forty-acre plots and sell them to the highest bidders. The proceeds of those sales would be used to pay for the pensions of Union soldiers, wartime damage done to the property of loyal men, and the national debt.[13]

Despite these grim possibilities, however, too many Confederates insisted on pointless resistance—what was called "kicking against the pricks."[14] Why? One major reason was that Northern Democrats were encouraging resistance and adamantly opposed to imposing black suffrage on the South.[15] "True, in the late war," wrote the editor of a Democratic Party organ in Illinois, "the negroes were the friends of the north and were loyal. So is my dog loyal. Is he, therefore, to vote?"[16] And Northern Democrats assured Southerners that the Republican Party was "fast undergoing the process of disintegration" and that not even a rejection of the Thirteenth Amendment would constitute a bar to the admission of Southern representatives to Congress.[17] Mobile novelist and Confederate propagandist Augusta Jane Evans wrote to J. L. M. Curry that when she traveled to New York with her brother, who was seeking medical care for his war wounds, she was told by Democratic Party leaders that the "entire west will repudiate the radical policy, unite with the South, and elect the next president." Democrat Benjamin Wood, the publisher of the *New York News*, assured her that the " 'balance of power will return to the hands of the South' and urged me to tell our people so."[18]

Evans did not fully accept this, but these messages resonated strongly with other former Confederates in Alabama. Democratic Party stalwart John Forsyth opened the ball on October 17 with an editorial attacking the congressional test oath that threatened to block Confederate Southerners from partnering with Northern Democrats in Congress. It "absolutely excludes from participation in the federal Government every man, with rare exceptions, who is worthy to take part in its administration." It was, he wrote, "a bar to the restoration of the Government of the Union." Taking his cue from Northern Democrats, Forsyth misadvised Alabamians to elect only men who could *not* take the oath. This would, Democrats maintained, force the Radical Republicans to reject them, thereby sparking a power struggle between them and the Northern conservatives.[19]

Some Southerners openly disagreed with this strategy. A Mobile newspaper published an editorial by a Virginia editor declaring that Northern radicals would be "overjoyed" if the "people of the South, smitten with judicial blindness, should send up to Congress as their representatives, the men who are most obnoxious and least likely to secure admission. It would be playing into their hands exactly."[20] But Alabama's political leadership ignored this warning.

Among the many Confederates who were boldly, recklessly coming forward to help produce the showdown men like Forsyth and Northern Democrats sought was C. C. Langdon, a Mobile newspaperman who had advocated the use of black flag tactics during the war and was very fortunate he had not so far been prosecuted for treason.[21] Candidates who could wore their dedication to the Confederacy as a badge of honor. One secessionist published a card in a newspaper proudly declaring that "I believed in the sovereignty of the States as taught by Jefferson and his illustrious compeers, and when the measure of our injuries was full, I followed the standard of my native state, and, along with you, fought to the last in support of the principles we cherished."[22] Some candidates also campaigned against Unionist candidates by expressly accusing them of having been traitors to the Confederacy during the war.[23]

Each of the three candidates for governor of Alabama, Robert Miller Patton, William Russell Smith, and Michael Jefferson Bulger, had supported the Confederacy to various degrees, although each now couched it in terms of having supported their state.[24] None were infected with Brownlowism, but the *Montgomery Advertiser* was taking no chances; it was backing the most conservative, eventual winner Robert Miller Patton. Among other things, Patton was absolutely opposed to black suffrage. The *Advertiser*'s editor also described Patton as having "no word of reproach for those [secessionists] who risked their reputations and their lives in the struggle they believed just and necessary."[25]

Forsyth was, meanwhile, attempting to influence the legislative elections by encouraging opposition to ratification of the Thirteenth Amendment. He charged that the second section of that measure, which gave Congress enforcement authority, was "a cunning and covert attack of the Radicals upon the essence of the State Rights principle." In particular, he argued, it "clothes the federal Congress with power over the black code in the States" and "is a crooked by-path to federal intermeddling with local police jurisdiction" and the imposition of black suffrage. For these reasons, he urged, "let the people bear this 'Trojan horse' of an amendment in mind when they select their representatives to the Legislature. It is filled with armed danger to the State Rights citadel."[26] As he had hoped, this issue became a decisive bone of contention between several candidates for the legislature.[27]

The reaction in the North to these trends was swift. On October 24, a Montgomery correspondent to the *New York Times* telegraphed a very widely circulated article about events in Alabama, which the *Times* published under the title "The South As It Is." This disturbing exposé described central and south Alabama as having "little or no patriotism" and "but very little love for the United States Government." The correspondent referred to what he called the "blood-and-thunder crowd," who "wish the infernal niggers were all dead, and the d____d Yankees all in h__l." The "next class of disloyalists," he continued, "are the ministers, of the Gospel," and another "disloyal gang are the editors of newspapers."[28] Alabama, as it was, was not a picture of loyalty.

The day after the transmission of that damning article, the Associated Press reported that the clerk of the US House of Representatives had decided not to enter the names of Southern congressmen-to-be on the House's roll when it convened in December. It was also reported that a joint committee of both houses would, instead, be appointed to investigate and decide whether any Southern representative would be admitted.[29] A Pennsylvania editor, summarizing the trend of events in Alabama and the rest of the South, concluded that "instead of admitting the rebel States back into the Union they must be remitted to a territorial condition, until their people can be educated into a proper conception of their condition and duties."[30]

Alabama governor Parsons was, at the time, attempting to sell a $1.5-million bond issue for the state in the Northeast, the proceeds of which were to be used to purchase sustenance for starving north Alabamians and thereby avert a human disaster of major proportions. While at a meeting in Boston, however, Parsons encountered US senator Charles Sumner who reportedly expressed confidence to him that not "a dollar would be invested by New England in Alabama bonds, so long as that 'State' denied civil and political rights to nearly one-half of its population." Sumner had reviewed Alabama's recently enacted constitutional ordinances and concluded that any justice to the freedmen was "founded on sand" and, therefore, "without justice." "There was no security; and security was the first requisite for such negotiations."[31]

Even President Johnson was beginning to have second thoughts about his restoration policy. On November 1, his Nashville organ warned that it was "beginning to be thought that offers of amnesty must be withdrawn and martial law and military rule must be executed with additional rigor."[32] Johnson's relatively liberal policies had seemingly begun to undermine the Confederate threat in Mexico, thereby giving him more leeway to apply a firmer hand to the increasingly recalcitrant South,[33] but with Maximilian still ensconced in Mexico, Johnson did nothing but stay the course.[34]

Men like Forsyth encouraged Alabamians to remain resolute. "Let the Radicals crack their whip and keep the breach open," he wrote. "But let us send no Jerry Sneaks" or wimps to Congress "to creep in by the back windows."[35] To the chagrin of many Northerners, Alabamians relied on this advice when they went to the polls on November 6. The result of the election confirmed what many Northerners already believed and what Alabama Unionists had feared.[36]

The *Cleveland Leader* decried that the "result of the recent Alabama election for Governor, State Legislature and Members of Congress, as indicated by the returns so far received, tells the same story as that of all previous elections under the reconstruction experiment. The most ultra rebel ticket in the field is successful." This, according to the editor, demonstrated that the "South is as haughty and rebellious as ever."[37] Southern sources confirmed the rout of Unionist candidates. The Montgomery correspondent of the New Orleans *Picayune* reported that "the 'soldiers' ticket' carried everything before it," electing Confederate veterans to many offices, including seats in the legislature.[38] Joseph C. Bradley of Huntsville wrote to Johnson blaming Parsons. The first sentence in his letter said it all: "Politically our state has gone wild." The legislature, he continued, "will be composed 3/4 of officers & privates from the Confederate Army. Every Member of Congress elected Cannot take the oath of office."[39] And as William Bibb Figures of the *Huntsville Advocate* put it, "our elections are just what the Radicals want them to be and have strengthened most wonderfully the hands of Chase, Sumner, Greeley, & Co."[40]

In the congressional races, Confederate congressman Thomas Jefferson Foster defeated wartime Unionist Charles Christopher Sheats in northwest Alabama.[41] At the other end of the state, C. C. Langdon beat wartime Unionist Thomas M. Mathews of Cahaba.[42] Confederate general Cullen Battle of Macon County won in southeast Alabama, and George Charles Freeman, a Confederate major who had lost a leg during the war, prevailed in the Montgomery district.[43] Confederate Joseph W. Taylor of Greene County defeated wartime Unionist Columbus Lea in the Tuscaloosa district.[44] Burwell T. Pope of St. Clair County was the lone winner who even claimed he could honestly take the test oath.[45]

Particularly galling for Ohioans was the result of the election for sheriff in Madison County.[46] There the voters selected Confederate captain Frank Gurley, the guerrilla leader who had shot and killed Gen. Robert McCook of Ohio in 1862. Gurley had been captured in 1863, tried before a military commission, found guilty of murder, and sentenced to be hanged, but the Lincoln administration had decided to commute the sentence to a five-year prison term. Gurley was, however, later accidentally included among several Confederate soldiers who were exchanged. When the Confederate armies surrendered, Gurley took the amnesty oath and returned to Madison County, where he lived in obscurity. Now he had been elected the chief law enforcement officer of an Alabama county. There was some solace for Northerners in the fact that Gurley's election brought him back to the attention of military authorities once again, and he was rearrested.[47]

At the same time an ominous reaction was taking place in the North. As Alabamians would soon read, elections that occurred in several key Northern states on November 7 were swept by the Republican Party. There was now not a single Northern state controlled by the Democratic Party, and even New Jersey was lost by the Democrats for the first time in recent memory.[48] Shortly after these elections, a correspondent wrote to the *Nashville Union* that the South's "manifestations of bad faith had discouraged, if they have not wholly destroyed the belief that generous treatment of the rebellious sections was the best policy." The Northern elections, he continued, had conclusively proved that the "overwhelming majority of the people of this country are resolved that all the vestiges and seed of the late rebellion shall be forever destroyed."[49] A Pennsylvania editor concurred in this assessment of Northern public opinion. "The people of large faith begin to see that it is idle to expect grapes from thorns or to look for figs from thistles. A bad tree, it is now plain, cannot bring forth good fruit."[50] Another Pennsylvania editor was just as emphatic. The election returns in the South "show that the rebellion is not yet closed. The war of bullets and bayonets may be over, but the war of ballots has just begun. It is only a change of tactics. The rebellion still lives, breathes and acts."[51]

Some in the North naively assumed that the jarring results in the Northern elections would convince the South to change its course. "It is to be hoped," wrote one editor "that the recent elections will open the eyes of the South to the delusiveness of any hopes founded on the triumph of Northern Democracy."[52] Johnson's policy was at stake, and as a Nashville editor warned, "Congress will soon meet, and it may take the matter out of the hands of the President."[53] On the economic front, Alabama businessmen continued to experience problems raising investment capital in the North,[54] but this did not bring enough of Alabama's political leaders to their senses. John Forsyth, who coveted a seat in the US Senate, immediately renewed his suicidal editorial campaign opposing the ratification of the Thirteenth Amendment. Under no circumstances was Congress, through the second section of that provision, to be empowered to interfere with the "Black codes" to be enacted by the Southern legislatures, he maintained.[55]

The perceived necessity for exclusive control of black labor through those codes was made even more acute by the embryonic unionization of the freedmen over the last several months.[56] According to a Columbus, Georgia, newspaper, "a league or union has been organized among the Freedmen of Montgomery for the purpose of fixing the rate of wages."[57] Without slavery, the power of the state was essential to break such a union. South Carolina, in Northern eyes the bad boy of the South, had recently adopted laws mandating that black people work, establishing mandatory apprenticeships for black youths and providing stiff penalties for vagrancy.[58] Forsyth and others wanted Alabama to follow suit.[59]

They also wanted freedom from federal intervention. Since the constitutional convention, Parsons, who also wanted a seat in the US Senate, had traveled to Washington, DC, where he met with Johnson to discuss future policy. The details of those discussions are, with two exceptions, unknown. One of Parsons's goals was to convince Johnson to remove federal occupation troops from Alabama.[60] Parsons also reportedly urged Johnson to block any efforts to amend the legislation establishing the Freedmen's Bureau to extend its life beyond one year.[61] The bureau was still providing rations to poor white and black north Alabamians in order to save them from starvation, and Parsons knew that north Alabama would soon experience a famine.[62] But Parsons and other planters seemed willing to sacrifice the poor in favor of their own financial interests. With the welfare provided by the bureau taken out of the equation, the black population would be forced to work for their bread in order to live and do so on terms dictated by the planters, who were in the process of conspiring to fix labor rates at a meeting of the newly formed Alabama State Agricultural Society.[63]

What had Johnson demanded in return? When the Alabama legislature convened on November 20, and with the eyes of the nation watching,[64] Parsons urged the legislators to ratify the Thirteenth Amendment, refrain from enacting any "Black Code," and simply adopt a race-neutral vagrancy law similar to that in force in Massachusetts, which merely penalized those who were both "idle *and* disorderly."[65] Some in the Alabama press criticized Parsons for this.[66] But a few days later, the legislature elected Parsons and prewar Unionist George Smith Houston of Limestone County to the US Senate, thereby rejecting Forsyth's provocative bid.[67] Then, under pressure from President Johnson, and on the assumption that it was the final step to the admission of Parsons, Houston, and the Alabama congressmen-elect to their seats in Congress, the legislature bit the bullet and ratified the Thirteenth Amendment on Saturday, December 2.[68]

As previously discussed, that amendment did not merely purport to abolish slavery and "involuntary servitude, except as a punishment for crime whereof the party shall have been duly convicted."[69] Section two also granted Congress unprecedented authority to enact legislation affecting legal relations within the states. It provided that "Congress shall have power to enforce this article by appropriate legislation."[70] The Alabama legislature attempted to limit that authority. Its joint resolution of ratification contained a proviso of questionable validity stating that it was adopted "with the understanding that it does not confer upon Congress the power to legislate upon the political status of freedmen in this State."[71] This was seemingly an exercise in futility. The death of the doctrine of states' rights, as still-imprisoned C. C. Clay conceded in a letter to Johnson, "has been established in the court of last resort—the field of battle—& its judgment is conclusive & final."[72] A Mobile editor agreed that the doctrine was now "exploded." The right to enforce the abolition of slavery, he wrote, implied the power to enact legislation to extinguish "all distinctions, political and social," which implied the further power to grant the freedmen "the highest privileges granted by a State to any of its citizens, and therefore, that the electoral franchise is one of these rights."[73]

But legislators, who were fearful of such an expansive interpretation of Congress's enforcement authority under section two of the amendment, may have received confidence from a totally unexpected source, Alabama's US district judge Richard Busteed. After convening his court for the first time in Mobile, Busteed had ruled that Johnson's continued suspension of the right of habeas corpus was unconstitutional.[74] Following his arrival in Montgomery, Busteed had delighted Confederate members of the Alabama legal profession when he agreed to entertain oral argument on the constitutionality of the test oath as applied to attorneys seeking to practice in federal courts.[75] For this, the members of the bar threw Busteed a lavish party at Montgomery's Exchange Hotel where he reportedly expressed opinions on racial matters consistent with those of his hosts.[76] Busteed, who did strike down the attorney test oath a few days later, could seemingly be counted on to protect Alabama from the Radical Republicans.[77] John Forsyth praised Busteed as "one of those rare champions of truth in an epoch of darkness and error."[78]

Parsons's telegram of December 2 to Johnson announcing the ratification began with the sentence: "'Tis done." Parsons did not mention the limiting proviso, but his prudence in this regard was immaterial.[79] Historian John Witherspoon DuBose wrote that "despite the good faith of the State, the doors of both branches of the Congress were closed to her."[80] But this is yet another of his inaccuracies. The die had been cast before the Alabama legislature had met,[81] and Alabama and the rest of the South had only themselves to blame.[82] Speaker of the House Colfax, a moderate Republican, had made specific reference to the election results in Alabama when he announced in a speech on November 18 that the pace of reconstruction had been dangerously swift. "Let us make haste slowly," he declared, and reconstruct the government "on the basis of indisputable loyalty."[83]

On the night of Parsons's telegram to Johnson, the Republican members of Congress met in a caucus to finalize their plan for the coming session. They formally agreed to the creation of a joint committee of fifteen members, who would investigate the Southern states and determine whether any were entitled to representation. No deadline was placed for the completion of this investigation, and it was decided that until the committee finished and reported its results, no Southern representative would be admitted.[84] The process of implementing this plan began when Congress convened on Monday, December 4. Not a single representative from Alabama or any other state of the former Confederacy was admitted.[85] Soon the fifteen-man Joint Committee on Reconstruction would begin an investigation, whose length was open ended.[86]

The bitter reaction among elites in Alabama was predictable.[87] To the editor of the *Mobile Times*, it was all part of a plan set in motion by the Radical Republicans before the assassination of Lincoln. They had felt, he wrote, a "secret joy" at having been "ridded of a man whose heart was known to be opened to the nobler instincts and inspirations of mercy and forgiveness." Deceived by his successor, those radicals had since "united in a league of crime and treason" to nullify Johnson's plan of restoration.[88] Senator-elect George Smith Houston wrote to Parsons predicting the "radicals intend to pass all obnoxious acts that they want before they let the Southern members have seats." This strategy, Houston correctly surmised, would allow the radicals to override Johnson's vetoes.[89]

Forsyth's initial public reaction was, by contrast, more measured and calculating. After all of his obstructionist machinations, he had fully expected Congress to balk at admitting the Southern representatives. Now, he wrote, the "question will go before the great tribunal of the American people at the polls in 1868—the question of constitutional freedom or of Radical higher law diabolism."[90] He, meanwhile, called on Johnson to "lead and champion" the nation's "true men in the struggle for right and law."[91] But Forsyth soon sought to imitate William Yancey, a man he had despised five years earlier and still blamed for the South's postwar crisis.[92] He claimed that there had been an "implied pledge at least, that having done all this—abolished slavery, ratified the Constitutional amendment, and repudiated her war debt—the other States would receive her back, in full fellowship, into the family of the Union, and a general and generous amnesty would obliterate the sad past." Then ignoring the fact that any such agreement had been made only with Johnson, he charged that the "Radical Congress pocketed the consideration of the bargain, on one side, and refused to fulfill the conditions on the other." Now, he continued, the radicals had "come forward with a long list of new conditions, stipulations and constitutional amendments, which must be complied with before the country can have the Union." But, he declared, "*we have done enough*. We owe it to ourselves, to our honest compatriots of the North, to the name of *Americans*, to do no more."[93] The *Montgomery Advertiser* agreed.[94] Too many Alabamians would take their advice to heart.

So did some Tennesseans who had lived under the repression of Brownlow's regime. A few even decided to fight back. Several former Confederate soldiers who lived in Pulaski, Tennessee, a short distance from the Alabama-Tennessee border, formed the Ku Klux Klan in December 1865. It would soon prove that terror could be used as a substitute for official state action.[95]

That was not yet necessary in Alabama. Indeed, one silver lining in the dark cloud for former—and current—Confederates in Alabama was the illusion that, other than the diminishing federal military presence and the hopefully soon to be extinct Freedman's Bureau, they had no effective constraints on their actions.[96] And Alabama's government officials were still trying to have both removed.[97] Alabama Unionists had already been the targets of repression by Confederates, and this was increasing. A retired Union army captain complained to Governor Parsons that the grand jury in Lawrence County had only indicted Union men. "If this is justice," he concluded, "loyal men will have to leave the country."[98] Other Unionists implored Parsons to authorize the formation of militia units led by Union men. A group from Jackson County warned that unless this was done, "union men can not live here any longer."[99] Hundreds of wary north Alabama Unionists signed and sent to Washington, DC, a controversial petition describing their plight attempting to live under the state and local governments controlled by their wartime adversaries, protesting the formation of new state militia units controlled by Confederates, and opposing the withdrawal of federal troops. If this were allowed, they warned, Unionists would be forced to leave the state. Jean Joseph Giers undertook the task of delivering the petition to Washington, DC.[100]

If the environment in Alabama was hostile for Unionists, it was toxic for the freedmen. And it went far beyond petty discrimination, such as the refusal of service to black people—even black Union troops—at public houses and inns.[101] A correspondent in Mobile wrote that "troops will be an absolute necessity here and elsewhere in this country longer than you or I shall live, or the entire generation of freedmen will pass away before the ruthless persecutions of their late masters. It is something entirely unaccountable to me," he continued, "that this poor, unfortunate race of people should be so thoroughly *hated* and persecuted unto death by those who so recently professed such unbounded love for, and interest in, them."[102]

As before the war, designing politicians were using racial paranoia to encourage white solidarity and racial repression. James Holt Clanton, now recovered from his war wounds and practicing law in Montgomery, wrote to Parsons with apparently accurate information he had received that freedmen were secretly "drilling at night" at a "secluded spot in the woods" of majority-black Macon County. One of the militant black members, according to Clanton, predicted "there would be a war between the Southern Whites & Blacks next Christmas where there would be worse times for this country than it had ever seen."[103]

More than anything else, their masters wanted to again control them and give them no option but to work on the land on the planters' terms. The editor of the *Montgomery Ledger* wrote that "we admit the importance of getting squarely back into the Union," but it was more important to "put the negro to work, and keep him in his place, than to secure the boon of the Union. We can well afford to stay out of the Union for twelve months, if by so doing, we can make a crop next year."[104] But to make that crop the planters needed to control the black laborers by what historian Ken Noe calls "pseudo-slavery."[105] Not surprisingly, many black residents began leaving the state.[106]

Those who remained faced a state government that was being mobilized for their subjugation and to force them to labor.[107] They were not given the right to vote—even on a conditional basis.[108] The only rights they were granted by the Alabama legislature were illusory. They were, for example, afforded the right to sue and testify in state courts—essential to the enforcement of legal rights. But as one observer sarcastically noted, with a "white judge, white lawyers, [and] white juries," "much good will it doubtless do" the freedmen.[109] In other words, judges and jurors might receive black testimony in a trial, but they were not required to listen or give it any weight in making decisions. And given the legislative history of this measure, there was no guarantee it was free from later repeal. According to a correspondent for the *Mobile Advertiser and Register*, after the bill was introduced it had met with heavy resistance and "had to 'run the gauntlet' of two Committees of Conference, and an avalanche of fiery declaration." There was, he continued, "a party in the Legislature who are radically in favor of depriving the freedman of all rights of any kind whatever."[110]

Despite reservations by some about the timing, the Alabama legislature dug the state an even deeper hole from a perception standpoint before its holiday recess on December 15. The legislators enacted several coercive laws to regulate the freedmen, the most significant of which were those addressing the issue of labor.[111] A key component of this set of legislation amounted to a revision of preexisting law outlawing vagrancy. Historian John Witherspoon DuBose justified it by claiming that the revision "was modeled on the Massachusetts law," while conceding that "the vagrant contemplated was the plantation negro."[112] But Alabama's new vagrancy law bore no resemblance whatsoever to the Massachusetts vagrancy statute. The basic definition of "vagrant" in Alabama law had been those who, "not having visible means to maintain himself, lives without employment."[113] The new law expanded this to include those who had a job but neglected it or were deemed "stubborn." Penalties for violation were also significantly increased.[114] The law may have facially been race neutral, but that did not fool Northerners. "Though color is not specified," wrote a skeptical Vermont editor, "it is pretty certain that white vagrants will not be thus dealt with."[115]

A second law required freedmen to enter into a contract of employment no later than January 8, 1866, unless they had a license to perform "irregular" work. Any freedman who abandoned his work or otherwise refused to perform it was guilty of vagrancy and subject to arrest.[116] A third law allowed black minors who lacked financial support to be involuntarily apprenticed by the county probate courts to third parties.[117] And to set the example for prosecuting attorneys (known as solicitors) around the state, the legislature elected archsecessionist and Confederate colonel John William Augustine Sanford as Alabama's attorney general.[118]

This body of legislation was yet another "product of political ineptitude," as historian Dan Carter called the passage of these laws at this critical point.[119] And at least one Alabama editor would have agreed with him. "Nothing," wrote the disapproving editor of the *Mobile Times*, "was better calculated to keep up together the several elements of Radicalism than a policy indicative of ill suppressed rancor at the present settlement of the great social issue of the war—slavery."[120] A Boston newspaper was already urging federal intervention and promoting the continued use of the Freedmen's Bureau to insure the freedom of the former slaves and to enforce the Thirteenth Amendment.[121]

Newly inaugurated governor Patton would later veto some of these measures but he approved the vagrancy law.[122] That law was enough to fulfill the earlier prediction of a Dallas County planter that the "nigger is going to be made a serf, sure as you live." Planters, he revealed, "will have an understanding among themselves: 'You won't hire my niggers, and I won't hire yours;' then what's left for them? They're attached to the soil, and we're as much their masters as ever."[123]

President Johnson nonetheless went further out on a political limb and authorized Parsons to turn over the governor's office to Patton.[124] This decision by Johnson led a dubious New York editor to wonder how the South would perceive Johnson's decision. Judging from past experience, he wrote, "the President's policy looks something like an attempt to check a refractory horse, by giving him a slack rein." But the editor's primary concern was how Congress would receive the end of provisional government in Alabama. He expected the worst. "It is not improbable," he continued, "that this Alabama affair may prove to be the rock that is destined to shiver the pretended friendship which has been so generally manifested by the politicians of all classes toward the President, and that the new formation of parties, which *must* come ere long, will be the result."[125]

In the short run, however, the governor's vetoes and the president's termination of the provisional government could not hide the fact that Alabama's legislature had adopted discriminatory laws oppressive to its black residents. Any objective observer had to wonder whether vetoes of such legislation would be forthcoming when efforts were made to pass similar laws in the future. And this possibility provided Radical Republicans with even more ammunition in their quest to impose black suffrage in the South whether Southerners agreed to it or not.[126] Most Alabama planters, however, do not appear to have been overly concerned about their political future, probably because they assumed that Johnson would use his veto power to protect them in lieu of the citadel of state sovereignty for which so many thousands of Alabamians had unsuccessfully fought in order to preserve the institution of slavery. But there were now calls for Johnson's impeachment even in the Tennessee press.[127]

If Johnson failed, John Forsyth had a surprising replacement as presidential nominee for the Democratic Party in 1868: Gen. U. S. Grant. The war hero had made a brief, cursory, inspection tour of conditions in a few Southern states (Virginia, North Carolina, South Carolina, and Georgia) and issued a report to Johnson concluding that "the mass of the thinking men of the South accept the present situation of affairs in good faith" and regard the issues of secession and slavery as having been "settled forever."[128] Tellingly, however, Grant did not recommend that all occupation troops be removed from the South (only all black troops) and he blocked efforts to have the federal government provide arms for use by the newly formed state militias.[129]

Some Alabamians were already preferring to look back instead of forward. Former governor Watts started that movement with the formation of a new historical society dedicated to the soldiers who had fought to uphold the Confederate cause,[130] an organization that some in the US military perceived as subversive.[131] Former governor Parsons later raised the ire of some in the North by referring to several Confederate flags stored at the Alabama capitol as "sacred souvenirs of the courage and endurance of those who went forth to battle under their folds, and who manfully upheld them with their life blood."[132] As the year came to a close, a Mobile editor called on the "kind-hearted ladies" of the city to do something toward "saving from desecration the heretofore neglected graves of the brave who fell in a noble, though ambitious, cause." "We cannot," he concluded, "forget the duty of reverence due the dead."[133] As the North would soon learn, the Alabama legislature would do its part by creating the first of several counties named for prominent Confederate military figures, the first being in honor of Patrick Cleburne, one of several generals killed just over a year earlier at the Battle of Franklin.[134]

The duty of reverence to the nation was a very different matter, at least among some Alabamians. On December 27, an incident seen by Northerners as emblematic of the South (as it seemingly was) occurred in a packed Mobile theater and created a national sensation. When the orchestra in the theater played "Yankee Doodle" as part of a medley of songs, some in the crowd hissed. As the *New York Times* reported, the song received the same disrespectful response the following night despite the presence of a number of federal soldiers in the audience.[135]

Since July, Carl Schurz, a retired Union general from Pennsylvania, had been commissioned by Johnson to investigate conditions in Alabama and several other Deep South states. All of the incidents since the surrender of the armies and the cessation of conventional warfare seemed to most objective Northern observers to confirm Schurz's controversial conclusions.[136] In his brutally frank and prescient forty-five page report, which Johnson reluctantly supplied to Congress near the close of the fateful year 1865, Schurz described a dangerous faction of Southern "incorrigibles," who "still indulge in the swagger which was so customary before and during the war, and still hope for a time when the Southern Confederacy will achieve its independence." These men, he wrote, "persecute Union men and negroes wherever they can do so with impunity, insist clamorously upon their 'rights,' and are extremely impatient of the presence of the federal soldiers." This faction, he continued, "is by no means unimportant; it is strong in numbers, deals in brave talk, addresses itself directly and incessantly to the passions and prejudices of the masses, and commands the admiration of the women."[137]

Schurz's suggested remedy? First, the control of the federal government over the Southern states must be continued. Second, "all the loyal and free labor elements of the South" must be enabled to "exercise a healthy influence upon legislation." Third, under no circumstances should the South be allowed to "build up another 'peculiar institution.'" On this latter point, Schurz predicted—quite accurately—that "attempts on the part of the Southern people to deprive the negro of his rights as a freedman may result in bloody collisions, and will certainly plunge Southern society into restless fluctuations and anarchical confusion."[138]

Reviewing all of the evidence provided on the temper of the South, an editor in Vermont spoke for many when he concluded that "we have not yet reached the era of good feeling throughout South and North. The South submits, as perforce it must, and with perhaps as good a grace as could be expected all things considered." But, he held, "Congress must exact full guarantees and clinch them by Constitutional amendments before full representation and power can be safely remitted to the hands that so lately strove to destroy the Union."[139] Those constitutional amendments, born of actions by hotheads and incorrigibles in Alabama and elsewhere in 1865, would further undermine the antebellum concept of state sovereignty and ultimately lead to many of the legal innovations and political and social changes in evidence today.

The average Alabamian did not foresee any of these impending changes when the year 1865 came to a close, but some recognized that unwanted change was ahead. Kate Cumming wrote that "this year has developed the fate of the South. Time has revealed the utter loss of all our hopes." She predicted that a change "must pass over every political and social idea, custom, and relation."[140] Some of those changes were already evident. On December 29, Sarah Espy fretted that her former house slaves had left, forcing her to set up "a new way of life." Having had "servants for 50 years I must now be my own servant or subject myself to having a stranger in the family which I do not by any means like." She must have assumed that would be the worst of her problems. On New Year's Eve, she wrote that she was "thankful for our peaceful condition, for our health, and that it is as well with us as it is in every respect. May we at the close of another year be as well off as we are now."[141] Bolstered by faith in God, planter James Mallory was also cautiously optimistic. "The close of the most eventful year, for war, death, and suffering that has ever been on this continent has closed[.] God in his mercy may have some wise purpose in the change of the relation of master and slave, it may be his time for their freedom and a more active life for whites [and] it may work well for us." Therefore, he concluded, "may we be thankful for past blessings and may we work hereafter for our good and Gods Glory."[142] Augustus Benners's last journal entry for 1865 more accurately reflected the future for Alabamians of all races and political persuasions. "Trouble on trouble—may God help us."[143]

17
The Legacy of 1865

The history of Alabama after 1865 is in many ways a consequence of what happened that year. In an editorial titled "Southern 'Hot-Heads' Injuring Themselves," the editor of the New York *Sun* wrote that the "implacable class of Southerners have made a mistake in not curbing their feelings until the Government should remove the restraints now imposed upon them. They could not wait until they had gone entirely through the process of reconstruction, and consequently they have been engaged in ventilating their feelings by persecuting Union men, ill-treating the freedmen, acting spitefully toward the Government, and in every possible way indicating that much of the 'old leaven' still remains in their composition." "We say," he concluded, "they have made a mistake in unveiling themselves thus early, because if they had patiently waited until the Government reins were withdrawn, they might have gratified their chivalric feelings with impunity. But they have awakened the suspicions of Congress, and have thus rendered their freedom from Government control somewhat indefinite."[1]

On December 19, 1865, the day after William Seward officially certified the ratification of the Thirteenth Amendment, Republicans in Congress began an unprecedented assault on discrimination.[2] Sen. Lyman Trumbull, a Republican from Illinois and the chairman of the Senate Judiciary Committee, announced that, in light of events in the South, legislation was necessary to make the amendment effective.[3] On January 5, 1866, he introduced a bill that would become the Civil Rights Act of 1866.[4] That extremely important law, which is now codified in part at 42 U.S.C. §§ 1981 and 1982, was intended to outlaw all "black codes," as well as other laws and private and public conduct denying equal economic rights.[5] It was designed to provide what one US Supreme Court associate justice described as "equal rights and treatment in the matrix of contractual and quasi-contractual relationships that form the economic sphere."[6] At least initially these rights were enforceable only by way of criminal prosecutions against state and local government officials and employees as well as private individuals.[7] Trumble naively assured that only one or two high-profile prosecutions in a state would be necessary to "break up this whole business."[8] President Johnson, with encouragement from Northern Democrats, attempted to block the law, but as Alabamians soon learned, his veto was narrowly overridden.[9]

There were concerns that this new law might be repealed by a later Congress or struck down as unconstitutional by unsympathetic judges.[10] In order to give the rights granted by the law a firmer foundation, and to aid Southern Unionists, Congressional Republicans decided that another constitutional amendment would be necessary.[11] A resolution proposing what became the Fourteenth Amendment was reported to both houses of Congress by the Reconstruction Committee of Fifteen on April 30, 1866.[12] Perhaps not coincidentally, this move was not made until after the French government officially notified the US government that its troops would be withdrawn from Mexico. This withdrawal was to occur in three stages, with the first occurring in November 1866 and the last in November 1867.[13] The process of adoption of the Fourteenth Amendment began less than thirty days after the French announcement.[14]

As finally approved by Congress and sent to the states for ratification in June 1866, that amendment contained a provision that would partially terminate the political rights of a group of Southern Confederates: "Section 3. No person shall be a Senator or Representative in Congress, or elector of President and Vice President, or hold any office, civil or military, under the United States, or under any State, who, having previously taken an oath, as a member of Congress, or as an officer of the United States, or as a member of any State legislature, or as an executive or judicial officer of any State, to support the Constitution of the United States, shall have engaged in insurrection or rebellion against the same, or given aid or comfort to the enemies thereof. But Congress may by a vote of two-thirds of each House, remove such disability."[15] Governor Patton estimated that if the amendment were ratified, it would affect 3,000 to 3,500 men.[16] It would not, however, prevent them from voting in state elections.

Significantly, the Fourteenth Amendment did not purport to supplement Unionist voting strength by granting suffrage rights to black citizens.[17] But it did deem them citizens of the nation—thereby overturning the dictum to the contrary in the US Supreme Court's prewar *Dred Scott* decision—and the state in which they resided.[18] It also limited even further the power of states to address internal matters: "Section 1. All persons born or naturalized in the United States, and subject to the jurisdiction thereof, are citizens of the United States and of the State wherein they reside. No State shall make or enforce any law which shall abridge the privileges or immunities of citizens of the United States; nor shall any State deprive any person of life, liberty, or property, without due process of law; nor deny to any person within its jurisdiction the equal protection of the laws."[19] One important effect of this provision was to constitutionally reaffirm the ban on "black codes"[20] and in essence overrule prior judicial decisions holding that the Bill of Rights were not binding on the states.[21] Thus, black and white citizens were guaranteed due process and equal protection of the laws,[22] and state and local governments and officials could not enact discriminatory laws or enforce laws in a discriminatory manner.[23]

The Fourteenth Amendment did use a carrot-and-stick approach to encourage the states to grant suffrage rights to their black residents or suffer a loss in congressional voting strength:

> Section 2. Representatives shall be apportioned among the several States according to their respective numbers, counting the whole number of persons in each State, excluding Indians not taxed. But when the right to vote at any election for the choice of electors for President and Vice President of the United States, Representatives in Congress, the Executive and Judicial officers of a State, or the members of the Legislature thereof, is denied to any of the male inhabitants of such State, being twenty-one years of age, and citizens of the United States, or in any way abridged, except for participation in rebellion, or other crime, the basis of representation therein shall be reduced in the proportion which the number of such male citizens shall bear to the whole number of male citizens twenty-one years of age in such State.[24]

Last, but certainly not least, the proposed amendment granted Congress the "power to enforce, by appropriate legislation, the provisions of this article."[25] Congress was thereby authorized to enact legislation like the Civil Rights Act of 1871—now codified at 42 U.S.C. § 1983—perhaps the most frequently used legal basis for attacking government action claimed to violate federal constitutional and statutory rights.[26]

None of those benefits would flow, however, unless the amendment was ratified. In order to spur Southern legislatures to further erode state sovereignty in this fashion, Radical Republicans in Congress began pushing for legislation that would abolish the existing state governments there and call for new constitutional conventions consisting of loyal men elected by a loyal, biracial electorate to create new governments.[27] Tennessee's governor Brownlow took no chances with the longevity of his regime or his state's growing economy. He quickly issued a proclamation calling his legislature into special session to ratify the amendment.[28] Alabama's governor Patton, however, initially bowed to fierce assaults against the amendment by Northern Democrats, Alabama Democrats, and the Alabama press and did not follow Brownlow's lead.[29] Thus, while Tennessee's legislature ratified the Fourteenth Amendment and Congress promptly admitted its senators and congressmen on July 23, 1866, Alabama remained on the outside looking in and threatened with black suffrage and a political upheaval,[30] as well as further reluctance by capital markets to commit economic resources to Alabama's redevelopment.[31] And even after the fall midterm elections in 1866 in the North were won by Republicans, thereby increasing the possibility of the adoption of the more radical reconstruction measure, Alabama Democrats unwisely continued their long pattern of political blunders by resolutely opposing ratification.[32] With encouragement from Northern Democrats, both houses of the Alabama legislature overwhelmingly voted to oppose ratification not once but twice despite a change of heart by Governor Patton.[33]

In response to this intransigence in Alabama and other Southern states, Congress enacted legislation designed to re-form and reorganize their governments, grant black suffrage, and disenfranchise a somewhat larger number of Confederates.[34] The *Montgomery Advertiser* sounded the alarm that forces were at work to organize a government in Alabama that would oppress and harass Confederates—one "as tyrannical as the one under which the people of Tennessee now groan."[35] But that did not change Alabama's course. The Republican-controlled legislature elected following this process in Alabama (only 28 of 131 legislators were black) ratified the Fourteenth Amendment in July 1868.[36] Shortly thereafter Alabama's senators and congressmen—all Republicans—were admitted to their seats in Congress on July 20.[37]

Alabama Republicans assured that the state's admission meant peace and prosperity. The editor of the Mobile *Nationalist* predicted that Alabama "will enter upon a career of prosperity to which it has heretofore been a stranger." Capital, he was certain, "will flow in to cultivate plantations now lying waste, dig out the coal and iron buried in our mountains, and make the streams now silent as the grave echo with the hum of industry."[38] The key was the ability to attract outside capital. Thomas Peters, who was elected in 1868 to a seat on the Alabama Supreme Court, wrote a public letter emphasizing the importance of Northern capital and labor to Alabama's economic aspirations. "These people," he wrote, "not only have the extra labor of the country, but they have more. They have the wealth of the country." Therefore, he concluded, "they are just the people we need among us in any numbers they wish to come."[39]

But the rise of Alabama Republicans to power, and the upcoming 1868 presidential election, incited Democrats to encourage white solidarity and attempt to suppress the black vote using violence and fraud.[40] Reports of the activities of the recently formed Ku Klux Klan filled the pages of Alabama newspapers.[41] A Montgomery editor and Klan member, former Confederate colonel Joseph Hodgson, declared that "as sure as the sun rises, the hatred which our people entertain towards the villains who are placed over us will grow day by day and month by month, until the spirit of vengeance beats a long roll in the throbbing veins of an outraged people."[42] In Tuscaloosa, one of Hodgson's Confederate subordinates, Ryland Randolph, called for the organization in every community of a Klan unit whose duty was the "condign cleansing of neighborhoods of all human impurities." Republicans, according to Randolph, should be hanged from every tree.[43]

These threats, and the acts of violence that followed, quickly came to the attention of the Northern public.[44] John Forsyth wrote from Washington, DC, that "large masses of Northern people on their farms and their workshops to-day believe that rebellion is as active in Southern hearts now as it was while the war was flagrant, and that only the sword stifles its outbreak." They further believed, he continued, that "we only await the restoration of State power to re-establish slavery," that "Union men are not safe amongst us;" and that "to murder negroes in cold blood is a pastime among us, only limited by dread of the federal soldiery."[45]

But this did not cause the Klan—the paramilitary wing of the Democratic Party—to pause. On the contrary, Ryland Randolph warned that once federal troops were withdrawn, the "carpet-baggers" would be left "to the mercy of unreconstructed rebels, and the negro voters to the influence of their former owners."[46] Other Democratic editors made similar threats.[47] In the coming months, local Republican officials were subjected to threats by the Klan if they did not resign,[48] alleged "uppity blacks" were lynched,[49] and the execution of "carpet-baggers and scalawags of the South" wherever found was pledged.[50]

The reaction in Northern money markets was almost fatal to the South's economic recovery. The influential *New York Times* was particularly damning:

The consequence is seen and read of all the world. Ruin still broods there, just as it did before peace. Industry does not revive. Enterprise stays dormant. Bankruptcy, public and private, is still the rule everywhere. Capital does not flow in, to take the place of that squandered in the war; it will not come, though the most valuable lands on the continent are offered for sale at the lowest price to attract it. Nor is there more than a trifle of that immigration which was so hopefully relied upon to recruit the wasted life-blood. Capitalists, whether American or European, send their means to the remotest corner of the earth rather than to that part of the American Union. Emigrants from Europe will starve and languish to the very death, sooner than cast their lots in that bloody land. Fortune hunters from the North will colonize new territories all along the line of the Pacific Railroad, exposing themselves and their families to Indian butchery, sooner than take their chances among their white fellow-countrymen south of the Potomac. The mercy of the Cheyennes and the Sioux is more trusted than that of the Ku Klux. Not even Northern Democrats, with their professed love of the South, will emigrate there if they can possibly avoid it. The section is as universally shunned as if the plague was rioting there. All men refuse to go to a region in which, as they hear, there is no security for property or life, where they would be exposed to the masked assassin at midnight, and to the ambushed murderer at noonday. Such a social state, we say, is dreaded more than the plague. When such desperate spirits are in the case, the universal feeling is that of the Hebrew King, Let me fall into the hands of God, not into those of men. It is impossible to imagine a more fatal combination of social and political evils than now afflict the South. It is a vital necessity to the South that their course be arrested. Left to themselves, they all the while only grow worse. It is doubtful even now whether they have not become incurably chronic.[51]

As a consequence, economic boosters in Alabama were forced to rely on the cash-starved state and local governments for investment capital. The main goal was to augment Alabama's transportation infrastructure, and these governmental entities not only purchased the stocks and bonds of private railroad corporations but also made them direct loans and endorsed their bonds, thereby incurring millions of dollars of direct and contingent liabilities if the railroads defaulted.[52]

At the same time, these governments were being targeted for destruction using the same vote-suppression tactics that had marred the 1868 presidential election. Some believed that the enforcement of voting rights would be enhanced if the right to vote were federalized, but since Connecticut voters had rejected a state constitutional amendment providing for black suffrage, other Northern states, Wisconsin, Ohio, Minnesota, as well as the Territory of Colorado and the District of Columbia, had rejected enfranchising proposals.[53] On February 26, 1869, however, Congress proposed to the states the

Fifteenth Amendment to the Constitution: "Section 1. The right of citizens of the United States to vote shall not be denied or abridged by the United States or by any State on account of race, color, or previous condition of servitude. Section 2. The Congress shall have power to enforce this article by appropriate legislation."[54]

In November 1869, the Alabama legislature approved that amendment.[55] Shortly after its final ratification in 1870, Congress passed the Enforcement Act of 1870, which made it a crime for public officers and private persons to obstruct individuals from exercising their right to vote. The statute was amended the following year to provide for close federal supervision of the electoral process from registration to the certification of returns.[56]

But these laws did not eliminate the violence, fraud, and coercion used to suppress Republican voting strength.[57] Moreover, in 1873 during the administration of Alabama Republican governor David Peter Lewis, the nation was struck by a depression that caused numerous businesses—including Alabama's railroad corporations—to fail and the foreclosure rate on farms to skyrocket.[58] This, in turn, caused Alabama's state and local governments to incur a multimillion dollar default on their bonds and endorsement liabilities.[59] Along with violence and election fraud, this allowed Alabama Democrats to "redeem"—as they called it—the state from the Republicans in the 1874 state elections.[60] No one who called himself a Republican would be elected governor of Alabama until 1986.[61]

Once in control, Alabama Democrats orchestrated the call of a constitutional convention in 1875, one of the purposes of which was to restrict financial incentives to private businesses and to prevent creditors of the state and local governments from using the federal court to force them to enact tax increases to pay their debts.[62] This was accomplished by, for the first time, placing caps on state and local taxes.[63] The delegates to the constitutional convention also dramatically restricted the authority of the state and local governments to incur debt and fund private business.[64] Even after the threat of bankruptcy ended, however, these restraints were maintained in Alabama's much-maligned 1901 Constitution.[65] Today, any efforts to make exceptions for economic incentives to lure particularly valuable economic projects require a constitutional amendment, explaining why Alabama's constitution is one of the most amended in the nation. Meanwhile, Alabama's government lacks the flexibility and nimbleness required in a competitive, global economy.[66] All are an indirect legacy of 1865.

Much of this could have been avoided if the right of all to vote had been readily enforceable. But as the US Supreme Court later observed, "as the years passed and fervor for racial equality waned, enforcement of the laws became spotty and ineffective," and most of their provisions were repealed in 1894.[67] The reasons for this have been the subject of numerous excellent studies.[68] But any lawyer would recognize that a major problem was that the federal judicial system and the US Justice Department were not equipped to address the violation of unpopular laws on such a massive, clandestine scale. Alabama, for example, had no more than one federal judge throughout the nineteenth century and well into the twentieth.[69]

Meanwhile, as historian Rob Riser and others have written, Alabama and other Southern states began enacting laws imposing literacy tests and other obstacles and devices to frustrate black suffrage.[70] Later federal voting rights laws proved to be no match for these tactics. As one judge noted, "attempts to cope with this vile infection resembled battling the Hydra. Whenever one form of voting discrimination was identified and prohibited others sprang up in its place."[71] And because of the time and expense involved, case-by-case litigation was inadequate to combat widespread and persistent discrimination in voting.[72]

But with the authority granted by the Fifteenth Amendment, and a renewed public will embodied in the civil rights movement to ensure the unfettered exercise of the right to vote, Congress finally moved forward in the 1960s to enact more effective legislation.[73] In the months leading up to the adoption of the landmark Voting Rights Act of 1965, Dallas County, Alabama, was repeatedly referred to in congressional debates and hearings as the "pre-eminent example of the ineffectiveness of existing legislation." After years of litigation, black registration in that county had risen from 156 to only 383, despite that there were approximately 15,000 African Americans of voting age residing there.[74] Under the new law, literacy tests and other similar voting qualifications were suspended, and any new voting regulations in nine states required federal preapproval before implementation. The use of federal examiners and poll watchers was authorized, as were civil and criminal sanctions.[75] Since then, registration ratios have increased dramatically, and minority candidates hold office at unprecedented levels.[76]

The last half of the twentieth century also saw the Fourteenth Amendment finally come into its own.[77] It was the basis for the US Supreme Court's landmark decision in *Brown v. Board of Education*, which called for the end of de jure segregation in the public schools of Alabama and throughout the nation.[78] The Fourteenth Amendment also provided constitutional authority for Congress to enact the Civil Rights Act of 1964 following racial violence in Birmingham, Alabama, in the wake of protests over equal access to hotels, restaurants, theaters, retail stores, and other private and public accommodations. In addition to addressing discrimination in that context, Congress included an extremely important provision in the law that prohibited discrimination in employment based on race, sex, religion, or national origin.[79]

There is sharp disagreement between historians regarding whether reconstruction efforts after the Civil War succeeded or failed. For example, Michael Fitzgerald calls them a "splendid failure;" Sarah Wiggins disagrees.[80] But both sides of this interpretational dispute are, in a sense, correct, depending on whether one judges success from the short or long term. Historian James McPherson notes that the Reconstruction era constitutional amendments "radically transformed the thrust of the Constitution from negative to positive liberty." He also suggests that without these amendments, "the United States might have developed into even more of an apartheid society in the twentieth century than it did."[81] Laws alone do not change what is in one's heart; they merely set a standard for conduct that may eventually gain traction. If Reconstruction was a "splendid failure" in the short run, much of the blame must be placed at the feet of the Democratic Party, which encouraged and countenanced Southern recalcitrance.[82] It was only much-delayed justice that that political party finally helped finish the push for equal rights and made Reconstruction a success.

No one can honestly maintain that, as of the present date, discrimination has been totally eliminated in the United States. However, the constitutional authority granted to Congress that breached the citadel of state rights and sovereignty set the stage for the enactment of federal laws that have reshaped our society in ways that Americans could not have foreseen in 1865. Demonstrating the role of contingency, one can only wonder what might have happened if events in 1865 had played out differently. What if Governor Watts had acceded to the pleas of Unionists in early 1865 to convene the legislature and reach a peace accord that included gradual emancipation and protection of the state's economic assets? What if President Lincoln had not been assassinated in April 1865 and the nation had remained cold to calls for the imposition of universal black suffrage? What if the Alabama Constitutional Convention of 1865 and the Alabama legislature had promptly fulfilled Northern expectations regarding minimal economic rights for its black population and perhaps limited suffrage rights? What if Confederates had refrained from antiblack and anti-Unionist violence as well as unnecessarily provocative demagoguery in 1865? What if Southerners had ignored the calls of Northern Democrats to elect congressmen and senators who could not take the test oath? It is at least arguable that Congress would have admitted those delegations to their seats, thereby providing an opportunity to uphold President Johnson's vetoes and block the adoption of the constitutional amendments offensive to Southern whites.

Much has been achieved from an economic standpoint in Alabama since then but much more could have been achieved if Alabama had been blessed with rational leaders in 1865. That was the critical year. And contrary to the myths spread by early historians like John DuBose and Walter Fleming, Alabamians need not have looked outside their state for villains.

Abbreviations

ADAH   Alabama Department of Archives and History, Montgomery, Alabama

ASCCLUNA   Archives and Special Collections, Collier Library, University of North Alabama, Florence, Alabama

HMCPL   Huntsville–Madison County Public Library, Huntsville, Alabama

OR   The War of the Rebellion: A Compilation of the Official Records of the Union and Confederate Armies

SHC   Southern Historical Collections, University of North Carolina, Chapel Hill

Notes

Introduction

1. John Witherspoon DuBose, *Alabama's Tragic Decade: Ten Years of Alabama, 1865–1874* (Birmingham, AL: Webb Book, 1940). See also Hugh C. Davis, "John W. DuBose: The Disillusioned Aristocrat," *Alabama Historical Quarterly* 27 (Fall and Winter, 1965): 167–90. Walter Fleming was also in the propagandist classification. Walter L. Fleming, *Civil War and Reconstruction in Alabama* (Spartanburg, SC: Reprint Co., 1978).

2. DuBose, *Alabama's Tragic Decade*, 7–8, 19–23, 26, 30–34, 38, 49–50.

3. Judge Walter Jones, "Alabama's Economic Loss Due to Reconstruction," *Alabama Lawyer* 14 (April 1953): 147–55; Sheldon Hackney, *Magnolias without Moonlight: The American South from Regional Confederacy to National Integration* (New Brunswick, NJ: Transaction Publishers, 2005), 18–19.

4. Richard Barksdale Harwell, ed., *Kate: The Journal of a Confederate Nurse* (Baton Rouge: Louisiana State University Press, 1998), 307.

5. Herbert James Lewis, *Clearing the Thickets: A History of Antebellum Alabama* (New Orleans: Quid Pro Books, 2013), 133–42.

6. Alasdair Roberts, *America's First Great Depression: Economic Crisis and Political Disorder after the Panic of 1837* (Ithaca, NY: Cornell University Press, 2012).

7. J. Mills Thornton, *Politics and Power in a Slave Society: Alabama, 1800–1860* (Baton Rouge: Louisiana State University Press, 1978), 460–61.

8. Robert Volney Riser, "Between Scylla and Charybdis: Alabama's 1901 Constitutional Convention Assesses the Perils of Disfranchisement," master's thesis, University of Alabama, 2000; Malcolm Cook McMillan, *Constitutional Development in Alabama, 1798–1901: A Study in Politics, the Negro, and Sectionalism* (Chapel Hill: University of North Carolina Press, 1955), v–xvi, 233–370.

9. Wayne Flynt, *Alabama in the Twentieth Century* (Tuscaloosa: University of Alabama Press, 2004), 367–68. Chris McNair of Jefferson County was the first African American elected to the Alabama legislature since Reconstruction.

10. Contrary to the startling declaration of another Alabama historian, the South did not "begin its move toward the Republican Party in 1865": Glenn Feldman, *The*

Irony of the Solid South: Democrats, Republicans, and Race, 1865–1944 (Tuscaloosa: University of Alabama Press, 2013), 3. Feldman's attempt to tie Republicanism to an economic paradigm where labor is exploited and his argument that Alabamians began moving in that direction after the Civil War ignore the fact that Alabama Democrats were practitioners and defenders of slavery, the most exploitive labor system. It also ignores the economic record of the postwar Bourbon Democrats in Alabama.

11. Thornton, *Politics and Power*, 312–15; Lewis, *Clearing the Thickets*, 4–5, 139–40, 229–45, 267–68.

12. Thornton, *Politics and Power*, 281; William Warren Rogers Sr., Robert David Ward, Leah Rawls Atkins and Wayne Flynt, *Alabama: The History of a Deep South State* (Tuscaloosa: University of Alabama Press, 2010), 174–81.

13. Ethel Armes, *The Story of Coal and Iron in Alabama* (Tuscaloosa: University of Alabama Press, 2011), 134–35; William Lindsey McDonald, *A Walk through the Past: People and Places of Florence and Lauderdale County Alabama* (Killen, AL: Heart of Dixie Publishing, 2003), 110–11; Richard C. Sheridan, "Civil War Manufacturing in the Tennessee Valley," *Journal of Muscle Shoals History* 15 (1999): 50, 56, 62–63.

14. Jay Sexton, *Debtor Diplomacy: Finance and American Foreign Relations in the Civil War Era 1837–1873* (New York: Clarendon Press, 2005), 79–80.

15. *Livingston* (AL) *Journal*, July 20, 1867, p. 2; (Tuscaloosa) *Independent Monitor*, March 25, 1868, p. 2; (Selma) *Alabama State Sentinel*, June 20, 1867, p. 2.

16. Armes, *Story of Coal and Iron in Alabama*, 179; Sheridan, "Civil War Manufacturing," 50, 56, 62–63; *Nashville News*, July 24, 1865, p. 2.

17. *Mobile News*, July 24, 1865, reprinted in (New Orleans) *Picayune*, July 27, 1865, p. 3.

18. Michael W. Fitzgerald, *Urban Emancipation: Popular Politics in Reconstruction Mobile, 1860–1890* (Baton Rouge: Louisiana State University Press, 2002), 84–87; Sarah Woolfolk Wiggins, ed., *The Journals of Josiah Gorgas 1857–1878* (Tuscaloosa: University of Alabama Press, 1995), 186.

Chapter 1

1. DuBose, *Alabama's Tragic Decade*, 3.

2. Jack Friend, *West Wind, Flood Tide: The Battle of Mobile Bay* (Annapolis, MD: Naval Institute Press, 2004); Chester G. Hearn, *Mobile Bay and the Mobile Campaign: The Last Great Battles of the Civil War* (Jefferson, NC: McFarland, 1993).

3. *Montgomery Mail*, December 29, 1864, p. 2. See generally Derek Smith, *In the Lion's Mouth: Hood's Tragic Retreat from Nashville, 1864* (Mechanicsburg, PA: Stackpole Books, 2011); Wiley Sword, *Embrace an Angry Wind: The Confederacy's Last Hurrah, Spring Hill, Franklin, and Nashville* (New York: Harper Collins, 1992).

4. Wiggins, *Journals of Josiah Gorgas*, 144.

5. Edward Norphlet Brown to Fannie Brown, December 24, 1864, Edward Norphlet Brown Letters, ADAH.

6. (Greensboro) *Alabama Beacon*, January 6, 1865, p. 2.

7. Private Journal of Sarah R. Espy, 92, ADAH.

NOTES TO PAGES 8–10 / 217

8. Grant Taylor to Malinda Taylor, January 24, 1865, in Ann Kicker Blomquist and Robert A. Taylor, eds., *This Cruel War: The Civil War Letters of Grant and Malinda Taylor* (Macon, GA: Mercer University Press, 2000), 327.

9. George Knox Miller to Celestine Miller, January 1, 1865, in Richard M. McMurry, ed., *An Uncompromising Secessionist: The Civil War of George Knox Miller, Eighth (Wade's) Confederate Cavalry* (Tuscaloosa: University of Alabama Press, 2007), 264.

10. Nancy M. Rohr, ed., *Incidents of the War: The Civil War Journal of Mary Jane Chadick* (Huntsville, AL: Silver Threads Publishing, 2005), 246.

11. Sarah Anne McClellan Davis to William Cowan McClellan, in John C. Carter, ed., *Welcome the Hour of Conflict: William Cowan McClellan and the 9th Alabama* (Tuscaloosa: University of Alabama Press, 2007), 274.

12. Diary of Miss Catherine M. Fennell, 54; HMCPL.

13. Harwell, *Kate*, 246.

14. Grady McWhiney, Warner O. Moore Jr., and Robert F. Pace, eds., *"Fear God and Walk Humbly": The Agricultural Journal of James Mallory, 1843–1877* (Tuscaloosa: University of Alabama Press, 1997), 343–44.

15. William Eppa Fielding, "William Eppa Fielding's Diary," in Faye Acton Axford, ed., *"To Lochaber Na Mair": Southerners View the Civil War* (Athens, AL: Athens Publishing, 1986), 136.

16. Wiggins, *Journals of Josiah Gorgas*, 147.

17. Diary of Sally Independence Foster, December 30, 1864, ASCCLUNA.

18. (Selma) *Chattanooga Rebel*, January 7, 1865, p. 1.

19. (Selma) *Mississippian*, January 3, 1865, reprinted in (Selma) *Chattanooga Rebel*, January 7, 1865, p. 2.

20. (Selma) *Chattanooga Rebel*, January 5, 1865, reprinted in *Macon Telegraph and Confederate*, January 9, 1865, p. 1; *Montgomery Mail*, reprinted in *New Orleans Times*, January 17, 1865, p. 1.

21. Edward Norphlet Brown to Fannie Brown, May 22, 1864, May 26, 1864, Edward Norphlet Brown Papers, ADAH.

22. See, e.g., *Cincinnati Enquirer*, January 6, 1865, p. 3; *New York Times*, January 6, 1865, pp. 1, 4; (Washington, DC) *National Intelligencer*, January 9, 1865. See also (Alexandria, Va.) *Soldiers Journal*, January 18, 1865, p. 4 (stating that Hood had "hunted ground" in Alabama to "rest and recruit his shattered army").

23. Jerry Keenan, *Wilson's Cavalry Corps: Union Campaigns in the Western Theatre, October 1864 through Spring 1865* (Jefferson, NC: McFarland, 1998), 124. See generally *New York Tribune*, January 12, 1865, p. 1; William J. Palmer to Major Moe, January 5, 1865, OR, Series 1, Vol. 45 (Part II), 521; W. J. Palmer to W. D. Whipple, January 7, 1865, OR, Series 1, Vol. 45 (Part II), 540–542; Smith, *In The Lion's Mouth*, 240–41.

24. The family of former presidential candidate John Bell of Tennessee also took refuge at Tuscaloosa at this time. *Cleveland Leader*, January 11, 1865.

25. *Chicago Journal*, reprinted in *Milwaukee Sentinel*, January 12, 1865, and *Cleveland Leader*, January 12, 1865, p. 3.

26. J. B. Hood to J. A. Seddon, January 3, 1865, OR, Series 1, Vol. 45 (Part II), 757;

Chicago Journal, reprinted in *Milwaukee Sentinel*, February 8, 1865; Smith, *In the Lion's Mouth*, 246.

27. R. Taylor to President Davis, January 9, 1865, OR, Series 1, Vol. 45 (Part II), 772.

28. R. Taylor to President Davis, January 15, 1865, OR, Series 1, Vol. 45 (Part II), 785. See generally Smith, *In the Lion's Mouth*, 251–52.

29. Richard A. Baumgartner, ed., *Blood and Sacrifice: The Civil War Journal of a Confederate Soldier*, by William Pitt Chambers. (Huntington, WV: Blue Acorn Press, 1994), 194–95, 197.

30. *Richmond Examiner*, January 23, 1865, p. 2.

31. (Montgomery) *Memphis Appeal*, January 2, 1864, p. 1.

32. *Mobile Advertiser and Register*, February 4, 1865, p. 2; (Greensboro) *Alabama Beacon*, February 17, 1865, p. 1.

33. *Mobile Advertiser and Register*, February 4, 1865, p. 2. Regarding Jemison, see Hermione Dannelly Jackson, "The Life and Times of Robert Jemison, Jr. during the Civil War and Reconstruction," master's thesis, University of Alabama, 1942.

34. *Mobile Advertiser and Register*, February 4, 1865, p. 2. Regarding Forsyth, see Lonnie R. Burnett, *The Pen Makes a Good Sword: John Forsyth of the "Mobile Register"* (Tuscaloosa: University of Alabama Press, 2006).

35. *New York Tribune*, reprinted in (Richmond) *Dispatch*, March 31, 1865, p. 2.

36. *Tuscaloosa Observer*, reprinted in *Mobile Advertiser and Register*, November 26, 1864, p. 1, and *Nashville Union*, November 29, 1864, p. 2, November 30, 1864, p. 2.

37. *Mobile Advertiser and Register*, November 16, 1864, p. 1.

38. Ibid., February 4, 1865, p. 2.

39. Walter C. Whitaker, *Richard Hooker Wilmer: Second Bishop of Alabama* (Philadelphia, PA: G. W. Jacobs, 1907), 108–9. See generally Ben H. Severance, *Portraits of Conflict: A Photographic History of Alabama in the Civil War* (Fayetteville University of Arkansas Press, 2012), 307, which includes an excellent biographical sketch of Wilmer.

40. *Mobile Advertiser and Register*, December 23, 1864, p. 2, reporting on a meeting of the "Mobile Conference recently held in Tuscaloosa in reference to the Orphans of Soldiers within its bounds"; December 28, 1864, p. 2, with an editorial expressing surprise regarding the significant support for orphan asylums in Alabama; January 13, 1865, p. 2.

41. *Montgomery Mail*, December 3, 1864, p. 2.

42. G. Ward Hubbs, *Voices from Company D: Diaries by the Greensboro Guards, Fifth Alabama Infantry Regiment, Army of Northern Virginia* (Athens: University of Georgia Press, 2003), 353.

43. Baumgartner, *Blood and Sacrifice*, 194.

44. *Selma Reporter*, January 19, 1865, p. 1.

45. *Mobile Advertiser and Register*, September 28, 1864, p. 1; *Columbus* (GA) *Enquirer*, October 9, 1864, p. 1.

46. W. J. Palmer to Major Moe, January 5, 1865, OR, Series 1, Vol. 45 (Part II), 521; *Montgomery Mail*, January 18, 1865, p. 2; *Montgomery Daily Advertiser*, January 30, 1865, p. 1.

NOTES TO PAGES 14–17 / 219

47. (Montgomery) *Memphis Appeal,* January 29, 1864, reprinted in *Mobile Advertiser and Register,* February 3, 1865, p. 1, stating that this raid occurred on January 10, 1865; *Richmond Whig,* cited in (New Orleans) *Times Picayune,* February 26, 1865, p. 2; Margaret M. Storey, *Loyalty and Loss: Alabama's Unionists in the Civil War and Reconstruction* (Baton Rouge: Louisiana State University Press, 2004), 166–67.

48. W. T. Sherman to Maj. Gen. George H. Thomas, January 21, 1865, OR, Series 1, Vol. 45 (Part II), 621–22. See also Rogers et al., *Alabama,* 219.

49. *Cleveland Leader,* January 9, 1865, p. 2, January 11, 1865, pp. 1–2; *New York Tribune,* January 11, 1865, p. 4, February 10, 1865, p. 4; *Milwaukee Sentinel,* March 4, 1865; *New York Times,* reprinted in *Nashville Times and True Union,* March 6, 1865, p. 2; *Philadelphia Press,* March 1, 1865, p. 1; *Chicago Tribune,* reprinted in *Charleston Mercury,* January 27, 1865, p. 1; *Boston Herald,* February 13, 1865, p. 4.

50. *Montgomery Mail,* January 24, 1865, p. 1. See also *Montgomery Advertiser,* March 3, 1865, p. 2; *Selma Reporter,* reprinted in (Grove Hill, AL) *Clarke County Journal,* January 26, 1865, p. 2; *Mobile Advertiser and Register,* February 7, 1865, p. 1. See also Glenn M. Linden and Virginia Linden, eds., *Disunion, War, Defeat, and Recovery in Alabama: The Journal of Augustus Benners, 1850–1885* (Macon, GA: Mercer University Press, 2007), 133, 136.

51. *Tuscaloosa Observer,* March 15, 1865, pp. 1–2.

52. (Montgomery) *Memphis Appeal,* reprinted in *Mobile Advertiser and Register,* February 18, 1865, p. 2.

53. *Cleveland Leader,* January 9, 1865, p. 2.

54. *Chicago Journal,* reprinted in *Milwaukee Sentinel,* February 8, 1865 and *New York Times,* February 8, 1865, February 10, 1865, p. 4.

55. Jefferson Davis to General Richard Taylor, January 12, 1865, OR, Series 1, Vol. 45 (Part II), 778–79.

56. *Chicago Journal,* reprinted in *Milwaukee Sentinel,* January 12, 1865. See also Bradley R. Clampitt, *The Confederate Heartland: Military and Civilian Morale in the Western Confederacy* (Baton Rouge: Louisiana State University Press, 2011), 124–32.

57. J. L. M. Curry to Governor Watts, January 23, 1865, quoted in Bessie Martin, *A Rich Man's War, A Poor Man's Fight: Desertion of Alabama Troops from the Confederate Army* (Tuscaloosa: University of Alabama Press, 2003), 157.

58. *Selma Reporter,* reprinted in *Selma Dispatch,* January 7, 1865, p. 2. See also (Montgomery) *Memphis Appeal,* reprinted in *Montgomery Mail,* January 27, 1865, p. 2.

59. *Mobile Advertiser and Register,* January 12, 1865, p. 2.

60. *Montgomery Mail,* January 3, 1865, quoted in Clampitt, *Confederate Heartland,* 126.

61. *Mobile Tribune,* September 10, 1863, p. 1.

62. William C. Harris, *Lincoln's Last Months* (Cambridge: MA: Belknap University Press, 2004), 5.

63. *Mobile Advertiser and Register,* September 13, 1864, p. 1.

64. Sister Sadie to Mary Emma Francis, January 18, 1865, in James P. Pate, ed., *When This Evil War Is Over: The Correspondence of the Francis Family, 1860–1865* (Tuscaloosa: University of Alabama Press, 2006), 206.

Chapter 2

1. *New York Tribune*, reprinted in (Richmond) *Dispatch*, March 31, 1865, p. 2. See also *Chicago Tribune*, reprinted in (Philadelphia) *North American and United States Gazette*, February 10, 1865.

2. Mildred Easby-Smith, *William Russell Smith of Alabama, His Life and Works* (Philadelphia: Dolphin Press, 1931), 158–60.

3. *Mobile Advertiser and Register*, February 14, 1865, p. 2. See also (Philadelphia) *North American and United States Gazette*, February 10, 1865.

4. Easby-Smith, *William Russell Smith of Alabama*, 161.

5. *Mobile Advertiser and Register*, January 25, 1865, p. 1, January 21, 1865, p. 1; (Montgomery) *Memphis Appeal*, reprinted in *Selma* (AL) *Reporter*, January 28, 1865, p. 2; *New York Tribune*, January 2, 1865, p. 4, January 10, 1865, p. 4, January 11, 1865, p. 4, January 13, 1865, p. 2, January 16, 1865, pp. 1–3; (Richmond) *Dispatch*, January 7, 1865, p. 2, January 13, 1865, p. 3, January 16, 1865, p. 3. See generally James B. Conroy, *Our One Common Country: Abraham Lincoln and the Hampton Roads Peace Conference of 1865* (Guilford, CT: Lyons Press, 2014), 78–90.

6. *Nashville Union*, December 27, 1864, p. 3, March 10, 1865, p. 2; *Lowell* (MA) *Citizen and News*, March 21, 1865 (Clemens applying for the position); *Mobile Advertiser and Register*, January 24, 1865, p. 2 (implying that Clemens had received the appointment); *Philadelphia Press*, March 21, 1865, p. 2; Jeremiah Clemens to William H. Seward, November 17, 1864, Lincoln Papers, Library of Congress; Jeremiah Clemens to William Seward, January 8, 1865, Papers of William H. Seward, Rush Rhees Library, University of Rochester.

7. *Mobile Advertiser and Register*, January 20, 1865, p. 2.

8. David Nathaniel Gellman, *Emancipating New York: The Politics of Slavery and Freedom, 1777–1827* (Baton Rouge: Louisiana State University Press, 2006).

9. Leroy P. Graf, Ralph W. Haskins, and Paul H. Bergeron, eds., *The Papers of Andrew Johnson*, vol. 7, *1864–1865* (Knoxville: University of Tennessee Press, 1986), 395–96.

10. (Richmond) *Dispatch*, February 14, 1865, p. 2; (New York) *World*, cited in (Portage) *Wisconsin State Register*, January 14, 1865, and (Athens, GA) *Southern Watchman*, February 1, 1865, p. 1; *Cleveland Leader*, January 13, 1865, p. 1; *New York Tribune*, January 17, 1865, p. 1.

11. Conroy, *Our One Common Country*, 99; Richard E. Beringer et al., *Why the South Lost the Civil War* (Athens: University of Georgia Press, 1991), 375. See also *New York Tribune*, January 17, 1865, p. 1 (quoting a report in the *Richmond Examiner* that "Mr. Blair told [Jefferson Davis] he could have peace on the basis of gradual emancipation.").

12. Doris Kearns Goodwin, *Team of Rivals: The Political Genius of Abraham Lincoln* (New York: Simon and Schuster, 2005), 459–60; James M. McPherson, *The Struggle for Equality: Abolitionists and the Negro in the Civil War and Reconstruction* (Princeton, NJ: Princeton University Press, 1964), 119–20.

13. William C. Harris, *With Charity for All: Lincoln and the Restoration of the Union* (Lexington: University of Kentucky Press, 1997), 85–86; Louis P. Masur, *Lincoln's Hundred Days: The Emancipation Proclamation and the War for the Union* (Cambridge, MA: Harvard University Press, 2012), 242–43.

14. *Montgomery Mail*, January 29, 1865, p. 1; (Richmond) *Dispatch*, January 13, 1865, p. 2; (New York) *World*, cited in (Portage) *Wisconsin State Register*, January 14, 1865; *Richmond Enquirer*, January 18, 1865; Jon L. Wakelyn, *Confederates against the Confederacy: Essays on Leadership and Loyalty* (Westport, CT: Praeger, 2002), 15, 135.

15. (Richmond) *Dispatch*, January 21, 1865, p. 1; *Cleveland Leader*, January 26, 1865, p. 2.

16. *Montgomery Mail*, reprinted in *Mobile Advertiser and Register*, February 17, 1865, p. 2.

17. *Richmond Sentinel*, January 14, 1865, reprinted in *Montgomery Advertiser*, January 29, 1865, p. 2 and *Nashville Union*, January 19, 1865, p. 2, January 28, 1865, p. 1. See also Wiggins, *Journals of Josiah Gorgas*, 149.

18. (Richmond) *Dispatch*, January 18, 1865, p. 2, January 21, 1865, p. 1; *Shreveport News*, February 14, 1865, p. 2; *Cleveland Leader*, January 20, 1865, p. 1, January 21, 1865, p. 3; (New Orleans) *Picayune*, January 31, 1865, p. 2; *Mobile Advertiser and Register*, January 31, 1865, p. 1.

19. (Richmond) *Dispatch*, January 21, 1865, p. 1.

20. Ibid., January 18, 1865, p. 2, January 21, 1865, p. 1; *Mobile Advertiser and Register*, January 31, 1865, p. 1, February 3, 1865, p. 1.

21. (New Orleans) *Picayune*, January 22, 1865, p. 4. Foote had lived in Tuscumbia in the 1820s.

22. *Selma Dispatch*, January 10, 1865, p. 2; *Montgomery Mail*, January 25, 1865, p. 2, February 1, 1865, p. 1; (Richmond) *Dispatch*, January 17, 1865, p. 3, January 19, 1865, pp. 2–3 (Foote was subsequently released); *Richmond Sentinel*, January 30, 1865, reprinted in (New Orleans) *Picayune*, February 17, 1865, p. 4; Conroy, *Our One Common Country*, 78–79.

23. *Mobile Advertiser and Register*, February 4, 1865, p. 2; (Greensboro) *Alabama Beacon*, February 17, 1865, p. 1.

24. If Smith had made it out of the Confederacy alive, it is unlikely that he would have attempted to communicate directly with Lincoln to discuss peace. Indeed, given one of Smith's literary productions earlier in the war, such an overture might have backfired. In 1863, Smith had written and published a five-act play titled *The Royal Ape: A Dramatic Poem*. The play, consisting of a biting parody of Northern Republicans in general and Lincoln and his family in particular, opened on the eve of the First Battle of Bull Run. Not only did Smith portray Lincoln's eldest son, Robert, as dressing in women's clothing to sneak out of Washington, DC, after the Confederate victory but he had Robert referring to his father, himself dressed in a "scotch cap and striped pants," as having "played the ape" to avoid detection. William Russell Smith, *The Royal Ape: A Dramatic Poem* (Richmond, VA: West and Johnston, 1863), 78–85.

222 / Notes to pages 22–25

25. William N. Bilbo to William H. Seward, February 14, 1865, Papers of William H. Seward, Rush Rhees Library, University of Rochester.

26. Paul D. Escott, *Many Excellent People: Power and Privilege in North Carolina, 1850–1900* (Chapel Hill: University of North Carolina Press, 1985), 50–51.

27. *Boston Advertiser*, January 25, 1865.

28. (New York) *World*, reprinted in (Millersburg, OH) *Holmes County Farmer*, February 9, 1865, p. 2.

29. Daily Journal of Joshua Burns Moore, 75, ADAH.

30. *Mobile Advertiser and Register*, January 20, 1865, p. 2, and reprinted in (New Orleans) *Picayune*, January 28, 1865, p. 1.

31. *Cleveland Herald*, January 20, 1865, p. 1; (New Orleans) *Picayune*, January 27, 1865, p. 2. The identity of these persons has not been determinable.

32. *Chicago Tribune*, reprinted in (Philadelphia) *North American and United States Gazette*, February 10, 1865. See also Daily Journal of Joshua Burns Moore, 75, ADAH (indicating that several Alabamians went to Washington, DC, on a peace mission at this time).

33. George H. Thomas to C. A. Dana, January 21, 1865, OR, Series 1, Vol. 45 (Part II), 622.

34. *Mobile Advertiser and Register*, November 20, 1864, p. 2.

35. J. J. Giers to Lt. Gen. U. S. Grant, January 26, 1865, OR, Series 1, Vol. 49 (Part I), 590–91.

36. J. J. Giers to Lt. Gen. U. S. Grant, January 26, 1865, OR, Series 1, Vol. 49 (Part I), 590–592. See also Fleming, *Civil War and Reconstruction*, 146–47.

37. W. J. Palmer to Brig. Gen. W. D. Whipple, January 7, 1865, OR, Series 1, Vol. 45 (Part II), 541; George H. Thomas to Brigadier General Hoffman, January 21, 1865, R. S. Granger to Brigadier Gen. P. D. Roddey, January 31, 1865, OR, Series 2, Vol. 8, 105, 157; P. D. Roddey to General Beauregard, February 3, 1865, OR, Series 2, Vol. 8, 179–80; P. D. Roddey to Brig. Gen. R. S. Granger, February 8, 1865, OR, Series 2, Vol. 8, 198–99; R. S. Granger to Brig. Gen. H. W. Wessells, February 14, 1865, OR, Series 2, Vol. 8, 220; R. S. Granger to Major-General Thomas, February 14, 1865, OR, Series 1, Vol. 49 (Part I), 713–14; William D. Whipple to Col. J. G. Parkhurst, February 17, 1865, OR, Series 2, Vol. 8, 244.

38. *Montgomery Mail*, reprinted in (New Orleans) *Picayune*, February 14, 1865, p. 1.

39. R. Taylor to General S. Cooper, January 21, 1865, OR, Series 1, Vol. 45 (Part II), 802. See also G. T. Beauregard to General Samuel Cooper, January 17, 1865, OR, Series 1, Vol. 45 (Part II), 789; Samuel Cooper to General G. T. Beauregard, January 19, 1865, OR, Series 1, Vol. 45 (Part II), 795; Richard Taylor to General Samuel Cooper, January 21, 1865, OR, Series 1, Vol. 45 (Part II), 802.

40. Jefferson Davis to Secretary of War, 1865, OR, Series 1, Vol. 45 (Part II), 790; Jefferson Davis to General R. Taylor, January 31, 1865, OR, Series 1, Vol. 49 (Part I), 946.

41. P. D. Roddey to Brig. Gen. W. H. Jackson, January 27, 1865, OR, Series 1, Vol. 49 (Part I), 938.

NOTES TO PAGES 25–29 / 223

42. P. D. Roddey to Brig. Gen. W. H. Jackson, January 27, 1865, OR, Series 1, Vol. 49 (Part I), 938.

Chapter 3

Epigraph 1. Private Journal of Sarah R. Espy, 93, ADAH.

Epigraph 2. Stouten Hubert Dent to "My Darling," February 1, 1865, in Gerald Ray Mathis and Douglas Clare Purcell, eds., *In the Land of the Living: Wartime Letters by Confederates from the Chattahoochee Valley of Alabama and Georgia* (Troy, AL: Troy State University Press, 1981), 121.

Epigraph 3. Civil War Diary of James Montgomery Lanning, 26, HMCPL.

Epigraph 4. Wiggins, *Journals of Josiah Gorgas*, 150.

Epigraph 5. Diary of Sally Independence Foster, February 1865, ASCCLUNA.

1. Grant Taylor to Malinda Taylor, December 29, 1864, in Blomquist and Taylor, *This Cruel War*, 319. See also Daily Journal of Joshua Burns Moore, 74, ADAH.

2. William L. Nugent to Nellie Nugent, December 26, 1864, in William M. Cash and Lucy Somerville Howorth, eds., *My Dear Nellie: The Civil War Letters of William L. Nugent to Eleanor Smith Nugent* (Jackson: University Press of Mississippi, 1977), 228–29.

3. *Mobile Advertiser and Register*, January 29, 1865, p. 2, February 8, 1865, p. 1; (Grove Hill, AL) *Clarke County Journal*, February 1, 1865, p. 2; (Washington, DC) *National Intelligencer*, February 1, 1865; (New Orleans) *Picayune*, January 27, 1865, p. 2, February 7, 1865, p. 2; *Cleveland Herald*, January 19, 1865; Conroy, *Our One Common Country*, 89, 107–11.

4. *Richmond Dispatch*, January 31, 1865, p. 2; *Mobile Advertiser and Register*, February 4, 1865, p. 2.

5. Conroy, *Our One Common Country*, 113–17; George C. Rable, *The Confederate Republic: A Revolution against Politics* (Chapel Hill: University of North Carolina Press, 1994), 292–93.

6. *New York Times*, cited in (New Orleans) *Picayune*, February 12, 1865, p. 2; *Nashville Press*, February 7, 1865, p. 1; *Cleveland Leader*, June 12, 1865, p. 1.

7. Paul J. Zingg, "John Archibald Campbell and the Hampton Road Conference: Quixotic Diplomacy, 1865," *Alabama Historical Quarterly* 36 (Spring 1974): 25–28.

8. *Mobile Advertiser and Register*, January 29, 1865, p. 2.

9. *Selma Reporter*, reprinted in (Grove Hill, AL) *Clarke County Journal*, February 9, 1865, p. 2.

10. (Richmond) *Dispatch*, reprinted in (New Orleans) *Picayune*, February 12, 1865, p. 3. See also Conroy, *Our One Common Country*, xxi.

11. Hubbs, *Voices from Company D*, 350.

12. Conroy, *Our One Common Country*, 176–78; David Herbert Donald, *Lincoln* (New York: Simon and Schuster, 1995), 557.

13. (New Orleans) *Picayune*, February 11, 1865, p. 2.

14. *Huntsville Advocate*, June 27, 1866, p. 2; *Nashville Union*, August 5, 1865, p. 2

(regarding Lincoln's offer of compensation); James W. Taylor to Abraham Lincoln, February 2, 1865, Papers of William H. Seward, Rush Rhees Library, University of Rochester (a letter from a Minnesotan to Lincoln outlining a plan for compensation that called for a payment of $87,016,000); Robert Saunders Jr., *John Archibald Campbell: Southern Moderate, 1811–1889* (Tuscaloosa: University of Alabama Press, 1997), 169–71; Thomas E. Schott, *Alexander H. Stephens of Georgia: A Biography* (Baton Rouge: Louisiana State University Press, 1988), 446; Donald, *Lincoln*, 558–61; Glyndon G. Van Deusen, *William Henry Seward* (New York: Oxford University Press, 1967), 382–88; John M. Taylor, *William Henry Seward: Lincoln's Right Hand* (Washington, DC: Potomac Books, 1991), 236; Beringer et al., *Why the South Lost*, 375; John C. Rodrigue, *Lincoln and Reconstruction* (Carbondale: Southern Illinois University Press, 2013), 118; Harris, *Lincoln's Last Months*, 116–21; Paul D. Escott, *"What Shall We Do with the Negro?": Lincoln, White Racism, and Civil War America* (Charlottesville: University of Virginia Press, 2009), 204–25; Conroy, *Our One Common Country*, 185–86, 188–89, 191–92, 196–97, 212–14; Michael Perman, *Reunion without Compromise: The South and Reconstruction: 1865–1868* (New York: Cambridge University Press, 1973), 46fn77. It must be acknowledged that a dwindling number of historians—particularly those who are protective of Lincoln's legacy—deny that he made these suggestions. Some now finesse the issue by omitting all mention of Hampton Roads. Richard Striner, *Father Abraham: Lincoln's Relentless Struggle to End Slavery* (New York: Oxford University Press, 2006). But despite the rumors that emanated before and after the conference, Lincoln never denied doing so and neither did Seward. As historian Doris Kearns Goodwin notes, Radical Republican leader Thaddeus Stevens feared that in order to achieve peace, Lincoln "would turn his back on emancipation" altogether (*Team of Rivals*, 694).

15. William E. Gienapp and Erica L. Gienapp, eds., *The Civil War Diary of Gideon Welles, Lincoln's Secretary of the Navy* (Urbana: Knox College Lincoln Studies Center and the University of Illinois Press, 2014), 581.

16. Horace Greeley to Abraham Lincoln, July 7, 1864, Abraham Lincoln Papers, Library of Congress, and reprinted in *Cleveland Leader*, April 3, 1865, p. 3, and (Washington, DC) *National Republican*, August 16, 1865, p. 1.

17. Edgar Thaddeus Welles, ed., *Diary of Gideon Welles: Secretary of the Navy under Lincoln and Johnson* (New York: W. W. Norton, 1911), 2:261, 271, 333; Paul Studenski and Herman Edward Krooss, *Financial History of the United States* (New York: McGraw-Hill, 1963), 160–61; *Annual Report of the Secretary of the Treasury on the State of the Finances, Statistical Appendix, 1980* (Washington, DC: Government Printing Office, 1980), 61; *Mobile Advertiser and Register*, October 14, 1865, p. 2.

18. *Chicago Tribune*, September 20, 1865, p. 2; *New York Times*, April 5, 1865, p. 4; Theodore Eli Grable, "Financial Policy of Hugh McCulloch," master's thesis, Indiana University, 1910, 5–9. Regarding Lincoln's secretary of the treasury at this time, see Robert J. Cook, *Civil War Senator: William Pitt Fessenden and the Fight to Save the Republic* (Baton Rouge: Louisiana State University Press, 2011), 184–87.

19. *Merchants' Magazine and Commercial Review*, January 1, 1865, p. 55. Some may

wonder how Lincoln could consider paying compensation to slaveholders under these circumstances. The answer is simple. The Treasury Department would continue its prior practice of borrowing or printing more money, but it would be used to pay for peace rather than war.

20. *Washington* (DC) *Chronicle,* March 24, 1865, quoted in *Bangor* (ME) *Whig and Courier,* March 27, 1865; Michael Vorenberg, "The Thirteenth Amendment Enacted," in Harold Holzer and Sara Vaughn Gabbard, eds., *Lincoln and Freedom: Slavery, Emancipation, and the Thirteenth Amendment* (Carbondale: Southern Illinois University Press, 2007), 188–90. Regarding Lincoln's emotional depression, see Michael Burlingame, *The Inner World of Abraham Lincoln* (Urbana: University of Illinois Press, 1994), 92–113.

21. *Memphis Bulletin,* reprinted in *Mobile Advertiser and Register,* January 29, 1865, p. 2.

22. *Cincinnati Gazette,* reprinted in *Nashville Times and True Union,* February 4, 1865, p. 2; (New York) *World,* reprinted in (Millersburg, OH) *Holmes County Farmer,* February 9, 1865, p. 2.

23. (New Orleans) *Picayune,* February 16, 1865, p. 2 (on Delaware); *Nashville Union,* February 24, 1865, p. 2 (on Kentucky); *Cleveland Leader,* February 25, 1865, p. 2.

24. *Nashville Press,* February 14, 1865, p. 2, February 20, 1865, p. 2.

25. *Mobile Advertiser and Register,* January 29, 1865, p. 2.

26. *St. Louis Republican,* February 3, 1865, reprinted in (New Orleans) *Picayune,* February 11, 1865, p. 2.

27. McElvain v. Mudd, 44 (Ala. 48 1870).

28. Saunders, *John Archibald Campbell,* 173.

29. See generally *Mobile Advertiser and Register,* February 11, 1865, p. 1; (New Orleans) *Picayune,* February 16, 1865, p. 2 (publishing the reports of the commissioners); *Cleveland Leader,* June 12, 1865, p. 1 (regarding Davis's instructions to the Confederate commissioners prior to the conference and efforts by them to change his mind); *Augusta* (GA) *Chronicle and Sentinel,* June 17, 1865 (publishing an article said to be based on Alexander Stephens's account of the conference), reprinted in *Nashville Union,* June 29, 1865, p. 1, and *Cleveland Leader,* June 26, 1865, p. 1; *Nashville Union,* March 30, 1866, p. 4 (publishing Seward's February 7, 1865, letter to Charles Francis Adams about the conference).

30. Conroy, *Our One Common Country,* 198–99.

31. Easby-Smith, *William Russell Smith of Alabama,* 161.

32. Diary of Sally Independence Foster, March 12, 1865, ASCCLUNA.

33. Ronald G. Griffin, *The 11th Alabama Volunteer Regiment in the Civil War* (Jefferson, NC: McFarland, 2012), 220.

34. Linden and Linden, eds., *Disunion, War, Defeat, and Recovery,* 130.

35. Lynda Lasswell Crist, ed., *The Papers of Jefferson Davis: 1861* (Baton Rouge: Louisiana State University Press, 1992), 11:575.

36. Edward Crenshaw, "Diary of Captain Edward Crenshaw of the Confederate States Army," *Alabama Historical Quarterly* 2 (Fall 1940): 376.

226 / Notes to pages 33–36

37. Daily Journal of Joshua Burns Moore, 76, ADAH.

38. *Mobile Advertiser and Register*, February 8, 1865, p. 1.

39. *Mobile Advertiser and Register*, January 21, 1865, p. 1.

40. *Mobile Advertiser and Register*, February 8, 1865, p. 1. Hook was a Revolutionary War–era merchant who—unpatriotically according to Patrick Henry—sued Continental Army officers to obtain payment for two steers of his that had been taken to feed the troops. George Morgan, *The True Patrick Henry* (Philadelphia: J. B. Lippincott, 1907), 376–77.

41. *Montgomery Mail*, quoted in *Mobile Advertiser and Register*, February 17, 1865, p. 2 and *Augusta* (GA) *Constitutionalist*, March 10, 1865, p. 1.

42. James Edmonds Saunders, *Early Settlers of Alabama* (Westminster, MD: Heritage Books, 2009), 129, 163–64; Willis Brewer, *Alabama, Her History, Resources, War Record, and Public Men: From 1540 to 1872* (Spartanburg, SC: Reprint Co., 1975), 683.

43. Fleming, *Civil War and Reconstruction*, 146; (New Orleans) *Picayune*, February 6, 1865, p. 2; *Chicago Tribune*, reprinted in (Philadelphia) *North American and United States Gazette*, February 10, 1865; *New York Times*, February 10, 1865, p. 4; *Chicago Journal*, reprinted in *Milwaukee Sentinel*, February 8, 1865; (New Orleans) *Picayune*, February 16, 1865, p. 2.

44. *Huntsville Advocate*, June 13, 1866, p. 2, June 27, 1866, p. 2.

45. *Chicago Journal*, reprinted in *Weekly Perrysburg* (OH) *Journal*, February 1, 1865, p. 2; *Cleveland Leader*, January 12, 1865, p. 2.

46. T. H. Watts to Gen. P. D. Roddey, February 14, 1865, Papers of Thomas Hill Watts, ADAH.

47. *Chicago Tribune*, reprinted in (Philadelphia) *North American and United States Gazette*, February 10, 1865.

48. *Montgomery Advertiser*, reprinted in (Greensboro) *Alabama Beacon*, February 24, 1865, p. 2.

49. Fleming, *Civil War and Reconstruction*, 146–47.

50. *St. Louis Republican*, reprinted in (New Orleans) *Picayune*, February 11, 1865, p. 1; (Philadelphia) *Bulletin*, March 21, 1865, p. 2; *Fremont* (OH) *Journal*, February 17, 1865, p. 1; *New York Times*, February 2, 1865, p. 1; and *Chattanooga Gazette*, February 5, 1865.

51. *Chicago Journal*, reprinted in *New York Times*, February 10, 1865, p. 4; *Milwaukee Sentinel*, February 8, 1865.

52. *Nashville Union*, February 4, 1865, p. 3.

53. J. H. Wilson to Capt. Robert H. Ramsey, February 2, 1865, OR, Series 1, Vol. 49 (Part I), 630–31.

54. R. S. Granger to Maj. Gen. Thomas, February 6, 1865, OR, Series 1, Vol. 49 (Part I), 662. See also R. R. Stewart to Major E. B. Beaumont, February 23, 1865, OR, Series 1, Vol. 49 (Part I), 50–51 (their headquarters was at Mount Hope).

55. (Montgomery) *Memphis Appeal*, reprinted in *Mobile Advertiser and Register*, February 18, 1865, p. 2. (Washington, DC) *National Tribune*, June 11, 1903, p. 3.

56. *Mobile Advertiser and Register*, February 8, 1865, p. 2.

NOTES TO PAGES 37–43 / 227

57. *Selma* (AL) *Dispatch*, reprinted in (Talladega, AL) *Democratic Watchtower*, February 14, 1865, p. 1.

58. (Selma, AL) *Chattanooga Rebel*, reprinted in (New Orleans) *Picayune*, February 17, 1865, p. 1.

59. *Mobile Advertiser and Register*, February 12, 1865, p. 1.

60. (Trenton, NJ) *State Gazette*, April 5, 1865, p. 2.

Chapter 4

1. *Mobile Advertiser and Register*, January 18, 1865, p. 2; (Richmond) *Dispatch*, January 28, 1865, p. 1. Regarding Forrest's nickname, see *Montgomery Mail*, January 13, 1864, p. 2, November 23, 1864, p. 2; *Edgefield* (SC) *Advertiser*, July 13, 1864, p. 1; *Fayetteville* (NC) *Observer*, June 9, 1864, p. 2; (Richmond) *Dispatch*, October 19, 1864, p. 1; *Camden* (SC) *Journal*, October 17, 1864, p. 1; *Yorkville* (SC) *Enquirer*, November 30, 1864, p. 2, February 15, 1866, p. 3.

2. (New Orleans) *Picayune*, January 21, 1865, p. 1.

3. *Albany* (GA) *Patriot*, January 4, 1865, p. 2; *Cleveland Leader*, January 9, 1865, p. 1.

4. (Richmond) *Dispatch*, February 3, 1865, p. 4.

5. N. B. Forrest to Lieut. Gen. R. Taylor, January 2, 1865, OR, Series 1, Vol. 45 (Part II), 756–57.

6. *Mobile Advertiser and Register*, February 28, 1865, p. 2.

7. Jack Hurst, *Nathan Bedford Forrest: A Biography* (New York: Random House, 1994), 246; (Richmond) *Dispatch*, February 28, 1865, p. 3.

8. *Cleveland Leader*, March 4, 1865, p. 1.

9. (Montgomery) *Memphis Appeal*, March 6, 1865, p. 1.

10. *Montgomery Advertiser*, reprinted in (Greensboro) *Alabama Beacon*, January 6, 1865, p. 1. See also *Mobile Advertiser and Register*, March 22, 1865, p. 2, March 30, 1865, p 1.

11. *Mobile Tribune*, reprinted in (New Orleans) *Picayune*, February 22, 1865, p. 1.

12. *Mobile Advertiser and Register*, February 12, 1865, p. 1.

13. *Montgomery Advertiser*, reprinted in *Columbus* (GA) *Enquirer*, December 29, 1864, p. 1.

14. *Richmond Enquirer*, January 11, 1865, p. 1; (Richmond) *Dispatch*, January 11, 1865, p. 1; *Mobile Advertiser and Register*, December 20, 1864, p. 1, December 23, 1864, pp. 1–2; *Montgomery Weekly Advertiser*, December 28, 1864, p. 2; *Selma* (AL) *Dispatch*, December 20, 1864, pp. 1–2.

15. *Selma* (AL) *Dispatch*, January 10, 1865, p. 2.

16. *Mobile Advertiser and Register*, January 13, 1865, p. 2.

17. Ibid., February 19, 1865, p. 2, March 22, 1865, p. 2; *Nashville Union*, March 11, 1865, p. 2; Martin, *Rich Man's War*, 86–89, 237.

18. Grant Taylor to Malinda Taylor, January 4, 1865, in Blomquist and Taylor, *This Cruel War*, 321.

19. (Richmond) *Dispatch*, January 30, 1865, p. 1; *Nashville Union*, March 11, 1865, p. 2.

228 / NOTES TO PAGES 43–46

20. *Montgomery Mail*, January 18, 1865, p. 2.

21. *Mobile News*, cited in *Cleveland Leader*, January 18, 1865, p. 2.

22. *Mobile Advertiser and Register*, reprinted in (New Orleans) *Picayune*, January 19, 1865, p. 1.

23. Captain Stouten Hubert Dent to his wife, February 10, 1865, in Mathis and Purcell, *In the Land of the Living*, 122.

24. *Mobile Advertiser and Register*, reprinted in (New Orleans) *Picayune*, January 19, 1865, p. 1.

25. *Raleigh Progress*, reprinted in *Nashville Union*, February 23, 1865, p. 1. Regarding Pennington, see William S. Powell, ed., *Dictionary of North Carolina Biography* (Chapel Hill: University of North Carolina Press, 1994), 5:67.

26. *Mobile Advertiser and Register*, February 7, 1865, p. 1, February 15, 1865, p. 2, February 24, 1865, p. 2.

27. *Huntsville Advocate*, June 13, 1866, p. 2, June 27, 1866, p. 2; Fleming, *Civil War and Reconstruction*, 316–17.

28. *Montgomery Advertiser*, March 3, 1865, p. 1. Regarding the rallies in Richmond, see Conroy, *Our One Common Country*, 216–25.

29. (Brattleboro) *Vermont Phoenix*, February 10, 1865, p. 2. See also Conroy, *Our One Common Country*, 228.

30. See, e.g., *Montgomery Advertiser*, January 30, 1865, p. 1, February 22, 1865, p. 2, March 3, 1865, p. 2, March 5, 1865, p. 2; *Tuscaloosa Observer*, March 8, 1865, p. 2. See generally Joseph T. Glatthaar, *The March To the Sea and Beyond: Sherman's Troops in the Savannah and Carolinas Campaigns* (Baton Rouge: Louisiana State University Press, 1985), 134–55.

31. William Stanley Hoole, *Alabama Tories: The First Alabama Cavalry, U.S.A., 1862–1865* (Tuscaloosa: Confederate Publishing, 1960), 43; Glenda McWhirter Todd, *First Alabama Cavalry, U.S.A: Homage to Patriotism* (Bowie, MD: Heritage Books, 1999), 12, 49–50.

32. *Montgomery Advertiser*, March 3, 1865, p. 2; *Mobile Advertiser and Register*, March 1, 1865, p. 1, March 2, 1865, p. 2, March 3, 1865, p. 1; *Anderson* (SC) *Intelligencer*, March 23, 1865, p. 2. See also James M. McPherson, *Battle Cry of Freedom: The Civil War Era* (New York: Oxford University Press, 1988), 825–30; William Gilmore Simms, *A City Laid Waste: The Capture, Sack, and Destruction of the City of Columbia* (Columbia: University of South Carolina Press, 2005); John G. Barrett, *Sherman's March through the Carolinas* (Chapel Hill: University of North Carolina Press, 1995), 61–93.

33. Samuel J. Martin: *"Kill-Cavalry": The Life of Union General Hugh Judson Kilpatrick* (Mechanicsburg, PA: Stackpole Books, 2000), 215.

34. Todd, *First Alabama Cavalry*, 50–51, 54.

35. *New York Times*, March 13, 1865, p. 2; *Cleveland Leader*, March 16, 1865, p. 2; Wager Swayne to Lt. A. C. Fenner, September 6, 1865, OR, Series 1, Vol. 38 (Part III), 514.

36. *Huntsville Advocate*, July 26, 1865, p. 3; Sarah Woolfolk Wiggins, *Scalawag in Alabama Politics: 1865–1881* (Tuscaloosa: University of Alabama Press, 1991), 11–13.

NOTES TO PAGES 46–50 / 229

37. Michael W. Fitzgerald, "Wager Swayne, the Freedmen's Bureau, and the Politics of Reconstruction in Alabama," *Alabama Review* 48 (July 1995): 188; John B. Myers, "The Alabama Freedmen and the Economic Adjustments during Presidential Reconstruction, 1865–1867," *Alabama Review* 26 (October 1973): 252–53.

38. See, e.g., *Mobile Advertiser and Register*, March 6, 1865, p. 2, March 8, 1865, p. 2; *Montgomery Advertiser*, February 22, 1865, p. 2, March 3, 1865, p. 2, March 5, 1865, p. 2.

39. Harwell, *Kate*, 258.

40. Linden and Linden, *Disunion, War, Defeat, and Recovery*, 131, 133.

41. Harwell, *Kate*, 271.

42. Private Journal of Sarah R. Espy, ADAH, 95.

43. McWhiney, Moore, and Pace, "*Fear God and Walk Humbly*," 346–47.

44. (New York) *World*, reprinted in *Nashville Press*, April 1, 1865, p. 2.

45. J. M. Withers to General J. C. Breckinridge, February 7, 1865, OR, Series 4, Vol. 3, 1064–65.

46. *Mobile Advertiser and Register*, February 5, 1865, p. 2, February 22, 1865, p. 2 (stating that Clay was in Macon, Georgia, on February 14); Ruth Ketring Nuermberger, *The Clays of Alabama: A Planter-Lawyer-Politician Family* (Tuscaloosa: University of Alabama Press, 2005), 262–64.

47. *Mobile Advertiser and Register*, February 24, 1865, p. 1.

48. (Montgomery) *Memphis Appeal*, February 18, 1865, p. 1.

49. *Mobile Advertiser and Register*, February 11, 1865, p. 2.

50. Ibid., February 15, 1865, pp. 1–2.

51. Ibid. See also (Mobile) *Army Argus and Crisis*, February 18, 1865, p. 5; *Meridian* (MS) *Clarion*, February 16, 1865, reprinted in *Nashville Press*, February 27, 1865, p. 1.

52. (Selma, AL) *Mississippian*, February 14, 1865, reprinted in *Mobile Advertiser and Register*, February 18, 1865, p. 2.

53. (New Orleans) *Picayune*, February 26, 1865, p. 2.

54. *Selma* (AL) *Dispatch*, reprinted in *Mobile Advertiser and Register*, February 18, 1865, p. 1.

55. (Talladega, AL) *Democratic Watchtower*, March 1, 1865, p. 2. See also *Mobile Advertiser and Register*, March 2, 1865, p. 2, March 21, 1865, p. 2, March 29, 1865, p. 2. Regarding White, see Sarah Woolfolk Wiggins, "Five Men Called Scalawags," *Alabama Review* 17 (January 1964): 45–55.

56. (Mobile) *Army Argus and Crisis*, reprinted in *Macon* (GA) *Telegraph and Confederate*, February 27, 1865, p. 2, and (New Orleans) *Picayune*, February 25, 1865, p. 2. See also *Mobile Advertiser and Register*, February 15, 1865, p. 1.

57. Martin, *Rich Man's War*, 195. See, generally *Montgomery Mail*, reprinted in *Mobile Advertiser and Register*, December 13, 1864, p. 1; *Mobile Advertiser and Register*, December 25, 1864, p. 1.

58. Gustavus Schnitzer to Lt. R. B. Avery, February 24, 1865, OR, Series 1, Vol. 49 (Part I), 52.

59. R. S. Granger to Brig. Gen. W. D. Whipple, March 25, 1865, OR, Series 1, Vol. 49 (Part II), 83.

230 / Notes to pages 50–54

60. (Selma, AL) *Mississippian*, reprinted in *Mobile Advertiser and Register*, February 15, 1865, p. 2, and *Edgefield* (SC) *Advertiser*, March 1, 1865, p. 1.

61. U. S. Grant to Maj. Gen. George H. Thomas, February 14, 1865, OR, Series 1, Vol. 49 (Part I), pp. 708–9, 716–17; *Mobile Advertiser and Register*, February 15, 1865, p. 2; James Pickett Jones, *Yankee Blitzkrieg: Wilson's Raid through Alabama and Georgia* (Lexington: University Press of Kentucky, 2000); Keenan, *Wilson's Cavalry Corps*; Rex Miller, *Croxton's Raid* (Fort Collins, CO: Old Army Press, 1979); T. Michael Parrish, *Richard Taylor: Soldier Prince of Dixie* (Chapel Hill: University of North Carolina Press, 1992), 432–33; Elbridge Colby, "Wilson's Cavalry Campaign of 1865," *Journal of the American Military History Foundation* 2 (Winter 1938): 204, 207.

62. James Harrison Wilson, *Under the Old Flag: Recollections of Military Operations in the War for the Union, the Spanish War, the Boxer Rebellion, etc.* (New York: D. Appleton, 1912), 2:205; William Lindsey McDonald, *Civil War Tales of the Tennessee Valley* (Killen, AL: Heart of Dixie Publishing, 2003), 93; Keenan, *Wilson's Cavalry Corps*, 138.

63. (Washington, DC) *National Tribune*, June 11, 1903, p. 3. See also *Louisville* (KY) *Journal*, March 17, 1865, p. 1 (one soldier charged that the real problem was that transports were being used to haul cotton). See generally Keenan, *Wilson's Cavalry Corps*, 145.

64. (Richmond) *Dispatch*, March 30, 1865, p. 2; N. B. Forrest to Lt. Gen. R. Taylor, March 6, 1865, OR, Series 1, Vol. 49 (Part I), pp. 1030–31; Keenan, *Wilson's Cavalry Corps*, 151–52.

65. Daily Journal of Joshua Burns Moore, 78–79, ADAH.

66. (Montgomery) *Memphis Appeal*, reprinted in *Mobile Advertiser and Register*, February 18, 1865, p. 2.

67. Hearn, *Mobile Bay*, 146–58; Sean Michael O'Brien, *Mobile 1865: Last Stand of the Confederacy* (Westport, CT: Praeger, 2001), 58–65; George S. Burkhardt, *Confederate Rage, Yankee Wrath: No Quarter in the Civil War* (Carbondale: Southern Illinois University Press, 2007), 236–37. See also (Montgomery) *Memphis Appeal*, reprinted in *Augusta* (GA) *Chronicle*, March 21, 1865, p. 3.

68. *Montgomery Advertiser*, reprinted in *Mobile Advertiser and Register*, March 1, 1865, p. 1.

69. *Montgomery Advertiser*, March 3, 1865, p. 1, March 5, 1865. See also William Warren Rogers Jr., *Confederate Home Front: Montgomery during the Civil War* (Tuscaloosa: University of Alabama Press, 1999), 385; Fleming, *Civil War and Reconstruction*, 341–42.

Chapter 5

1. *Montgomery Advertiser*, March 3, 1865, p. 2; *Mobile Advertiser and Register*, February 24, 1865, p. 2. See also *Mobile Advertiser and Register*, February 26, 1865, p. 2, March 19, 1865, p. 2.

2. *Mobile Advertiser and Register*, January 12, 1865, p. 2.

3. Ibid., January 13, 1865, p. 2.

NOTES TO PAGES 54–56 / 231

4. *Richmond Sentinel*, reprinted in *Nashville Press*, February 23, 1865, p. 2. Regarding guerrilla warfare in the Civil War, see Daniel E. Sutherland, *A Savage Conflict: The Decisive Role of Guerrillas in the American Civil War* (Chapel Hill: University of North Carolina Press, 2009), 265–75. Historians appear to disagree regarding whether Davis favored guerrilla warfare. See Herman Hattaway and Richard Beringer, *Jefferson Davis, Confederate President* (Lawrence: University of Kansas Press, 2002), 166 (yes); William B. Feis, "Jefferson Davis and the 'Guerrilla Option': A Reexamination," in *The Collapse of the Confederacy*, ed. Mark Grimsley and Brooks D. Simpson (Lincoln: University of Nebraska Press, 2001), 104–105 (no); Jay Winik, *April 1865: The Month That Saved America* (New York: HarperCollins, 2006) (yes); Emory M. Thomas, "Ambivalent Visions of Victory: Davis, Lee, and Confederate Grand Strategy," in *Jefferson Davis' Generals*, ed. Gabor S. Boritt (New York: Oxford University Press, 1999), 32–33 (yes); William J. Cooper, *Jefferson Davis: American* (New York: Vintage Books, 2001), 566 (no); Sutherland, *A Savage Conflict*, 267 (no).

5. *Anderson* (SC) *Intelligencer*, March 23, 1865, p. 2; *Mobile Advertiser and Register*, March 25, 1865, p. 2.

6. *Brownlow's Knoxville Whig, and Rebel Ventilator*, March 15, 1865, p. 2; *Nashville Dispatch*, reprinted in (Richmond) *Dispatch*, March 27, 1865, p. 2; *Nashville Press*, April 1, 1865, p. 1.

7. *Edgefield* (SC) *Advertiser*, March 29, 1865, p. 1.

8. W. T. Sherman to George H. Thomas, January 21, 1865, OR, Series 1, Vol. 4 (Part II), 621–22; William T. Sherman to U. S. Grant, April 25, 1865, in John Y. Simon, ed., *The Papers of Ulysses S. Grant* (Carbondale: Southern Illinois University Press, 1984), 14:425–26 ("I now apprehend that the Rebel Armies will disperse; and instead of dealing with six or seven states, we will have to deal with numberless bands of desperadoes headed by such men as Mosby, Forrest, Red Jackson, & others who know not, and care not for danger or its consequences."). Regarding Lincoln's fears of guerrilla warfare, see Donald, *Lincoln*, 574.

9. *Mobile Advertiser and Register*, February 28, 1865, p. 2.

10. *Shreveport Semi-Weekly News*, April 6, 1865, p. 1; *Columbia* (SC) *Phoenix*, March 30, 1865, p. 3; (Richmond) *Dispatch*, March 24, 1865, p. 4.

11. *Mobile Advertiser and Register*, March 29, 1865, p. 1.

12. Ibid.

13. See, e.g., *Columbus* (GA) *Enquirer*, January 28, 1864, February 14, 1864, May 25, 1864, June 12, 1864, June 26, 1864, July 12, 1864, July 14, 1864, July 30, 1864, August 13, 1864, August 23, 1864, September 4, 1864; (Richmond) *Dispatch*, January 7, 1865, p. 1, January 31, 1864, p. 2, February 3, 1865, p. 2, February 6, 1865, p. 1; *Montgomery Advertiser*, February 3, 1865, p. 1. See generally Howard Jones, *Crucible of Power: A History of American Foreign Relations to 1913* (Lanham, MD: Rowman and Littlefield Publishers, 2009), 234–36; Alfred Jackson Hanna and Kathryn Abbey Hanna, *Napoleon III and Mexico: American Triumph over Monarchy* (Chapel Hill: University of North Carolina Press, 1971), 131–66; Dean B. Mahin, *One War at a Time: The International Dimensions of the American Civil War* (Washington, DC: Brassey's, 1999), 275–

77; William E. Hardy, "South of the Border, Ulysses S. Grant and the French Intervention," *Civil War History* 54 (March 2008): 63, 69, 73; John Mason Hart, *Empire and Revolution: The Americans in Mexico since the Civil War* (Berkeley: University of California Press, 2002), 9–14.

14. *Mobile Advertiser and Register*, January 13, 1865, p. 2.

15. Ibid., February 28, 1865, p. 1 (publishing a resolution supporting these efforts), March 2, 1865, p. 2, March 3, 1865, p. 2, March 10, 1865, p. 1, March 22, 1865, p. 2, April 8, 1865, p. 2.

16. *Mobile Advertiser and Register*, April 8, 1865, p. 2. The idea of Confederate societies appears to have originated in Mississippi in 1863. See *Mobile Advertiser and Register*, October 6, 1863, p. 2, October 6, 1863, p. 2.

17. (Troy, AL) *Southern Advertiser*, April 21, 1865, p. 2.

18. *Mobile Advertiser and Register*, March 3, 1865, p. 1, March 19, 1865, p. 2.

19. *Mobile Advertiser and Register*, March 3, 1865, p. 2.

20. (Washington, DC) *National Republican*, March 25, 1864, p. 1; *Cleveland Leader*, April 14, 1865, p. 2; McPherson, *Battle Cry of Freedom*, 273.

21. *Selma* (AL) *Dispatch*, December 1, 1864, reprinted in *Cleveland Leader*, January 23, 1865, p. 2, among many others.

22. *Mobile Advertiser and Register*, April 8, 1865, p. 2.

23. See, e.g., *Mobile Advertiser and Register*, October 2, 1863, p. 2, December 20, 1863, p. 2.

24. Ibid., November 20, 1864, p. 1.

25. Ibid., December 7, 1864, p. 1.

26. Ibid., January 6, 1865, p. 2.

27. Ibid., January 20, 1865, p. 2.

28. Ibid., February 8, 1865, p. 2.

29. Ibid., March 3, 1865, p. 1.

30. See generally Ronald C. White, *Lincoln's Greatest Speech: The Second Inaugural* (New York: Simon and Schuster, 2003).

31. *Nashville Press*, March 4, 1865, p. 2.

32. Jeremiah Clemens to Benjamin F. Butler, November 16, 1864, Lincoln Papers, Library of Congress.

33. *Mobile Advertiser and Register*, March 3, 1865, p. 1.

34. *New York Herald*, reprinted in *Cleveland Leader*, March 11, 1865, p. 2.

35. *Jacksonville* (AL) *Republican*, March 16, 1865, p. 1; *Mobile Advertiser and Register*, March 12, 1865, p. 1, March 14, 1865, p. 2. See also Harry S. Stout, *Upon the Altar of the Nation: A Moral History of the American Civil War* (New York: Penguin Books, 2007), 425–28.

36. *New York Times*, March 2, 1865, p. 4 (vehemently opposing it); *New York Tribune*, reprinted in *Xenia* (OH) *Sentinel*, March 10, 1865, p. 2 (favoring black suffrage but not as a precondition to peace).

37. Compare with *Chattanooga Gazette*, January 27, 1865 (declaring that the power of Southern elites should be broken), February 1, 1865 (same). See generally David

NOTES TO PAGES 59–62 / 233

Johnson, *Decided on the Battlefield: Grant, Sherman, Lincoln, and the Election of 1864* (Amherst, NY: Prometheus Books, 2012), 252–55.

38. *Belmont* (OH) *Chronicle*, March 9, 1865, p. 2.

39. Genesis, 22:15, quoted in (Hillsborough, OH) *Highland Weekly News*, March 9, 1865, p. 2.

40. *New York Tribune*, reprinted in *Burlington* (VT) *Free Press*, March 10, 1865, p. 2.

41. *New York Tribune*, March 22, 1865, p. 4.

42. (Virginia City) *Montana Post*, March 11, 1865, p. 2.

43. *Fremont* (OH) *Journal*, March 10, 1865, p. 2; *Cleveland Leader*, March 6, 1865, p. 2.

44. (Washington, DC) *National Intelligencer*, March 6, 1865.

45. *Sunbury* (PA) *American*, March 11, 1865, p. 2.

46. William C. McClellan to Robert McClellan, March 24, 1865, in Carter, *Welcome the Hour of Conflict*, 275–76.

47. (Washington, DC) *National Republican*, March 17, 1865, p. 2.

48. (Brookville, PA) *Jeffersonian*, March 23, 1865, p. 1.

49. *Nashville Union*, March 11, 1865, p. 2. See, e.g., *Nashville Union*, March 18, 1865, p. 3. Regarding other reports of desertion in the aftermath of Lincoln's address, see, e.g., *Nashville Union*, March 18, 1865, p. 3; *Nashville Times and True Union*, March 31, 1865, p. 1; *Memphis Bulletin*, March 28, 1865, reprinted in (Washington, DC) *National Republican*, April 7, 1865, p. 2.

50. Edward Norphlet Brown to Fannie Brown, March 4, 1865, Edward Norphlet Brown Letters, 337, ADAH.

51. Henry Groves Connor, *John Archibald Campbell* (Clark, NJ: Lawbook Exchange, 2004), 174; Conroy, *Our One Common Country*, 243.

52. Conroy, *Our One Common Country*, 231–34.

53. *Richmond Enquirer*, March 7, 1865, reprinted in *Burlington* (VT) *Free Press*, March 17, 1865, p. 2. See also *Richmond Sentinel*, March 9, 1865, reprinted in *Nashville Union*, March 19, 1865, p. 1.

54. (Richmond) *Dispatch*, March 22, 1865, p. 1 (publishing a card from Hunter).

55. Wiggins, *Journals of Josiah Gorgas*, 174.

56. *Cleveland Leader*, March 20, 1865, p. 2.

57. (Portage) *Wisconsin State Register*, March 11, 1865.

58. *Nashville Union*, April 18, 1865, p. 2.

59. *Cleveland Leader*, April 18, 1865, p. 1; *Raleigh Standard*, April 18, 1865, reprinted in (Washington, DC) *National Republican*, April 27, 1865, p. 2; *Cincinnati Commercial*, reprinted in (Millersburg, OH) *Holmes County Farmer*, April 27, 1865, p. 3; *Xenia* (OH) *Sentinel*, April 28, 1865, p. 3; *Richmond Whig*, cited in (Millersburg, OH) *Holmes County Farmer*, May 4, 1865, p. 1.

60. (Brookville, PA) *Jeffersonian*, April 27, 1865, p. 2.

61. *Nashville Union*, March 10, 1865, p. 2; (New Orleans) *Picayune*, March 28, 1865, p. 3; *Mobile Advertiser and Register*, March 29, 1865, p. 2; *Nashville Times and True Union*, March 30, 1865, p. 2; *Nashville Union*, April 15, 1865, p. 2.

234 / Notes to pages 63–65

62. *Jackson* (MS) *News*, reprinted in (Selma, AL) *Mississippian*, reprinted in *Mobile Advertiser and Register*, March 12, 1865, p. 1.

63. *Montgomery Advertiser*, March 12, 1865, p. 1.

64. *Montgomery Mail*, reprinted in *Mobile Advertiser and Register*, March 24, 1865, p. 2. See also *Montgomery Mail*, February 24, 1865, p. 2.

65. *Mobile Advertiser and Register*, March 24, 1865, p. 1.

66. (Mobile) *Army Argus and Crisis*, April 8, 1865, p. 4.

67. *Tuscaloosa Observer*, March 8, 1865, p. 1.

68. Ibid. See also ibid., March 15, 1865, p. 1.

69. His first grandson, future Arkansas lawyer Wolsey Randall Martin, had been born to his daughter Lucy and Confederate quartermaster John Mason Martin on February 6, 1865. John Hallum, *Biographical and Pictorial History of Arkansas* (Albany, NY: Weed, Parsons, 1887), 378–80.

70. Wilson, *Under the Old Flag*, 183.

71. Todd, *First Alabama Cavalry*, 238. The soldier, Jason Guin, was a direct ancestor of US district judge J. Foy Guin, who was appointed to the bench of the Northern District of Alabama by Republican president Richard Nixon in 1973.

72. *Mobile Advertiser and Register*, March 14, 1865, p. 1.

73. Ibid., p. 2.

74. Ibid., March 18, 1865, p. 1.

75. Ibid., March 21, 1865, p. 2.

76. *Tuscaloosa Observer*, March 15, 1865, p. 1.

77. *Mobile Advertiser and Register*, April 1, 1865, p. 1. *Tuscaloosa Observer*, March 15, 1865, p. 1. It is submitted that one key to understanding the behavior of Robert Jemison and others who had opposed secession at the outset was that their financial future was now inextricably entwined with the Confederacy, not only because it served as a bulwark for slavery but also because it was the only entity that was obligated to pay the war bonds and treasury notes they held. Without those assets, they would turn into paupers unless the state could later somehow be forced to compensate them. As will be seen, this particular issue would become very significant in the months after the war ended. In addition, as the post quartermaster in Tuscaloosa, Jemison's younger brother had a cushy and highly desirable bombproof position, and it is possible Jemison did not want to jeopardize that by refusing to demonstrate his loyalty to the cause in this empty way.

78. *Mobile Advertiser and Register*, March 24, 1865, p. 2 (Augusta, Georgia), March 29, 1865, p. 1 (Canton, Mississippi), April 4, 1865, p. 1 (the "Forrest Society of Loyal Confederates" was formed at Demopolis, Alabama), April 5, 1865, p. 1 (Greensboro, Alabama), April 9, 1865, p. 2 ("Ladies Society of Loyal Confederates" in Mobile). See generally Anne S. Rubin, *A Shattered Nation: The Rise and Fall of the Confederacy, 1861–1868* (Chapel Hill: University of North Carolina Press, 2005), 57; H.E. Sterkx, *Partners In Rebellion: Alabama Women in the Civil War* (Rutherford, NJ: Farleigh Dickinson University Press, 1970), 19.

79. Betty J. Ownsbey, *Alias "Paine": Lewis Thornton Powell, The Mystery Man of the*

NOTES TO PAGES 65–68 / 235

Lincoln Conspiracy (Jefferson, NC: McFarland, 1993) 56–57; Michael W. Kauffman, *American Brutus: John Wilkes Booth and the Lincoln Conspiracies* (New York: Random House, 2004), 179; Kate Clifford Larson, *The Assassin's Accomplice: Mary Surratt and the Plot to Kill Abraham Lincoln* (New York: Basic Books, 2008), 62–65, 66–70.

80. Keenan, *Wilson's Cavalry Corps*, 152; George F. Pearce, *Pensacola during the Civil War: A Thorn in the Side of the Confederacy* (Gainesville: University Press of Florida, 2000), 225–27.

Chapter 6

1. Daily Journal of Joshua Burns Moore, 85, ADAH.

2. Joseph W. Danielson, *War's Desolating Scourge: The Union's Occupation of North Alabama* (Lawrence: University Press of Kansas, 2012), 151–54.

3. *Nashville Times and True Union*, March 31, 1865, p. 1.

4. Daily Journal of Joshua Burns Moore, 85, ADAH.

5. *Nashville Times and True Union*, March 31, 1865, p. 1.

6. McDonald, *Walk through the Past*, 110–11; G. M. Dodge to Capt. S. Wait, May 5, 1863, OR, Series 1, Vol. 23 (Part I), 246, 249; *Huntsville Confederate*, May 30, 1863, p. 2, June 5, 1863, p. 2; Sheridan, "Civil War Manufacturing," 50, 56, 62–63; Severance, *Portraits of Conflict*, 307.

7. *Mobile Advertiser and Register*, March 25, 1865, p. 1.

8. *Montgomery Advertiser*, March 28, 1865. See also *Macon (GA) Telegraph and Confederate*, March 29, 1865, p. 2.

9. Keenan, *Wilson's Cavalry Corps*, 152; Jones, *Yankee Blitzkrieg*, 13, 27–29; Rogers et al., *Alabama*, 220; Charles A. Misulia, *Columbus, Georgia, 1865: The Last True Battle of the Civil War* (Tuscaloosa: University of Alabama Press, 2010), 13; Thomas Crofts, *History of the Service of the Third Ohio Veteran Volunteer Cavalry in the War for the Preservation of the Union from 1861–1865* (Toledo, OH: Stoneman Press, 1910), 188; Benjamin F. McGee, *History of the 72d Indiana Volunteer Infantry of the Mounted Lightning Brigade* (Lafayette, IN: S. Vater Printers, 1882), 519–27.

10. *Edgefield (SC) Advertiser*, March 29, 1865, p. 1; *Mobile Advertiser and Register*, March 22, 1865, p. 2.

11. *Columbia (SC) Phoenix*, March 30, 1865, p. 1.

12. *Philadelphia Press*, March 25, 1865, p. 2.

13. Thomas Jordan and J. P. Pryor, *The Campaigns of Lieut.-Gen. N. B. Forrest, and of Forrest's Cavalry* (New Orleans: Blelock, 1868), 659–61.

14. *Tuscaloosa Observer*, March 30, 1865, reprinted in *Mobile Advertiser and Register*, April 5, 1865, p. 2.

15. (Mobile) *Army Argus and Crisis*, April 8, 1865, p. 4.

16. Regarding Hardcastle, see *Confederate Veteran* 23, no. 7 (July 1915): 325; Bruce S. Allardice, *Confederate Colonels: A Biographical Register* (Columbia: University of Missouri Press, 2008), 179–80 (Hardcastle was born on July 5, 1836, in Maryland, graduated from West Point in 1861, and was disabled during the war when his leg was bro-

ken in Kentucky); Michael Ronald Hardcastle, *The Roots of the Hardcastles: "An old Yorkshire Family"* (self-published, 2009), 130–31.

17. J. H. Wilson to Brig. Gen. William D. Whipple, May 3, 1865, OR, Series 1, Vol. 49 (Part I), 350.

18. *Tuscaloosa Observer*, March 30, 1865, reprinted in *Mobile Advertiser and Register*, April 5, 1865, p. 2.

19. (Mobile) *Army Argus and Crisis*, April 8, 1865, p. 4.

20. *Tuscaloosa Observer*, March 30, 1865, reprinted in *Mobile Advertiser and Register*, April 5, 1865, p. 2.

21. E. Surget to Brig. Gen. D. W. Adams, March 28, 1865, OR, Series 1, Vol. 49 (Part II), 1170 ("Kentucky brigade will strike enemy's rear from Tuscaloosa").

22. Jordan and Pryor, *Campaigns of Lieut.-Gen. N. B. Forrest*, 661.

23. Keenan, *Wilson's Cavalry Corps*, 162.

24. A. B. Hardcastle to General D. W. Adams, April 2, 1865, reprinted in Hardcastle, *Roots of the Hardcastles*, 130. The telegram does not appear in the OR.

25. (Washington, DC) *National Tribune*, April 23, 1891, p. 1, February 16, 1911, p. 2. See also Waldon Spicer Loving, *Coming Like Hell: The Story of the 12th Tennessee Cavalry* (San Jose, CA: Writers Club Press, 2002), 138; *Columbia* (SC) *Phoenix*, April 10, 1865, p. 2.

26. A. B. Hardcastle to Major John Rawl, April 11, 1865, reprinted in Thomas P. Clinton, "The Military Operations of General John T. Croxton In West Alabama, 1865," in *Transactions of the Alabama Historical Society 1899–1903*, ed. Thomas McAdory Owen, (Montgomery: Alabama Historical Society, 1904), 4:459–60. This report does not appear in the OR.

27. Regarding ownership of the bridge, see Kenneth D. Willis, *Spanning the Black Warrior River: Seven Bridges between Tuscaloosa and Northport, Alabama* (n.p., 2010), 4–12; John S. Lupold and Thomas L. French Jr., *Bridging Deep South Rivers: The Life and Legend of Horace King* (Athens: University of Georgia Press, 2004), 85–86, 103–4, 207.

28. *Nashville Union*, May 27, 1865, p. 2 (regarding that student, Leonidas Waldemar Alston of Marengo County), May 28, 1865, p. 2 (same); *Montgomery Advertiser*, December 6, 1865, p. 2 (regarding the investment). See also Thomas C. McCorvey, "Southern Cadets in Action," *Century* 39 (November 1889): 152–53.

29. James Benson Sellers, *History of the University of Alabama* (Tuscaloosa: University of Alabama Press, 1953), 275.

30. *Mobile Advertiser and Register*, October 7, 1864, p. 1. See also *Nashville Union*, May 28, 1865, p. 2; David J. Langum and Howard P. Walthall, *From Maverick to Mainstream: Cumberland School of Law, 1847–1997* (Athens: University of Georgia Press, 1997), 49–50 (the university building that was destroyed, University Hall, had been used as a barracks to house black Union soldiers).

31. *Columbus* (GA) *Enquirer*, July 10, 1864, p. 2.

32. Jones, *Yankee Blitzkrieg*, 52, 60, 148–49; Rogers et al., *Alabama*, 220.

33. John T. Croxton to Maj. John M. Bacon, May 1865, OR, Series 1, Vol. 49 (Part I), 418–19 (hereinafter Croxton's Report); Miller, *Croxton's Raid*, 29; Jones, *Yankee Blitzkrieg*, 59–60.

34. On his way from Elyton, Croxton had skirmished with Red Jackson's much larger force near what is now Vance on the morning of April 1 before turning back and moving north toward the Black Warrior River. Croxton's Report, 420–21; (Greensboro) *Alabama Beacon*, April 5, 1865, p. 2.

35. (Washington, DC) *National Tribune*, April 23, 1891, p. 1; Croxton's Report, 421.

36. Matthew William Clinton, *Matt Clinton's Scrapbook* (Northport, AL: Portals, 1979), 170; Miller, *Croxton's Raid*, 37–43; Jones, *Yankee Blitzkrieg*, 150; Keenan, *Wilson's Cavalry Corps*, 206; Wilson, *Under the Old Flag*, 206.

37. *Tuscaloosa News*, July 23, 1989, p. 3F (quoting a letter from a woman who had attended the party).

38. *Montgomery Mail*, February 3, 1865, p. 1 (publishing an article regarding a surge in marriages in Mobile).

39. (Washington, DC) *National Tribune*, April 23, 1891, p. 1.

40. Clinton, "Military Operations," 452–53.

41. Miller, *Croxton's Raid*, 51–52; Sellers, *History of the University of Alabama*, 284.

42. Croxton's Report, 421. See also Miller, *Croxton's Raid*, 37; Jones, *Yankee Blitzkrieg*, 147.

43. Miller, *Croxton's Raid*, 37; Jones, *Yankee Blitzkrieg*, 148.

44. (Washington, DC) *National Tribune*, April 23, 1891, p. 1. See also Hardcastle, *Roots of the Hardcastles*, 130–31 (reprinting a telegram dated April 12, 1865, stating that in addition to the post commander, Colonel Hardcastle, they captured nine officers and sixty-three enlisted men).

45. (Washington, DC) *National Tribune*, July 23, 1891, p. 3.

46. Croxton's Report, 421.

47. Miller, *Croxton's Raid*, 38; Jones, *Yankee Blitzkrieg*, 150–51.

48. Miller, *Croxton's Raid*, 51; Keenan, *Wilson's Cavalry Corps*, 206.

49. Sellers, *History of the University of Alabama*, 275, 285–87; Miller, *Croxton's Raid*, 46–49; Jones, *Yankee Blitzkrieg*, 151; Clark E. Center Jr., "The Burning of the University of Alabama," *Alabama Heritage* 16 (Spring, 1990): 30; Robert O. Mellown and Gene Byrd, "F. A. P. Barnard and Alabama First Observatory," *Journal of the Alabama Academy of Science* 57 (January 1986): 39–44; Rogers et al., *Alabama*, 220.

50. *Mobile Advertiser and Register*, April 9, 1865, p. 2.

51. Robert O. Mellown, "Construction of the Alabama Insane Hospital, 1852–1861," *Alabama Review* 38 (April 1985): 102–103; Clinton, *Matt Clinton's Scrapbook*, 159, 163, 165; Croxton's Report, 421.

52. Miller, *Croxton's Raid*, 51–52; Jones, *Yankee Blitzkrieg*, 152.

53. (Greensboro) *Alabama Beacon*, April 5, 1865, p. 2; Miller, *Croxton's Raid*, 53–54; Jones, *Yankee Blitzkrieg*, 153; Keenan, *Wilson's Cavalry Corps*, 207 (also noting that the Pickens County courthouse at Carrollton was later burned by Wilson's men); Lupold, *Bridging Deep South Rivers*, 207–8 (the bridge was later rebuilt by the famous black bridge builder, Horace King). See also Scott W. Owens, "The Federal Invasion of Pickens County, April, 1865: Croxton's Sipsey River Campaign," *Alabama Review* 62 (April 2009): 83–112 (discussing the activities of Croxton's raiders after they left Tuscaloosa).

238 / NOTES TO PAGES 74–76

54. Miller, *Croxton's Raid*, 54; Jones, *Yankee Blitzkrieg*, 153.

55. (Washington, DC) *National Tribune*, April 23, 1891, p. 1.

Chapter 7

Epigraph. Axford, "*To Lochaber Na Mair*," 157–58.

1. Brian Steel Wills, "The Confederate Sun Sets on Selma: Nathan Bedford Forrest and the Defense of Alabama in 1865," in *The Yellowhammer War: The Civil War and Reconstruction in Alabama*, ed. Kenneth W. Noe (Tuscaloosa: University of Alabama Press, 2013), 71–84.

2. Joseph H. Woodward II, *Alabama Blast Furnaces* (Tuscaloosa: University of Alabama Press, 2007), 46–47, 83, 138; William N. Still, "Selma and the Confederate States Navy," *Alabama Review* 15 (January 1962), 19–37; W. David Lewis, *Sloss Furnaces and the Rise of the Birmingham District: An Industrial Epic* (Tuscaloosa: University of Alabama Press, 1994), 34–38; Richard J. Stockham, "Alabama Iron for the Confederacy: The Selma Works," *Alabama Review* 21 (July 1969): 163–72; James Sanders Day, *Diamonds in the Rough: A History of Alabama's Cahaba Coal Field* (Tuscaloosa: University of Alabama Press, 2013).

3. Woodward, *Alabama Blast Furnaces*, 122, 126.

4. Wiggins, *Journals of Josiah Gorgas*, 178; Woodward, *Alabama Blast Furnaces*, 82–84, 106–107; Armes, *Story of Coal and Iron*, 185–87; Jones, *Yankee Blitzkrieg*, 63; James R. Bennett and Karen R. Utz, *Iron and Steel: A Guide to Birmingham Area Industrial Heritage Sites* (Tuscaloosa: University of Alabama Press, 2010), 52–61.

5. Armes, *Story of Coal and Iron*, 186; Jones, *Yankee Blitzkrieg*, 64; Woodward, *Alabama Blast Furnaces*, 136–39, 160; Bennett and Utz, *Iron and Steel*, 1–15.

6. Wiggins, *Journals of Josiah Gorgas*, 189–90; Armes, *Story of Coal and Iron*, 69, 177, 186; Woodward, *Alabama Blast Furnaces*, 121–26; Lewis, *Clearing the Thickets*, 304; Bennett and Utz, *Iron and Steel*, 41–43.

7. Woodward, *Alabama Blast Furnaces*, 46–48, 97–99; Rhonda Coleman Ellison, *Bibb County Alabama: The First Hundred Years, 1818–1918* (Tuscaloosa: University of Alabama Press, 1984), 129–32; Jones, *Yankee Blitzkrieg*, 63–64; Armes, *Story of Coal and Iron*, 186; Bennett and Utz, *Iron and Steel*, 48–51; Frank E. Vandiver, "Josiah Gorgas and the Brierfield Iron Works," *Alabama Review* 3 (January 1950): 5–21; David L. Nolen, "Wilson's Raid on the Coal and Iron Industry in Shelby County," master's thesis, University of Alabama, Birmingham, 1988.

8. Walter W. Stephen, "The Brooke Guns From Selma," *Alabama Historical Quarterly* 29 (Fall 1958): 462–75; Armes, *Story of Coal and Iron*, 143–38; Charles S. Davis, *Colin J. McRae: Confederate Financial Agent* (Tuscaloosa: Confederate Publishing, 1961); Alston Fitts III, *Selma: Queen City of the Black Belt* (Selma, AL: Clairmont Press, 1989), 49–54; W. T. Sherman to Maj. Gen. H. W. Halleck, November 18, 1863, OR, Series 1, Vol. 31 (Part III), 185; Lovell H. Rousseau to Maj. Gen. W. T. Sherman, June 19, 1864, OR, Series 1, Vol. 38 (Part IV), 530–31.

9. Ernest Barnwell Johnston Jr., "Selma, Alabama, As a Center of Confederate

NOTES TO PAGES 76–78 / 239

War Production, 1860–1865," bachelor's thesis, Harvard College, 1952; Armes, *Story of Coal and Iron*, 135; *New York Herald*, reprinted in *Macon* (GA) *Telegraph*, May 21, 1865, p. 1.

10. (Selma, AL) *Chattanooga Rebel*, April 1, 1865, reprinted in *Mobile Advertiser and Register*, April 5, 1865, p. 2; (Greensboro) *Alabama Beacon*, April 5, 1865, p. 2; J. H. Wilson to Brig. Gen. William D. Whipple, May 3, 1865, OR, Series 1, Vol. 49 (Part I), 350–51 (hereinafter Wilson's Report).

11. Jones, *Yankee Blitzkrieg*, 81.

12. Ibid., 82; Hurst, *Nathan Bedford Forrest*, 250; Walter M. Jackson, *The Story of Selma* (Birmingham, AL: Birmingham Print, 1954), 215.

13. *New York Herald*, April 22, 1865, p. 8; *Macon* (GA) *Telegraph*, May 21, 1865, p. 1; J. H. Wilson to Brig. Gen. William D. Whipple, June 29, 1865, OR, Series 1, Vol. 49 (Part I), 360–61; Jones, *Yankee Blitzkrieg*, 79–80.

14. (Mobile) *Army Argus and Crisis*, April 8, 1865, p. 4. See also Jones, *Yankee Blitzkrieg*, 82; Fitts, *Selma*, 58; Jackson, *Story of Selma*, 215–16.

15. Fitts, *Selma*, 57–58; Jackson, *Story of Selma*, 215–16; Parrish, *Richard Taylor*, 434–35; Jones, *Yankee Blitzkrieg*, 82–83; Hurst, *Nathan Bedford Forrest*, 251. Regarding Mayor Henry, see *Selma* (AL) *Messenger*, May 15, 1867, p. 3; (Mobile) *Nationalist*, March 14, 1867, p. 2.

16. (Selma) *Chattanooga Rebel*, April 1, 1865, reprinted in *Mobile Advertiser and Register*, April 5, 1865, p. 2.

17. (Selma) *Chattanooga Rebel*, April 27, 1865, p. 1.

18. *Selma* (AL) *Union*, reprinted in (New Orleans) *Picayune*, April 23, 1865, p. 3; Fitts, *Selma*, 57–58; Keenan, *Wilson's Cavalry Corps*, 169; Parrish, *Richard Taylor*, 435; Jackson, *Story of Selma*, 216.

19. Richard R. Hancock, *Hancock's Diary: A History of the Second Tennessee Confederate Cavalry* (Nashville: Brandon Print, 1887), 558.

20. *Macon* (GA) *Telegraph and Confederate*, April 6, 1865, p. 2; *Augusta* (GA) *Chronicle*, April 9, 1865, p. 12; *Columbia* (SC) *Phoenix*, April 10, 1865, p. 3; (Columbus, GA) *Sun*, April 5, 1865, reprinted in *Edgefield* (SC) *Advertiser*, April 12, 1865, p. 1.

21. John T. Trowbridge, *The Desolate South 1865–1866: A Picture of the Battlefields and of the Devastated Confederacy* (New York: Duell, Sloan and Pearce, 1956), 226.

22. *New York Herald*, April 22, 1865, p. 8; *Selma* (AL) *Union*, reprinted in (New Orleans) *Picayune*, April 23, 1865, p. 2; *Mobile News*, July 13, 1865, p. 4. For a list of casualties among the defenders, see *Montgomery Mail*, April 21, 1865, p. 2.

23. *New York Herald*, April 13, 1865, p. 1; (Washington, DC) *National Intelligencer*, April 13, 1865; *New Haven* (CT) *Palladium*, April 12, 1865; *Cleveland Leader*, April 14, 1865, p. 2.

24. *Louisville* (KY) *Journal*, April 30, 1865, p. 1; *Columbia* (SC) *Phoenix*, April 10, 1865, p. 3; *New York Herald*, April 13, 1865, p. 1; *Boston Herald*, April 24, 1865, p. 4; Jones, *Yankee Blitzkrieg*, 90; Hurst, *Nathan Bedford Forrest*, 251–53; Jackson, *Story of Selma*, 218; Wilson's Report, 351.

25. Wilson's Report, 351.

240 / NOTES TO PAGES 78–81

26. *Montgomery Mail*, April 7, 1865, reprinted in *Augusta* (GA) *Constitutionalist*, April 12, 1865, p. 1; *Edgefield* (SC) *Advertiser*, April 19, 1865, p. 4 (citing the comments of a woman who escaped Selma); (Selma, AL) *Chattanooga Rebel*, April 14, 1865, reprinted in (Greensboro) *Alabama Beacon*, April 21, 1865, p. 2; *Mobile Advertiser and Register*, April 9, 1865, p. 2; *Columbia* (SC) *Phoenix*, April 10, 1865, p. 3.

27. *Edgefield* (SC) *Advertiser*, April 12, 1865, p. 1, April 19, 1865, p. 4 (citing the contents of a letter). See generally Jones, *Yankee Blitzkrieg*, 90–95; Fitts, *Selma*, 59–60; Keenan, *Wilson's Cavalry Corps*, 172–73.

28. Rogers et al., *Alabama*, 221; Jones, *Yankee Blitzkrieg*, 95–100; Keenan, *Wilson's Cavalry Corps*, 175–76; Fitts, *Selma*, 60; Wilson's Report, 351; Wiggins, *Journals of Josiah Gorgas*, 183–84.

29. *Selma* (AL) *Federal Union*, reprinted in *New Orleans Times*, April 25, 1865, p. 7. See also Whitelaw Reid, *After the War: A Southern Tour: May 1, 1865, to May 1, 1866* (London: Sampson Low, Son, and Marston, 1866), 384–85.

30. Daily Journal of Joshua Burns Moore, 85, ADAH.

31. Diary of A. H. Whetstone, July 1864–December 1865, A. S. Williams III, Americana Collection, Gorgas Library, University of Alabama.

32. (Mobile) *Army Argus and Crisis*, April 8, 1865, p. 4; *Columbia* (SC) *Phoenix*, April 10, 1865, p. 3; (Columbus, GA) *Sun*, reprinted in *Anderson* (SC) *Intelligencer*, April 20, 1865, p. 1 ("well informed men believe that neither Chalmer's nor Jackson's divisions had gotten to Selma when the place was attacked.").

33. *Meridian* (MS) *Clarion*, April 4, 1865, reprinted in *Mobile Advertiser and Register*, April 5, 1865, p. 2, and *Shreveport News*, April 25, 1865, p. 1. The *Selma* (AL) *Federal Union* later claimed that Forrest choked General Chalmers at some point during or after the battle, May 1, 1865, p. 2, reprinted in (Washington, DC) *National Republican*, May 16, 1865, p. 2.

34. (Mobile) *Army Argus and Crisis*, April 8, 1865, pp. 1, 4.

35. *Washington* (DC) *Chronicle*, March 24, 1865, quoted in *Bangor* (ME) *Whig and Courier*, March 27, 1865, and cited in *Mobile Advertiser and Register*, March 29, 1865, p. 2; *Columbia* (SC) *Phoenix*, March 30, 1865, p. 1.

36. *New York Times*, March 23, 1865, p. 4, March 29, 1865, p. 4; *New York Tribune*, March 24, 1865, p. 4. See also *Nashville Union*, March 30, 1865, p. 2 (stating that Lincoln's prior amnesty proclamation "is a failure"); (Washington, DC) *National Republican*, April 7, 1865, April 13, 1865, p. 1; *Boston Advertiser*, March 28, 1865.

37. *Montgomery Mail*, April 7, 1865, p. 1; *Mobile News*, April 17, 1865, p. 2; Winik, *April 1865*, 73–172; Conroy, *Our One Common Country*, 256–59.

38. *New York Tribune*, April 6, 1865, p. 4. See also *New York Times*, April 5, 1865, p. 4 (calling for clemency to the South).

39. *Augusta* (GA) *Constitutionalist*, April 28, 1865, p. 3; Wilson's Report, 351. See, e.g., Hurst, *Nathan Bedford Forrest*, 253; Jones, *Yankee Blitzkrieg*, 98–99; Keenan, *Wilson's Cavalry Corps*, 178–79; Fitts, *Selma*, 60–61; Jackson, *Story of Selma*, 218.

40. Jackson, *Story of Selma*, 218; Wills, "Confederate Sun Sets on Selma," 84–85.

41. (Mobile) *Army Argus and Crisis*, April 8, 1865, p. 1; (Troy, AL) *Southern Adver-*

NOTES TO PAGES 81–83 / 241

tiser, April 21, 1862, p. 2. See also *Mobile Advertiser and Register*, April 5, 1865, p. 2; (Columbus, GA) *Sun*, reprinted in *Augusta Chronicle*, April 13, 1865, p. 3.

42. Hurst, *Nathan Bedford Forrest*, 253–58.

43. W. T. Sherman to George H. Thomas, January 21, 1865, OR, Series 1, Vol. 45 (Part II), 621–22; *Cleveland Leader*, April 14, 1865, p. 2.

44. (Indianapolis, IN) *State Sentinel*, October 30, 1865, p. 2.

45. *New York Herald*, May 15, 1865, p. 1, reprinted in *Boston Herald*, May 17, 1865, p. 5; (Columbus, GA) *Sun*, April 12, 1865, reprinted in *Edgefield* (SC) *Advertiser*, April 19, 1865, p. 1; Jones, *Yankee Blitzkrieg*, 103–4; Keenan, *Wilson's Cavalry Corps*, 180–81; William Stanley Hoole, ed., *History of the Seventh Alabama Cavalry Regiment Including Capt. Charles P. Storrs's Troop of University of Alabama Cadet Volunteers* (Tuscaloosa: Confederate Publishing, 1984), 8.

46. *Montgomery Mail*, April 9, 1865, p. 1.

47. Ibid., April 11, 1865, April 18, 1865, p. 2. See also (Columbus, GA) *Sun*, April 6, 1865, reprinted in *Anderson* (SC) *Intelligencer*, April 20, 1865, p. 1; *Augusta* (GA) *Chronicle*, April 11, 1865, p. 2.

48. *Montgomery Advertiser*, April 18, 1865, p. 2.

49. (Columbus, GA) *Sun*, April 6, 1865, reprinted in *Anderson* (SC) *Intelligencer*, April 20, 1865, p. 1, and *Augusta* (GA) *Constitutionalist*, April 12, 1865, p. 1.

50. (Troy, AL) *Southern Advertiser*, April 21, 1865, p. 2; (Columbus, GA) *Sun*, April 5, 1865, reprinted in *Edgefield* (SC) *Advertiser*, April 12, 1865, p. 1; (Columbus, GA) *Sun*, April 12, 1865, reprinted in *Edgefield* (SC) *Advertiser*, April 19, 1865, p. 1; *Augusta* (GA) *Chronicle and Sentinel*, April 16, 1865; *Montgomery Advertiser*, April 18, 1865, p. 2; *Mobile News*, May 4, 1865, p. 1; *New York Herald*, May 15, 1865, p. 1, reprinted in *Boston Herald*, May 17, 1865, p. 5; *Nashville Press*, April 25, 1865, p. 1; *New York Herald*, reprinted in *Cleveland Leader*, May 16, 1865, p. 1 ("Fortunately the wind was from the east, and blew the flames away from the City"); Rogers, *Confederate Home Front*, 145–47.

51. *New York Herald*, reprinted in *Cleveland Leader*, May 16, 1865, p. 1.

52. *Montgomery Advertiser*, April 18, 1865, p. 2. See also *Montgomery Mail*, April 17, 1865, p. 1; *New York Herald*, May 15, 1865, p. 1, reprinted in *Boston Herald*, May 17, 1865, p. 5. See generally Rogers, *Confederate Home Front*, 145–47.

53. The delegation included Coleman, Milton Saffold, Saffold's brother-in-law, Dr. James Berney, businessman Josiah Morris, and others. *Montgomery Advertiser*, April 18, 1865, p. 2.

54. Rogers, *Confederate Home Front*, 147; Jones, *Yankee Blitzkrieg*, 111–12; Malcolm Cook McMillan, *The Alabama Confederate Reader* (Tuscaloosa: University of Alabama Press, 1963), 420–21; Wilson's Report, 352.

55. *New York Herald*, May 15, 1865, p. 1, reprinted in *Boston Herald*, May 17, 1865, p. 5, and *Milwaukee Sentinel*, May 19, 1865. See also (Selma, AL) *Chattanooga Rebel*, April 15, 1865, reprinted in *Montgomery Mail*, April 21, 1865, p. 1.

56. *New York Herald*, May 15, 1865, p. 1.

57. *Montgomery Advertiser*, April 18, 1865, p. 3. See also Malcolm Cook McMillan,

The Disintegration of a Confederate State: Three Governors and Alabama's Wartime Home Front, 1861–1865 (Macon, GA: Mercer University Press, 1986), 119–20; Keenan, *Wilson's Cavalry Corps*, 182; Jones, *Yankee Blitzkrieg*, 111.

58. Wilson's Report, 352; *Montgomery Advertiser*, April 18, 1865, p. 2.

59. *Montgomery Advertiser*, April 18, 1865, p. 2.

60. Ibid.

61. Ibid., April 22, 1865, p. 2; see also (Troy, AL) *Southern Advertiser*, April 28, 1865, p. 2. Wilson abandoned the town when he moved on to Columbus, and it would not be permanently occupied until April 24 when forces under the command of General A. J. Smith finally arrived from Mobile. *Nashville Union*, May 16, 1865, p. 1; *Montgomery Mail*, April 24, 1865, p. 1.

62. (Columbia) *South Carolinian*, March 31, 1865.

63. (Mobile) *Army Argus and Crisis*, April 1, 1865, p. 1, April 8, 1865, p. 1; *Milwaukee Sentinel*, April 14, 1865; *Charleston Courier*, April 20, 1865, p. 1; Severance, *Portraits of Conflict*, 300.

64. *Mobile Advertiser and Register*, April 5, 1865, p. 2.

65. Burkhardt, *Confederate Rage*, 237–39; Severance, *Portraits of Conflict*, 302–3; Michael W. Fitzgerald, "Another Kind of Glory: Black Participation and Its Consequences in the Campaign for Confederate Mobile," *Alabama Review* 54 (October 2001): 243, 256–61; Fitzgerald, *Urban Emancipation*, 25.

66. *New York Times*, April 24, 1865, p. 1; *Mobile News*, April 13, 1865; (Washington, DC) *National Intelligencer*, April 19, 1865, April 27, 1865; *Montgomery Advertiser*, April 22, 1865, p. 2; *Cleveland Leader*, April 27, 1865, p. 1 (publishing the mayor's letter); *Charleston Courier*, April 27, 1865, p. 1; (Washington, DC) *National Republican*, May 1, 1865, p. 2; Burnett, *Pen Makes a Good Sword*, 144–46.

67. (Washington, DC) *National Republican*, April 7, 1865, p. 2.

68. *Charleston Courier*, April 27, 1865, p. 1; *Shreveport News*, May 2, 1865, p. 2.

69. *Mobile News*, April 13, 1865, reprinted in *New York Tribune*, May 2, 1865, p. 7 (reporting the surrender and urging the citizens to "submit cheerfully" to Yankee occupation).

70. *Montgomery Advertiser*, April 22, 1865, p. 2; *Montgomery Mail*, April 24, 1865, p. 2, April 26, 1865, p. 1, April 27, 1865, p. 1; *New York Times*, April 10, 1865, p. 4, April 14, 1865, p. 1 (describing the surrender); Elizabeth R. Varon, *Appomattox: Victory, Defeat, and Freedom at the End of the Civil War* (New York: Oxford University Press, 2014), 56–59.

71. John A. Eidsmoe, "Warrior, Statesman, Jurist for the South: The Life, Legacy, and Law of Thomas Goode Jones," *Jones Law Review* 5, no. 1 (Spring 2001): 51, 86–91. See also *New York Times*, April 10, 1865, p. 4; *Belmont* (OH) *Chronicle*, April 13, 1865, p. 2; Stout, *Upon the Altar of the Nation*, 439–42.

72. Wiggins, *Journals of Josiah Gorgas*, 167.

73. Elizabeth Avery Meriwether, *Recollections of 92 Years, 1824–1916* (Nashville: Tennessee Historical Commission, 1958), 158–59. See also (Selma, AL) *Chattanooga Rebel*, April 19, 1865, reprinted in *Montgomery Daily Mail*, April 22, 1865, p. 1.

NOTES TO PAGES 85–92 / 243

74. Diary of Sally Independence Foster, April 9, 1865, ASCCLUNA.

75. Rohr, *Incidents of the War*, 282.

76. Harwell, *Kate*, 275.

77. *Demopolis* (AL) *Herald*, April 25, 1865, reprinted in *Cleveland Leader*, June 23, 1865, p. 2. The editor had an ulterior motive. He concluded that as a consequence of this turn of events, "there is no man who can or will deny that Confederate notes will greatly enhance in value, and finally command coin at but a small discount, if not at par." Given this and the state of Alabama's guarantee of that currency, he asked, "why should the people, then, be afraid to take their own money?"

78. Daily Journal of Joshua Burns Moore, 85–86, ADAH.

79. Wiggins, *Journals of Josiah Gorgas*, 162; *Raleigh* (NC) *Progress*, May 1, 1865, reprinted in (Washington, DC) *Star*, May 9, 1865, p. 4.

80. (Brattleboro) *Vermont Transcript*, May 5, 1865, p. 2.

81. *Bedford* (PA) *Inquirer*, May 5, 1865, p. 3.

82. *Montgomery Mail*, May 29, 1865, p. 1, June 5, 1865, p. 2.

Chapter 8

Epigraph. 1. McWhiney, Moore, and Pace, "*Fear God and Walk Humbly,*" 348.

Epigraph 2. Baumgartner, *Blood and Sacrifice*, 216.

Epigraph 3. Alexander Beaufort Meek, "The Martyrs of the South," reprinted in *Selma* (AL) *Reporter*, June 4, 1864, p. 2; *Columbia* (SC) *Phoenix*, December 1, 1865, p. 4.

1. *Montgomery Advertiser*, reprinted in *Columbus* (GA) *Enquirer*, May 14, 1864, p. 2.

2. Thornton, *Politics and Power*, 281.

3. Gregor Dallas, *1945: The War That Never Ended* (New Haven, CT: Yale University Press, 2005), 84–86, 369, 371–72.

4. Armes, *Story of Coal and Iron*, 195.

5. *Cincinnati Commercial*, reprinted in (Washington, DC) *National Republican*, June 26, 1865, p. 5.

6. Wiggins, *Journals of Josiah Gorgas*, 189.

7. (Milledgeville, GA) *Southern Recorder*, May 9, 1865, p. 2.

8. *Mobile News*, June 5, 1865, p. 4; *Nashville Union*, April 13, 1865, p. 2; (Washington, DC) *National Republican*, April 13, 1865, p. 1.

9. Stanly Coben, "Northeastern Business and Radical Reconstruction: A Reexamination," *Journal of American History* 46 (June 1959): 83–84. "Southrons" is a now-obsolete word that was common during the period as an alternate way to refer to Southerners.

10. A. W. Spies to Governor Patton, November 30, 1866, Robert Miller Patton Papers, ADAH.

11. Cf. *Montgomery Mail*, April 27, 1865, p. 1 (attempting, unsuccessfully, to encourage optimism even after Lincoln's very untimely death).

12. Escott, "*What Shall We Do With the Negro?,*" 223–27.

13. United States v. George Washington Gayle et al., Criminal Case # 1073, US

District Court for the Middle District of Alabama, 1866 Term, National Archives, Atlanta, Georgia.

14. *Selma* (AL) *Dispatch*, December 1, 1864, reprinted in *New York Herald*, January 21, 1865, p. 1; *Providence* (RI) *Press*, January 23, 1865, p 2; (Newark, NJ) *Centinel of Freedom*, January 24, 1865, p. 3; *Philadelphia Inquirer*, January 26, 1865, p. 2; *Cleveland Leader*, January 23, 1865, p. 2; *Fremont* (OH) *Journal*, January 27, 1865, p. 2; (Brookville, PA) *Jeffersonian*, February 16, 1865, p. 1; *Albany* (NY) *Journal*, January 21, 1865, p. 2; *Hartford* (CT) *Courant*, January 23, 1865, p.3; *Jamestown* (NY) *Journal*, February 3, 1865, p. 2, and many other newspapers.

15. (Washington, DC) *National Republican*, April 15, 1865, p 2; (Milledgeville, GA) *Southern Recorder*, April 25, 1865, p. 2. See generally Terry Alford, *Fortune's Fool: The Life of John Wilkes Booth* (New York: Oxford University Press, 2015).

16. *New York Post*, cited in *Nashville Press*, April 10, 1865, p. 1; (Washington, DC) *National Intelligencer*, April 8, 1865; *Montgomery Mail*, April 24, 1865, p. 2.

17. Saunders, *John Archibald Campbell*, 78–85; Perman, *Reunion without Compromise*, 46fn77. See generally (Petersburg, VA) *Daily Express*, April 15, 1865; *Nashville Union*, April 9, 1865, p. 1, April 13, 1865, p. 1; *Cleveland Leader*, April 10, 1865, p. 1, April 11, 1865, p. 2; *Nashville Press*, April 10, 1865, p. 1, April 13, 1865, p. 1; *New York Times*, April 6, 1865, p. 4, April 8, 1865, p. 1, April 10, 1865, p. 1, April 11, 1865, p. 4, April 15, 1865, p. 4; *Richmond Whig*, April 7, 1865, reprinted in *New York Times*, April 10, 1865, p. 4, and (Washington, DC) *National Intelligencer*, April 10, 1865; *New York Tribune*, April 14, 1865, p. 4; *Anderson* (SC) *Intelligencer*, April 13, 1865, p. 2; *New York Tribune*, quoted in *Burlington* (VT) *Free Press*, April 14, 1865, p. 3; (Greensboro) *Alabama Beacon*, May 5, 1865, p. 1; *Mobile News*, May 5, 1865, p. 2.

18. *Nashville Press and Times*, June 3, 1865, p. 2 (publishing a petition from "Loyal Citizens of Alabama"); *Nashville Union*, June 23, 1865, p. 1; *Mobile News*, June 8, 1865, p. 2, June 30, 1865, p. 1.

19. *New York Herald*, March 30, 1865, reprinted in *Richmond Examiner*, April 3, 1865, p. 1; Roy Basler and Carl Sandburg, eds., *Abraham Lincoln: His Speeches and Writings* (Cleveland, OH: World Publishing, 1946), 163–65.

20. *Montgomery Weekly Advertiser*, February 23, 1862, March 16, 1862, March 26, 1862, April 13, 1862, August 10, 1862; *Mobile Advertiser and Register*, April 16, 1862, p. 1, May 7, 1862, p. 2, May 11, 1862, p. 1, June 6, 1862, p. 1; (New Orleans) *Picayune*, August 7, 1862, p. 1; *Selma* (AL) *Reporter*, August 13, 1862, p. 1, July 12, 1863, p. 2.

21. *Selma* (AL) *Reporter*, August 16, 1862, pp. 1, 2 (regarding Union general Robert L. McCook, who was killed on August 5, 1862); (New Orleans) *Picayune*, August 18, 1862, p. 2.

22. *Selma* (AL) *Reporter*, August 18, 1862, p. 1.

23. (Selma, AL) *Chattanooga Rebel*, January 7, 1865, p. 2; *Augusta* (GA) *Chronicle*, March 1, 1865, p. 3; *Macon* (GA) *Telegraph and Confederate*, March 2, 1865, p. 1; *Hartford* (CT) *Courant*, April 7, 1865, p. 3; (New Orleans) *Times Picayune*, April 15, 1865, p. 1; Ethan Sepp Rafuse, *Robert E. Lee and the Fall of the Confederacy, 1863–1865* (Lanham, MD: Rowman and Littlefield Publishers, 2008), 252.

NOTES TO PAGES 93–96 / 245

24. *Milwaukee Sentinel*, April 7, 1865, p. 2.

25. Stout, *Upon the Altar of the Nation*, 430, 444; Thomas, "Ambivalent Visions of Victory," 32–33. But see Feis, "Jefferson Davis," 105 (asserting that Davis did not advocate guerrilla warfare).

26. Brandon H. Beck, ed., *Third Alabama!: The Civil War Memoir of Brigadier General Cullen Andrews Battle, CSA* (Tuscaloosa: University of Alabama Press, 2000); (Richmond) *Dispatch*, April 30, 1886, p. 3 (Davis's speech in Montgomery, Alabama in 1886); Crist, *Papers of Jefferson Davis*, 12:505.

27. *New York Herald*, April 1, 1865, p. 4, April 6, 1865, p. 4; *Providence* (RI) *Press*, March 1, 1865, p. 3; Hurst, *Nathan Bedford Forrest*, 255–58; William Stanley Hoole, *History of Shockley's Alabama Escort Company* (Tuscaloosa, AL: Confederate Publishing, 1983), 13–15; *Columbia* (SC) *Phoenix*, May 20, 1865, p. 2; M. H. Chrysler to Maj. S. L. Woodward, May 15, 1865, OR, Series 1, Vol. 49 (Part II), 796–97 (reporting rumors of French involvement); Andrew F. Rolle, *The Lost Cause: The Confederate Exodus to Mexico* (Norman: University of Oklahoma Press, 1962), 46; W. C. Nunn, *Escape from Reconstruction* (Fort Worth: Texas Christian University Press, 1962); Gerard A. Patterson, *From Blue to Gray: The Life of Confederate General Cadmus M. Wilcox* (Mechanicsburg, PA: Stackpole, 2001), 96–101; Sutherland, *Savage Conflict*, 268–70, 273–74; M. T. Mahoney and Marjorie Locke Mahoney, *Mexico and the Confederacy, 1860–1867* (San Francisco, CA: Austin and Winfield, 1998); Todd W. Wahlstrom, *The Southern Exodus to Mexico: Migration across the Borderlands after the American Civil War* (Lincoln: University of Nebraska Press, 2015).

28. See generally Jones, *Crucible of Power*, 234–36; Hanna and Hanna, *Napoleon III and Mexico*, 131–66; *Jacksonville* (AL) *Republican*, January 9, 1864, p. 2.

29. (Selma, AL) *Mississippian*, January 20, 1865, reprinted in *Macon* (GA) *Telegraph and Confederate*, January 24, 1865, p. 2; *Selma* (AL) *Dispatch*, quoted in *Macon* (GA) *Telegraph and Confederate*, February 6, 1865, p. 1; (New Orleans) *Picayune*, February 26, 1865, p. 4; (Selma, AL) *Chattanooga Rebel*, April 27, 1865, p. 1; *Huntsville Confederate*, reprinted in *Columbus* (GA) *Enquirer*, January 28, 1864, p. 1, October 23, 1864, p. 1.

30. See, e.g., Hanna and Hanna, *Napoleon III and Mexico*, 116–27, 141–42, 155–80; (Philadelphia) *Age*, March 1, 1865, p. 2.

31. Mahin, *One War at a Time*, 275–77; Jones, *Crucible of Power*, 235; Hanna and Hanna, *Napoleon III and Mexico*, 209–38; Hardy, "South of the Border," 63, 69, 73.

32. *New York Times*, April 5, 1865, p. 4.

33. *New York Commercial*, reprinted in (Washington, DC) *National Intelligencer*, April 15, 1865; William G. Thomas, *The Iron Way: Railroads, the Civil War, and the Making of Modern America* (New Haven, CT: Yale University Press, 2011).

34. See generally *New York Times*, March 27, 1865, p. 1; Donald C. Pfanz, *Petersburg Campaign: Abraham Lincoln at City Point, March 20–April 9, 1865* (Lynchburg, VA: H. E. Howard, 1989), 4.

35. Goodwin, *Team of Rivals*, 713, 732; Stout, *Upon the Altar of the Nation*, 430; Donald, *Lincoln*, 574, 582–84; William S. McFeely, *Grant: A Biography* (New York: W. W. Norton, 1981), 212–13; Pfanz, *Petersburg Campaign*, 4–29; Johnson, *Decided on*

the Battlefield, 247–29; *New York Herald*, March 30, 1865, reprinted in *Richmond Examiner*, April 3, 1865, p. 1; (Washington, DC) *National Intelligencer*, April 15, 1869 (publishing a letter by Sherman regarding this meeting). See generally Chester G. Hearn, *Lincoln, the Cabinet, and the Generals* (Baton Rouge: Louisiana State University Press, 2010), 287–92; Varon, *Appomattox*, 115–16.

36. Conroy, *Our One Common Country*, 259–62, 265–73.

37. Ibid., 273–75.

38. *Cleveland Leader*, April 14, 1865, p. 2. See also *New York Times*, April 10, 1865, p. 1.

39. W. C. Bibb to Abraham Lincoln, April 12, 1865, Lincoln Papers, Library of Congress; Saunders, *Early Settlers of Alabama*, 439–40 (Bibb succeeded in meeting with Lincoln). John Witherspoon DuBose claims that Lincoln revealed to Bibb his intention to allow the existing governments of all of the Southern states to remain in place. DuBose, *Alabama's Tragic Decade*, 34–37.

40. *Nashville Union*, April 15, 1865, p. 2; *Nashville Times and True Union*, March 30, 1865, p. 2 (publishing a letter from Daniel Havens Bingham); Robert S. Tharin to Abraham Lincoln, October 3, 1862, Abraham Lincoln Papers, Library of Congress; *New York Herald*, reprinted in *Mobile News*, June 30, 1865, p. 1 (publishing another letter from Daniel Havens Bingham).

41. *Nashville Union*, April 15, 1865, p. 2.

42. Conroy, *Our One Common Country*, 276–85.

43. *New York Tribune*, cited in *Burlington* (VT) *Free Press*, April 7, 1865, p. 3. This process would later be used by Andrew Johnson.

44. *New York Times*, March 30, 1865, p. 1, March 30, 1865, p. 1, March 31, 1865, p. 4, April 1, 1865, p. 1, April 10, 1865, p. 4; *Bangor* (ME) *Whig and Courier*, March 27, 1865. See also Pfanz, *Petersburg Campaign*, 31–36, 79–80. Seward arrived at City Point on March 30 and left for Washington, DC, on April 1. *Washington* (DC) *Chronicle*, April 12, 1865; *New York Times*, March 31, 1865, p. 4.

45. Welles, *Diary of Gideon Welles*, 2:279–80.

46. *Mobile Advertiser and Register*, April 8, 1865, p. 2. There is evidence that money to pay the assassins was also being raised in other parts of the country (William C. Edwards and Edward Steers Jr., eds., *The Lincoln Assassination: The Evidence* [Urbana: University of Illinois Press, 2009], 916, 1087–91, 1096–97), probably explaining why Lewis Powell would, prior to his execution, reveal that insofar as the government's arrest of conspirators, "you have not got half of them," ibid., xxiv.

47. Clinton, "Military Operations," 460–61.

48. Edwards and Steers, *Lincoln Assassination*, 268, 270, 303, 315, 789, 1000; Kauffman, *American Brutus*, 189–90.

49. Kauffman, *American Brutus*, 171.

50. Ibid., 151.

51. Edwards and Steers, *Lincoln Assassination*, 1042.

52. *Richmond Whig*, April 7, 1865, reprinted in *New York Tribune*, April 10, 1865, p. 1; *New York Times*, April 10, 1865, p. 1.

53. *New York Times*, April 5, 1865, p. 4.

54. *Washington* (DC) *Chronicle*, April 4, 1865, reprinted in *Cleveland Leader*, April

NOTES TO PAGES 98–101 / 247

6, 1865, p. 2, and *Milwaukee Sentinel*, April 8, 1865. See generally *Mobile News*, April 17, 1865, p. 2, April 25, 1865, p. 2.

55. *New York Times*, February 6, 1865, p. 4.

56. Rohr, *Incidents of the War*, 275; *Mobile Advertiser and Register*, March 18, 1865, p. 1, March 26, 1865, p. 1, March 30, 1865, p. 1; Johnson, *Decided on the Battlefield*, 250–52.

57. *Mobile Advertiser and Register*, March 30, 1865, p. 1.

58. *Milwaukee Sentinel*, March 15, 1865; (Concord) *New Hampshire Statesman*, March 24, 1865; (Boston) *Liberator*, April 7, 1865, p. 54; *Frank Leslie's Illustrated Newspaper*, April 15, 1865, p. 50. See also *New York Times*, March 14, 1865, p. 1, March 20, 1865, p. 4; *Mobile News*, May 21, 1865, p. 2; White, *Lincoln's Greatest Speech*, 37–39.

59. *Holmes County* (OH) *Farmer*, March 23, 1865, p. 3; *Urbana* (OH) *Union*, March 29, 1865, p. 1.

60. *Cincinnati Commercial*, reprinted in *Mobile Advertiser and Register*, March 26, 1865, p. 1. See generally Howard Means, *The Avenger Take His Place: Andrew Johnson and the 45 Days That Changed the Nation* (Orlando, FL: Harcourt, 2006), 86–96.

61. *New York Times*, April 10, 1865, p. 4, April 11, 1865, p. 4; *Cleveland Leader*, April 11, 1865, p. 1; (Montpelier) *Vermont Watchman and State Journal*, April 14, 1865, p. 2.

62. (Washington, DC) *National Republican*, April 11, 1865, p. 2; *Cleveland Leader*, April 11, 1865, p. 1; *Nashville Press*, April 13, 1865, p. 1; *Montgomery Mail*, April 24, 1865, p. 2; Conroy, *Our One Common Country*, 280.

63. House Report 7, 40 Cong., 1 Session (1867), 674.

64. Kauffman, *American Brutus*, 205, 207.

65. William A. Blair, *With Malice toward Some: Treason and Loyalty in the Civil War Era* (Chapel Hill: University of North Carolina Press, 2014), 234–67.

66. *Lowell* (MA) *Citizen and News*, January 11, 1865; (Philadelphia) *North American and United States Gazette*, January 14, 1865; (Washington, DC) *National Intelligencer*, January 13, 1865; *New York Times*, January 30, 1865, p. 1; Chester G. Hearn, *When the Devil Came down to Dixie: Ben Butler in New Orleans* (Baton Rouge: Louisiana State University Press, 1997), 1–2, 5, 10–17, 29, 236–37; Edward G. Longacre, *Army of Amateurs: General Benjamin F. Butler and the Army of the James, 1863–1865* (Mechanicsburg, PA: Stackpole Books, 1997); Richard West Jr., *Lincoln's Scapegoat General: A Life of Benjamin F. Butler, 1818–1893* (Boston: Houghton Mifflin, 1965), 38–75, 290–92; Johnson, *Decided on the Battlefield*, 234–35.

67. *Athens* (TN) *Post*, October 31, 1862, p. 1; *Memphis Appeal*, December 30, 1862, p. 2; West, *Lincoln's Scapegoat General*, 143; Hearn, *When the Devil Came*, 90–109, 174.

68. George Fort Milton, *The Age of Hate: Andrew Johnson and the Radicals* (Hamden, CT: Archon Books, 1965), 25.

69. *Cleveland Leader*, April 13, 1865, p. 2. See also (Brattleboro) *Vermont Phoenix*, April 14, 1865, p. 2 (calling it a "good speech"); *Cleveland Herald*, April 11, 1865; *New York Times*, April 11, 1865, p. 4; *Cleveland Leader*, April 11, 1865, p. 1; *Brooklyn Eagle*, April 11, 1865; (Atchison, KS) *Freedom's Champion*, April 27, 1865. Butler's description of his plan inexplicably did not include white Southern Unionists.

70. *Cincinnati Gazette*, reprinted in *Milwaukee Sentinel*, April 15, 1865.

71. *New York Tribune*, April 12, 1865, p. 4.

72. Phillip W. Magness, "Benjamin Butler's Colonization Testimony Reevaluated," *Journal of the Abraham Lincoln Association* 29 (Winter 2008): 1, 7–8, 10.

73. *New York Tribune*, reprinted in *Cleveland Leader*, April 15, 1865, p. 1.

74. Benjamin F. Butler, *Autobiography and Personal Reminiscences of Major General Benjamin F. Butler* (Boston: A. M. Thayer, 1892), 903–4. See also *New York Tribune*, June 27, 1886, p. 10. Many excellent historians have maintained that Lincoln would not have discussed colonization with Butler at this point because he had supposedly discarded that concept after issuing his Emancipation Proclamation. See, e.g., William Lee Miller, *Lincoln's Virtues: An Ethical Biography* (New York: Vintage Books, 2003); Mark E. Neely, "Abraham Lincoln and Black Colonization: Benjamin Butler's Spurious Testimony," *Civil War History* 25 (March 1979): 77–83. However, there is important evidence to the contrary on this issue, particularly an article authored by one of Lincoln's cabinet members, Secretary of the Navy Gideon Welles, in the *Galaxy* magazine twelve years after Lincoln's death. According to Welles, who wrote that "the truth need not be suppressed," emancipation "had constituted no part of the policy of the president at the time of his inauguration, and when finally decreed he connected with it, as an essential and indispensable part of his policy, a plan of deportation of the colored population." This, said Welles, stemmed from "a conviction that the white and black races could not abide together on terms of social and political equality" and a belief that they could not peaceably occupy the same territory—that one must dominate the other." Lincoln, wrote Welles, also believed that "the Africans were mentally an inferior race" and that any attempt to make them and the whites one people would tend to the degradation of the whites without materially elevating the blacks, but that separation would promote the happiness and welfare of each." In sum, according to Welles, Lincoln "believed it would be best for both the whites and blacks that the latter should leave the country." Gideon Welles, "Administration of Abraham Lincoln," *The Galaxy* 23 (October 1877): 438, 444, discussed in (Washington, DC) *National Tribune*, November 1, 1877, p. 3, and Henry Louis Gates Jr., ed., *Lincoln on Race and Slavery* (Princeton, NJ: Princeton University Press, 2009), iv–lviii. See also Phillip W. Magness and Sebastian Page, *Colonization after Emancipation: Lincoln and the Movement for Black Resettlement* (Columbia: University of Missouri Press, 2011), 109–127; *St. Louis Globe-Democrat*, October 14, 1875, p. 2 (discussing Lincoln's statements to black people regarding his colonization plans); *Washington* (DC) *Post*, April 14, 1889, p. 10 (quoting a former senator familiar with Lincoln who confirmed that "Lincoln had no idea that the negroes were to live among us as freedmen with equal rights."). It is telling that no evidence has apparently been found that others who knew Lincoln ever disputed these recollections.

75. (Washington, DC) *National Intelligencer*, February 6, 1865; *New York Times*, February 6, 1865, p. 5, March 6, 1865, p. 1; (Panama City, Panama) *Mercantile Chronicle*, February 13, 1865; (Baltimore) *Sun*, February 6, 1865, p. 2; *Hartford* (CT) *Courant*, February 7, 1865, p. 2. See generally Eric Foner, *The Fiery Trial: Abraham Lincoln and American Slavery* (New York: W. W. Norton, 2010), 402 (attempting to discredit the

existence of this colonization project but failing to explain why the Panama newspapers would falsify the story).

76. *New York Times*, March 6, 1865, p. 1; *New York Herald*, March 6, 1865, p. 1; *Hartford (CT) Courant*, March 6, 1865, p. 3; *Boston Herald*, March 7, 1865, p. 2.

77. Sickles was still in Central America in May after Lincoln's assassination. *New York Times*, May 16, 1865, p. 8, May 28, 1865, p. 3; (Baltimore) *Sun*, May 16, 1865, p. 1.

78. Magness, "Benjamin Butler's Colonization Testimony Reevaluated," 8, 10.

79. Varon, *Appomattox*, 116–20.

80. *New York Tribune*, April 12, 1865, p. 1; *New York Times*, April 12, 1865, p. 1; *Nashville Press*, April 14, 1865, p. 2; *Milwaukee Sentinel*, April 14, 1865; *Mobile News*, April 20, 1865, p. 1.

81. See, e.g., *New York Times*, April 10, 1865, p. 4; Varon, *Appomattox*, 126, 131.

82. *New York Tribune*, April 13, 1865, p. 4.

83. Escott, "*What Shall We Do With the Negro?*," 102–5.

84. *New York Tribune*, April 12, 1865, p. 1; *Mobile News*, April 20, 1865, p. 1. In early 1864, Lincoln had privately suggested, but did not request or require, that the Louisiana constitutional convention adopt a form of limited black suffrage. Brian R. Dirck, *Lincoln and the Constitution* (Carbondale: Southern Illinois University Press, 2012), 127.

85. (New York) *Army and Navy Journal*, reprinted in *Burlington (VT) Free Press*, April 14, 1865, p. 2.

86. Many Lincoln historians and others have sought to put different words in his mouth. Virtually all have suggested that Lincoln actually advocated universal suffrage and that this had incited John Wilkes Booth—for the first time—to form the intent to murder Lincoln. See, e.g., Michael Burlingame, *Lincoln and the Civil War* (Carbondale: Southern Illinois University Press, 2011), 128; Kauffman, *American Brutus*, 210; James L. Swanson, *Manhunt: The 12-Day Chase for Lincoln's Killer* (New York: HarperCollins, 2007), 6; Donald, *Lincoln*, 588; Thomas Goodrich, *The Darkest Dawn: Lincoln, Booth, and the Great American Tragedy* (Bloomington: Indiana University Press, 2005), 42; James M. McPherson, *Abraham Lincoln* (New York: Oxford University Press, 2009), 61; Bill O'Reilly and Martin Dugard, *Killing Lincoln: The Shocking Assassination That Changed America* (New York: St. Martin's Press, 2015), 109; Harris, *Lincoln's Last Months*, 224; Elizabeth D. Leonard, *Lincoln's Avengers: Justice, Revenge, and Reunion after the Civil War* (New York: W. W. Norton, 2004), 56–57; Varon, *Appomattox*, 137; Conroy, *Our One Common Country*, 281. This myth can be traced to no writing of Booth's. It, instead, comes from a work of historical fiction published in 1886. George Townsend, *Katy of Catoctin; or, The Chain-Breakers; a National Romance* (New York: D. Appleton, 1886), 490. See also William H. Herndon and Jesse W. Weik, *Abraham Lincoln: The True Story of a Great Life* (New York: D. Appleton, 1909), 2:289.

87. *New York Tribune*, April 12, 1865, p. 4. See also Varon, *Appomattox*, 125; McPherson, *Struggle for Equality*, 314.

88. John Niven, ed., *The Salmon P. Chase Papers: Journals, 1829–1872* (Kent, OH: Kent State University Press, 1993), 1:527.

250 / Notes to pages 105–110

89. (Washington, DC) *National Intelligencer*, April 13, 1865.

90. *New Haven* (CT) *Palladium*, April 12, 1865.

91. *New York Times*, February 10, 1865, p. 4. See also *New York Times*, February 4, 1865, p. 4. See generally Esther Marguerite Hall Albjerg, "A Critique of the New York Daily Press during Reconstruction, 1865–1869," PhD diss., University of Wisconsin-Madison, 1925, 110.

92. *New York Times*, April 13, 1865, p. 4.

93. *New York Tribune*, April 12, 1865, p. 4. See also *Milwaukee Sentinel*, April 14, 1865.

94. *Cleveland Leader*, April 12, 1865, p. 2.

95. *New York Tribune*, April 14, 1865, p. 4.

96. Ibid.

97. J. E. Johnston to Maj. Gen. W. T. Sherman, April 14, 1865, OR, Series 1, Vol. 47 (Part III), 206–7; Craig L. Symonds, *Joseph E. Johnston: A Civil War Biography* (New York: W. W. Norton, 1992), 354–55.

98. (Washington, DC) *National Intelligencer*, April 14, 1865.

99. Don E. Fehrenbacher and Virginia Fehrenbacher, eds., *Recollected Words of Abraham Lincoln* (Stanford, CA: Stanford University Press, 1996), 485–86; Gideon Welles, "Lincoln and Johnson: Their Plan of Reconstruction and the Resumption of National Authority," *Galaxy* 13 (April 1872): 526.

100. Varon, *Appomattox*, 118; Conroy, *Our One Common Country*, 286.

101. McPherson, *Struggle for Equality*, 308–9, 311, 314–15; Xi Wang, *Trial of Democracy: Black Suffrage and Northern Republicans, 1860–1910* (Athens: University of Georgia Press, 1997), 19, 315n66.

102. John W. Blassingame and John R. McKivigan, eds., *The Frederick Douglass Papers* (New Haven, CT: Yale University Press, 1991), 4:76–78.

103. Charles Sumner to Salmon Chase, April 10, 1865, reprinted in Beverly Wilson Palmer, ed., *The Selected Letters of Charles Sumner* (Boston: Northeastern University Press, 1990), 2:282–85.

104. McPherson, *Struggle for Equality*, 311–15; (New York) *World*, reprinted in *Nashville Times and True Union*, May 16, 1865, p. 1; *Bangor* (ME) *Whig and Courier*, June 12, 1865. See also Varon, *Appomattox*, 135–45.

105. Varon, *Appomattox*, 146; Perman, *Reunion without Compromise*, 3.

106. *Charleston Courier*, April 18, 1865, p. 4. See also McPherson, *Struggle for Equality*, 311–15. Abolitionist Wendell Phillips also opposed capital punishment but advocated banishment and confiscation. *Mobile News*, May 16, 1865, p. 2.

107. McWhiney, Moore, and Pace, "*Fear God and Walk Humbly*," 349.

Chapter 9

1. *Montgomery Mail*, April 24, 1865, p. 1.

2. (Selma, AL) *Chattanooga Rebel*, April 19, 1865, reprinted in *Montgomery Mail*, April 22, 1865, p. 1.

3. (Selma, AL) *Chattanooga Rebel*, April 20, 1865, reprinted in *Mobile News*, May

NOTES TO PAGES 110–111 / 251

5, 1865, p. 1, *Milwaukee Sentinel*, May 11, 1865, *Cleveland Leader*, May 10, 1865, p. 1, and *Boston Herald*, May 12, 1865, p. 4. See also *Cleveland Leader*, June 3, 1865, p. 2 ("The Selma (AL) Rebel, after shouting over the murder of Mr. Lincoln, immediately lay down, kicked a little, gasped, rolled up its eyes and died.").

4. Danielson, *War's Desolating Scourge*, 157–58. But see *Montgomery Mail*, April 24, 1865, p. 1 (condemning the assassinations on the day occupation forces arrived in Montgomery).

5. *Demopolis* (AL) *Herald*, reprinted in (Greensboro) *Alabama Beacon*, April 21, 1865, p. 2. The editor of the *Herald* had been killed in the trenches at Selma. *New Orleans Times*, April 25, 1865, p. 7. See also Carolyn L. Harrell, *When the Bell Tolls for Lincoln: Southern Reaction to the Assassination* (Macon, GA: Mercer University Press, 1997), 69–75.

6. *Demopolis* (AL) *Herald*, April 25, 1865, reprinted in *Cleveland Leader*, June 23, 1865, p. 2.

7. See generally Harriet E. Amos Doss, "Every Man Should Consider His Own Conscience: Black and White Alabamians' Reactions to the Assassination of Abraham Lincoln," in *The Yellowhammer War: The Civil War and Reconstruction in Alabama*, ed. Kenneth W. Noe (Tuscaloosa: University of Alabama Press, 2013), 165–76; Ben Ames Williams, ed., *A Diary from Dixie by Mary Boykin Chesnut* (Cambridge, MA: Harvard University Press, 1980), 522.

8. Ironically, on the day of Lincoln's assassination, a grand flag-raising ceremony had taken place at Union-occupied Fort Sumter as part of efforts to put closure on the bloody conflict. *Charleston Courier*, April 15, 1865.

9. *New York Tribune*, April 18, 1865, p. 4.

10. *Cleveland Leader*, May 18, 1865, p. 1.

11. George C. Rable, *God's Almost Chosen People: A Religious History of the American Civil War* (Chapel Hill: University of North Carolina Press, 2010), 376–87. But see Harris, *Lincoln's Last Months*, 230–33 (providing evidence of Protestant ministers calling for Old Testament retribution).

12. Winik, *April 1865*, 259–61, 353–63; Harris, *Lincoln's Last Months*, 229–30; Thomas Reed Turner, *Beware the People Weeping: Public Opinion and the Assassination of Abraham Lincoln* (Baton Rouge: Louisiana State University Press, 1982), 18–23.

13. (Philadelphia) *North American and United States Gazette*, April 15, 1865. See also (Washington, DC) *National Intelligencer*, April 17, 1865.

14. *New York Evening Post*, reprinted in (Washington, DC) *National Intelligencer*, April 17, 1865.

15. *Gallipolis* (OH) *Journal*, April 20, 1865, p. 2. See also Varon, *Appomattox*, 144–50, 175; Edward J. Blum, *Reforging the White Republic: Race, Religion, and American Nationalism, 1865–1898* (Baton Rouge: Louisiana State University Press, 2005), 20–27, 32.

16. Carole Emberton, "Reconstructing Loyalty: Love, Fear, and Power in the Postwar South," in *The Great Task Remaining before Us: Reconstruction as America's Continuing Civil War*, ed. Paul A. Cimbala and Randall M. Miller (New York: Fordham University Press, 2010), 180.

252 / Notes to pages 111–114

17. *Mobile News*, April 20, 1865; *Montgomery Mail*, April 24, 1865, p. 1; May 1, 1865, p. 1. See also (Washington, DC) *National Republican*, April 15, 1865, p. 2; (Washington, DC) *National Intelligencer*, April 16, 1865.

18. *Mobile Advertiser and Register*, June 14, 1864, p. 2, June 23, 1864, p. 1.

19. James S. Jones, *Life of Andrew Johnson, Seventeenth President of the United States* (New York: AMS Press, 1975), 76–104, 106; Paul H. Bergeron, *Andrew Johnson's Civil War and Reconstruction* (Knoxville: University of Tennessee Press, 2011), 68; Conroy, *Our One Common Country*, 288–89. See also *Nashville Union*, January 13, 1865, p. 2; *Brownlow's Knoxville Whig, and Rebel Ventilator*, January 25, 1865, p. 1.

20. Derek W. Frisby, "A Victory Spoiled: West Tennessee Unionists during Reconstruction," in *Great Task Remaining before Us*, ed. Cimbala and Miller, 12–21.

21. (Philadelphia) *North American and United States Gazette*, November 18, 1865; *Milwaukee Sentinel*, November 20, 1865; (New Orleans) *Picayune*, November 25, 1865, p. 3; *Nashville Press and Times*, November 18, 1865, p. 2.

22. *Brownlow's Knoxville Whig, and Rebel Ventilator*, January 11, 1865, p. 1, January 25, 1865, p. 1, February 1, 1865, p. 2, March 1, 1865, p. 2, April 19, 1865, p. 1, May 17, 1865, p. 1, June 7, 1865, p. 2, June 21, 1865, pp. 2–3; *Mobile Advertiser and Register*, December 5, 1865, p. 2. See also Ben H. Severance, *Tennessee's Radical Army: The State Guard and Its Role in Reconstruction, 1867–1869* (Knoxville: University of Tennessee Press, 2005), 5.

23. (Washington, DC) *National Intelligencer*, April 16, 1865.

24. Associated Press, quoted in *Cleveland Herald*, April 17, 1865. See also *New York Evening Post*, reprinted in (Washington, DC) *National Intelligencer*, April 17, 1865; Varon, *Appomattox*, 142–45, 175.

25. (St. Clairsville, OH) *Belmont Chronicle*, May 11, 1865, p. 2.

26. Daily Journal of Joshua Burns Moore, 84–85, ADAH. See also *Brownlow's Knoxville Whig, and Rebel Ventilator*, May 3, 1865, p. 2.

27. Martha Hodes, *Mourning Lincoln* (New Haven, CT: Yale University Press, 2015); Harris, *Lincoln's Last Months*, 227–28; Varon, *Appomattox*, 142; *Pomeroy* (OH) *Weekly Telegraph*, May 18, 1865, p. 2; Eric Foner, *Reconstruction: America's Unfinished Revolution, 1863–1877* (New York: Perennial Classics, 2002), 178; Michael Green, "Reconstructing the Nation, Reconstructing the Party: Postwar Republicans and the Evolution of a Party," in *Great Task Remaining before Us*, ed. Cimbala and Miller, 191.

28. *New York Tribune*, reprinted in *Lowell* (MA) *Citizen and Morning News*, April 19, 1865, and *Cleveland Leader*, April 20, 1865, p. 2; *Montgomery Mail*, May 6, 1865, p. 2.

29. Hearn, *When the Devil Came*, 237 (Butler later helped lead the fight for Johnson's impeachment); (Boston) *Liberator*, April 28, 1865, p. 66.

30. *New York Times*, April 29, 1865, p. 4.

31. Ibid., May 5, 1865, p. 4.

32. *New York Herald*, May 3, 1865, quoted in *Nashville Press and Times*, May 16, 1865, p. 1, *Lowell* (MA) *Citizen and News*, May 5, 1865, and *Cleveland Herald*, May 12, 1865. See also Douglas Fermer, *James Gordon Bennett and the "New York Herald": A Study of Editorial Opinion in the Civil War Era 1854–1867* (London: Royal Historical Society, 1986), 1, 297–99. See also Leonard, *Lincoln's Avengers*, 148, 199.

NOTES TO PAGES 114–116 / 253

33. Israel Washburn to William H. Seward, May 20, 1865, and Charles Dunscombe to William H. Seward, June 5, 1865, Papers of William Seward, Rush Rhees Library, University of Rochester; (Columbus) *Weekly Ohio Statesman*, May 13, 1865, p. 2; (Montpelier) *Vermont Watchman and State Journal*, June 23, 1865, p. 1; (Mobile) *Nationalist*, June 18, 1868, p. 2; Turner, *Beware the People Weeping*, 18–23, 52, 78, 127; Blair, *With Malice toward Some*, 268–69; Blum, *Reforging the White Republic*, 21, 38, 41–42; Wang, *Trial of Democracy*, 19.

34. Blassingame and McKivigan, *Frederick Douglass Papers*, 4: 76–78.

35. *Charleston Courier*, May 13, 1865, p. 2 (reporting on a speech by Gen. Rufus Saxton).

36. (Washington, DC) *National Intelligencer*, July 28, 1865.

37. Jones, *Life of Andrew Johnson*, 104–6; John Cimprich, "The Beginning of the Black Suffrage Movement in Tennessee, 1864–65," *Journal of Negro History* 65 (Summer 1980): 189–90. See also *Brownlow's Knoxville Whig, and Rebel Ventilator*, January 25, 1865, p. 2.

38. *Chicago Tribune*, April 17, 1865; Foner, *Reconstruction*, 180.

39. W. T. Sherman to Generals Johnston and Hardee, April 23, 1865, OR, Series 1, Vol. 47 (Part III), 287.

40. Memorandum between Sherman and Johnston dated April 18, 1865, OR, Series 1, Vol. 47 (Part III), 243–44. See also *New York Times*, April 23, 1865, p. 1; *Charleston Courier*, April 27, 1865, p. 1; *Cleveland Leader*, May 2, 1865, p. 2. See also Conroy, *Our One Common Country*, 289–90; Varon, *Appomattox*, 151–53; (Selma, AL) *Chattanooga Rebel*, April 27, 1865, p. 1.

41. Alabama Confederates were likely aware of reports that Tennessee Unionists had recently succeeded in creating a proverbial "tort hell" in that state, where civil lawsuits were being filed by Unionists against Confederates for such torts as assault and battery and false imprisonment, and juries composed of Unionists were awarding large verdicts against them. See, e.g., *Nashville Union*, March 7, 1865, p. 1; *Brownlow's Knoxville Whig, and Rebel Ventilator*, February 22, 1865, p. 2, March 1, 1865, p. 2, March 15, 1865, p. 2; *Nashville Times and True Union*, March 13, 1865, p. 1; *Milwaukee Sentinel*, March 28, 1865; *Cleveland Leader*, June 1, 1865, p. 2.

42. *Nashville Press and Times*, June 3, 1865, p. 2 (publishing a petition to Johnson from "Loyal Citizens of Alabama").

43. W. T. Sherman to General Webster, April 17, 1865, OR, Series 1, Vol. 47 (Part III), 237. See also *New York Times*, June 1, 1865, p. 2 (publishing Sherman's later testimony before the Committee on the Conduct of the War); (Washington, DC) *National Intelligencer*, November 30, 1868, April 15, 1869.

44. Edward Crenshaw, "Diary of Captain Edward Crenshaw of the Confederate States Army," *Alabama Historical Quarterly* 2 (Fall 1940): 469.

45. W. T. Sherman to Brig. Gen. L. S. Baker, April 19, 1865, OR, Series 1, Vol. 47 (Part III), 249–50.

46. Special Field Orders, No. 57, April 18, 1865, OR, Series 1, Vol. 47 (Part III), 246. Regarding Justice Henry Hitchcock, see Lewis, *Clearing the Thickets*, 33, 71, 106, 116, 121–22, 134–36.

47. W. T. Sherman to General Easton, April 18, 1865, OR, Series 1, Vol. 47 (Part III), 246.

48. Edwin M. Stanton to Major-General Dix, April 22, 1865, OR, Series 1, Vol. 47 (Part III), 285.

49. *Charleston Courier*, April 26, 1865, p. 1. See generally Means, *Avenger Takes His Place*, 123–26, 142, 180–82; Harris, *Lincoln's Last Months*, 234–39.

50. *Charleston Courier*, April 22, 1865, p. 1; *Mobile News*, April 20, 1865, p. 2.

51. *New York Herald*, April 24, 1865, reprinted in *Charleston Courier*, April 28, 1865, p. 1, and *Nashville Press*, April 28, 1865, p. 1; Means, *Avenger Take His Place*, 120.

52. Edwin M. Stanton to Lt. Gen. Grant, April 21, 1865, OR, Series 1, Vol. 47 (Part III), 263; Conroy, *Our One Common Country*, 290.

53. U. S. Grant to Maj. Gen. W. T. Sherman, April 21, 1865, OR, Series 1, Vol. 47 (Part III), 263–64; U. S. Grant to E. M. Stanton, April 24, 1865, OR, Series 1, Vol. 47 (Part III), 293 (an apparently false report by Grant regarding this episode); *New York Times*, May 12, 1865, p. 2.

54. *New York Times*, April 24, 1865, p. 4; (Washington, DC) *National Intelligencer*, April 25, 1865; *Mobile News*, May 4, 1865, p. 2. H. W. Halleck to E. M. Stanton, April 22, 1865, OR, Series 1, Vol. 47 (Part III), 277; *New York Herald*, reprinted in *Macon* (GA) *Telegraph and Georgia Journal and Messenger*, May 25, 1865. See generally Means, *Avenger Takes His Place*, 139–46.

55. William T. Sherman to U. S. Grant, April 25, 1865, in *Papers of Ulysses S. Grant*, ed. Simon, 14:425–26.

56. *Columbus* (GA) *Enquirer*, June 5, 1865, p. 1 (publishing a letter from Sherman to a friend in which he castigated the War Department).

57. Daily Journal of Joshua Burns Moore, 85, ADAH.

58. Ibid.

59. Ibid., 90.

60. *Nashville Union*, June 23, 1865, p. 1.

61. See generally (Washington, DC) *National Intelligencer*, May 13, 1865.

62. A. Lincoln to Major General McClernand, January 8, 1863 in Roy P. Basler, ed., *The Collected Works of Abraham Lincoln* (New Brunswick, NJ: Rutgers University Press, 1953), 6:48–49.

63. Foner, *Reconstruction*, 165.

64. *New York Herald*, July 23, 1865, p. 1.

65. Williams, *Diary from Dixie*, 529.

66. Statutes at Large, vol. 13, p. 507 (March 3, 1865). See generally Jason J. Battles, "Labor, Law, and the Freedmen's Bureau in Alabama, 1865–1867," in *Yellowhammer War*, ed. Noe, 241–57; George R. Bentley, *A History of the Freedmen's Bureau* (New York: Octagon Books, 1974), 44–49; Foner, *Reconstruction*, 69, 151–52; *Mobile News*, June 14, 1865, p. 2 (publishing an account of this story by Francis B. Carpenter, a portrait painter who had lived in the White House for six months while painting a portrait of Lincoln), July 2, 1865, p. 1 (publishing another account of Lincoln's remarks). See also Fehrenbacher and Fehrenbacher, *Recollected Words of Abraham Lincoln*, 78–79, 89 (discussing Carpenter and this anecdote).

NOTES TO PAGES 119–121 / 255

67. See, e.g., (Jackson) *Mississippian*, August 13, 1865; (Little Rock) *Arkansas Gazette*, September 5, 1865; *New Orleans Times*, quoted in *Milwaukee Sentinel*, March 28, 1866; *Bangor* (ME) *Whig and Courier*, August 17, 1865 (giving statistics supporting this theory); *Milwaukee Sentinel*, August 25, 1865 (suggesting the existence of a conspiracy to exterminate the entire race); *Chicago Times*, reprinted in *Mobile News*, June 20, 1865, p. 3.

68. *New York Herald*, quoted in *Huntsville Advocate*, July 19, 1865, p. 2.

69. See generally Jim Downs, *Sick from Freedom: African-American Illness and Suffering during the Civil War and Reconstruction* (New York: Oxford University Press, 2012).

70. (Washington, DC) *National Intelligencer*, July 28, 1865 (discussing majority-black counties and states); Varon, *Appomattox*, 150.

Chapter 10

Epigraph. Baumgartner, *Blood and Sacrifice*, 220.

1. For comparative studies of postwar transitions, see Edward L. Ayers, *What Caused the Civil War? Reflections on the South and Southern History* (New York: W. W. Norton, 2005), 146–66; William A. Blair, "Why Didn't the North Hang Some Rebels? The Postwar Debate Over Punishment For Treason," in *More Than a Contest between Armies: Essays on the Civil War Era*, ed. James Marten and A. Kristen Foster (Kent, OH: Kent State University Press, 2008), 189–218; Sarah Woolfolk Wiggins, "Alabama's Reconstruction after 150 Years," in *Yellowhammer War*, ed. Noe, 180.

2. Maya Jasanoff, *Liberty's Exiles: American Loyalists in the Revolutionary World* (New York: Random House, 2011), 68–69, 220; Phyllis R. Blakely and John N. Grant, *Eleven Exiles: Accounts of Loyalists of the American Revolution* (Toronto: Dundurn, 1982), 13–22; Ruma Chopra, *Unnatural Rebellion: Loyalists in New York City During the Revolution* (Charlottesville: University of Virginia Press, 2011), 210–26.

3. Grant Foreman, *Indian Removal: The Emigration of the Five Civilized Tribes of Indians* (Norman: University of Oklahoma Press, 1932).

4. Dallas, *1945*, 610, 612; Richard Bessel, *Germany 1945: From War to Peace* (London: Simon and Schuster UK, 2009), 199–200, 206–9, 250–51.

5. *Chicago Tribune*, April 17, 1865; Charles Marvine to William H. Seward, May 27, 1865, Papers of William Seward, Rush Rhees Library, University of Rochester.

6. (Oskaloosa, KS) *Independent*, May 27, 1865, p. 2.

7. Margaret M. Storey, "The Crucible of Reconstruction: Unionists and the Struggle for Alabama's Postwar Home Front," in *Great Task Remaining before Us*, ed. Cimbala and Miller, 75.

8. Kauffman, *American Brutus*, 335; Hans L. Trefousse, *Andrew Johnson: A Biography* (New York: W. W. Norton, 1989), 211; Varon, *Appomattox*, 191.

9. *Mobile News*, May 12, 1865, p. 2; *Charleston Courier*, May 16, 1865, p. 1; *Nashville Press*, May 1, 1865, p. 2; *Burlington* (VT) *Free Press*, June 9, 1865, p. 2.

10. (Columbus) *Weekly Ohio Statesman*, May 4, 1865, p. 3; (Washington, DC) *Star*, May 9, 1865, p. 4; *Edgefield* (SC) *Advertiser*, May 10, 1865, p. 1.

11. *Mobile News*, May 17, 1865, pp. 1–2; *Montgomery Mail*, May 22, 1865, p. 1;

Nashville Times and True Union, May 16, 1865, p. 2; *Charleston Courier*, May 19, 1865, p. 1; Means, *Avenger Takes His Place*, 151–55; Thomas Goodrich and Debra Goodrich, *The Day Dixie Died: Southern Occupation 1865–1866* (Mechanicsburg, PA: Stackpole Books, 2001), 33–62; Hattaway and Beringer, *Jefferson Davis, Confederate President*, 427–29; Varon, *Appomattox*, 192. Texas was reportedly his destination. *Montgomery Mail*, May 16, 1865, p. 1; Mark K. Ragan, *Confederate Saboteurs: Building the Hunley and Other Secret Weapons of the Civil War* (College Station: Texas A&M University Press, 2015), 170, 174.

12. *Mobile News*, May 17, 1865, p. 2; *Mobile News*, May 20, 1865, p. 2; *Nashville Press and Times*, May 24 1865, p. 1; Nuermberger, *Clays of Alabama*, 264–67.

13. *Boston Journal*, reprinted in *Bangor* (ME) *Whig and Courier*, May 12, 1865, *Nashville Union*, May 19, 1865, p. 2 and (Montpelier) *Vermont Watchman and State Journal*, May 19, 1865, p. 1.

14. *Nashville Press*, May 8, 1865, p. 1; *Nashville Press and Times*, May 27, 1865, p. 1, May 29, 1865, p. 1; *Nashville Union*, May 7, 1865, p. 1; *Mobile News*, May 31, 1865, p. 1, June 3, 1865, p. 4. See also *New York Times*, May 7, 1865, p. 1, May 16, 1865, p. 1, May 21, 1865, p. 1; Means, *Avenger Takes His Place*, 82–183.

15. *New York Times*, June 6, 1865, p. 1.

16. *New York Times*, April 16, 1865, p. 6, May 8, 1865, p. 2, May 12, 1865, p. 8, May 13, 1865, p. 1, May 23, 1865, p. 4. See also *New York Times*, April 8, 1865, p. 3 (discussing the Cahaba prison); Means, *Avenger Takes His Place*, 187–89 (discussing the reaction in the North).

17. Regarding the *Sultana* disaster, see generally William O. Bryant, *Cahaba Prison and the Sultana Disaster* (Tuscaloosa: University of Alabama Press, 2001); Alan Huffman, *Sultana: Surviving Civil War, Prison, and the Worst Maritime Disaster in American History* (New York: Harper, 2009); Means, *Avenger Takes His Place*, 178–80, 195.

18. *Nashville Times and True Union*, March 30, 1865, p. 2 (publishing a letter from Alabama Unionist Daniel Havens Bingham); *New York Herald*, reprinted in *Mobile News*, June 30, 1865, p. 1 (publishing another letter from Bingham); James Alex Baggett, *The Scalawags: Southern Dissenters in the Civil War and Reconstruction* (Baton Rouge: Louisiana State University Press, 2003), 161–64.

19. *Cleveland Leader*, May 18, 1865, p. 2.

20. *New York Times*, May 1, 1865. See also Goodrich and Goodrich, *Day Dixie Died*, 73; Dan T. Carter, *When the War Was Over: The Failure of Self-Reconstruction in the South, 1865–1867* (Baton Rouge: Louisiana State University Press, 1985), 56.

21. *Mobile News*, reprinted in *Cleveland Leader*, May 4, 1865, p. 2.

22. *Montgomery Weekly Post*, January 8, 1861.

23. Captain Hanson to Lt. Col. J. Hough, May 25, 1865, OR, Series 1, Vol. 49 (Part II), 909; Lt. Christensen to Maj. A. Fredenberg, May 30, 1865, OR, Series 1, Vol. 49 (Part II), 934; Malcolm C. McMillan, "Alabama," in *The Confederate Governors*, ed. Wilfred Buck Yearns (Athens: University of Georgia Press, 1985), 21.

24. McMillan, "Alabama," 21–30.

25. *Mobile News*, June 17, 1865, p. 3; McMillan, *Disintegration of a Confederate State*,

NOTES TO PAGES 123–125 / 257

120 (stating that Watts was arrested at Union Springs, Alabama, and then sent to Macon, Georgia, where he was released); *Montgomery Mail*, May 6, 1865 (Watts returned to Montgomery on May 5).

26. (Montgomery) *Alabama State Journal*, October 21, 1868, p. 2.

27. Varon, *Appomattox*, 56–59.

28. *Mobile News*, May 6, 1865, p. 1; *Pomeroy* (OH) *Weekly Telegraph*, May 11, 1865, p. 2; *Cleveland Leader*, May 16, 1865, p. 1.

29. *Macon* (GA) *Telegraph*, June 1, 1865, p. 2; Charles Anthony Smith, *The Rise and Fall of War Crimes Trials: From Charles I to Bush II* (New York: Cambridge University Press, 2012), 55; Goodrich and Goodrich, *Day Dixie Died*, 78, 156–59. See also (New Orleans) *Picayune*, May 26, 1865, p. 2 (Gen. Joe Wheeler arrested); *Mobile News*, June 8, 1865, p. 2 (Lee arrested); (Greensboro) *Alabama Beacon*, June 23, 1865, p. 2.

30. Kauffman, *American Brutus*, 337.

31. Although Wirz was ultimately tried by a military tribunal, Lee and others arrested on treason charges the following month were indicted by a federal grand jury in Norfolk, Virginia, and therefore had the right to be tried by a jury composed of Virginia residents. (Washington, DC) *National Republican*, June 20, 1865, p. 2; (New Orleans) *Picayune*, June 29, 1865, p. 2.

32. (Columbus) *Weekly Ohio Statesman*, May 13, 1865, p. 2.

33. *Cleveland Leader*, May 16, 1865, p. 2. See also *Montgomery Mail*, July 1, 1865, p. 3.

34. *Montgomery Mail*, April 21, 1865, p. 1.

35. Wiggins, *Journals of Josiah Gorgas*, 174.

36. *New York Tribune*, reprinted in *Cleveland Leader*, May 17, 1865, p. 1.

37. *Mobile News*, June 3, 1865, p. 2 (publishing a letter from Curry), July 21, 1865, p. 2; *Nashville Union*, June 17, 1865, p. 2; *Columbia* (SC) *Phoenix*, June 27, 1865, p. 2. See also Means, *Avenger Take His Place*, 184–85.

38. *Selma Times*, reprinted in *Charleston Courier*, August 14, 1865, p. 4.

39. *New York Times*, reprinted in *Huntsville Advocate*, July 19, 1865, p. 3; *Mobile News*, July 21, 1865, p. 2.

40. Daily Journal of Joshua Burns Moore, 85, ADAH.

41. *Nashville Union*, June 16, 1865, p. 2. See also (Washington, DC) *National Republican*, June 23, 1865, p. 2 (reminding the public of Walker's 1861 speech in Montgomery assuring that "the Confederate flag would wave not only over the Capitol at Washington, but over Faneuil Hall"), June 26, 1865, p. 2 (publishing a letter regarding Walker's efforts to bring about Tennessee's secession); *Nashville Union*, June 27, 1865, p. 1 (reporting support among Alabama Unionists for Walker's pardon); *Mobile News*, June 27, 1865, p. 2 (same), July 2, 1865, p. 1 (same); (Montpelier) *Vermont Watchman and State Journal*, June 30, 1865, p. 1; (New Orleans) *Picayune*, June 30, 1865, p. 1.

42. Testimony of E. Woolsey Peck, November 3, 1871, US Congress, *Testimony Taken by the Joint Select Committee to Inquire into the Condition of Affairs in the Late Insurrectionary States: Alabama* (Washington: Government Printing Office, 1872) (hereinafter Alabama Testimony), 1:1851. J. J. Giers gave the same testimony. Perman, *Reunion without Compromise*, 20.

43. *New York Herald*, July 30, 1865, p. 1. See also *Mobile News*, July 25, 1865, p. 2.

44. Fleming, *Civil War and Reconstruction*, 308.

45. (Greensboro) *Alabama Beacon*, May 5, 1865, p. 1; R. S. Granger to Brig. Gen. William D. Whipple, OR, Series 1, Vol. 49 (Part II), p. 820; *New York Tribune*, June 23, 1865, p. 4; *Louisville (KY) Journal*, June 24, 1865, p. 1; *Cleveland Leader*, June 24, 1865, p. 1. But see *Macon (GA) Telegraph*, reprinted in *Nashville Union*, July 16, 1865, p. 2 (denying this allegation).

46. S. Jones to Major-General Steele, May 2, 1865, OR, Series 1, Vol. 49 (Part II), 576–77; *Mobile News*, May 4, 1865, p. 1, May 5, 1865, p. 2; *New York Herald*, May 12, 1865, p. 5; (Philadelphia) *North American and United States Gazette*, May 16, 1865.

47. George W. Howard to Brig. Gen. R. S. Granger, July 1, 1865, OR, Series 1, Vol. 49 (Part II), 1057.

48. *Mobile News*, May 2, 1865, p. 2.

49. *Anderson (SC) Intelligencer*, April 20, 1865, p. 1; *Weekly Perrysburg (OH) Journal*, May 10, 1865, p. 3; *Columbia (SC) Phoenix*, May 20, 1865, p. 2; Hart, *Empire and Revolution*, 9–14.

50. Varon, *Appomattox*, 156, 188; Hardy, "South of the Border," 63, 69, 73; Mahin, *One War at a Time*, 270–72.

51. Private Journal of Sarah R. Espy, 98, ADAH.

52. Cynthia Deltaven Pitcock and Bill L. Gurley, eds., *I Acted from Principle: The Civil War Diary of Dr. William M. McPheeters, Confederate Surgeon in the Trans-Mississippi* (Fayetteville: University of Arkansas Press, 2002), 300.

53. *Mobile News*, May 6, 1865, p. 1; *Cleveland Leader*, May 16, 1865, p. 1.

54. Parthenia Antoinette Hague, *A Blockaded Family: Life in Southern Alabama during the Civil War* (Boston: Houghton Mifflin, 1988), 164; Goodrich and Goodrich, *Day Dixie Died*, 111–23. There is evidence that Taylor's soldiers were already deserting at a rate of one thousand each night even before the formal surrender. (New Orleans) *Picayune*, June 18, 1865, p. 6.

55. Eric T. Dean Jr., "Post-Traumatic Stress," in *The Civil War Veteran: A Historical Reader*, ed. Larry M. Logue and Michael Barton (New York: New York University Press, 2007), 11.

56. (Tuscaloosa) *Independent Monitor*, September 13, 1871, p. 2. See generally Eric T. Dean, *Shook over Hell: Post-Traumatic Stress, Viet Nam, and the Civil War* (Cambridge, MA: Harvard University Press, 1997), 233–35. The asylum in Tuscaloosa averaged fewer than a hundred patients during the war. *Mobile Tribune*, November 11, 1862, p. 2; *Mobile Advertiser and Register*, November 13, 1863, p. 1; *Montgomery Advertiser*, November 13, 1863, p. 2.

57. Wiggins, *Journals of Josiah Gorgas*, 190; Peter Bryce to Governor Parsons, September 11, 1865, Papers of Lewis E. Parsons, ADAH.

58. Baumgartner, *Blood and Sacrifice*, 222–23.

59. Williams, *Diary from Dixie*, 519, 523, 528; Jason Phillips, *Diehard Rebels: The Confederate Culture of Invincibility* (Athens: University of Georgia Press, 2010), 181; Ragan, *Confederate Saboteurs*, 173–74, 179–81.

NOTES TO PAGES 127–129 / 259

60. Williams, *Diary from Dixie*, 519, 523.

61. A. Ackerman to William H. Seward, July 8, 1865, Papers of William Seward, Rush Rhees Library, University of Rochester.

62. *Houston Tri-Weekly Telegraph*, May 10, 1865, quoted in Varon, *Appomattox*, 165–66.

63. *Cleveland Leader*, May 10, 1865, p. 1.

64. *Mobile News*, May 7, 1865, p. 2.

65. Hubbs, *Voices from Company D*, 381.

66. *Dallas* (TX) *Herald*, May 18, 1865, p. 2.

67. *Shreveport Semi-Weekly News*, May 11, 1865, p. 1.

68. Clayton Jewett, ed., *Rise and Fall of the Confederacy: The Memoir of Senator Williamson S. Oldham, CSA* (Columbia: University of Missouri Press, 2006), 209–14 (Oldham remained in Mexico through part of 1866).

69. Axford, "*To Lochaber Na Mair,*" 159.

70. McWhiney, Moore, and Pace, "*Fear God and Walk Humbly,*" 349.

71. Trowbridge, *Desolate South*, 231.

72. Harwell, *Kate*, 299.

73. William Edgar Hughes, ed., *W. E. H. Gramp, The Journal of a Grandfather* (St. Louis, MO: W. E. Hughes, 1912), 113–14, 116–17.

74. U. S. Grant to Andrew Johnson, June 19, 1865, in Paul H. Bergeron, *Papers of Andrew Johnson*, vol. 8, *May–August 1986* (Knoxville: University of Tennessee Press, 1989), 257.

75. U. S. Grant to Maj. Gen. Philip H. Sheridan, May 17, 1865, in Simon, *Papers of Ulysses S. Grant*, 15:43–45. See generally Hardy, "South of the Border," 73–75; Hanna and Hanna, *Napoleon III and Mexico*, 216–39; Brooks D. Simpson, *Let Us Have Peace: Ulysses S. Grant and the Politics of War and Reconstruction, 1861–1868* (Chapel Hill: University of North Carolina Press, 1991), 103, 112.

76. Jewett, *Rise and Fall of the Confederacy*, 67.

77. Hardy, "South of the Border," 66, 76–77; Hanna and Hanna, *Napoleon III and Mexico*, 236–47.

78. Regarding that search and the resulting speculation about Johnson's motives, see Annette Gordon-Reed, *Andrew Johnson* (New York: Henry Holt, 2011), 99–103; Trefousse, *Andrew Johnson*, 228; Varon, *Appomattox*, 194–95; Blair, "Why Didn't the North Hang Some Rebels?," 196–97; Eric L. McKitrick, *Andrew Johnson and Reconstruction* (New York: Oxford University Press, 1988), 134–41; Foner, *Reconstruction*, 191; LaWanda Cox and John Cox, *Politics, Principle, and Prejudice, 1865–1866: Dilemma of Reconstruction America* (New York: Free Press of Glencoe, 1963), 44–45, 97–99.

79. Varon, *Appomattox*, 209.

80. Blair, "Why Didn't the North Hang Some Rebels?," 197. See also Blair, *With Malice toward Some*, 243.

81. See, e.g., *Montgomery Mail*, June 8, 1865, p. 3, July 12, 1865, p. 4; *Chattanooga Gazette*, reprinted in (Philadelphia) *New Age*, June 6, 1865, p. 2; *Huntsville Advocate*, July 19, 1865, p. 2; *Mobile Advertiser and Register*, February 2, 1866, supplement, p. 1,

February 10, 1866, p. 2; (Washington, DC) *National Republican*, May 26, 1865, p. 2; *Nashville Union*, June 18, 1865, p. 3; (Nashville) *Republican Banner*, July 18, 1865, p. 2. See generally Wahlstrom, *Southern Exodus to Mexico*; George D. Harmon, "Confederate Migrations To Mexico," *Hispanic American Historical Review* 17 (November 1937): 458; Hanna and Hanna, *Napoleon III and Mexico*, 221–35; Mahoney and Mahoney, *Mexico and the Confederacy*, 75–155; Daniel E. Sutherland, *The Confederate Carpetbaggers* (Baton Rouge: Louisiana State University Press, 1988), 14; Nunn, *Escape from Reconstruction*, 25–102; Rolle, *Lost Cause*, 17–55, 79–91.

82. *Huntsville Advocate*, October 12, 1865, p. 4. See generally Larry David Stephens, *John P. Gatewood: Confederate Bushwhacker* (Gretna, LA: Pelican Publishing, 2012).

83. Regarding Gatewood, see also *Mobile Advertiser and Register*, October 30, 1864, p. 2; *Columbus* (GA) *Enquirer*, November 4, 1864, p. 2; *Vicksburg* (MS) *Daily Herald*, March 25, 1864, p. 2. "Black flag" tactics meant giving no mercy—a "take-no-prisoners" approach.

84. (Montpelier) *Vermont Watchman and State Journal*, June 16, 1865, p. 2; *Cleveland Leader*, June 5, 1865, p. 2; *Burlington* (VT) *Free Press*, June 30, 1865, p. 4.

85. *Cleveland Leader*, June 13, 1865, p. 3.

86. Forrest had a lot of people gunning for him in Tennessee, including black troops in Memphis determined to obtain revenge for the Fort Pillow massacre. (Washington, DC) *National Intelligencer*, May 23, 1865.

87. *Mobile Advertiser and Register*, February 24, 1866, supplement, p. 1; (New Orleans) *Picayune*, February 25, 1866, p. 5.

88. (New Orleans) *Bee*, reprinted in *Norfolk* (VA) *Post*, January 9, 1866, p. 1.

89. Diary of Jason Niles, May 6, 1865, SHC, as quoted in Carter, *When the War Was Over*, 9.

90. *Nashville Union*, May 30, 1865, p. 1.

91. *Mobile News*, May 13, 1865, p. 1 (publishing Forrest's May 9 letter to his men); *Montgomery Mail*, May 24, 1865, p. 2 (same); *Columbus* (GA) *Enquirer*, June 5, 1865, p. 1; *Mobile News*, May 13, 1865, p. 1; (Grove Hill, AL) *Clarke County Journal*, May 25, 1865, p. 1; *Nashville Union*, May 24, 1865, p. 1.

92. Hurst, *Nathan Bedford Forrest*, 254–65; *New York Times*, May 25, 1865, p. 4. See also *Columbus* (GA) *Enquirer*, June 5, 1865, p. 1 (publishing Forrest's final address to his men, which occurred on May 9 at Gainesville, Alabama); *Nashville Union*, May 21, 1865, p. 1; *Chicago Tribune*, reprinted in (New Orleans) *Picayune*, June 9, 1865, p. 1 (Forrest reportedly said that he was now "as good a Union man as anybody" and that the South was "whipped," and he "was going to support the federal government as heartily as anyone could."). *Nashville Times*, reprinted in *Brownlow's Knoxville Whig, and Rebel Ventilator*, May 3, 1865, p. 1 (reporting that the Tennessee legislature was considering a bill to establish a state militia that Brownlow assured would be used against "rebels").

93. Hoole, *History of the Seventh Alabama Cavalry*, 8. See generally Parrish, *Richard Taylor*, 441 (stating that more than forty thousand men were paroled at Meridian, Mississippi, alone during this period).

NOTES TO PAGES 131–135 / 261

94. Donald C. Simmons Jr., *Confederate Settlements in British Honduras* (Jefferson, NC: McFarland, 2001), 12–13 (connecting mild reconstruction policy to the decisions of Southerners to remain in the United States); Anthony James Jones, *America and Guerrilla Warfare* (Lexington: University Press of Kentucky, 2000), 98–101 (same); Storey, "Crucible of Reconstruction," 75.

Chapter 11

1. Earl J. Hess, *The Civil War in the West: Victory and Defeat from the Appalachians to the Mississippi* (Chapel Hill: University of North Carolina Press, 2012), 291–92, 295–96, 299.

2. Proclamation of R. S. Granger, OR, Series 1, Vol. 49 (Part II), 506.

3. Proclamation of George H. Thomas to the Citizens of Morgan, Marshall, Lawrence Counties, AL, April 12, 1865, in OR, Series 1, Vol. 49 (Part II), 506, and reprinted in *Nashville Union*, May 6, 1865, p. 3.

4. *Montgomery Mail*, April 21, 1865, p. 1. See also *Montgomery Mail*, April 24, 1865, p. 1 (occupation troops finally arrived in Montgomery on April 24).

5. *Charleston Courier*, May 16, 1865, p. 1.

6. See also *Mobile News*, May 17, 1865, p. 2 (Alexander Stephens), June 8, 1865, p. 2 (Lee, Judah P. Benjamin, Gov. Joe Brown of Georgia); (Grove Hill, AL) *Clarke County Journal*, June 8, 1865, p. 2 (former secretary of war Seddon).

7. *Mobile News*, May 9, 1865, p. 1.

8. Daily Journal of Joshua Burns Moore, 85, ADAH.

9. *Nashville Union*, May 9, 1865, p. 3.

10. *Weekly Perrysburg (OH) Journal*, May 24, 1865, p. 3.

11. Proclamation of R. S. Granger, April 20, 1865, OR, Series 1, Vol. 49 (Part II), 506.

12. *Montgomery Mail*, May 29, 1865, p. 2.

13. J. J. Giers to R. S. Granger, May 10, 1865, OR, Series 1, Vol. 49 (Part II), 703–7.

14. *Nashville Union*, May 16, 1865, p. 1.

15. Ibid.

16. Ibid., Roddey surrendered and received his parole at Courtland on May 17, 1865. John H. Eicher and David J. Eicher, *Civil War Commands* (Stanford, CA: Stanford University Press, 2001), 458.

17. *Memphis Bulletin*, May 22, 1865, p. 2; *Louisville (KY) Journal*, May 19, 1865, p. 1.

18. Regarding other meetings in north Alabama, see generally *Philadelphia Bulletin*, May 25, 1865, p. 1.

19. Edward Hatch to Brig. Gen. W. D. Whipple, June 8, 1865, OR, Series 1, Vol. (Part II), 971–72; Journal of Joshua Burns Moore, 88, ADAH.

20. *Mobile News*, May 6, 1865, p. 1.

21. (Washington, DC) *National Intelligencer*, April 27, 1865.

22. *Raleigh Register*, April 1, 1834, November 8, 1836; (Tuscaloosa) *Alabama Intelligencer and States Rights Expositor*, December 5, 1835 (publishing a report by Bing-

ham); (Jackson) *Mississippian*, January 27, 1837; *Raleigh Register*, December 13, 1867; (Little Rock) *Arkansas State Gazette*, December 11, 1846, July 7, 1848, July 21, 1848, August 4, 1848; Wiggins, *Scalawag in Alabama Politics*, 26; *New York Times*, August 1, 1865, p. 1; (Mobile) *Nationalist*, December 20, 1866, p. 2.

23. *New York Herald*, reprinted in *Mobile News*, June 30, 1865, p. 1; *Huntsville Advocate*, July 12, 1865, p. 1.

24. *Mobile News*, July 25, 1865, p. 6.

25. *New York Tribune*, January 29, 1866, p. 1. See also *Dallas* (TX) *Herald*, December 9, 1865, p. 2 (expressing fear that proscription of Confederates would occur in Texas).

26. *Nashville Times and True Union*, March 30, 1865, p. 2.

27. Jeremiah Clemens to Andrew Johnson, November 19, 1864, Graf, *Papers of Andrew Johnson*, 7:304.

28. Jeremiah Clemens to Andrew Johnson, April 21, 1865, ibid., 7:599.

29. Jeremiah Clemens, *Tobias Wilson: A Tale of the Great Rebellion* (Philadelphia: J. B. Lipincott, 1865), 16, 25. See also W. Stanley Hoole, "Jeremiah Clemens, Novelist," *Alabama Review* 18 (January 1965): 23; Wallace T. Hettle, *The Peculiar Democracy: Southern Democrats in Peace and Civil War* (Athens: University of Georgia Press, 2001), 122–41; *Montgomery Mail*, May 3, 1865, p. 1.

30. *Nashville Union*, April 15, 1865, p. 2 (publishing a letter from Clemens).

31. Rohr, *Incidents of the War*, 300; *New York Tribune*, May 23, 1865, p. 4; *New York Times*, May 23, 1865, p. 1, August 17, 1865, p. 1 (reporting that one of Clemens's children was part black); *Philadelphia Press*, May 26, 1865, p. 2; *Philadelphia Bulletin*, May 23, 1865, p. 4; *Cleveland Leader*, May 23, 1865, p. 1; (Grove Hill, AL) *Clarke County Journal*, June 8, 1865, p. 2; Hoole, "Jeremiah Clemens," 34–35.

32. *Nashville Union*, May 25, 1865, p. 2.

33. (Montgomery) *Alabama State Sentinel*, July 4, 1867, p. 1; (Montgomery) *Alabama State Journal*, October 16, 1874, p. 2; Wiggins, *Scalawag in Alabama Politics*, 39, 57–61; (Stevenson, AL) *Jackson County News*, June 10, 1865, p. 1; Richard Nelson Current, *Lincoln's Loyalists: Union Soldiers from the Confederacy* (Boston: Northeastern University Press, 1992), 170–73; John Craig Stewart, *The Governors of Alabama* (Gretna, LA: Pelican, 1975), 101, 107, 110, 116; Regarding Spencer, see Terry L. Seip, "Of Ambition and Enterprise: The Making of Carpetbagger George E. Spencer," in *Yellowhammer War*, ed. Noe, 191–219; Rogers et al., *Alabama*, 249.

34. *Charleston Courier*, June 14, 1865, p. 1. See also (Stevenson, AL) *Jackson County News*, June 10, 1865, p. 1.

35. Baggett, *Scalawags*, 161; Marjorie Howell Cook, "Restoration and Innovation: Alabamians Adjust to Defeat: 1865–1867," PhD diss., University of Alabama, 1968), 11–12. See also *Mobile News*, June 9, 1865, p. 1 (discussing Smith's qualifications), June 17, 1865, p. 3; (New York) *World*, reprinted in (Little Rock) *Arkansas State Gazette*, June 13, 1865.

36. *Mobile News*, September 21, 1865, p. 2 (referring to the state of affairs in Tennessee); *Dallas* (TX) *Herald*, December 9, 1865, p. 2 (same).

NOTES TO PAGES 139–143 / 263

37. F. Steele to Col. C. T. Christensen, May 1, 1865, OR, Series 1, Vol. 49 (Part II), 560–61.

38. See generally Cook, "Restoration and Innovation," 8–9 and 8n8.

39. E. R. S. Canby to Secretary of War, May 7, 1865, OR, Series 1, Vol. 49 (Part II), 658.

40. Regarding Byrd, see Thomas McAdory Owen, *History of Alabama and Dictionary of Alabama Biography* (Spartanburg, SC: Reprint Co.), 3:277.

41. *Mobile News*, May 12, 1865, p. 2. See also *Mobile News*, May 13, 1865, p. 1; *Boston Herald*, May 24, 1865, p. 4.

42. C. C. Andrews to Col. C. T. Christensen, May 11, 1865, OR, Series 1, Vol. 49 (Part II), 727.

43. Perman, *Reunion without Compromise*, 39.

44. *Mobile News*, May 19, 1865, p. 2.

45. *Mobile News*, May 19, 1865, p. 2; *Opelika* (AL) *Union*, June 1, 1865; Cook, "Restoration and Innovation," 9–10.

46. *Mobile News*, May 19, 1865, p. 2. See also *Montgomery Mail*, May 1, 1865, p. 2; *Nashville Press and Times*, May 31, 1865, p. 2; Perman, *Reunion without Compromise*, 50.

47. *Mobile News*, May 17, 1865, p. 1, May 19, 1865, p 3.

48. *Mobile News*, May 17, 1865, p. 1, May 19, 1865, p. 3, May 20, 1865, p. 2, May 24, 1865, p. 2, June 9, 1865, p. 1; *Charleston Courier*, June 7, 1865, p. 1 (reporting their arrival in New York City and departure for Washington, DC).

49. *Mobile News*, May 17, 1865, p. 1. See also *Nashville Press and Times*, June 3, 1865, p. 2.

50. George E. Spencer to Andrew Johnson, June 2, 1865, Bergeron, *Papers of Andrew Johnson*, 8:172. See generally Perman, *Reunion without Compromise*, 36.

51. Jean J. Giers to Andrew Johnson, May 30, 1865, Bergeron, *Papers of Andrew Johnson*, 8:145.

52. *Nashville Press and Times*, May 31, 1865, pp. 1–2.

53. *Montgomery Advertiser*, November 13, 1866, p. 2; *Nashville Press and Times*, June 9, 1865, p. 1; *Charleston Courier*, June 14, 1865, p. 1.

54. *Nashville Press and Times*, June 9, 1865, p 1; *Charleston Courier*, June 14, 1865, p. 1.

Chapter 12

Epigraph. Phillips, *Diehard Rebels*, 56–57.

1. See, e.g., Gordon-Reed, *Andrew Johnson*, 3–7; David Warren Bowen, *Andrew Johnson and the Negro* (Knoxville: University of Tennessee Press, 1989), 123–24; McKitrick, *Andrew Johnson and Reconstruction*, 3–14.

2. Rogers et al., *Alabama*, 230; *Nashville Union*, June 29, 1865, p. 2.

3. Foner, *Reconstruction*, 180; Perman, *Reunion without Compromise*, 71, 75, 81; Cox and Cox, *Politics, Principle, and Prejudice*, 157.

4. Perman, *Reunion without Compromise*, 37.

5. *New York Times*, January 17, 1866, p. 4.

6. Storey, "Crucible of Reconstruction," 75.

7. Michael C. C. Adams, *Living Hell: The Dark Side of the Civil War* (Baltimore, MD: Johns Hopkins University Press, 2014), 182–205.

8. Hague, *Blockaded Family*, 164.

9. *Montgomery Mail*, May 1, 1865; (Montgomery) *Mobile News*, May 4, 1865, p. 1 (Selma), May 5, 1865, p. 2; DuBose, *Alabama's Tragic Decade*, 3–8.

10. William H. Brantley, *Chief Justice Stone of Alabama* (Birmingham: Birmingham Publishing, 1943), 175–76.

11. *New York News*, reprinted in *Mobile News*, May 11, 1865, p. 2.

12. *Mobile News*, July 1, 1865, p. 2.

13. *Mobile Advertiser and Register*, November 22, 1865, p. 2. Regarding Busteed, see Christopher Lyle McIlwain Sr., "United States District Judge Richard Busteed and the Alabama Klan Trials of 1872," *Alabama Review* 65 (October 2012): 263–89.

14. *New York Times*, March 3, 1865, p. 4; *Mobile News*, July 18, 1865, p. 2; *New York Times*, July 23, 1865, p. 5; (New Orleans) *Picayune*, July 26, 1865, p. 2. Intensifying interest among Southern lawyers in the content and philosophy of postwar state governments, some states had adopted similar requirements for practice in state courts. (San Francisco) *Evening Bulletin*, February 27, 1864. The Tennessee legislature was considering a law requiring a test oath not only from lawyers but also doctors, ministers, and public officials. *New York Times*, May 25, 1865, p. 4.

15. *Columbus* (GA) *Enquirer*, November 5, 1863, p. 2.

16. (New Orleans) *Picayune*, June 23, 1865, p. 2.

17. *Columbus* (GA) *Enquirer*, November 5, 1863, p. 2.

18. *Shreveport Semi-Weekly News*, May 16, 1865, p. 2; *New York Herald*, reprinted in *Nashville Union*, May 25, 1865, p. 2 (reporting that in Mobile, "one lot" consisting of a thousand Confederate dollars "sold for fifty cents, as a curiosity.").

19. S. J. McMorris to Lewis Parsons, September 11, 1865, Papers of Lewis E. Parsons, ADAH.

20. *Mobile News*, May 12, 1865, p. 2.

21. *Milwaukee Sentinel*, May 13, 1865. See also Louis M. Kyriakoudes, "The Rise of Merchants and Market Towns in Reconstruction-Era Alabama," *Alabama Review* 49 (April 1996): 83.

22. Harwell, *Kate*, 305.

23. Mary Ann Hall to Sister, July 4, 1865, Alexander K. Hall Family Papers, ADAH.

24. James M. Williams to Elizabeth Rennison, May 21, 1865, in John Kent Folmar, ed., "Post Civil War Mobile: The Letters of James M. Williams, May–September, 1865," *Alabama Historical Quarterly* 32 (Fall and Winter 1970): 186–98.

25. Linden and Linden, *Disunion, War, Defeat, and Recovery*, 137.

26. James Robert Maxwell, *Autobiography of James Robert Maxwell of Tuskaloosa, Alabama* (Baltimore, MD: Gateway Press, 1996), 286.

27. Ibid., 286, 294; *Huntsville Advocate*, July 26, 1865, p. 3.

28. *Mobile News*, June 24, 1865, p. 2.

29. *Mobile News*, July 24, 1865, reprinted in (New Orleans) *Picayune*, July 27, 1865, p. 3. Although it would turn out to be the quiet before the storm, one reason for the absence of noise was the loss of so many Alabamians during the war. According to Lewis Parsons, "about 122,000 of her sons have been carried to the field of battle, 35,000 of whom will never return; and it is probably an equal or larger number are permanently injured by wounds or disease while in the service," *Montgomery Advertiser*, July 22, 1865, p. 3.

30. *New York Herald*, July 23, 1865, p. 1; Maxwell, *Autobiography*, 294.

31. *Montgomery Mail*, June 5, 1865, p. 3.

32. *Mobile News*, June 22, 1865, p. 4. See also *Huntsville Advocate*, July 26, 1865, p. 3; (New Orleans) *Picayune*, July 27, 1865, p. 1, May 9, 1866, p. 9.

33. (Millersburg, OH) *Holmes County Farmer*, June 15, 1865, p. 3; *Cleveland Leader*, June 15, 1865, p. 3.

34. *New York Herald*, cited in *Nashville Union*, May 30, 1865, p. 3. See also *New York Times*, reprinted in *Cleveland Leader*, June 15, 1865, p. 3; (New York) *World*, reprinted in *Milwaukee Sentinel*, July 22, 1865; *Cleveland Leader*, July 28, 1865, p. 2 (Mobile); *Montgomery Mail*, July 8, 1865, p. 2.

35. *New York Times*, quoted in *Milwaukee Sentinel*, November 4, 1865, p. 3. See also *Selma Times*, cited in *Cincinnati Enquirer*, February 10, 1866, p. 2, and quoted in *New York Tribune*, February 12, 1866, p. 4; *Providence* (RI) *Press*, February 12, 1866, p. 3.

36. The second-greatest number of rations were distributed in Alabama, 65 percent of which went to white people. Denise E. Wright, "'Objects of Humanity': The White Poor in Civil War and Reconstruction Georgia," in *Great Task Remaining before Us*, ed. Cimbala and Miller, 108. See also Severance, *Portraits of Conflict*, 308.

37. *Burlington* (VT) *Free Press*, June 9, 1865, p. 1.

38. See, e.g., (Greensboro) *Alabama Beacon*, June 2, 1865, p. 2; *Mobile News*, July 6, 1865, p. 2; (New Orleans) *Picayune*, August 22, 1865, p. 2; *Cleveland Leader*, June 10, 1865, p 2.

39. *Nashville Union*, July 27, 1865, p. 3, July 30, 1865, p. 3; (New Orleans) *Picayune*, August 25, 1865, p. 6. See generally Goodrich and Goodrich, *Day Dixie Died*, 151–52.

40. Barksdale, *Kate*, 302; *New York Times*, reprinted in *Nashville Union*, June 13, 1865, p. 1; *Cleveland Leader*, June 15, 1865, p. 3.

41. See, e.g., *Nashville Union*, May 19, 1865, p. 4 (reporting the apprehension and execution of a gang of bushwhackers near Florence); *Nashville Press and Times*, May 22, 1865, p. 2 (same); *Mobile News*, May 25, 1865, p. 1, June 24, 1865, p. 2; Maxwell, *Autobiography*, 299–305; Carter, *When the War Was Over*, 15.

42. Harwell, *Kate*, 284. See also Douglas A. Blackmon, *Slavery by Another Name: The Re-Enslavement of Black Americans from the Civil War to World War II* (New York: Doubleday, 2008), 24–26.

43. Maxwell, *Autobiography*, 294; (Greensboro) *Alabama Beacon*, June 2, 1865, p. 2; *Huntsville Advocate*, July 26, 1865, p. 2.

44. (Washington, DC) *National Intelligencer*, May 23, 1865 (discussing an incident in Memphis).

266 / Notes to pages 147–148

45. *Mobile News*, May 4, 1865, p. 2, May 6, 1865, p. 1, June 3, 1865, p. 2; *Nashville Press*, May 6, 1865, p. 3, May 19, 1865, p. 2.

46. Michael W. Fitzgerald, "From Unionists to Scalawags: Elite Dissent in Civil War Mobile," *Alabama Review* 55 (April 2002): 117 (discussing successful efforts to hide and preserve cotton from destruction in Mobile when Confederate forces withdrew).

47. *Shreveport News*, June 6, 1865, p. 1.

48. Wiggins, *Journals of Josiah Gorgas*, 182; *Mobile News*, June 3, 1865, p. 2 (reporting government sales of two thousand bales of cotton from South Carolina); *Cleveland Leader*, May 17, 1865, p. 1 (General Canby issued an order prohibiting the sale or transfer of Confederate cotton to anyone except federal officers), June 16, 1865, p 1; (New Orleans) *Picayune*, August 1, 1865, p. 6. See generally Arlie R. Slabaugh, *Confederate States Paper Money: Civil War Currency from the South* (Iola, WI: Krause Publications, 2012), 15–16.

49. L. F. Hubbard to Capt. W. H. F. Randall, May 20, 1865, OR, Series 1, Vol. 49 (Part II), 854–55.

50. *Selma* (AL) *Messenger*, July 8, 1865, reprinted in *Mobile News*, July 13, 1865, p. 4 (reporting that "some officer of the army and some citizen are jointly engaged in this traffic" and that evidence of bribery and corruption "has come to light"); *New York Herald*, July 23, 1865, p. 1 (same); *Mobile News*, July 30, 1865, p. 2; *Hartford* (CT) *Courant*, July 24, 1865, p. 3; *Cincinnati Enquirer*, July 25, 1865, p. 2; *Cleveland Leader*, July 25, 1865, p. 1. See also John Kent Folmar, ed., *From That Terrible Field: Civil War Letters of James M. Williams, Twenty-First Alabama Infantry Volunteers* (Tuscaloosa: University of Alabama Press, 1981), 155 (complaining of "loyal Confederates" in Mobile hiding cotton near the end of the war).

51. *Cleveland Leader*, June 16, 1865, p. 1.

52. Hilary Abner Herbert, "Grandfather Talks about His Life under Two Flags: Reminiscences," 172, in Sarah Espy Papers, ADAH. Regarding Herbert, see Hugh C. Davis, "Hilary A. Herbert: Bourbon Apologist," *Alabama Review* 20 (July 1967): 216. See also Richard W. Griffen, "Cotton Fraud and Confiscations in Alabama, 1863–1866," *Alabama Review* 7 (October 1954): 265–76.

53. *Augusta* (GA) *Constitutionalist*, reprinted in *Edgefield* (SC) *Advertiser*, June 6, 1865, p. 1; *Anderson* (SC) *Intelligencer*, June 22, 1865, p. 2 (reporting from Montgomery).

54. John S. Kennedy to Governor Parsons, September 23, 1865, Papers of Lewis E. Parsons, ADAH (regarding purchases of cotton in west Alabama by George E. Spencer).

55. Maxwell, *Autobiography*, 307.

56. (Tuscumbia) *North Alabamian*, quoted in (New Orleans) *Picayune*, July 15, 1865, p. 2; (New Orleans) *Picayune*, July 27, 1865, p. 1; (Grove Hill, AL) *Clarke County Journal*, August 10, 1865, p. 2; *Mobile Advertiser and Register*, August 8, 1865, reprinted in (New Orleans) *Picayune*, August 12, 1865, p. 2.

57. See, e.g., *Montgomery Mail*, July 28, 1865, reprinted in (New Orleans) *Picayune*, August 4, 1865, p. 3 (Montgomery and West Point Railroad; Alabama and Florida

NOTES TO PAGES 148–150 / 267

Railroad); *Mobile News*, May 2, 1865, p. 2 (Mobile and Ohio Railroad), June 5, 1865, p. 4; *New York Herald*, May 4, 1865, p. 5 (Alabama and Tennessee Railroad); *Nashville Press and Times*, June 13, 1865, p. 1 (Selma and Meridian Railroad); *Huntsville Advocate*, July 12, 1865, p. 2 (Memphis and Charleston Railroad).

58. *Mobile News*, June 27, 1865, p. 2; *Mobile Advertiser and Register*, August 6, 1865, p. 1; *Huntsville Advocate*, July 12, 1865, p. 2.

59. See, e.g., F. Steele to Col. C. T. Christensen, May 1, 1865, May 9, 1865, J. Hough to Brevet Maj. Gen. G. H. Grierson, May 9, 1865; Ed. R. S. Canby to Lt. Gen. Grant, May 7, 1865, M. H. Chrysler to Maj. S. L. Woodward, May 15, 1865, J. McArthur to Lt. Col. Hough, June 9, 1865, OR, Series 1, Vol. 49 (Part II), 560–61, 658–59, 698, 796–97, 975–76; *Cleveland Leader*, June 15, 1865, p. 2.

60. *Weekly Perrysburg* (OH) *Journal*, May 24, 1865, p. 3.

61. As one frustrated Alabama editor would lament seven years later, "any man can see at once, that if all the articles worn and used by us, were manufactured in our midst, they would be infinitely cheaper. The raw material for *every one of them* is around us in *abundance*, but our cotton is not made into goods, our iron ore is not smelted, and our coal is not mined, because the capital is not here to forward it. Capital is not here, because there is not sufficient outlet for the manufactured article." The remedy, he urged, was to construct more railroads. "Open up your arteries of trade, give free vent to commerce by Rail and River, show a country with demand asking for supply, and capital *will* come. You cannot do this without Railroads. Just as well try to send blood through a man's body without veins and arteries." *Lauderdale* (AL) *Times*, October 31, 1871, p. 2.

62. *Nashville Union*, June 24, 1865, p. 2.

63. *Selma Times*, reprinted in *Mobile News*, July 6, 1865, p. 3, and (New Orleans) *Picayune*, July 12, 1865, p 1.

64. *Montgomery Advertiser*, April 17, 1866, p. 4, April 24, 1866, p. 1; (New Orleans) *Picayune*, June 23, 1865, p. 2, April 19, 1866, p. 2.

65. Linden and Linden, *Disunion, War, Defeat, and Recovery*, 137; *Mobile News*, May 12, 1865, p. 2, June 9, 1865, p. 2 (discussing efforts to establish national banks in Selma and Montgomery); *Mobile Advertiser and Register*, January 24, 1866, supplement, p. 1 (discussing per acre costs of production); *Montgomery Advertiser*, April 13, 1866, p. 5 (discussing a continuing shortage of agricultural capital).

66. *Mobile News*, June 9, 1865, p. 2, June 22, 1865, p. 4; *Huntsville Advocate*, July 26, 1865, p. 3; *Nashville Union*, July 29, 1865, p. 3.

67. Sylvia H. Krebs, "'Will the Freedmen Work?' White Alabamians Adjust to Free Black Labor," *Alabama Historical Quarterly* 36 (Summer 1974): 151–63.

68. Wiggins, *Journal of Josiah Gorgas*, 175.

69. *Selma Times*, reprinted in *Mobile Daily News*, July 6, 1865, p. 3.

70. Linden and Linden, eds., *Disunion, War, Defeat, and Recovery*, 138–39.

71. McWhiney, Moore, and Pace, "*Fear God and Walk Humbly*," 349–50.

72. Robert Jemison to Col. Thomas, June 21, 1865, Robert Jemison Jr. Papers, Hoole Special Collections Library, University of Alabama.

73. *Macon* (GA) *Telegraph*, reprinted in *Edgefield* (SC) *Advertiser*, June 21, 1865, p. 1. See also *Nashville Press and Times*, June 13, 1865, p. 1 (reporting on the situation in Selma); *Columbia* (SC) *Phoenix*, June 27, 1865, p. 2 (discussing the work ethic of freed slaves in Mobile).

74. *Mobile News*, May 30, 1865, p. 4, July 18, 1865, p. 1; (Greensboro) *Alabama Beacon*, June 2, 1865, p. 2 (Gainesville); *Huntsville Advocate*, July 19, 1865, p. 2; *Cleveland Leader*, June 30, 1865, p. 2; Fitzgerald, *Urban Emancipation*, 27–30; Michael W. Fitzgerald, *Splendid Failure: Postwar Reconstruction in the American South* (Chicago: Ivan R. Dee, 2007), 31–32; William Cohen, *At Freedom's Edge: Black Mobility and the Southern White Quest for Racial Control, 1861–1915* (Baton Rouge: Louisiana State University Press, 1991), 11–12.

75. Basil Manly to Jane Smith, June 8, 1865, Basil Manly Papers, Hoole Special Collections Library, University of Alabama.

76. (Greensboro) *Alabama Beacon*, June 23, 1865, p. 2. See also *Mobile News*, June 23, 1865, p. 4 (regarding an order issued by the commander at Selma prohibiting his men from "creating dissatisfaction between the negroes on the plantation and the planter"); (New Orleans) *Picayune*, June 27, 1865, p. 1 (refusal of the Freedmen's Bureau to adopt minimum wage requirements).

77. *Selma Federal Union*, reprinted in (Grove Hill, AL) *Clarke County Journal*, June 29, 1865, p. 2; C. C. Andrews to the Freedmen of Selma and Vicinity, May 9, 1865, OR, Series 1, Vol. 49 (Part II), 728–29 (reprinting a copy of his speech). See generally Peter Kolchin, *First Freedom: The Responses of Alabama's Blacks to Emancipation and Reconstruction* (Westport, CT: Greenwood Press, 1972), 4–6.

78. *Montgomery Mail*, May 26, 1865, p. 2; *Mobile News*, reprinted in (New Orleans) *Picayune*, June 13, 1865, p. 5. Cf., (Troy, AL) *Southern Advertiser*, September 16, 1865, p. 2 (indicating that this measure may have been effective). However, they did not countenance unusually cruel punishment. A Selma man, William H. Gordon, was found guilty by a military commission on a charge of "cruelly treating negroes" and thereby "causing one Green Hooper, a negro, to be drowned" and was "sentenced to be hung." (Washington, DC) *National Republican*, August 1, 1865, p. 2. See generally Myers, "Alabama Freedmen and Economic Adjustment," 252.

79. (Greensboro) *Alabama Beacon*, June 23, 1865, p. 2; *Mobile News*, July 2, 1865, p. 4; *New York Herald*, cited in *Nashville Union*, July 18, 1865, p. 3 ("many of them have yet to be taught that freedom and idleness are not synonymous"); *Cincinnati Enquirer*, August 5, 1865, p. 3. But see *Montgomery Mail*, reprinted in (New Orleans) *Picayune*, June 25, 1865, p. 4.

80. Petition of Lawrence County Residents to Governor Parsons, September 26, 1865, Lewis E. Parsons Papers, ADAH.

81. Diary of Miss Catherine M. Fennell, 57–58, Heritage Room, HMCPL.

82. John B. Myers, "Reaction and Adjustment: The Struggle of Alabama Freedmen in Post-Bellum Alabama, 1865–1867," *Alabama Historical Quarterly* 32 (Spring and Summer 1970): 5–22.

83. *Selma Mirror*, August 15, 1865, reprinted in *Cincinnati Enquirer*, September 11, 1865, p. 2.

NOTES TO PAGES 151–152 / 269

84. *Plymouth* (IN) *Weekly Democrat*, November 9, 1865, p. 2; Blum, *Reforging the White Republic*, 39.

85. *Mobile News*, July 24, 1865, reprinted in (New Orleans) *Picayune*, July 27, 1865, p. 3.

86. *New York Tribune*, June 3, 1865, p. 4.

87. Ibid. See also *New York Herald*, May 12, 1865, p. 5 (describing the reaction of slaves to gunboats of the Union navy moving up the Alabama River from Mobile). The knowledge that the Union army was the catalyst for their freedom was understandably common throughout the black community in Alabama. According to an 1865 Nashville newspaper, a "negro woman who was baptized a few Sundays ago at Huntsville, Ala., came forth from the water shouting—'freed from slavery, freed from sin—bless God and General Grant.'" *Nashville Union*, July 30, 1865, p. 2. Hence, later efforts were doomed to failure as Alabama Democrats tried to convince the black population that white Southerners were not fighting to preserve the institution of slavery and had instead championed its abolition.

88. *New York Times*, April 20, 1865, p. 5; (Washington, DC) *National Intelligencer*, reprinted in *Huntsville Advocate*, July 26, 1865, p. 1.

89. *Nashville Press and Times*, May 5, 1865, p. 1.

90. *New York Herald*, reprinted in *Mobile News*, July 4, 1865, p. 2.

91. *Huntsville Advocate*, July 26, 1865, p. 1.

92. (Washington, DC) *National Intelligencer*, reprinted in *Huntsville Advocate*, July 26, 1865, p. 1.

93. *Montgomery Mail*, reprinted in *Mobile Advertiser and Register*, September 7, 1865, p. 2. See also *Montgomery Advertiser*, January 14, 1866, p. 2 (reporting international production figures).

94. *New York Herald* ("many planters contend that the day of cotton planting is passed"), reprinted in *Huntsville Advocate*, July 26, 1865, p. 2.

95. *New York Herald*, July 23, 1865, p. 1, reprinted in *Nashville Press and Times*, July 25, 1865, p. 1. See also *Hartford* (CT) *Courant*, July 24, 1865, p. 3. See also Reid, *After the War*, 381.

96. *New York Herald*, reprinted in *Mobile News*, June 3, 1865, p. 3.

97. *New York Times*, reprinted in *Mobile News*, June 8, 1865, p. 2. See also *New York Commercial and Advertiser*, reprinted in *Columbia* (SC) *Phoenix*, June 8, 1865, p. 3 (discussing emigration to the South); *New York Herald*, reprinted in *Nashville Union*, June 10, 1865, p. 1.

98. *New York Herald*, reprinted in *Milwaukee Sentinel*, July 22, 1865, and (New Orleans) *Picayune*, July 29, 1865, p. 3.

99. *New York Herald*, May 4, 1865, p. 5; *Mobile News*, May 4, 1865, p. 1; *Nashville Press*, May 5, 1865, p. 1.

100. Vandiver, "Josiah Gorgas," 5–21; Wiggins, *Journals of Josiah Gorgas*, 189–197; (New York) *World*, reprinted in (New Orleans) *Picayune*, July 21, 1865, p. 3, August 30, 1865, p. 7; *Mobile Advertiser and Register*, September 7, 1865, p. 2; *Mobile News*, June 5, 1865, p. 4; *Huntsville Advocate*, July 26, 1865, p. 2; (New Orleans) *Picayune*, June 9, 1865, p. 2. See also Milton Brown to Andrew Johnson, July 18, 1865, Bergeron, *Pa-*

pers of Andrew Johnson, 8:425; (New Orleans) *Daily Picayune*, August 30, 1865, p. 7; (Washington, DC) *National Intelligencer*, September 15, 1865, p. 2; *Selma Messenger*, September 28, 1865, reprinted in *Augusta* (GA) *Constitutionalist*, October 11, 1865, p. 1; *Montgomery Mail*, reprinted in *New Orleans Times*, September 9, 1865, supplement, p. 1.

101. See generally Andrew McFarland Davis, *The Origin of the National Banking System* (Washington, DC: Government Printing Office, 1910), 155–97; Irwin Unger, *The Greenback Era: A Social and Political History of American Finance, 1865–1879* (Princeton, NJ: Princeton University Press, 1968), 18–19; Carter, *When the War Was Over*, 100; Louis M. Hacker, *The Triumph of American Capitalism: The Development of Forces in American History to the End of the Nineteenth Century* (New York: McGraw-Hill, 1965), 365–68.

102. (Columbus, GA) *Sun*, November 4, 1865, p. 2; *Mobile News*, July 19, 1865, p. 2.

103. See *Mobile News*, June 9, 1865, p. 2, June 14, 1865, p. 2, June 22, 1865, p. 4, July 19, 1865, p. 2, September 12, 1865, p. 1; (Grove Hill, AL) *Clarke County Journal*, November 9, 1865, p. 2; (Greensboro) *Alabama Beacon*, June 16, 1865, p. 2; *Mobile Advertiser and Register*, September 13, 1865, p. 2, November 5, 1865, p. 2, November 22, 1865, p. 2; *New York Herald*, July 30, 1865, p. 1; *Huntsville Advocate*, August 31, 1865, p. 3, October 12, 1865, p. 3, November 9, 1865, p. 3 and supplement; (New Orleans) *Picayune*, June 20, 1865, p. 1, and supplement, August 27, 1865; *Cleveland Leader*, June 19, 1865, p. 4.

104. *Montgomery Mail*, May 16, 1865, p. 2; Fleming, *Civil War and Reconstruction*, 316–17.

105. *Montgomery Mail*, May 15, 1865, p. 2.

106. Axford, *"To Lochaber Na Mair,"* "Mary Fielding's Diary," 159.

107. Harwell, *Kate*, 302.

108. Wendy Hamand Venet, ed., *Sam Richard's Civil War Diary: A Chronicle of the Atlanta Home Front (Athens: University of Georgia Press, 2009)*, 270. See also Williams, Williams, and Carlson, *Rich Man's War*, 126. As has been noted by others, myths regarding constitutional issues and states' rights were publicly used to obscure the preservation of slavery as the real purpose of the war. See Beringer et al., *Why the South Lost*, 403–17.

109. Linden and Linden, *Disunion, War, Defeat, and Recovery*, 137.

110. Dwight Franklin Henderson, ed., *The Private Journal of Georgiana Gholson Walker 1862–1865 with Selections from the Post-War Years, 1865–1876* (Tuscaloosa, AL: Confederate Publishing, 1963), 110.

111. Donald E. Collins, *The Death and Resurrection of Jefferson Davis* (Lanham MD: Rowan and Littlefield Publishers, 2005), 17–18.

112. Virginia K. Jones, ed., "The Journal of Sarah G. Follansbee," *Alabama Historical Quarterly* 27 (Fall and Winter 1965): 241.

113. Daily Journal of Joshua Burns Moore, 84, ADAH.

114. Wiggins, ed., *Journals of Josiah Gorgas*, 175.

115. McWhiney, Moore, and Pace, *"Fear God and Walk Humbly,"* 343.

NOTES TO PAGES 154–157 / 271

116. Private Journal of Sarah R. Espy, 97, ADAH.

117. *Montgomery Mail*, May 15, 1865.

118. Hague, *Blockaded Family*, 162. See also Sutherland, *Savage Conflict*, 275.

119. See generally Michael W. Fitzgerald, "Radical Republicanism and the White Yeomanry during Alabama Reconstruction, 1865–1868," *Journal of Southern History* 54 (November 1988): 565. See also *Asheville* (AL) *Vidette*, reprinted in *Meridian* (MS) *Clarion*, March 28, 1865, p. 2.

120. *Nashville Union*, May 30, 1865, p. 3.

121. Harwell, *Kate*, 284.

122. A. Asboth to Lt. Col. C. T. Christensen, May 17, 1865, OR, Series 1, Vol. 49 (Part II), 826–827. See also Allen W. Jones, "Unionism and Disaffection in South Alabama: The Case of Alfred Holley," *Alabama Review* 24 (April 1971): 114–32.

123. Private Journal of Sarah R. Espy, 100, ADAH.

124. Jewett, *Rise and Fall of the Confederacy*, 53, 208.

125. *Buffalo Advertiser*, reprinted in *Mobile News*, July 21, 1865, p. 6, (New Orleans) *Picayune*, July 25, 1865, p. 6, and *Boston Herald*, July 11, 1865, p. 4; *Mobile News*, June 24, 1865, p. 2, *Howard* (MO) *Union*, July 20, 1865, p. 1, *Ashtabula* (OH) *Weekly Telegraph*, July 22, 1865, p. 2. See also John McArthur to Lt. Col. J. Hough, June 9, 1865, OR, Series 1, Vol. 49 (Part II), 976.

126. *Montgomery Mail*, May 31, 1865, p. 2.

127. Ellen Blue, "Diary of Ellen Blue," in Mary Ann Neeley, ed., *The Works of Matthew Blue, Montgomery's First Historian* (Montgomery, AL: NewSouth Books, 2010), 394.

128. Turner, *Beware the People Weeping*, 18–23, 52, 78, 127; Blum, *Reforging the White Republic* 22, 38, 41–42; Susanna Michele Lee, *Claiming the Union: Citizenship in the Post–Civil War South* (New York: Cambridge University Press, 2014), 12–38.

129. *New York Times*, May 2, 1865, p. 8; *Boston Advertiser*, May 3, 1865; *Lowell* (MA) *Citizen and News*, May 3, 1865, May 4, 1865; (Washington, DC) *National Intelligencer*, May 3, 1865; *Bangor* (ME) *Whig and Courier*, May 5, 1865; (Boston) *Congregationalist*, May 5, 1865, p. 71; *Milwaukee Sentinel*, May 8, 1865; (Windsor) *Vermont Chronicle*, May 13, 1865, p. 4.

130. *New York Times*, June 19, 1865, p. 1; (Boston) *Liberator*, June 23, 1865, p. 98; (San Francisco) *Evening Bulletin*, July 18, 1865. See also *Lowell* (MA) *Citizen and News*, September 18, 1865; *Milwaukee Sentinel*, September 27, 1865; *New York Tribune*, June 30, 1865, p. 4.

131. Rohr, *Incidents of the War*, 296. Lee gave this warning in a newspaper interview. Perman, *Reunion without Compromise*, 34.

132. Harwell, *Kate*, 290.

133. Jeffrey W. Hunt, *The Last Battle of the Civil War: Palmetto Ranch* (Austin: University of Texas Press, 2002), 5.

134. George Robertson to Julia, May 8, 1865, quoted in ibid., 49.

135. Steve Cottrell, *Civil War in Texas and New Mexico Territory* (Gretna, LA: Pelican, 1998), 109–11.

272 / NOTES TO PAGES 157–159

136. (Washington, DC) *National Republican*, May 29, 1865, p. 2; *Montgomery Mail*, May 26, 1865, p. 2, May 29, 1865, p. 1.

137. *Mobile News*, May 26, 1865, p. 2; (New Orleans) *Picayune*, October 27, 1865, p. 4.

138. *Mobile News*, May 26, 1865, p. 2.

139. Ibid., May 30, 1865, p. 4.

140. Ibid., May 25, 1865, and May 26, 1865, p. 2; (New Orleans) *Daily Picayune*, May 26, 1865, reprinted in *Cleveland Leader*, June 3, 1865, p. 2 (publishing a letter from Mobile). See also (Washington, DC) *National Republican*, May 29, 1865, p. 2, May 30, 1865, p. 2; *Nashville Union*, May 30, 1865, p. 1; *Columbia* (SC) *Daily Phoenix*, June 8, 1865, p. 2, June 10, 1865, p. 2, June 27, 1865, p. 2 (putting the death toll at over one thousand). See generally Fitzgerald, *Urban Emancipation*, 30; Norman Andre Trudeau, *Out of the Storm: The End of the Civil War, April–June 1865* (Boston: Little, Brown, 1991), 324–34; Mrs. Hugh C. Bailey, "Mobile's Tragedy: The Great Magazine Explosion of 1865," *Alabama Review* 21 (January 1968): 40.

141. *Mobile News*, May 26, 1865, p. 2; *Highland* (OH) *Weekly News*, June 15, 1865, p. 2; (New Orleans) *Picayune*, May 27, 1865, p. 2; *Cincinnati Enquirer*, July 25, 1865, p. 2. Given the amount of death and destruction, proving this was almost impossible.

142. *New Orleans Times*, June 6, 1865, and June 7, 1865, cited in *New York Times*, June 12, 1865, p. 1, June 18, 1865, p. 1; (Washington, DC) *National Republican*, June 12, 1865, p. 2; *Boston Advertiser*, June 13, 1865; *Lowell* (MA) *Citizen and News*, June 13, 1865; (Washington, DC) *National Intelligencer*, June 13, 1865; *Cleveland Herald*, June 19, 1865. See also *Mobile News*, May 31, 1865, reprinted in (New Orleans) *Picayune*, June 3, 1865, p. 2; *Mobile News*, June 8, 1865, reprinted in (New Orleans) *Picayune*, June 10, 1865, p. 1; *Cincinnati Gazette*, reprinted in *Cleveland Leader*, June 13, 1865, p. 1 (reporting the arrest of a man named John Jackson who admitted his involvement); *White Cloud Kansas Chief*, June 15, 1865, p. 2; *Belmont* (OH) *Chronicle*, June 22, 1865, p. 2; (Oskaloosa, KS) *Independent*, June 24, 1865, p. 2; *Columbia* (SC) *Phoenix*, June 27, 1865, p. 2, June 29, 1865, p 2. The court of inquiry appointed to investigate the incident later concluded that the cause of the explosion could not be determined. (Washington, DC) *National Intelligencer*, July 27, 1865; (Washington, DC) *National Republican*, July 25, 1865, p. 2.

143. *Belmont* (OH) *Chronicle*, June 22, 1865, p. 2. See also *White Cloud Kansas Chief*, June 15, 1865, p. 2; (Oskaloosa, KS) *Independent*, June 24, 1865, p. 2.

144. *Burlington* (VT) *Free Press*, May 26, 1865, p. 3; (New Orleans) *Picayune*, June 22, 1865, p. 4; *Dayton* (OH) *Empire*, September 23, 1865, p. 1.

145. Welles, *Diary of Gideon Welles*, 333.

146. Jewett, *Rise and Fall of the Confederacy*, 82.

147. Cox and Cox, *Politics, Principle, and Prejudice*, 163; Blum, *Reforging the White Republic*, 23–24, 38–39. Compare *Harper's Weekly*, reprinted in *Belmont* (OH) *Chronicle*, June 22, 1865, p. 2 ("we are in no danger of treating any body too severely"); (Montpelier) *Vermont Watchman and State Journal*, June 23, 1865, p. 1 ("rebels are rebels still" and if not allowed "'states rights,' and other popular aristocratic dogmas, they will

fight again"); (Oskaloosa, KS) *Independent*, June 24, 1865, p. 2 (calling for the execution of Davis, Lee, General Johnston, and "most of the ringleaders of the rebellions"); *Gallipolis* (OH) *Journal*, June 29, 1865, p. 1; *Cleveland Leader*, June 30, 1865, p. 2; and *Belmont* (OH) *Chronicle*, July 27, 1865, p. 1 (arguing for black suffrage); (Millersburg, OH) *Holmes County Farmer*, June 22, 1865, p. 2 (calling allegations against the South "purely false and slanderous"); *Albany Journal*, reprinted in *Nashville Union*, June 25, 1865, p. 2 (praising Johnson's more moderate approach); *New York Herald*, reprinted in *Nashville Union*, June 28, 1865, p. 1 (also praising Johnson and attacking "the Jacobin element of the North" who were raising "a row about negro suffrage"); *Nashville Union*, July 29, 1865, p. 2 (opposing universal black suffrage); (New York) *World*, reprinted in *Mobile News*, July 19, 1865, p. 2 (opposing black suffrage).

Chapter 13

1. McKitrick, *Andrew Johnson and Reconstruction*, 7–8.

2. Wiggins, *Journals of Josiah Gorgas*, 175, 183; Williams, *Diary from Dixie*, 539; *Montgomery Mail*, June 5, 1865, p. 3.

3. *Mobile News*, June 3, 1865, p. 2, June 6, 1865, p. 2, June 13, 1865, p. 4; (Greensboro) *Alabama Beacon*, June 16, 1865, p. 2; (Grove Hill, AL) *Clarke County Journal*, June 15, 1865, p. 2; *New York News*, June 3, 1865, reprinted in (Greensboro) *Alabama Beacon*, June 23, 1865, p. 2. See also Varon, *Appomattox*, 192–93; Jonathan Truman Dorris, *Pardon and Amnesty under Lincoln and Johnson: The Restoration of the Confederates to Their Rights and Privileges, 1861–1898* (Chapel Hill: University of North Carolina Press, 1953), 111–13; Foner, *Reconstruction*, 183.

4. *Mobile News*, June 6, 1865, p. 3; *Huntsville Advocate*, July 12, 1865, p. 2; Means, *Avenger Takes His Place*, 201–3; Brooks D. Simpson, Leroy P. Graf, John Muldowny, eds., *Advice after Appomattox: Letters to Andrew Johnson 1865–1866* (Knoxville: University of Tennessee Press, 1987), 61.

5. James Oakes, *The Radical and the Republican: Frederick Douglass, Abraham Lincoln, and the Triumph of Anti-Slavery Politics* (New York: W. W. Norton, 2007), 250–54 (he at one point claimed it was a fear that forcing black suffrage would spark a race war but did not mention that it would encourage continued armed resistance to federal authority).

6. Perman, *Reunion without Compromise*, 3–4.

7. Foner, *Reconstruction*, 180; (New York) *World*, reprinted in *Huntsville Advocate*, August 17, 1865, p. 4; *New York Herald*, reprinted in *Mobile News*, June 25, 1865, p. 2; *Boston Advertiser*, June 26, 1865.

8. *New York Times*, reprinted in *Mobile Daily News*, July 7, 1865, p. 3; *New York News*, reprinted in *Mobile News*, July 18, 1865, p. 2; (New York) *World*, reprinted in *Mobile News*, July 19, 1865, p. 2. See also Means, *Avenger Takes His Place*, 212–16.

9. Journal of Joshua Burns Moore, 90, ADAH. See generally Foner, *Reconstruction*, 186–90; Edward L. Gambill, *Conservative Ordeal: Northern Democrats and Reconstruction, 1865–1868* (Ames: Iowa State University Press, 1981), 27–28.

10. James N. Leiker, *Racial Borders: Black Soldiers along the Rio Grande* (College Station: Texas A&M University Press, 2002), 28; James K. Bryant II, *The 36th Infantry United States Colored Troops in the Civil War: A History and Roster* (Jefferson, NC: McFarland, 2012), 119–21. See also Clyde McQueen, *The Black Army Officer* (Bloomington, IN: Authorhouse, 2009), 2 (stating that 19,768 black troops were still in Texas in January 1866); Edward A. Miller Jr., *The Black Civil War Soldiers of Illinois: The Story of the Twenty-Ninth U.S. Colored Infantry* (Columbia: University of South Carolina Press, 1998), 152–67; William A. Dobak, *Freedom by the Sword: The U.S. Colored Troops, 1862–1867* (Washington, DC, US Army Center of Military History 2011), 437–47 (noting that Frederick Steele's force had been sent from Alabama); Richard M. Reid, *Freedom for Themselves: North Carolina's Black Soldiers in the Civil War Era* (Chapel Hill: University of North Carolina Press, 2008), 54–62 (noting considerable discontent among black troops over this deployment); William L. Richter, *The Army in Texas during Reconstruction, 1865–1870* (College Station: Texas A&M University Press, 1987), 17.

11. (Troy, AL) *Southern Advertiser*, September 16, 1865, p. 2; *New York Times*, May 16, 1865, p. 8, May 28, 1865, p. 3, June 9, 1865, p. 1, June 26, 1865, p. 1 (Sickles finally left Panama on June 10, apparently unsuccessful in his endeavor); *Washington* (DC) *Chronicle*, reprinted in *Chicago Tribune*, July 14, 1865, p. 3. For the debate among historians regarding Sickles's mission, see Foner, *Fiery Trial*, 402 (noting that Sickles publicly denied that his mission to Central America related to colonization); Thomas Keneally, *American Scoundrel: The Life of the Notorious Civil War General Dan Sickles* (New York: Nan A. Talese/Doubleday, 2002), 310–15 (maintaining that colonization was part of Sickles's mission).

12. Jones, *Life of Andrew Johnson*, 106 ("I hope the Negro will be transferred to Mexico, or some other country congenial to his nature"); LeRoy P. Graf and Ralph W. Haskins, eds., *Papers of Andrew Johnson*, vol. 6, *1862–1864* (Knoxville, University of Tennessee Press), li.

13. Cox and Cox, *Politics, Principle, and Prejudice*, 55–56.

14. *Nashville Union*, June 23, 1865, p. 1; Hubbs, *Voices from Company D*, 384.

15. (Clearfield, PA) *Raftsman's Journal*, May 10, 1865, p. 2.

16. Chester Hearn, *The Impeachment of Andrew Johnson* (Jefferson, NC: McFarland, 2000), 60; *New York Tribune*, January 29, 1866, p. 1 (publishing a letter from William Brownlow).

17. Jean Joseph Giers to Andrew Johnson, May 30, 1865, in Bergeron, *Papers of Andrew Johnson*, 8:145.

18. Jeremiah Clemens to Andrew Johnson, November 19, 1864, and April 21, 1865, Graf, *Papers of Andrew Johnson*, 7:302–4, 598–600; Richard H. Barham to Andrew Johnson, April 30, 1865, ibid., 7:670–72; (New York) *Sun*, January 20, 1866, p. 2.

19. *Bangor* (ME) *Whig and Courier*, June 5, 1865.

20. *Augusta* (GA) *Constitutionalist*, July 8, 1865, reprinted in Bergeron, *Papers of Andrew Johnson*, 8:183–84. Johnson took the same position in response to requests from groups in other Southern states. Perman, *Reunion without Compromise*, 42–44, 57–58.

NOTES TO PAGES 163–164 / 275

21. *Augusta* (GA) *Constitutionalist*, July 8, 1865, p. 2.

22. *Mobile News*, June 11, 1865, p. 2.

23. *Selma* (AL) *Reporter*, September 24, 1863, p. 2; *Boston Herald*, January 12, 1864; *Nashville Press*, April 18, 1865, p. 3.

24. *Huntsville Advocate*, July 12, 1865, p. 3; *Hartford* (CT) *Courant*, July 10, 1865, p. 2; *Mobile Advertiser and Register*, July 22, 1865, p. 2; *Louisville* (KY) *Journal*, July 10, 1865, p. 1; Lewis E. Parsons, Joseph C. Bradley, and James Q. Adams to Andrew Johnson, May 15, 1865, in Graf, *Papers of Andrew Johnson*, 7:75; Milo Howard Jr., "John Hardy and John Reid: Two Selma Men of Letters," *Alabama Review* 22 (January 1969): 44, 50; John Hardy, *Selma: Her Institutions, and Her Men* (Selma, AL: Bert Neville and Clarence DeBray, 1957), xi.

25. Charles David Greer, *Why Texans Fought in the Civil War* (College Station: Texas A&M University Press, 2013), 32–33; Carl H. Moneyhon, *Republicanism in Reconstruction Texas* (College Station: Texas A&M University Press, 1980), 21–24.

26. Carl H. Moneyhon, *Texas After the Civil War: The Struggle of Reconstruction* (College Station: Texas A&M University Press, 2004), 40–41; Richter, *Army in Texas during Reconstruction*, 22, 46; *Montgomery Advertiser*, August 24, 1866, p. 2, August 25, 1866, p. 1; *Dallas* (TX) *Herald*, August 5, 1865, p. 2, August 12, 1865, p. 1; *Eufaula* (AL) *News*, October 14, 1865, p. 2; James Alex Baggett, "Origins of Early Texas Republican Party Leadership," *Journal of Southern History* 40 (August 1974): 441.

27. *Mobile News*, June 30, 1865, p. 1. But it is very possible that Parsons had closer wartime ties to Johnson and his Unionist political machine in Nashville than we will ever know. It is striking that James Quinton Smith, another Alabama member of that machine, wrote to Johnson on June 6 endorsing Parsons's selection as provisional governor. James Q. Smith to Andrew Johnson, June 6, 1865, cited in Wiggins, *Scalawag in Alabama Politics*, 157n15. Parsons may have served as a secret Union agent during at least the latter part of the war and, if so, Johnson and James Quinton Smith may have been aware of this. One wonders what promises had been made to Parsons in exchange for his activities. If Parsons was a secret agent, that fact was never made known.

28. *Mobile News*, June 16, 1865, p. 2, June 17, 1865, p. 3, June 29, 1865, July 7, 1865, p. 1; *Cincinnati Enquirer*, July 25, 1865, p. 2; *New York Herald*, reprinted in *Mobile News*, June 30, 1865, p. 1 (publishing a letter to the editor by Daniel Havens Bingham); *Nashville Press and Times*, July 4, 1865, p. 1; (New Orleans) *Picayune*, July 8, 1865, p. 1; *Huntsville Advocate*, July 12, 1865, p. 1; (Grove Hill, AL) *Clarke County Journal*, July 13, 1865, p. 1. See also Fleming, *Civil War and Reconstruction*, 347, 352; Wiggins, *Scalawag in Alabama Politics*, 10–11.

29. *Mobile News*, June 29, 1865, p. 2. Regarding Parsons's acts of wartime disloyalty to the Union, see (Washington, DC) *National Republican*, January 11, 1866, p. 1.

30. Perman, *Reunion without Compromise*, 62, 66.

31. (Greensboro) *Alabama Beacon*, June 30, 1865, p. 2; *Selma Messenger*, reprinted in *Mobile News*, July 13, 1865, p. 2; *Mobile News*, July 19, 1865, p. 2; (New Orleans) *Picayune*, July 30, 1865, p. 8.

32. *Mobile News*, July 6, 1865, p. 2; *Montgomery Mail*, July 8, 1854, p. 2.

276 / Notes to pages 164–166

33. *Selma Messenger*, cited in (Jackson) *Mississippian*, July 20, 1865; (Greensboro) *Alabama Beacon*, June 2, 1865, p. 2.

34. *New York Tribune*, reprinted in (Portage) *Wisconsin State Register*, June 3, 1865; *New York Times*, June 7, 1865, p. 4; *Mobile News*, June 12, 1865, p. 1, June 15, 1865, p. 2; *Boston Post*, reprinted in *Bangor* (ME) *Whig and Courier*, June 8, 1865; *Mobile News*, June 11, 1865, p. 2; Means, *Avenger Takes His Place*, 204.

35. *New Haven* (CT) *Palladium*, June 22, 1865; (Greensboro) *Alabama Beacon*, June 2, 1865, p. 2; *Mobile News*, June 3, 1865, p. 2, June 28, 1865, p. 2; *New York Times*, June 3, 1865, p. 4; (Concord) *New Hampshire Statesman*, June 2, 1865; *Boston Advertiser*, June 6, 1865; Means, *Avenger Takes His Place*, 206; McPherson, *Struggle for Equality*, 321.

36. And this coalition between the two groups and disillusioned Northerners would ultimately form. Michael W. Fitzgerald, *The Union League Movement in the Deep South: Politics and Agricultural Change during Reconstruction* (Baton Rouge: Louisiana State University Press, 1989), 42–43.

37. Perman, *Reunion without Compromise*, 122; *New York Times*, July 2, 1865, p. 6; (Greensboro) *Alabama Beacon*, July 14, 1865, p. 2; *Huntsville Advocate*, July 19, 1865, pp. 1–2, July 26, 1865, p. 2.

38. (New Orleans) *Picayune*, June 25, 1865, p. 1 (former vice president and Confederate general John Breckenridge); *Huntsville Advocate*, July 12, 1865, p. 3, July 19, 1865, p. 2 (politicians and military officials including Gen. Kirby Smith and two former Louisiana governors), July 26, 1865, p. 2 (Judah Benjamin); *Cincinnati Enquirer*, July 7, 1865, p. 3; *New York Herald*, reprinted in (Sandusky, OH) *Commercial Register*, July 27, 1865, p. 2; Dorris, *Pardon and Amnesty*, 116 (Breckinridge, Judah Benjamin, Robert Toombs); *Nashville Union*, reprinted in *Huntsville Advocate*, July 19, 1865, p. 1; *Nashville Press and Times*, July 28, 1865, p. 2.

39. *Selma* (AL) *Messenger*, reprinted in *Augusta* (GA) *Constitutionalist*, August 5, 1865, p. 3; *Selma* (AL) *Messenger*, September 24, 1865, p. 2. See also Peter A. Brannon, "Southern Emigration to Brazil," *Alabama Historical Quarterly* 1 (Summer, Fall, Winter 1930): 74–96, 280–305, 467–488; Julia L. Keyes, "Our Life in Brazil," *Alabama Historical Quarterly* 28, nos. 3–4 (Fall and Winter 1966): 129–339.

40. (New Orleans) *Picayune*, June 27, 1865, p. 1. See also *Providence* (RI) *Press*, June 21, 1865, p. 3; *New York Tribune*, June 22, 1865, p, 4; *Mobile News*, June 29, 1865, p. 2; (Washington, DC) *National Intelligencer*, June 22, 1865; *Milwaukee Sentinel*, June 24, 1865. Ruffin blew the "upper portion of his head . . . entirely off." *Richmond Republican*, June 20, 1865, reprinted in *Columbia* (SC) *Phoenix*, July 4, 1865, p. 2; *Nashville Union*, June 24, 1865, p. 1; *Burlington* (VT) *Free Press*, June 30, 1865, p. 4; (New Orleans) *Picayune*, June 27, 1865, p. 1, June 29, 1865, p. 6; *Milwaukee Sentinel*, June 24, 1865.

41. *Huntsville Advocate*, July 19, 1865, p. 2.

42. Daily Journal of Joshua Burns Moore, 103, ADAH.

43. *Huntsville Advocate*, July 19, 1865, p. 2; Stephen A. Townsend, *Yankee Invasion of Texas* (College Station: Texas A&M University Press, 2006), 137–38; Blair, *With Malice toward Some*, 243; Robert L. Kerby, *Kirby Smith's Confederacy: The Trans-Mississippi South, 1863–1865* (New York: Columbia University Press, 1972), 428–29; Lewis L.

Gould, *Alexander Watkins Terrell: Civil War Soldier, Texas Lawmaker, American Diplomat* (Austin: University of Texas Press, 2004), 48; Anthony Arthur, *General Jo Shelby's March* (New York: Random House, 2010), 61–82; *Mobile Advertiser and Register*, February 2, 1866, supplement, p. 1 (listing the many Confederate officers in Mexico), February 10, 1866, p. 2 (reporting the arrival of Gen. Jubal Early).

44. Cadmus Wilcox to Major Robertson, October 8, 1865, in *Selma Times*, reprinted in *Memphis Avalanche*, February 9, 1866, p. 1.

45. Gould, *Alexander Watkins Terrell*, 49.

46. Means, *Avenger Take His Place*, 203, 223–25; Dorris, *Pardon and Amnesty*, 135–45. Under intense press scrutiny, the president had already begun issuing pardons to wealthy, somewhat prominent men excepted from his amnesty proclamation (see, e.g., *Louisville* [KY] *Journal*, June 24, 1865, p. 1), triggering a stampede of former Confederates to Washington, DC. (Grove Hill, AL) *Clarke County Journal*, June 15, 1865, p. 2. Most early recipients of a pardon were small fish, but then word that former Confederate secretary of war Leroy Pope Walker was seeking a pardon hit the New York press and was flashed across the nation by telegraph. *Mobile News*, June 27, 1865, p. 2, July 2, 1865, p. 1; (New Orleans) *Picayune*, June 30, 1865, p. 1.

47. *Providence* (RI) *Press*, September 14, 1865, p. 2, quoting William Shakespeare, *Othello*, Act 4, Scene 2, p. 8.

48. See generally *Huntsville Advocate*, July 19, 1865, p. 2.

49. *Mobile Advertiser and Register*, August 8, 1865, August 15, 1865, p. 2, August 27, 1865, p. 2; *Selma Times*, August 12, 1865, quoted in (New Orleans) *Picayune*, August 16, 1865, p. 1, August 29, 1865, p. 6.

50. *Mobile Advertiser and Register*, August 27, 1865, p. 2.

51. *New York Herald*, reprinted in *Mobile News*, June 25, 1865, p. 2.

52. John W. Ford to Andrew Johnson, June 29, 1865, Graf, *Papers of Andrew Johnson*, 7:312–13. See also John J. Siebels to Andrew Johnson, June 30, 1865, Bergeron, *Papers of Andrew Johnson*, 8:322–24.

53. *Mobile Advertiser and Register*, August 27, 1865, p. 2.

54. (New Orleans) *Picayune*, June 23, 1865, p. 2.

Chapter 14

Epigraph. *Nashville Union*, November 19, 1865, p. 1.

1. *Bangor* (ME) *Whig and Courier*, October 3, 1865, October 31, 1865; *Milwaukee Sentinel*, September 28, 1865; James Michael Quill, *Prelude to the Radicals: The North and Reconstruction* (Washington, DC: University Press of America, 1980), 122–35; Perman, *Reunion without Compromise*, 145.

2. Perman, *Reunion without Compromise*, 188–89.

3. *New York Times*, November 20, 1865, p. 1 (publishing a speech by the Speaker of the House); *Huntsville Advocate*, November 30, 1865, p. 1 (same); David B Chesebrough, *No Sorrow Like Our Sorrow: Northern Protestant Ministers and the Assassination of Lincoln* (Kent, OH: Kent State University Press, 1994), 53–65.

4. *Chattanooga Gazette*, October 3, 1865, reprinted in *Nashville Press and Times*,

October 6, 1865, p. 2, and *Milwaukee Sentinel*, October 14, 1865, p. 2; Herold Melvin Hyman, *The Era of the Oath: Northern Loyalty Tests during the Civil War and Reconstruction* (Philadelphia: University of Pennsylvania Press, 1954), xi–xiv; Robert Dixon Sawrey, *Dubious Victory: The Reconstruction Debate in Ohio* (Lexington: University Press of Kentucky, 1992), 12–13.

5. (Bellow Falls) *Vermont Chronicle*, August 5, 1865, p. 5; *Boston Advertiser*, May 7, 1865. See also Wiggins, *Scalawag in Alabama Politics*, 12 (referring to Carl Schurz in Alabama); John Richard Dennett, *The South As It Is: 1865–1866* (Tuscaloosa: University of Alabama Press, 2010), xi; John R. McKivigan, *Forgotten Firebrand: James Redpath and the Making of Nineteenth-Century America* (Ithaca, NY: Cornell University Press, 2008), 113.

6. Testimony of E. Woolsey Peck, November 3, 1871, Alabama Testimony, 1871.

7. See, e.g., Orville Eastland to Andrew Johnson, September 3, 1865, September 8, 1865, Bergeron, *Papers of Andrew Johnson*, 9:16–18, 44–46. See also *Dayton* (OH) *Empire*, July 31, 1865, p. 3; John Hope Franklin, *Reconstruction after the Civil War* (Chicago: University of Chicago Press, 1994), 32.

8. Williams, *Diary from Dixie*, 533.

9. George W. Howard to Brig. Gen. R. S. Granger, July 1, 1865, OR, Series 1, Vol. 49 (Part II), 1057; Storey, "Crucible of Reconstruction," 74.

10. (Tuscumbia) *North Alabamian*, quoted in (New Orleans) *Picayune*, July 15, 1865, p. 2.

11. Anthony W. Dillard to Andrew Johnson, August 14, 1865, Bergeron, *Papers of Andrew Johnson*, 8:582–83. See also Michael W. Fitzgerald, "'He Was Always Preaching the Union': The Wartime Origins of White Republicanism during Reconstruction," in *Yellowhammer War*, ed. Noe, 234.

12. Gregory P. Downs, *After Appomattox: Military Occupation and the Ends of the War.* (Cambridge, MA: Harvard University Press, 2015), 66.

13. *Milwaukee Sentinel*, July 22, 1865, August 17, 1865; (Philadelphia) *North American and United States Gazette*, August 19, 1865, p. 135; *New York Times*, August 22, 1865, p. 1; *Cleveland Leader*, August 18, 1865, p. 2; Carl Schurz to Andrew Johnson, August 29, 1865, Bergeron, *Papers of Andrew Johnson*, 8:671; Henry Wilson to William H. Seward, June 15, 1865, Papers of William H. Seward, Rush Rhees Library, University of Rochester; Glenn Feldman, *The Irony of the Solid South: Democrats, Republicans, and Race, 1865–1944* (Tuscaloosa: University of Alabama Press, 2013), 4–5, 7.

14. *New Orleans Tribune*, reprinted in (Boston) *Liberator*, August 25, 1865, p. 135.

15. (Washington, DC) *National Republican*, January 22, 1866, p. 1.

16. S. S. Houston to Lewis Parsons, August 29, 1865, Papers of Governor Lewis Parsons, ADAH. See generally Wiggins, *Scalawag in Alabama Politics*, 40–42, 56–61; George C. Rable, *But There Was No Peace: The Role of Violence in the Politics of Reconstruction* (Athens: University of Georgia Press, 2007); Allen W. Trelease, *White Terror: The Ku Klux Klan Conspiracy and Southern Reconstruction* (New York: Harper and Row, 1971); Kimberly Menaster, "Political Violence in the American South: 1882–1890," master's thesis, Massachusetts Institute of Technology, 2009; Carole Ember-

NOTES TO PAGE 170 / 279

ton, *Beyond Redemption: Race, Violence, and the American South after the Civil War* (Chicago: University of Chicago Press, 2013); Ray Granade, "Violence: An Instrument of Policy in Reconstruction Alabama," *Alabama Historical Quarterly* 30 (Fall–Winter 1968): 181; William Warren Rogers Jr., "The Boyd Incident: Black Belt Violence during Reconstruction," *Civil War History* 21 (December 1975): 308; William Warren Rogers Jr., *Black Belt Scalawag: Charles Hays and the Southern Republicans in the Era of Reconstruction* (Athens: University of Georgia Press, 1993); John Z. Sloan, "The Ku Klux Klan and the Alabama Election of 1872," *Alabama Review* 18 (April 1965): 113; Melinda M. Hennessey, "Political Terrorism in the Black Belt: The Eutaw Riot," *Alabama Review* 33 (January 1980): 35; Gene L. Howard, *Death at Cross Plains: An Alabama Reconstruction Tragedy* (Tuscaloosa: University of Alabama Press, 1984); Richard Bailey, *Neither Carpetbaggers Nor Scalawags: Black Officeholders during the Reconstruction of Alabama, 1867–1878* (Montgomery, AL: R. Bailey Publishers, 1991); Michael W. Fitzgerald, "Extralegal Violence and the Planter Class: The Ku Klux Klan in the Alabama Black Belt during Reconstruction," in *Local Matters: Race, Crime, and Justice in the Nineteenth-Century South*, ed. Christopher Waldrep and Donald G. Nieman (Athens: University of Georgia Press, 2001); McIlwain, "United States District Judge," 263–89.

17. *New York Herald*, reprinted in (New Orleans) *Picayune*, July 29, 1865, p. 3; *New York Times*, October 28, 1865, p. 2; (New Orleans) *Picayune*, August 1, 1865, p. 6.

18. E. C. Cabell to Lewis Parsons, September 29. 1865, Papers of Lewis E. Parsons, ADAH. For a similar letter, see F. A. Redington to Lewis Parsons, September 4, 1865, ibid.

19. *New York Tribune*, September 9, 1865, p. 4; *New York Times*, August 2, 1865, p. 1. See also (New Orleans) *Picayune*, July 15, 1865, p. 3, August 1, 1865, p. 7; *Charleston Courier*, September 12, 1865, p. 1; *Huntsville Advocate*, July 19, 1865, p. 2; *Sunbury* (PA) *American*, September 23, 1865, p. 1; Ben C. Truman to Andrew Johnson, October 13, 1865, in Simpson, Graf, and Muldowny, *Advice after Appomattox*, 186. See also J. Barry Vaughn, *Bishops, Bourbons, and Big Mules: A History of the Episcopal Church in Alabama* (Tuscaloosa: University of Alabama Press, 2013), 58–62; Fleming, *Civil War and Reconstruction*, 325–29; Severance, *Portraits of Conflict*, 298.

20. *Montgomery Mail*, September 22, 1865, p. 2, September 26, 1865, p. 2; *Mobile Advertiser and Register*, September 23, 1865, p. 2, January 10, 1866, p. 2, January 13, 1866, p. 4; (New Orleans) *Picayune*, September 24, 1865, p. 7, January 9, 1866, p. 6; (Philadelphia) *North American and United States Gazette*, October 4, 1865; *Montgomery Advertiser*, January 6, 1866, p. 2; *Huntsville Advocate*, October 4, 1865, p. 3; *Nashville Press and Times*, October 6, 1865, p. 2; (Petersburg, VA) *Express*, October 6, 1865; *Mobile Tribune*, October 7, 1865, p. 4; *Milwaukee Sentinel*, October 14, 1865, p. 2; *Cleveland Leader*, October 7, 1865, p. 1; *New York Tribune*, October 10, 1865, p. 4; (Washington, DC) *Star*, October 27, 1865, p. 1; *New York Times*, January 7, 1866, p. 3; Wiggins, *Journals of Josiah Gorgas*, 179, 188.

21. Forsyth resumed publication of the *Mobile Register* in mid-July, 1865. (New Orleans) *Picayune*, July 6, 1865, p. 4, July 18, 1865, p. 4; Burnett, *Pen Makes A Good*

280 / Notes to pages 170–172

Sword, 148; John Kent Folmar, "Reaction to Reconstruction: John Forsyth and the *Mobile Advertiser and Register*, 1865–1867," *Alabama Historical Quarterly* 37 (Winter 1975): 245–64.

22. *Mobile News*, July 7, 1865, p. 2.

23. (Washington, DC) *National Republican*, January 29, 1866, p. 2.

24. Thomas M. Peters to Thaddeus Stevens, February 22, 1866, in Beverly Wilson Palmer, ed., *The Selected Papers of Thaddeus Stevens, vol. 2, April 1865–August 1868* (Pittsburgh: University of Pittsburgh Press, 1998), 88–90.

25. *Mobile News*, July 22, 1865, p. 3.

26. *Mobile News*, July 25, 1865, p. 2. See also Baggett, *Scalawags*, 162.

27. *Milwaukee Sentinel*, August 8, 1865. See also *Boston Advertiser*, August 10, 1865.

28. Perman, *Reunion without Compromise*, 117–18.

29. *Huntsville Advocate*, August 17, 1865, p. 2; *Mobile News*, July 22, 1865, p. 3; *New York Herald*, July 30, 1865. See generally Fitzgerald, "Radical Republicanism," 569; Baggett, *Scalawags*, 162; Fleming, *Civil War and Reconstruction*, 353–54.

30. *Huntsville Advocate*, August 17, 1865, p. 1. See also Joseph C. Bradley to Andrew Johnson, September 8, 1865, Bergeron, *Papers of Andrew Johnson*, 9:44–46; Cook, "Restoration and Innovation," 17–18; Wiggins, *Scalawag in Alabama Politics*, 11.

31. *New York Herald*, July 3, 1865, p. 1.

32. *Mobile Advertiser and Register*, August 15, 1865, p. 2, August 16, 1865, p. 2, August 17, 1865, p. 1, August 22, 1865, p. 2; *Mobile News*, August 15, 1865, p. 2; (New Orleans) *Picayune*, August 4, 1865, p. 7, August 19, 1865, p. 1; (Philadelphia) *North American and United States Gazette*, August 31, 1865; Burnett, *Pen Makes a Good Sword*, 150–51. See also Gustavus W. Horton to Lewis Parsons, August 1, 1865, Papers of Lewis E. Parsons, ADAH; Fitzgerald, *Urban Emancipation*, 44–45; Donald G. Nieman, ed., *Freedom, Racism, and Reconstruction: Collected Writings of LaWanda Cox* (Athens: University of Georgia Press, 1997), 188–92. During Congressional Reconstruction, Mobile Unionist Gustavus Horton was appointed mayor of Mobile. Harriet E. Amos, "Trials of a Unionist: Gustavus Horton, Military Mayor of Mobile during Reconstruction," *Gulf Coast Historical Review* 4 (Spring 1989): 134–51. On the other hand, Parsons also appointed William Hugh Smith to the post of circuit judge. *Montgomery Mail*, August 8, 1865, p. 2.

33. Lewis E. Parsons to Andrew Johnson, August 24, 1865, Bergeron, *Papers of Andrew Johnson*, 8:648. See also Fitzgerald, "Radical Republicanism," 569–71; *Montgomery Mail*, reprinted in *Mobile News*, September 8, 1865, p. 2.

34. Anthony W. Dillard to Andrew Johnson, August 14, 1865, Bergeron, *Papers of Andrew Johnson*, 8:582–83.

35. Bergeron, *Andrew Johnson's Civil War*, 79–80.

36. Fleming, *Civil War and Reconstruction*, 353–54; Perman, *Reunion without Compromise*, 125, 130.

37. *Montgomery Mail*, September 22, 1865, p. 2 (James Gilchrist); *Mobile Advertiser and Register*, July 28, 1865, p. 2; (Grove Hill, AL) *Clarke County Journal*, August 3, 1865, p. 1; *Huntsville Advocate*, August 17, 1865, p. 1.

NOTES TO PAGES 172–175 / 281

38. Wiggins, *Journals of Josiah Gorgas*, 184.

39. *Huntsville Advocate*, August 31, 1865, p. 2; *Mobile Advertiser and Register*, September 6, 1865, p. 2; (New Orleans) *Picayune*, September 16, 1865, p. 2; *New York Times*, August 24, 1865, p. 1, September 7, 1865, p. 1; Lewis Parsons to Andrew Johnson, September 11, 1865; Bergeron, *Papers of Andrew Johnson*, 9:63; Cook, "Restoration and Innovation," 23–24; Lewis Parsons to George Goldthwaite and Henry Semple, August 22, 1865, Papers of Lewis E. Parsons, ADAH.

40. Wiggins, *Journals of Josiah Gorgas*, 186; Danielson, *War's Desolating Scourge*, 156; Robert S. Rhodes, "The Registration of Voters and the Election of Delegates to the Reconstruction Convention in Alabama," *Alabama Review* 8 (April 1955): 119–42.

41. (Grove Hill, AL) *Clarke County Journal*, August 10, 1865, p. 2; *Mobile Advertiser and Register*, July 28, 1865, p. 2, August 17, 1865, p. 2, August 23, 1865, p. 2, August 31, 1865, p. 2.

42. (Jackson) *Mississippian*, September 5, 1865.

43. *Montgomery Weekly Advertiser*, September 24, 1867, p. 2.

44. *Mobile Advertiser and Register*, July 28, 1865, p. 2; see also July 30, 1865, p. 2, August 17, 1865, p. 2, August 23, 1865, p. 2.

45. Douglas B. Ball, *Financial Failure and Confederate Defeat* (Urbana: University of Illinois Press, 1991), appendix L.

46. *Washington* (DC) *Chronicle*, reprinted in *Mobile News*, September 16, 1865, p. 1; *New York Tribune*, September 20, 1865, p. 4.

47. Joseph C. Bradley to Andrew Johnson, September 8, 1865; Bergeron, *Papers of Andrew Johnson*, 9:44–46.

48. Charles Pelham to Governor Parsons, September 11, 1865, Lewis E. Parsons Papers, ADAH.

49. *Mobile Advertiser and Register*, August 22, 1865, p. 2, September 12, 1865, p. 2, September 17, 1865, p. 2, September 30, 1865, p. 2; McMillan, *Constitutional Development in Alabama*, 99–101; Fleming, *Civil War and Reconstruction*, 361.

50. *Huntsville Advocate*, August 17, 1865, p. 2.

51. Ibid.

52. Charles Pelham to Governor Parsons, September 17, 1865, Papers of Lewis E. Parsons, ADAH.

53. *New York Times*, July 12, 1865, p. 1.

54. Joseph C. Bradley to Andrew Johnson, September 8, 1865; Bergeron, *Papers of Andrew Johnson*, 9:44–46; Sidney C. Posey to Andrew Johnson, June 26, 1865; ibid., 9: 16–18; (New Orleans) *Picayune*, September 19, 1865, p. 1; *Mobile Advertiser and Register*, September 20, 1865, p. 2; *Huntsville Advocate*, October 12, 1865, p. 4; McMillan, *Constitutional Development in Alabama*, 95–97.

55. *Mobile Tribune*, quoted in *Nashville Press and Times*, September 2, 1865, p. 2; *New York Times*, September 30, 1865, p. 1; McMillan, *Constitutional Development in Alabama*, 95n28.

56. *Mobile News*, September 26, 1865, p. 1.

57. *Mobile Tribune*, reprinted in the *Nashville Press and Times*, September 1, 1865,

p. 2; *Mobile News*, September 13, 1865, p. 2, September 22, 1865, p. 1; *Mobile Tribune*, reprinted in (New Orleans) *Picayune*, September 19, 1865, pp. 1, 6; McMillan, *Constitutional Development in Alabama*, 95–97 and 95n28.

58. Joseph C. Bradley to Andrew Johnson, September 8, 1865; Bergeron, *Papers of Andrew Johnson*, 9:44–46.

59. *Mobile Tribune*, reprinted in *Nashville Press and Times*, September 1, 1865, p. 2. Much to the chagrin of north Alabama Unionists, this sentiment was said to have cost David Campbell Humphreys a seat in the convention when his opponent reportedly "took decided grounds against amending the Constitution of the United States abolishing Slavery." Joseph C. Bradley to Andrew Johnson, September 8, 1865; Bergeron, *Papers of Andrew Johnson*, 9:44–46. Humphreys would not be the last political victim of the ghosts of Confederate soldiers or the planter class.

60. *Selma Times*, reprinted in *New York Times*, July 25, 1865, p. 2, August 17, 1865, p. 1; *Mobile News*, September 13, 1865, p. 2; *Mobile Advertiser and Register*, July 28, 1865, p. 2, October 8, 1865, p. 1.

61. *New York Times*, September 17, 1865, p. 5. See also *Mobile Advertiser and Register*, September 8, 1865, p. 2.

62. *Huntsville Advocate*, July 12, 1865, p. 3, July 19, 1865, p. 2; *Mobile News*, July 13, 1865, p. 4, July 25, 1865, p. 7; *Mobile Advertiser and Register*, July 26, 1865, p. 2; (New Orleans) *Picayune*, July 9, 1865, p. 2, July 28, 1865, p. 1; *New York Times*, July 9, 1865, p. 1.

63. Rev. J. A. Swan to William H. Seward, June 19, 1865, Papers of William Seward, Rush Rhees Library, University of Rochester.

64. *New York Times*, July 15, 1865, p. 4. See generally McPherson, *Struggle for Equality*, 321–33.

65. William H. Seward to John Bigelow, July 1, 1865, Papers of William Seward, Rush Rhees Library, University of Rochester.

66. (New York) *World*, reprinted in *Bedford* (PA) *Inquirer*, September 8, 1865, p. 3; *Huntsville Advocate*, July 19, 1865, p. 2; *Mobile Advertiser and Register*, July 20, 1865, p. 2; *Montgomery Advertiser*, July 22, 1865, p. 3; Gambill, *Conservative Ordeal*, 25–37.

67. *Mobile Advertiser and Register*, July 20, 1865, p. 2; see also July 22, 1865, p. 2.

68. Ibid., September 25, 1864, p. 2, November 9, 1864, p. 2.

69. Ibid., August 30, 1865, p. 2. See also *Mobile News*, September 21, 1865, p. 1.

Chapter 15

1. *Philadelphia Inquirer*, November 24, 1865, p. 1 (also expressing concern that the South could "filibuster away" an entire session of Congress).

2. *Bedford* (PA) *Inquirer*, September 8, 1865, p. 3.

3. *Philadelphia Inquirer*, November 24, 1865, p. 1. Regarding expressions of concern about renewed Southern political power, see *Burlington* (VT) *Free Press*, September 1, 1865, p. 1; (Montpelier) *Vermont Watchman and State Journal*, September 1, 1865, p. 2; (Chardon, OH) *Jeffersonian Democrat*, September 8, 1865, p. 2; *New York Tribune*, September 20, 1865, p. 4.

NOTES TO PAGES 178–180 / 283

4. (Montpelier) *Vermont Watchman and State Journal*, September 1, 1865, p. 2. See also (Washington, DC) *National Republican*, October 25, 1865, p. 2.

5. Wiggins, *Journals of Josiah Gorgas*, 186.

6. DuBose, *Alabama's Tragic Decade*, 45.

7. A. L. Jeffries to Lewis Parsons, September 6, 1865, Lewis E. Parsons Papers, ADAH; *Montgomery Mail*, September 9, 1865, reprinted in *New Orleans Times*, September 15, 1865, p. 6; *Mobile Tribune*, reprinted in (Columbus, GA) *Sun*, September 6, 1865, p. 2; Linden and Linden, *Disunion, War, Defeat, and Recovery*, 142; G. Ward Hubbs, *Guarding Greensboro: A Confederate Company in the Making of a Southern Community* (Athens: University of Georgia Press, 2003), 208–9.

8. Hubbs, *Guarding Greensboro*, 209. See also Wiggins, *Journals of Josiah Gorgas*, 185–86.

9. (New York) *Sun*, September 20, 1865, p. 1; *New York Tribune*, September 20, 1865, p. 1; (Hillsborough, OH) *Highland Weekly News*, September 7, 1865, p. 2; *Mobile News*, September 12, 1865, p. 1; *New Orleans Times*, September 15, 1865, p. 6; (Washington, DC) *National Intelligencer*, September 20, 1865. See also letter to President Johnson from Citizens of Cherokee County, Alabama, September, 1865, Bergeron, *Papers of Andrew Johnson*, 9:3–4; DuBose, *Alabama's Tragic Decade*, 25–26.

10. *New York Herald*, September 17, 1865, p. 2; *Mobile Advertiser and Register*, September 6, 1865, p. 1.

11. *Mobile News*, September 22, 1865, p. 3; Wiggins, *Scalawag in Alabama Politics*, 12; McMillan, *Constitutional Development in Alabama*, 91.

12. *New York Times*, November 20, 1865, p. 1. Part of the problem was that arrangements were not made in all precincts to administer the requisite amnesty oath. Journal of Joshua Burns Moore, 97, ADAH; (Tuscumbia) *North Alabamian*, November 17, 1865, p. 3.

13. Storey, *Loyalty and Loss*, 175.

14. Joseph C. Bradley to Lewis Parsons, September 4 and September 5, 1865, Lewis E. Parsons Papers, ADAH.

15. John Whiting to Lewis Parsons, September 14, 1865, ibid.

16. Levi Lawler to Governor Parsons, September 11, 1865, ibid.

17. (Troy, AL) *Southern Advertiser*, September 16, 1865, p. 2.

18. *Mobile Advertiser and Register*, September 8, 1865, p. 2, September 9, 1865, p. 2, September 15, 1865, p. 1; (Moulton, AL) *Christian Herald*, September 8, 1865, p. 2, September 14, 1865, p. 2; *Huntsville Advocate*, October 4, 1865; *Montgomery Advertiser*, October 1, 1865, reprinted in *Mobile Times*, October 5, 1865, p. 7; *Nashville Union*, September 5, 1865, p. 2; McMillan, *Constitutional Development in Alabama*, 92–93; J. Mills Thornton, "Alabama Emancipates," in *Dixie Redux: Essays in Honor of Sheldon Hackney*, ed. Raymond Arsenault and Orville Burton (Montgomery, AL: NewSouth Books, 2013), 80; Storey, *Loyalty and Loss*, 175; Wiggins, *Scalawag in Alabama Politics*, 12; Baggett, *Scalawags*, 162–63. Some Unionists claimed that secessionists in towns had been allowed to vote, but that Unionists in rural areas were not because arrangements had not been made to administer the requisite oath to them. Carter, *When the War Was Over*, 64.

284 / Notes to pages 181–182

19. *Nashville Union*, September 10, 1865, p. 2.

20. *Mobile News*, September 13, 1865, p. 2, September 16, 1865, p. 6; *Mobile Advertiser and Register*, September 15, 1865, p. 1. Regarding Fitzpatrick, see Severance, *Portraits of Conflict*, 39; Samuel L. Webb and Margaret E. Armbrester, *Alabama Governors: A Political History of the State* (Tuscaloosa: University of Alabama Press, 2001), 54–57.

21. *Nashville Union*, August 17, 1865, p. 1; *Cincinnati Gazette* reprinted in *Providence* (RI) *Press*, October 11, 1865, p. 3. See also (New Orleans) *Picayune*, September 13, 1865, p. 3; *Mobile News*, September 14, 1865, p. 6.

22. Journal of Joshua Burns Moore, 98, ADAH. See generally Foner, *Reconstruction*, 193.

23. *Mobile Advertiser and Register*, September 15, 1865, p. 1.

24. Ibid., September 19, 1865, p. 2 (listing the names of several reporters).

25. *Washington* (DC) *Chronicle*, cited in *Mobile News*, September 16, 1865, p. 1, September 29, 1865, p. 2; *New York Times*, September 25, 1865, p. 1; (New Orleans) *Picayune*, September 19, 1865; *Mobile Advertiser and Register*, September 20, 1865, p. 2; Storey, *Loyalty and Loss*, 177–78.

26. *Cleveland Leader*, September 18, 1865, p. 1; *New York Tribune*, September 20, 1865, p. 4; (Washington, DC) *National Republican*, September 18, 1865, p. 2; *Mobile News*, September 23, 1865, p. 3; *Mobile Advertiser and Register*, September 21, 1865, p. 2.

27. *New York Tribune*, September 20, 1865, p. 4.

28. (Washington, DC) *National Republican*, September 18, 1865, p. 2.

29. *Nashville Press and Times*, September 20, 1865, p. 2.

30. *Cleveland Leader*, September 19, 1865, p. 1; (New Orleans) *Picayune*, September 19, 1865, p. 6; *Mobile Advertiser and Register*, September 20, 1865, p. 2; *Mobile News*, September 20, 1865, p. 2, September 21, 1865, p. 1.

31. *New York Tribune*, September 28, 1865, p. 4, October 3, 1865, p. 4; (Washington, DC) *National Intelligencer*, September 23, 1865; *New York Times*, September 30, 1865, p. 1; *Milwaukee Sentinel*, September 29, 1865; *New York Times*, September 30, 1865, p. 1, October 15, 1865, p. 3; *Mobile Advertiser and Register*, September 22, 1865, p. 1, October 8, 1865, p. 1; *Mobile News*, September 22, 1865, p. 1; Thornton, "Alabama Emancipates," 82. Regarding some of White's wartime activities, see (New Orleans) *Picayune*, February 26, 1865, p. 2; (Talladega, AL) *Democratic Watchtower*, March 1, 1865, p. 2.

32. *Mobile News*, September 19, 1865, p. 1, September 20, 1865, p. 2, September 21, 1865, p. 1, September 29, 1865, p. 2; *Mobile Advertiser and Register*, September 20, 1865, p. 2; *New York Times*, September 25, 1865, p. 1, September 27, 1865, p. 1; *Milwaukee Sentinel*, September 28, 1865; Storey, *Loyalty and Loss*, 176–77.

33. (Washington, DC) *National Intelligencer*, September 23, 1865; *New York Times*, September 30, 1865, p. 1. The contents of the petition may be found in *Norfolk* (VA) *Post*, October 14, 1865, p. 2, and Bergeron, *Papers of Andrew Johnson*, 9:134–35.

34. *Huntsville Advocate*, October 12, 1865, p. 2.

35. *New York Journal*, reprinted in (Columbia, SC) *Phoenix*, September 30, 1865, p. 2. See also (New Orleans) *Picayune*, October 14, 1865, p 8.

Notes to pages 182–183 / 285

36. F. W. Sykes, L. P. Walker, etc., to Lewis Parsons and Benjamin Fitzpatrick, September 19, 1865, reprinted in Perman, *Reunion without Compromise*, 73–74, 102.

37. *Montgomery Mail*, September 26, 1865, p. 3; *Selma* (AL) *Messenger*, September 23, 1865, reprinted in *Mobile Advertiser and Register*, September 29, 1865, p. 2, October 6, 1865, p. 2; *Huntsville Advocate*, October 4, 1865, p. 3; *Mobile News*, September 30, 1865, p. 2; (New Orleans) *Picayune*, September 27, 1865, p. 3; *Mobile Tribune*, October 4, 1865, p. 2.

38. *Montgomery Mail*, September 22, 1865, p. 2; (Troy, AL) *Southern Advertiser*, September 16, 1865, p. 2; *Mobile Tribune*, September 25, 1865, reprinted in (New Orleans) *Picayune*, September 27, 1865, p. 3, October 7, 1865, p. 1; *Huntsville Advocate*, September 28, 1865, p. 3; *Mobile Advertiser and Register*, September 29, 1865, p. 2.

39. Charles Pelham to Governor Parsons, September 17, 1865, and G. D. Shortridge to Governor Parsons, November 1, 1865, Papers of Lewis E. Parsons, ADAH.

40. *Montgomery Mail*, September 26, 1865, p. 2; *Mobile News*, September 23, 1865, p. 3, September 26, 1865, p. 2, September 27, 1865, p. 2, September 29, 1865, p. 2; *Mobile Advertiser and Register*, September 23, 1865, p. 2, September 26, 1865, p. 2, September 29, 1865, p. 2, September 30, 1865, p. 2, October 12, 1865, p. 2; *Mobile Tribune*, October 12, 1865, p. 5; *Milwaukee Sentinel*, September 28, 1865, October 11, 1865; *New York Times*, September 24, 1865, p. 1, September 27, 1865, p. 1; Thornton, "Alabama Emancipates," 82–83; Wiggins, *Scalawag in Alabama Politics*, 12; J. W. Shepherd, *The Constitution, and Ordinances Adopted by the State Convention of Alabama Which Assembled at Montgomery on the Twelfth Day of September, A.D. 1865, with Index, Analysis, and Table of Titles* (Montgomery, AL: Gibson and Whitfield, State Printers, 1865), 45 (slavery), 48 (secession), 53–54 (war debt).

41. *Huntsville Advocate*, October 4, 1865, p. 3; (New Orleans) *Picayune*, October 14, 1865, p. 1.

42. William H. Seward to Henry Shelton Sanford, September 22, 1865, Papers of William Seward, Rush Rhees Library, University of Rochester.

43. *New York Tribune*, September 26, 1865, p. 5, September 28, 1865, p. 4, October 3, 1865, p. 4; (Clearfield, PA) *Raftsman's Journal*, October 11, 1865, pp. 1–2.

44. *New York Tribune*, September 28, 1865, p. 4. See also *Milwaukee Sentinel*, September 28, 1865; *Bangor* (ME) *Whig and Courier*, October 3, 1865.

45. Blair, *With Malice toward Some*, 268–69; (Montpelier) *Vermont Watchman and State Journal*, September 29, 1865, p. 1; (Washington, DC) *National Republican*, October 3, 1865, p. 2; *New York Times*, October 3, 1865, p. 4; *New York Independent*, reprinted in (Boston) *Liberator*, October 13, 1865.

46. *New York Tribune*, October 3, 1865, p. 4.

47. DuBose, *Alabama's Tragic Decade*, 46. Walter Fleming also made this erroneous assertion. Fleming, *Civil War and Reconstruction*, 367.

48. (New Orleans) *Picayune*, October 7, 1865, p. 1.

49. *Selma Times*, reprinted in (New Orleans) *Picayune*, September 22, 1865, p. 2; *Huntsville Advocate*, September 28, 1865, p. 2.

50. John B. Myers, "The Freedmen and the Law in Post-Bellum Alabama, 1865–1867," *Alabama Review* 23 (January 1970): 56–69.

286 / Notes to pages 183–184

51. Shepherd, *Constitution and Ordinances*, 45; (Moulton, AL) *Christian Herald*, September 22, 1865, p. 2, September 29, 1865, p. 2; (New Orleans) *Daily Picayune*, September 22, 1865, p. 2; *Burlington* (VT) *Free Press*, October 6, 1865, p. 4; *New York Times*, September 24, 1865, p. 1; *Huntsville Advocate*, September 28, 1865, pp. 2–3; *Milwaukee Sentinel*, September 28, 1865; *Mobile Advertiser and Register*, September 20, 1865, p. 2; *Mobile News*, September 21, 1865, p. 1.

52. *Milwaukee Sentinel*, September 26, 1865. See also *Milwaukee Sentinel*, September 28, 1865; *New York Tribune*, October 3, 1865, p. 4.

53. W. E. B. Du Bois, *Black Reconstruction in America: Toward a History of the Part Which Black Folk Played in the Attempt to Reconstruct Democracy in America, 1860–1880* (New Brunswick, NJ: Transaction Publishers, 2012), 166. Johnson would have agreed with Du Bois on the effect of qualified black suffrage on Northern public opinion. Johnson had telegraphed Mississippi's provisional governor that its adoption would "completely" foil the Radicals in their attempt to prevent the admission of Southerners into Congress. LaWanda Cox and John H. Cox, "Johnson and the Negro," in *Reconstruction: An Anthology of Revisionist Writings*, ed. Kenneth M. Stampp and Leon F. Litwack (Baton Rouge: Louisiana State University Press, 1969), 65–66.

54. (New York) *Sun*, October 2, 1865, p. 1; *New York Times*, October 1, 1865, p. 1; (Washington, DC) *National Republican*, October 3, 1865, p. 2; (Washington, DC) *National Intelligencer*, October 3, 1865.

55. Lewis Parsons to Andrew Johnson, October 2, 1865, Papers of Governor Lewis Parsons, ADAH; (Grove Hill, AL) *Clarke County Journal*, October 12, 1865, p. 2; *Mobile Advertiser and Register*, October 17, 1865, p. 1; *Mobile Times*, October 17, 1865, p. 1, October 26, 1865, p. 8, October 27, 1865, p. 3, October 31, 1865, p. 3. Ironically, Johnson had unwisely suggested this. Andrew Johnson to Lewis E. Parsons, September 1, 1865, in Bergeron, *Papers of Andrew Johnson*, 9:12; Downs, *After Appomattox*, 80–81; Perman, *Reunion without Compromise*, 136. See generally Clyde E. Wilson, "State Militia of Alabama during the Administration of Lewis E. Parsons, Provisional Governor June 21st 1865 to December 18, 1865," *Alabama Historical Quarterly* 14, nos. 3 and 4 (1952): 301–22; Dan T. Carter, "The Anatomy of Fear: The Christmas Day Insurrection Scare of 1865," *Journal of Southern History* 42 (August 1976): 345–49 (fear of an insurrection by the freedmen likely led to calls for the reinstitution of the militia).

56. Shepherd, *Constitution and Ordinances*, 70–71; (New York) *Sun*, October 2, 1865, p. 1; *New York Times*, October 1, 1865, p. 1; (Washington, DC) *National Republican*, October 3, 1865, p. 2; (Indianapolis, IN) *State Sentinel*, October 4, 1865, p. 3; *Mobile Advertiser and Register*, October 4, 1865, p. 2.

57. Andrew Johnson to Lewis E. Parsons, October 3, 1865, in Bergeron, *Papers of Andrew Johnson*, 9:182; Andrew Johnson to Lewis Parsons, October 4, 1865, Papers of Governor Lewis E. Parsons, ADAH; *Huntsville Advocate*, October 12, 1865, p. 3.

58. *New York Independent*, reprinted in (Boston) *Liberator*, October 13, 1865.

59. *New York Times*, September 25, 1865, p. 4. See also *Charleston Courier*, October 3, 1865, supplement, p. 3; *Boston Advertiser*, September 30, 1865.

NOTES TO PAGES 185–187 / 287

60. *Mobile News*, September 29, 1865, p. 2; *New York Times*, October 3, 1865, p. 5, October 10, 1865, p. 5; *Mobile Tribune*, October 13, 1865, p. 2; Storey, *Loyalty and Loss*, 177; Fleming, *Civil War and Reconstruction*, 365–66.

61. *New York Times*, November 20, 1865, p. 1. See also *Louisville Journal*, reprinted in *Huntsville Advocate*, November 23, 1865, p. 2.

62. *Bangor* (ME) *Whig and Courier*, October 3, 1865. This metaphor was in frequent use during this period. (New Orleans) *Picayune*, October 11, 1865, p. 2; (Clearfield, PA) *Raftsman's Journal*, October 11, 1865, pp. 1–2.

63. *New York Times*, October 3, 1865, p. 4.

64. *Montgomery Mail*, July 30, 1865, reprinted in *Mobile Advertiser and Register*, August 6, 1865, p. 6.

65. *Montgomery Mail*, September 12, 1865, reprinted in *Milwaukee Sentinel*, September 27, 1865; (Mobile) *Nationalist*, December 28, 1865, p. 2; Fitzgerald, *Urban Emancipation*, 42, 50–53, 61.

66. *Mobile Daily Times*, October 26, 1865, p. 8 (Athens barber John McCormick); (New Orleans) *Picayune*, September 30, 1865, p. 1 (future Louisiana Republican Pinckney Benton Stewart Pinchback); (Columbus, GA) *Sun*, October 12, 1865, p. 1; (Mobile) *Nationalist*, March 22, 1866, p. 3.

67. *Huntsville Advocate*, November 9, 1865, p. 3; Carter, *When the War Was Over*, 194–95; *Bangor* (ME) *Whig and Courier*, October 31, 1865.

68. *Mobile Advertiser and Register*, November 5, 1865, p. 5, November 12, 1865, p. 2; (Columbus, GA) *Sun*, November 24, 1865; *Mobile Daily Times*, November 26, 1865, p. 2.

69. *Mobile Advertiser and Register*, November 12, 1865, p. 2. See also *Mobile Times*, November 26, 1865, p. 2.

70. *New York Tribune*, November 15, 1865, reprinted in Donna L. Dickerson, *The Reconstruction Era: Primary Documents on Events from 1865 to 1877* (Westport, CT: Greenwood Press, 2003), 19–21.

Chapter 16

Epigraph. *Montgomery Ledger*, reprinted in (Washington, DC) *National Republican*, January 5, 1866, p. 2.

1. *New York Times*, October 3, 1865, p. 4, October 4, 1865, p. 4; (New Orleans) *Picayune*, October 3, 1865, p. 1, October 11, 1865, p. 2, October 14, 1865, p. 1; *Washington* (DC) *Chronicle*, reprinted in *Huntsville Advocate*, October 12, 1865, p. 2, October 19, 1865, p. 2, and (Moulton, AL) *Christian Herald*, October 27, 1865, p. 2; *Pomeroy* (OH) *Weekly Telegraph*, October 26, 1865, p. 2; *Mobile Advertiser and Register*, November 11, 1865, p. 2.

2. *Mobile Times*, October 4, 1865, p. 1, October 5, 1865, p. 1, October 6, 1865, p. 2, October 13, 1865, p. 2, October 15, 1865, p. 1, October 27, 1865, p. 4; *Mobile Advertiser and Register*, September 26, 1865, p. 2, October 4, 1865, pp. 1–2, October 20, 1865, p. 2, October 28, 1865, p. 1; (New Orleans) *Picayune*, October 14, 1865, p. 8, October

288 / NOTES TO PAGES 187–190

17, 1865, p. 7; *New York Tribune*, October 3, 1865, p. 4; (St. Clairsville, OH) *Belmont Chronicle*, May 11, 1865, p. 2; Gambill, *Conservative Ordeal*, 37–38.

3. *Mobile Advertiser and Register*, September 26, 1865, p. 2, October 20, 1865, p. 2.

4. *Philadelphia Ledger*, reprinted in (Indianapolis, IN) *State Sentinel*, October 19, 1865, p. 2.

5. (New Orleans) *Picayune*, October 27, 1865, p. 9; *Mobile Advertiser and Register*, October 27, 1865, p. 1, October 22, 1865, p. 1; (Jackson) *Mississippian*, November 1, 1865.

6. *Huntsville Advocate*, October 12, 1865, p. 2.

7. Ibid., pp. 2–3.

8. *Montgomery Mail*, September 30, 1865, p. 3.

9. Quoted in *Mobile Advertiser and Register*, September 21, 1865, p. 1.

10. *Mobile News*, September 17, 1865, p. 2.

11. *Mobile Times*, October 5, 1865, p. 2, October 10, 1865, p. 2.

12. (Columbus, GA) *Sun*, October 6, 1865, p. 4, October 24, 1865, p. 2.

13. *Mobile Tribune*, October 6, 1865, p. 2; *Mobile News*, September 28, 1865, p. 2; (New Orleans) *Picayune*, September 22, 1865, p. 1; *Mobile Advertiser and Register*, September 22, 1865, p. 2; Foner, *Reconstruction*, 235–36.

14. (Mobile) *Nationalist*, March 28, 1867, p. 2; *Montgomery Advertiser*, May 30, 1867, p. 2; (Columbia, SC) *Phoenix*, September 17, 1865, p. 1. This is a biblical phrase from the Book of Acts, 9:5.

15. Perman, *Reunion without Compromise*, 166.

16. *Ottawa* (IL) *Free Trader*, September 30, 1865, p. 2.

17. (New Orleans) *Picayune*, November 1, 1865, supplement, November 5, 1865, p. 2; *New York News*, reprinted in (Grove Hill, AL) *Clarke County Journal*, November 9, 1865, p. 2; *Mobile Advertiser and Register*, November 2, 1865, p. 4; *Chicago Times*, reprinted in *Mobile Advertiser and Register*, November 4, 1865, p. 2; (Wheeling, WV) *Intelligencer*, November 8, 1865, p. 2; *Louisville* (KY) *Journal*, reprinted in *Huntsville Advocate*, November 16, 1865, p. 2.

18. Augusta Jane Evans to J. L. M. Curry, October 7, 1865, in Rebecca Grant Sexton, ed., *A Southern Woman of Letters: The Correspondence of Augusta Jane Evans Wilson* (Columbia: University of South Carolina Press, 2002), 108.

19. *Mobile Advertiser and Register*, October 17, 1865, p. 2. See also *Mobile Advertiser and Register*, October 29, 1865, p. 2, November 2, 1865, p. 4; Perman, *Reunion without Compromise*, 166.

20. *Lynchburg Virginian*, reprinted in *Mobile Times*, October 5, 1865, p. 7.

21. *Mobile Advertiser and Register*, July 11, 1863, p. 2. See also *Mobile Times*, October 17, 1865, p. 1, October 20, 1865, p. 4; *Mobile Advertiser and Register*, July 11, 1863, p. 2, October 7, 1865, p. 2; *New York Times*, October 31, 1865, p. 1.

22. *Mobile Advertiser and Register*, October 20, 1865. See also *Mobile Times*, October 26, 1865, p. 8 (Cullen Battle); (Grove Hill, AL) *Clarke County Journal*, November 2, 1865, p. 2; *Mobile Advertiser and Register*, October 27, 1865, p. 2.

NOTES TO PAGES 190–191 / 289

23. Joseph C. Bradley to Andrew Johnson, November 15, 1865, in Bergeron, *Papers of Andrew Johnson*, 9:385; George E. Spencer to Grenville Dodge, October 14, 1865, quoted in Richard Nelson Current, *Those Terrible Carpetbaggers* (New York: Oxford University Press, 1988), 31.

24. *Mobile Times*, October 1, 1865, p. 1, October 4, 1865, p. 1, October 10, 1865, p. 5, October 17, 1865, pp. 1 and 4, October 19, 1865, pp. 1 and 7, October 25, 1865, p. 4, October 29, 1865, p. 1, November 3, 1865, p. 1, November 5, 1865, p. 4; *Mobile Advertiser and Register*, October 14, 1865, p. 1, October 17, 1865, p. 2, November 5, 1865, p. 2; *Huntsville Advocate*, October 19, 1865, pp. 2–3; (Grove Hill, AL) *Clarke County Journal*, October 26, 1865, p. 2; (New Orleans) *Picayune*, November 3, 1865, supplement; *Cleveland Leader*, November 6, 1865, p. 2; *New York Times*, October 30, 1865, p. 8, October 31, 1865, p. 1; (Greensboro) *Alabama Beacon*, October 27, 1865, p. 2.

25. *Montgomery Advertiser*, reprinted in *Mobile Advertiser and Register*, October 14, 1865, p. 1. See also *Milwaukee Sentinel*, November 2, 1865, p. 1; *New York Times*, October 30, 1865, p. 8; (Washington, DC) *National Republican*, January 11, 1866, p. 1; Storey, *Loyalty and Loss*, 179; Wiggins, *Scalawag in Alabama Politics*, 13; Carter, *When the War Was Over*, 258; Perman, *Reunion without Compromise*, 171.

26. *Mobile Advertiser and Register*, October 31, 1865, p. 2. See also *Mobile Advertiser and Register*, November 17, 1865, p. 2; *Brownlow's Knoxville Whig, and Rebel Ventilator*, November 22, 1865, p. 2.

27. *Huntsville Advocate*, November 9, 1865, p. 3, November 16, 1865, p. 2; Thornton, "Alabama Emancipates," 83–84.

28. *New York Times*, October 31, 1865, p. 1, reprinted in *Indianapolis* (IN) *Herald*, November 1, 1865, p. 3, *Cleveland Leader*, November 1, 1865, p. 1 (Wheeling, WV) *Intelligencer*, November 3, 1865, p. 1, *Milwaukee Sentinel*, November 4, 1865, p. 3, *Huntsville Advocate*, November 9, 1865, supplement, November 30, 1865, supplement; *Sunbury* (PA) *American*, November 25, 1865, p. 2. See also *New York Times*, November 2, 1865, p. 1.

29. (New Orleans) *Picayune*, October 26, 1865, p. 6. See also (New Orleans) *Picayune*, November 3, 1865, p. 1, November 5, 1865, p. 2, November 7, 1865, p. 1, November 21, 1865, p. 2; *Mobile Advertiser and Register*, reprinted in (Grove Hill, AL) *Clarke County Journal*, November 9, 1865, p. 2; *Huntsville Advocate*, November 23, 1865, p. 1; Cox and Cox, *Politics, Principle, and Prejudice*, 139–42.

30. *Pittsburgh Gazette*, reprinted in (Butler, PA) *American Citizen*, November 8, 1865, p. 1.

31. (Boston) *Liberator*, December 1, 1865. See also *Cleveland Leader*, November 29, 1865, p. 3, *Norfolk* (VA) *Post*, November 25, 1865, p. 1. Regarding conditions in Alabama, see *New York Times*, December 8, 1865, p. 1; (Bloomsburg, PA) *Star of the North*, October 25, 1865, p. 1; Storey, *Loyalty and Loss*, 182–87.

32. *Nashville Union*, November 1, 1865, p. 2; see also November 24, 1865, p. 2.

33. *Huntsville Advocate*, November 23, 1865, p. 3.

34. There were reports that Maximilian subsequently legalized a form of slavery

to encourage Confederates to colonize in Mexico. *New York Times*, January 3, 1866, p. 4. Some Confederates attempted to do so. *Mobile Advertiser and Register*, January 17, 1866, p. 2.

35. *Mobile Advertiser and Register*, reprinted in (Grove Hill, AL) *Clarke County Journal*, November 9, 1865, p. 2. The reference to "Jerry Sneaks" is from a British song titled "Jerry Sneak's at Home" regarding men who appear very powerful in public but meekly submitted to their wives in their own homes. George Cruikshank, Robert Cruikshank, and J. R. Marshall, *The Universal Songster; or, Museum of Mirth* (London: Jones, 1834), 3:189.

36. Storey, "Crucible of Reconstruction," 76.

37. *Cleveland Leader*, November 10, 1865, p. 1. See also *New York Times*, November 20, 1865, p. 1; *New York Tribune*, November 16, 1865, p. 4 (citing a letter received from north Alabama); Storey, *Loyalty and Loss*, 178–79; J. Mills Thornton III, "Alabama's Presidential Reconstruction Legislature," in *A Political Nation: New Directions in Mid-Nineteenth-Century American Political History*, ed. Gary W. Gallagher and Rachel A. Shelden (Charlottesville: University of Virginia Press, 2012), 167–87.

38. (New Orleans) *Picayune*, November 14, 1865, p. 2. See also (Lafayette, AL) *Chambers Tribune*, reprinted in (Columbus, GA) *Sun*, November 21, 1865, p. 2; *Nashville Union*, November 11, 1865, p. 1, November 18, 1865, p. 2, November 23, 1865, p. 2; Thornton, "Alabama's Presidential Reconstruction Legislature," 168–70.

39. Joseph C. Bradley to President Johnson, November 15, 1865, in Bergeron, *Papers of Andrew Johnson*, 9:383. See also Baggett, *Scalawags*, 164.

40. *Huntsville Advocate*, November 16, 1865, p. 2.

41. Ibid., p. 3; *Nashville Union*, November 23, 1865, p. 2; (Grove Hill, AL) *Clarke County Journal*, November 23, 1865, p. 2; *Chattanooga Gazette*, reprinted in (Little Rock) *Arkansas Gazette*, December 8, 1865.

42. *Huntsville Advocate*, November 16, 1865, p. 2, November 23, 1865, p. 3; *Nashville Union*, November 23, 1865, p. 2; (Grove Hill, AL) *Clarke County Journal*, November 16, 1865, p. 2; *Chattanooga Gazette*, reprinted in (Little Rock) *Arkansas Gazette*, December 8, 1865; DuBose, *Alabama's Tragic Decade*, 61.

43. *Huntsville Advocate*, November 16, 1865, p. 2, November 23, 1865, p. 3; *Nashville Union*, November 23, 1865, p. 2; (Grove Hill, AL) *Clarke County Journal*, November 23, 1865, p. 2; *Chattanooga Gazette*, reprinted in (Little Rock) *Arkansas Gazette*, December 8, 1865.

44. (Grove Hill, AL) *Clarke County Journal*, November 23, 1865, p. 2; *Huntsville Advocate*, November 23, 1865, p. 3.

45. *Montgomery Advertiser*, November 30, 1865, p. 2; *Huntsville Advocate*, November 30, 1865, p. 2.

46. *Fremont (OH) Journal*, November 24, 1865, p. 2; *Urbana (Ohio) Union*, November 29, 1865, p. 2; *Cleveland Leader*, November 30, 1865, p. 2; (Hillsboro, OH) *Highland Weekly News*, November 30, 1865, pp. 1 and 2.

47. *Mobile Advertiser and Register*, December 5, 1865, p. 2; *Mobile Times*, December

NOTES TO PAGES 193–194 / 291

5, 1865, p. 4, December 7, 1865, p. 2, December 22, 1865, p. 6; *Nashville Union*, November 30, 1865, p. 2; (Washington, DC) *Star*, December 1, 1865, p. 1.

48. *Mobile Advertiser and Register*, October 17, 1865, p. 1, October 24, 1865, p. 2; *Mobile Tribune*, October 17, 1865, p. 2; (New Orleans) *Picayune*, November 12, 1865, p. 1; Gambill, *Conservative Ordeal*, 38–39.

49. *Nashville Union*, November 19, 1865, p. 1.

50. *Pittsburgh Gazette*, reprinted in (Butler, PA) *American Citizen*, November 8, 1865, p. 1.

51. *Edensburg* (PA) *Alleghanian*, December 7, 1865, p. 2.

52. (Wheeling, WV) *Intelligencer*, November 8, 1865, p. 2.

53. *Nashville Union*, November 24, 1865, p. 2.

54. *Huntsville Advocate*, November 9, 1865, p. 3 (reporting John W. Lapsley's lack of success in acquiring capital for projects in Dallas County). But see *Huntsville Advocate*, November 9, 1865, p. 2 (funding was obtained for the extension of the Alabama and Tennessee Rivers Railroad from Blue Mountain to the Georgia state line).

55. *Mobile Advertiser and Register*, November 17, 1865, p. 2. See also Burnett, *Pen Makes a Good Sword*, 152. Regarding Forsyth's quest for the senate, see *Mobile Advertiser and Register*, November 25, 1865, p. 2.

56. *Mobile Times*, November 15, 1865, p. 6; (New Orleans) *Picayune*, November 29, 1865, p. 2.

57. (Columbus, GA) *Sun*, November 18, 1865, p. 1. Regarding a "Convention of Colored People at Mobile" on November 23, 1865, see *Mobile Advertiser and Register*, November 24, 1865, pp. 2–3, November 25, 1865, p. 2; *Mobile Times*, November 25, 1865, p. 2, November 26, 1865, p. 2.

58. *New York Tribune*, reprinted in (Boston) *Liberator*, November 24, 1865; *Boston Journal*, reprinted in (Boston) *Liberator*, November 24, 1865; *New Haven* (CT) *Palladium*, December 6, 1865.

59. *Selma Times*, November 17, 1865, reprinted in *Nashville Press and Times*, November 29, 1865, p. 2; *Nashville Union and American*, December 12, 1865, p. 2.

60. George W. Parsons to Mr. Strudwick and others, November 1, 1865, Lewis E. Parsons Papers, ADAH.

61. (Washington, DC) *Star*, October 30, 1865, p. 2, November 2, 1865, p. 2; *Cleveland Leader*, November 3, 1865, p. 1.

62. (Mobile) *Nationalist*, January 11, 1866, p. 1; (Tuscumbia) *North Alabamian*, reprinted in *Montgomery Advertiser*, January 13, 1866, p. 2; *Montgomery Advertiser*, reprinted in (Columbus) *Weekly Ohio Statesman*, December 11, 1865, p. 2; (Washington, DC) *Star*, December 19, 1865, p. 2; *New York Times*, November 14, 1865, p. 1.

63. *Mobile Times*, November 26, 1865, p. 1; *Nashville Union and American*, December 12, 1865, p. 2; *Montgomery Mail*, reprinted in *Mobile Advertiser and Register*, October 29, 1865, p. 4 (referring to "concert of action"); Reid, *After the War*, 373.

64. *Middlebury* (VT) *Register*, November 29, 1865, p. 2.

65. *Mobile Times*, November 26, 1865, p. 1. See also *New York Times*, November 24,

1865, p. 1, November 25, 1865, December 3, 1865, p. 3; (Washington, DC) *National Intelligencer*, November 29, 1865; (Grove Hill, AL) *Clarke County Journal*, November 30, 1865, p. 2; Thornton, "Alabama Emancipates," 83. The Massachusetts law penalized being "an idle and disorderly person." Commonwealth v. Sullivan, 5 Allen 511, 1862 WL 3955 (Mass., 1862).

66. *Montgomery Mail*, reprinted in (Washington, DC) *National Republican*, November 30, 1865, p. 2.

67. *Montgomery Advertiser*, November 29, 1865, p. 2; *Huntsville Advocate*, December 14, 1865, p. 2; (Greensboro) *Alabama Beacon*, December 8, 1865, p. 2; *Mobile Advertiser and Register*, December 1, 1865, p. 1 (Forsyth claimed that Houston tried to prevent Parsons's selection), December 5, 1865, p. 1; *Mobile Times*, December 2, 1865, p. 6, December 5, 1865, p. 2, December 6, 1865, p. 2; *New York Times*, December 1, 1865, p. 1, December 5, 1865, pp. 1 and 4; *New York Tribune*, December 1, 1865, p. 4; (Washington, DC) *National Intelligencer*, December 5, 1865.

68. *Mobile Advertiser and Register*, December 5, 1865, p. 1; *Mobile Times*, December 6, 1865, p. 2; *New York Times*, December 10, 1865, p. 1, December 25, 1865, p. 4; *Natchez* (MS) *Courier*, December 12, 1865; Thornton, "Alabama's Presidential Reconstruction Legislature," 173.

69. U.S. Const. amend. XIII, § 1.

70. Ibid., § 2.

71. *Mobile Advertiser and Register*, December 5, 1865, p. 1.

72. Clement C. Clay Jr. to Andrew Johnson, November 23, 1865, in Bergeron, *Papers of Andrew Johnson*, 9:420–23.

73. *Mobile Times*, December 7, 1865, p. 2. See also *New York Times*, December 25, 1865, p. 4.

74. *New York Times*, November 27, 1865, p. 1; (Washington, DC) *National Intelligencer*, November 27, 1865; *Mobile Advertiser and Register*, December 12, 1865, p. 2.

75. *Montgomery Advertiser*, November 30, 1865, p. 2, December 2, 1865; *New York Times*, December 10, 1865, p. 3.

76. *Mobile Times*, December 5, 1865, p. 2.

77. *In re Shorter*, 22 F.Cas. 16 (DC, Ala., 1865); *Mobile Advertiser and Register*, December 17, 1865, p. 2.

78. *Mobile Advertiser and Register*, December 12, 1865, p. 2.

79. Lewis E. Parsons to Andrew Johnson, December 2, 1865, in Bergeron, *Papers of Andrew Johnson*, 9:455; (New Orleans) *Picayune*, December 12, 1866, p. 4; *Mobile Advertiser and Register*, December 12, 1865, p. 2.

80. DuBose, *Alabama's Tragic Decade*, 60.

81. (Washington, DC) *National Republican*, November 20, 1865, p. 2, cited in *Mobile Times*, December 7, 1865, p. 2; *Mobile Times*, December 1, 1865, p. 2; *New York Times*, December 3, 1865, p. 1. As historian Ben Severance once noted to me, even unconditional Unionists from Tennessee were denied admission to Congress.

82. (Washington, DC) *National Republican*, December 4, 1865, p. 2; (New York) *Sun*, January 20, 1866, p. 2.

NOTES TO PAGES 196–197 / 293

83. *New York Times*, November 20, 1865, p. 1; *Huntsville Advocate*, November 30, 1865, p. 1.

84. *New York Times*, December 3, 1865, p. 1; (New Orleans) *Picayune*, December 10, 1865, p. 1; *Mobile Advertiser and Register*, December 13, 1865, p. 2.

85. *Mobile Advertiser and Register*, December 7, 1865, p. 2, December 28, 1865, p. 2; *Mobile Times*, December 16, 1865, p. 4, December 20, 1865, pp. 1 and 7; (Grove Hill, AL) *Clarke County Journal*, January 18, 1866, p. 2; Wiggins, *Scalawag in Alabama Politics*, 14.

86. (New Orleans) *Picayune*, January 30, 1866, p. 10; Foner, *Reconstruction*, 239.

87. Reid, *After the War*, 380.

88. *Mobile Times*, December 7, 1865, p. 2. See also *Mobile Times*, December 14, 1865, p. 1.

89. George S. Houston to Lewis Parsons, December 25, 1865, quoted in Perman, *Reunion without Compromise*, 177.

90. *Mobile Advertiser and Register*, December 9, 1865, p. 2.

91. Ibid., December 13, 1865, p. 2, see also December 20, 1865, p. 2.

92. Ibid., December 15, 1866, p. 2.

93. Ibid., December 24, 1865, p. 2. Forsyth's diatribe was criticized in the North. (Wheeling, WV) *Intelligencer*, December 16, 1865, p. 2.

94. *Montgomery Advertiser*, December 17, 1865, p. 2.

95. Hurst, *Nathan Bedford Forrest*, 278–79; David Chalmers, "The Klan Rides, 1865–71," in *Terrorism: Critical Concepts in Political Science*, ed. David C. Rapoport (New York: Routledge, 2006), 48–49; Severance, *Tennessee's Radical Army*, 6–11; Susan Lawrence Davis, *Authentic History Ku Klux Klan, 1865–1877* (New York: American Library Service, 1924), 6, 35–37.

96. (Grove Hill, AL) *Clarke County Journal*, January 18, 1866, p. 2; *Montgomery Mail*, reprinted in *Plymouth* (IN) *Weekly Democrat*, November 23, 1865, p. 2. See also (Richmond) *Dispatch*, December 22, 1865, p. 2.

97. *Nashville Union and American*, December 20, 1865, p. 1; (Washington, DC) *Star*, December 22, 1865, p. 2.

98. D. J. Burke to Governor Parsons, October 4, 1865, Papers of Lewis E. Parsons, ADAH. Discriminatory prosecutions were also taking place in Lauderdale County. S. C. Posey to Governor Parsons, November 18, 1865, ibid.

99. J. A. Hammond et al. to Governor Parsons, October 9, 1865, ibid.

100. (Philadelphia) *North American and United States Gazette*, January 20, 1866; *New York Times*, January 23, 1866, p. 4; (New York) *Sun*, January 20, 1866, p. 2; *Brownlow's Knoxville Whig, and Rebel Ventilator*, January 24, 1866, p. 2; *New York Tribune*, January 25, 1866, p. 6, January 26, 1866, p. 1; (Brattleboro) *Vermont Phoenix*, January 26, 1866, p. 2; *Nashville Press and Times*, January 15, 1866, reprinted in *Montgomery Advertiser*, January 24, 1866, p. 2; *Huntsville Advocate*, January 18, 1866, p. 3. See generally Fitzgerald, "Radical Republicanism," 570–71; US Congress, *Report of the Joint Committee on Reconstruction*, 39th Cong., 1st sess., pt. 3 (Washington, DC: Government Printing Office, 1966).

101. (Nashville) *Union and American*, January 27, 1866, p. 2.

102. (Washington, DC) *National Republican*, January 22, 1866, p. 1.

103. James H. Clanton to Governor Parsons, October 20, 1865, Papers of Lewis E. Parsons, ADAH. Regarding Clanton's reputed involvement with the Klan, see Davis, *Authentic History Ku Klux Klan*, 61.

104. *Montgomery Ledger*, reprinted in (Charleston) *South Carolina Leader*, December 23, 1865, p. 2. See generally Michael W. Fitzgerald, "'To Give Our Votes to the Party': Black Political Agitation and Agricultural Change in Alabama," *Journal of American History* 76 (September 1989): 489–90; Foner, *Reconstruction*, 198–99.

105. Noe, *Yellowhammer War*, 8.

106. (Washington, DC) *National Intelligencer*, January 19, 1866; (Philadelphia) *North American and United States Gazette*, January 20, 1866; *Columbus* (GA) *Enquirer*, reprinted in *Dayton* (OH) *Empire*, November 29, 1865, p. 1.

107. Foner, *Reconstruction*, 198.

108. A proposal for qualified suffrage was tabled by this legislature. Fleming, *Civil War and Reconstruction*, 388–90.

109. *Washington* (DC) *Chronicle*, reprinted in (Raleigh) *Weekly North Carolina*, January 3, 1866, p. 4.

110. *Mobile Advertiser and Register*, December 15, 1865, p. 2.

111. George A. Wood, "The Black Code of Alabama," *South Atlantic Quarterly*, 13 (October 1914): 350–60; Burnett, *Pen Makes a Good Sword*, 153–54; Wiggins, *Scalawag in Alabama Politics*, 16; (Moulton, AL) *Christian Herald*, January 5, 1866, p. 3, January 12, 1866, p. 2; *Mobile Times*, December 6, 1865, p. 2, December 9, 1865, p. 4, December 10, 1865, p. 1, December 14, 1865, pp. 1 and 4, December 15, 1865, pp. 1 and 6, December 20, 1865, p. 2, January 24, 1866, p. 2; *Mobile Advertiser and Register*, December 10, 1865, p. 1, December 14, 1865, p. 2, December 15, 1865, p. 2, December 16, 1865, pp. 2 and 4, December 17, 1865, p. 1; *Montgomery Advertiser*, December 14, 1865, supplement, December 17, 1865, p. 2.

112. DuBose, *Alabama's Tragic Decade*, 55–56.

113. The prewar Alabama Code also included within the definition of the term "vagrant" those who abandoned their families, prostitutes and keepers of houses of prostitution, beggars, and gamblers. A first offense conviction required incarceration for ten days. A second offense brought twenty days in jail. AL Code § 3794 (1852), 664.

114. AL Acts, nos. 107 and 112, pp. 116, 119–21 (1865); Those convicted of a violation by a justice of the peace could be incarcerated for up to three months in the county house of corrections, if one existed, or the county jail. Repeat offenders could be given up to thirty-nine lashes on his or her back. *Mobile Times*, December 10, 1865, p. 1. See also Fleming, *Civil War and Reconstruction*, 382.

115. (Montpelier) *Vermont Watchman and State Journal*, December 29, 1865. Alabama historian Walter Fleming concedes this point. Fleming, *Civil War and Reconstruction*, 383.

Notes to pages 199–201 / 295

116. *Mobile Advertiser and Register*, December 10, 1865, p. 1; *Montgomery Advertiser*, December 14, 1865, supplement.

117. AL Acts, nos. 103 and 120, pp. 114, 128–31 (1865); *Montgomery Advertiser*, December 14, 1865, supplement; *Mobile Advertiser and Register*, December 16, 1865, p. 4; Fleming, *Civil War and Reconstruction*, 381–82.

118. *Mobile Times*, December 2, 1865, p. 1, December 5, 1865, p. 2; *Mobile Advertiser and Register*, December 5, 1865, p. 1. Regarding Sanford, see Julie Novkov, *Radical Union: Law, Intimacy, and the White State in Alabama, 1865–1954* (Ann Arbor: University of Michigan Press, 2008), 141; DuBose, *Alabama's Tragic Decade*, 59–60.

119. Carter, *When the War Was Over*, 177.

120. *Mobile Times*, December 14, 1865, p. 4.

121. *Boston Advertiser*, December 28, 1865.

122. *Mobile Advertiser and Register*, December 17, 1865, p. 1, December 19, 1865, pp. 1–2; Theodore B. Wilson, *The Black Codes of the South* (Tuscaloosa: University of Alabama Press, 1965), 75–77; Perman, *Reunion without Compromise*, 79.

123. Trowbridge, *Desolate South*, 223.

124. (New York) *Weekly Sun*, December 30, 1865, p. 2.

125. (New York) *Sun*, January 20, 1866, p. 2.

126. *Mobile Times*, December 14, 1865, p. 4; (Montpelier) *Vermont Watchman and State Journal*, December 29, 1865; *Boston Advertiser*, December 28, 1865; *Milwaukee Sentinel*, December 29, 1865; *Mobile Advertiser and Register*, January 23, 1866, p. 1. See also Thornton, "Alabama's Presidential Reconstruction Legislature," 175–77.

127. (Nashville) *Union and American*, December 30, 1865, p. 1.

128. *Mobile Advertiser and Register*, December 16, 1865, p. 2; *New York Times*, December 20, 1865, p. 4; (New Orleans) *Picayune*, December 28, 1865, p. 2; *Mobile Times*, December 28, 1865, p. 1.

129. Simon, *Papers of Ulysses S. Grant*, 16:54; Downs, *After Appomattox*, 106.

130. (Columbus, GA) *Sun*, November 29, 1865, p. 1. This had not benefitted Watts in his own quest for a seat in the US Senate. *Mobile Advertiser and Register*, December 1, 1865, pp. 1–4 (Watts received only seventeen votes).

131. Testimony of Gen. Benjamin Grierson, in US Congress, *Report of the Joint Committee on Reconstruction*, 121–23.

132. *Milwaukee Sentinel*, December 11, 1865.

133. *Mobile Times*, December 28, 1865, p. 5; *Mobile Advertiser and Register*, April 17, 1866, p. 2.

134. *Cleveland Leader*, January 31, 1866, p. 2.

135. *New York Times*, January 14, 1866, p. 2; (Philadelphia) *Telegraph*, January 3, 1866, p. 1.

136. John H. Mahaffey, ed., "Carl Schurz Letter from Alabama, August 15–16, 1865," *Alabama Review* 3 (April 1950): 134–45.

137. Senate Ex. Docs., 39th Cong., 1st sess., no. 2, pp. 2–46 (ser. 1237). See also *Cleveland Leader*, December 28, 1865, p. 2; *Norfolk* (VA) *Post*, December 28, 1865,

296 / Notes to pages 202–204

p. 2; *Burlington* (VT) *Free Press*, December 29, 1865, p. 2; *Nashville Union and American*, December 29, 1865, p. 2; (Raleigh) *North Carolina Standard*, January 3, 1866, p. 2; *Fremont* (OH) *Journal*, January 5, 1866, p. 1; *New York Times*, December 20, 1865, p. 4. Regarding Schurz's investigation, see Simpson, Graf, and Muldowny, *Advice after Appomattox*, 68–77.

138. Senate Ex. Docs., 39th Cong., 1st sess., no. 2, pp. 2–46.

139. *Burlington* (VT) *Weekly Free Press*, January 5, 1866, p. 2.

140. Harwell, *Kate*, 307.

141. Private Journal of Sarah R. Espy, 106, ADAH.

142. McWhiney, Moore, and Pace, "*Fear God and Walk Humbly*," 354–55.

143. Linden and Linden, *Disunion, War, Defeat, and Recovery*, 145.

Chapter 17

1. (New York) *Sun*, January 20, 1866, p. 2. Similar expressions can be found in the Southern press. Perman, *Reunion without Compromise*, 147.

2. Foner, *Reconstruction*, 243–51; Perman, *Reunion without Compromise*, 187.

3. Jones v. Alfred H. Mayer Co., 392 U.S. 409, 431 (1968); *Congressional Globe*, 39th Cong., 1st sess., 77. See generally Alexander Tsesis, *The Thirteenth Amendment and American Freedom: A Legal History* (New York: New York University Press, 2004); G. Sidney Buchanan, "The Quest for Freedom: A Legal History of the Thirteenth Amendment," *Houston Law Review* 12 (1974–1975): 1; George Rutherglen, *Civil Rights in the Shadow of Slavery: The Constitution, Common Law, and the Civil Rights Act of 1866* (New York: Oxford University Press, 2013).

4. Jones v. Alfred H. Mayer Co., 392 U.S., 431; *Congressional Globe*, 39th Cong., 1st sess., 129.

5. *Congressional Globe*, 39th Cong., 1st sess., 474; Runyon v. McCrary, 427 U.S. 160, 179 (1976); City of Memphis v. Greene, 451 U.S. 100, 125n38 (1981); Jones v. Alfred H. Mayer Co., 392 U.S., 437–38; Griffin v. Breckinridge, 403 U.S., 88, 105 (1971).

6. Goodman v. Lukens Steel Co., 482 U.S. 656, 676 (1987).

7. 18 U.S.C. § 241. Civil claims were later authorized by what is now 42 U.S.C. § 1983. See generally Risa L. Goluboff, "The Thirteenth Amendment and the Lost Origins of Civil Rights," *Duke Law Journal* 50, no. 6 (2001): 1609–85.

8. *Congressional Globe*, 39th Cong., 1st sess., 475.

9. *Montgomery Advertiser*, April 8, 1866, p. 4, April 10, 1866, p. 4; McPherson, *Struggle for Equality*, 350; Gambill, *Conservative Ordeal*, 53–55.

10. John W. Burgess, *Reconstruction and the Constitution, 1866–1876* (Whitefish, MT: Kessinger Publishing, 2007), 73–74; Rogers et al., *Alabama*, 241.

11. McDonald v. City of Chicago, Ill., 561 U.S. 742 (2010); Gambill, *Conservative Ordeal*, 59–61. See generally Foner, *Reconstruction*, 251–71; Perman, *Reunion without Compromise*, 234–65.

12. Reynolds v. Sims, 377 U.S. 533, 595 (1964).

Notes to pages 204–206 / 297

13. (New Orleans) *Picayune*, April 26, 1866, p. 3, May 3, 1866, p. 6; *New York Times*, March 8, 1866, p. 5, April 5, 1866, p. 5, April 17, 1866, p. 4, April 20, 1866, p. 1; Mahin, *One War at a Time*, 276.

14. *Mobile Advertiser and Register*, May 6, 1866, p. 5, May 16, 1866, supplement, p. 1, June 24, 1866, supplement, p. 2; *Montgomery Advertiser*, May 16, 1866, p. 3, May 23, 1866, p. 2, June 15, 1866, p. 2; *Huntsville Advocate*, May 2, 1866, p. 2, May 16, 1866, p. 2, May 19, 1866, p. 3, June 13, 1866, p. 2, June 27, 1866, p. 2, June 30, 1866, p. 2, July 18, 1866, p. 2.

15. U.S. Const. amend. XIV, § 3.

16. *Huntsville Advocate*, reprinted in *Montgomery Advertiser*, January 1, 1867, p. 2.

17. Oregon v. Mitchell, 400 U.S. 112 (1970); Reynolds v. Sims, 377 U.S. 533, 599 (1964).

18. Scott v. Sandford, 60 U.S. 393 (1857).

19. U.S. Const. amend. XIV, § 1.

20. Hurd v. Hodge, 334 U.S. 24, 32 (1948).

21. Barron ex rel. Tiernan v. Mayor of Baltimore, 7 pet. 243 (1833).

22. *Montgomery Advertiser*, June 23, 1866, p. 2.

23. Richard L. Aynes, "Unintended Consequences of the Fourteenth Amendment," in *Unintended Consequences of Constitutional Amendment*, ed. David E. Hyvig (Athens: University of Georgia Press, 2000), 110–40.

24. U.S. Const. amend. XIV, § 2.

25. Ibid., § 5. The amendment also allayed fears of Northerners and Southern Unionists that, once the Southern states had run the gauntlet to admission to Congress, they would repeal state law prohibitions adopted in 1865 on payment of war debts incurred by the Confederacy and the states:

> Section 4. The validity of the public debt of the United States, authorized by law, including debts incurred for payment of pensions and bounties for services in suppressing insurrection or rebellion, shall not be questioned. But neither the United States nor any State shall assume or pay any debt or obligation incurred in aid of insurrection or rebellion against the United States, or any claim for the loss or emancipation of any slave; but all such debts, obligations and claims shall be held illegal and void. (U.S. Const. amend. XIV, § 4)

26. Jett v. Dallas, 491 U.S. 701, 723 (1989); City of Memphis v. Greene, 451 U.S. 100, 120 (1981).

27. *Montgomery Advertiser*, June 3, 1866, p. 2, June 22, 1866, p. 2; Foner, *Reconstruction*, 273–77; Perman, *Reunion without Compromise*, 265–71.

28. *Mobile Advertiser and Register*, June 24, 1866, supplement, p. 1; *Montgomery Advertiser*, June 24, 1866, p. 3, June 27, 1866, p. 2, July 10, 1866, p. 2.

29. *Montgomery Mail*, reprinted in *Mobile Advertiser and Register*, June 24, 1866, supplement, p. 2; (Grove Hill, AL) *Clarke County Journal*, June 28, 1866, p. 2; *Montgomery Advertiser*, June 10, 1866, p. 2, June 15, 1866, p. 2, September 29, 1866, p. 2, October 19, 1866, p. 2; *Mobile Advertiser and Register*, June 12, 1866, p. 2, July 1, 1866, p. 2,

October 4, 1866, p. 2, October 30, 1866, p. 2; *Huntsville Advocate*, July 11, 1866, p. 3; (New York) *World*, reprinted in *Mobile Advertiser and Register*, October 21, 1866, p. 2; Gambill, *Conservative Ordeal*, 77–80; James Edward Bond, *No Easy Walk to Freedom: Reconstruction and the Ratification of the Fourteenth Amendment* (Westport, CT: Praeger, 1997), 101–14.

30. (Moulton, AL) *Christian Herald*, July 27, 1866, p. 2; *Huntsville Advocate*, July 28, 1866, pp. 2–3, August 1, 1866, p. 3; Rogers et al., *Alabama*, 241.

31. *Mobile Advertiser and Register*, May 16, 1866, supplement, p. 1, June 15, 1866, p. 2; (New Orleans) *Picayune*, May 20, 1866, p. 10.

32. *Montgomery Advertiser*, November 4, 1866, p. 2, November 9, 1866, p. 2, January 1, 1867, p. 2; *Mobile Advertiser and Register*, November 14, 1866, p. 1.

33. *Montgomery Advertiser*, December 8, 1866, p. 2, February 15, 1867, p. 2, February 19, 1867, p. 2; *Mobile Advertiser and Register*, December 8, 1866, p. 2, February 17, 1867, p. 2, February 21, 1867, p. 2; Fleming, *Civil War and Reconstruction*, 394–98; Perman, *Reunion without Compromise*, 256–65.

34. *Mobile Advertiser and Register*, February 21, 1867, p. 2, February 22, 1867, p. 2; *Montgomery Advertiser*, February 19, 1867, p. 2, February 27, 1867, p. 2. See also Foner, *Reconstruction*, 274–80; Rogers et al., *Alabama*, 241–42.

35. *Montgomery Advertiser*, March 6, 1867, p. 2.

36. Ala. Acts, Joint Resolutions, pp. 137–39 (July 13, 1868); *Selma* (AL) *Times and Messenger*, July 15, 1868, pp. 1–2; Wiggins, *Scalawag in Alabama Politics*, 38–39; Joseph Bliss James, *The Ratification of the Fourteenth Amendment* (Macon, GA: Mercer University Press, 1984).

37. *New York Times*, August 6, 1868, p. 6 (they were admitted on July 20, 1868). See generally Terry L. Seip, *The South Returns to Congress: Men, Economic Measures, and Intersectional Relationships, 1868–1879* (Baton Rouge: Louisiana State University Press, 1983).

38. (Mobile) *Nationalist*, June 18, 1868, p. 2.

39. *Huntsville Advocate*, reprinted in (Montgomery) *Alabama State Journal*, June 3, 1869, p. 1.

40. *Mobile Register*, July 27, 1868, p. 2, July 31, 1868, p. 2; Wiggins, *Scalawag in Alabama Politics*, 41–42.

41. (Tuscaloosa) *Independent Monitor*, March 18, 1868, p. 2; *Moulton* (AL) *Advertiser*, March 20, 1868, p. 2, April 10, 1868, p. 3; *Montgomery Advertiser*, March 1, 1868, p. 4, March 6, 1868, p. 3, March 11, 1868, p. 2; (Greensboro) *Alabama Beacon*, March 28, 1868, p. 2, March 28, 1868, p. 3; *Livingston* (AL) *Journal*, March 28, 1868, pp. 2–3; *Mobile Register*, March 23, 1868, p. 2, April 15, 1868, p. 4, July 27, 1868, p. 2.

42. *Montgomery Mail*, reprinted in *Mobile Register*, March 16, 1868, p. 2.

43. (Tuscaloosa) *Independent Monitor*, March 18, 1868, p. 2. Regarding Randolph, see G. Ward Hubbs, *Searching for Freedom after the Civil War: Klansman, Carpetbagger, Scalawag, and Freedman* (Tuscaloosa: University of Alabama Press, 2015); Sarah Woolfolk Wiggins, "The Life of Ryland Randolph as Seen through His Letters to John DuBose," *Alabama Historical Quarterly* 30 (Fall and Winter 1968): 145–80.

NOTES TO PAGES 207–209 / 299

44. *Harper's Weekly*, March 28, 1868, reprinted in (Tuscaloosa) *Independent Monitor*, April 1, 1868, p. 2; *Milwaukee Sentinel*, April 23, 1868; *New York Tribune*, reprinted in (Ripley, OH) *Independent Press*, April 24, 1868; (Philadelphia) *Northern American and United States Gazette*, reprinted in (New Orleans) *Picayune*, April 26, 1868, p. 1; *Cincinnati Commercial*, reprinted in *New York Times*, May 1, 1868, p. 11.

45. *Mobile Register*, May 9, 1868, p. 2.

46. (Tuscaloosa) *Independent Monitor*, June 9, 1868, p. 2.

47. *Moulton* (AL) *Advertiser*, July 10, 1868, p. 2; *Mobile Register*, July 23, 1868, p. 2, July 27, 1868, p. 2, July 31, 1868, p. 2.

48. (Selma) *Alabama State Sentinel*, reprinted in *Mobile Register*, August 7, 1868, p. 2; (Tuscaloosa) *Independent Monitor*, August 11, 1868, p. 3.

49. *Decatur Republican*, reprinted in *Bangor* (ME) *Whig and Courier*, August 25, 1868; (Tuscaloosa) *Independent Monitor*, September 1, 1868, p. 2.

50. (Tuscaloosa) *Independent Monitor*, August 25, 1868, p. 2.

51. *New York Times*, September 4, 1868, p. 4. See also *New York Citizen*, reprinted in (Tuscaloosa) *Independent Monitor*, September 22, 1868, p. 1.

52. Allen Johnston Going, *Bourbon Democracy in Alabama* (Tuscaloosa: University of Alabama Press, 1992), 61–65, 76–78; Fleming, *Civil War and Reconstruction*, 587–605; Wiggins, *Scalawag in Alabama Politics*, 42–45.

53. Oregon v. Mitchell, 400 U.S. 112, 156–57 (1970); *Mobile Advertiser*, February 13, 1868, p. 2.

54. U.S. Const. amend. XV. See generally William Gillette, *The Right to Vote: Politics and Passage of the Fifteenth Amendment* (Baltimore, MD: Johns Hopkins University Press, 1965).

55. Ala. Acts, Joint Resolution, no. 1 (November 24, 1869).

56. Hanes Walton, Sherman C. Puckett, Donald Richard Deskins, *The African American Electorate: A Statistical History* (Thousand Oaks, CA: CQ Press, 2012), 364; Bernard Grofman, Lisa Handley, Richard G. Niemi, *Minority Representation and the Quest for Voting Equality* (New York: Cambridge University Press, 1992), 5; Rutherglen, *Civil Rights*, 80.

57. Everette Swinney, *Enforcing the Fifteenth Amendment, 1870–1877* (Baton Rouge, Louisiana State University Press, 1962); Lou Falkner Williams, *The Great South Carolina Ku Klux Klan Trials, 1871–1872* (Athens: University of Georgia Press, 2004); Rogers et al., *Alabama*, 251; Walton, Puckett, and Deskins, *African American Electorate*, 364; Grofman, Handley, and Niemi, *Minority Representation*, 5; Rutherglen, *Civil Rights*, 80.

58. Wiggins, *Scalawag in Alabama Politics*, 86, 104–105; Going, *Bourbon Democracy in Alabama*, 10, 61, 65–66. Regarding the Panic of 1873, which was followed by over two decades of economic depression in the South, see M. John Lubetkin, *Jay Cooke's Gamble: The Northern Pacific Railroad, the Sioux, and the Panic of 1873* (Norman: University of Oklahoma Press, 2014).

59. Going, *Bourbon Democracy in Alabama*, 65–66; Rogers et al., *Alabama*, 252–54.

60. Wiggins, *Scalawag in Alabama Politics*, 86–103; Going, *Bourbon Democracy in Ala-*

bama, 9–18, 61, 68; Fleming, *Civil War and Reconstruction*, 771–95; Rogers et al., *Alabama*, 257–58, 260–64.

61. Patrick R. Cotter, *After Wallace: The 1986 Contest for Governor and Political Change in Alabama* (Tuscaloosa: University of Alabama Press, 2013), 218.

62. *Tuscaloosa Times*, September 15, 1875, p. 2; *Mobile Register*, June 15, 1875, p. 3; Going, *Bourbon Democracy in Alabama*, 70–78 (noting that this gave state negotiators leverage to negotiate a reduction in the debt). For examples of this type of litigation, see Hoffman v. City of Quincy, 71 U.S. 535 (1866); Heine v. Levee Commissioners, 86 U.S. 655 (1873); Chisholm v. Montgomery, 5 F.Cas. 635 (M.D. Ala., 1875).

63. Going, *Bourbon Democracy in Alabama*, 24, 71, 83, 153; Ala. Const. art. XI, §§ 4, 5 and 7 (1875).

64. Going, *Bourbon Democracy in Alabama*, 24; Ala. Const., art IV, § 54, and art. XI, § 3 (1875); Rogers et al., *Alabama*, 264–68.

65. Ala. Const., §§ 213, 214, 215, 216, 224, and 225 (1901); Wayne Flynt, *Alabama in the Twentieth Century* (Tuscaloosa: University of Alabama Press, 2004), 10.

66. Flynt, *Alabama in the Twentieth Century*, 10–11.

67. State of South Carolina v. Katzenbach, 383 U.S. 301, 310 (1966). See also Shelby County, Ala. v. Holder, 133 S.Ct. 2612, 2619 (2013).

68. Frank J. Scaturro, *The Supreme Court's Retreat from Reconstruction: A Distortion of Constitutional Jurisprudence* (Westport, CT: Greenwood Press, 2000); David W. Blight, *Race and Reunion: The Civil War in American Memory* (Cambridge, MA: Harvard University Press, 2001), 130–32; William Alan Blair, "The Use of Military Force to Protect the Gains of Reconstruction," *Civil War History* 51 (December 2005): 388–402; Robert Cook, "Unfinished Business: African Americans and the Civil War Centennial," in *Legacy of Disunion: The Enduring Significance of the American Civil War*, ed. Susan-Mary Grant and Peter J. Parish (Baton Rouge: Louisiana State University Press, 2003), 49; William Gillette, *Retreat from Reconstruction, 1869–1879* (Baton Rouge: Louisiana State University Press, 1979), 363–80; LaWanda Cox, "From Emancipation to Segregation: National Policy and Southern Blacks," in *Interpreting Southern History: Essays in Honor of Sanford W. Higginbotham*, edited by John B. Boles and Evelyn Thomas Nolen, 199–253 (Baton Rouge: Louisiana State University Press, 1987); Robert J. Kaczorowski, *The Politics of Judicial Interpretation: The Federal Courts, Department of Justice and Civil Rights, 1866–1876* (New York: Fordham University Press, 2005).

69. Wiggins, *Scalawag in Alabama Politics*, 139–42; Paul M. Pruitt Jr., *Taming Alabama: Lawyers and Reformers, 1804–1929* (Tuscaloosa: University of Alabama Press, 2010), 63–73 (after Richard Busteed resigned, he was replaced by John Bruce in 1875 and, upon Bruce's death, Bruce was replaced by Thomas Goode Jones in 1901).

70. State of South Carolina v. Katzenbach, 383 U.S., 310–11; R. Volney Riser, *Defying Disfranchisement: Black Voting Rights Activism in the Jim Crow South, 1890–1908* (Baton Rouge: Louisiana State University Press, 2010), 112–37.

71. Shelby County, Ala. v. Holder, 133 S.Ct., 2633.

72. State of South Carolina v. Katzenbach, 383 U.S., 328.

73. Shelby County, AL v. Holder, 133 S.Ct., 2619; City of Rome v. United States, 446 U.S. 156, 173–78 (1980). See generally Gary May, *Bending toward Justice: The Voting Rights Act and the Transformation of American Democracy* (Washington, DC: Basic Books, 2013).

74. State of South Carolina v. Katzenbach, 383 U.S., 314.

75. Ibid., 315–16.

76. Northwest Austin Mun. Utility Dist. No. One v. Holder, 557 U.S. 193, 202–3 (2009).

77. Patricia Lucie, "The Enduring Significance of the Civil War Constitutional Amendments," in *Legacy of Disunion*, ed. Grant and Parish, 171–87.

78. Brown v. Board of Education, 347 U.S. 483 (1954).

79. For an excellent collection of essays, see Bernard Grofman, ed., *Legacies of the 1964 Civil Rights Act* (Charlottesville: University of Virginia Press, 2000).

80. Fitzgerald, *Splendid Failure*; Wiggins, "Alabama's Reconstruction," 186. Walter Fleming saw it as a failure too. Fleming, *Civil War and Reconstruction*, 801–3.

81. James M. McPherson, "'For a Vast Future Also': Lincoln and the Millennium," in *Legacy of Disunion*, ed. Grant and Parish, 143, 146.

82. Lawrence Grossman, *The Democratic Party and the Negro: Northern and National Politics 1868–1892* (Urbana: University of Illinois Press, 1976); Gambill, *Conservative Ordeal*; Susan M. Glisson, ed., *The Human Tradition in the Civil Rights Movement* (Lanham, MD: Rowman and Littlefield Publishers, 2006), 49; Oakes, *Radical and the Republican*, 280; Bruce R. Bartlett, *Wrong on Race: The Democratic Party's Buried Past* (New York: Palgrave Macmillan, 2008), 23–42; Jean H. Baker, *Affairs of the Party: The Political Culture of the Northern Democrats in the Mid-Nineteenth Century* (New York: Fordham University Press, 1998), 353–54; Erik Benjamin Alexander, "'A Revival of the Old Organization': Northern Democrats and Reconstruction, 1868–1876," PhD diss., University of Virginia, 2010.

Bibliography

Primary Sources

UNPUBLISHED

Alabama Department of Archives and History

Alpheus Baker Diary
Zillah Haynie Brandon Diary
Edward Norphlet Brown Letters
John Joel Chappell Diary
Edward Crenshaw Diary
Sarah Lowe Davis Diary
Sarah R. Espy Journal
Thomas L. Faulkner Diary
John Jefferson Flowers Diary
Margaret Josephine Miles Gillis Diary
Alexander K. Hall Family Papers
Hilary Abner Herbert Papers
Andrew Barry Moore Papers
Joshua Burns Moore Journal
Lewis E. Parsons Papers
Robert Miller Patton Papers
John Gill Shorter Papers
Leroy Pope Walker Papers
Thomas Hill Watts Papers

Archives and Special Collections, Collier Library, University of North Alabama

Sally Independence Foster Diary

A. S. Williams III, Americana Collection, Gorgas Library, University of Alabama

Diary of A. H. Whetstone

Auburn University Library of Special Collections and Archives

Elizabeth Rhodes Diary

304 / Bibliography

David M. Rubenstein Rare Book and Manuscript Library, Duke University

C. C. Clay Jr. Papers
John Forsyth Papers
George S. Houston Papers
Henry Watson Papers

Hoole Special Collections Library, University of Alabama, Tuscaloosa

Robert Jemison Jr. Papers
Basil Manly Papers

Huntsville–Madison County Public Library, Huntsville, Alabama

Daniel Coleman Diary
Catherine M. Fennell Diary
James Montgomery Lanning Diary

Lawrence County, Alabama Archives

Hubbard Family File

Library of Congress, Washington, DC

Abraham Lincoln Papers

National Archives, Atlanta, Georgia

Confederate Papers Relating to Citizens or Business Firms, 1861–65

Rush Rhees Library, University of Rochester, New York

William H. Seward Papers

Southern Historical Collection, Wilson Library, University of North Carolina, Chapel Hill

John Archibald Campbell Papers
James Harrison Papers
Mary Elizabeth Mitchell Journal
Spring Family Papers
Frances Woolfolk Wallace Diary

Published

Axford, Faye Acton, ed. *"To Lochaber Na Mair": Southerners View the Civil War*. Athens, AL: Athens Publishing, 1986.

Basler, Roy P., ed. *The Collected Works of Abraham Lincoln*. 9 vols. New Brunswick, NJ: Rutgers University Press, 1953.

Basler, Roy, and Carl Sandburg, eds. *Abraham Lincoln: His Speeches and Writings*. Cleveland, OH: World Publishing, 1946.

Bates, William, ed. *The Stars and Stripes in Rebeldom: A Series of Papers Written by Federal Prisoners in Richmond, Tuscaloosa, New Orleans and Salisbury, N.C.* Boston: T. O. H. P. Burnham, 1862.

BIBLIOGRAPHY / 305

Baumgartner, Richard A., ed. *Blood and Sacrifice: The Civil War Journal of a Confederate Soldier*. By William Pitt Chambers. Huntington, WV: Blue Acorn Press, 1994.

Beck, Brandon H., ed. *Third Alabama!: The Civil War Memoir of Brigadier General Cullen Andrews Battle, CSA*. Tuscaloosa: University of Alabama Press, 2000.

Bergeron, Paul H., ed. *The Papers of Andrew Johnson*. Vol. 8, *May–August 1865*. Knoxville: University of Tennessee Press, 1989.

———, ed. *The Papers of Andrew Johnson*. Vol. 9, *September 1865–January 1866*. Knoxville: University of Tennessee Press, 1991.

Bird, Edgeworth, and John Rozier. *The Granite Farm Letters: The Civil War Correspondence of Edgeworth and Sallie Bird*. Athens: University of Georgia Press, 1988.

Blassingame, John W., and John R. McKivigan. *The Frederick Douglass Papers*. 9 vols. New Haven, CT: Yale University Press, 1991.

Blomquist, Ann Kicker, and Robert A. Taylor, eds. *This Cruel War: The Civil War Letters of Grant and Malinda Taylor, 1862–1865*. Macon, GA: Mercer University Press, 2000.

Brown, Kathleen S. *Family History: Kuhns—Koon—Koons—Kohn—Coon Kith and Kin*. Gordo, AL: self-published, 1990.

Butler, Benjamin F. *Autobiography and Personal Reminiscences of Major General Benjamin F. Butler*. Boston: A. M. Thayer, 1892.

Carter, John C., ed. *Welcome the Hour of Conflict: William Cowan McClellan and the 9th Alabama*. Tuscaloosa: University of Alabama Press, 2007.

Cash, William M., and Lucy Somerville Howorth, eds. *My Dear Nellie: The Civil War Letters of William L. Nugent to Eleanor Smith Nugent*. Jackson: University Press of Mississippi, 1977.

Clemens, Jeremiah. *Tobias Wilson: A Tale of the Great Rebellion*. Philadelphia: J. B. Lipincott, 1865.

Cooper, William J., Jr., ed. *Jefferson Davis: The Essential Writings*. New York: Random House, 2004.

Crenshaw, Edward. "Diary of Captain Edward Crenshaw of the Confederate States Army." *Alabama Historical Quarterly* 2 (Fall 1940): 465–82.

Crist, Lynda Lasswell, ed. *The Papers of Jefferson Davis: 1861*. 14 vols. Baton Rouge: Louisiana State University Press, 1992.

Crowson, Noel, and John V. Brogden, eds. *Bloody Banners and Barefoot Boys: "A History of the 27th Regiment Alabama Infantry CSA," The Civil War, Memoirs and Diary Entries of J. P. Cannon, M.D.* Shippensburg, PA: Burd Street Press, 1997.

Cruikshank, George, Robert Cruikshank, and J. R. Marshall. *The Universal Songster; or, Museum of Mirth*. Vol. 3. London: Jones, 1834.

Cutrer, Thomas W., ed. *Oh, What a Loansome Time I Had: The Civil War Letters of Major William Morel Moxley, Eighteenth Alabama Infantry, Emily Beck Moxley*. Tuscaloosa: University of Alabama Press, 2002.

Dickerson, Donna L. *The Reconstruction Era: Primary Documents on Events from 1865 to 1877*. Westport, CT: Greenwood Press, 2003.

DuBose, John Witherspoon, *Alabama's Tragic Decade: Ten Years of Alabama 1865–1874*. Birmingham: Webb Book, 1940.

Edwards, William C., and Edward Steers Jr., eds. *The Lincoln Assassination: The Evidence*. Urbana: University of Illinois Press, 2009.

Fehrenbacher, Don E., and Virginia Fehrenbacher, eds. *Recollected Words of Abraham Lincoln*. Stanford, CA: Stanford University Press, 1996.

Folmar, John Kent, ed. *From That Terrible Field: Civil War Letters of James M. Williams, Twenty-First Alabama Infantry Volunteers*. Tuscaloosa: University of Alabama Press, 1981.

————, ed. "Post Civil War Mobile: The Letters of James M. Williams, May–September, 1865." *Alabama Historical Quarterly* 32 (Fall and Winter 1970): 186–98.

Genoways, Ted, and Hugh H. Genoways. *A Perfect Picture of Hell: Eyewitness Accounts by Civil War Prisoners from the 12th Iowa*. Iowa City: University of Iowa Press, 2001.

Gienapp, William E., and Erica L. Gienapp, eds. *The Civil War Diary of Gideon Welles, Lincoln's Secretary of the Navy*. Urbana: Knox College Lincoln Studies Center and the University of Illinois Press, 2014.

Goethe, Johann Wolfgang von, *Goethe's Travels in Italy*. London: George Bell and Sons, 1885.

Graf, LeRoy P., ed. *The Papers of Andrew Johnson*. Vol. 7, *1864–1865*. Knoxville: University of Tennessee Press, 1986.

Graf, LeRoy P., and Ralph W. Haskins, eds. *The Papers of Andrew Johnson*. Vol. 6, *1862–1864*. Knoxville: University of Tennessee Press, 1983.

Griffith, Lucille, ed. *Yours till Death: Civil War Letters of John W. Cotton*. Tuscaloosa: University of Alabama Press, 1951.

Hague, Parthenia. *A Blockaded Family: Life in Southern Alabama during the Civil War*. Boston: Houghton Mifflin, 1988.

Hallock, Judith Lee, ed. *The Civil War Letters of Joshua K. Callaway*. Athens: University of Georgia Press, 1997.

Hancock, Richard R. *Hancock's Diary: A History of the Second Tennessee Confederate Cavalry*. Nashville: Brandon Print, 1887.

Hardy, John. *Selma: Her Institutions, and Her Men*. Selma, AL: Bert Neville and Clarence DeBray, 1957.

Harwell, Richard Barksdale, ed. *Kate: The Journal of a Confederate Nurse*. Baton Rouge: Louisiana State University Press, 1998.

Henderson, Dwight Franklin, ed. *The Private Journal of Georgiana Gholson Walker 1862–1865 with Selections from the Post-War Years, 1865–1876*. Tuscaloosa, AL: Confederate Publishing, 1963.

Herndon, William H., and Jesse W. Weik, *Abraham Lincoln: The True Story of a Great Life*. Vol. 2. New York: D. Appleton, 1909.

Hubbs, G. Ward. *Voices from Company D: Diaries by the Greensboro Guards, Fifth Alabama Infantry Regiment, Army of Northern Virginia*. Athens: University of Georgia Press, 2003.

Hughes, William Edgar, ed. *W. E. H. Gramp, the Journal of a Grandfather*. St. Louis, MO: W. E. Hughes, 1912.

Jewett, Clayton E., ed., *Rise and Fall of the Confederacy: The Memoir of Senator Williams S. Oldham, CSA*. Columbia: University of Missouri Press, 2006.

BIBLIOGRAPHY / 307

Johnson, Rossiter, and John Howard Brown, eds. *The Twentieth Century Biographical Dictionary of Notable Americans*. Boston: Biographical Society, 1904.

Jones, John Beauchamp. *A Rebel War Clerk's Diary at the Confederate States Capital*. Philadelphia: J. B. Lippincott, 1866.

Jones, Virginia K., ed. "The Journal of Sarah G. Follansbee." *Alabama Historical Quarterly* 27 (Fall and Winter 1965): 213–58.

Jordan, Thomas, and J. P. Pryor. *The Campaigns of Lieut.-Gen. N. B. Forrest, and of Forrest's Cavalry*. New Orleans: Blelock, 1868.

Linden, Glenn, and Virginia Linden, eds. *Disunion, War, Defeat, and Recovery in Alabama: The Journal of Augustus Benners, 1850–1885*. Macon, GA: Mercer University Press, 2007.

Livingston, John. *Portraits of Eminent Americans Now Living: With Biographical and Historical Memoirs of Their Lives and Actions*. New York: Cornish, Lamport, 1853–54.

Lowe, Richard, ed., *A Texas Cavalry Officer's Civil War: The Diary and Letters of James C. Bates*. Baton Rouge: Louisiana State University Press, 1999.

Mahaffey, John H., ed., "Carl Schurz Letter from Alabama, August 15–16, 1865." *Alabama Review* 3 (April 1950): 134–45.

Mathis, Gerald Ray, and Douglas C. Purcell. *In the Land of the Living: Wartime Letters by Confederates from the Chattahoochee Valley of Alabama and Georgia*. Troy, AL: Troy State University Press, 1981.

Maxwell, James Robert. *Autobiography of James Robert Maxwell of Tuskaloosa, Alabama*. Baltimore, MD: Gateway Press, 1996.

McMurry, Richard M., ed. *An Uncompromising Secessionist: The Civil War of George Knox Miller, Eighth (Wade's) Confederate Cavalry*. Tuscaloosa: University of Alabama Press, 2007.

McWhiney, Grady, Warner O. Moore Jr., and Robert F. Pace, eds. *"Fear God and Walk Humbly": The Agricultural Journal of James Mallory, 1843–1877*. Tuscaloosa: University of Alabama Press, 1997.

Meek, Alexander Beaufort. "The Martyrs of the South." In *Selma Morning Reporter*, June 4, 1864, p. 2.

Meriwether, Elizabeth Avery. *Recollections of 92 Years, 1824–1916*. Nashville: Tennessee Historical Commission, 1958.

Murphree, Joel, ed. "Autobiography and Civil War Letters of Joel Murphree of Troy, Alabama, 1864–1865." *Alabama Historical Quarterly* 19 (Spring, 1957): 170–208.

Neeley, Mary Ann, ed., *The Works of Matthew Blue, Montgomery's First Historian*. Montgomery, AL: NewSouth Books, 2010.

Niven, John, ed. *The Salmon P. Chase Papers: Journals, 1829–1872*. 2 vols. Kent, OH: Kent State University Press, 1993.

Noy, Gary. *Distant Horizon: Documents from the Nineteenth Century American West*. Lincoln: University of Nebraska Press, 1999.

Official Proceedings of the National Democratic Convention. Dayton, OH: Daily Journal Book and Job Rooms, 1882.

Palmer, Beverly Wilson, ed. *The Selected Papers of Charles Sumner*. 2 vols. Boston: Northeastern University Press, 1990.

———, ed. *The Selected Papers of Thaddeus Stevens*. Vol. 2, *April 1865–August 1868*. Pittsburgh: University of Pittsburgh Press, 1998.

Pate, James P., ed. *When This Evil War Is Over: The Correspondence of the Francis Family, 1860–1865*. Tuscaloosa: University of Alabama Press, 2006.

Pfanz, Donald C., ed. *"The Letters of General Richard S. Ewell: Stonewall's Successor.* Knoxville: University of Tennessee Press, 2012.

Phillips, John R., ed. "The Diary of a Union Soldier from Alabama." *Alabama Heritage* 28 (Spring 1993): 20–25.

Pitcock, Cynthia Deltaven, and Bill L. Gurley, eds. *I Acted from Principle: The Civil War Diary of Dr. William M. McPheeters, Confederate Surgeon in the Trans-Mississippi*. Fayetteville: University of Arkansas Press, 2002.

Redkey, Edwin S., ed. *A Grand Army of Black Men: Letters from African American Soldiers in the Union Army, 1861–1865*. Cambridge, MA: Cambridge University Press, 1992.

Reid, Whitelaw. *After the War: A Southern Tour: May 1, 1865, to May 1, 1866*. London: Sampson Low, Son, and Marston, 1866.

Rohr, Nancy M., ed. *Incidents of the War: The Civil War Journal of Mary Jane Chadick*. Huntsville, AL: Silver Threads Publishing, 2005.

Sexton, Rebecca Grant, ed. *A Southern Woman of Letters: The Correspondence of Augusta Jane Evans Wilson*. Columbia: University of South Carolina Press, 2002.

Simon, John Y., ed. *The Papers of Ulysses S. Grant*. 24 vols. Carbondale: Southern Illinois University Press, 1967–1984.

Smith, William Russell. *The Royal Ape: A Dramatic Poem*. Richmond, VA: West and Johnston, 1863.

Townsend, George. *Katy of Catoctin; or, The Chain-Breakers; A National Romance*. New York: D. Appleton, 1886.

Trowbridge, John T. *The Desolate South 1865–1866: A Picture of the Battlefields and of the Devastated Confederacy*. New York: Duell, Sloan and Pearce, 1956.

Venet, Wendy Hamand, ed. *Sam Richard's Civil War Diary: A Chronicle of the Atlanta Home Front*. Athens: University of Georgia Press, 2009.

Welles, Edgar Thaddeus. *Diary of Gideon Welles, Secretary of the Navy under Lincoln and Johnson*. Vol. 2. New York: W. W. Norton, 1911.

Welles, Gideon. "Administration of Abraham Lincoln." *Galaxy* 23 (October 1877): 437–50.

———. "Lincoln and Johnson: Their Plan of Reconstruction and the Resumption of National Authority." *Galaxy* 13 (April 1872): 521–32.

Wiggins, Sarah Woolfolk, ed. *The Journals of Josiah Gorgas 1857–1878*. Tuscaloosa: University of Alabama Press, 1995.

Wilson, Gary, ed. "The Diary of John S. Tucker: Confederate Soldier from Alabama." *Alabama Historical Quarterly* 43 (Spring 1981): 5–33.

Wilson, James Harrison. *Under the Old Flag: Recollections of Military Operations in the War for the Union, the Spanish War, the Boxer Rebellion, etc.* 2 vols. New York: D. Appleton, 1912.

BIBLIOGRAPHY / 309

Woodward, C. Vann, ed., *Mary Chesnut's Civil War*. New Haven, CT: Yale University Press, 1981.

PUBLIC DOCUMENTS

Alabama House Journal

Alabama Senate Journal

Annual Report of the Secretary of the Treasury on the State of the Finances, Statistical Appendix, 1980. Washington, DC: Government Printing Office, 1980.

Congressional Globe. Washington, DC: Congressional Globe Office, 1865 Executive Documents of the House of Representatives for the Second Session of the Forty-Ninth Congress 1886–87. Washington, DC: Government Printing Office, 1887.

Official Journal of the Constitutional Convention of Alabama, 1861. Montgomery, AL: Shorter and Reid, State Printers, 1861.

Ordinances and Constitution of the State of Alabama, with the Constitution of the Provisional Government of the Confederate States of America. Montgomery, AL: Shorter and Reid, State Printers, 1861.

Shepherd, J. W. *The Constitution, and Ordinances Adopted by the State Convention of Alabama Which Assembled at Montgomery on the Twelfth Day of September, A.D. 1865, with Index, Analysis, and Table of Titles.* Montgomery, AL: Gibson and Whitfield, State Printers, 1865.

US Congress. *Joint Select Committee to Investigate the Affairs of the Late Insurrectionary States, United States Senate Reports.* No. 22, "Alabama Testimony in Ku Klux Klan Report." Second sess., 42nd Cong., vol. 9. Washington, DC: Government Printing Office, 1872.

———. *Report of the Joint Committee on Reconstruction.* First sess., 39th Congress, part 3. Washington, DC: Government Printing Office, 1966.

———. *Testimony Taken by the Joint Select Committee to Inquire into the Condition of Affairs in the Late Insurrectionary States: Alabama.* 13 vols. Washington, DC: Government Printing Office, 1872.

US Senate Executive Journal. Washington, DC: Government Printing Office, 1872.

The War of the Rebellion: A Compilation of the Official Records of the Union and Confederate Armies. Washington, DC: Government Printing Office, 1887.

NEWSPAPERS

Albany (GA) Patriot

Albany (NY) Advertiser

Albany (NY) Argus

Albany (NY) Journal

Alexandria (VA) Gazette Advertiser

Alexandria (VA) Herald

(Alexandria, VA) *Soldiers Journal*

American Beacon and Norfolk (VA) and Portsmouth Advertiser

(Amherst, NH) *Farmers' Cabinet*

Anderson (SC) Intelligencer
Arkansas Gazette
Asheville (AL) *Vidette*
Ashtabula (OH) *Weekly Telegraph*
(Atchison, KS) *Freedom's Champion*
Athens (AL) *Herald*
Athens (AL) *Republican*
(Athens, GA) *Athenian*
(Athens, GA) *Southern Banner*
(Athens, GA) *Southern Watchman*
(Athens, GA) *Union Banner*
Athens (TN) *Post*
Atlanta Confederacy
Atlanta Intelligencer
Augusta (GA) *Chronicle*
Augusta (GA) *Chronicle and Georgia Advertiser*
Augusta (GA) *Chronicle and Sentinel*
Augusta (GA) *Constitutionalist*
(Baltimore) *Exchange*
Baltimore Patriot and Mercantile Advertiser
(Baltimore) *Pilot and Transcript*
(Baltimore) *Sun*
Bangor (ME) *Whig and Courier*
Barre (MA) *Gazette*
Bedford (PA) *Inquirer*
(Belfast, ME) *Waldo Patriot*
(Bellows Falls) *Vermont Chronicle*
Belmont (OH) *Chronicle*
(Bennington) *Vermont Gazette*
(Bloomsburg, PA) *Star of the North*
Boston Advertiser
Boston Atlas
Boston Commercial Gazette
(Boston) *Congregationalist*
Boston Herald
(Boston) *Liberator*
(Boston) *New-England Palladium*
Boston Recorder
Brandon (MS) *Republican*
(Brattleboro) *Vermont Phoenix*
Brattleboro (VT) *Semi-Weekly Eagle*
Brooklyn Eagle
(Brookville, PA) *Jeffersonian*

Brownlow's Knoxville Whig, and Rebel Ventilator
Buffalo Advertiser
Burlington (VT) *Free Press*
(Butler, PA) *American Citizen*
(Cahawba, AL) *Dallas Gazette*
Cahawba (AL) *Gazette*
Cahawba (AL) *Press and Alabama State Intelligencer*
(Cahawba, AL) *Southern Democrat*
Camden (SC) *Gazette*
Camden (SC) *Journal*
Canton (MS) *Citizen*
(Carrollton) *West Alabamian*
(Chardon, OH) *Jeffersonian Democrat*
(Charleston) *City Gazette and Commercial Advertiser*
Charleston Courier
Charleston Mercury
(Charleston) *South Carolina Leader*
(Charlotte, NC) *Western Democrat*
Chattanooga Gazette
Chattanooga Rebel
Chicago Journal
Chicago Post
Chicago Times
Chicago Tribune
(Chillicothe, OH) *Weekly Recorder*
Cincinnati Commercial
Cincinnati Enquirer
Cincinnati Gazette
Cincinnati Press
City of Washington (DC) *Gazette*
(Clarksville, TN) *Town Gazette and Farmers Register*
(Clarksville, TN) *Weekly Chronicle*
Clayton (AL) *Banner*
(Clearfield, PA) *Raftsman's Journal*
Cleveland Herald
Cleveland Leader
Columbia Democrat and Bloomsburg (PA) *General Advertiser*
Columbia (SC) *Phoenix*
(Columbia) *South Carolinian*
Columbia Tennessee Democrat
(Columbiana, AL) *Shelby County Guide*
Columbus (GA) *Enquirer*
Columbus (GA) *Sentinel*

(Columbus, GA) *Sun*
Columbus (GA) *Times*
Columbus (IN) *Republic*
(Columbus) *Weekly Ohio Statesman*
(Concord) *New Hampshire Patriot and State Gazette*
(Concord) *New Hampshire Statesman*
(Cooperstown, NY) *Otsego Herald*
(Cooperstown, NY) *Watch-Tower*
Courtland (AL) *Herald*
Dadeville (AL) *Banner*
Dallas (TX) *Herald*
Dayton (OH) *Empire*
Decatur (AL) *Clarion*
(Decatur, AL) *Morgan Observer*
Decatur (AL) *Register*
Demopolis (AL) *Herald*
(Easton, MD) *Republican Star and General Advertiser*
Edensburg (PA) *Alleghanian*
Edgefield (SC) *Advertiser*
Eufaula (AL) *News*
(Eufaula, AL) *Spirit of the South*
Eutaw (AL) *Whig*
Eutaw (AL) *Whig and Observer*
Fayetteville (NC) *Observer*
Florence (AL) *Enquirer*
Florence (AL) *Gazette*
Florence (AL) *Journal*
(Florence, AL) *Times Daily*
Frank Leslie's Illustrated (NY) *Newspaper*
Fremont (OH) *Journal*
Gainesville (AL) *Independent*
Gallipolis (OH) *Journal*
(Georgetown, DC) *National Messenger*
Glasgow (MO) *Weekly Times*
(Greensboro) *Alabama Beacon*
Greenville (SC) *Mountaineer*
(Grove Hill, AL) *Clarke County Journal*
(Hallowell, ME) *American Advocate and Kennebec Advertiser*
Harper's Weekly
(Hartford) *Connecticut Mirror*
Hartford (CT) *Courant*
Hartford (CT) *Press*
(Haverhill, MA) *Essex Gazette*

BIBLIOGRAPHY / 313

Hayneville (AL) *Chronicle*
Highland (OH) *Weekly News*
(Hillsborough, OH) *Highland Weekly News*
Holmes County (OH) *Farmer*
Howard (MO) *Union*
Huntsville Advocate
Huntsville Alabamian
Huntsville Chronicle
Huntsville Confederate
(Huntsville) *Democrat*
Huntsville Independent
Huntsville Republican
(Huntsville) *Southern Advocate*
Indianapolis (IN) *Herald*
(Indianapolis, IN) *State Sentinel*
Ithaca (NY) *Herald*
(Jackson) *Mississippian*
Jackson (MS) *News*
Jacksonville (AL) *Republican*
Jamestown (NY) *Journal*
(Keene) *New Hampshire Sentinel*
Lauderdale (AL) *Times*
Liberty (MO) *Tribune*
(Little Rock) *Arkansas Gazette*
(Little Rock) *Arkansas State Gazette*
(Little Rock) *Arkansas Times*
(Little Rock) *Arkansas Weekly Gazette*
Livingston (AL) *Independent*
Livingston (AL) *Journal*
London Standard
(London, England) *Times*
Louisville (KY) *Courier*
Louisville (KY) *Journal*
Lowell (MA) *Citizen and News*
Lynchburg (VA) *Gazette*
Macon (GA) *Confederate*
Macon (GA) *Telegraph*
Macon (GA) *Telegraph and Confederate*
Macon (GA) *Telegraph and Georgia Journal and Messenger*
Macon (GA) *Weekly Telegraph*
(Marion, AL) *American*
Marion (AL) *Commonwealth*
Marion (AL) *Review*

Memphis Appeal
Memphis Avalanche
Memphis Bulletin
(Memphis) *Western Times*
Meridian (MS) *Clarion*
Middlebury (VT) *Register*
(Middleton, CT) *Middlesex Gazette*
Milledgeville (GA) *Confederate Union*
(Milledgeville) *Georgia Journal*
(Milledgeville, GA) *Reflector*
(Milledgeville, GA) *Southern*
(Milledgeville, GA) *Southern Recorder*
Milledgeville (GA) *Statesman*
(Millersburg, OH) *Holmes County Farmer*
Milwaukee Sentinel
Missouri Republican
Mobile Advertiser
Mobile Advertiser and Register
(Mobile) *Army Argus and Crisis*
(Mobile) *Banner of Reform*
Mobile Commercial Register
Mobile Commercial Register and Patriot
Mobile Daily Times
Mobile Mercury
(Mobile) *Nationalist*
Mobile News
Mobile Register
Mobile Register and Journal
Mobile Times
Mobile Tribune
(Mobile) *Weekly Herald and Tribune*
Montgomery Advertiser
Montgomery Advertiser and Mail
(Montgomery) *Advertiser and Mail*
(Montgomery) *Advertiser and State Gazette*
(Montgomery) *Alabama Journal*
(Montgomery) *Alabama State Journal*
(Montgomery) *Alabama State Sentinel*
Montgomery Atlas
(Montgomery) *Confederation*
Montgomery Flag and Advertiser
Montgomery Ledger
Montgomery Mail

BIBLIOGRAPHY / 315

(Montgomery) *Memphis Appeal*
(Montgomery) *Tri-Weekly Flag and Advertiser*
Montgomery Weekly Advertiser
(Montgomery) *Weekly Alabama Journal*
Montgomery Weekly Mail
Montgomery Weekly Post
(Montpelier) *Vermont Watchman and State Journal*
Moulton (AL) Advertiser
Moulton (AL) Banner and Lawrence Enquirer
(Moulton, AL) *Christian Herald*
Moulton (AL) Democrat
Moulton (AL) Flag
Nashville Clarion
Nashville Democrat
Nashville News
Nashville Patriot
Nashville Press
Nashville Press and Times
Nashville Republican and State Gazette
(Nashville) *Republican Banner*
Nashville Tennessean
Nashville Times and True Union
Nashville Union
Nashville Union and American
Nashville Whig
Nashville Whig and Tennessee Advertiser
Natchez (MS) *Courier*
(Natchez, MS) *Ariel*
(Natchez) *Mississippi Free Trader*
(Natchez) *Mississippi State Gazette*
National Banner and Nashville Whig
(Newark, NJ) *Centinel of Freedom*
Newark (OH) Advocate
Newbern (NC) *Weekly Progress*
Newburyport (MA) *Herald*
New Haven (CT) *Palladium*
New Orleans Argus
(New Orleans) *Bee*
New Orleans Era
(New Orleans) *Jeffersonian*
(New Orleans) *Louisiana Advertiser*
(New Orleans) *Picayune*
(New Orleans) *Republican*

New Orleans Times
(New Orleans) *Times Picayune*
(New Orleans) *True American*
Newport (MA) *Herald*
Newport (RI) *Mercury*
(Newport) *Rhode Island Republicans*
New York Advertiser
(New York) *American*
(New York) *Columbian*
New York Commercial
New York Commercial and Advertiser
New York Courier
New York Essex Patriot
New York Evening Post
New York Express
New York Herald
New York Journal of Commerce
(New York) *Mercantile Advertiser*
(New York) *Merchants' Magazine and Commercial Review*
(New York) *National Advocate*
New York Observer
New York Post
New York Spectator
New York Times
New York Transcript
New York Tribune
(New York) *Sun*
(New York) *Weekly Sun*
(New York) *World*
(Norfolk, VA) *American Beacon and Commercial Diary*
Norfolk (VA) *Post*
Norwich (CT) *Courier*
Opelika (AL) *Union*
Opelika (AL) *Weekly Southern Era*
(Oskaloosa, KS) *Independent*
(Ossining, NY) *Hudson River Chronicle*
Ottawa (IL) *Free Trader*
(Panama City, Panama) *Mercantile Chronicle*
(Petersburg, VA) *American Star*
(Petersburg, VA) *Daily Express*
Philadelphia Bulletin
Philadelphia Inquirer
(Philadelphia) *New Age*
(Philadelphia) *North American and United States Gazette*

BIBLIOGRAPHY / 317

(Philadelphia) *Pennsylvania Inquirer and National Gazette*
Philadelphia Press
(Philadelphia) *Telegraph*
(Pittsfield, MA) *Berkshire County Whig*
Pittsfield (MA) *Sun*
Plymouth (IN) *Weekly Democrat*
Pomeroy (OH) *Weekly Telegraph*
(Pontotoc, MS) *Chickasaw Union*
(Pontotoc, MS) *Spirit of the Times*
(Portage) *Wisconsin State Register*
(Port Allen, LA) *Sugar Planter*
Portland (ME) *Advertiser*
Portland (ME) *Eastern Argus*
(Portsmouth) *New Hampshire Gazette*
Portsmouth (NH) *and Great Falls Journal of Literature and Politics*
Portsmouth (NH) *Journal and Rockingham Gazette*
Portsmouth (NH) *Journal of Literature and Politics*
(Poughkeepsie, NY) *Independence*
Providence (RI) *Patriot*
Providence (RI) *Patriot and Columbian Phenix*
Providence (RI) *Press*
(Providence) *Rhode Island American and Gazette*
(Providence) *Rhode Island American and General Advertiser*
(Raleigh) *North Carolina Standard*
Raleigh (NC) *Progress*
Raleigh (NC) *Register*
Raleigh (NC) *Standard*
(Raleigh) *Weekly North Carolina*
Richmond Compiler
(Richmond) *Dispatch*
Richmond Enquirer
Richmond Examiner
Richmond Sentinel
Richmond Whig
Ripley (OH) *Bee*
(Ripley, OH) *Independent Press*
(Russellville, AL) *Franklin Democrat*
(Salem, MA) *Essex Register*
Salem (MA) *Gazette*
(Sandusky, OH) *Commercial Register*
(San Francisco) *Evening Bulletin*
(Savannah, GA) *Morning News*
Savannah Georgian
Savannah (GA) *Republican*

Scioto (OH) *Gazette*
(Selma) *Alabama State Sentinel*
(Selma, AL) *Chattanooga Rebel*
Selma (AL) *Courier*
Selma (AL) *Dispatch*
Selma (AL) *Federal Union*
Selma (AL) *Free Press*
Selma (AL) *Messenger*
(Selma, AL) *Mississippian*
Selma (AL) *Reporter*
(Selma, AL) *Southern Argus*
Selma (AL) *Times and Messenger*
Selma (AL) *Union*
Selma (AL) *Weekly Issue*
Semi-Weekly Raleigh (NC) *Register*
(Shelbyville) *Tennessee Herald*
Shreveport News
Shreveport Semi-Weekly News
(Shreveport) *South-Western*
(St. Albans) *Vermont Transcript*
St. Cloud (MN) *Democrat*
(St. Clairsville, OH) *Belmont Chronicle*
St. Louis Globe-Democrat
St. Louis Republican
(St. Stephens, AL) *Halcyon and Tombeckbe Public Advertiser*
(Statesville, NC) *Iredell Express*
(Stevenson, AL) *Jackson County News*
(Stroundsburg, PA) *Jeffersonian Republican*
Sunbury (PA) *American*
(Talladega, AL) *Democratic Watchtower*
Talladega (AL) *Reporter*
(Trenton, NJ) *State Gazette*
(Troy, AL) *Southern Advertiser*
(Tuscaloosa) *Alabama Intelligencer and States Rights Expositor*
(Tuscaloosa) *Alabama State Intelligencer*
(Tuscaloosa) *Blade*
(Tuscaloosa) *Chronicle*
(Tuscaloosa) *Flag of the Union*
(Tuscaloosa) *Independent Monitor*
Tuscaloosa Inquirer
Tuscaloosa News
Tuscaloosa Observer
(Tuscaloosa) *Spirit of the Age*
Tuscaloosa Times

BIBLIOGRAPHY / 319

(Tuscaloosa) *Tuskaloosa Gazette*
Tuscumbia (AL) *Advertiser*
Tuscumbia (AL) *Constitution*
(Tuscumbia, AL) *North Alabamian*
(Tuscumbia, AL) *North Alabamian and Times*
Tuscumbia (AL) *Patriot*
Tuscumbia (AL) *Telegraph*
Urbana (OH) *Union*
Vermont Intelligencer and Bellows Falls Advertiser
Vicksburg (MS) *Daily Herald*
Vicksburg (MS) *Sentinel*
(Virginia City) *Montana Post*
(Warren, OH) *Western Reserve Chronicle*
Washington City (DC) *Weekly Gazette*
Washington (DC) *Chronicle*
(Washington, DC) *Globe*
Washington (DC) *Herald*
(Washington, DC) *National Intelligencer*
(Washington, DC) *National Republican*
(Washington, DC) *National Tribune*
(Washington, DC) *Niles Register*
Washington (DC) *Post*
Washington (DC) *Southern Press*
Washington (DC) *Star*
(Washington, DC) *United States Telegraph*
Weekly Perrysburg (OH) *Journal*
Weekly Raleigh (NC) *Register*
(Wheeling, WV) *Intelligencer*
White Cloud Kansas Chief
(Wilmington) *American Watchman and Delaware Republican*
Winchester (TN) *Bulletin*
(Windsor) *Vermont Chronicle*
Worchester (MA) *Palladium*
Xenia (OH) *Sentinel*
Yorkville (SC) *Enquirer*

Secondary Sources

BOOKS, DISSERTATIONS, AND THESES

Abernethy, Thomas P. *The South in the New Nation*. Baton Rouge: Louisiana State University Press, 1961.

Adams, Michael C. C. *Living Hell: The Dark Side of the Civil War*. Baltimore, MD: Johns Hopkins University Press, 2014.

Alabama Writers Program, *Alabama: A Guide to the Deep South*. New York: R. A. Smith, 1941.

Alasdair, Roberts. *America's First Great Depression: Economic Crisis and Political Disorder after the Panic of 1837*. Ithaca, NY: Cornell University Press, 2012.

Albjerg, Esther Marguerita Hall. "A Critique of the New York Daily Press during Reconstruction, 1865–1869." PhD diss., University of Wisconsin-Madison, 1925.

Alexander, Bevin. *How the South Could Have Won the Civil War: The Fatal Errors That Led to Confederate Defeat*. New York: Crown Publishers, 2007.

Alexander, Erik Benjamin. "'A Revival of the Old Organization': Northern Democrats and Reconstruction, 1868–1876." PhD diss., University of Virginia, 2010.

Alford, Terry. *Fortune's Fool: The Life of John Wilkes Booth*. New York: Oxford University Press, 2015.

Allardice, Bruce S. *Confederate Colonels: A Biographical Register*. Columbia: University of Missouri Press, 2008.

Allmendinger, David F., Jr. *Nat Turner and the Rising in Southhampton County*. Baltimore, MD: Johns Hopkins University Press, 2014.

Armes, Ethel Marie. *The Story of Coal and Iron in Alabama*. Tuscaloosa: University of Alabama Press, 2011.

Arthur, Anthony. *General Jo Shelby's March*. New York: Random House, 2010.

Ash, Stephen V., ed. *Secessionists and Other Scoundrels: Selections from Parson Brownlow's Book*. Baton Rouge: Louisiana State University Press, 1999.

——. *When the Yankees Came: Conflict and Chaos in the Occupied South, 1861–1865*. Chapel Hill: University of North Carolina Press, 1995.

Ashdown, Paul, and Edward Caudill. *The Myth of Nathan Bedford Forrest*. Lanham, MD: Rowman and Littlefield, 2005.

Ayers, Edward L. *What Caused the Civil War? Reflections on the South and Southern History*. New York: W. W. Norton, 2005.

Baggett, James Alex. *The Scalawags: Southern Dissenters in the Civil War and Reconstruction*. Baton Rouge: Louisiana State University Press, 2003.

Bailey, Anne J. *The Chessboard of War: Sherman and Hood in the Autumn Campaigns of 1864*. Lincoln: University of Nebraska Press, 2000.

Bailey, Richard. *Neither Carpetbaggers Nor Scalawags: Black Officerholders during the Reconstruction of Alabama, 1867–1878*. Montgomery, AL: R. Bailey Publishers, 1991.

Baker, Jean H. *Affairs of the Party: The Political Culture of the Northern Democrats in the Mid-Nineteenth Century*. New York: Fordham University Press, 1998.

Ball, Douglas B. *Financial Failure and Confederate Defeat*. Urbana: University of Illinois Press, 1991.

Ballantyne, Jane C., Scott M. Fishman, and James P. Rathmell. *Bonica's Management of Pain*. Philadelphia: Lippincott, Williams, and Williams, 2010.

Ballard, Michael B. *The Civil War in Mississippi: Major Campaigns and Battles*. Jackson: University Press of Mississippi, 2011.

Balleison, Edward J. *Navigating Failure: Bankruptcy and Commercial Society in Antebellum America*. Chapel Hill: University of North Carolina Press, 2001.

BIBLIOGRAPHY / 321

Baptist, Edward E. *The Half Has Never Been Told: Slavery and the Making of American Capitalism*. New York: Basic Books, 2014.

Barney, William L. *The Road to Secession: A New Perspective on the Old South*. New York: Praeger, 1972.

———. *The Secessionist Impulse in Alabama and Mississippi in 1860*. Tuscaloosa: University of Alabama Press, 2004.

Barnwell, John. *Love of Order: South Carolina's First Secession Crisis*. Chapel Hill: University of North Carolina Press, 1982.

Barrett, John G. *Sherman's March through the Carolinas*. Chapel Hill: University of North Carolina Press, 1995.

Bartlett, Bruce R. *Wrong on Race: The Democratic Party's Buried Past*. New York: Palgrave Macmillan, 2008.

Bartlett, Irving H. *John C. Calhoun: A Biography*. New York: W. W. Norton, 1993.

Bateman, Fred, and Thomas Weiss. *Deplorable Scarcity: The Failure of Industrialization in the Slave Economy*. Chapel Hill: University of North Carolina Press, 2002.

Bauer, K. Jack. *Zachary Taylor: Soldier, Planter, Statesman of the Old Southwest*. Baton Rouge: Louisiana State University Press, 1993.

Baxter, Maurice G. *Henry Clay and the American System*. Lexington: University Press of Kentucky, 2004.

Beckert, Sven. *Empire of Cotton: A Global History*. New York: Vintage Books, 2014.

Bell, Robert K. "Reconstruction in Tuscaloosa County." Master's thesis, University of Alabama, 1933.

Bennett, James R. *Tannehill and the Growth of the Alabama Iron Industry: Including the Civil War in West Alabama*. Saline, MI: Alabama Historic Ironworks Commission, 1999.

Bennett, James R., and Karen R. Utz. *Iron and Steel: A Guide to Birmingham Area Industrial Heritage Sites*. Tuscaloosa: University of Alabama Press, 2010.

Bentley, George R. *A History of the Freedmen's Bureau*. New York: Octagon Books, 1974.

Bergeron, Arthur W. "The Confederate Defense of Mobile, 1861–1865." PhD diss., Louisiana State University, 1980.

———. *Confederate Mobile*. Jackson: University Press of Mississippi, 1991.

Bergeron, Paul H. *Andrew Johnson's Civil War and Reconstruction*. Knoxville: University of Tennessee Press, 2011.

Beringer, Richard E., Herman Hattaway, Archer Jones, and William N. Still. *The Elements of Confederate Defeat: Nationalism, War Aims, and Religion*. Athens: University of Georgia Press, 1988.

Beringer, Richard E., Herman Hattaway, Archer Jones, William N. Still Jr. *Why the South Lost the Civil War*. Athens: University of Georgia Press, 1991.

Berlin, Ira, *Many Thousands Gone: The First Two Centuries of Slavery in North America*. Cambridge, MA: Belknap Press of Harvard University Press, 1998.

———. *Slaves without Masters: The Free Negro in the Antebellum South*. New York: Pantheon Books, 1974.

Berney, Saffold. *Handbook of Alabama: A Complete Index to the State, with Map.* Spartanburg, SC: Reprint Co., 1975.

Berry, Stephen W. *House of Abraham: Lincoln and the Todds, a Family Divided by War.* Boston: Mariner Books, 2009.

Berry, Thelma Caine. "The Life of Edmund Winston Pettus." Master's thesis, Auburn University, 1944.

Bessel, Richard. *Germany 1945: From War to Peace.* London: Simon and Schuster UK, 2009.

Black, Robert C. *Railroads of the Confederacy.* Chapel Hill: University of North Carolina Press, 1998.

Blackmon, Douglas A. *Slavery by Another Name: The Re-Enslavement of Black Americans from the Civil War to World War II.* New York: Doubleday, 2008.

Blair, William A. *With Malice toward Some: Treason and Loyalty in the Civil War Era.* Chapel Hill: University of North Carolina Press, 2014.

Blakely, Phyllis R., and John N. Grant. *Eleven Exiles: Accounts of Loyalists of the American Revolution.* Toronto: Dundurn, 1982.

Blight, David W. *Race and Reunion: The Civil War in American Memory.* Cambridge, MA: Harvard University Press, 2001.

Blum, Edward J. *Reforging the White Republic: Race, Religion, and American Nationalism, 1865–1898.* Baton Rouge: Louisiana State University Press, 2005.

Bodenhorn, Howard. *State Banking in Early America: A New Economic History.* New York: Oxford Press, 2003.

Bolton, Charles C. *Poor Whites of the Antebellum South: Tenants and Laborers in Central North Carolina and Northeast Mississippi.* Durham, NC: Duke University Press, 1996.

Bond, James Edward. *No Easy Walk to Freedom: Reconstruction and the Ratification of the Fourteenth Amendment.* Westport, CT: Praeger, 1997.

Bordewich, Fergus M. *America's Great Debate: Henry Clay, Stephen A. Douglas, and the Compromise That Preserved the Union.* New York: Simon and Schuster, 2012.

Borritt, Gabor S., ed. *Jefferson Davis's Generals.* New York: Oxford University Press, 1999.

Bowen, David Warren. *Andrew Johnson and the Negro.* Knoxville: University of Tennessee Press, 1989.

Boyko, John. *Blood and Daring: Canada and the American Civil War.* Toronto: Alfred A. Knopf, 2013.

Bradley, George C., and Richard L. Dahlen. *From Conciliation to Conquest: The Sack of Athens and the Court Martial of Colonel John B. Turchin.* Tuscaloosa: University of Alabama Press, 2006.

Brands, H. W. *Andrew Jackson: His Life and Times.* New York: Anchor Books, 2005.

Brant and Fuller. *Memorial Record of Alabama: A Concise Account of the State's Political, Military, Professional and Industrial Progress, Together with the Personal Memoirs of Many of Its People.* Spartanburg, SC: Reprint Co., 1976.

Brantley, William H. *Chief Justice Stone of Alabama.* Birmingham, AL: Birmingham Publishing, 1943.

BIBLIOGRAPHY / 323

Brewer, Willis. *Alabama, Her History, Resources, War Records, and Public Men: From 1540 to 1872*. Spartanburg, SC: Reprint Co., 1975.

Bryant, James K., II. *The 36th Infantry United States Colored Troops in the Civil War: A History and Roster*. Jefferson, NC: McFarland, 2012.

Bryant, William O. *Cahaba Prison and the Sultana Disaster*. Tuscaloosa: University of Alabama Press, 2001.

Bungay, George W. *Traits of Representative Men*. New York: Fowler and Wells, 1882.

Burgess, John W. *Reconstruction and the Constitution, 1866–1876*. Whitefish, MT: Kessinger Publishing, 2007.

Burkhardt, George S. *Confederate Rage, Yankee Wrath: No Quarter in the Civil War*. Carbondale: Southern Illinois University Press, 2007.

Burlingame, Michael. *Abraham Lincoln: A Life*. Baltimore, MD: Johns Hopkins University Press, 2008.

———. *The Inner World of Abraham Lincoln*. Urbana: University of Illinois Press, 1994.

———. *Lincoln and the Civil War*. Carbondale: Southern Illinois University Press, 2011.

Burnett, Lonnie A. *The Pen Makes a Good Sword: John Forsyth of the "Mobile Register."* Tuscaloosa: University of Alabama Press, 2006.

Cabaniss, Allen. *The University of Mississippi: Its First Hundred Years*. Hattiesburg: University College Press of Mississippi, 1971.

Campbell, R. Thomas. *Hunters of the Night: Confederate Torpedo Boats in the War between the States*. Shippensburg, PA: Burd Street Press, 2001.

Carnahan, Burrus M. *Act of Justice: Lincoln's Emancipation Proclamation and the Law of War*. Lexington: University Press of Kentucky, 2007.

Carroll, Joseph Cephas. *Slave Insurrections in the United States, 1800–1865*. Mineola, NY: Dover Publications, 2004.

Carter, Dan T. *When the War Was Over: The Failure of Self-Reconstruction in the South, 1865–1867*. Baton Rouge: Louisiana State University Press, 1985.

Carter, Davis Blake. *The Story Uncle Minyard Told: A Family's 200 Year Migration across the South*. Spartanburg, SC: Reprint Co., 1994.

Castel, Albert. *Decision in the West: The Atlanta Campaign of 1864*. Lawrence: University Press of Kansas, 1992.

Cauthen, Charles Edward. *South Carolina Goes to War, 1860–1865*. Columbia: University of South Carolina Press, 2005.

Chesebrough, David B. *Clergy Dissent in the Old South, 1830–1865*. Carbondale: Southern Illinois University Press, 1996.

———. *No Sorrow Like Our Sorrow: Northern Protestant Ministers and the Assassination of Lincoln*. Kent, OH: Kent State University Press, 1994.

Chodes, John J. *Jabez L. M. Curry: Confederate Educator, Trojan Horse*. New York: Algora Publishing, 2005.

Chopra, Ruma. *Unnatural Rebellion: Loyalists in New York City during the Revolution*. Charlottesville: University of Virginia Press, 2011.

Cimbala, Paul A., and Randall M. Miller, eds. *The Great Task Remaining before Us: Reconstruction as America's Continuing Civil War*. New York: Fordham University Press, 2010.

Cimprich, John. *Slavery's End in Tennessee, 1861–1865*. Tuscaloosa: University of Alabama Press, 2002.

Clampitt, Bradley R. *The Confederate Heartland: Military and Civilian Morale in the Western Confederacy*. Baton Rouge: Louisiana State University Press, 2011.

Clark, James Harold. "History of the North East and South West Railroad to 1872." Master's thesis, University of Alabama, 1949.

Clark, John B. *Populism in Alabama*. Auburn, AL: Auburn Print, 1927.

Clark, John Elwood. *Railroads in the Civil War: The Impact of Management on Victory and Defeat*. Baton Rouge: Louisiana State University Press, 2004.

Clay-Clopton, Virginia. *A Belle of the Fifties: Memoirs of Mrs. Clay of Alabama*. Tuscaloosa: University of Alabama Press, 1999.

Cline, Wayne. *Alabama Railroads*. Tuscaloosa: University of Alabama Press, 1997.

Clinton, Mathew William. *Matt Clinton's Scrapbook*. Northport, AL: Portals, 1979.

Cohen, William. *At Freedom's Edge: Black Mobility and the Southern White Quest for Racial Control, 1861–1915*. Baton Rouge: Louisiana State University Press, 1991.

Cole, Arthur Charles. *The Whig Party in the South*. Glouchester, MA: P. Smith, 1962.

Collins, Donald E. *The Death and Resurrection of Jefferson Davis*. Lanham, MD: Rowman and Littlefield Publishers, 2005.

Connor, Henry Groves. *John Archibald Campbell*. Clark, NJ: Lawbook Exchange, 2004.

Conrad, Alfred H., and John R. Meyer. *The Economics of Slavery and Other Studies in Econometric History*. Chicago: Aldine Publishing, 1964.

Conroy, James B. *Our One Common Country: Abraham Lincoln and the Hampton Roads Peace Conference of 1865*. Guilford, CT: Lyons Press, 2014.

Cook, Marjorie Howell. "Restoration and Innovation: Alabamians Adjust to Defeat: 1865–1867." PhD diss., University of Alabama, 1968.

Cook, Robert J. *Civil War Senator: William Pitt Fessenden and the Fight to Save the Republic*. Baton Rouge: Louisiana State University Press, 2011.

Cooling, Benjamin Franklin. *To the Battles of Franklin and Nashville and Beyond: Stabilization and Reconstruction in Tennessee and Kentucky, 1864–1866*. Knoxville: University of Tennessee Press, 2011.

Cooper, William J., Jr. *Jefferson Davis: American*. New York: Vintage Books, 2001.

———. *Jefferson Davis and the Civil War Era*. Baton Rouge: Louisiana State University Press, 2008.

———. *The South and the Politics of Slavery, 1828–1856*. Baton Rouge: Louisiana State University Press, 1978.

Corlew, Robert E. *Tennessee: A Short History*. Knoxville: University of Tennessee Press, 1981.

Cotter, Patrick R. *After Wallace: The 1986 Contest for Governor and Political Change in Alabama*. Tuscaloosa: University of Alabama Press, 2013.

Cottrell, Steve. *Civil War in Texas and New Mexico Territory*. Gretna, LA: Pelican, 1998.

Cox, Karen L. *Dixie's Daughter: The United Daughters of the Confederacy and the Preservation of Confederate Culture*. Gainesville: University Press of Florida, 2003.

Cox, LaWanda C. Fenlason and John H. Cox. *Politics, Principle, and Prejudice, 1865–1866: Dilemma of Reconstruction America*. New York: Free Press of Glencoe, 1963.

BIBLIOGRAPHY / 325

Craton, Michael. *Slavery, Abolition and Emancipation*. London: Longman, 1976.

Crofts, Thomas. *History of the Service of the Third Ohio Veteran Volunteer Cavalry in the War for the Preservation of the Union from 1861–1865*. Toledo, OH: Stoneman Press, 1910.

Current, Richard Nelson. *Lincoln's Loyalists: Union Soldiers from the Confederacy*. Boston: Northeastern University Press, 1992.

——. *Those Terrible Carpetbaggers*. Oxford University Press, 1998.

Dallas, Gregor. *1945: The War That Never Ended*. New Haven, CT: Yale University Press, 2005.

Daniel, Larry J. *Soldiering in the Army of Tennessee: A Portrait of Life in the Confederate Army*. Chapel Hill: University of North Carolina Press, 1991.

Danielson, Joseph W. *War's Desolating Scourge: The Union's Occupation of North Alabama*. Lawrence: University Press of Kansas, 2012.

Dattel, Gene. *Cotton and Race in the Making of America: The Human Cost of Economic Power*. Lanham, MD: Ivan R. Dee, 2009.

Davis, Andrew McFarland. *The Origin of the National Banking System*. Washington, DC: Government Printing Office, 1910.

Davis, Charles S. *Colin J. McRae: Confederate Financial Agent*. Tuscaloosa, AL: Confederate Publishing, 1961.

Davis, David Brion. *Inhuman Bondage: The Rise and Fall of Slavery in the New World*. Oxford: Oxford University Press, 2006.

Davis, Stephen. *Atlanta Will Fall: Sherman, Joe Johnston, and the Yankee Heavy Battalions*. Wilmington, DE: Scholarly Resources, 2001.

Davis, Susan Lawrence. *Authentic History Ku Klux Klan, 1865–1877*. New York: American Library Service, 1924.

Davis, William C., ed. *The Confederate General*. New York: National Historical Society, 1991.

——. *Look Away: A History of the Confederate States of America*. New York: Free Press, 2002.

——. *Rhett: The Turbulent Life and Times of a Fire-Eater*. Columbia: University of South Carolina Press, 2009.

Day, James Sanders. *Diamonds in the Rough: A History of Alabama's Cahaba Coal Field*. Tuscaloosa: University of Alabama Press, 2013.

Dean, Eric T., Jr. *Shook over Hell: Post-Traumatic Stress, Viet Nam, and the Civil War*. Cambridge, MA: Harvard University Press, 1997.

DeBlack, Thomas A. *With Fire and Sword: Arkansas, 1861–1874*. Fayetteville: University of Arkansas Press, 2003.

Deland, T. A., and A. Davis Smith. *North Alabama: Historical and Biographical*. Birmingham, AL: Smith and Deland, 1888.

Denman, Clarence Phillips. *The Secession Movement in Alabama*. Montgomery, AL: Alabama State Department of Archives and History, 1933.

Dennett, John Richard. *The South As It Is: 1865–1866*. Tuscaloosa: University of Alabama Press, 2010.

Dirck, Brian R. *Lincoln and the Constitution*. Carbondale: Southern Illinois University Press, 2012.

Dobak, William A. *Freedom by the Sword: The U.S. Colored Troops, 1862–1867.* Washington, DC: US Army Center of Military History, 2011.

Dodd, Donald B. "Unionism in Confederate Alabama." PhD diss., University of Georgia, 1969.

Dodd, Donald B., and Wynelle S. Dodd. *Winston: An Antebellum and Civil War History of a Hill County of North Alabama.* Jasper, AL: C. Elliot, 1972.

Donald, David Herbert. *Lincoln.* New York: Simon and Schuster, 1995.

Dorman, Lewy. *Party Politics in Alabama from 1850 through 1860.* Tuscaloosa: University of Alabama Press, 1995.

Dorris, Jonathan Truman. *Pardon and Amnesty under Lincoln and Johnson: The Restoration of the Confederates to Their Rights and Privileges, 1861–1898.* Chapel Hill: University of North Carolina Press, 1953.

Dowdey, Clifford. *Death of a Nation: The Story of Lee and His Men at Gettysburg.* New York: Knopf, 1958.

Downs, Gregory P. *After Appomattox: Military Occupation and the Ends of the War.* Cambridge, MA: Harvard University Press, 2015.

Downs, Jim. *Sick from Freedom: African-American Illness and Suffering during the Civil War and Reconstruction.* New York: Oxford University Press, 2012.

Dubay, Robert W. *John Jones Pettus, Mississippi Fire-Eater: His Life and Times, 1813–1867.* Jackson: University Press of Mississippi, 2008.

Du Bois, W. E. B. *Black Reconstruction in America: Toward a History of the Part of Which Black Folk Played in the Attempt to Reconstruct Democracy in America, 1860–1880.* New Brunswick, NJ: Transaction Publishers, 2012.

Dunnavant, Robert. *Decatur, Alabama: Yankee Foothold in Dixie, 1861–1865.* Athens, AL: Pea Ridge Press, 1995.

———. *The Railroad War: N. B. Forrest's 1864 Raid through Northern Alabama and Middle Tennessee.* Athens, AL: Pea Ridge Press, 1994.

Dupre, Daniel S. *Transforming the Cotton Frontier: Madison County, Alabama 1800–1840.* Baton Rouge: Louisiana State University Press, 1997.

Durham, David I. *A Southern Moderate in Radical Times: Henry Washington Hilliard, 1808–1892.* Baton Rouge: Louisiana State University Press, 2008.

Easby-Smith, Mildred. *William Russell Smith of Alabama, His Life and Works.* Philadelphia: Dolphin Press, 1931.

Edwards, Laura F. *A Legal History of the Civil War and Reconstruction: A Nation of Rights.* New York: Cambridge University Press, 2015.

Egerton, Douglas R. *Gabriel's Rebellion: The Virginia Slave Conspiracies of 1800 and 1802.* Chapel Hill: University of North Carolina Press, 1993.

Eicher, John H., and David J. Eicher. *Civil War Commands.* Stanford, CA: Stanford University Press, 2001.

Ellis, Barbara G. *The Moving Appeal: Mr. McClanaham, Mrs. Dill, and The Civil War's Great Newspaper Run.* Macon, GA: Mercer University Press, 2003.

Ellis, Richard E. *The Union at Risk: Jacksonian Democracy, States' Rights and the Nullification Crisis.* New York: Oxford University Press, 1987.

BIBLIOGRAPHY / 327

Ellison, Rhonda Coleman. *Bibb County Alabama: The First Hundred Years, 1818–1918.* Tuscaloosa: University of Alabama Press, 1984.

Emberton, Carole. *Beyond Redemption: Race, Violence, and the American South after the Civil War.* Chicago: University of Chicago Press, 2013.

English, Bertis. "Civil Wars and Civil Beings: Violence, Religion, Race, Politics, Education, Culture and Agrarianism in Perry County, Alabama, 1860–1875." PhD diss., Auburn University, 2006.

English, Bethe Anne. *A Common Thread: Labor, Politics and Capital Mobility in the Textile Industry.* Athens: University of Georgia Press, 2006.

Escott, Paul D. *The Confederacy: The Slaveholders Failed Venture.* Santa Barbara, CA: Praeger, 2010.

———. *Many Excellent People: Power and Privilege in North Carolina, 1850–1900.* Chapel Hill: University of North Carolina Press, 1985.

———. *Military Necessity: Civil-Military Relations in the Confederacy.* Westport, CT: Praeger Security International, 2006.

———. *"What Shall We Do with the Negro?": Lincoln, White Racism, and Civil War America.* Charlottesville: University of Virginia Press, 2009.

Evans, Clement A., ed. *Confederate Military History: A Library of Confederate States History.* Atlanta: Confederate Publishing, 1899.

Evans, Curtis J. *The Conquest of Labor: Daniel Pratt and Southern Industrialization.* Baton Rouge: Louisiana State University Press, 2001.

Feis, William B. *Grant's Secret Service: The Intelligence War from Belmont to Appomattox.* Lincoln: University of Nebraska Press, 2004.

Feldman, Glenn. *The Irony of the Solid South: Democrats, Republicans and Race, 1865–1944.* Tuscaloosa: University of Alabama Press, 2013.

Fermer, Douglas. *James Gordon Bennett and the "New York Herald": A Study of Editorial Opinion in the Civil War Era 1854–1867.* London: Royal Historical Society, 1986.

Fidler, William Perry. *Augusta Evans Wilson, 1835–1909: A Biography.* Tuscaloosa: University of Alabama Press, 1951.

Fisher, Noel C. *War at Every Door: Partisan Politics and Guerrilla Violence in East Tennessee, 1860–1869.* Chapel Hill: University of North Carolina Press, 1997.

Fitts, Alston, III. *Selma: Queen City of the Black Belt.* Selma, AL: Clairmont Press, 1989.

Fitzgerald, Michael W. *Splendid Failure: Postwar Reconstruction in the American South.* Chicago: Ivan R. Dee, 2007.

———. *The Union League Movement in the Deep South: Politics and Agricultural Change during Reconstruction.* Baton Rouge: Louisiana State University Press, 1989.

———. *Urban Emancipation: Popular Politics in Reconstruction Mobile, 1860–1890.* Baton Rouge: Louisiana State University Press, 2002.

Fleming, Thomas J. *A Disease in the Public Mind: A New Understanding of Why We Fought the Civil War.* New York: Da Capo Press, 2013.

Fleming, Walter Lynwood. *Civil War and Reconstruction in Alabama.* Spartanburg, SC: Reprint Co., 1978.

Flynt, Wayne. *Alabama in the Twentieth Century*. Tuscaloosa: University of Alabama Press, 2004.

Foner, Eric. *The Fiery Trial: Abraham Lincoln and American Slavery*. New York: W. W. Norton, 2010.

—— *Reconstruction: America's Unfinished Revolution, 1863–1877*. New York: Perennial Classics, 2002.

Foner, Philip S. *A History of Cuba and Its Relations with the United States, 1845–1895. 2 vols*. New York: International Publishers, 1963.

Forbes, Robert Pierce. *The Missouri Compromise and Its Aftermath: Slavery and the Meaning of America*. Chapel Hill: University of North Carolina Press, 2007.

Ford, Lacy K. *Origins of Southern Radicalism: The South Carolina Upcountry, 1800–1860*. New York: Oxford University Press, 1988.

Foreman, Grant. *Indian Removal: The Emigration of the Five Civilized Tribes of Indians*. Norman: University of Oklahoma Press, 1932.

Franklin, John Hope. *Reconstruction after the Civil War*. Chicago: University of Chicago Press, 1994.

Franklin, John Hope, and Loren Schwenginger. *Runaway Slaves: Rebels on the Plantation*. New York: Oxford University Press, 1999.

Freehling, William W. *The Road to Disunion: Secessionists at Bay 1776–1854*. New York: Oxford University Press, 1990.

——. *The South vs. the South: How Anti-Confederate Southerners Shaped the Course of the Civil War*. New York: Oxford University Press, 2001.

Frey, Jerry. *Three Quarter Cadillac: Common Sense for the Common Good*. Sandy, UT: Aardvark Global Publishing, 2008.

Friend, Jack. *West Wind, Flood Tide: The Battle of Mobile Bay*. Annapolis, MD: Naval Institute Press, 2004.

Fry, Joseph A. *John Tyler Morgan and the Search for Southern Autonomy*. Knoxville: University of Tennessee Press, 1992.

Fuller, A. James. *Chaplain to the Confederacy: Basil Manly and Baptist Life in the Old South*. Baton Rouge: Louisiana State University Press, 2000.

Gallagher, Gary W. *The Confederate War*. Cambridge, MA: Harvard University Press, 1997.

Gallagher, Gary W., and Alan T. Nolan, eds. *The Myth of the Lost Cause and Civil War History*. Bloomington: Indiana University Press, 2001.

Gambill, Edward L. *Conservative Ordeal: Northern Democrats and Reconstruction, 1865–1868*. Ames: Iowa State University Press, 1981.

Garrett, Jill K. *A History of Florence, Alabama*. Columbia, TN: J. K. Garrett, 1968.

Garrett, William. *Reminiscences of Public Men in Alabama*. Atlanta: Plantation Publishing Company Press, 1872.

Gates, Henry Louis, ed. *Lincoln on Race and Slavery*. Princeton, NJ: Princeton University Press, 2009.

Geggus, David P. *The Impact of the Haitian Revolution in the Atlantic World*. Columbia: University of South Carolina Press, 2001.

BIBLIOGRAPHY / 329

Gellman, David Nathaniel. *Emancipating New York: The Politics of Slavery and Freedom, 1777–1827*. Baton Rouge: Louisiana State University Press, 2006.

Gillette, William. *Retreat from Reconstruction, 1869–1879*. Baton Rouge: Louisiana State University Press, 1979.

———. *The Right to Vote: Politics and Passage of the Fifteenth Amendment*. Baltimore, MD: Johns Hopkins University Press, 1965.

Gladstone, William Ewart. *J. L. M. Curry*. Richmond: B. V. Johnson, 1891.

Glatthaar, Joseph T. *The March to the Sea and Beyond: Sherman's Troops in the Savannah and Carolinas Campaigns*. Baton Rouge: Louisiana State University Press, 1985.

Glisson, Susan M., ed. *The Human Tradition in the Civil Rights Movement*. Lanham, MD: Rowan and Littlefield Publishers, 2006.

Goethe, Johann Wolfgang von. *Goethe's Travels in Italy*. London: George Bell and Sons, 1885, 408.

Going, Allen Johnston. *Bourbon Democracy in Alabama*. Tuscaloosa: University of Alabama Press, 1992.

Going, Charles Buxton. *David Wilmot, Free-Soiler: A Biography of the Great Advocate of the Wilmot Proviso*. Gloucester, MA: P. Smith, 1966.

Goodrich, Thomas. *The Darkest Dawn: Lincoln, Booth, and the Great American Tragedy*. Bloomington: Indiana University Press, 2005.

Goodrich, Thomas, and Debra Goodrich Bisel. *The Day Dixie Died: Southern Occupation, 1865–1866*. Mechanicsburg, PA: Stackpole Books, 2001.

Goodwin, Doris Kearns. *Team of Rivals: The Political Genius of Abraham Lincoln*. New York: Simon and Schuster, 2005.

Gordon-Reed, Annette. *Andrew Johnson*. New York: Henry Holt, 2011.

Gott, Kendall D. *Where the South Lost the War: An Analysis of the Fort Henry–Fort Donelson Campaign, February 1862*. Mechanicsburg, PA: Stackpole Books, 2003.

Gould, Lewis L. *Alexander Watkins Terrell: Civil War Soldier, Texas Lawmaker, American Diplomat*. Austin: University of Texas Press, 2004.

Grable, Theodore Eli. "Financial Policy of Hugh McCulloch." Master's thesis, Indiana University, 1910.

Grant, Susan-Mary, and Peter J. Parish, eds. *Legacy of Disunion: The Enduring Significance of the American Civil War*. Baton Rouge: Louisiana State University Press, 2003.

Greenberg, Amy S. *A Wicked War: Polk, Clay, Lincoln, and the 1846 U.S. Invasion of Mexico*. New York: Vintage Books, 2012.

Greer, Charles David. *Why Texans Fought in the Civil War*. College Station: Texas A&M University Press, 2013.

Griffin, Ronald G. *The 11th Alabama Volunteer Regiment in the Civil War*. Jefferson, NC: McFarland, 2012.

Griffith, Lucille. *Alabama: A Documentary History to 1900*. Tuscaloosa: University of Alabama Press, 1968.

Grimsley, Mark. *The Hard Hand of War: Union Military Policy toward Southern Civilians (1861–1865)*. Cambridge: Cambridge University Press, 1995.

Grofman, Bernard, ed. *Legacies of the 1964 Civil Rights Act*. Charlottesville: University of Virginia Press, 2000.

Grofman, Bernard, Lisa Handley, and Richard G. Niemi. *Minority Representation and the Quest for Voting Equality*. New York: Cambridge University Press, 1992.

Groom, Winston. *Vicksburg, 1863*. New York: Alfred A. Knopf, 2009.

Grossman, Lawrence. *The Democratic Party and the Negro: Northern and National Politics 1868–1892*. Urbana: University of Illinois Press, 1976.

Guelzo, Allen C. *Fateful Lightning: A New History of the Civil War and Reconstruction*. New York: Oxford University Press, 2012.

Hacker, Louis M. *The Triumph of American Capitalism: The Development of Forces in American History to the End of the Nineteenth Century*. New York: McGraw-Hill, 1965.

Hackney, Sheldon. *Magnolias without Moonlight: The American South from Regional Confederacy to National Integration*. New Brunswick, NJ: Transaction Publishers, 2005.

Hall, Clifton R. *Andrew Johnson: Military Governor of Tennessee*. Princeton, NJ: Princeton University Press, 1916.

Hallum, John. *Biographical and Pictorial History of Arkansas*. Albany, NY: Weed, Parsons, 1887.

Halperin, Rick. "Leroy Pope Walker and the Problems of the Confederate War Department, 1861." PhD diss., Auburn University, 1978.

Hammond, John Craig. *Slavery, Freedom, and Expansion in the Early American West*. Charlottesville: University of Virginia Press, 2007.

Hanna, Alfred Jackson, and Kathryn Abbey Hanna. *Napoleon III and Mexico: American Triumph over Monarchy*. Chapel Hill: University of North Carolina Press, 1971.

Hardcastle, Michael Ronald. *The Roots of the Hardcastles: "An old Yorkshire Family."* Self-Published, 2009.

Hardin, David. *After the War: The Lives and Images of Major Civil War Figures after the Shooting Stopped*. Lanham, MD: Rowman and Littlefield Publishing Group, 2010.

Harncourt, Paul. *The Planter's Railway: Excitement and Civil War Years*. Arab, AL: Heritage, 1995.

Harrell, Carolyn L. *When the Bell Tolls for Lincoln: Southern Reaction to the Assassination*. Macon, GA: Mercer University Press, 1997.

Harris, William C. *Leroy Pope Walker: Confederate Secretary of War*. Tuscaloosa: Confederate Publishing, 1962.

———. *Lincoln's Last Months*. Cambridge, MA: Belknap Press, 2004.

———. *With Charity for All: Lincoln and the Restoration of the Union*. Lexington: University of Kentucky Press, 1997.

Hart, John Mason. *Empire and Revolution: The Americans in Mexico since the Civil War*. Berkeley: University of California Press, 2002.

Hartnett, Stephen John. *Democratic Dissent and the Cultural Fictions of Antebellum America*. Urbana: University of Illinois Press, 2002.

Hattaway, Herman, and Richard Beringer. *Jefferson Davis, Confederate President*. Lawrence: University of Kansas Press, 2002.

Haulman, Clyde A. *Virginia and the Panic of 1819: The First Great Depression and the Commonwealth*. London: Routledge, 2008.

BIBLIOGRAPHY / 331

Haynes, Robert V. *The Mississippi Territory and the Southwest Frontier 1795–1817*. Lexington: University Press of Kentucky, 2010.

Hearn, Chester G. *The Impeachment of Andrew Johnson*. Jefferson, NC: McFarland, 2000.

———. *Lincoln, the Cabinet, and the Generals*. Baton Rouge: Louisiana State University Press, 2010.

———. *Mobile Bay and the Mobile Campaign: The Last Great Battles of the Civil War*. Jefferson, NC: McFarland, 1993.

———. *When the Devil Came down to Dixie: Ben Butler in New Orleans*. Baton Rouge: Louisiana State University Press, 1997.

Henneman, John Bell, ed. *The South in the Building of the Nation: Political History of the Southern States*. Gretna, LA: Pelican Publishing, 2002.

Herr, Kincaid A. *The Louisville and Nashville Railroad, 1850–1963*. Lexington: University Press of Kentucky, 2000.

Hess, Earl J. *The Civil War in the West: Victory and Defeat from the Appalachians to the Mississippi*. Chapel Hill: University of North Carolina Press, 2012.

Hesseltine, William Best. *Civil War Prisons: A Study in War Psychology*. Columbus: Ohio State University Press, 1930.

———. *Three against Lincoln: Murat Halstead Reports the Caucuses of 1860*. Baton Rouge: Louisiana State University Press, 1960.

Hettle, Wallace. *The Peculiar Democracy: Southern Democrats in Peace and Civil War*. Athens: University of Georgia Press, 2001.

Heyman, Max L. Jr. *Prudent Soldier: A Biography of Major General E. R. S. Canby 1817–1873*. Glendale, CA: Arthur H. Clark, 1959.

Heyse, Amy L. *Teachers of the Lost Cause: The United Daughters of the Confederacy and the Rhetoric of Their Catechisms*. College Park: University of Maryland, 2006.

Hodes, Martha. *Mourning Lincoln*. New Haven, CT: Yale University Press, 2015.

Holt, Michael K. *The Rise and Fall of the American Whig Party: Jacksonian Politics and the Outset of the Civil War*. New York: Oxford University Press, 1999.

Holzer, Harold, Edna Greene Medford, and Frank J. Williams. *The Emancipation Proclamation: Three Views*. Baton Rouge: Louisiana State University Press, 2006.

Hood, John Bell. *Advance and Retreat: Personal Experiences in the United States and Confederate States Armies*. New Orleans: Hood Orphan Memorial Fund, 1880.

Hood, Stephen M. *John Bell Hood: The Rise, Fall, and Resurrection of a Confederate General*. El Dorado Hills, CA: Savas Beatie, 2013.

Hoole, William Stanley. *Alabama Tories, The First Alabama Cavalry, U.S.A., 1862–1865*. Tuscaloosa, AL: Confederate Publishing, 1960.

———, ed. *History of the Seventh Alabama Cavalry Regiment Including Capt. Charles P. Storrs's Troop of University of Alabama Cadet Volunteers*. Tuscaloosa, AL: Confederate Publishing, 1984.

———. *History of Shockley's Alabama Escort Company*. Tuscaloosa, AL: Confederate Publishing, 1983.

Hoole, William Stanley, and Elizabeth Hoole McArthur. *The Yankee Invasion of West Alabama, March–April, 1865*. Tuscaloosa, AL: Confederate Publishing, 1985.

Horwitz, Tony. *Midnight Rising: John Brown and the Raid That Sparked the Civil War.* New York: Henry Holt, 2011.

Howard, Gene L. *Death at Cross Plains: An Alabama Reconstruction Tragedy.* Tuscaloosa: University of Alabama Press, 1984.

Hubbs, G. Ward. *Guarding Greensboro: A Confederate Company in the Making of a Southern Community.* Athens: University of Georgia Press, 2003.

———. *Searching for Freedom after the Civil War: Klansman, Carpetbagger, Scalawag, and Freedman.* Tuscaloosa: University of Alabama Press, 2015.

———. *Tuscaloosa: Portrait of An Alabama County: An Illustrated History.* Northridge, CA: Windsor Publications, 1987.

———. *Voices from Company D: Diaries by the Greensboro Guards, Fifth Alabama Infantry Regiment, Army of Northern Virginia.* Athens: University of Georgia Press, 2003.

Huffman, Alan. *Sultana: Surviving Civil War, Prison, and the Worst Maritime Disaster in American History.* New York: Harper, 2009.

Hummel, Jeffrey Rogers. *Emancipating Slaves, Enslaving Free Men: A History of the American Civil War.* Chicago: Open Court, 1996.

Hunt, Alfred N. *Haiti's Influence on Antebellum America.* Baton Rouge: Louisiana State University Press, 1988.

Hunt, Jeffrey W. *The Last Battle of the Civil War: Palmetto Ranch.* Austin: University of Texas Press, 2002.

Hurst, Jack. *Nathan Bedford Forrest: A Biography.* New York: Random House, 1994.

Huston, James L. *Calculating the Value of the Union: Slavery, Property Rights, and the Economic Origins of the Civil War.* Chapel Hill: University of North Carolina Press, 2003.

Hyman, Herold Melvin. *The Era of the Oath: Northern Loyalty Tests during the Civil War and Reconstruction.* Philadelphia: University of Pennsylvania Press, 1954.

Iowa Adjutant General's Office. *Roster and Record of Iowa Soldiers In Miscellaneous Organizations of the Mexican War, Indian Campaigns, War of the Rebellion, and the Spanish-American and Philippine Wars: Together With Historical Sketches of Volunteer Organizations, 1861–1866.* Des Moines, IA: E. H. English, State Printer, E. D. Chassell, State Binder, 1910.

Jack, Theodore Henley. "Sectionalism and Party Politics in Alabama 1819–1842." PhD diss., University of Chicago, 1919.

Jackson, Hermoine Dannelly. "The Life and Times of Robert Jemison, Jr., during the Civil War and Reconstruction." Master's thesis, University of Alabama, 1942.

Jackson, Walter M. *The Story of Selma.* Birmingham, AL: Birmingham Print, 1954.

James, Joseph Bliss. *The Ratification of the Fourteenth Amendment.* Macon, GA: Mercer University Press, 1984.

Jasanoff, Maya. *Liberty's Exiles: American Loyalists in the Revolutionary World.* New York: Random House, 2011.

Jenkins, Jeffery A., and Charles Haines Stewart. *Fighting for the Speakership: The House and the Rise of Party Government.* Princeton, NJ: Princeton University Press, 2012.

John, Reinhard O. *The Liberty Party, 1840–1848: Antislavery Third-Party Politics in the United States.* Baton Rouge: Louisiana State University Press, 2009.

Johns, George Sibley. *Philip Henson, the Southern Union Spy.* St. Louis, MO: Nixon-Jones Print, 1887.

Johnson, David. *Decided on the Battlefield: Grant, Sherman, Lincoln, and the Election of 1864.* Amherst, NY: Prometheus Books, 2012.

Johnston, Ernest Barnwell, Jr. "Selma, Alabama, as a Center of Confederate War Production, 1860–1865." Bachelor's thesis, Harvard College, 1952.

Johnston, Rev. Milus E. *The Sword of "Bushwacker" Johnston.* Huntsville, AL: Flint River Press, 1992.

Jones, Anthony James. *America and Guerrilla Warfare.* Lexington: University Press of Kentucky, 2000.

Jones, Howard. *Blue and Gray Diplomacy: A History of Union and Confederate Foreign Relations.* Chapel Hill: University of North Carolina Press, 2010.

———. *Crucible of Power: A History of American Foreign Relations to 1913.* Lanham, MD: Rowman and Littlefield Publishers, 2009.

Jones, James P. *Yankee Blitzkrieg: Wilson's Raid through Alabama and Georgia.* Lexington: University Press of Kentucky, 2000.

Jones, James S. *Life of Andrew Johnson, Seventeenth President of the United States.* New York: AMS Press, 1975.

Jordan, Winthrop. *White over Black: American Attitudes toward the Negro, 1550–1812.* Chapel Hill: University of North Carolina Press, 1968.

Kaczorowski, Robert J. *The Politics of Judicial Interpretation: The Federal Courts, Department of Justice and Civil Rights, 1866–1876.* New York: Fordham University Press, 2005.

Kammen, Michael. *Mystic Chords of Memory: The Transformation of Tradition in American Culture.* New York: Knopf, 1991.

Kane, Harnett T. *Spies for the Blue and Gray.* Garden City, NY: Hanover House, 1954.

Kaplan, Edward. *The Bank of the United States and the American Economy.* Westport, CT: Greenwood Press, 1999.

Kauffman, Michael W. *American Brutus: John Wilkes Booth and the Lincoln Conspiracies.* New York: Random House, 2004.

Keehn, David C. *Knights of the Golden Circle: Secret Empire, Southern Secession, Civil War.* Baton Rouge: Louisiana State University Press, 2013.

Keenan, Jerry. *Wilson's Cavalry Corps: Union Campaigns in the Western Theatre, October 1864 through Spring 1865.* Jefferson, NC: McFarland, 1998.

Keneally, Thomas. *American Scoundrel: The Life of the Notorious Civil War General Dan Sickles.* New York: Nan A. Talese/Doubleday, 2002.

Kerby, Robert L. *Kirby Smith's Confederacy: The Trans-Mississippi South, 1863–1865.* New York: Columbia University Press, 1972.

Kinchen, Oscar A. *Confederate Operations in Canada and the North.* North Quincy, MA: Christopher Publishing House, 1970.

Kirkland, Edward C. *Peacemakers of 1864.* New York: MacMillan Company, 1927.

Klingaman, William K. *Abraham Lincoln and the Road to Emancipation 1861–1865.* New York: Viking, 2001.

Klingberg, Frank W. *The Southern Claims Commission*. Berkeley: University of California Press, 1955.

Kohl, Lawrence Frederick. *The Politics of Individualism: Parties and the American Character in the Jacksonian Era*. New York: Oxford University Press, 1989.

Kolchin, Peter. *First Freedom: The Responses of Alabama's Blacks to Emancipation and Reconstruction*. Westport, CT: Greenwood Press, 1972.

Kvach, John F. *DeBow's Review: The Antebellum Vision of the New South*. Lexington: University Press of Kentucky, 2013.

Langum, David J., and Howard P. Walthall. *From Maverick to Mainstream: Cumberland School of Law, 1847–1997*. Athens: University of Georgia Press, 1997.

Larson, Kate Clifford. *The Assassin's Accomplice: Mary Surratt and the Plot to Kill Abraham Lincoln*. New York: Basic Books, 2008.

Lauderdale, Clara Mary. "Population of Alabama between 1860 and 1870." Master's thesis, University of Wisconsin, 1912.

Leckie, William H., and Shirley A. Leckie. *Unlikely Warriors: General Benjamin H. Grierson and His Family*. Norman: University of Oklahoma Press, 1984.

Lee, Susanna Michele. *Claiming the Union: Citizenship in the Post–Civil War South*. New York: Cambridge University Press, 2014.

Leftwich, Nina. *Two Hundred Years at Muscle Shoals*. Tuscumbia, AL: Viewpoint Press, 1935.

Leiker, James N. *Racial Borders: Black Soldiers along the Rio Grande*. College Station: Texas A&M University Press, 2002.

Leonard, Elizabeth D. *Lincoln's Avengers: Justice, Revenge, and Reunion after the Civil War*. New York: W. W. Norton, 2004.

Lepa, Jack H. *Breaking the Confederacy: The Georgia and Tennessee Campaigns of 1864*. Jefferson, NC: McFarland, 2005.

Lepler, Jessica M. *The Many Panics of 1837: People, Politics, and the Creation of a Transatlantic Financial Crisis*. New York: Cambridge University Press, 2013.

Levine, Bruce. *Confederate Emancipation: Southern Plans to Free and Arm Slaves during the Civil War*. New York: Oxford University Press, 2006.

———. *The Fall of the House of Dixie: The Civil War and the Social Revolution That Transformed the South*. New York: Random House, 2013.

Lewis, Herbert James. *Clearing the Thickets: A History of Antebellum Alabama*. New Orleans: Quid Pro Books, 2013.

———. *Lost Capitals of Alabama*. Charleston, SC: History Press, 2014.

Lewis, W. David. *Sloss Furnaces and the Rise of the Birmingham District: An Industrial Epic*. Tuscaloosa: University of Alabama Press, 1994.

Livermore, Thomas Leonard. *Numbers and Losses in the Civil War in America, 1861–1865*. Bloomington: Indiana University Press, 1957.

Longacre, Edward G. *Army of Amateurs: General Benjamin F. Butler and the Army of the James, 1863–1865*. Mechanicsburg, PA: Stackpole Books, 1997.

———. *A Soldier to the Last: Maj. Gen. Joseph Wheeler in Blue and Gray*. Washington, DC: Potomac Books, 2007.

BIBLIOGRAPHY / 335

Loving, Waldon Spicer. *Coming Like Hell: The Story of the 12th Tennessee Cavalry, Richardson's Brigade, Forrest's Cavalry Corps, Confederate States Army, 1862–1865.* San Jose, CA: Writers Club Press, 2002.

Lubetkin, M. John, *Jay Cooke's Gamble: The Northern Pacific Railroad, the Sioux, and the Panic of 1873.* Norman: University of Oklahoma Press, 2014.

Lupold, John S., and Thomas L. French Jr. *Bridging Deep South Rivers: The Life and Legend of Horace King.* Athens: University of Georgia Press, 2004.

Magee, James J. *Freedom of Expression.* Westport, CT: Greenwood Press, 2002.

Magness, Phillip W., and Sebastian Page. *Colonization after Emancipation: Lincoln and the Movement for Black Resettlement.* Columbia: University of Missouri Press, 2011.

Mahin, Dean B. *One War at a Time: The International Dimensions of the American Civil War.* Washington, DC: Brassey's, 1999.

Mahoney, M. T., and Marjorie Locke Mahoney. *Mexico and the Confederacy, 1860–1867.* San Francisco, CA: Austin and Winfield, 1998.

Martin, Bessie. *Desertion of Alabama Troops from the Confederate Army: A Study in Sectionalism.* New York: Columbia University Press, 1932.

——. *A Rich Man's War, A Poor Man's Fight: Desertion of Alabama Troops from the Confederate Army.* Tuscaloosa: University of Alabama Press, 2003.

Martin, Samuel J. *"Kill-Cavalry": The Life of Union General Hugh Judson Kilpatrick.* Mechanicsburg, PA: Stackpole Books, 2000.

Marvel, William. *Andersonville: The Last Depot.* Chapel Hill: University of North Carolina Press, 1994.

Maslowski, Peter. *Treason Must Be Made Odious, Military Occupation and Wartime Reconstruction in Nashville, Tennessee, 1862–65.* Millwood, NY: KTO Press, 1978.

Massey, Mary Elizabeth. *Refugee Life in the Confederacy.* Baton Rouge: Louisiana State University Press, 2001.

Masur, Louis P. *Lincoln's Hundred Days: The Emancipation Proclamation and the War for the Union.* Cambridge, MA: Harvard University Press, 2012.

May, Gary. *Bending toward Justice: The Voting Rights Act and the Transformation of American Democracy.* Washington, DC: Basic Books, 2013.

Mayer, Henry. *All on Fire: William Lloyd Garrison and the Abolition of Slavery.* New York: W. W. Norton, 1998.

McClintock, Russell. *Lincoln and the Decision for War: The Northern Response to Secession.* Chapel Hill: University of North Carolina Press, 2008.

McCrary, Peyton. *Abraham Lincoln and Reconstruction: The Louisiana Experiment.* Princeton, NJ: Princeton University Press, 1978.

McDonald, William Lindsey. *Civil War Tales of the Tennessee Valley.* Killen, AL: Heart of Dixie Publishing, 2003.

——. *A Walk through the Past—People and Places of Florence and Lauderdale County, Alabama.* Killen, AL: Heart of Dixie Publishing, 2003.

McDonough, James Lee, and James Pickett Jones. *War So Terrible: Sherman and Atlanta.* New York: Norton, 1987.

McFeely, William S. *Grant: A Biography.* New York: W. W. Norton, 1981.

McGee, Benjamin F. *History of the 72d Indiana Volunteer Infantry of the Mounted Lightning Brigade*. LaFayette, IN: S. Vater Printers, 1882.

McGrane, Reginald Charles. *The Panic of 1837: Some Financial Problems of the Jacksonian Era*. Chicago: University of Chicago Press, 1965.

McKitrick, Eric L. *Andrew Johnson and Reconstruction*. New York: Oxford University Press, 1988.

McKiven, Henry M. *Iron and Steel: Class, Race, and Community in Birmingham, Alabama, 1875–1920*. Chapel Hill: University of North Carolina Press, 1995.

McKivigan, John R. *Forgotten Firebrand: James Redpath and the Making of Nineteenth-Century America*. Ithaca, NY: Cornell University Press, 2008.

McLaughlin, James Fairfax. *The American Cyclops: The Hero of New Orleans, and Spoiler of Silver Spoons*. Baltimore, MD: Kelly and Piet, 1868.

McMillan, Malcolm Cook. *The Alabama Confederate Reader*. Tuscaloosa: University of Alabama Press, 1963.

———. *Constitutional Development in Alabama, 1798–1901: A Study in Politics, the Negro, and Sectionalism*. Chapel Hill: University of North Carolina Press, 1955.

———. *The Disintegration of a Confederate State: Three Governors and Alabama's Wartime Home Front, 1861–1865*. Macon, GA: Mercer University Press, 1986.

———. *The Land Called Alabama*. Austin, TX: Steck-Vaughn, 1968.

McMurry, Richard M. *Atlanta 1864: Last Chance for the Confederacy*. Lincoln: University of Nebraska Press, 2000.

McNeely, Patricia G., Debra Redding van Tuyll, and Henry H. Schulte. *Knights of the Quill: Confederate Correspondents and Their Civil War Reporting*. West Lafayette, IN: Purdue University Press, 2010.

McPherson, Edward. *The Political History of the United States of America during the Great Rebellion*. Washington, DC: Philip and Solomons, 1865.

McPherson, James M. *Abraham Lincoln*. New York: Oxford University Press, 2009.

———. *Battle Cry of Freedom: The Civil War Era*. New York: Oxford University Press, 1988.

———. *The Struggle for Equality: Abolitionists and the Negro in the Civil War and Reconstruction*. Princeton, NJ: Princeton University Press, 1964.

———. *War on the Waters: The Union and Confederate Navies, 1861–1865*. Chapel Hill: University of North Carolina Press, 2012.

McQueen, Clyde. *The Black Army Officer*. Bloomington, IN: Authorhouse, 2009.

McWhiney, Grady. *Braxton Bragg and Confederate Defeat*. New York: Columbia University Press, 1969.

Means, Howard B. *The Avenger Takes His Place: Andrew Johnson and the 45 Days That Changed the Nation*. Orlando, FL: Harcourt, 2006.

Memorial Record of Alabama. Spartanburg, SC: Reprint Co., 1976.

Menaster, Kimberly. "Political Violence in the American South: 1882–1890." Master's thesis, Massachusetts Institute of Technology, 2009.

Merry, Robert W. *A Country of Vast Designs: James K. Polk, the Mexican War, and the Conquest of the American Continent*. New York: Simon and Schuster, 2009.

BIBLIOGRAPHY / 337

Mieczkowski, Yanek. *The Routledge Historical Atlas of Presidential Elections*. New York: Routledge, 2001.

Miller, Edward A., Jr. *The Black Civil War Soldiers of Illinois: The Story of the Twenty-Ninth U.S. Colored Infantry*. Columbia: University of South Carolina Press, 1998.

Miller, Randall Martin. *The Cotton Mill Movement in Antebellum Alabama*. New York: Arno Press, 1978.

Miller, Rex. *Croxton's Raid*. Fort Collins, CO: Old Army Press, 1979.

Miller, William Lee. *Arguing about Slavery: The Great Battle in the United States Congress*. New York: Vintage, 1996.

———. *Lincoln's Virtues: An Ethical Biography*. New York: Vintage Books, 2003.

Milton, George Fort. *The Age of Hate: Andrew Johnson and the Radicals*. Hamden, CT: Archon Books, 1965.

Misulia, Charles A. *Columbus, Georgia, 1865: The Last True Battle of the Civil War*. Tuscaloosa: University of Alabama Press, 2010.

Mize, Joel Sanford. *Unionists of the Warrior Mountains of Alabama*. Lakewood, CO: Dixie Historical Research and Education Publication, 2004.

Moneyhon, Carl H. *Republicanism in Reconstruction Texas*. College Station: Texas A&M University Press, 1980.

———. *Texas after the Civil War: The Struggle of Reconstruction*. College Station: Texas A&M University Press, 2004.

Moore, Albert Burton. *Conscription and Conflict in the Confederacy*. New York: MacMillan, 1924.

———. *History of Alabama*. Tuscaloosa: Alabama Book Store, 1951.

Morales, William R. *The 41st Alabama Infantry Regiment, Confederate States of America: A Narrative of the Civil War Regiment from West Central Alabama*. Wyandotte, OK: Gregath Publishing, 2001.

Moreau, Joseph. *Schoolbook Nation: Conflicts over American Textbooks from the Civil War to the Present*. Ann Arbor: University of Michigan Press 2003.

Morgan, George. *The True Patrick Henry*. Philadelphia: J. B. Lippincott, 1907.

Mushkat, Jerome. *Fernando Wood: A Political Biography*. Kent, OH: Kent State University Press, 1990.

Musicant, Ivan. *Divided Waters: The Naval History of the Civil War*. New York: Castle Books, 2000.

Neely, Mark E. *Southern Rights: Political Prisoners and the Myth of Confederate Constitutionalism*. Charlottesville: University Press of Virginia, 1999.

Nelson, Larry E. *Bullets, Ballots, and Rhetoric: Confederate Policy for the United States Presidential Contest of 1864*. Tuscaloosa: University of Alabama Press, 1980.

Nevins, Allan. *The Emergence of Lincoln*. New York: Scribner, 1950.

Novkov, Julie. *Radical Union: Law, Intimacy, and the White State in Alabama, 1865–1954*. Ann Arbor: University of Michigan Press, 2008.

Newman, Jennifer Ann. "Writing, Religion and Women's Identity in Civil War Alabama." PhD diss., Auburn University, 2009.

Nieman, Donald G., ed. *Freedom, Racism, and Reconstruction: Collected Writings of LaWanda Cox*. Athens: University of Georgia Press, 1997.

Niven, John. *John C. Calhoun and the Price of Union: A Biography*. Baton Rouge: Louisiana State University Press, 1988.

Noe, Kenneth W., ed. *The Yellowhammer War: The Civil War and Reconstruction in Alabama*. Tuscaloosa: University of Alabama Press, 2013.

Nolen, David L. "Wilson's Raid on the Coal and Iron Industry in Shelby County." Master's thesis, University of Alabama, Birmingham, 1988.

Novak, Daniel A. *The Wheel of Servitude: Black Forced Labor after Slavery*. Lexington: University Press of Kentucky, 1978.

Nuermberger, Ruth Ketring. *The Clays of Alabama: A Planter-Lawyer-Politician Family*. Tuscaloosa: University of Alabama Press, 2005.

Nunn, W. C. *Escape from Reconstruction*. Fort Worth: Texas Christian University Press, 1962.

Oakes, James. *Freedom National: The Destruction of Slavery in the United States, 1861–1865*. New York: W. W. Norton, 2013.

———. *The Radical and the Republican: Frederick Douglass, Abraham Lincoln, and the Triumph of Anti-Slavery Politics*. New York: W. W. Norton, 2007.

O'Brien, Sean Michael. *Mobile 1865: Last Stand of the Confederacy*. Westport, CT: Praeger, 2001.

———. *Mountain Partisans: Guerrilla Warfare in the Southern Appalachians, 1861–1865*. Westport, CT: Praeger, 1999.

Oldshue, Jerry C. "The Secession Movement in Tuscaloosa County, Alabama." Master's thesis, University of Alabama, 1961.

Onofrio, Jan. *Alabama Biographical Dictionary*. St. Clair Shores, MI: Somerset Publishers, 1998.

O'Reilly, Bill, and Martin Dugard. *Killing Lincoln: The Shocking Assassination That Changed America*. New York: St. Martin's Press, 2015.

Ott, Thomas O. *The Haitian Revolution, 1789–1804*. Knoxville: University of Tennessee Press, 1973.

Otte, Herman Frederick. *Industrial Opportunity in the Tennessee Valley of Northwestern Alabama*. New York: Columbia University Press, 1940.

Owen, Thomas McAdory. *History of Alabama and Dictionary of Alabama Biography*. 4 vols. Spartanburg, SC: Reprint Co., 1978.

Ownsbey, Betty J. *Alias "Paine": Lewis Thorton Powell, The Mystery Man of the Lincoln Conspiracy*. Jefferson, NC: McFarland, 1993.

Parks, Joseph H. *Joseph E. Brown of Georgia*. Baton Rouge: Louisiana State University Press, 1977.

Parrish, T. Michael. *Richard Taylor: Soldier Prince of Dixie*. Chapel Hill: University of North Carolina Press, 1992.

Patterson, Gerard A. *From Blue to Gray: The Life of Confederate General Cadmus M. Wilcox*. Mechanicsburg, PA: Stackpole, 2001.

Pearce, George F. *Pensacola during the Civil War: A Thorn in the Side of the Confederacy.* Gainesville: University Press of Florida, 2000.

Perman, Michael. *Reunion without Compromise: The South and Reconstruction 1865–1868.* New York: Cambridge University Press, 1973.

Perret, Geoffrey. *Lincoln's War: The Untold Story of America's Greatest President as Commander in Chief.* New York: Random House, 2004.

Pfanz, Donald C. *Petersburg Campaign: Abraham Lincoln at City Point, March 20–April 9, 1865.* Lynchburg, VA: H. E. Howard, 1989.

———. *Richard S. Ewell: A Soldier's Life.* Chapel Hill: University of North Carolina Press, 1998.

Phillips, Jason. *Diehard Rebels: The Confederate Culture of Invincibility.* Athens: University of Georgia Press, 2010.

Powell, William S., ed. *Dictionary of North Carolina Biography.* Vol. 5. Chapel Hill: University of North Carolina Press, 1994.

Pruitt, Paul M., Jr. *Taming Alabama: Lawyers and Reformers, 1804–1929.* Tuscaloosa: University of Alabama Press, 2010.

Quill, James Michael. *Prelude to the Radicals: The North and Reconstruction.* Washington, DC: University Press of America, 1980.

Rable, George C., *But There Was No Peace: The Role of Violence in the Politics of Reconstruction.* Athens: University of Georgia Press, 2007.

———. *Civil Wars: Women and the Crisis of Southern Nationalism.* Urbana: University of Illinois Press, 1989.

———. *The Confederate Republic: A Revolution against Politics.* Chapel Hill: University of North Carolina Press, 1994.

———. *God's Almost Chosen Peoples: A Religious History of the American Civil War.* Chapel Hill: University of North Carolina Press, 2010.

Rafuse, Ethan Sepp. *Robert E. Lee and the Fall of the Confederacy, 1863–1865.* Lanham, MD: Rowman and Littlefield Publishers, 2008.

Ragan, Mark K. *Confederate Saboteurs: Building the Hunley and Other Secret Weapons of the Civil War.* College Station: Texas A&M University Press, 2015.

Randolph County Heritage Book Committee. *The Heritage of Randolph County, Alabama.* Randolph County, AL: Heritage Publishing Consultants, 1998.

Reid, Richard M. *Freedom for Themselves: North Carolina's Black Soldiers in the Civil War Era.* Chapel Hill: University of North Carolina Press, 2008.

Rice, Charles. *Hard Times: The Civil War in Huntsville and North Alabama.* Huntsville, AL: Old Huntsville, 1995.

Rice, Jessie Pearl. *J. L. M. Curry: Southerner, Statesman and Educator.* New York: Kings Crown Press, 1949.

Richter, William L. *The Army in Texas during Reconstruction, 1865–1870.* College Station: Texas A&M University Press, 1987.

Riser, Robert Volney. "Between Scylla and Charybdis: Alabama's 1901 Constitutional Convention Assesses the Perils of Disfranchisement." Master's thesis, University of Alabama, 2000.

———. *Defying Disfranchisement: Black Voting Rights Activism in the Jim Crow South, 1890–1908.* Baton Rouge: Louisiana State University Press, 2010.

Roberts, Alasdair. *America's First Great Depression: Economic Crisis and Political Disorder after the Panic of 1837.* Ithaca, NY: Cornell University Press, 2012.

Rodrigue, John C. *Lincoln and Reconstruction.* Carbondale: Southern Illinois University Press, 2013.

Rogers, William Warren, Jr. *Black Belt Scalawag: Charles Hays and the Southern Republicans in the Era of Reconstruction.* Athens: University of Georgia Press, 1993.

———. *Confederate Home Front: Montgomery during the Civil War.* Tuscaloosa: University of Alabama Press, 1999.

Rogers, William Warren, Sr. *The One-Gallused Rebellion: Agrarianism in Alabama, 1865–1896.* Baton Rouge: Louisiana State University Press, 1970.

Rogers, William Warren, Sr., Robert David Ward, Leah Rawls Atkins, and Wayne Flynt. *Alabama: The History of a Deep South State.* Tuscaloosa: University of Alabama Press, 2010.

Rolle, Andrew R. *The Lost Cause: The Confederate Exodus to Mexico.* Norman: University of Oklahoma Press, 1962.

Rothman, Adam. *Slave Country: American Expansion and the Origins of the Deep South.* Cambridge, MA: Harvard University Press, 2005.

Rothman, Joshua D. *Flush Times and Fever Dreams: A Story of Capitalism and Slavery in the Age of Jackson.* Athens: University of Georgia Press, 2012.

Rowland, Dunbar. *Jefferson Davis: Constitutionalist.* Jackson: Printed for the Mississippi Department of Archives and History, 1923.

Rubin, Anne S. *A Shattered Nation: The Rise and Fall of the Confederacy, 1861–1868.* Chapel Hill: University of North Carolina Press, 2005.

Ruhlman, Fred F. *Captain Henry Wirz and Andersonville Prison: A Reappraisal.* Knoxville: University of Tennessee Press, 2006.

Rumore, Pat Boyd. *From Power to Service: The Story of Lawyers in Alabama.* Montgomery: Alabama State Bar, 2010.

Rutherglen, George. *Civil Rights in the Shadow of Slavery: The Constitution, Common Law, and the Civil Rights Act of 1866.* New York: Oxford University Press, 2013.

Saunders, James Edmonds. *Early Settlers of Alabama.* Westminster, MD: Heritage Books, 2009.

Saunders, Robert, Jr. *John Archibald Campbell, Southern Moderate: 1811–1889.* Tuscaloosa: University of Alabama Press, 1997.

Sawrey, Robert Dixon. *Dubious Victory: The Reconstruction Debate in Ohio.* Lexington: University Press of Kentucky, 1992.

Scaturro, Frank J. *The Supreme Court's Retreat from Reconstruction: A Distortion of Constitutional Jurisprudence.* Westport, CT: Greenwood Press, 2000.

Schermerhorn, Calvin, Michael Plunkett, and Edward Gaynor, eds. *Rambles of a Runaway from Southern Slavery: Henry Goings.* Charlottesville: University of Virginia Press, 2012.

BIBLIOGRAPHY / 341

Schlesinger, Arthur M., Jr., ed. *History of American Presidential Elections, 1789–1968.* New York: Chelsea House, 1971.

Schoen, Brian. *The Fragile Fabric of Union: Cotton, Federal Politics, and the Global Origins of the Civil War.* Baltimore, MD: Johns Hopkins University Press, 2009.

Schott, Thomas E. *Alexander H. Stephens of Georgia: A Biography.* Baton Rouge: Louisiana State University Press, 1988.

Schwab, John Christopher. *The Confederate States of America 1861–1865: A Financial and Industrial History of the South during the War.* New York: Burt Franklin, 1968.

Scott, William Forse. *The Story of a Cavalry Regiment: The Career of the Fourth Iowa Veteran Volunteers from Kansas to Georgia, 1861–1865.* New York: G. P. Putnam, 1892.

Seip, Terry L. *The South Returns to Congress: Men, Economic Measures, and Intersectional Relationships, 1868–1879.* Baton Rouge: Louisiana State University Press, 1983.

Sellers, Charles. *The Market Revolution: Jacksonian America 1815–1846.* New York: Oxford University Press, 1991.

Sellers, James Benson. *History of the University of Alabama.* Tuscaloosa: University of Alabama Press, 1953.

——. *The Prohibition Movement in Alabama, 1702–1943.* Chapel Hill: University of North Carolina Press, 1943.

——. *Slavery in Alabama.* Tuscaloosa: University of Alabama Press, 1950.

Severance, Ben H. *Portraits of Conflict: A Photographic History of Alabama in the Civil War.* Fayetteville: University of Arkansas Press, 2012.

——. *Tennessee's Radical Army: The State Guard and Its Role in Reconstruction, 1867–1869.* Knoxville: University of Tennessee Press, 2005.

Sexton, Jay. *Debtor Diplomacy: Finance and American Foreign Relations in the Civil War Era 1837–1873.* New York: Clarendon, 2005.

Shields, Johanna Nichol. *Freedom in a Slave Society: Stories from the Antebellum South.* Cambridge: Cambridge University Press, 2012.

Silver, James W. *Confederate Morale, and Church Propaganda.* Tuscaloosa: Confederate Publishing, 1957.

Simmons, Donald C., Jr. *Confederate Settlements in British Honduras.* Jefferson, NC: McFarland, 2001.

Simms, William Gilmore. *A City Laid Waste: The Capture, Sack, and Destruction of the City of Columbia.* Columbia: University of South Carolina Press, 2005.

Simpson, Brooks D. *Let Us Have Peace: Ulysses S. Grant and the Politics of War and Reconstruction, 1861–1868.* Chapel Hill: University of North Carolina Press, 1991.

Simpson, Brooks D., Leroy P. Graf, and John Muldowny, eds. *Advice after Appomattox: Letters to Andrew Johnson, 1865–1866.* Knoxville: University of Tennessee Press, 1987.

Sinha, Manisha. *Counterrevolution of Slavery: Politics and Ideology in Antebellum South Carolina.* Chapel Hill: University of North Carolina Press, 2000.

Slabaugh, Arlie R. *Confederate States Paper Money: Civil War Currency from the South.* Iola, WI: Krause Publications, 2012.

Smith and Deland. *North Alabama, Historical and Biographical*. Birmingham: Smith and Deland, 1888.

Smith, Andrew F. *Starving the South: How the North Won the Civil War*. New York: St. Martin's Press, 2011.

Smith, Charles Anthony. *The Rise and Fall of War Crimes Trials: From Charles I to Bush II*. New York: Cambridge University Press, 2012.

Smith, Derek. *In the Lion's Mouth: Hood's Tragic Retreat from Nashville, 1864*. Mechanicsburg, PA: Stackpole Books, 2011.

Smith, John David, and J. Vincent Lowery. *The Dunning School: Historians, Race, and the Meaning of Reconstruction*. Lexington: University Press of Kentucky, 2013.

Smith, Page. *A People's History of the Antebellum Years: The Nation Comes of Age*. New York: McGraw-Hill, 1981.

Stampp, Kenneth Milton. *The Peculiar Institution: Slavery in the Antebellum South*. New York: Knopf, 1956.

Stephens, Larry David. *John P. Gatewood, Confederate Bushwhacker*. Gretna, LA: Pelican Publishing, 2012.

Sterkx, H. E. *Partners in Rebellion: Alabama Women in the Civil War*. Rutherford, NJ: Farleigh Dickinson University Press, 1970.

Stewart, John Craig. *The Governors of Alabama*. Gretna, LA: Pelican, 1975.

Stoker, Donald. *The Grand Design: Strategy and the U.S. Civil War*. New York: Oxford University Press, 2010.

Storey, Margaret M. *Loyalty and Loss: Alabama's Unionists in the Civil War and Reconstruction*. Baton Rouge: Louisiana State University Press, 2004.

Stout, Harry S. *Upon the Altar of the Nation: A Moral History of the American Civil War*. New York: Penguin Books, 2007.

Striner, Richard. *Father Abraham: Lincoln's Relentless Struggle to End Slavery*. New York: Oxford University Press, 2006.

Strode, Hudson. *Jefferson Davis: Tragic Hero*. New York: Harcourt, Brace, 1964.

Studenski, Paul, and Herman Edward Krooss. *Financial History of the United States*. New York: McGraw-Hill, 1963.

Sutherland, Daniel E. *The Confederate Carpetbaggers*. Baton Rouge: Louisiana State University Press, 1988.

———. *A Savage Conflict: The Decisive Role of Guerrillas in the American Civil War*. Chapel Hill: University of North Carolina Press, 2009.

Swanson, James L. *Manhunt: The 12-Day Chase for Lincoln's Killer*. New York: HarperCollins, 2007.

Sweikart, Larry. *Banking in the American South from the Age of Jackson to Reconstruction*. Baton Rouge: Louisiana State University Press, 1987.

Swinney, Everette. *Enforcing the Fifteenth Amendment, 1870–1877*. Baton Rouge: Louisiana State University Press, 1962.

Sword, Wiley. *Embrace an Angry Wind: The Confederacy's Last Hurrah: Spring Hill, Franklin, and Nashville*. New York: Harper Collins, 1992.

BIBLIOGRAPHY / 343

Symonds, Craig L. *Joseph E. Johnston: A Civil War Biography*. New York: W. W. Norton, 1992.

Tap, Bruce. *Over Lincoln's Shoulder: The Committee on the Conduct of the War*. Lawrence: University of Kansas Press, 1998.

Tatum, Georgia Lee. *Disloyalty in the Confederacy*. Lincoln: University of Nebraska Press, 2000.

Taylor, Alan. *The Internal Enemy: Slavery and War in Virginia, 1772–1832*. New York: W. W. Norton, 2013.

Taylor, Frazine K. *Researching African American Genealogy in Alabama: A Resource Guide*. Montgomery, AL: NewSouth Books, 2008.

Taylor, John M. *William Henry Seward: Lincoln's Right Hand*. Washington, DC: Potomac Books, 1981.

Taylor, Richard. *Destruction and Reconstruction: Personal Experiences of the Late War*. Edinburgh: Blackwood and Sons, 1879.

Thomas, Emory M. *The Confederacy as a Revolutionary Experience*. Englewood Cliffs, NJ: Prentice-Hall, 1971.

Thomas, William G. *The Iron Way: Railroads, the Civil War, and the Making of Modern America*. New Haven, CT: Yale University Press, 2011.

Thornton, J. Mills. *Politics and Power in a Slave Society: Alabama, 1800–1860*. Baton Rouge: Louisiana State University Press, 1978.

Todd, Glenda McWhirter. *First Alabama Cavalry, U.S.A.: Homage to Patriotism*. Bowie, MD: Heritage Books, 1999.

Towns, Peggy Allen. *Duty Driven: The Plight of North Alabama's African Americans during the Civil War*. Bloomington, IN: AuthorHouse, 2012.

Townsend, Stephen A. *The Yankee Invasion of Texas*. College Station: Texas A&M University Press, 2006.

Trefousse, Hans L. *Andrew Johnson: A Biography*. New York: W. W. Norton, 1989.

Trelease, Allen W. *White Terror: The Ku Klux Klan Conspiracy and Southern Reconstruction*. New York: Harper and Row, 1971.

Trudeau, Noah Andre. *Out of the Storm: The End of the Civil War, April–June, 1865*. Boston: Little, Brown, 1991.

——. *Southern Storm: Sherman's March to the Sea*. New York: Harper, 2008.

Tsesis, Alexander. *The Thirteenth Amendment and American Freedom: A Legal History*. New York: New York University Press, 2004.

Tucker, Spencer. *Andrew Foote: Civil War Admiral on Western Waters*. Annapolis, MD: Naval Institute Press, 2000.

Turner, Thomas Reed. *Beware the People Weeping: Public Opinion and the Assassination of Abraham Lincoln*. Baton Rouge: Louisiana State University Press, 1982.

Unger, Irwin. *The Greenback Era: A Social and Political History of American Finance, 1865–1879*. Princeton, NJ: Princeton University Press, 1968.

Urwin, Gregory J. W. *Black Flag over Dixie: Racial Atrocities and Reprisals in the Civil War*. Carbondale: Southern Illinois University Press, 2004.

US Congress. *Biographical Directory of the American Congress, 1774–1949.* Washington, DC: US Government Printing Office, 1950.

Van Deusen, Glyndon G. *William Henry Seward.* New York: Oxford University Press, 1967.

Vandiver, Frank Everson. *Ploughshares into Swords: Josiah Gorgas and Confederate Ordinance.* Austin: University of Texas Press, 1952.

Varon, Elizabeth R. *Appomattox: Victory, Defeat, and Freedom at the End of the Civil War.* New York: Oxford University Press, 2014.

Vaughn, J. Barry. *Bishops, Bourbons, and Big Mules: A History of the Episcopal Church in Alabama.* Tuscaloosa: University of Alabama Press, 2013.

Wahlstron, Todd W. *The Southern Exodus to Mexico: Migration across the Borderlands after the American Civil War.* Lincoln: University of Nebraska Press, 2015.

Wakelyn, Jon L. *Confederates against the Confederacy: Essays on Leadership and Loyalty.* Westport, CT: Praeger, 2002.

Walker, Henry James. *Let Us Keep the Feast: The History of Christ Episcopal Church, Tuscaloosa, Alabama, 1828–1998.* Tallahassee, FL: Sentry Press, 2000.

Walther, Eric H. *The Fire-Eaters.* Baton Rouge: Louisiana State University Press, 1992.

———. *William Lowndes Yancey and the Coming of the Civil War.* Chapel Hill: University of North Carolina Press, 2006.

Walton, Hanes, Sherman C. Puckett, and Donald Richard Deskins. *The African American Electorate: A Statistical History.* Thousand Oaks, CA: CQ Press, 2012.

Walvin, James. *England, Slaves and Freedom, 1776–1838.* Jackson: University Press of Mississippi, 1986.

Wang, Xi. *Trial of Democracy: Black Suffrage and Northern Republicans, 1860–1910.* Athens: University of Georgia Press, 1997.

Ward, Andrew. *River Run Red: The Fort Pillow Massacre in the American Civil War.* New York: Viking, 2005.

Warner, Ezra J., and W. Buck Yearns. *Biographical Register of the Confederate Congress.* Baton Rouge: Louisiana State University Press, 1975.

Warren, Robert Penn. *The Legacy of the Civil War.* Lincoln: University of Nebraska Press, 1998.

Webb, Sam L., and Margaret E. Armbrester, *Alabama Governors: A Political History of the State.* Tuscaloosa: University of Alabama Press, 2001.

Weitz, Mark A. *More Damning Than Slaughter: Desertion in the Confederate Army.* Lincoln: University of Nebraska Press, 2005.

Welsh, Jack D. *Two Confederate Hospitals and Their Patients: Atlanta to Opelika.* Macon, GA: Mercer University Press, 2005.

Werlich, Robert. *"Beast" Butler: The Incredible Career of Major General Benjamin Franklin Butler.* Washington, DC: Quaker Press, 1962.

Wesley, Timothy L. *The Politics of Faith during the Civil War.* Baton Rouge: Louisiana State University Press, 2013.

BIBLIOGRAPHY / 345

West, Richard, Jr. *Lincoln's Scapegoat General: A Life of Benjamin F. Butler, 1818–1893*. Boston: Houghton Mifflin, 1965.

Whitaker, Walter C. *Richard Hooker Wilmer: Second Bishop of Alabama*. Philadelphia: G. W. Jacobs, 1907.

White, Ronald C. *Lincoln's Greatest Speech: The Second Inaugural*. New York: Simon and Schuster, 2003.

Wiggins, Sarah Woolfolk. *The Scalawag in Alabama Politics, 1865–1881*. Tuscaloosa: University of Alabama Press, 1991.

Wiggins, Sarah Woolfolk, and Ruth Smith Truss, eds. *The Journal of Sarah Haynsworth Gayle, 1827–1835: A Substitute for Social Intercourse*. Tuscaloosa: University of Alabama Press, 2013.

Wiley, Bell I. *Life of Johnny Reb: The Common Soldier of the Confederacy*. Baton Rouge: Louisiana State University Press, 2000.

Williams, Ben Ames, ed. *A Diary from Dixie by Mary Boykin Chesnut*. Cambridge, MA: Harvard University Press, 1980.

Williams, David. *Bitterly Divided: The South's Inner Civil War*. New York: New Press, 2008.

Williams, David, Teresa Drips Williams, and David Carlson. *Plain Folk in a Rich Man's War: Class and Dissent in Confederate Georgia*. Gainesville: University Press of Florida, 2002.

———. *Rich Man's War: Class, Caste, and Confederate Defeat in the Lower Chattahoochee Valley*. Athens: University of Georgia Press, 1998.

Williams, George Washington. *A History of the Negro Troops in the War of Rebellion*. New York: Bergman Publishers, 1968.

Williams, Lou Falkner. *The Great South Carolina Ku Klux Klan Trials, 1871–1872*. Athens: University of Georgia Press, 2004.

Williams, T. Harry. *P. G. T. Beauregard: Napoleon in Gray*. Baton Rouge: Louisiana State University Press, 1955.

Willis, Kenneth D. *Spanning the Black Warrior River: Seven Bridges between Tuscaloosa and Northport, Alabama*. N.p., 2010.

Wills, Brian Steel. *A Battle from the Start: The Life of Nathan Bedford Forrest*. New York: Harper Perennial, 1993.

———. *The River Was Dyed with Blood: Nathan Bedford Forrest and Fort Pillow*. Norman: University of Oklahoma Press, 2014.

Wilson, Keith P. *Campfires of Freedom: The Camp Life of Black Soldiers during the Civil War*. Kent, OH: Kent State University Press, 2002.

Wilson, Theodore B. *The Black Codes of the South*. Tuscaloosa: University of Alabama Press, 1965.

Winik, Jay. *April 1865: The Month That Saved America*. New York: HarperCollins, 2006.

Winkle, Kenneth. *Lincoln's Citadel: The Civil War in Washington, DC*. New York: W. W. Norton, 2013.

Wolfe, Suzanne Rau. *The University of Alabama, A Pictorial History*. Tuscaloosa: University of Alabama Press, 1983.

Wood, Forrest G. *Black Scare: The Racist Response to Emancipation and Reconstruction*. Berkeley: University of California Press, 1970.

Wood, W. J. *Civil War Generalship: The Art of Command*. Westport, CT: Praeger, 1997.

Woodward, Joseph H., II. *Alabama Blast Furnaces*. Tuscaloosa: University of Alabama Press, 2007.

Woodward, Colin Edward. *Marching Masters: Slavery, Race, and the Confederate Army during the Civil War*. Charlottesville: University of Virginia Press, 2014.

Woodward, C. Vann. *The Burden of Southern History*. Baton Rouge: Louisiana State University Press, 2008.

Wright, Gavin. *Slavery and American Economic Development*. Baton Rouge: Louisiana State University Press, 2006.

Wyeth, John Allan. *That Devil Forrest: Life of General Nathan Bedford Forrest*. Baton Rouge: Louisiana State University Press, 1989.

Periodicals and Essays

Amos, Harriet, E. "Trials of a Unionist: Gustavus Horton, Military Mayor of Mobile during Reconstruction." *Gulf Coast Historical Review* 4 (Spring 1989): 134–51.

Aynes, Richard L. "Unintended Consequences of the Fourteenth Amendment." In *Unintended Consequences of Constitutional Amendment*, edited by David E. Hyvig, 110–40. Athens: University of Georgia Press, 2000.

Baggett, James Alex. "Origins of Early Texas Republican Party Leadership." *Journal of Southern History* 40 (August 1974): 441–54.

Bailey, Fred Arthur. "The Textbooks of the Lost Cause: Censorship and the Creation of Southern State Histories." *Georgia Historical Quarterly* 75 (Fall 1991): 507–33.

Bailey, Hugh C. "Disloyalty in Early Confederate Alabama." *Journal of Southern History* 23 (November 1957): 522–28.

Bailey, Mrs. Hugh C. "Mobile Tragedy: The Great Magazine Explosion of 1865." *Alabama Review* 21 (January 1968): 40–52.

Battles, Jason J. "Labor, Law, and the Freedmen's Bureau in Alabama, 1865–1867." In *The Yellowhammer War: The Civil War and Reconstruction in Alabama*, edited by Kenneth W. Noe, 240–57. Tuscaloosa: University of Alabama Press, 2013.

Beal, Mildred. "Charles Teed Pollard: Industrialist." *Alabama Historical Quarterly* 2 (Summer 1940): 494–505.

Bearss, Edwin C. "A Federal Raid up the Tennessee River." *Alabama Review* 17 (October 1964): 261–70.

———. "Rousseau's Raid on the Montgomery and West Point Railroad," *Alabama Historical Quarterly* 25 (Spring and Summer 1963): 7–48.

Blair, William Alan. "The Use of Military Force to Protect the Gains of Reconstruction." *Civil War History* 51 (December 2005); 388–402.

———. "Why Didn't the North Hang Some Rebels? The Postwar Debate over Punishment for Treason." In *More Than a Contest between Armies: Essays on the Civil*

War Era, edited by James Marten and A. Kristen Foster, 189–218. Kent, OH: Kent State University Press, 2008.

Brannon, Peter A. "Southern Emigration to Brazil." *Alabama Historical Quarterly* 1 (Summer, Fall, Winter 1930): 74–96, 280–305, 467–88.

Buchanan, G. Sidney. "The Quest for Freedom: A Legal History of the Thirteenth Amendment." *Houston Law Review* 12 (1974–1975): 1–34, 331–78, 592–639, 843–89, 1069–85.

Burnett, Lonnie A. "Precipitating a Revolution: Alabama's Democracy in the Election of 1860." In *The Yellowhammer War: The Civil War and Reconstruction in Alabama*, edited by Kenneth W. Noe, 15–33. Tuscaloosa: University of Alabama Press, 2013.

Carter, Dan T. "The Anatomy of Fear: The Christmas Day Insurrection Scare of 1865." *Journal of Southern History* 42 (August 1976): 345–64.

Center, Clark E., Jr. "The Burning of the University of Alabama." *Alabama Heritage* 16 (Spring 1990): 30–45.

Chalmers, David. "The Klan Rides, 1865–71." In *Terrorism: Critical Concepts in Political Science*, edited by David C. Rapoport, 48-60. New York: Routledge, 2006.

Cimprich, John. "The Beginning of the Black Suffrage Movement in Tennessee, 1864–65." *Journal of Negro History* 65 (Summer 1980): 185–95.

Clinton, Thomas P. "The Military Operations of General John T. Croxton in West Alabama, 1865." In *Transactions of the Alabama Historical Society 1899–1903*, edited by Thomas McAdory Owen. Vol. 4. Montgomery, AL: Alabama Historical Society, 1904.

Coben, Stanley. "Northeastern Business and Radical Reconstruction: A Re-examination." *Journal of American History* 46 (June 1959): 67–90.

Colby, Eldridge. "Wilson's Cavalry Campaign of 1865." *Journal of American Military History Foundation* 2 (Winter 1938): 204–21.

Cook, Robert. "Unfinished Business: African Americans and the Civil War Centennial." In *Legacy of Disunion: The Enduring Significance of the American Civil War*, edited by Susan-Mary Grant and Peter J. Parish, 48–64. Baton Rouge: Louisiana State University Press, 2003.

Cox, LaWanda. "From Emancipation to Segregation: National Policy and Southern Blacks." In *Interpreting Southern History: Essays in Honor of Sanford W. Higginbotham*, edited by John B. Boles and Evelyn Thomas Nolen, 199–253. Baton Rouge: Louisiana State University Press, 1987.

Cox, LaWanda, and John H. Cox. "Johnson and the Negro." In *Reconstruction: An Anthology of Revisionist Writings*, edited by Kenneth M. Stampp and Leon F. Litwack, 59–84. Baton Rouge: Louisiana State University Press, 1969.

Culver, Emma Beall. "Thomas Hill Watts, A Statesman of the Old Regime." In *Transactions of the Alabama Historical Society 1899–1903*, edited by Thomas McAdory Owen IV, 415–39. Montgomery, AL: n.p., 1904.

Davidson, William H. "Brigadier General James Holt Clanton: Alabama's Rash Gallant." *Alabama Lawyer* 20 (July 1959): 285–96.

Davis, Hugh C. "Hilary A. Herbert: Bourbon Apologist," *Alabama Review* 20 (July 1967): 216–25.

———. "John W. Dubose: The Disillusioned Aristocrat." *Alabama Historical Quarterly* 27 (Fall and Winter 1965): 167–90.

Dean, Eric T. "Post-Traumatic Stress." In *The Civil War Veteran: A Historical Reader*, edited by Larry M. Logue and Michael Barton, 126–45. New York: New York University Press, 2007.

Doss, Harriet E. Amos. "Every Man Should Consider His Own Conscience: Black and White Alabamians' Reaction to the Assassination of Abraham Lincoln." In *The Yellowhammer War: The Civil War and Reconstruction in Alabama*, edited by Kenneth W. Noe, 165–77. Tuscaloosa: University of Alabama Press, 2013.

Draughon, Ralph. "Some Aspects of the History of Alabama Bond Issues." *Alabama Review* 6 (July 1953): 163–74.

Eckinger, Helen. "The Militarization of the University of Alabama." *Alabama Review* 66 (July 2013): 163–85.

Edwards, Elisabeth L. "La Grange College." *Alabama Historical Quarterly* 14, nos. 1 and 2 (1952): 149–55.

Eidsmoe, John A. "Warrior, Statesman, Jurist for the South: The Life, Legacy, and Law of Thomas Goode Jones." *Jones Law Review* 5, no. 1 (2001): 51–225.

Emberton, Carole. "Reconstructing Loyalty: Love, Fear, and Power in the Postwar South." In *The Great Task Remaining before Us: Reconstruction as America's Continuing Civil War*, edited by Paul A. Cimbala and Randall M. Miller, 173–82. New York: Fordham University Press, 2010.

English, Bertis. "Freedom's Church: Sociocultural Construction, Reconstruction, and Post-Reconstruction in Perry County, Alabama's African American Churches." In *The Yellowhammer War: The Civil War and Reconstruction in Alabama*, edited by Kenneth W. Noe, 258–80. Tuscaloosa: University of Alabama Press, 2013.

Feis, William B. "Jefferson Davis and the 'Guerrilla Option': A Reexamination." In *The Collapse of the Confederacy*, edited by Mark Grimsley and Brooks D. Simpson, 104–28. Lincoln: University of Nebraska Press, 2001.

Fitzgerald, Michael W. "Another Kind of Glory: Black Participation and Its Consequences in the Campaign for Confederate Mobile." *Alabama Review* 54 (October 2001): 243–75.

———. "Extralegal Violence and the Planter Class: The Ku Klux Klan in the Alabama Black Belt during Reconstruction." In *Local Matters: Race, Crime, and Justice in the Nineteenth-Century South*, edited by Christopher Waldrep and Donald G. Nieman, 155–71, Athens: University of Georgia Press, 2001.

———. "From Unionists to Scalawags: Elite Dissent in Civil War Mobile." *Alabama Review* 55 (April 2002): 106–21.

———. "'He Was Always Preaching the Union': The Wartime Origins of White Republicanism during Reconstruction." In *The Yellowhammer War: The Civil War and Reconstruction in Alabama*, edited by Kenneth W. Noe, 220–39. Tuscaloosa: University of Alabama Press, 2013.

—. "Radical Republicanism and the White Yeomanry during Alabama Reconstruction, 1865–1868." *Journal of Southern History* 54 (November 1988): 565–96.

—. "Republican Factionalism and Black Empowerment: The Spencer-Warner Controversy and Alabama Reconstruction, 1868–1880." *Journal of Southern History* 64 (August 1998): 473–94.

—. "'To Give Our Votes to the Party': Black Political Agitation and Agricultural Change in Alabama." *Journal of American History* 76 (September 1989): 489–505.

—. "Wager Swayne, the Freedmen's Bureau, and the Politics of Reconstruction in Alabama." *Alabama Review* 48 (July 1995): 188–232.

Fleming, Walter L. "The Peace Movement in Alabama during the Civil War." *South Atlantic Quarterly* 2 (April and July 1903): 114–24, 246–60.

Folmar, John Kent. "Reaction to Reconstruction: John Forsyth and the *Mobile Advertiser and Register*, 1865–1867." *Alabama Historical Quarterly* 37 (Winter 1975): 245–64.

Frisby, Derek W. "A Victory Spoiled: West Tennessee Unionists during Reconstruction." In *The Great Task Remaining before Us: Reconstruction as America's Continuing Civil War*, edited by Paul A. Cimbala and Randall M. Miller, 9–29. New York: Fordham University Press, 2010.

Goluboff, Risa L. "The Thirteenth Amendment and the Lost Origins of Civil Rights." *Duke Law Journal* 50, no. 6 (2001): 1609–85.

Granade, Ray. "Violence: An Instrument of Policy in Reconstruction Alabama." *Alabama Historical Quarterly* 30 (Fall–Winter 1968): 181–202.

Green, Michael. "Reconstructing the Nation, Reconstructing the Party: Postwar Republicans and the Evolution of a Party." In *The Great Task Remaining before Us: Reconstruction as America's Continuing Civil War*, edited by Paul A. Cimbala and Randall M. Miller, 183–204. New York: Fordham University Press, 2010.

Griffen, Richard W. "Cotton Fraud and Confiscations in Alabama, 1863–1866." *Alabama Review* 7 (October 1954): 265–76.

Gross, Jennifer Lynn. "Augusta Jane Evans: Alabama's Confederate *Macaria*." In *The Yellowhammer War: The Civil War and Reconstruction in Alabama*, edited by Kenneth W. Noe, 125–48. Tuscaloosa: University of Alabama Press, 2013.

Hacker, J. David. "A Census-Based Count of the Civil War Dead." *Civil War History* 57 (December 2011): 307–48.

Hardy, William E. "South of the Border, Ulysses S. Grant and the French Intervention." *Civil War History* 54 (March 2008): 63–86.

Harmon, George D. "Confederate Migrations to Mexico." *Hispanic American Historical Review* 17 (November 1937): 458–87.

Hassan, Gail S. "Health and Welfare of Freedmen in Reconstruction Alabama." *Alabama Review* 35 (April 1982): 94–110.

Hennessey, Melinda M. "Political Terrorism in the Black Belt: The Eutaw Riot." *Alabama Review* 33 (January 1980): 35–48.

Hoole, W. Stanley. "Jeremiah Clemens, Novelist." *Alabama Review* 18 (January 1965): 5–36.

Horton, Paul. "The Culture, Social Structure and Political Economy of Antebellum Lawrence County, Alabama," *Alabama Review* 41 (October 1988): 243–70.

——. "Lightning Rod Scalawag: The Unlikely Political Career of Thomas Minnott Peters." *Alabama Review* 64 (April 2011): 116–42.

——. "Submitting to the Shadow of Slavery: The Secession Crisis and Civil War in Alabama's Lawrence County." *Civil War History* 44 (June 1988): 111–36.

Howard, Milo, Jr. "John Hardy and John Reid: Two Selma Men of Letters." *Alabama Review* 22 (January 1969): 44–52.

Jones, Allen W. "Unionism and Disaffection in South Alabama: The Case of Alfred Holley." *Alabama Review* 24 (April 1971):114–32.

Jones, Judge Walter. "Alabama's Economic Loss Due to Reconstruction." *Alabama Lawyer* 14 (April 1953): 147–55.

Keyes, Julia L. "Our Life in Brazil." *Alabama Historical Quarterly* 28, nos. 3–4 (Fall and Winter 1966): 129–339.

Kitchens, Joel D. "E. W. Peck: Alabama's First Scalawag Chief Justice." *Alabama Review* 54 (January 2001): 3–32.

Krebs, Sylvia H. "'Will the Freedmen Work?' White Alabamians Adjust to Free Black Labor." *Alabama Historical Quarterly* 36 (Summer 1974): 151–63.

Kyriakoudes, Louis M. "The Rise of Merchants and Market Towns in Reconstruction-Era Alabama." *Alabama Review* 49 (April 1996): 83–107.

Logue, Cal M. "Rhetorical Ridicule of Reconstruction Blacks." *Quarterly Journal of Speech* 62 (December 1976): 400–409.

Lucie, Patrica. "The Enduring Significance of the Civil War Constitutional Amendments." In *Legacy of Disunion: The Enduring Significance of the American Civil War*, edited by Susan-Mary Grant and Peter J. Parish, 171–87. Baton Rouge: Louisiana State University Press, 2003.

Magness, Phillip W. "Benjamin Butler's Colonization Testimony Reevaluated." *Journal of the Abraham Lincoln Association* 29 (Winter 2008): 1–28.

McConnell, Roland C. "From Preliminary to Final Emancipation Proclamation: The First Hundred Days." *Journal of Negro History* 48 (October 1963): 260–76.

McCorvey, Thomas C. "Southern Cadets in Action." *Century* 39 (November 1889): 152–53.

McDonald, William L. "The Day They Set Fire to the Mills." *Journal of Muscle Shoals History* 7 (1979): 61–64.

McIlwain, Christopher Lyle, Sr. "United States District Judge Richard Busteed and the Alabama Klan Trials of 1872." *Alabama Review* 65 (October 2012): 263–89.

McKenzie, Robert H. "Reconstruction of the Alabama Iron Industry, 1865–1880." *Alabama Review* 25 (July 1972): 178–91.

McMillan, Malcolm C. "Alabama." In *The Confederate Governors*, edited by Wilfred Buck Yearns, 15–40. Athens: University of Georgia Press, 1985.

McPherson, James M. "'For a Vast Future Also': Abraham and the Millennium." In *Legacy of Disunion: The Enduring Significance of the American Civil War*, edited by

Susan-Mary Grant and Peter J. Parish, 134–48. Baton Rouge: Louisiana State University Press, 2003.

Mellown, Robert O. "Alabama's Fourth Capital: The Construction of the State House in Tuscaloosa. *Alabama Review* 40 (October 1987): 259–83.

———. "Construction of the Alabama Insane Hospital 1852–1861." *Alabama Review* 38 (April 1985): 83–104.

Mellown, Robert O., and Gene Byrd. "F. A. P. Barnard and Alabama's First Observatory." *Journal of Alabama Academy of Science* 57 (January 1986): 39–44.

Miller, Randall M. "Daniel Pratt's Industrial Urbanism: The Cotton Mill Town in Ante-Bellum Alabama." *Alabama Historical Quarterly* 34 (Spring 1972): 5–35.

Myers, John B. "The Alabama Freedmen and Economic Adjustment during Presidential Reconstruction, 1865–1867." *Alabama Review* 26 (October 1973): 252–66.

———. "The Freedmen and the Law in Post-Bellum Alabama, 1865–1867." *Alabama Review* 23 (January 1970): 56–69.

———. "Reaction and Adjustment: The Struggle of Alabama Freedmen in Post-Bellum Alabama, 1865–1867." *Alabama Historical Quarterly* 32 (Spring and Summer 1970): 5–22.

Neely, Mark E. "Abraham Lincoln and Black Colonization: Benjamin Butler's Spurious Testimony." *Civil War History* 25 (March 1979): 77–83.

Owen, Thomas McAdory. *Basil Manly: The Founder of the Alabama Historical Society.* In *Transactions of the Alabama Historical Society 1899–1903*, edited by Thomas McAdory Owen IV, 125–40. Montgomery, AL: n.p., 1904.

Owens, Scott W. "The Federal Invasion of Pickens County, April, 1865: Croxton's Sipsey River Campaign." *Alabama Review* 62 (April 2009): 83–112.

Owsley, Frank L. "Defeatism in the Confederacy." *North Carolina Historical Review* 3 (July 1926): 446–56.

Panhorst, Michael. "Devotion, Deception, and the Ladies Memorial Association, 1865–1898: The Mystery of the Alabama Confederate Monument." *Alabama Review* 65 (July 2012): 182–200.

Pruitt, Paul M., Jr. "The Life and Times of Legal Education in Alabama, 1819–1897." *Alabama Law Review* 49 (Fall 1997): 281–321.

———. "Scalawag Dreams: Elisha Wolsey Peck's Career, and Two of His Speeches, 1867–1869." *Alabama Review* 66 (July 2013): 211–39.

Rable, George C. "Despair, Hope, and Delusion: The Collapse of Confederate Morale Reexamined." In *The Collapse of the Confederacy*, edited by Mark Grimsley and Brooks D. Simpson, 129–67. Lincoln: University of Nebraska Press, 2001.

Rhodes, Robert S. "The Registration of Voters and the Election of Delegates to the Reconstruction Convention in Alabama." *Alabama Review* 8 (April 1955): 119–42.

Rogers, William Warren, Jr. "The Boyd Incident: Black Belt Violence during Reconstruction." *Civil War History* 21 (December 1975): 309–29.

———. "Safety Lies Only in Silence: Secrecy and Subversion in Montgomery's Unionist Community." In *Enemies of the Country: New Perspectives on Unionists in the Civil*

War South, edited by John C. Inscoe and Robert C. Kenzer, 172–87. Athens: University of Georgia Press, 2001.

Scott, William C., Jr. "Phillip Dale Roddey: Confederate General from Alabama." *Journal of Muscle Shoals History* 15 (1999): 37–49.

Seip, Terry L. "Of Ambition and Enterprise: The Making of Carpetbagger George E. Spencer." In *The Yellowhammer War: The Civil War and Reconstruction in Alabama*, edited by Kenneth W. Noe, 191–219. Tuscaloosa: University of Alabama Press, 2013.

Sheridan, Richard C. "Civil War Manufacturing in the Tennessee Valley." *Journal of Muscle Shoals History* 15 (1999): 50–68.

Simpson, Brooks D. "Continuous Hammering and Mere Attrition: Lost Cause Critics and the Military Reputation of Ulysses S. Grant." In *The Myth of the Lost Cause and Civil War History*, edited by Gary W. Gallagher and Alan T. Nolan, 147–69. Bloomington: Indiana University Press, 2000.

Sloan, John Z. "The Ku Klux Klan and the Alabama Election of 1872." *Alabama Review* 18 (April 1965): 113–23.

Stephen, Walter W. "The Brooke Guns from Selma." *Alabama Historical Quarterly* 29 (Fall 1958): 462–75.

Still, William W. "Selma and the Confederate States Navy." *Alabama Review* 15 (January 1962): 19–37.

Stockham, Richard J. "Alabama Iron for the Confederacy: The Selma Works." *Alabama Review* 21 (July 1969): 163–72.

Storey, Margaret M. "The Crucible of Reconstruction: Unionists and the Struggle for Alabama's Postwar Home Front." In *The Great Task Remaining before Us: Reconstruction as America's Continuing Civil War*, edited by Paul A. Cimbala and Randall M. Miller, 69–87. New York: Fordham University Press, 2010.

Summersell, Charles G. "Kolb and the Populist Revolt as Viewed by Newspapers." *Alabama Historical Quarterly* 19 (Fall and Winter 1957): 375–94.

Thomas, Emory M. "Ambivalent Visions of Victory: Davis, Lee, and Confederate Grand Strategy." In *Jefferson Davis's Generals*, edited by Gabor S. Boritt, 27–45. New York: Oxford University Press, 1999.

Thornton, J. Mills, III. "Alabama Emancipates." In *Dixie Redux: Essays in Honor of Sheldon Hackney*, edited by Raymond Arsenault and Orville Burton, 80–100. Montgomery, AL: NewSouth Books, 2013.

———. "Alabama's Presidential Reconstruction Legislature." In *A Political Nation: New Directions in Mid-Nineteenth-Century American Political History*, edited by Gary W. Gallagher and Rachel A. Sheldon, 167–87. Charlottesville: University of Virginia Press, 2012.

Upchurch, Thomas Adams. "Senator John Tyler Morgan and the Genesis of Jim Crow Ideology, 1889–1891." *Alabama Review* 57 (April 2004): 110–31.

Vandiver, Frank E. "Josiah Gorgas and the Brierfield Iron Works," *Alabama Review* 3 (January 1950): 5–21.

Vorenberg, Michael. "The Thirteenth Amendment Enacted." In *Lincoln and Freedom: Slavery, Emancipation, and the Thirteenth Amendment*, edited by Harold Holzer and

Sara Vaughn Gabbard, 180–94. Carbondale: Southern Illinois University Press, 2007.

Waters, Zack C., "General Philip D. Roddey: 'Defender of North Alabama.'" *Alabama Heritage* 110 (Fall 2013): 24–33.

Weiner, Jonathan. "Female Planters and Planters' Wives in Civil War and Reconstruction: Alabama, 1850–1870." *Alabama Review* 30 (April 1977): 135–49.

———. "Planter Persistence and Social Change: Alabama, 1850–1870." *Journal of Interdisciplinary History* 7 (Autumn 1976): 235–60.

Wiggins, Sarah Woolfolk. "Alabama's Reconstruction after 150 Years." In *The Yellowhammer War: The Civil War and Reconstruction in Alabama*, edited by Kenneth W. Noe, 177–91. Tuscaloosa: University of Alabama Press, 2013.

———. "Five Men Called Scalawags." *Alabama Review* 17 (January 1964): 45–55.

———. "The Life of Ryland Randolph as Seen through His Letters to John DuBose." *Alabama Historical Quarterly* 30 (Fall and Winter 1968): 145–80.

Wills, Brian Steele. "The Confederate Sun Sets on Selma: Nathan Bedford Forrest and the Defense of Alabama in 1865." In *The Yellowhammer War: The Civil War and Reconstruction in Alabama*, edited by Kenneth W. Noe, 71–89. Tuscaloosa: University of Alabama Press, 2013.

Wilson, Clyde E. "State Militia of Alabama during the Administration of Lewis E. Parsons, Provisional Governor June 21st 1865 to December 18, 1865." *Alabama Historical Quarterly* 14, nos. 3 and 4 (1952): 301–22.

Wood, George A. "The Black Code of Alabama." *South Atlantic Quarterly* 13 (October 1914): 350–60.

Woolfolk, Sarah Van V. "George E. Spencer: A Carpetbagger in Alabama." *Alabama Review* 19 (January 1966): 41–52.

Wright, Denise E. "'Objects of Humanity': The White Poor in Civil War and Reconstruction Georgia." In *The Great Task Remaining before Us: Reconstruction as America's Continuing Civil War*, edited by Paul A. Cimbala and Randall M. Miller, 101–21. New York: Fordham University Press, 2010.

Zingg, Paul J. "John Archibald Campbell and the Hampton Roads Conference: Quixotic Diplomacy, 1865." *Alabama Historical Quarterly* 36 (Spring 1974): 21–34.

Index

abolitionists, 19, 22, 104, 108, 114, 123, 151, 188, 250n106

Adams, Daniel W., 68–69, 82

African Methodist Episcopal Church, 185

Alabama, admitted to Union, 1; agricultural economy, 2; capital shortage, 2, 91; debts to Northern creditors, 91; industrial economy, 2, 89; mineral wealth, 2, 90, 91

Alabama Constitution: adjournment of convention, 184; of 1865, 170, 173; election of delegates to convention, 179–80; emancipation, 182, 190; fears of Brownlowism, 173; freedmen's rights, 183; loss by Unionists, 179–80; opposition to Thirteenth Amendment, 181; pressure from Andrew Johnson, 180; ratification, 184–85; reaction of freedmen, 185; registration for election of delegates, 173, 179; right of secession, 182; the war debt, 173, 181, 182

Alabama Constitution of 1875, 209

Alabama Constitution of 1901, 1, 209

Alabama Democrats and Democratic Party, 200, 206–7; "Redemption," 209

Alabama elections, 188, 189, 190, 191–93, 195–96

Alabama Historical Society, 200–201

Alabama Hospital for the Insane, 74, 126, 258n56

Alabama legislature, 185, 194; Black Code legislation, 194, 197–99, 294n113, n114; black suffrage, 294n108; civil rights, 198; creation of counties named for Confederates, 201; election of US senators, 194; Patton vetoes, 199; Thirteenth Amendment, 194–95

Alabama militia, 96, 184, 185, 197

Alabama, postwar conditions, 92; banking system, 152–53, 267n65; black code, 149, 150, 175, 190, 193, 292n65; capital shortage, 152, 179, 180, 191, 193, 267n61, 267n65; cotton, 147–48, 151–52, 266n46, 266n48, 266n50, 266n54; court system, 144; credit system, 149, 152–53; crops, 146, 148–50; currency, 145–46, 153, 243n77, 264n18; death toll, 265n29; destruction, 146, 152; fears of a race war, 147, 185, 198; individual debts, 144, 149; inflation, 144–45; internal conflict about process of reconstruction, 135–42, 162; labor system, 149–51, 193–94, 268n76, 268nn78–79; land values, 152, 267n65; laws, 132; lawyers, 144, 195, 264n14; medical care, 147; mineral wealth, 152; orphans, 12–13, 218n40; poverty, 145–46; public meetings, 133–34, 135, 139–40, 141; railroads, 148, 266n57, 267n61; relationships with occupation troops, 147; starvation 145, 146–47, 191, 194, 265n36; state debt, 126, 175; suicide, 165; support for continuing the war, 128–29, 131–32, 156; Unionist sentiment, 132, 133–34, 135, 136; violence, 125, 133, 147, 154, 155, 156, 157–58, 169, 179, 265n41

Alabama Republican Party, 71, 206, 209; effect of Panic of 1873, 209

Alabama River, 76, 81, 125, 269n87

Alabama State Agricultural Society, 194

356 / INDEX

Alabama Supreme Court, 144, 206

Alabama's Tragic Decade: Ten Years of Alabama, 1865–1874 (John Witherspoon Du-Bose), 1, 7

Alabama Unionists, 96, 117–18, 121, 162, 164; reaction to presidential reconstruction, 161, 164, 166

Alexandria, Alabama, 174

Allen, Henry W., 128

American Revolutionary War, 63

amnesty and pardon, 80, 104, 105

Andersonville, Georgia, 121, 123

apprenticeship, 19, 24, 104, 114, 118, 194, 199

Army and Navy Journal, 104

Army of Northern Virginia, 13, 29, 33, 60, 84, 123

Army of Tennessee, 7, 9, 11, 12, 15, 16, 47, 123

Ashville, Alabama, 35

Athens Herald, 135

Autauga County, Alabama, 79, 182

Bainbridge, Alabama, 7

Baldwin, Marion A., 140

Barnard, F. A. P., 74

Battle, Cullen A., 93, 192

Battle House Hotel, 85

Battle of Ebenezer Church, 76

Battle of Fort Blakely, 84

Battle of Franklin, 201

Battle of Mobile Bay, 7

Battle of Nashville, 7, 13, 91

Battle of Selma, 77–78

Battle of Shiloh, 68

Battle of Spanish Fort, 84

Beauregard, P. G. T., 25

Beecher, Henry Ward, 108–9

Bell, John, 217n24

Benners, Augustus, 33, 46, 146, 149, 154, 202

Berney, Dr. James, 241n53

Berry, Obediah, 63, 73

Bibb Naval Furnace, 76

Bibb, William C., 96, 246n39

Bibb, William J., 140

Bingham, Daniel H., 135–36, 137, 164

Birmingham *Age-Herald*, 1

"black codes," 175, 185, 190, 193, 194, 203, 205

Black Reconstruction in America (W. E. B. Du Bois) 183, 286n53

black suffrage, 97, 105–6, 107, 118, 183, 208

Black Warrior River, 10, 64, 67, 68, 69, 148, 237n34; toll bridge, 10, 67, 70, 73, 74

Blair, Montgomery, 161

Blair, Sr., Francis P., 18, 19, 20, 26, 220n11

Blair, William, 129

Blue Mountain, Alabama, 90, 128, 291n54

Blue, Ellen, 155–56

"Bonnie Blue Flag," 74

Book of Judges, 109

Booth, John Wilkes, 65, 92, 98, 100, 101, 114, 121, 133, 249n86

Boston Herald, 102

Boston Journal, 121

Botts, John M., 118

Bradley, Joseph C., 34, 139, 140, 141, 174, 175, 179–80, 192

Brazil, 165

Breckinridge, John C., 47

Brierfield, Alabama, 76

Brooklyn, New York, 109

Brooks, William M., 124

Brown v. Board of Education, 210

Brown, Edward Norphlet, 7, 9, 61

Brown, Fannie, 7

Brownlow, William G., 111–12, 115, 136, 164, 188, 205–6, 260n92; Brownlowism, 111–12, 135, 136, 138, 140, 173, 188, 190, 197, 253n81

Brown, Neil Smith, 12

Bruce, John, 300n69

Bulger, Michael J., 190

Burnsville, Alabama 78

Busteed, Richard, 144, 195, 300n69

Butler, Benjamin F., 100, 101–3, 113, 114, 115, 156, 247n69, 248n74, 252n29

Byrd, William M., 139

Cahaba, Alabama, 15, 57, 80, 92, 121, 125, 192

Cahawba Iron Works, 75

Calhoun County, Alabama, 174

Campbell, John A., 27–32, 61, 92, 96

Canada, 47, 91, 121

Canby, Edward S., 15, 52, 67, 126, 135, 139, 158

Canby's invasion, 52, 83–84; Fort Blakely, 84;

INDEX / 357

Mobile, Alabama, 83–84; Pollard, Alabama, 83; Spanish Fort, 83–84
Carpenter, Francis B., 254n66
Carpenter, James A., 72
Carpenter-Leach wedding, 72–73
Carrollton, Alabama, 237n53
Carter, Dan, 199
Catoma Creek, 82
Central America, 103
Central Rolling Mill, 76
Chadick, Mary, 85, 156
Chalmers, James R., 79, 240n32–33
Chambers County, Alabama, 128
Chambers, William Pitt, 89, 120
Chase, Salmon P., 105, 108, 111, 192
Chattanooga Rebel, 9, 37, 48, 77, 78, 110, 251n3
Cherokee County, Alabama, 130, 179
Chesnut, Mary Boykin, 127
Chicago Journal, 10, 35
Chicago Tribune, 23, 34, 120
Chilton, William Parish, 64
Cincinnati Commercial, 90, 99, 101
Cincinnati Gazette, 30
Citronelle, Alabama, 123
City Point, Virginia, 95
Civil Rights Act of 1866, 203–4
Civil Rights Act of 1871 (42 U.S.C. § 1983), 205
Civil Rights Act of 1964, 210–11
Civil War and Reconstruction in Alabama (Walter Fleming), 125
Civil War Alabama; class conflict, 9, 33, 43, 154–55; conscription, 42; desertions, 33, 43, 56, 60–61, 66, 258n54; destruction of Alabama's industries, 2, 66–67; destruction of cotton, 78, 82; drunkenness, 43; guerrilla warfare, 49, 53–54, 130, 231n4; inflation, 144–45; peace sentiment, 16, 20, 21–22, 23, 24–25, 33–34, 35, 36–37, 43, 46–47, 56, 60, 62, 63, 155; prisons, 121, 123; reaction to surrenders, 84–85; regrets, 150–51, 153; slavery, 16; slave soldiers, 44, 62–63; spies, 64; war meetings, 48–49, 52, 63, 64
Clanton, James Holt, 36, 42–43, 166, 198, 294n103

Clarke County, Alabama, 89
Clay, C. C., 47, 86, 91, 121, 133, 195, 229n46
Clay, J. Withers, 179
Cleburne, Patrick, 201
Clemens, Jeremiah, 18, 58, 62, 96–97, 136–37, 220n6
Cleveland Leader, 62, 96, 106, 192
Clitherall, Alexander B., 139
Coleman, Walter L., 82, 241n53
Colfax, Schuyler, 185, 195
Confederate Congress, 18
Confederate propaganda, 79, 85
Confederate States of America; Confederate Congress, 11, 18, 20–21; failure to pay soldiers, 43, 56; propaganda, 79, 85
Columbia, South Carolina, 45–46, 70
Columbus, Georgia, 82, 83
Columbus, Mississippi, 25
Connecticut, 187, 208
Corinth, Mississippi, 8, 41
Courtland, Alabama, 10, 133
Covington County, Alabama, 155
Cramer, Francis L., 44
Crenshaw, Edward, 33
Croxton, John T., 71–74, 75, 237n34, 237n53
CSS *Alabama*, 91
CSS *Tuscaloosa*, 91
Cumberland, Tennessee, 93
Cumberland University, 70, 236n30
Cumming, Kate, 46, 85, 128, 145, 147, 153–54, 155, 156, 202
Curry, J. L. M., 15–16, 49, 86, 124, 189

Dale County, Alabama, 49, 78
Dallas County, Alabama, 146
Darwinism, 119
Davis, Jefferson, 10, 14, 15, 20, 25, 26, 32, 54, 61, 63, 80, 85, 93, 107, 109, 121, 123, 135, 154, 182, 231n4, 256n11
Davis, Nicholas, 141
Declaration of Independence, 120
Democratic Party (North), 161, 174, 176–77, 189, 193, 204, 206, 207, 211
Demopolis, Alabama, 85, 125, 147–48
Demopolis Herald, 110, 251n5
depression of 1837, 1, 7
depression of 1873, 299n58

"Dixie," 74, 78
Dodge, Grenville, 137
Douglas, Stephen A., 176
Douglass, Frederick, 108, 114, 124
Drake, John, 179
Du Bois, W. E. B., 183, 286n53
DuBose, John W., 1, 3, 7, 110, 125, 179, 183, 195, 199, 212, 246n39
Durham Station, North Carolina, 116

Eastport, Mississippi, 14–15, 23
Egypt, 152
Eldridge, Alabama, 69
elections, presidential: 1864, 98
Elyton, Alabama, 67, 68, 69, 71, 237n34
Emancipation Proclamation, 32, 174
Espy, Sarah, 26, 46, 126, 154, 155, 202
Eufaula, Alabama, 82
Evans, Augusta J., 189
Exchange Hotel, 82, 195

Fairbanks, William H., 134
Faneuil Hall, 165, 257n41
Federal Union, 78, 150
Fennell, Catherine, 150–51
Fielding, Mary, 75, 153
Fifteenth Amendment, 209–10
Fifteenth Army Corps, 146
Figures, William B., 174, 192
Finch's Ferry, Alabama, 68
First Alabama Cavalry, USA, 44, 64, 137
Fitzgerald, Michael, 155, 211
Fitzpatrick, Benjamin, 61, 140, 181, 182
Fleming, Walter, 125, 212, 215n1, 285n47, 294n115, 301n80
Florence, Alabama, 14, 33, 66, 146
Follansbee, Sarah, 82, 154
Foote, Henry S., 21, 22, 221nn21–22
Forrest, Nathan Bedford, 36, 41, 54–55, 67, 68, 69, 76, 77, 78, 79, 80–81, 125, 130, 131, 260n86, 260nn91–92
Forsyth, John, 12, 18, 21–23, 36, 43, 48, 53, 55, 57, 67, 84, 85, 86, 97, 99, 111, 167, 170, 172, 173, 176, 185, 189, 190, 191, 193, 196, 200, 207, 279n21, 291n55, 292n67, 293n93
Fort Blakely, 52

Fort Gaines, 122
Fort Morgan, 122
Fort Pillow massacre, 81, 84, 130, 260n86
Fort Pulaski, 122
Fort Sumter, 91, 110, 251n8
Foster, Charles, 70, 74
Foster, Sally Independence, 26, 85
Foster, Thomas J., 192
Fourteenth Amendment, 204–5, 206, 210, 297n25
France, 63, 93, 127, 143, 158, 176, 204
Frankfort, Alabama, 135
Franklin County, Alabama, 22, 117, 135, 181
freedmen, 100, 149–51, 193–94, 269n87; colonization, 102–3; land for, 150; mortality rate, 151; right to testify, 172; suffrage rights, 2, 97, 104–6, 107–8, 113–14, 176
Freedmen's Bureau, 46, 118–19, 150, 194, 199
Freeman, George C., 192

Gainesville, Alabama, 81, 131, 157
Garland, Landon C., 13, 14, 70, 73, 74
Garrett, William, 172–73
Gatewood, John P., 130
Gayle, George Washington, 57, 92, 97–98, 101, 116
Georgia, 7, 11, 13, 70
germ warfare, 121
Giers, Jean Joseph (J. J.), 24, 34, 133–34, 141, 162, 197, 257n42
Gilchrist, James G., 56
Goldthwaite, George, 140
Gorgas, Josiah, 7, 26, 62, 84, 124, 149, 154, 172, 179
gradual emancipation, 19, 117
Granger, Gordon, 84, 85
Granger, Robert S., 49, 132, 133
Grant, Ulysses S., 14, 24, 44, 50, 52, 80, 84, 93, 95, 100, 101, 103, 110, 116–17, 123, 126, 129, 130, 137, 158, 200, 231n8, 254n53, 269n87
Gravelly Springs, Alabama, 15, 50
Greely, Horace, 30, 185, 192
Greensboro, Alabama, 8, 33, 179
Greenville, Alabama, 83
guerrilla warfare, 3, 14, 35, 49–50, 53–54, 58, 80, 93, 192

INDEX / 359

Guin, Jason, 234n71
Guin, J. Foy, 234n71
Guntersville, Alabama, 150
Gurley, Frank, 192–93

Hague, Parthenia, 154
Hall, Mary Ann, 146
Hamilton, Andrew J., 164
Hampton Roads Peace Conference, 27–33, 36, 96, 119, 224n16, 225n29
Hardcastle, Aaron B., 67–69, 72, 235n16, 237n44
Hardy, John, 62–63, 163–64, 182
Hartford Courant, 102
Haynesville, Alabama, 82
Helena, Alabama, 76
Henry, John H., 76
Herbert, Hillary, 148
Hitchcock, Henry, 116
Hodgson, Joseph, 207
Holly, Alfred, 155
Hood, John Bell, 7, 8, 9, 10, 11, 14, 41, 75, 215n22
Horton, Gustavus, 280n32
Houston, George Smith, 50, 141, 194, 196, 292n67
Hubbard, David, 65
Hubbs, G. Ward, 179
Humphries, David C., 141, 179–80, 282n59
Hunter, Robert M. T., 27, 61–62
Huntsville Advocate, 171, 174, 188, 192
Huntsville, Alabama, 85, 110, 148, 156, 171
Huntsville Confederate, 179
Huntsville Independent, 179
Hurricane Creek, 73

India, 152

Jackson, Mississippi, 62
Jackson *Mississippian*, 9, 48, 50
Jackson News, 62
Jackson, William H. "Red," 68, 69, 72, 79, 117, 231n8, 237n34, 240n32
Jacksonville, Alabama, 49
Jamaica, 185
Jasper, Alabama, 14
Jefferson County, Alabama, 10, 68

Jemison, Robert, 11–12, 14, 18, 64–65, 70, 72, 150, 234n77
Johnson, Andrew, 3, 19, 46, 50, 85, 93, 97, 99, 114, 129, 131, 132, 135–36, 175, 179, 186, 191, 192, 193, 195–97, 200, 212, 246n43, 252n29, 259n78, 274n20, 275n27; Alabama, 138, 140, 141, 142, 163, 164–65, 172, 174, 180, 184, 194, 201, 204, 253n42; assassination plot, 57, 92, 93, 98, 110; black suffrage, 160–61, 176, 178, 183, 273n147, 286n53; cabinet, 158; colonization, 274n12; confiscation, 165; disenfranchisement, 165; inauguration, 111, 120; militia, 286n55; pardons, 160, 166, 172–73, 181, 182, 277n46; reconstruction policies, 112, 113, 114, 115, 116–17, 121, 123, 128, 140, 142, 143, 156, 159, 160–62, 165–67, 168, 169, 173, 176, 191, 200
Johnston, Joseph E., 47, 85, 107, 115–16, 123
Jones, Thomas G., 84, 300n69
Jones, William Giles, 48
Juarez, Benito Pablo, 94, 129, 161

Kelley, William D., 178
Kilpatrick, Judson, 45, 107
King George III, 120
King, Horace, 237n53
Kirkwood Hotel, 111
Ku Klux Klan, 131, 207, 294n103; proto-Klan, 169, 197

LaGrange College, 70
Langdon, C. C., 190, 192
Lapsley, John W., 291n54
Lawler, Levi, 180
Lawrence County, Alabama, 150, 197
Lea, Columbus, 192
Leach and Avery Foundry, 70, 74
Leach-Carpenter wedding, 72
Leach, Sewell J., 70, 72
Lebanon, Tennessee, 70
Lee, Robert E., 13, 14, 80, 84–85, 93, 103, 123, 156, 257n29, 257n31
Lewis, David P., 141, 209
Limestone County, Alabama, 141
Lincoln, Abraham, 3, 31, 92, 95, 99–100, 103, 109, 143, 221n24, 224n14, 224n18, 224–

25n19, 231n8, 233n49, 243n11, 246n39, 254n66; Alabama, 18; apprenticeship, 104, 118; black suffrage, 104–5, 107, 249n84, 249n86; City Point meeting, 95–96; colonization, 102, 248n74; compensated emancipation, 20, 224n14, 224–25n19; emancipation proclamation, 12, 16, 19, 248n74; emotional state, 225n20; goals for postwar period, 96, 107; gradual emancipation, 19–20, 22, 29; last speech, 103–7, 249n86; second inaugural address, 59–60, 62, 79; Thirteenth Amendment, 16, 102, 104

Lincoln assassination, 3, 57–58, 65, 92, 97–98, 100, 110, 156, 246n46, 249n77, 249n86, 251nn3–4, 251n8; effect on black suffrage, 105, 113–14; Northern reaction, 3, 110–23, 123; reaction in Alabama, 110, 124, 125, 140; trial of the conspirators, 121, 133

Little Cahaba Furnace, 76

Louisiana, 104, 128

Louisville Journal, 135

Loyal League, 156

Lyon, Hylan, 51

Macon County, Alabama, 192, 198

Madison County, Alabama, 192

Magruder, John B., 127–28

Mallory, James, 46, 89, 109, 128, 149–50, 154, 202

Manly, Reverend Basil, 150

Marion, Alabama, 78

Martin, John M., 234n69

Massachusetts, 100

Mathews, Thomas M., 80, 192

Maximilian, Ferdinand, 56, 93–94, 127, 143, 156, 161, 178, 191, 289–90n34

Maxwell, James R., 146

McClellan, Robert, 60

McClellan, William, 60

McCook, Edward, 82

McCook, Robert L., 93, 192

McCullough, Hugh, 158

McNair, Chris, 215n9

McPherson, James, 211

Meek, Alexander B., 89

Memphis and Charleston Railroad, 66

Memphis Appeal, 15, 42, 48, 51

Merchants Magazine and Commercial Review, 30

Meridian, Mississippi, 15, 260n93

Meridian (Mississippi) *Clarion*, 79

Meriwether, Elizabeth, 84–85

Mexico, 56, 93–94, 204; Confederate exodus to, 85, 93, 127, 128, 129–31, 143, 158, 165–66, 176, 178, 182, 191; threat of Confederate resurgence, 127, 129, 131

militia, 184, 185

Milton, Florida, 52

Milton, John, 122

Mississippi, 13, 70

Mobile Advertiser and Register, 11–12, 16, 57, 70, 84, 198

Mobile, Alabama, 1, 10, 48, 83–84, 139, 145, 157

Mobile *Army Argus and Crisis*, 79

Mobile Bay, 52

Mobile News, 84, 126, 127, 133, 141, 145, 164, 170, 171

Mobile Times, 196, 199

Mobile Tribune, 42, 175

Monroe Doctrine, 94

Montgomery Advertiser, 42, 52, 67, 83, 89, 132, 190, 197, 206

Montgomery, Alabama, 15, 42, 44, 64, 81–83, 139–40, 146–47, 155

Montgomery Ledger, 198

Montgomery Mail, 15, 16, 20, 34, 63, 80, 124, 132–33, 152, 153, 154, 155, 188

Montgomery Weekly Advertiser, 173

Moore, Andrew B., 122

Moore, Joshua Burns, 22, 33, 51, 66, 78, 85, 112–13, 117–18, 124–25, 133, 154, 161, 165, 181

Morgan County, Alabama, 135

Morris, Josiah, 244n53

Mosby, John S., 53, 65, 117, 231n8

Moulton, Alabama, 24, 117, 135

Mount Vernon arsenal, 122

Mudd, William S., 71, 72

Murfee, James T., 73

Napoleon III, 74, 103, 160

Nashville Times and True Union, 136

Nashville Union, 36, 61, 62, 131, 134, 193
national debt, 30, 91, 92, 189
Native Americans, 119, 120, 205, 208
Nauvoo, Alabama, 14
New Orleans, Louisiana, 100
New Orleans *Picayune*, 192
New Orleans Times, 158
New York Evening Post, 111
New York Herald, 58, 82, 102, 113–14, 119; 135, 146, 152
New York Journal, 182
New York Times, 95, 102, 105–6, 113, 116–17, 143, 147, 152, 158, 161, 164, 175, 176, 184, 185, 190–91, 201
New York Tribune, 12, 59, 80, 97, 103, 106, 151, 164, 181, 185
New York *World*, 19, 22, 47
niter factory, 74
North Alabama, 132
North Carolina, 107, 160
Northern capital, 119
Northport, Alabama, 10, 67, 70, 72, 73
Nugent, William, 26

Oldham, Williamson S., 128, 259n68
Olmstead, Elisha S., 70, 73
Orr, Jehu, 20, 21

Palmetto Ranch, Texas, 156
Panama, 161
Parsons, Lewis E., 139, 140, 141, 163, 164, 167, 169, 170–71, 174, 179, 180, 182, 183, 184, 185, 191, 192, 195, 196, 201, 265n29, 275n27, 280n32; appointment as provisional governor, 164, 165, 166; election as US senator, 184, 194, 196, 292n67; policies as provisional governor, 164, 170–72, 191, 194, 200, 197; Unionist opposition, 170–72, 179, 275n29; Unionist support, 275n27
Patton, Robert M., 190, 199–200, 204, 206
Pearl Harbor, 110
Peck, E. W., 64, 70, 71, 72, 125, 169
Peck, Lydia, 72
Pennington, John, 44
Pensacola, Florida, 52
Perry County, Alabama, 78

Peters, Thomas M., 117, 134, 135, 170, 206
Phelan, John D., 141
Phillips, Phillip, 121
Phillips, Wendell, 123, 188, 250n106
Pickens County, Alabama, 237n53
Pickens, Samuel, 13, 29
Pickett, Richard O., 134
Pierpont, Francis, 93
Plantersville, Alabama, 76, 78
Plymouth Church, 109
Pollard, Alabama, 42–43, 52, 83
Pope, Burwell T., 192
Powell, Lewis Thornton, 65, 100
Pratt, Daniel, 182
presidential election of 1868, 163, 196, 200, 207, 208
Price, Sterling, 178
Protestant Episcopal Church, 170

Quinn, Jerome, 50–51

railroads, 2, 52; Alabama and Florida Railroad, 83; Alabama and Tennessee Rivers Railroad, 76; bankruptcy, 209; government aid, 208, 209; Montgomery and West Point Railroad, 90; Selma and Meridian Railroad, 125; Tennessee and Alabama Central Railroad, 135
Randolph County, Alabama, 137, 155
Randolph, Ryland, 207
Reconstruction (Congressional): admission of Southern representatives, 191, 195–97, 200; black suffrage, 183, 184, 185, 187, 189, 204; confiscation, 189; constitutional amendments, 202; disenfranchisement, 204; economic sanctions, 191, 193, 207; impeachment of President Johnson, 200; Joint Committee on Reconstruction, 196; legislation, 203; Lincoln assassination as a factor, 168, 174, 196; loyalty as a factor, 162, 168, 171–72, 173–74, 178, 179–180, 181, 183, 184, 185–86, 187, 188, 191, 192, 193, 195–96, 201; Reconstruction Acts, 206; report of Charles Shurz as a factor, 201; support for immediate uncompensated emancipation as a factor, 173, 174, 175–76, 180–81, 182, 187, 190,

193; treatment of freedmen and white Unionists as a factor, 163, 169, 185–86, 191, 197–99, 200, 201, 207–8, 293n98; treatment of northerners as a factor, 169–70; Unionist sentiment as a factor, 197

Reconstruction (Presidential), 92–93; colonization, 102, 103, 161; effect of Lincoln assassination, 110–19, 120–22, 123, 156; effect of national debt, 94, 158; fears of Franco-Mexican intervention, 94, 129, 131, 143, 156–57; fears of guerrilla warfare, 93, 94, 97, 115–16, 117, 126, 128, 131; gradual emancipation, 143; Northern public opinion, 79–80, 93, 95, 98, 100, 103, 105–7, 108–9, 110–19, 122, 123, 158, 159, 180; provisional governments, 97, 143; Southern propaganda, 55, 156–57; ten percent plan, 104–5; Thirteenth Amendment, 143; and Unionists, 293n98

Red Mountain Iron and Coal Company, 75

Republican Party (Northern), 1, 19, 22, 93, 99, 100, 101, 102, 103, 156, 176, 185, 193, 216n10; equal rights for freedmen, 100, 156, 165, 176, 178, 180

Rice, Samuel Farrow, 52, 64, 141

Richmond *Dispatch*, 12, 28

Richmond Enquirer, 61

Richmond Sentinel, 20, 54

Richmond, Virginia, 7, 80, 90, 92

Roddey, Philip D., 24–25, 34–35, 36, 49, 50, 66, 76, 78, 80, 125, 134, 261n16

Rodes, Robert, 65

Roupes Valley Iron Works, 75–76

Ruffin, Edmund G., 165, 276n40

Russellville, Alabama, 10

Saffold, Milton J., 82, 139, 140, 241n53

Sanford, John W. A., 199

Savannah, Georgia, 33–34, 46, 70, 122

Schurz, Carl, 201–2

secession and secessionists, 1, 22, 34, 78, 96, 117, 124, 136, 140; postwar criticism of, 136, 154–55

Second Treaty of Paris, 120

Seibles, J. J., 140

Selma, Alabama, 10, 14, 48, 76, 83, 92, 110,

139, 155, 173; military-industrial complex, 14, 75, 76–78

Selma Dispatch, 36, 43, 57, 92

Selma Mirror, 151

Selma Reporter, 16, 28

Selma Times, 124, 149

Seventh Alabama Cavalry, 81

Severance, Ben, 218n39, 292n81

Seward, William H., 29–30, 97, 182, 203, 224n14, 246n44; assassination plot, 57, 92, 120, 121, 133; failed assassination, 110, 140; threat from French-backed Confederates in Mexico, 127, 129, 160, 176

Sheats, Charles C., 139, 192

Shelby County, Alabama, 10, 76

Shelby County Iron Manufacturing Company, 76

Sheridan, Philip H., 129

Sherman, William T., 11, 13, 14, 34, 44, 54, 70, 81, 107, 109, 116–17

Shorter, John G., 70, 122, 140, 174

Sickles, Daniel, 102–3, 161, 249n77, 274n11

Skinner, William, 117

slavery, 2, 24–25, 37

slaves, 74

Slough, Robert H., 84, 172

Smith, A. J., 242n61

Smith, James Q., 163, 182, 275n27

Smith, Kirby, 127, 128, 131, 165, 276n38

Smith, William Hugh, 137–38, 163, 164, 280n32

Smith, William Russell, 18–19, 20, 21–22, 27, 32, 190, 221n24; *The Royal Ape: A Dramatic Poem*, 221n24

Society of Loyal Confederates, 53, 56, 58, 64–65, 97, 232n16

Somerville, Alabama, 135

South Carolina, 44

Southern Unionists, 80, 93

Spanish Fort, 52

Spencer, George E., 44–45, 137, 141

St. Clair County, Alabama, 192

Stanton, Alabama, 76

Stanton, Edwin, 92, 117, 139

Steele, Frederick, 52, 84, 125, 138–39, 274n10

Stephens, Alexander, 26–27, 61, 225n29

INDEX / 363

Stevens, Thaddeus, 101, 170, 189, 224n14
Streight, Abel, 81
Streight's Raid, 81
Sultana disaster, 256n17
Sumner, Charles, 97, 100–101, 108, 191, 192
Surratt, Mary, 65
surrender terms, 84, 103, 114–16, 123, 135
Swayne, Noah, 45
Swayne, Wager T., 45–46
Swoope, Rev. E. M., 134

Talladega, Alabama, 155
Talladega *Democratic Watchtower*, 49
Taylor, Grant, 26, 43
Taylor, Joseph W., 192
Taylor, Richard, 10, 15, 25, 41, 73, 76–77, 85,
   123, 126–27, 135, 144, 157, 258n54
temperance, 81
Tennessee, 7, 98, 205
Tennessee River, 7, 14, 24
test oath, 144, 187, 189, 192, 195, 211,
   264n14
Texas, 127–28, 129, 143, 164
Thirteenth Amendment, 16, 22, 29–30, 96,
   102, 143, 190
Thomas, George Henry, 7, 10, 14, 15, 23–24,
   35, 36, 50, 132, 133, 134
Townsend, George, 249n36
Tredegar Works, 90
Tupelo, Mississippi, 10
Tuscaloosa, Alabama, 10, 11, 12–13, 14, 15,
   17, 18, 20, 25, 34, 36, 49, 50, 63–65, 67–
   74, 75, 76, 77, 78, 83, 85, 98, 123, 125,
   126, 146, 148, 150, 169, 192, 207, 217n24,
   218n40, 234n77, 237n53, 258n56
Tuscaloosa Observer, 12, 63, 67, 68
Tuscumbia, Alabama, 66
Tuscumbia *North Alabamian*, 169

Unionists, 2, 14, 18, 32–35, 44, 47, 48, 49,
   50, 52, 58, 62, 63, 64, 69, 71, 80, 82, 85,
   89, 93, 96–97, 111, 112, 115, 117, 118,
   119, 121, 122, 125, 130–42, 155, 162,
   163–64, 165, 167, 168, 169, 171–72, 174,
   175, 179, 181–82, 190, 192, 194, 197, 204,
   211, 247n69, 253n41, 257n41, 275n27,

280n32, 282n59, 283n18, 292n81,
   297n25
United States, 91; national debt, 91, 92
University of Alabama, 7, 10, 13, 62, 68, 70–
   71, 73, 74; its cadets, 71, 72, 73
US Colored Troops, 52, 84, 130, 147
US Congress, 16, 29
US Customs House, 158
US Justice Department, 209–10
US Military Academy at West Point, 68
US Supreme Court, 30–32, 45–46, 105, 174–
   75, 204, 209–10
US Treasury Department, 102, 135, 179

Vance, Alabama, 69, 237n34
Virginia legislature, 93, 96, 97
voting fraud, 209
voting rights, 208–9; Enforcement Acts of
   1870 and 1871, 209; obstruction, 210;
   Voting Rights Act of 1865, 210

Wade-Davis bill, 107
Walker, Georgiana, 154
Walker, Leroy Pope, 91, 125, 182, 257n41
Wall, John J., 158
Warren, James, 112, 134
Washington County, Alabama, 169
Washington, DC, 98
Washington (DC) *Chronicle*, 79–80, 98, 173–74
Washington (DC) *National Intelligencer*,
   105, 107
Washington (DC) *National Republican*, 84, 181
Watts, Thomas Hill, 16, 24, 34–35, 43, 44,
   51, 64, 81–82, 86, 117, 122–23, 134, 138,
   140, 166, 200, 257n25, 295n130
Wedowee, Alabama, 155
Welles, Gideon, 29, 97, 107, 158, 248n74
West Point, Mississippi, 67
Wheeler, Joseph, 70, 257n29
"When this Cruel War is Over," 89
Whetstone, A. H., 79
White, Alexander, 48
"white man's government," 176
Whiting, John, 180
Wiggins, Sarah, 211
Wilcox, Cadmus, 166

Willard's Hotel, 100
Williams, James M., 146
Wilmer, Bishop Richard Hooker, 12–13, 170, 218n39
Wilson, James H., 14, 50, 71, 80–81, 121, 123
Wilson's Raid, 50–52, 67; Bibb County, Alabama, 75, 76; Elyton, Alabama, 68, 71; Irondale, Alabama, 75; Jasper, Alabama, 67; Jefferson County, Alabama, 75; Lowndes County, Alabama, 81; Montgomery, Alabama, 71, 81–83, 242n61; Northport, Alabama, 72, 73; Oxmoor, Alabama, 75; Selma, Alabama 68, 76–79, 81–83; Shelby County, Alabama, 75, 76; Tannehill, Alabama, 75; Tuscaloosa, Alabama, 67–74, 237n53
Wirz, Henry, 123, 257n31
Withers, Jones Mitchell, 47
Wood, Benjamin, 189
World War II, 120

Yancey, William Lowndes, 1, 86, 124, 136, 164, 196
"Yankee Doodle," 201